CITY & PARASITE

CITY WITHOUT SUBURB

CITY WITH SUBURB

SUBURB WITHOUT CITY

CITIES WITHIN THE CITY

NEW URBANISM AND BEYOND

DESIGNING CITIES FOR THE FUTURE

NEW URBANISM AND BEYOND

DESIGNING CITIES FOR THE FUTURE

EDITED BY
TIGRAN HAAS

RIZZOLI NEW YORK

First published in the United States of America in 2008 by
Rizzoli International Publications, Inc.
300 Park Avenue South
New York, NY 10010
www.rizzoliusa.com

ISBN-13: 978-0-8478-3111-1
LCCN: 2007943410

Distributed to the U.S. trade by Random House, New York

Design: ABIGAIL STURGES

Front cover: Seaside, Florida, photo © Steven Brooke

Printed and bound in China

2009 2009 2010 2011 2012/ 10 9 8 7 6 5 4 3 2 1

CONTENTS

NEW URBANISM & BEYOND / 9
TIGRAN HAAS

PART I
THEORIES OF URBAN FORM / 14

I.1 GENERATIVE CODES: The Path to Building Welcoming,
Beautiful, Sustainable Neighborhoods / 14
CHRISTOPHER ALEXANDER

I.2 THE NEW SCIENCE OF SPACE AND THE ART OF PLACE:
Toward a Space-led Paradigm for Researching and
Designing the City / 30
BILL HILLIER

I.3 THREE URBANISMS: New, Everyday, and Post / 40
DOUGLAS KELBAUGH

I.4 URBAN RENAISSANCE, URBAN VILLAGES, SMART GROWTH:
Find the Differences / 48
PETER HALL

I.5 SETTLEMENTS OF THE FUTURE / 52
LÉON KRIER

I.6 SOMETHING LIVED, SOMETHING DREAMED:
Principles and Poetics in Urban Design / 58
WILLIAM McDONOUGH

PART 2
EXPLORING NEW URBANISM / 64

2.1 THE TRADITIONAL NEIGHBORHOOD
AND URBAN SPRAWL / 64
ANDRÉS DUANY AND ELIZABETH PLATER-ZYBERK

2.2 THE URBAN NETWORK / 67
PETER CALTHORPE

2.3 NEW URBANISM: A Forum, Not a Formula / 70
ELLEN DUNHAM-JONES

2.4 MAKING CLOTH FROM THREADS / 74
DANIEL SOLOMON

2.5 THE UNBEARABLE LIGHTNESS OF NEW URBANISM / 77
EMILY TALEN

2.6 THE CHALLENGES OF ACHIEVING SOCIAL OBJECTIVES
THROUGH MIXED USE / 80
JILL GRANT

PART 3
SUBURBIA, SPRAWL,
AND URBAN DECLINE / 86

3.1 THE SUBURBAN CITY / 86
DOLORES HAYDEN

3.2 SPEED, SIZE, AND THE DESTRUCTION OF CITIES / 89
DOM NOZZI

3.3 RESTRAINING SPRAWL: A Common Interest to Enhance
the Quality of Life for All / 93
LOUISE NYSTRÖM

3.4 THE EMERGENCE OF MIXED-USE TOWN CENTERS
IN THE UNITED STATES / 98
TOM MARTINEAU

3.5 URBAN DESIGN AND THE METROPOLIS / 103
ROBERT BEAUREGARD

**PART 4
STREETS, TRANSPORT,
AND PUBLIC REALM** / 106

4.1 LIVELY, ATTRACTIVE, AND SAFE CITIES—BUT HOW? / 106
JAN GEHL

4.2 GREAT STREETS AND CITY PLANNING / 109
ALLAN JACOBS

4.3 TRUE URBANISM AND THE EUROPEAN SQUARE:
Catalyst for Social Engagement and Democratic Dialogue / 112
SUZANNE CROWHURST LENNARD

4.4 URBANISM AND THE ARTICULATION OF THE BOUNDARY / 117
ALI MADANIPOUR

4.5 THE NEW URBANISM AND PUBLIC SPACE / 120
GEORGE BAIRD

4.6 TRANSIT-ORIENTED DEVELOPMENT IN AMERICA:
Strategies, Issues, Policy Directions / 124
ROBERT CERVERO

**PART 5
THE ELEMENTS OF URBAN DESIGN** / 130

5.1 RECOMBINANT URBANISM / 130
DAVID GRAHAME SHANE

5.2 SPATIAL CAPITAL AND HOW TO MEASURE IT:
An Outline of an Analytical Theory of Urban Form / 135
LARS MARCUS

5.3 CENTRALITY AND CITIES: Multiple Centrality Assessment
as a Tool for Urban Analysis and Design / 140
SERGIO PORTA AND VITO LATORA

5.4 INTEGRATED APPROACHES AND DYNAMIC PROCESSES / 146
ARUN JAIN

5.5 PLANNING FOR WALKABLE STREETS / 153
RICK HALL

**PART 6
REAL ESTATE, CITY MARKETING,
AND CULTURE** / 158

6.1 URBAN RETAIL PLANNING PRINCIPLES
FOR TRADITIONAL NEIGHBORHOODS / 158
ROBERT GIBBS

6.2 CONFRONTING THE QUESTION OF MARKET DEMAND
FOR URBAN RESIDENTIAL DEVELOPMENT / 163
LAURIE VOLK AND TODD ZIMMERMAN

6.3 THE NEED FOR PATIENT EQUITY
IN CREATING GREAT PLACES / 167
CHRISTOPHER B. LEINBERGER

6.4 A CHANGED FOCUS ON RETAIL
AND ITS IMPLICATIONS ON PLANNING / 173
ANDERS ALMÉR

6.5 THE ROLE OF CULTURE IN URBAN DEVELOPMENT / 176
GÖRAN CARS

6.6 HERITAGE MANAGEMENT IN URBAN DEVELOPMENT
PLANNING / 182
KRISTER OLSSON

**PART 7
SUSTAINABILITY, TECHNOLOGY,
AND THE ENVIRONMENT** / 186

7.1 DOES NEW URBANISM REALLY OVERCOME
AUTOMOBILE DEPENDENCE? / 186
PETER NEWMAN

7.2 GREEN URBANISM: A Manifesto for Re-Earthing Cities / 189
TIMOTHY BEATLEY

7.3 ECO-TECH URBANISM:
Towards the Green and Smart City / 197
DUSHKO BOGUNOVICH

7.4 ON COMMUNITY (from Zoon Politikon to Multitude) / 201
LARS LERUP

7.5 PETROCOLLAPSE AND THE LONG EMERGENCY / 204
JAMES HOWARD KUNSTLER

**PART 8
URBAN DIGITAL SPACES
AND CYBER CITIES** / 208

8.1 CONNECTIVITY AND URBAN SPACE / 208
WILLIAM MITCHELL

8.2 URBAN NETWORK ARCHITECTURES
AND THE STRUCTURING OF FUTURE CITIES / 212
STEPHEN GRAHAM

8.3 LOCATIVE MEDIA URBANISM / 218
MALCOLM McCULLOUGH

8.4 WHAT IS THE INTERNET DOING TO COMMUNITY—
AND VISA VERSA / 221
BARRY WELLMAN

8.5 THE SANTA FE–ING OF THE URBAN AND URBANE / 225
JOEL GARREAU

PART 9
SOCIAL CAPITAL AND
MUTUAL BENEFIT / 232

9.1 CREATING COMMON SPACES: Urban Planning,
Local Media, and Technology / 232
ROBERT PUTNAM AND LEWIS FELDSTEIN

9.2 THE THIRD PLACE: A Belated Concept / 234
RAY OLDENBURG

9.3 DEMOCRACY AND "NEIGHBORLY COMMUNITIES":
Some Theoretical Considerations on
the Built Environment / 238
KEVIN LEYDEN AND PHILIP MICHELBACH

9.4 SPRAWLING CITIES / 244
KARL OLOV ARNSTBERG

9.5 BEYOND THE NEIGHBORHOOD:
New Urbanism as Civic Renewal / 249
DAVID BRAIN

9.6 URBAN DESIGN AND DEVELOPMENT
IN THE SWEDISH TRADITION / 255
KNUT STRÖMBERG

PART 10
COMPLEXITY SCIENCE
AND NEW URBAN FORMS / 258

10.1 HIERARCHY, SCALE, AND COMPLEXITY
IN URBAN DESIGN / 258
MICHAEL BATTY

10.2 GROWING SUSTAINABLE SUBURBS: An Incremental
Strategy for Reconstructing Modern Sprawl / 262
LUCIEN STEIL, NIKOS A. SALINGAROS,
AND MICHAEL MEHAFFY

10.3 COMPLEX SYSTEMS THINKING AND NEW URBANISM / 275
T. IRENE SANDERS

10.4 NEW SCIENCE, NEW ARCHITECTURE . . . NEW URBANISM? / 280
MICHAEL MEHAFFY

10.5 QUANTUM URBANISM:
Urban Design in the Post-Cartesian Paradigm / 288
AYSSAR ARIDA

PART 11
BEYOND URBANISM AND
THE FUTURE OF CITIES / 292

11.1 ANOTHER NEW URBANISM / 292
EDWARD SOJA

11.2 NEW URBANISM IN THE AGE OF RE-URBANISM / 296
ROBERT FISHMAN

11.3 THE NEW URBANISM IN THE TWENTY-FIRST CENTURY:
Progress or Problem? / 299
EDWARD ROBBINS

11.4 MAKING PUBLIC INTERVENTIONS
IN TODAY'S MASSIVE CITIES / 303
SASKIA SASSEN

11.5 THE WORLD IS SPIKY: Globalization Has Changed
the Economic Playing Field, but Hasn't Leveled It / 309
RICHARD FLORIDA

11.6 SPACE OF FLOWS, SPACE OF PLACES: Materials for
a Theory of Urbanism in the Information Age / 314
MANUEL CASTELLS

NOTES / 322

CONTRIBUTORS / 338

ACKNOWLEDGMENTS / 340

INDEX / 341

CREDITS / 348

NEW URBANISM & BEYOND

TIGRAN HAAS

A hundred years after we are gone and forgotten,
those who never heard of us will be living
with the results of our actions.
— Oliver Wendell Holmes

The contributions of the New Urbanism within the architectural, urban planning, and urban design discourse and practice have been multiple and invaluable. The New Urbanism has skillfully come to grips with very complex issues of urbanism, and presented them in a pragmatic way not just to professionals, but also to the layperson. The last ten years have seen a resurgence in the urban design debate and its rise from a marginalized, still fairly undefined discipline to a mainstream, tour-de-force, "talk of the town" issue. That notwithstanding, there is still an ongoing (and what at times seems and feels like an *ad infinitum* and *ad nauseam*) debate and discourse surrounding the discipline of urban design—since at least 1956, at the Harvard Graduate School of Design conference on urban design, a gathering intended to shape, define, and find a niche for the field. Some fifty years later, there is still discussion and confusion over the discipline, not to mention criticism and praise over a single movement that has taken the limelight and the field of theory and practice by storm; that of New Urbanism. It is crucial to understand that this movement is a continuation and (contemporary) amalgamation of those ideas in urbanism that have always championed the notion of looking at people first, and that the power of physical design is a formidable force that can enable positive change to the built environment, as well as contribute to the social life of a community. The proponents of this movement have reiterated on many occasions that their set of ideas and practices has a history that long predates this planning and design movement. The New Urbanism rests on shoulders of great individuals and the theories, practices, and tools they have developed throughout the history of urbanism.

The main ideas of the New Urbanism—about the relationship of urban land to the hinterland, the relation of the city to its transportation infrastructure, neighborhoods that are diverse and support appropriate planning and architecture, the link of the city to its own history and cultural heritage, the important role of public space in the urban socioculture of the city, and the emphasis on the human being as the measure of all things—came together long before the Congress of the New Urbanism (CNU) was brought to life. What New Urbanism did was build a popular movement with global spillover effects, one that would comprehensively advance a coherent theory of urbanism, a solid conceptual framework, and a new, revised set of tools and techniques. As Stephen (Steve) Bantu Biko said, "the power of a movement lies in the fact that it can indeed change the habits of people. This change is not the result of force but of dedication, of moral persuasion." The coalition assembled under the umbrella of New Urbanism sees the movement not as a panacea, but more as an arena—one that fosters a plethora of contemporary and future ideas of good urbanism for our cities and regions.

There are certainly commonalities and differences in the way the universal principles of good urbanism are understood and implemented in the United States and Europe. Nonetheless, they both share the same values of traditional urbanism and civic life; from the Aristotelian ideas of livable communities for all citizens, to the works and thoughts on urban design formulated in the writings and practices of Camillo Sitte, Gordon Cullen, Kevin Lynch, Léon Krier, Colin Rowe, Jane Jacobs, Christopher Alexander, and others. The New Urbanism movement has only forwarded the idea of good urbanism principles onto the contemporary planning agenda. It is really nothing more than traditional urbanism advocated and pursued in the economic, legal, social, political, and cultural context of post-World War II planning and sprawl. Rampant development of the periphery of cities, linked with disinvestment in older urban centers, resulted in a destructive and unsustainable combination. This has been most evident in the United States, where since the 1950s, Americans have been moving away from the cores of their cities to suburbia. The middle class thought it was simply opting for larger houses, bigger yards, less crime, a better environment, less pollution, and better schools. The darker side of this flight brought a malignancy, especially in the complete dominance of the automobile. New Urbanism provided an alternative to the suburban development that has dominated American life and physical landscape over the past fifty years, with its anonymous houses and alienated households; congested intersections of tangled, spaghetti-like lanes; rising edge cities; and cavernous, soulless shopping malls. The diffuse pattern of urban growth in the United States is partly a consequence of particular geographic conditions, cultural characteristics, and raw market forces, but it is also an accidental outcome of certain government policies.

Even though there are fundamentally different aspects assigned to the shaping of European cities, there are obviously a lot of similarities, which are favorable to the inclusion of New Urbanism's line of thought. Western Europe and the United States are highly developed postindustrial civilizations—universal in a truly global sense—on the brink of becoming network-mobile, highly urbanized societies, with the high prosperity of their mass-consumerist citizens placing enormous pressures on cities. The creation of places relieved of city core pressures, with higher security and proximity to cleaner environments, coupled with the expansion of multinational companies (and the creation of edge cities, clusters, huge retail centers, etc.), have supported the use of automobiles and the creation of vast arterials and highway networks. The major challenges that face us today are associated with social and urban inequality, where planning problems are often connected with uneven development, decay, and a deterioration in the quality of urban life—including social, ethnic, and economic stratification; wasteful consumption of resources; transportation congestion; and environmental degradation. The rampant development of city peripheries, together with disinvestment in older urban cores, presents a destructive and unsustainable combination. Movements like New Urbanism conceive communities that are balanced in function (housing and services), create inclusive housing that supports home-based businesses (in vogue with information technology and the demands of the mobile society we live in), spatially define the public realm as a key element, facilitate pedestrian accessibility and "walkability," minimize and put into perspective automobile use, and support public transportation—the promotion and increased use of trains and light rail, instead of more highways and roads. The popularity and acceptance of this movement, as well as the global adoption of its principles, have shown that we are dealing with universal problems in our urban conditions. Nonetheless, each geographic and cultural context and matrix requires sensitivity and specificity when dealing with the complexities of urban form.

The idea behind the New Urbanism design philosophy is to identify and deliver solutions that work in a twofold manner: first by defining sustainable and identifiable urban forms; and secondly by establishing and then supporting a real sense of vibrant, livable communities. Within these concepts and solutions the neighborhood center becomes both a civic focal point and an informal gathering place for the community's people. The idea is that the long-term functional viability of New Urbanist projects is secured by the inclusion of some critical components: the principle of mixed use, which states that a variety of uses—such as shopping, leisure, and community facilities—should exist alongside housing units, which should also offer diversity in housing types and a choice of tenures, both residential and commercial. Even though places should be compact, in the aim of creating a recognizable neighborhood, such density of development should be designed to encourage all of the above nonhousing activities. Walkability, discouraging excessive car use, and a strong sense of place are relevant. At the core of this idea lies the commitment to the concepts of strong citizen participation (in the planning process), affordable housing, and socioeconomic diversity. In a nutshell, the movement offers a completely new reconsideration of contemporary architecture, design, planning, and policy making, as well as ways to revitalize and repair our cities. All of this evolves in a sustainable metropolitan vision where cities would be ecologically, socially, and spatially *acceptable* again. Good urbanism is not about superficial style, but about pragmatic function. In most criticism of the New Urbanism, superficial appearances are often confused with fundamental precepts. Good neighborhoods and towns are based on fundamental principles—on how they provide for living, not how they look. The alignment of professionals assembled under the banner of New Urbanism has turned to examples of urban design that have survived the test of time—thriving over the centuries—and adapted them for the contemporary era.

Peter Calthorpe (a cofounder of New Urbanism) remarked recently that "aside from its principles, New Urbanism is a unique coalition, a coalition of many different individuals, professions, and vantage points." The reputation of the New Urbanism movement today is undisputable—it is not an American phenomenon anymore; it is a global one, and as such is a cutting-edge trend in urban planning and design due to its systemic, all-encompassing approach to problems in the natural and built environment. The greatest misconception today has to do with the incorrect interpretations, interventions, and applications within urban design and its continuous replacement by architectural design— in most cases, avant-garde architecture. This is largely due to the attitude of some of the leading contemporary architects, carried on the wings of popular architectural and design media and supported by most architecture schools and their curricula, in not seeing the fundamental differences between architecture and urbanism.

As Andrés Duany and Dan Solomon (both also cofounders of New Urbanism) have reiterated on numerous occasions, "the attitude of the architects is that they hold the sacred, untouchable ground, with their impenetrable architectural *masterpieces*—works of art. Their buildings have the sole function of defining space by their sheer presence and domination, and if done *beautifully* and attractively enough, they will suffice as the sole magnets and attractors of everyday citizens. The composition and the surroundings will not matter anymore; even if they exist, they will be just a supporting act for the main, grandiose spectacle in space—their building." As Duany reflected in an interview, "traditionalists and those associated with good urbanism hold people's hearts, while critics, modernists, and other avant-garde individualists (architects) command most of the intellectual territory with an aggressiveness that urbanists do not have, aggressiveness that captures new territory and dominates the discourses." The heaviest criticism of New Urbanism falls into the categories of its supposed "style," "conservatism," "utopianism," "communitarianism," and "refusal to confront the political economy of power." It is often looked at as "more ideology than theory," criticized for its unrealistic and idealistic philosophy. It is also picked apart for the purported lack of authenticity in its products and its pragmatic, normative design stance. Finally, there is a common perception that the movement's mythos is concentrated in the idea that changing people's physical environment (*the shaping of spatial order*) will take care of the social inequalities that pressure their livelihoods and can also be the foundation of a new moral and aesthetic order.

Even though New Urbanism, as a major design and social movement, was initiated and is led primarily by architects, the hardest and most abrasive criticism comes precisely from architects with diametrically opposed, entrenched hard-core views and ideas of what our cities and communities are and should be. The spearhead of these attacks (often hidden under the guise of general criticism of urbanism or urban design) is led by a number of elite architectural schools, their "*wise old men and women*," and an array of disciples and allies in both academia and practice alike. At first glance their criticism seems to have strong intellectual vigor, solid thematic and didactic critiques, and some unusual democratic (at times revolutionary) critical stances. In their essence, however, they lack coherence, both rational and theoretical argumentation, and pragmatic value. To examine them more closely is not our concern here, but a few hints shall suffice. The fact that criticism predominates over construction in the debates surrounding New Urbanism would not be as much of a problem if it were constructive: indeed, it should be welcomed. Unfortunately, the present criticism is often featured in flawed arguments (with various strains of logical fallacies), unclear conceptual frameworks, and inconsistent categories of theoretical thought. Moreover, a lot of the unfavorable judgment centers on the fixation that urbanism (i.e., the New Urbanism) has failed and "disappeared as a profession," or that—in order to survive—it should invent a kind of universal formula or "golden key" for solving most of the acute global problems we are faced with today. At the same time, urbanism has to attain some paragon state, with a just society and equality for all (enhancing equity, diversity, and ultimately the survival of the planet) in its capacity to support humanity. As a matter of fact, urbanism (including architecture, planning, and urban design) *can* support these noble goals and work towards providing a good quality of life for all—but urbanism alone is not and cannot be concerned with devising the means to do this. This is not its task; rather, it is the task of sociotechnology and social policymaking.

More to the point, such sheer utopianism, abstract humanism, and ethical romanticism forces urbanism into some areas that are simply unacceptable. Furthermore, they are impossible to resolve within the field. We also come across superficial, high-sounding words for small matters—pomposity shrouding trivialities—in attempts to discredit the principles and ideas of New Urbanism. We are also offered muddled and wishful thinking, voluntarism combined with awkward analogies, and even more logical fallacies. It should be noted that at times the arguments of its critics are embedded or hidden in rhetorical patterns that obscure the logical connections between their statements; however, it is not difficult to spot the fallacies in these arguments. What is most disturbing, however, is the lack of understanding of the complexity of urbanism as a discipline, as well as what appears to be a conscious ignorance of all the positive achievements within the New Urbanist movement. Charles E. Schumer was correct when he said that "A culture of inertia has set in. Criticism predominates over construction; critics are given more weight than those trying to build. It doesn't matter how small a constituency or flawed an argument the critic possesses. He or she always seems to predominate in political circles, in the news media, and in the public debate." The sad fact is that in the epoch of semantic innovations (as well as semantic tricks), mere linguistic phrases have taken priority over real, substantive problems, ideas, and new methodological possibilities. Some critics demand such things as "imagining a new newness," "developing a sophisticated awareness of the global condition," "exploring the ethics and expression of consent and diversity," "embracing human diversity of all kinds," an ability to "apply a wide-angle lens to the many issues . . . ," etc. The trouble is that these critics have no effective solutions for the real and pressing problems facing urbanism today. Ironically and paradoxically (and rather unfairly) they brand New Urbanism with accusations of utopianism, idealism, and unrealistic ideas while it is *their* unrealistic, idealistic, and somewhat grotesque outcries that certainly pass for the essential ingredients of pure utopianism—a "definitive global triumph of lunacy." Certain critics of New Urbanism have sometimes co-opted its concepts and ideas: they hide this by using their own terminology, not that developed for New Urbanism. However, they appear not to notice this, and continue their criticism of the structure even while using it themselves. They are writing about urbanism without really being urbanists, and thus belong to the category of "literary intellectuals." Such critics are busy telling us that urbanism is not urbanism, and what it *cannot* or should not do, or that it does not exist anymore. Yet at the same time these critics explain to us what urbanism *must* do. This is simply a contradiction *in adjecto*.

Urbanism is the study of cities—their inner structures and environments as well as developments and processes within. It is also the practice of planning, arranging, designing, and creating human communities. It is, therefore, a discipline that is here for the long haul. The notion of time as an important dimension is essential; everything that is accomplished now is done for the future, as yesterday is gone, today is already here, and we only have tomorrow. This moment—the here and now—is not the sole factor, and urbanism cannot be judged *only* by its present results. The key to its success lies in the long run and in the understanding of the complexities and realities on the ground, while having a realistic vision of the future in mind. Urbanism is a historical, sequential, and extremely complex discipline. Robert Fishman pointed out recently that the "urban past is also an integral part of the urban future, and that the traditional vocabulary of urban design [that New Urbanism uses], which gave identity and permanence to our cities throughout history, is as much part of our future as the urban past." History, identity, permanence, and complexity are all beasts of the long span, not a ballyhoo moment of avant-gardism, as many of the critics of New Urbanism would like to see it.

Although urbanism is, as pointed out before, the study of cities—their economic, political, social, and cultural environments and processes, as well as the practice of creating human communities—abstract concepts such as justice, ethics, solidarity, equality, diversity, and the more sophisticated developments of them lie beyond the confines of urbanism. More precisely, they are indispensable categories of social, moral, and political thought, but they are devoid of meaning or application until specific content is put into them. What should be stressed here is the impossibility of inventing an abstract, supersocial, superhistorical standard by which all urban endeavors can be judged. Urbanism is a complex discipline in flux. It has nothing to do with final solutions, catastrophes, deaths, endings, etc. Rather, it is involved with values, complexities, dynamics, etc.—which imply comparison and cautious relativism. That is why urbanists tend to express their judgments (moral/social ones) in words of a comparative nature, with terms such as *modern, new, traditional, conservative,* etc., rather than in uncompromising absolutes like *just, unjust, good, bad,* etc.

The current processes of globalization, city marketing, localization, commercialization, and medialization are, via fascinating new forms of visual phenomena and marketing energies, transforming and reurbanizing cities across the globe. The challenges that will shape the outcome of our cities will be experienced through a wave of exploding population growth, transformation of networks, and economic disparity and prosperity where consequences for the environment and on the long-term social well-being of inhabitants will become primary. Changes and advancements are already at our doorstep in the form of global philosophies, technologies, economics, communications, infrastructure, and in rapid demographic shifts, not to mention shifts in people's attitudes and behavior. As Manuel Castells points out, "we are currently contemplating the emergence of new social landscapes, in which individualized persons strive to cope with the responsibility of constructing their networks of communication on the basis of who they are and what they want." The emerging economic, demographic, social, and market trends will affect major cities, which will in turn automatically have an impact on regions and communities, altering the requisites for future urban planning and design. People will still continue to move to our towns and cities from the hinterlands. There are many factors in play here, so many "knowables," but also many "unknowables" that will

alter the way we think and the way we shape our cities. The ability of urbanism to globally cope with the impact of high-energy demands and high fuel costs may call for new urban design approaches and adaptations—a change in both the concept and layout of cities as we know them.

Urbanism as a discipline is needed: it is needed to assist, train, and facilitate people and communities, as well as manage change with all the planning and design skills it possesses. It needs to enable an environment that will forge professionals into a cadre, a coalition for urban change that can merge development, design, and planning tools into new integrative systems. It has to establish itself as a discipline of new problem-solving paradigms that can equip architects, planners, and urban designers with sophisticated tools and a sharper cultural awareness so that they can practice planning and development anywhere in the world. If such professionals and decision makers are not able to combat and respond to this crisis in a proper way, then the prospect of making liveable cities and sustainable communities will not succeed in the long run. Even though we might have technological breakthroughs, the future will not allow us to keep using and abusing our natural resources and environment in the extravagant ways we have become accustomed to in the last millennium.

The future of Urbanism holds a vision of a long-term, integrated, systems approach to developing and achieving healthy cities and communities by jointly addressing physical, economic, environmental, and social issues. What we need is a broad coalition of progressive ideas at a systems level—one that will offer a synthesis of skills, innovation, and knowledge. This coalition needs to recognize and handle the dynamics of human change and diversity in the built environment on all scales—from urban to regional to global. We also need stronger, more clear-cut urban planning and design theories, procedures, and tools for dealing with the uncertainties of the future. Yet, maybe the most significant conclusion here would be that the majority of our real-world problems do not fit into the domain of just one discipline. To solve this and break through the traditional boundaries between architecture, planning, and urban design, new cross-disciplinary, collaborative, and integrated approaches need to be developed if we are going to achieve the goal of a more sustainable urban condition. Hopefully this book represents an important effort towards that goal. What we do today will surely affect tomorrow, and future generations will be living with the results of our actions. So, simply put, we cannot afford the luxury of failure.

The aim of this book is to provide a comprehensive, state-of-the-art overview of ideas and thoughts on urbanism—architecture, planning, and urban design—from some of the leading urban minds of today. New Urbanism is taken as the *leitmotif,* as it is an international, cutting-edge movement to reform the design of our built environment by raising the quality of life and standard of living through creating better urban places. The texts herein also aim to offer a better understanding of how cities can thrive in a new era; their timeliness goes directly in line with the current efforts to sensitize—as well as establish guidelines and tips for—city leaders, community activists, business people, researchers, students, and regular citizens who seek to understand and improve the status of their cities, communities, neighborhoods, and other urban places.

New Urbanism & Beyond concentrates on cardinal issues confronting contemporary urbanism, urban and town planning and design, and focuses on the key topics that will be of value to scholars, undergraduate, and graduate students, as well as professionals and decision makers, in this and all fields related to urban studies. The contributions come from major theoreticians and practitioners in the field today. The intention was to produce a first-class work of urban planning and design reference, with New Urbanism as the recurring theme. This advanced primer will be both an essential resource for practice as well as a useful aid in academic teaching: a solid, provocative starting point for wider exploration of the subject. In the past two decades in particular, urban design emerged as an academic specialty akin to, but somewhat distinct from, traditional architecture and urban planning. Again, there are strong differences of opinion on whether or not it is an autonomous professional and academic field, separate from planning and architecture. New Urbanism, as the movement that has revived urban design, has attracted attention in the academic literature of several other disciplines and in popular literature. All of that has been followed by a remarkable number of publications that have emerged from all sides to theorize and analyze the urban condition, proposing new approaches to its design challenges.

This is a unique collection of essays—untarnished, in their raw form—coming from some of the leading urban thinkers of today. This group of authors originates from an array of disciplines akin to urbanism, including advocates and sound critics of New Urbanism, as well as those who lie somewhere in between. The book is organized into eleven topical sections grouped according to pertinent, contemporary themes ranging from theories of urban form, explorations of new urbanism, suburbia, transportation, real estate, social capital, elements of urban design, sustainability and technology, complexity science, and the future of cities. These essential readings show that we have not come to the "end of urbanism" as some would like us to believe. On the contrary, we are in many ways at the beginning of something new. These diverging and dynamic essays cover issues within the fields in which urbanism operates: architecture, planning and urban design, landscape architecture, ecology, urban development, and social and natural science in general. At times they expose the highly varied modes of thinking that are consistent with the multidimensional complexity and considerations of our cities—along with their many layers of social, political, cultural, economic, technological, legal, experiential, and aesthetic meanings.

New Urbanism & Beyond is the result of the summer course, conference, and debates on New Urbanism held in October of 2004 at the Royal Institute of Technology in Stockholm. This was the largest ever gathering (after the famous Exploring New Urbanism conference at the Harvard Graduate School of Design in 1999) of what Professor Manuel Castells has called "some of the brightest urban minds of today." This work has even gone a step further, and assembled *almost all* the brightest urban minds of today. This is not an anticipatory work, a book of dreams, or a nostrum for the future design of cities and our communities; it is simply a solidly grounded collection of ideas and thoughts addressing our urban condition (and beyond) written by an exceptional group of individuals never assembled before in one place. It is a coherent and consistent series of proactive lessons on how the evolution of urbanism will alter the way we live, work, build, and communicate in our cities, communities, and neighborhoods—an unpretentious, balanced set of essays with a vision of contemporary and future urban form and its influence on everyday life patterns in our brave new twenty-first-century world.

April 2007, Stockholm

PART 1: THEORIES OF URBAN FORM

GENERATIVE CODES

THE PATH TO BUILDING WELCOMING, BEAUTIFUL, SUSTAINABLE NEIGHBORHOODS

CHRISTOPHER ALEXANDER

WITH RANDY SCHMIDT, BRIAN HANSON, MAGGIE MOORE ALEXANDER, AND MICHAEL MEHAFFY

A Simple Question: What Is It That We Really Need From The Neighborhood Where We Live?

Most of us share a general, intuitive understanding of the qualities we would like to have in the neighborhood around us. It is not very complicated.

A sense of privacy—we are left alone when we want to be alone. Friendly people who know you, and whom you greet and occasionally talk to. Safety—safety from violence, from theft. Physical safety from traffic and noise. Safety for children. Safety at night. A beautiful place—one that lifts your heart when you walk around or look out of the window. Intimate and personal. Trees and gardens. Water, perhaps. A place to sit in public that is really a wonderful place. Streets and public places where everyone feels at home, instead of ones where no one feels at home. A uniqueness of the neighborhood, so we know it both when we are home and when we get home.

And, of course, we also hope for these qualities in a newly built neighborhood, or in a refurbished neighborhood. This is the dream, one might say, of every developer. A developer with a conscience, who dreams of building neighborhoods, who hopes and wishes to build something for people that has these qualities.

Yet we all know that developers rarely—if we are more honest, perhaps never—reach this ideal. There is something about the way that things are set up in the contemporary process of building houses that prevents it, perhaps even virtually forbids it.

The reason is not hard to find. Making a neighborhood that has these qualities is a human process. It is generated by a long chain of human events, involving respect for people, respect for one another, respect for land and place, and respect for age-old ways of making things: the origin of every genuine human structure. Above all it comes from the land, and it comes from the people.

When successful, it binds land and people together into a social-spatial fabric or tapestry. The list of qualities at the beginning of this section are that fabric or tapestry of which we are dreaming. We will never get that kind of neighborhood unless we consciously set out to make that fabric. The fabric must be generated by the processes we use, and in the processes we support, which try to build houses and public space and neighborhoods—it is this fabric that must be generated. Without it, nothing valuable can ensue. With it, the neighborhood has a very strong chance of life.

Building that fabric—successfully, in modern society—is what this paper is about.

What is a Generative Code?

A generative code is a system of explicit steps for creating such a fabric. It defines the end product, not by specifying the end product itself, but by defining the steps that must be used to *reach* it. Unlike a process that defines the end product and then leaves the details of getting there to the developer, the processes initiated by a generative code assure that the end product will be unique each time it occurs, and will be unique in exactly the ways that matter.[1]

The generative codes we are concerned with here are the processes specific to the environment—our world and its construction, especially in areas that we may roughly call "neighborhoods." They are, to be more precise, codes that are capable of driving or guiding the organic unfolding of a neighborhood (new, existing, or partly existing, greenfield or brown field) in such a way that the neighborhood and the people who do and will live and work in it have a good chance of flourishing personally, economically, and ecologically. Like the example of biological generative code, such a code is necessarily highly complex (in its effects) though simple (in its structure). It is *necessarily* dynamic. It specifies processes, happening under a variety of types of control, that will contribute to the proper unfolding of the whole, and delineates the interaction of the people concerned in such a way that what results may, with good fortune, become a living neighborhood.

An example of a generative code in another context is the thing known in surgical medicine as a "procedure." It defines a surgical operation in such a way that it can be learned and transmitted. Those who have learned it are able to apply the procedure to widely different individuals, each with unique circumstances, producing unique results according to the idiosyncrasies of the patient.

FIG. 1 Eishin Campus, street entrance.

FIG. 2 Eishin garden with cherry trees.

Another generative code is the system that allows a plant to unfold from a seed—a system not yet understood in full detail. It used to be thought that the genetic information in the plant's DNA was all that you needed to define the process, and so the end product. It is now known that the situation is much more complicated, and consists of interlocking processes taking place in different organs and organelles, chemical concentrations, enzymes, and interlocking sequences of action and production.

At one time in our recent history as a people we underestimated the complexity of ecological systems, and only recently found out that crude mechanical methods of agriculture kill living systems and destroy living species. In the same fashion we have, during the last fifty years, lived through an era where crude methods of urban development have given the impression of a capacity to create our built environment. We are now entering a new era in which the delicacy of this operation and the delicacy of the procedures we must use to do it are first becoming visible and practicable. If we are careful, in the next ten years we may find that we *do* have the capacity to generate living neighborhoods on earth. But the techniques we use will turn out to be very different, and more subtle, than we previously thought. Like the other examples cited, the code itself is simple. But the result

of its interacting elements can be complex and beautiful.

The word "generative" also has an additional, crucial meaning. In a generative code there is *always* a sequence, an order, to the instructions. The specifications provided by the code not only describe geometrical features (as in a form-based code like a zoning ordinance), but also describe the approximate sequence in which these features must be introduced to help the neighborhood become whole. This aspect of generative codes, novel for urban codes, may be described as the specification of an unfolding.

The idea of unfolding is entirely straightforward. It simply acknowledges what has not been acknowledged up until now in urban codes—namely, that the *order* in which things are introduced is as vital as the specification of the geometrical features. This is both common sense and ordinary. It is a natural part of the specification of a surgical procedure wherein sequence is paramount. It is a feature of virtually all biological specification and coding, where it is now known that DNA alone bears partial responsibility for the ensuing form, and that the larger part is borne of the unfolding processes inherent in cell dynamics.[2] Unfolding sequence is even a natural feature of a recipe for baking a cake. There we are very familiar with the fact that an approximate adherence to the right *sequence* is at least as important as adherence to the ingredient *specifications*, if not more important.

So this generative feature of urban codes—that the code must contain a description of the approximate sequence in which the elements of the code are best brought forth in order that a living whole may unfold successfully from them—is natural and ordinary. It is surprising that it has not previously been noticed, or implemented on a significant scale in anything we currently view as an urban code. Yet this sequence is the decisive aspect that allows a code to give life to a neighborhood.[3] An urban code may only be defined as generative when it has this feature.

When generative codes are used in a process of development, the following characteristics typically get woven into the social-spatial fabric:

1. A more beautiful and coherent geometric form that is natural to the land.

2. More probable successful integration and adaptation to plants, trees, animals, and land forms, resulting in communities and built areas that, like traditional towns and villages, seem part of nature.

3. Successful fine-tuning and deep adaptation.

4. More successful integration with living processes in the daily life of the inhabitants.

5. Better fit with individual, local needs of any given building, garden, space, or enclosure.

6. Far greater likelihood that genuine community will emerge in the new place.

7. More uniqueness of each place, street, building, and project.

8. More profound linkage to sustainability and environmental objectives.

9. An easier path to the desired end state described above.

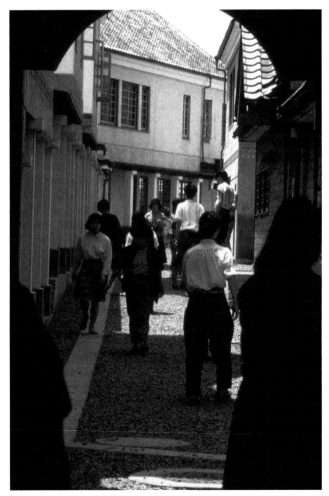

FIG. 3 Archway and pedestrian street.

FIG. 4 The farmer's market in Fresno, California.

Historical Background

In the modern era the first conscious, deliberately thought-out efforts to guide and control neighborhoods were already types of code: the zoning ordinances introduced in Chicago in the last decade of the nineteenth century. New York City adopted the first citywide zoning regulations in 1916 as a reaction to construction of the Equitable Building (which still stands today, at 120 Broadway).[4] The advent of building codes, in their modern form, also started in the nineteenth century; yet what is generally accepted as the first building code was part of the Code of Hammurabi, dating back to 1700 BCE. Legal covenants, attached by deed trust to a particular piece of land, are also used in many countries, and may also be viewed as a type of code.

In all these cases the essence of the code was that it described and defined certain *geometrical* or *configurational* features, and then required that they be present in the finished product.

Gradually, during the last two or three decades of the twentieth century, the shortcomings of this prevailing, "old" system of urban codes became clear and inspired a number of major changes. The big innovation came in the late '70s and early '80s from Christopher Alexander's pattern languages, and from Andrés Duany's subsequent effort to introduce form-based codes similar to patterns as tools for guiding development in cities and neighborhoods. At first this "new urbanism" movement (by now world-wide), focused on the inadequacy and poverty of the older code elements themselves, and replaced them with rules dealing with sidewalks, front yards, windows, building facades, street widths, parking, mixed use, and so forth. Many of these rules represent a distinct functional improvement over previously existing ideas of development, suburban tracts, and urban housing. But, like the elements of existing building codes and zoning ordinances, the elements of these New Urbanism codes are rules enforced by law, which require that a certain number of *geometric* conditions are met within a neighborhood.

The built result is often more like a carefully plotted piece of fiction than real life. For a time you might be fooled into thinking this is real, but sooner or later its artificiality can be glimpsed. Indeed, the ultimate effect of these form-based codes on built projects is by no means universally liked or accepted. A deep fear and suspicion of them pervades our culture—as demonstrated by *The Truman Show* and the "Arcadia" episode from the sixth season of *The X-Files*—for fairly understandable reasons. The application of these codes, although intended to help developers do a better job of building neighborhoods, in fact, has too little effect on certain other, deeper things that matter more. The qualities listed at the beginning of this paper—simple, basic qualities that all people desire—are still lacking, and though they may appear in developers' stated ambitions, those same developers rarely have any capacity for achieving them. The places built are, after all, still "developer built," and thus, typically still have the inevitable taint of rigidity, sometimes coupled with a large dose of commercialism. The people who live in these places inevitably feel like the inhabitants of a "machine for living." Negative qualities occur and are felt by inhabitants, despite the fact that the architects of the new form-based codes rightly see themselves as crusaders battling this very problem.

In short, the step of outlining the new form-based codes, as far as it has gone to date, has not been strong enough to make a real difference in the process of creating vibrant and healthy neighborhoods that people genuinely care for. The difference between these new form-based urban codes and older building codes and zoning ordinances is somewhat positive. New Urbanism projects do make practical advances in pedestrian space, the placing of cars, and mixed-use development. The rules have changed, becoming more complex, and now pay greater attention to important practical aspects of the habitable character of the ensuing neighborhoods. This is all positive, in principle, though sometimes too rigid. The *geometry* therefore becomes more different, more complex, more interesting, and possibly more useful, too. Such change is highly desirable since, without a doubt, one of the things wrong with twentieth-century cities lies in the fact that their geometry and layout emphasized cars in undesirable ways, and their buildings were faceless, too slick, too gigantic, and tired.

Despite these advances, the products of New Urbanism, in their geometry, still make only very small improvements to the human condition. The emergence of living structure, of real social life, is not really more firmly guaranteed by these new urban codes than it was by the earlier, less pleasant combinations of zoning and building codes. Despite greater sophistication, the results still tend to be lifeless; the shapes are different, but the inner social character, and the emotional health of the inhabitants, has not really become better. It is true that they slightly resemble traditional buildings, but not for any obviously good reason, and the wholeness—of work, of spirit, of plants and animals and people—that was felt in traditional society has not yet come into being in the products of New Urbanism.

In short, you cannot change the soul of a person by putting on lipstick, nor can you do this with architecture. You cannot make the world a better place to live in by changing the style of the buildings. The products of the new form-based codes have so far still been primarily stylistic. Although they also contain certain practical benefits for living, they are fundamentally making changes only in the *appearance*, not in the underlying substance or social-spatial fabric, of the communities they create.

What does make a neighborhood a good place to live in is the experience of inner psychological freedom, the freedom in the air, the possibility of unconstrained activity and interaction, emotionally satisfying work, an atmosphere of enjoyment, and the invitation to be alive. It includes a certain friendliness. It includes the sum of the activities and interactions that occur there. It includes ownership by everyone in some degree, a situation in which streets and blocks control their own destinies.

Actual freedom, this liberating and nourishing kind of freedom, does not come from the style of the buildings; it comes from the way people feel ownership of the place, and that, in turn, comes from *the way the place has been generated*, and by the way it is continuously being generated as its life goes forward.

Specifically we may say that this nourishing quality will arise in a place to the extent that three things are respected:

1. The land: What is built preserves and extends the deep structure of what is there already.[5]

2. The people: What is built comes from the actions and wishes of the people who live and work there, not from a faceless corporation.

3. The communal spirit that is felt: The work of generating the place comes from the heart, and has at its root a spirit of communality and love of life that is palpable, and can be experienced because it is visible, and above all, because it is truly there. The social life of a neighborhood comes about from the existence of a profound, articulate public structure in the space, which bestows community, and the opportunity for community, on the people who live there.

We believe that certain recent experiments have now begun to demonstrate—at least on a preliminary basis—that newly built neighborhoods created in this better and more generative way fundamentally alter how people living and working there feel about the place and about themselves.

We are very much afraid, however, that—although they are vitally important—these three considerations have so far been almost altogether missing from contemporary development, including New Urbanist development.

That is because New Urbanism and its experiments, just like virtually all other contemporary forms of architecture, have been built on the foundation of modern development as a *mechanical process*, without sufficiently questioning the assumptions underlying this process or getting to the root of these assumptions. Because the New Urbanists have so intensely desired to succeed in a practical way, and implement large areas of built projects, they have embraced, without enough critical awareness, the machinery and the monetary and control structures of the modern developer, lock, stock, and barrel. That is to say, they have embraced the very thing that was, and is, the origin of a great part of our environmental ills in the first place.

In addition, they are also trying to solve the problem at the level of physical design, which requires some kind of perfect blueprint executed by a faithful builder or developer. But what we are learning now is that nature doesn't work that way, and the best projects are generative and continually adaptive, not master planned. The solution is going to have

FIG. 5A AND 5B Stakes for house lots, streets, and building masses in a neighborhood in Santa Rosa de Cabal, Columbia, and the site plan arising from this process. All these stakes were placed by family members themselves with help and guidance from Center for Environmental Structure staff.

to be a new kind of evolving, adaptive, generative, design-build approach.

History of Experimental Projects with Generative Codes at the Center for Environmental Structure

Work on generative codes, mainly in private contexts, began in the late 1970s at the University of California and the Center for Environmental Structure (CES) in Berkeley. The following is a summary of our experiences in these kinds of projects.

Since the appearance of *A Pattern Language* in the late 1970s, Alexander and his colleagues have been engaging in a long series of experimental projects, all designed to deliver communities and neighborhoods that are more "real"—that is to say, more focused on the human aspects of spatial and social structure, and how real people actually feel about their environment—and endeavoring to produce a built environment that truly makes people happy in their day-to-day lives. All these projects have been designed to overcome the shortcomings of modernistic architectural development projects, largely because they have used entirely different means of design, planning, production, and procurement.[6] In recent years we have also been working rather consciously to make progress in the very direction where we observed our colleagues working on New Urbanism, and its form-based codes, most seriously at fault.

Unfortunately, the difficulties and challenges involved increase exponentially with an increase in scale. To obtain projects that would demonstrate these concepts on a larger scale, therefore, requires certain agencies being willing to create a bubble in which pilot projects can take place.

To do this we have taken an intuitive approach, in which we place the feelings of people at center stage, and allow that to guide a process of design and construction that is able to produce the real thing.[7] This means that we try to shape our procurement processes in ways that improve human beings' sense of belonging to the communities that are created. This simple rule of thumb, this attitude, has guided most of our choices, and insofar as it has been practically possible, we have taken every step to make this one aim has been the center target.

To achieve these results we, like Andrés Duany and his colleagues, took off from our own findings in *A Pattern Language*. But the directions we took were different.[8] Duany and his colleagues, in their form-based codes, made the attempt to codify and *require* that pattern-like entities be embodied in the geometry of the design, in the form of simply expressed and rigidly enforced rules, *while leaving the process of procurement largely unchanged*. In our work at CES we paid as much attention as possible to the process and tried to create (new) formal ways of supporting a more humane and more involved process, which included the inhabitants and neighbors of the project in hand, and had the intrinsic quality that its steps would heal the surroundings and heal the community itself. Thus we consciously focused on the process that would *generate* the deep structure of the world we were responsible for, and it was this generative emphasis that gave our work its meaning and result. Hence the term *generative codes* has gradually emerged as the best descriptor of all the work we have been doing.

The following table shows a strong correlation between two variables:

A. The number of generative features present in the development process by which each one was created, and

B. The success of the different CES projects, in creating life, as judged by people familiar with the project.

See the last two columns in the table.[9]

The two evaluations of the nineteen projects were submitted to a rank-order correlation test.[29] Spearman's correlation coefficient (rho) is 0.67, which is very high for such a small sample. This degree of correlation among nineteen items is significant at the 0.002 level, meaning that a correlation this high would have occurred by chance only two times out of every thousand random trials.

The nine columns (3–11) stand for nine features of the procurement process, present or absent, in the way each of these projects was handled. One may say that these various projects turned out well in rough proportion to the number of YES indications that appear next to them. Turning out well, in this sense, means that in the resulting environment there is, to a strong degree, human satisfaction: the place is considered beautiful or pleasant; people report a wholesome feeling from being in the place.

It appears, then, that the presence of these features in the procurement process correlates positively with the success of the ensuing project. So, after several decades of such experiments, we may now say that our evidence strongly suggests that the following aspects of the procurement process play a vital role in people's satisfaction with the results:

• The creation of a neighborhood always starts with respect for, engagement in, and careful enhancement of the community life of the neighborhood, even in its smallest details.

• Clients and users had a major part in the creation of the pattern language that was the basis for the generative code.

• To feel genuine satisfaction and identity with a neighborhood, the clients themselves and users must physically play a significant role in laying out buildings, streets, dwellings, and public spaces.

• Further, it makes a real difference when people do this on the ground, walking around together on the land itself, placing strings, stakes, and markers, reaching a mental state where they almost feel that the buildings are already there.

• It also makes an enormous difference to the success of the project if the plans are drawn *from* the stakes left in the ground (the opposite of what happens in typical production processes and housing construction procurement today). This can be achieved economically by use of high-tech surveying methods that allow a direct translation of the field position of a stake to the digital drawing that defines the project.

SOME OF THE EXPERIMENTAL PROJECTS DONE BY CES

A This column shows the number of generative features (from the nine features in columns 1-9) that are present in the process that formed each project – the number of YES's in the row.

B These numbers show our own intuitive evaluation of the finished environment in each project, in human terms and when judged as a healthy and wholesome place to live, on a scale of 1 to 10 (10 being the highest).

FEATURES OF THE PROCUREMENT PROCESS		Primary focus on growth of community as the main object of procurement process	Pattern language by clients	Layout by clients	Layout on the ground	Drawings done after layout (not before)	Direct construction management	Budget under our control	Subs directly controlled	Focus on well-being of the human community guided every phase of work	A	B
PROJECTS												
Modesto[10]	1975	YES	YES	YES	YES	YES	NO	NO	NO	NO	5	2
Mexicali[11]	1978	YES	NO	YES	YES	YES	YES	YES	YES	YES	8	7
University of Oregon[12]	1981	YES	YES	YES	NO	NO	NO	NO	NO	NO	3	4
Shorashim[13]	1982	YES	NO	YES	YES	YES	NO	NO	NO	NO	4	3
Sala[14]	1983	YES	YES	YES	YES	YES	YES	YES	YES	YES	9	6
Guasare, Venezuela[15]	1983	YES	NO	YES	YES	YES	UNKNOWN	NO	YES	NO	5	4
Fresno[16]	1985	YES	NO	NO	YES	NO	YES	YES	YES	NO	5	6
Eishin[17]	1985	YES	YES	YES	YES	YES	YES	NO	YES	YES	8	9
Pasadena ordinance[18]	1987	NO	YES	YES	YES	NO	NO	NO	NO	NO	3	3
Whidbey Island[19]	1988	YES	YES	YES	YES	YES	YES	YES	YES	YES	9	10
Emoto[20]	1989	NO	NO	NO	NO	YES	YES	NO	YES	NO	3	6
San Jose[21]	1990	YES	YES	YES	NO	NO	YES	YES	YES	YES	7	7
Colombia[22]	1991	YES	YES	YES	YES	YES	YES	YES	YES	NO	8	5
Upham[23]	1992	NO	NO	YES	YES	YES	YES	YES	YES	NO	6	8
Agate housing[24]	1993	NO	NO	NO	YES	YES	YES	NO	NO	NO	3	5
Texas[25]	1994	YES	NO	YES	YES	YES	YES	YES	YES	YES	8	8
West Dean[26]	1995	YES	NO	YES	YES	YES	YES	YES	YES	YES	8	10
Sullivan[27]	2000	YES	NO	YES	YES	YES	YES	YES	YES	YES	8	7
Sanders[28]	2004	YES	NO	YES	YES	YES	NO	NO	NO	YES	5	7

FIG. 6 One of the alcoves in the Linz Café, Linz, Austria.

- Possibly the biggest single factor is the control of the project through construction management, not by a general contractor, but by a project manager who directly controls budgets and subcontractors, and who is in touch all the time with the members of the community.
- Further, it makes a great difference if money explicitly enters into the process, such that the contract documents control the total contract price but also allow flexible reassignment of line item costs while the process moves forward, so that matters of importance can be addressed during construction without raising costs.
- It is also vital that subcontractors are directly controlled by the architect and local families, under the supervision of a project manager, so that many hundreds of small adaptations can be made as the project advances without causing delays or cost overruns.
- In conclusion, we believe that even when housing has to be built without community and without real people as clients, the creation of the housing must be handled in a form that introduces community and unfolding from the first minute of the first day. And the project as a whole is seen as a human endeavor, not as a technical endeavor, and that this human endeavor has as its continuing, principal object the day-to-day enhancement of each individual in the community, so that they can then give back to the community, the well-being that they have received from it.

These nine features summarize the content of columns 3–11 in the table. We believe, and to a first approximation have now demonstrated, that these nine aspects of project management and procurement play a key role in allowing people to feel affection for the places where they live and work, generating a community atmosphere, enhancing the degree of life experienced, and encouraging positive feelings among neighbors and respect for the place they live in.

The fact of a high rank-order correlation of 0.67 between the presence of these nine features of a development process, and the experienced quality of life in the finished projects, with the correlation deemed statistically significant at the 0.002 level, CANNOT BE UNDERESTIMATED. For the first time, we believe we have the bedrock of an empirical finding, which opens the door to empirical and practical reassessment of the entire modern process of environmental development.

The Process of Procurement

From the very beginning of our experiments, the most important lesson we learned over and over again was that it is the process of procurement, above all, that *must* be modified. By procurement we mean the *entire process*, from beginning to end, starting with the first conception of the project and including: the involvement of clients and potential inhabitants; design and planning; obtaining permits and budgeting; project management, construction management, and management of contracts and subcontracts; and finally the physical construction, plant life, and ecology. Design is only a very small part of all that. It is vitally important, but not nearly as important as the process of procurement as a whole.

The reason for placing such importance on the procurement process as a whole is easy to explain. In the normal procurement process—the one that is standard for modern developers—the sequences of the project are rigidly divided into phases. Each of these phases is begun, completed, and then handed on to the next process. Because this entire present-day procedure is mechanical, the result, not surprisingly, is mechanical as well.

In the kind of procurement we have practiced, the different players pass in and out of the overall procurement procedure, much like threads of a multicolored skein of wool, where the different colored threads pass in and out and in again, while together the threads all run through the skein from beginning to the end, always focused on the well-being of the whole.

Consider the following players in a typical community:
- Individuals who live there, initially, already
- Individuals, families, and businesses who are likely to enter the new community
- Planning officials of the local authority
- Architects who work with the community
- Developers who provide some capital for the construction
- Engineers who deal with soils and/or other existing conditions requiring remedial action

- The project manager who oversees the process in its entirety
- Community advocates who play a role in helping make sure that individual persons are represented and involved all the way along
- Banks or lenders who have a financial stake in the new neighborhood
- Construction contractors and subcontractors
- Craftsmen
- Children of the families
- Ecologists taking care of the existing fauna and flora
- Local business support services

In a successful project, one which captures the qualities we listed at the beginning, all these different types of persons and professionals are involved, and must be involved. But it is not sufficient for them to be involved merely at the beginning, in a token meeting or *charette*—one meeting is not enough. All of these individuals need to pass in and out of the process, continually, as it moves along. They contribute when they have something to contribute or when they are needed. Their timely involvement in the project is manageable—and as we ourselves have seen on various occasions, it can be managed successfully, in practice.

For coherence of organization, the entry of all these different people into the project needs to be orchestrated by a designated project manager, who works for a fee, not for profit, and under the guidance of a generative code. Most important, and perhaps most notable, the developer is not the primary player, but rather just one of the players whose interest in the project is financial. His financial interest does not give him the right to control the situation. Rather, he must play his role appropriately and help to nurture the complex process that is going on. In our view, it is the project manager who has the primary responsibility for bringing the different players in, at different times and on many different occasions, as required. It is also his responsibility to safeguard the coherent unfolding and the myriad internal adaptations of the whole.

The generative code is the document that oversees this process and provides the chart and organizational backbone for the project manager's actions, as well as the weaving in and out of different players at appropriate moments in the process. This code sets out, as clearly as possible, the steps that must be taken, in their rough order, and the people who are most appropriate for each step. Each element of the code embodies a decision that unfolds the whole, at its proper place and time, and this generative code is constructed so that the whole—the neighborhood, all its personal and individual details, all its subtle adaptations of buildings to one another and to the land—is taken care of, gently, by the way construction management and contracts are handled.

FIG. 7 A festival in Eishin Square.

FIG. 8 Students in an arcade.

These are examples of how generative code unfolds the whole:

• Existing businesses within the neighborhood are protected and the community integrated into the new construction so that current jobs and economic flows are protected, so the community grows as a whole.

• Unfortunate housing and vulnerable families are supported by inclusion in the new neighborhood, and their unique characteristics are encouraged to become part of what emerges next.

• Main pedestrian places are chosen by community members walking the site and looking at the most beautiful places, views, and spots that have a settled feeling.

• Gardens are chosen, when possible, by the families themselves, so that their house is related to a piece of land they like.

• The internal layout of each house is made (whenever possible) by the family who will first live there, and they do this by placing blocks on the slab, so that interior walls and partitions are based on the real feeling that has been verified in the actual place.

• Windows are placed from the inside of each dwelling, after rooms have been decided, so that views and light are as beautiful as possible for each room in the house.

• Ornament is done in brickwork, leadwork, and interior plaster: inexpensive ornamentation is provided by the craftsmen within a tight budget provided by the project manager.

• Outdoor walls, balustrades, seats, and fountains are provided from a community budget: householders in the vicinity decide on the layout, and provision comes from a line item in the budget allocated to this purpose.

• Public gardens and main pedestrian thoroughfares are laid out with walks, trees, low walls, seats, fountains, and views over local landscapes.

This is where the depth and power of the generative code comes from.

If we hope for a better architecture, we must learn, and acknowledge, that the subtle structure of a created environment depends almost entirely on the key features of the procurement process. Generative code drastically changes, redirects, and improves the procurement process so that the better architecture we hope for can be achieved.

Operational Underpinning of a Generative Code:
Independent, Community-Oriented Project Management

How then, is this to work? Most important, how does a generative code make it work?

The motive for making money must be tempered by a motive to create a beautiful and healthy neighborhood with a coherent, integrated, caring attitude toward community that brings quality of life to its inhabitants. All this must be done through a new and presently unfamiliar organizational configuration.

In order to understand this, let us review the most basic project management tool: a PERT (program evaluation and review technique) chart. A PERT chart describes the events that will occur in a complex project, the length of time each event is likely to take till completion, the time sequence in which these events must occur, and, most specifically, the precedence relation between events (e.g., event A must be completed before event B can start).

In the field of construction these events are usually confined to the actual construction itself—although certain non-construction preliminaries (such as getting permits) may also appear on the chart—mainly because they have a crucial capacity for damaging effective completion if not taken into account and undertaken in time.

Now, in pure building construction itself, it is perfectly obvious that different events or jobs are interdependent, and that the emerging whole we think of as the building is unfolding gradually. This is in no way mysterious, and no one expects that the building is going to appear magically on a certain day. But in community building, when we make a neighborhood, we face a different, more complicated task. The idea that planning, design, community building, adaptation, and so forth are all necessary events, and necessarily part of the work of community building and healing the environment, which must continue through the procurement of a building, is not yet familiar. Yet when we think logically about the myriad decisions that *must*, in a sensibly conceived neighborhood building project, occur in an interdependent and partially sequential fashion, then the idea of design, planning, and even wider fields of expertise and cooperation as part of a network of interrelated actions, begins to appear perfectly sensible, necessary, and indeed inevitable in a building project.

The items that appear in a generative code are capable, for the first time in any forceful public instrument, of dealing explicitly with the codecision making of people in a community. They deal, explicitly, with the priority of community and individual values, and with the idea that these human values must have priority over all development policies and over all methods of development that may be put forward.

We must now face the issue of money and profit, and focus especially on the current confusion between privatized action on behalf of social values, and the potential risks and realities of this proposal.

The focus on community, and the necessity of careful attention to many vital community issues *that do not gener-*

ate profit, has not been adequately discussed. It is no secret that developers are motivated, in most cases, by the opportunity to make money out of land by increasing its monetary value. Most often this has been accepted by local governments and national governments who seek to justify and benefit, second hand, from the developer's profit motive, by being able to rely on said developers to do what the government cannot do or no longer wishes to do—that is, provide the needed capital for the huge investments required.

However, there are abundant examples of ways in which this kind of policy has backfired in recent years. The fiasco of private developers who were encouraged to take over public education at the elementary and secondary level is an excellent example. The developers rapidly moved to place priority on profit, ahead of educational aims, causing a shabby education for students. The romantic image of old-fashioned private schools as a source of excellence has no reality in these recently created schools, as present-day values do not correspond to the values built into those historic institutions, which were solid, and untainted by the desire to accumulate wealth. The modern version of this idea, using developers who have no history of educational wisdom as money-making protagonists who do it for profit, from a distance, just does not work.

A similar problem has arisen in many cities, where property developers opt for massive land clearance instead of selective infill. This has caused anguish among communities who see their own heritage, no matter how poor, being torn up by developers for whom it is less trouble to raze communities and build from scratch than to build and heal, through carefully poised improvements and infill buildings, which require more discussion; this is inconvenient for the money-oriented machine.

Simply put, all community building, and, in particular, the kind of community building supported by the use of generative codes, requires an independent and scrupulously professional project manager as the chief of operations, for several reasons:

First, the subtle interweaving of decisions, made by different interested parties in a community, can only be undertaken with success by a person dedicated to *this* task—not only to the bottom line. The field of project management, especially if coupled with people from a social service background—anthropologists, community field workers, and so on—can deliver the community project in a way that does achieve a built and grown community.

Second, it is the specialized field of project management that trains people to thread their way through such complexity while holding fast to cost and time targets.

Third, even this will only work when the project manager, or project management team, is independent: that means able to stand completely outside the profit cycle, and untainted by the mixture of motives that present-day construction and development are inevitably subject to. Indeed, it is not only the overall process set in place by the generative code that must be handled on a project management basis. We believe that the construction activities

FIG. 9 The Upham House, Berkeley, California.

FIG. 10 Bridge with students.

themselves must be run by an independent project manager who controls subcontractors directly, not thorough the conduit of a general contractor.

Fourth, the project managers can only be placed in a reliable and ethically sound position by a fixed-fee form of payment, the fee set as a flat percentage of the project cost. It is our experience that this arrangement generates trust and, of course, has the effect that all money saved is placed back into the project construction funds and then accrues to tangible improvements in the project. Any form of arrangement by developers, contractors, or project managers that allows savings in the project to go to the pockets of the individuals and companies concerned, works against the community, and ultimately robs it of just that increased value that the project management plus generative code are capable of bringing in.

It is also our sad experience, gained on many continents, that whenever standard contracting or development arrangements are in place, whenever an opportunity arises for money to supersede human values and the human value of the community building process, then sooner or later the project goes wrong. Whether it is small-scale petty thievery (eighty

sheets of plywood double billed on successive invoices), medium-scale (routinely tripling cost proposals for change orders), or large-scale (motivations for land deals that encourage a developer to make inappropriate suggestions of land coverage and density in order to further their own financial aims)—the result is always the same. It is not only the petty and major thievery that causes harm. What causes the most harm is that, in such a climate, no one associated with those motives can maintain clean hands, and the really important issues—of individual participation, community trust, the health and welfare of land, trees, houses, windows, paths, gardens, and even seats—all become tainted and ultimately destroyed. This is not a pretty picture, but it is familiar to all of us, from countless development projects, in countless nations.

For these very reasons we at the Center for Environmental Structure have operated for thirty years as nonprofit contractors and developers. People have trusted us because we wished to strengthen the basis for strong communities, which became possible only because we operated outside the predominant system.

Of course, the all-important question remains: What is to

FIG. 11 Yellow boat made by the students in front of the student cafeteria, which they also helped to lay out.

be developers source of capital? It is very clear that the emphasis on community described here cannot be accomplished through the goals and attitudes that large-scale developers typically hold today. Their role needs to change and other sources of capital must be found. There are a number of possible solutions:

1. Developers are invited to take part as financiers, but the return on their investment is carefully regulated. They are not entrusted with running the development process itself unless they can demonstrate an understanding of how to implement generative code. They are not allowed to tamper with the community-inspired aspects of the process.

2. Government finds ways of providing loans to other institutional entities at the community level, such as loans to nonprofit land trusts and groups of individual house owners.

3. In the United States, at least, a tradition of nonprofit developers has been growing up. It is in its infancy, but it creates an industry-wide precedent for development that is fee based, not profit based, and professionally committed to healing the earth and making good environments. The experience of these nonprofits demonstrates that there is no nec-

essary functional linkage between good neighborhood management and the making of profit, and therefore no reason to go on relying on commerce and profit as the necessary underpinning of successful neighborhood development. The belief that this is inevitable and necessary is little more than an old wives' tale.

4. Patient money is obtained from long-term investors, and from investors who require a moral commitment to positive healing of the earth from their investments.

5. It appears very likely, to us, that the key issue, at root, may be the present coupling of land speculation with zoning ordinances. It is a fact that most present-day developers make their money not by providing a service that heals communities and land, but by buying land cheap, manipulating the zoning process to gain permission for greatly increased land use, and by cashing in the surplus. This process, even when engaged by benign and altruistic people and companies, cannot help being steered towards the increase of land-use density as the principal goal—something usually irrelevant to the best interest of the community. Careful analysis of this topic can lead to entirely new forms of finance and investment, separated from the glitter of cash and

oriented towards the real goal of a healthy environment.

Undoubtedly other solutions can be found by industry players who are committed to building vibrant, sustainable communities and choose to support such ventures both at home and abroad.

But it is in any case imperative that the dangerous effects of the commercial system presently in place be understood, and that the community building motive, paid by a fixed, contracted fee, be allowed to take its place ahead of any profit motive. Our experience suggests some promising avenues to explore. As a starting point, independent, community-oriented project management must be supported as the major tool of development, in a way that is coupled with generative codes of the type we have described.

Placing Practical Emphasis on Respect for Individuals, Respect For Land, and Respect for Continuity

To further explain our misgivings about the current procurement process, we offer this analysis. The standard process, which has been in place for about half a century, works through a very limited kind of efficiency that is, at its core, mechanical. It uses mechanical forms of cost accounting, mechanical approaches to human work, and mechanical approaches to profit. In order to achieve the results we have been able to achieve, we had to intervene in the procurement process. We did this, essentially, by starting from scratch and by rebuilding the procurement process from the ground up. We did not do this by appealing to any theory or to any pre-established notion of how it should be done. Rather, we simply did it by doing whatever seemed intuitively *necessary* to do to get the right results—results that were intuitively wholesome, which engaged people's affections, and which led to results that made people happy and the environment healthy.

Our experiments in procurement were, in many cases, risky since we needed the courage to try methods in which we had little experience. It was part of the given that we had to take control of decisions we had not been trained to take, and we had to try methods and procedures that were, in many, many cases, untried. We had to risk failure; we had to use the compass of instinct even when those who believed they "knew better" advised us against what we were doing on the grounds that it was risky.

- We did our own contracting.
- We used new kinds of contracts.
- We worked to fixed costs.
- We engaged the people we were working for in the initial pattern languages.
- We engaged people in the actual layout process.
- We used physical models and full-size cardboard and tape mock-ups to settle difficult points.
- When necessary we modified building code requirements on our own steam.
- Staying within budget was always a vital part of the process.
- We allowed time to slip when that was necessary.
- The one thing that led us was always *the health of the whole*. This took priority over everything else.

From what has been said before, the morphogenetic sequence—the sequence that permits coherent unfolding of the whole—does not easily fit together with the present practice of development, whether this be free private enterprise development as practiced in the United States and Western Europe, or the kind of government-sponsored housing undertaken by local authorities or federal and state governments.[30]

In either case, the developer takes the risk, the bank lends money against this risk, and the insurance against risk—which both developers and banks experience—is provided by a highly rigid and mechanical process. Unfortunately, that makes the recipients of the housing—the public who walk and use the land within these areas—pay an immense price for this insurance: namely, they have an inhuman, sterile, and impersonal environment, thus disconnecting people from society and from land.

A Decisive and Lasting Change

This decisive change, if it is to take root, cannot avoid a confrontation with the issue of development, as we currently understand it, and developers.

In the last fifty years it has almost always been assumed that the way to get construction of neighborhoods to meet the growing world population is through the "good offices" of a developer: a person, or an institution who is willing to take the financial risk, undertake the huge effort of management, and who will, in short, get things done.

This is, of course, a rampant nod to commercialism, which, if we did not live in such a commercial era, would be seen for what it is. The life of a community cannot be held hostage by a person or corporation who seeks to make money and profit from the construction of its streets and buildings. The streets and buildings are part of the neighborhood's lifeblood, the city's lifeblood, and they must be interwoven with the activities and life of the people themselves. Anything less leads inevitably to drug abuse, crime, teenage violence, anomie, and despair—the very earmarks of twentieth-century urbanism.

This mistake was so deep-seated in the United Kingdom, for example, that the Labor government, and specifically the office of deputy prime minister John Prescott, laid their entire housing program on the foundation of development as usual, and on the primary role of the commercially motivated developer.[31] In the programs this Labor government set in place from 2000–2005, it was therefore the developers who told the cities what to do and how to do it within the commercial system they were used to. The people in their natural communities were bought and sold, and held hostage, by a very few developers who were far too careless with the lives of those for whom they were

FIG. 12 Some of the seventy families working on their houses in a new neighborhood.

ostensibly working.

A successful policy in which developers play a major role in the future can only be trusted if it is coupled with the reorganization of the development community along professional, fee-based, nonprofit lines. The reorganization of development, creation of new legal controls and guidelines that fundamentally alter the way a developer enters into the growth process of a community, must be the bottom line of a successful policy for building and rebuilding neighborhoods. Generative codes, together with the radical shifts in power and control, and changes in responsibility of planning officers, inhabitants, and builders alike, are—in one form or another, we believe— the only possible foundation for the way successful neighborhoods can be created.

It is the generative codes *themselves*, their widespread use, and the widespread acceptance of the vision these new codes embody that matters most. The use of these codes, if properly done, will include vast changes in our view of land, changes in our way of caring for both urban

and rural land, and massive involvement of communities and businesses in the planning, construction, and repair of neighborhoods. In all likelihood, in the long run, it will wash away the system of zoning and its ills, and replace both that system and the operational behavior of city planners with new visions.

But to be quite honest, we do not yet know which group of people in society are most likely to emerge as leaders of this new kind of generative process. Where will these leaders, competent and inspired to use generative codes for the widespread benefit of society, come from? They could conceivably be architects—unlikely, but possible. They could be a new breed of developer, with a more actively engaged moral sense. They could be community leaders. Or, as suggested above, they could be project management engineers, infused with a strong dose of anthropology and people-oriented skills.

It is too early to tell. But in any case, it is the opinion of this group of authors, that generative codes, and all that they stand for and make possible, will lie at the core of a new era

THE NEW SCIENCE OF SPACE AND THE ART OF PLACE

TOWARD A SPACE-LED PARADIGM FOR RESEARCHING AND DESIGNING THE CITY

BILL HILLIER

The City as Object

Looked at naively, the city seems to be a special kind of object: a network of linear spaces linking a large and dense collection of buildings. This dual form is what we see when we look down on the city, what we use when we occupy it, what we experience as we move in it, what we draw when we represent it, and what we change when we design it. In all these senses, the city *as object* seems to *be* the city. It commands the attention of those who use the city as much as those who design and plan our interventions in its form and functioning (figure 1).

It is an odd reflection, then, that it was only in the final decades of the twentieth century that the city as object began to feature seriously in the reflection and research that must accompany planning and design. Early commentators had noted or advocated its geometrical properties, or lack of them, and others—preeminently Sitte[1]—had noted local properties of the building space relation as the raw material out of which the city as object is constructed. But the form of the object as a whole eluded analytic commentary.

In the more cerebral twentieth century, intellectual fashion led us away from the city as object and towards the study of the city as one or other kind of abstraction. We saw the rise of the *analogy*: the city as machine, as organism, or as text, all of which set the city as object at a distance from reflection because the city is not really like any of these things. We also saw the rise to dominance of the social sciences, which, pointing to social, economic, and psychological processes in cities—whose complexity exceeds that even of the spatial and physical city—demanded paradigms of study in which the city as object is seen as the spatial and physical output of these processes. But it is not, of course; the city as object does not arise directly from social and economic processes, but from the *act of building* in light of these processes. So the social sciences came to see the city as object as an epiphenomenon, a product of the processes that make the city, but not a necessary manifestation of them. In the

social-science paradigms of the city, which have dominated the second half of the twentieth century, the city as object all but disappears.

Originating in the last quarter of the twentieth century the aim of the *space syntax* movement was to bring together the study of the city as object with the study of social, economic, and cultural processes, and so, show these processes to be spatial in an architectural way, and allow us to bring together urban design with urban reflection and research.[2] Space syntax addresses the city naively, as what it seems to be: a network of spaces created by successive acts of building. The syntactic *space-led* approach to the city, often thought of simply as a method of urban analysis, has, through the efforts of a large and growing research community, become a new kind of theory of the city, one which shows the formal and functional processes of the city to be unique and so not tractable to treatment by analogy with other kinds of system.

The Fundamental Urban Relation

Why then should the network of space preoccupy us to the point where we seek to make it the centerpiece of theory? The answer is that syntactic studies of cities as networks of space have, in recent years, brought to light a fundamental link between the form of cities and their functioning, one which affects our whole approach to the city: that the *configuration of the space network is, in and of itself, a primary shaper of the pattern of movement*. This is not simply a technical observation. In shaping movement, space also shapes the patterns of human *copresence*—and of course *coabsence*—that seem to be the key to our sense that good cities are human and social, as well as physical, things. This effect arises not from the properties of individual spaces, or even from their local connections, but from the whole configuration of the network at a nonlocal scale. The implication is that the large-scale architecture of the urban spatial network, which has been neglected for decades by *both research and practice,*

FIG. 1 Aerial view of part of west London.

matters much more than we thought to the life of the city and how it comes into existence.

The idea is, of course, not really new. Most designers believe that we can manipulate space to create emergent human patterns, although there are conflicting views on how this can and should be done. What is new is the idea that this is a *scientific proposition*. The idea does not feature significantly, for example, in most engineering-based movement models, where movement is seen as a matter of attraction: locations attract movement according to the "mass" of their attractions, such as the shopping floor area, and the space network is the means of getting there. The models work by analogy with a Newtonian physical system, and this is where the core idea of attraction comes from. As with planetary bodies, attraction is seen as proportionate to the combined "mass" of areas and inverse to some definition of distance. Such models can of course be made to work, but they can never be true theoretical models because attraction is not primary. The space network, by shaping movement, also shapes the pattern of attractors, since attractor activities like retail follow the patterns of movement already created by the network. So if we want a theoretical understanding of the city, we should not start with the distribution of attraction, since this is in good part an emergent product of the network. The shift to a network view of the city, as implied by space syntax, is then also a paradigm change. It puts the phenomena of the city into a different order.

Once we understand the relation between the network configuration and movement, we can begin to see how cities come to be as they are and how they work. In particular, we can begin to understand why and how cities, if they are allowed to, tend to self-organize into a *polycentric* pattern, by creating a network of linked centers and subcenters at all scales, from a couple of shops and a cafe to whole sub-cities, all set into a background of residential space. This is the nature of the organic city, which evolves over tens or hundreds of years to form the seamless web of busy and quiet places, with everything seeming to be in the right place. So what we are talking about here is a theory of the self-evolving city. A key element in this is that the process by which cities create themselves is about the *relation between scales*: that how local places arise in cities depends as much on how they are embedded in their larger-scale context as in their intrinsic properties.

The Architecture of the Network Shapes Movement

As the argument is founded on the link between space configuration and movement, the reader must, at the outset, be convinced that this is the case. First, we can show it is common sense. Consider the simple grid in figure 2a, with a main street, cross street, side streets, and backstreets. Imagine that all the streets are lined with houses, and people are moving between the houses by the most direct routes they can find: Several things are intuitively clear: more people will pass through the main street than the side streets or back streets;

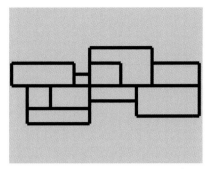

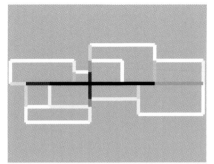

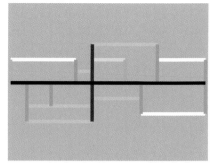

FIG. 2A A notional grid with a horizontal main street, cross street, and side and back streets.

FIG. 2B Notional grid: pattern of "integration" values, or the closeness of each line to all others, from dark for highest to light for lowest.

FIG. 2C Notional grid: pattern of "choice" values, or the degree to which each line lies on the simplest paths from each line to all others, from dark for highest to light for lowest.

more people will pass through the central bits of the main street than the peripheral bits. The main street is easier to get to than other streets—it is more accessible. The cross street will also get a good deal of movement—but more than the main street? It is hard to be sure. What is clear is that we intuitively expect the position of each street in the overall grid to affect both *to-* and *through-movement* patterns and flows. It is not a matter of psychology, but instead has to do with the way the grid is put together.

Now to- and through-movement are the two components of human movement. For every trip, we select a destination to go *to*, and a series of spaces to pass *through* on the way. Both obviously matter to how cities work. For example, over time we are likely to go to more near than far destinations, so if some locations are in some sense "nearer" to *all* locations within a certain radius than others, as in figure 2a, this gives these locations greater potential as destinations than simply by virtue of them having greater ease of accessibility. If we want to open a shop, for example, it would make more sense to put it on the main street than on one of the side streets. Similarly, if routes between all origin destination pairs pass through some spaces more than others, as is clearly the case, it will likewise be sensible to locate the shop in one of those spaces, though it may not always be intuitively obvious which these spaces are. The point is that these are objective properties of spatial layouts.

So if we can measure these properties, then we would know something very useful about grids: the *to-* and *through-movement* potentials of each space. In fact, in any network that can be represented as a graph of elements and relations, it is easy to calculate both the *closeness* of each element to all others, that is, the accessibility for *to-movement*, and the degree to which each element lies on paths *between* elements, that is, its potential for *through-movement*. In syntax, we call the closeness of each element to all others the *integration value*, and color them from dark, for high integration, to light for low, as in figure 2b, so we can see the different potentials of each street as a kind of pattern in the whole. The *betweenness* property, the propensity of spaces to lie on paths between pairs of elements, we call *choice* value, meaning how likely each space is to be chosen on paths from all elements to all others. We color them as

before from dark for high to light for low, as in figure 2c, so we can see the pattern. Traffic engineers are familiar with both of these measures, but they have never, to my knowledge, applied them to the street networks considered as geometric configurations in their own right—they never considered them architecturally.

But there is a concealed assumption in what we are saying: how people calculate distance. In figure 2a we have assumed that what matters is the least number of lines we must use to go from one line to another. We call this the *fewest turns* distance. Two decades have passed since space syntax first showed that simply by representing the urban grid as a network of the fewest and longest lines that would cover it, as we have in figure 2, and calculating integration and choice values for each line on the basis of the fewest turns, there would be something between a 60% and 80% agreement between the spatial values and the observed movement flows. Such "least line" maps have been the basis of a very large number of urban studies, and have been applied with success on a large number of real projects.[3]

But what if the angle of the turn also matters? And what about simple metric distance? Surely people simply try to minimize this in making spatial (as opposed to temporal) judgments about routes? In fact, evidence suggests that, although people judge short linear distances well—for example we can throw a missile so that its parabola leads it to hit a target—in more complex, nonlinear spaces, our notions of distance are severely compromised by such factors as the number and angle of turns.[4] To solve this problem, we have developed a major refinement of the space syntax technique. Starting from the *least line* map, we divide each line into its segments (between intersections) and represent the segments as the nodes of a graph with the intersections as links. We then assign *integration* and *choice* measures using different definitions of distance: *shortest path* (metric), *least angle change* (geometric), *fewest turns* (topological), and weightings to relations between each segment and all others, and we apply them at different radii from each segment, also defining radii for shortest paths, least angle change paths, and fewest turns paths. This yields a matrix of configurational measures, which we can use to see and explore how people actually move in urban grids.[5]

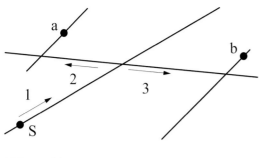

(a) line model

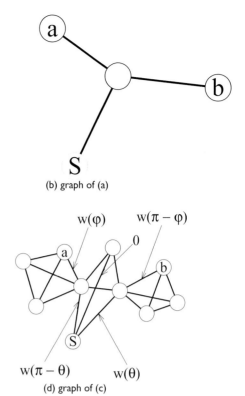

(b) graph of (a)

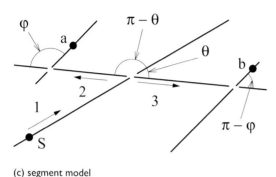

(c) segment model

(d) graph of (c)

FIG. 3 Street segment-based syntactic analysis.

It works very simply. With these techniques, we can make different analyses of the same urban grid, and then ask which analysis agrees best with the observed pattern of movement (figure 3). In a recent study of four different urban areas of London, the answer was unambiguous: *least angle* analysis is the best predictor of movement, followed closely by *fewest turns*, with metric *shortest path* analysis well back in third place. The only plausible interpretation of this result is that people do not navigate with a mental model of metric distances, but with a geometric and angular model of how the alignments of the grid are connected to each other. As cognitive scientists have long suspected, but been unable to prove, we navigate with an *architectural* model in our heads, not a simple account of metric distances. This has major implications for how we design cities.

The Shape of Cities

If the *shape* of space in the city shapes movement, then what is that shape like, and how does it come to be like that? First we can use the analysis to show how cities acquire a certain type of large-scale structure. For example, if we take a small town in France (figure 4), represent its street structure as a simple line map, analyze its integration pattern (in this case

FIG. 4 The plan of a town in the south of France and its integration map.

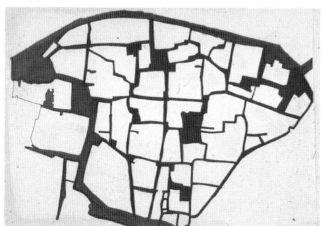

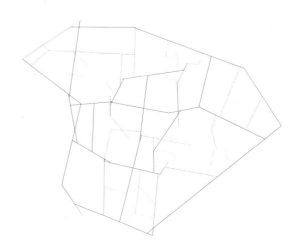

is going on in the social and economic life of the town.

While not universal, the deformed wheel pattern is found again and again in the large-scale structure of cities. Figure 5 shows it in the central areas of Atlanta. More remarkably, figure 6 shows it in a more complex form with multiple rims in the metropolitan area of Tokyo, a much larger system. We find the same underlying pattern in Venice, even without the canals, and in London we find it approximated at two levels: that of the metropolitan area as a whole, the largest system so far studied, as in figure 7, and at the level of the local area. This is why people think of London as a set of urban villages. Its "villages" are usually the hubs of local deformed wheels, with the spoke acting as strong linkages to the supergrid, providing locally the strong center-to-edge links that the large-scale deformed wheel provides for the city as a whole.

Why the deformed wheel? The answer is simple. It is a way of overcoming the natural tendency for centers to become segregated as the city grows around them by linking centers to edges, thereby allowing strangers access to the heart of the system and inhabitants access to the edges. This deep structure of the city is a *spatial* phenomenon, but one which is shaped by the city as a *social* thing.

The *integration* patterns we are finding, it will be recalled, measure the accessibility of street segments as destinations, and so, can be thought of as recording the *to-movement* structure of the city. If we look at the patterns formed by the *choice* measure, we are, of course, looking at the *through-movement* patterns, and we find these, while often overlapping with the deformed wheels, are rather different and always take the form of a network. Figure 8 shows on the left the *choice* structure of metropolitan Tokyo, and on the right that of London. The two measures can be used separately or in combination to examine the structures of different cities. More importantly, they can be applied at different scales by restricting the radius at which the measures are applied. For example, as Peponis suggests,[6] the choice measure at the level of the whole city often identifies the natural boundaries of areas, but by restricting the radius to which it is applied, the measure brings to light a much finer scale

using either line fewest turns analysis or segment least angle analysis), and color it up from dark to light in the usual way, we find the darker lines—the main "integrators" in syntax—form a striking pattern: a kind of *deformed wheel*. There is a hub, or at least an intersection, of integrated lines at or near the center, integrated spokes which link center to edge, and sometimes we also find integrated rims, or edge lines. The wheel forms the dominant pattern of public space, where most of the shops are, while the lighter areas in the interstices are predominantly residential, though, of course, with gradations between the two. So this means that the structure is not purely formal matter. It has to do with what

FIG. 6 The deformed wheel pattern in the metropolitan area of Tokyo.

FIG. 7 London within the M25 with its approximation of the deformed wheel.

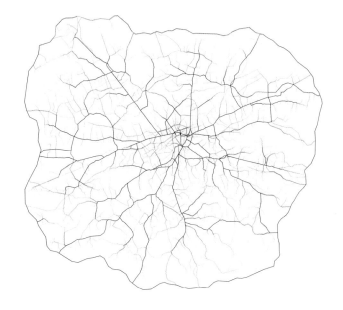

FIG. 8 The choice, or through-movement structures of Tokyo and London.

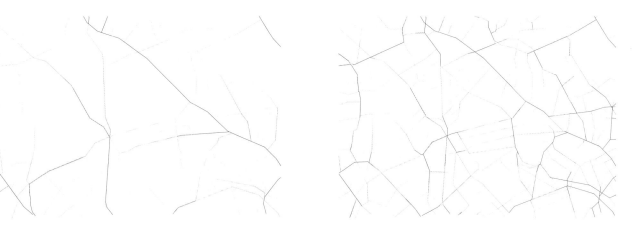

FIG. 9 Choice analysis of part of northwest London for trips of any length (left) and for trips up to 1.25 kilometers (right).

structure, reflecting the fact that shorter trips will tend to prioritize more local spaces. Figure 9 shows part of northwest London analyzed first (left) for trips of any length (hence longer trips, for the most part) and then (right) for trips up to 1.25 km (0.75 mi). The right figure picks out core spaces of several "urban villages."

The Dual City

But we have generated a puzzle. Cities are geometrically very different—a city in the Arab world, for example, will have little in common geometrically with a North American city—so how do they come up with similar large-scale patterns? Do cities, in spite of their differences, have certain commonalities in how they are generated? Our studies suggest that cities in general are created by a dual process, and each side of the duality exploits the relation between space and movement in a different way. On the one hand, there is a *public space* process, which is about bringing people together and therefore orders space in such a way as to maximize the reach of spaces and so maximize movement and co-presence. This process is largely driven by microeconomic factors, and tends to be invariant across cultures, as trade and exchange always work the same way. The public space process gives rise to the global structure of the city, which is usually some variant on the deformed wheel.

On the other hand, there is a *residential space* process, which uses space to restrain and structure movement in the image of a residential culture of some kind, seeking perhaps to structure relations between inhabitants and strangers, men and women, near and far kin, and so on. Domestic space and its environs are usually the richest

expression of culture in space, and, of course, they differ across regions, and even within regions. This is why we find such great differences in the fabric of the background space of the city—its geometry, connectivity, openness or "closedness"—in contrast to the tendency of global structures towards universality.

We can illustrate this dual process with singular clarity in a city with more than one culture (now unfortunately separated): Nicosia, on the island of Cyprus. In figure 10 (left) of Old Nicosia within the walls, top right is the Turkish quarter, and bottom left the Greek quarter. Their line geometry is different. In the Turkish quarter, lines are shorter, their angles of incidence have a different range, there is much less tendency for lines to pass through each other, and there is a much greater tendency for lines to form distinct local groups. The integration analysis (right) confirms the differences. Syntactically, the Turkish area is much less integrated than the Greek area. We can also show that it is less intelligible and has less synergy between scales[7] between the local and global aspects of space. Yet in spite of these strong cultural differences in the tissue of space, we still find Nicosia as a whole is held together by a clear, deformed wheel structure. The deformed wheel, as it were, overrides the cultural differences in the residential fabric of space, and creates the global system of spaces where cultures come together.

The Polycentric City

So how, against this dual background, do cities acquire their generic *polycentric* form, that is, the evolution of a network of linked, differently scaled centers, set against the background of residential space? In figure 11 we see the distribu-

FIG. 10 Old Nicosia within the walls (left) and integration analysis (right).

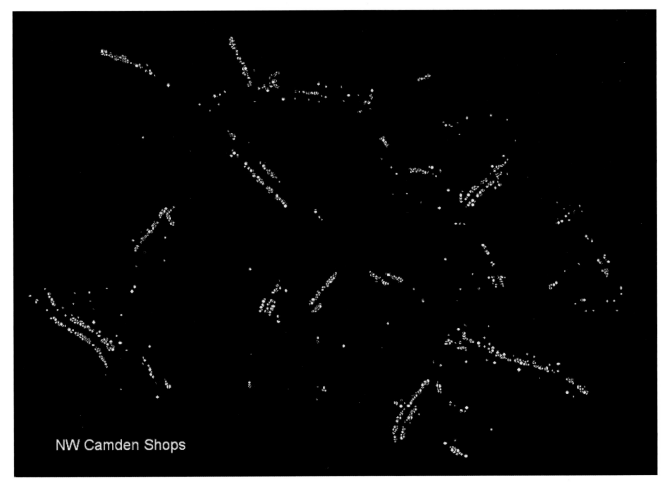

NW Camden Shops

FIG. 11 The distribution of shops in part of the area of northwest London shown in Figure 9.

tion of shops, restaurants, and bars in part of northwest London. We see centers at all scales, and with a certain geometric logic to their scaling and spacing. How does this happen? The process[8] is something like this:

• As the city grows through the accumulation of buildings and areas, a street network emerges which links it all together, and through its structure the emergent street network shapes a pattern of "natural movement," making some spaces higher in copresence than others.

• Movement-seeking land uses then migrate to movement-rich locations, while others, perhaps residential, tend to migrate to less movement-rich locations—if movement-seeking land uses locate in the wrong locations, or if something changes the network, then they probably don't succeed—so there is a selection mechanism in our evolutionary process.

• The presence of shops in locations that are already movement rich attract more movement, so there is a multiplier effect on the movement already there.

• This then attracts more—and more diverse—land uses, which seek to take advantage of the enriched copresence in the location.

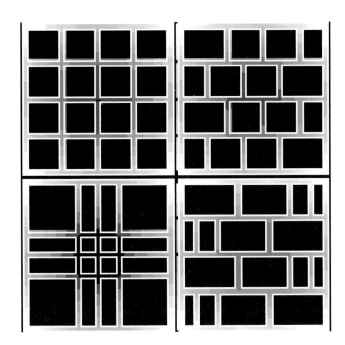

FIG. 12 Four grids in which the mean trip length from all points to all others is shown from dark (for least) to light (for most).

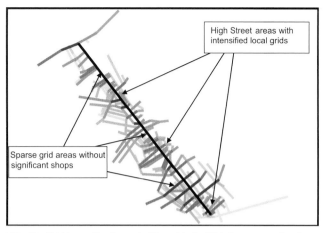

FIG. 13 Grid intensification coincides with the High Street areas in a London alignment.

High Street areas with intensified local grids

Sparse grid areas without significant shops

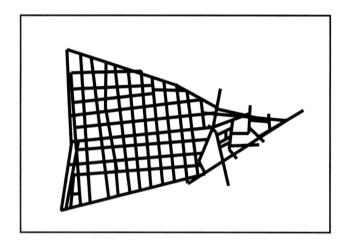

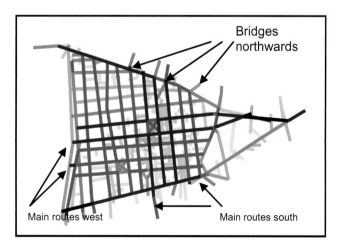

Bridges northwards

Main routes west

Main routes south

FIG. 14 The intensification of the original Spanish grid of Santiago within the area defined by the main routes in and out.

Virginia Highland 1872

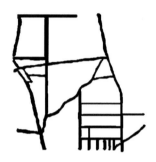

Virginia Highland 1893

Virginia Highland 1921

Virginia Highland 1993

FIG. 15 The historical evolution of a local center, the Virginia Highland, in Atlanta, Georgia, from 1872 to 1993, showing how global (the intersection of two main boulevards, Virginia and Highland) and local (the grid intensification around the intersection) factors combine to form the live center.

- This process will then stabilize at a certain level related to the original grid properties that generated the natural movement in the first place.
- But in other locations, again dependent on the strength of the original conditions, the growth of the center feeds back onto the structure of the grid—for example, to subdivide blocks to improve interaccessibility and increase the quantity and diversity of the "shopping surface." We call this process *grid intensification*.

Grid Intensification

Grid intensification can be both the cause and the effect of center formation, and, as either, it is of particular interest because, unlike the larger-scale processes, it is essentially a metric process. It is little appreciated that the placing and shaping of blocks can have critical effects on the length of trips from all points in a system to all others, a property we call *metric integration*. In figure 12, for example, we show four grids with the same land coverage and the same travelable distance in each case, with mean trip length from all points to all others shown from black for least to white for most.

The grid with small central blocks (bottom left) has a shorter mean trip length, and is therefore more trip efficient than the regular grid; this is a pervasive phenomenon in center formation in cities.[9] For example, if we take the alignment linking the center of London to its northwest edge (figure 13). Or consider the change over time of the original Spanish grid of Santiago, Chile (figure 14). The grid intensification by the construction of a system of arcades occurs within the region of the grid defined by the main connections north, south, and west, and little occurs outside this envelope. This illustrates how local and global factors interact in the creation of centers. We can see the same interaction between scales creating live local places even in American cities in the evolution over a century of Virginia Highland, in Atlanta, as in figure 15.

The Architecture of the City

This, then, is the reasoning behind the space syntax definition of the city as a *network of linked centers at different scales set into a background of residential space*. All cities seem to evolve toward some interpretation of this form if they are allowed to. One implication of this stands out above all others. The architecture of the urban grid—its geometry, angularity, and connectedness—which has been neglected for decades by both practice and research, is one of the primary sources of the differentiation between places—both busy and quiet, and often in close proximity—that is the defining feature of the self-organized city. The architecture of the urban grid as a whole, and even more so at the level where the local area links to the global structure, must be reclaimed by urban design.

Other principles can also be extracted to clarify the centrality and complexity of the role of space in urban design. First, the analysis makes it clear that space can be used generatively to create life in cities, and conservatively to support cultures, by engineering space to create *copresence* through *movement* to varying degrees in different kinds of areas. How cities balance these between the live network and the residential areas is one of the prime sources of the individuality of cities. Second, the relation between activity and space is not direct, but generic. It passes through the demands that different activities make on *movement* and *copresence*. This is why new patterns of activity can so often be absorbed into existing urban spaces. Third, and perhaps most importantly, for decades we have, through the influence of both traffic engineering and architectural preconceptions, thought of movement as being between places, thereby mentally separating movement from place. Here we have shown that movement, engineered by the grid, is intrinsic to place, to the point where it is probably the final arbiter of the character of place. We can no longer separate the issue of movement, in all its subtlety and grid dependency, from the creation of urban places.

Finally, it is clear that the art of place creation should interact with the emerging *science of space*, so that we can learn to design *with* the self-organizing principles of cities rather than against them. Intuition is a reasonable guide to the local properties of space, but at the level of interaction between local and global scales through which urban *place* happens, the art of urban design can and should call on the new science if it is to succeed in its aim of reinterpreting the concept for the twenty-first century. The techniques explained here, and other emerging techniques, are already being applied on a large number of projects by young companies[10] in many parts of the world, including the United Kingdom, Europe, Japan, and Australia, and also form the basis of a growing research field highlighted in a symposium held every two years. In the long run, both the art and the science will stand or fall together.

THREE URBANISMS

NEW, EVERYDAY, AND POST

DOUGLAS KELBAUGH

Without community we are doomed to insular, private worlds. As our society becomes more privatized and our culture more narcissistic, there is a greater need and desire to be part of something bigger than our individual selves. A shared history or hoped-for future may provide the sense of a greater whole for some members of society. For some people, religion may fulfill this psychological and social need. For others, it may be group recreation, team or spectator sports, or social organizations. For many people, however, belonging to a community is the highest expression and fulfillment of this need. Humans are social and cultural animals, and the desire to share our lives and to connect with others makes some form of community a *sine qua non* of sane existence. On the other hand, humans also have a fundamental urge to express themselves, individuate themselves psychologically and socially, compete, excel, and rise above the crowd. A community must therefore, nurture both a respect for group values and a tolerance for individuality, even eccentricity. This dialectic between community norms and the individual human spirit will always require societal adjustments and cultural inflections, as will the tension between a community's past and its future.

A true community must deal with the full range of human nature, including its own dark side. If it projects its own shortcomings and pathologies onto an outside enemy or stigmatized minority, it is not fully facing itself. Typically, the unity in community is bought at the price of identifying competitors and enemies, who are sure to return the favor. If this competition and hostility are an inevitable part of the human condition, the question arises as to what the most hospitable scale for social harmony and unity—and the least hospitable scale for hostility and enmity—could be. At what physical scale, and what social granularity, are justice and community best fostered in a given society or culture? Although these questions are probably unanswerable, some urbanists claim the walkable neighborhood of a half mile on each side is still the most effective size to engender physical community and build social capital. Others point out that the metropolitan region is now the most competitive unit in the global economy, and therefore, the optimum scale for governance, planning, and a sense of sociopolitical unity. Still others cling to the nation-state as the right scale for culture and political allegiance and unity.

Few of us would deny the value of a robust public realm, as well as the importance of mutual respect and tolerance. Many contemporary critics, however, question the notion of traditional community. They posit that communities of interest and of practice, notably ones enabled by modern transportation and electronic communications, have supplanted what used to be communities of propinquity and place, which they claim are slowly atrophying. It comes as no surprise that automobiles, airplanes, telecommunications, and computers have profoundly changed our lives for better and for worse, and will continue to do so. However, it is not evident that they have reduced our need for contiguous community. Indeed, being stuck in traffic, or an airport, or facing a computer screen all day with a telephone or iPod to your ear and a radio or television in the background increases the appetite for *place*—physical as opposed to virtual place. The habitual and addictive mix of instant communication and physical mobility have also changed our sense of *time*. The ubiquitous communications network has forced us to be "on" 24/7, whether we like it or not. Slow Food, Slow Cities, and Slow Trams are examples of countermovements that social and technology pundits like John Thackara contend are more than passing fads.

It is in this changing social and technological milieu that we design and build our physical environments. Contemporary architecture and urbanism have evolved in radically different ways to respond to these and other forces. Beyond the conventional "market urbanism" that is fast changing the face of American downtowns and suburbs, there are at least three self-conscious schools of urbanism: New Urbanism, Everyday Urbanism, and Post-urbanism. These three approaches represent the cutting edge of theoretical and professional activity in so-called Western architecture and urbanism. They are probably inevitable and necessary developments in the

FIG. 1A Denver's former Stapleton Airport is being converted into a large 4,700-acre New Urbanist community with 12,000 homes planned by Calthorpe Associates and developed by Forest City Enterprises, Inc.

FIG. 1B Mixed-use buildings at Stapleton designed in a background, but contemporary architectural style, are built to the sidewalk to define a continuous street wall, while placing residential units above retail shops—a traditional but still effective if elusive urban configuration.

evolution of cities. All three have their merits and demerits, but not in equal proportion. Because the built environment is arguably the biggest and longest-lived investment that a society makes, it behooves us to examine these three syndromes, their overlaps and oppositions, and their ramifications and outcomes.

New Urbanism

New Urbanism is both idealistic and pragmatic. It represents a peculiarly American mix of noble objectives and commercial means, high-striving and lofty in its communitarian objectives but practical in its methods. Unlike the other two urbanisms, it is an organized movement with the Congress for the New Urbanism (CNU) to promote and defend its tenets. Its charter aspires to almost utopian goals, more than its proponents have been able to achieve on the ground: to equitably mix people of different income, ethnicity, race, and age; to build public architecture and public space that make citizens feel they are part of, and proud of, a culture and community that adds up to more than the sum of its private worlds; to be a responsible ecological force; to weave a tighter urban fabric that mixes land of different uses and buildings of different architectural types within a well-connected network of streets and green spaces; to utilize regional public transit, revenue sharing, planning, and governance to better tie together the metropolitan area.

Countering the physical fragmentation, social polarization, and functional compartmentalization of the modern city, it attempts to better integrate physical and social environments. It maintains that there is a structural relationship between social behavior and physical form, although it recognizes that the connection has its limits, and can be subtle and elusive. It posits that good design can have a measurably positive effect on one's sense of place and community. The basic physical model is a compact, transit-friendly, walkable city with a hierarchy of private and public buildings and places that promote face-to-face social interaction and daily physical activity. It is not dense by European and Asian standards, but denser than conventional American sprawl (albeit marginally so in too many cases). The urban hierarchy runs the gamut from background housing and private yards to foreground civic and institutional buildings, with public squares and parks that are reminiscent of the City Beautiful tradition. And its urban centers are surrounded by open space and low-density housing that recalls the Garden City tradition. Its architecture is typically derivative in style, typology, and materials—to use a word of its own making, neo-traditional.

New Urbanists are committed to reversing sprawl, which they demonstrate wastes land, energy, and time. In particular, they resist single-use zoning, which has come to dominate development on the suburban fringe of cities in North America and elsewhere. They promote mixed-use zoning with low- and mid-rise buildings that form a continuous street wall, hard against the sidewalk, and that put offices and housing above retail shops. They seek more patient capital, i.e., investors who are in a project for the long haul. They want to reform contemporary financial and banking practices that encourage developers to build and quickly "flip" projects for profits. And they lament the way Wall Street has limited the architectural palette by only investing in a reduced number of standard "product" types. New Urbanism fights auto-dependency with Transit-Oriented Development (TOD) and Traditional Neighborhood Development (TND) on urban infill and suburban greenfield and grayfield sites. The "transect" has been more recently developed to order the cross-section of a town or city, with a gradient of six zones of gradually increasing density from the natural hinterlands to the urban core (figures 1a and 1b).

Everyday Urbanism

Everyday Urbanism is not as utopian as New Urbanism, nor is it as tidy or doctrinaire. It celebrates and builds on everyday, ordinary life and reality, with little pretense about the possibility of building a perfectible or ideal environment. Its proponents are open to and incorporate "the elements that remain elusive: ephemerality, cacophony, multiplicity, and simultaneity."[1] This openness to populist and grassroots informality makes Everyday Urbanism more conversational and bottom-up than inspirational and top-down. Unlike New Urbanism, it downplays the relationship between physical design and social behavior. For instance, it celebrates the way indigenous and migrant groups informally respond in resourceful and imaginative ways to their ad hoc conditions and marginal spaces. It admires and tries to help people adapt and improvise *in spite of* available physical design and planning. Appropriating space for informal commerce in parking and vacant lots, as well as private driveways and yards for garage sales, is urban design by default rather than by design. Vernacular and street architecture in vibrant, ethnic neighborhoods such as the barrios of Los Angeles (with public markets rather than chain stores and street murals rather than civic art) is championed.

Everyday Urbanism could be confused with conventional real estate development (or "ReUrbanism" if it is of sufficient quality and sophistication to deserve this more generous title recently coined by Robert Fishman). However, it is more intentional and democratic than the generic residential and commercial "product" that mainstream developers, bankers, and Wall Street have commodified and builders supply en masse to a market of anonymous consumers. As Chris Leinberger has pointed out, the bundling of diverse projects for Wall Street investors has reduced the number of residential and commercial building types that are regularly and easily financed to a much smaller number than in the past.[2] This sanctioning of diminished variety, coupled with a short-term investment mentality that is blind to financial returns beyond the first five to seven years, has architecturally dumbed down our built environment. Admirably, Everyday Urbanism tends to work below this financial system to empower disadvan-

FIG. 2 Parking lots, sidewalks, and vacant lots are temporarily but productively taken over by informal markets in Everyday Urbanism.

taged and disenfranchised people and communities by working in the gaps and on the margins (figure 2).

Post-urbanism

Post-urbanism, popular among many design professionals and academicians, tends to be heterotopian, provocative, and sensational. It is not a true movement or even a widely used term. Landscape Urbanism or Infrastructure Urbanism, which also tend to take a post-structuralist view of the world, are better known. Post-urbanism is difficult to characterize physically, but it favors disconnected, broken, fractal, or flowing forms. It often accepts an automobile and consumer-based urbanism. It argues that shared values or metanarratives are no longer possible in a world that is increasingly fragmented and composed of ghettoes of the "other" (e.g., the homeless, the poor, minorities) and mainstream zones of consumers, internet surfers, and free-range tourists. These liminal and exciting zones of taboo and fantasy, and these commercial zones of unfettered consumption, are viewed as liberating because they allow "for new forms of knowledge, new hybrid possibilities, new unpredictable forms of freedom."[3] It criticizes New Urbanist communities based on physical place and propinquity for being nostalgic, stultifying, and irrelevant in light of modern technology and telecommunications.

Post-urbanism attempts to impress an increasingly sophisticated consumer of the built environment with ever-wilder and more provocative architecture and urbanism. Examples are the Case Western Reserve Business School in Cleveland, the Experience Music Project in Seattle by Frank Gehry, and the former Guggenheim Museum in Las Vegas by Rem Koolhaas. Like modernism, its architectural language is usually abstract, with little reference to surrounding physical or historical context. It also continues the modernist project of shock tactics, no matter how modest the building site or program. It is sometimes difficult to know if it is neo-avant-garde or truly avant-garde—whether it employs shock for its own sake or whether the principal motive is to inspire genuine belief in the possibility of changing the status quo and resisting conventions and limits that are thought to be too predictable and restrictive. It's equally difficult to decide when it's innocently flirting with the media and the marketplace or complicit in spurious corporate branding and advertising.

Some Post-urbanists describe discordant insertions into the city as examples of open, democratic urbanism, despite the fact they tend to ignore or overpower local settings and sensibilities. Projects are usually physically self-contained, if not self-centered, seemingly with little faith in the work of others to complete the urban fabric, even the dynamic, fragmented one that they defend as authentic and appropriate to the zeitgeist. Signature buildings are more self-referential than contextual, and sprawling, auto-centric cities like

FIG. 3A The BMW plant by Zaha Hadid not only embodies but expresses the laminar flows of industrial assembly manufacturing processes. The Post-urbanist architecture is visually dynamic, with its stream forms frozen around existing buildings like solidified lava.

FIG. 3B Los Angeles, a city not known for an intense, walkable downtown, is attempting to establish a vibrant 24/7 mixed-use district with almost 2,500 residential units on Grand Avenue. Frank Gehry, who designed the popular Disney Concert Hall across this major street, has proposed an informal mix of low- and high-rise buildings (prejumbled and fractured as if by an earthquake), a mixed-use project that is pedestrian-oriented if not street-oriented.

Atlanta, Houston, and Las Vegas are held up as models (although the very idea of a standard model might be rejected outright by some Post-urbanists). The orderliness and tidiness of New Urbanism are considered an attempted revival of a past that never existed, and Post-urbanists might applaud Everyday Urbanism for being less uniform, scenographic, and predictable than New Urbanism.

Sensibilities and Methodologies

The differences in these three architectures and urbanisms probably start with the designers' aesthetic *sensibilities*, which arguably run deeper than design *values*, which are more slowly inculcated and largely solidified in architecture school (figures 3a and 3b). Sensibilities, including phobias and philias, supposedly arise from one's early experiences and deep-seated memories (such as parental behavior, toilet training, and childhood play). If so, this psychological foundation is less conscious and harder to change than acquired knowledge, learned values, and taste. How messy and complex a world designers can tolerate is therefore more hardwired than how much social injustice bothers them. Where designers fit on the spectrum of the three urbanisms may be revealed by where they are most comfortable and prefer to spend their time: for instance, around the grand monuments and leafy boulevards of nineteenth-century Paris, in the narrow medieval streets and buildings of its Marais district, or in the modernist high-rise complex of La Defense. (They may, in

fact, enjoy all of these places, depending on mood, time of day, etc., but a single designer's portfolio rarely, if ever, spans this architectural and urban range.) Social and ethical values, of course, temper these visceral design sensibilities, but the gut often prevails.

These urbanisms also utilize different methodologies. New Urbanism is the most precedent-based (figure 4a). It tries to learn and extrapolate from enduring architectural types, as well as historical examples and traditions as they intersect contemporary environmental, technological, social, and economic practices. It is the most normative, often drafting prescriptive, form-based codes rather than proscriptive, function-based zoning (e.g., it prefers the "build-to line" of form-based codes to the "set-back line" of conventional zoning). Coherence, legibility, and human scale in architecture and urbanism are highly valued, and a diversity of uses and users is sought, if not often achieved on the ground. As has been noted, New Urbanism is also realistic and pragmatic in the sense that it works with, while also trying to reform, standard development and financing mechanisms. Politically savvy, it has built coalitions with other movements, such as Smart Growth, and other organizations, such as the Urban Land Institute (which has given it clout in the post-Katrina planning of the Gulf Coast).

New Urbanists believe that a coherent hierarchy of architectural types, street types, and public spaces—with a clear distinction between foreground and background buildings—can best sort out and make legible the complex mixture of land uses and building functions that cities had always possessed until post–World War II zoning separated them. As American cities move back to mixed-use urbanism, with its walkability and chance encounters—*the one tendency that everyone from Léon Krier to Rem Koolhaas embraces*—architectural type becomes more effective than zoning as an ordering device (figure 4b). Typology can promote a richer and more understandable urban order than zoning, which singles out and isolates land uses as if it is unable to juggle more than one variable at a time. And it can dignify the many ordinary buildings that are not vying with honorific buildings for the center of attention.

Everyday Urbanism is the most populist of the three urbanisms, with the designer seen as an empirical student of the common and popular rather than the ideal and elite. It harkens back to and grows out of the community design movement of the 1970s, which has stubbornly survived and recently reinvigorated itself. The design professional has fewer conceits and is more of a participant than leader in the public dialogue. Citizen participation is the most open-ended and democratic of the three. It is less normative and doctrinaire than New Urbanism, because it is more about celebrating and capitalizing on existing, everyday conditions, such as public markets and street life, than overturning them and starting over with a different model. It is also the most modest, incremental, and compassionate of the paradigms, with the strongest commitment to social and economic justice. However, if the New Urbanist romanticizes a nostalgic past, the Everyday Urbanist overestimates the mythic aspect of the ordinary and commonplace.

Post-urbanism accepts and expresses the techno-flow of a global world, both real and virtual. It is experimental rather than normative, and often relishes overturning design guidelines and zoning codes, as well as subverting common expectations. Post-urbanists don't engage the public as directly in open dialogue, perhaps because they feel the traditional

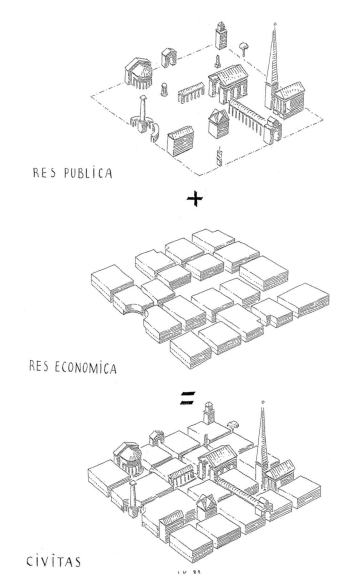

RES PUBLICA

+

RES ECONOMICA

=

CIVITAS

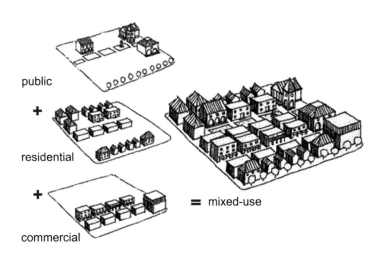

public

+

residential

+

commercial

= mixed-use

FIG. 4A Léon Krier's mixed-use diagram illustrates the clarity of a typological urbanism, albeit in a neoclassical idiom, with elaborate foreground and simple background buildings. The former are reserved for civic and institutional uses and the latter for residential and commercial uses, which typically make up 80% of the urban fabric. With the network of small blocks of low-rise, street-oriented structures, New Urbanism strives to be more human-scaled and pedestrian-friendly than the single-use super-blocks of Post Urbanism or the parking lots of Everyday Urbanism.

FIG. 4B This American adaptation of Krier's diagram illustrates the same point less dramatically, with less formal architecture for more modest public foreground buildings and with background residential and commercial buildings that are more free-standing and varied architecturally.

"polis" is increasingly obsolete and its civic institutions too calcified to promote new possibilities. They are usually the most talented and celebrated designers, who are increasingly treated by the media as solo artists or lone geniuses despite the fact a large multidisciplinary team is needed to develop and execute the work. (There may be nothing wrong per se with the media turning individual architects into stars—it's not unprecedented and it raises the profession's public confidence and profile—but it must be asked whether excessive celebrity has become a corrupting influence on the practice of architecture.)

The quintessential Post-urbanist is Rem Koolhaas, the vanguard Dutch designer and brilliant provocateur. He has proclaimed, perhaps as a trope, that urbanism is dead, and that there is no longer any hope of achieving urban coherence or unity. Post-urbanist form is rigorously consistent within its own architectural vocabulary and syntax (algorithm may be a more apt and descriptive term). Externally, however, the designs are formally indifferent to—or at odds with—their surroundings, and demonstrate little interest in making a consistent or coherent urban fabric; it's as if the design is surrounded by an invisible envelope, with extreme attention to formal consistency within it, and almost zero attention to formal issues outside of it. Nonetheless, a virtuoso project like Gehry's Disney Hall in Los Angeles, which is a freestanding sculptural object, successfully counterpoints its existing context of modernist buildings.

Post-urbanist projects tend to be large, denatured, deracinated, esoteric, and confrontational with their contexts. Like early modernist buildings, they want to make an entirely new start on architecture and the city. Some are a spatial and formal tour de force and powerful foreground architecture that enriches the city. (We academics forget just how hard it is to consistently produce good buildings, especially given the increased velocity of the process and the economic pressures from clients.) If the New Urbanist tends to hold too high the best practices of the past and the Everyday Urbanist overrates a prosaic present, the Post-urbanist is overcommitted to an endlessly exciting and audacious future.

Outcomes

The three paradigms lead to very different physical outcomes. New Urbanism, with its Latinate clarity and order, achieves the most aesthetic unity and coherent community, while it also mixes different uses at a human scale in familiar architectural types and styles. However, its architectural harmony is usually achieved with historical styles that lack tectonic integrity. This pastiche is more understandable for the developer-built speculative housing that must sell in the marketplace, but is inexcusable for the nonresidential buildings and especially the public structures, which are typically allowed to break the design code. Its connective grids of pedestrian- and traffic-calmed streets look better from the ground than from the air, where they can look formulaic and generic. (Ironically, the curvy cul-de-sacs of suburbia look elegant from the air, in spite of their shortcomings on the ground.)

Everyday Urbanism, which is the least driven by design, has trouble achieving as much aesthetic coherence—day or night, micro or macro. But it is egalitarian and lively on the street. Post-urbanist site plans look the most exciting, with their laser-like vectors, fractal geometries, and sweeping arcs and flows of circulatory systems. However, they are often overscaled and empty of pedestrians. Tourists in rental cars experiencing the architecture and urbanism through their windshields may be a better-served audience than residents for whom there is less human-scale nuance and architectural detail to reveal itself over the years. Local citizens become tourists in their own city, just as tourists become citizens of the world.

Everyday Urbanism may make the most sense in developing countries where global cities are mushrooming with informal squatter settlements that defy government control and planning, and where the underclass simply wants a stake in the economic system and the city. But it doesn't make much sense in the cities of Europe, where a wealthier citizenry has the luxury of punctuating a dense urban fabric with modernist commercial and institutional buildings as counterpoint to the traditional architecture. The conventional masonry fabric sets off light, crystalline buildings better than the more open fabric and the glass curtain-wall buildings of North American cities. Because North American cities lack the thick fabric of European cities, and are typically underprogrammed and sometimes almost empty, New Urbanist infill usually makes the most sense.

In an ecology of cities, it might be said that development in the third world (and in poor American neighborhoods) represents early successional growth, the beginnings of a forest. Middle-aged North American cities are thickening and diversifying their stand of midsuccessional growth with mixed-use infill development in their downtowns and first-ring suburbs. The gridded American city is like a tree plantation or orchard with its single species in a Cartesian layout that, like single-use zoning, is being replaced by more diverse ecologies. European cities are akin to late successional or climax forests, with their historic centers like mature beech forests, where there is little room for growth except in clearings carefully made for new, more exotic plantings.

Everyday Urbanism is too often an urbanism of default rather than design. It is a bottom-up approach that is "too much bottom, not enough up," to use Michael Speaks' words.[4] Post-urbanism is too often an urbanism of trophy buildings, of which a city needs, and can absorb, only so many. Americans can build a more physically ordered and architecturally ambitious commons than Everyday Urbanism offers, and a more humane commons than Post-urbanism promises. Although Europe may delight in avant-garde Post-urbanist design and the developing world may embrace informal Everyday Urbanism, the typical American metropolis would benefit most from New Urbanism at this point in its evolution. (American cities need some rules to prove the exceptions, rather than exceptions to prove the rule.) It represents the responsible middle path, less glamorous than Post-urbanism and more ambitious than Everyday Urbanism.

New Urbanism is not an absolute or ultimate fix. Like all movements, it will ossify and lose its meaning and value as it runs the inevitable historical course from archetype to type to stereotype. However, it is urbanistically and environmentally superior to what now passes for conventional or "market" brownfield, grayfield, and greenfield development in America today. A big question is whether its exemplary urban principles will be realized in more contemporary architecture, especially public and institutional buildings. Another big question is whether New Urbanism is flexible enough to tap into and harness new economic forces in the emergent global economy, rather than rely on formal templates, regulatory codes, and moral mandates. As Jane Jacobs points out in *Dark Age Ahead*, sprawl will only densify and diversify if underlying economic and social forces make it a natural, voluntary, and sustainable process.

Many Difficult Questions

Traditional notions of the city and of community and its pubic realm are forever being challenged and replaced by new design ideologies and new technologies. The quickening pace of change is as disorienting as it is exhilarating. As the world turns faster, we need to step back more frequently to examine what drives us as designers. Are architects too enthralled by the invention of form and change for its own sake, rather than by innovation that solves real problems? (Is art and design being confused and conflated with technology, where progress does depend on perpetual innovation?) Is the mandate for originality—or worse, for novelty—devaluing architecture and urbanism? On the other hand, is the natural human desire to question and experiment being squelched by neotraditional design attitudes? Could New Urbanism be less sentimental in its architectural language and less restrained in its urban form and still sell in the market? Does Everyday Urbanism underestimate the value and pleasure that architectural and urban form can add to our lives? Is Post-urbanism turning downtowns into spaces of infotainment and spectacle? Are New Urbanist public realms as authentic and egalitarian as claimed? And, like Post-urbanism, is it party to the neoconservative love affair with privatization and its blind embrace of the market? Which of these urban paradigms makes sense—when, where, and why?

As a society, there are equally large urban questions and challenges. Can we reduce the amount of land, energy, and time that is wasted in suburban sprawl? Can we make our lifestyles of automobile and air travel sufficiently sustainable to stop global warming? More specifically, can we reduce the structural need in contemporary lifestyles to move further, faster, and more frequently, or are we already so invested in our low-density pattern of infrastructure and settlement that it has reached the point of no return? Can we rebuild our hollowed-out central cities? Can regional cooperation emerge to unify our polarized metropolitan areas? Are we too seduced by personal pleasures and private wealth to cultivate a truly democratic public realm that challenges us to rub shoulders with people from all walks of life? Can the human spirit and imagination better align themselves with the planetary supply of natural resources and the carrying capacity of our biosphere? Can we significantly reduce global poverty and inequities? Or will technology, the market, and the media simply push and pull us when and where they want? These are questions that urbanism must address and help answer.

URBAN RENAISSANCE, URBAN VILLAGES, SMART GROWTH

FIND THE DIFFERENCES

PETER HALL

Recent years have seen a constant two-way flow of planners, and planning ideas, across the Atlantic. Urban villages were invented in England, by planners close to Prince Charles, and crossed the water to crossbreed with American notions, producing the New Urbanism. Smart growth became an American mantra, at least on the east and west coasts, but the basic idea was one familiar to European, especially British or Swedish, land use planning. The British Urban Task Force report in 1999, reflected this approach but blended concepts from New Urbanism into it. New Urbanism arrived most definitively on the European stage in 2005, when it became the major theme of the United Kingdom Urban Summit. Every planner and every plan repeats the same mantra: compact urban places, designed for walking and cycling and public transport; densities to support that objective; mixed uses, especially in and around town centers; a return to traditional urban designs with sidewalks and street blocks.

And yet, analyzing the plans and their outcomes more deeply, there are differences. The New Urbanist designs are very often just that: architectural design concepts, often of a high quality, but divorced from wider planning contexts. The critical needs are densities to ensure shops within walking distance and good access to transit: what the Californian New Urbanist Peter Calthorpe calls TODs (Transit-Oriented Developments), and Michael Bernick and Robert Cervero call transit villages.[1] But developments like Seaside or Celebration in Florida, Kentlands in Maryland (outside Washington, DC) (figure 3), or Laguna West in California (figure 1) tend to be isolated from any wide metropolitan context; they are either self-contained and isolated settlements, or outer suburbs lacking any coherent connection by public transport to wider metropolitan employment or service opportunities. Just a few developments, like Peter Calthorpe's The Crossings at Mountain View in Silicon Valley (figure 2) or his much larger master plan for the old Stapleton Airport site in Denver, Colorado, consciously address these wider issues. Furthermore, densities in many of these developments remain generally lower than would be necessary to support good transit service—certainly, much lower than their European equivalents.

Smart growth tries to address these limitations by introducing negative growth controls on the European model, such as the Portland, Oregon Urban Growth Boundary. But there are arguments about its effectiveness. A related device is the Urban Service Boundary (USB), which restricts extensions of infrastructure like water or sewer service, as in Sacramento, California, and the entire state of Maryland. Variants of this have been adopted in Florida and New Jersey.

An important exception, it could be argued, is the recent trend in both North America and Europe for apartment construction in and around city centers, catering to a new market of singles and childless couples who seek an almost antisuburban lifestyle. As exemplified in the centers of Manchester and Leeds in England, Philadelphia or Chicago in the United States, Vancouver in Canada, and Pasadena in Southern California, these aim to provide a deliberately urban ambience based on access to traditional shopping centers (now relabeled "Lifestyle Centers"), cultural facilities, restaurants, bars, and gyms; invariably they are supported by—and reciprocally help to support—mixed-use zoning, form-based codes to promote New Urbanist designs, and a high-quality transit service.[2] But these deliberately target niche markets, and though they form a significant element in the regeneration of many cities, there is some emerging evidence that their occupants do not stay in them very long before moving out in search of more conventional, family-oriented housing (figures 4 and 5).

Conversely, the general emphasis in northern Europe on tightly controlled urban development, invariably supported by existing or planned transport infrastructure, has no real parallel in North America. Though North American cities have also invested, especially in light rail, this does not seem to have had any evident effect on patterns of planned urban growth. It is perhaps significant that in Edmonton, Alberta, a Canadian city that has invested more generously than is usual in light rail, a new extension is being planned that skirts new low-density suburbs without attempting directly to exploit the potential market they offer. The same could be found in many other similar cases over the last decade; there is a lack of integration.

No greater contrast could be found than with the new transit-based developments in the neighboring cities of Strasbourg in France and Freiburg in Germany, to name only two examples. Furthermore, almost without exception the European examples are developed at higher densities than the American ones—sometimes very much higher—and sometimes with a high proportion of apartments. In England, the archetype of suburban nations, planning authorities have accepted a government "White Paper" recommendation for a minimum average density of new developments of thirty dwellings per hectare (twelve houses per acre): around four times or more than the average recent American suburban development, which often has more garage floor space than the total American home area of sixty years ago.[3] Local authorities do this because in Britain the NIMBY (not in my backyard) principle looms large: countryside dwellers are fiercely opposed to any new development that might spoil their view or introduce unacceptable neighbors.

Behind these differences, of course, lies a wealth of historical influence. Europe offers a whole host of such different influences, going back as far as a century: the original English garden cities as advocated by Ebenezer Howard, and their realization as the new towns after World War II; their equivalents in Germany, France, and Sweden, which commonly (with a few early exceptions) were garden suburbs or satellites rather than true garden cities on the Howard model; the Corbusian model of high-rise blocks in a parkland setting, which became so pervasive (and so degraded) in the great urban renewal schemes of the 1960s; and the transit-based satellite towns as developed around Stockholm in the 1950s and (on a far larger scale) around Paris in the 1960s. All these continued to have an influence, often a very direct influence, on actual urban developments, years or even decades after they were first formulated—for good and, not infrequently, for ill.

What is relatively new is the opportunity for large-scale urban regeneration in so many cities, both in North America and Europe, as a result of wholesale deindustrialization and parallel changes—the closure of urban docks and railway freight yards—in the 1980s and 1990s, as well as the need in some cases to rectify the mistakes made in an earlier wave of rebuilding thirty years before. This has led to the creation of new urban quarters, often in inner districts close to city centers, where the ideas of the urban village, or New Urbanism, have come into play. But even here, it can be argued that some of the key influences have been far from entirely new. Often, the resulting urban forms—traditional apartment blocks on traditional streets—bear a close relationship to very traditional ones, ranging from nineteenth-century rebuilding by pioneers like Cerdà in Barcelona or Haussmann in Paris to early twentieth-century schemes like that of Berlage in Amsterdam. And the ideas of Jane Jacobs, who in 1961 advocated a return to such traditional forms, have proved extremely persuasive: as frequent commentaries suggest, they represent an attack on the entire modernist idiom that dominated urban design from the 1920s to the 1970s.

FIG. 1 Laguna West, California

FIG. 2 The Crossings, Mountain Valley, California

FIG. 3 Kentlands, Maryland

This is to speak of changing fashions in architectural urban form: in particular, the counterattack, which Jacobs led, on Corbusier's ideas of ending the tyranny of the corridor street. But the location of the new developments, though it may have been contingent on external circumstances, was significant. They happened in parts of the city that either had an existing infrastructure of public transport, or could fairly easily have such an infrastructure injected (London's Docklands, the Kop van Zuid in Rotterdam, Tolbiac in Paris). This, plus the fact that the land was accessible and potentially

FIG. 4 Java Island, Amsterdam, Netherlands

valuable, meant that higher densities were a logical and accepted consequence. Add to this the fact of a new niche market for apartments arising from sociodemographic change—the growth of huge student colonies around the expanding urban universities, the parallel development of dual-career households, and the resultant pattern of delayed childbearing (or even no childbearing at all), the reaction against suburban lifestyles on the part of so many who had experienced a suburban childhood—and it was perfectly logical that these quarters should become the location of the new urban lifestyles.

As already noted, the phenomenon was fairly universal because the motives were the same: it could be observed as much in Chicago as in Cologne, in Sydney as in Stuttgart. But there was a key difference: no part of any European city had ever seen such catastrophic decay and abandonment as was found on the south side of Chicago or the north side of Philadelphia. As a result, an urban renaissance was easier to forge in Europe—or in Australia, where paradoxically the suburbs, or more precisely some outer suburbs, had long been viewed as unfashionable in comparison with inner-city

FIG. 5 Millennium Village, Greenwich, England

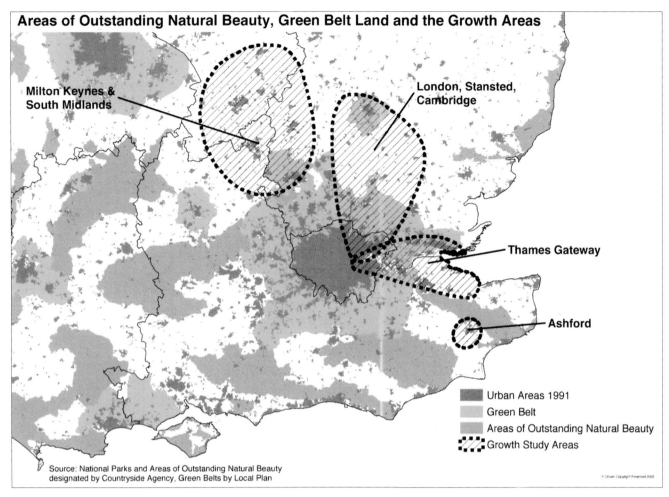

Areas of Outstanding Natural Beauty, Green Belt Land and the Growth Areas

Milton Keynes & South Midlands

London, Stansted, Cambridge

Thames Gateway

Ashford

Urban Areas 1991
Green Belt
Areas of Outstanding Natural Beauty
Growth Study Areas

Source: National Parks and Areas of Outstanding Natural Beauty designated by Countryside Agency, Green Belts by Local Plan

© Crown Copyright Reserved 2002

FIG. 6 Sustainable Communities diagram

nineteenth-century suburbs like Paddington in Sydney or Carlton in Melbourne.

The critical question now is whether, out of these very different initiatives, a new urban form is truly being born—or is capable of being born. Such a form would be a hybrid: it would take the best urban design features of the American New Urbanism and transplant them into new suburban locations which would cater to the emerging demand for family-friendly housing, consequent to the aging of the inner-city apartment generation and their need for space in which to rear children, in communities that offer sustainable access to local facilities on foot and to citywide jobs and services by good public transport. There are emerging signs of this in Europe, particularly the designs for new developments in the United Kingdom government's Sustainable Communities strategy, which takes the form of urban extensions along high-speed rail extensions with feeder bus services: Ingress Park in the Thames Gateway, close to the new Ebbsfleet train

station and connected to it by the new Fastrack busway system; Northstowe new town on the planned Cambridgeshire busway linked to a new train station on the edge of Cambridge City; and major new extensions like Oakgrove in Milton Keynes and Upton in Northampton, within easy bus rides of city-center stations (figure 6).

These, and others to follow, offer real promise that we can return to a previous age of sustainable, public-transit-based suburbs. But they do demand a special relationship between the private sector, which will build them, and the public sector, which will have to help fund the necessary infrastructure—almost certainly through some way of capturing the resultant rise in value for the community. There are challenges here for planners at every scale of planning, from the strategic to the local, and in every kind of specialization, from architectural to transport engineering to financial. The question is whether we can find or train all these talents in time to meet the scale of these challenges.

SETTLEMENTS OF THE FUTURE

LÉON KRIER

1

Today we can fairly safely affirm that the city of the future, or more correctly, the cities of the future, will not conform to a single and unified vision of whatever kind.

2

There exist universal principles to build good cities and villages. They transcend ages, climates, and continents. They are essentially anthropological principles, related to the habitual capacities of the human skeleton, body, and mind. Settlements must be able to function by muscular pedestrian motion horizontally (surface limitation) and vertically (limited number of floors):

- streets and squares;
- cities, villages, and urban quarters;
- development programs and plots;
- building methods and architecture—of a certain type, size, character, aesthetic, density, and functional complexity—are the critical axioms of urbanism. They are not to be confounded with the axioms of suburbanism.

The principles of traditional architecture and urbanism are not merely historical phenomena; they cannot, therefore, simply be declared outdated. They are practical and aesthetic responses to practical problems of settling and building. They are as timeless as the principles of musical harmony, language, science, gastronomy. Modernism's philosophic fallacy lies in the infantile ambition to replace these fundamental principles in their entirety. Those architects who claim today to be inventing the architecture and urbanism of the twenty-first century are clearly even more foolish than the masters of historic "modernism." Modernism can no longer proclaim itself, against worldwide evidence, to be the sole legitimate representative and embodiment of modernity. Modernity and modernism are clearly distinct phenomena *and must not* be confused or amalgamated. Modernism is, like so many -isms, born out of an excessive, possibly pathological desire for modernity. Like all forms of fundamental-

ism, it is reductive and tyrannical in its essence. If modernism wants to become a constructive part of the modern democratic worlds, it has to learn, at long last, that democracy is based on *tolerance* and *plurality*. That democratic tolerance, also in matters of architecture and urbanism, is indeed based on a constitutionally founded reciprocity. Short of this change of attitude, modernism will become an item of outdated twenty-first-century ideology.

3

Urban space is a void—a structural and structuring void; it has a hierarchy, it has dimensions and character, it cannot be just a leftover between haphazard building operations. Too much of it is a waste, a false luxury; too little of it is a false economy. All buildings have a public facade, acting positively or negatively on public space, enriching or impoverishing it. Streets, squares, and their numerous declinations are the optimum forms of collective space. Neither public nor private enterprise produces a robust public space naturally, as a mere byproduct of their activities. Public space and the public realm in general—their form, aesthetic quality, and socializing power—are never a result of accident, but are instead the result of a civilizing vision and intentional will.

It is not age, but rather the genetic capacities of its founding principles that ensure the quality of public space. Even one thousand years of suburban expansions will never parallel the civilizing power of urban foundations.

Urban centers are not called historic, because of their age, but because of the maturity and structuring power of their organizing principles. These principles are transcendent and timeless—they are known to us; we can, if we so wish, build urban centers that will instantly have the qualities of so-called historic centers.

Today there also exist, in all modern societies, public and private buildings, sacred and profane buildings, buildings for assemblies or for single individuals, for rest and industry, for music and silence, for honoring or punishing, for hiding or displaying, for production or consumption, for commercial

Mature CITY

Mature CITY

Organic EXPANSION through DUPLICATION

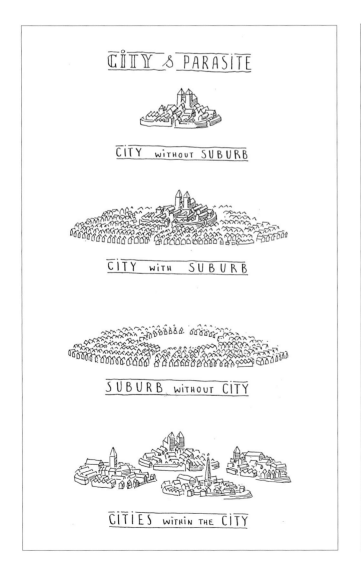

CITY & PARASITE

CITY without SUBURB

CITY with SUBURB

SUBURB without CITY

CITIES within the CITY

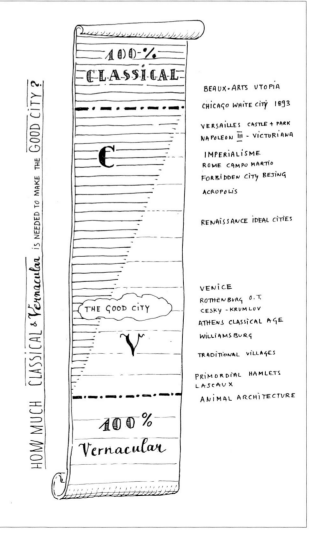

HOW MUCH CLASSICAL & Vernacular IS NEEDED TO MAKE THE GOOD CITY?

100 % CLASSICAL

C

THE GOOD CITY

V

100 % Vernacular

BEAUX-ARTS UTOPIA

CHICAGO WHITE CITY 1893

VERSAILLES CASTLE + PARK
NAPOLEON III - VICTORIANA

IMPERIALISME
ROME CAMPO MARTIO
FORBIDDEN CITY BEJING
ACROPOLIS

RENAISSANCE IDEAL CITIES

VENICE
ROTHENBURG O.T.
CESKY - KRUMLOV
ATHENS CLASSICAL AGE
WILLIAMSBURG

TRADITIONAL VILLAGES

PRIMORDIAL HAMLETS
LASCAUX

ANIMAL ARCHITECTURE

A FUNCTIONAL **ZONE**
admits
*one single quality (function) of a City
at the exclusion of all others*

EXCLUSIVE

All that is not specifically obligatory is strictly forbidden

AN URBAN **QUARTER**
CONtains and PROmotes
all the Qualities of a
CITY

IN - CLUSIVE

*All is Permitted & Promoted
that is not strictly forbidden*

CORRECT ZONING OF LARGE EMPLOYMENT

DISPERSAL

MISTAKEN ZONING OF LARGE EMPLOYMENT

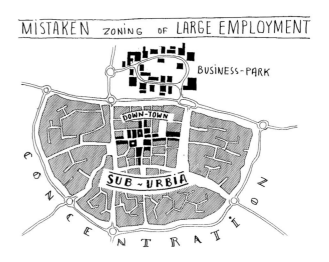

MISTAKEN ZONING OF LARGE EMPLOYMENT

BUSINESS-PARK

DOWN-TOWN

SUB-URBIA

CONCENTRATION

and institutional purposes, for defense and for war. Truly, the scaleless uniformity, aesthetic poverty, and general vulgarity of contemporary settlements are not due to a reduced social intercourse, but to a global metaphysical crisis. The exponential growth of industrial activities and power, brought about by the generalized use of fossil fuels, may indeed be the prime cause of an all-encompassing hubris.

Functional zoning is the instrument of this mental and environmental catastrophe. A deconstructional operation, which under the guise of planning literally destructures our

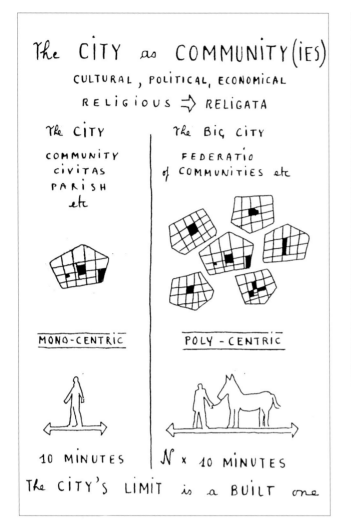

The CITY as COMMUNITY(IES)

CULTURAL, POLITICAL, ECONOMICAL
RELIGIOUS ⇒ RELIGATA

The CITY

COMMUNITY
CIVITAS
PARISH
etc

The BIG CITY

FEDERATIO
of COMMUNITIES etc

MONO-CENTRIC   POLY-CENTRIC

10 MINUTES   N x 10 MINUTES

The CITY'S LIMIT is a BUILT one

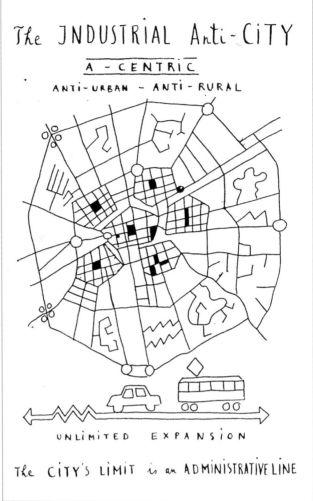

The INDUSTRIAL Anti-CITY

A-CENTRIC
ANTI-URBAN - ANTI-RURAL

UNLIMITED EXPANSION

The CITY'S LIMIT is an ADMINISTRATIVE LINE

society's and the planet's future, ensures the maximum wastage of land, time, and energies in everyday social performances. It also leads to a radical semantic deconstruction of urbanism and architecture—in short, to suburbanism and modernism. Horizontal and vertical sprawl, the futureless, monocord overexpansion and poorly chosen location of cities, their hyper-scaled, single-use buildings and zones—in the form of skyscrapers, landscaped strip malls, and residential ghettoes—are the dinosaurs of an ending fossil-fuel-based age. They represent vertical and horizontal forms of overdevelopment, of logistic overextension, of runaway entropy; they are asocial, unecological, and attractive only from an Olympian distance.

Traditional urban design and architecture instead allow for the articulation and organization of contrasting social activities into coherent, meaningful, and ecological organisms. They become second nature, without explanations and justifications; their techniques transcend time and space, and are universal constituents of all enduring civilizations.

4

The science and art of building cities, on the one hand, and the science and art of building suburbs, on the other, are fully known to us. Opting for one or the other is not a matter of historic fate, but rather one of cultural and political choice. There exist no valid excuses of any kind—neither social, economic, political, cultural, psychological, religious, historical, nor simply human—for building suburbs, spoiling both cities and land.

Building traditional cities is a responsible, ecological form of economic development; building suburbs is a corrupt form of economic development. Overpopulation, suburbanism, and industrialism are epiphenomena of the fossil-fuel age. With the decline of fossil fuel availability our notions of economic growth—and hence of the planet's carrying capacity—will change radically, as J. H. Kunstler demonstrates in "The Long Emergency," and we will have to return to traditional forms of settlement, agriculture, and building whether we like it or not. The notions of sustainability will turn from being political facts to principles of existential necessity.

5

It is not history and age, but rather structure, ideas, and ecology that confer quality on an urban context. We are not interested in historic centers and architecture because of their age and history, but because of their actuality and their relevance,

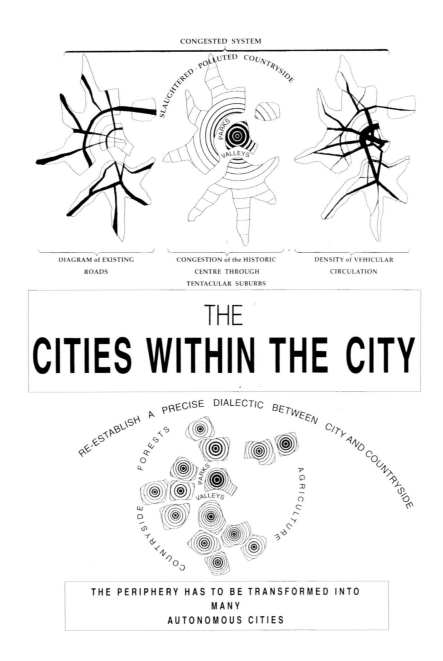

CONGESTED SYSTEM

SLAUGHTERED · POLLUTED COUNTRYSIDE

PARKS

VALLEYS

DIAGRAM of EXISTING
ROADS

CONGESTION of the HISTORIC
CENTRE THROUGH
TENTACULAR SUBURBS

DENSITY of VEHICULAR
CIRCULATION

THE
CITIES WITHIN THE CITY

RE-ESTABLISH A PRECISE DIALECTIC BETWEEN CITY AND COUNTRYSIDE

FORESTS

PARKS

VALLEYS

COUNTRYSIDE

AGRICULTURE

THE PERIPHERY HAS TO BE TRANSFORMED INTO
MANY
AUTONOMOUS CITIES

their ancient modernity. Whether a traditional structure is five hundred years of age or only one year of age does not make a fundamental difference to its quality. It is its structure, scale, composition, materials, and design that are decisive, not its age or "historicity." The originality of a great building lies not in the oldness of its building material, but, as J. Fest explains, in the originality of its project.

6

In matters of architecture and urbanism, fundamental principles are of universal value, but realizations are always local and regional, adapted to specific climates, topography, social habits, materials, and industry—i.e., to geographic/ecological and cultural contexts. Only classical architecture tends to transcend its regional origins. Even though it is anchored to the vernacular of the region (Tuscan, Doric, Ionian, and so

on) or rooted in the style of a dynasty or sovereign, the artistic elaboration and symbolic codification of monumental architecture transcends place and origin and allows for a new, universal application; it represents a truly international style. Its power and validity are maintained only by strictly controlling its proliferation, using it exclusively for exceptional and symbolically outstanding buildings.

7

A common mistake of fossil-fuel age "thinking" is to distinguish between "high" and "low" technologies. Human "technology" will be ecological or it won't have a future to speak of. Sustainable means ecological, and has nothing to do with progress, modernism, ideology, advanced or reactionary attitudes, creativity, industry, or economy as they have been propagated for the last two centuries.

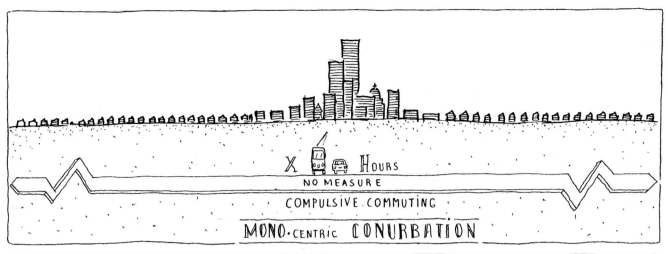

X 🚎 🚗 HOURS
NO MEASURE
COMPULSIVE COMMUTING

MONO·centric **CONURBATION**

10 🚶 MINUTES
‹The STANDARD MEASURE›

POLY·centric **FEDERATION**

TYPOLOGIES of ROOMS or CORRIDORS
of cellular or arterial structures

not to be confused EVER AGAIN ! ! ! ! ! please

DOMINANT VOLUME & ROOM CORRESPOND
perceivable at one glance

BUILDINGS AS LABYRINTHINE
circulation structures

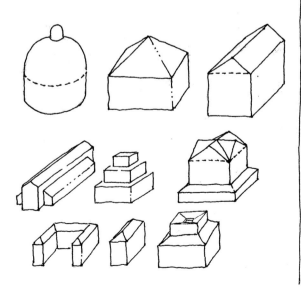

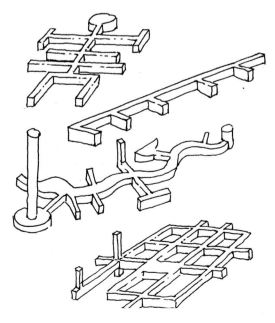

SOMETHING LIVED, SOMETHING DREAMED

PRINCIPLES AND POETICS IN URBAN DESIGN

WILLIAM McDONOUGH

After a prolific decade of writing and public speaking, William McDonough is perhaps as well known for his eloquence and ideas as he is for his groundbreaking work in architecture, community design, and urban planning—and rightly so. While McDonough pushes the limits of architecture with designs for "buildings like trees," green-roofed factories, and sustainable cities, the hopeful, life-affirming prose of his manifesto, Cradle to Cradle, *has inspired a generation of designers to "remake the way we make things." The bridge between the two—what makes the words and deeds equally effective—is McDonough's adherence to enduring principles. In* The Hannover Principles *we are asked "to insist on the right of humanity and nature to coexist in a healthy, supportive, diverse, and sustainable condition." In* Cradle to Cradle, *the laws of nature become a framework for good design as McDonough shows how human creations can be as beautiful, effective, and beneficial as new growth in the natural world. And in this essay, which was first published as a limited edition book by the University of Utah's Red Butte Press, McDonough applies ecological principles to urban design. Exploring the poetics of place, he suggests how architects and planners can enrich urban life by recognizing how deeply our cities are embedded in the natural world. Beyond the structural transformations of New Urbanism he sees cities designed to create "a vital, soulful rapport between nature and culture." The essay is focused on the American West, but its appeal is universal. For McDonough, that's the point: Everywhere, truly great twenty-first-century cities will grow out of a keen attention to the "evocative geography" of distinct locales, the particular way in which the forces of geology and climate, evolution, and cultural history shape each landscape. With McDonough, one stands at the intersection of these forces, applying principle to place and imagining urban landscapes that celebrate nature and rhyme with our hopes and dreams.*

— The Editor

Just over twenty years ago the celebrated journalist John McPhee began a series of now-famous trips across the United States on Interstate 80 in search of the "annals of the former world," the geological story of North America. McPhee and the geologists he traveled with were drawn to the interstate because road cuts provide an unrivaled window into geological history, revealing millions of years of volatile flux—pulsing glaciers and colliding tectonic plates, the thrust of mountain ranges, and the force of molten matter, all of it there in the exposed roadside rock. McPhee was especially drawn to the Great Basin of the American West. While the geology of the eastern United States was certainly interesting, he found the forces at work there had grown "stable and conservative." Meanwhile, the "far-out stuff was in the Far West of the country—wild, weirdsman, a leather-jacket geology in mirrored shades, with its welded tufts and Franciscan mélange . . . its strike-slip faults and falling buildings, its boiling springs and fresh volcanics, its extensional disassembling of the earth." In other words, geologically speaking, the West is where it's at: mountain building in all its forceful glory is happening *today*. It is, as the East had been so long ago, "radical . . . unstable, reformist, revolutionary." One could say the same about the *urban* West. While the shifting faults of the Great Basin and range put on their dynamic, earth-splitting show, fast-growing cities like Denver, Salt Lake City, Phoenix, and Seattle are creating a new western topography all their own. In a very real way they, too, are disassembling the earth.

Consider Las Vegas; booming in the southern reaches of the Great Basin, Las Vegas is the fastest-growing city in the United States, with twenty thousand housing starts annually and new acreage coming under development every day. If the city's growth represented a thoughtful response to the western landscape, it might well be worth celebrating. Instead, we see housing tract after housing tract planted with irrigated turf, each lot projecting onto the desert the grassy, pastoral world of another time and place. We see the sheep meadows of Scotland shrunk to half-acre lots, each with a miniature barn and a miniature tractor. We see the English heath on arid ground, watered greens and fairways replacing the sagebrush steppe, golfers roaming the rolling hills like bored shepherds, whacking stones with their staffs—one geologic province overlaid upon another.

Projecting other worlds onto the American West is nothing new. When Brigham Young led Mormon pioneers into the Great Basin Desert in 1847, he scanned the valley of the Great Salt Lake and famously declared, "This is the place!" But the place he *saw* was not the place before him, and he immediately began to change it.

In *Cadillac Desert,* Marc Reisner observes that "within hours of ending their ordeal, the Mormons were digging shovels into the earth beside the streams draining the Wasatch Range, leading canals into the surrounding desert which they would convert to fields. . . . Without realizing it, they were laying the foundation for the most ambitious desert civilization the world has seen." By the mid-1960s, when the Bureau of Reclamation's ostentatious century of dam building came to a close, the great rivers of the West had been marshaled for irrigation and power generation, and "great valleys and hemispherical basins" across millions of acres of the region "metamorphosed from desert blond to semitropic green."

To nineteenth-century American minds, Young and the Mormons were simply exercising their frontier rights and following established patterns of orderly settlement, both of which were cultural imperatives in the West. Indeed, long before the Mormons laid down the canals and gridiron streets of their ideal city, the Public Land Survey System had set the course for westward expansion and town planning. Established by the United States Congress in 1785, the survey system was designed to equitably distribute land to settlers. Ultimately, however, it flattened the western landscape into a one-dimensional map, projecting onto all geographies a rigid, standardized grid that is still used for dividing and developing property. As landscape historian J. B. Jackson wrote, the National Survey "determined the character of our whole rural landscape" and became "the characteristic national design for the environment."

The grid was a Jeffersonian idea. Believing that "small landowners are the most precious portion of the state," Jefferson thought a formalized system for surveying and selling small parcels of government land in the western states and territories was the surest way to create a class of the ideal American citizen—the independent yeoman. The system he embraced surveyed land in a north-south, east-west rectangular grid, mapping 640-acre sections within thirty-six-square-mile townships. Sections were sold for as little as a dollar an acre and, following the Homestead Act of 1862, quarter sections were virtually given away. While selling land, granting homesteads, and establishing towns on the grid did help put land into the hands of the common man and woman, it also made the mapmaker's projection the foundation of western settlement. Prairie and desert were

"conquered" section by section, lot by lot in the service of an ideal, regardless of the qualities of the land. Just so, western cities grew block by block across the land—surveyor's cities.

As the grid determined patterns of settlement it became an enduring landscape feature—not just a mark on the terrain, but cultural history writ large, the trace of a way of seeing. Landscape architect Elizabeth Meyer has noted that land in America is often seen as empty and ripe for the taking, rather than full and fully realized in and of itself—it exists to be transformed. In the late nineteenth century this was gospel; Western boosters took up the slogan "rain follows the plow," which came to define the American stance toward the arid West. It is gospel still, in rural and urban places alike. Looking at a desert lot on the edge of a booming western metropolis, conventional developers tend not to see a living place with an age-old evolutionary history, a place once inhabited by Arapaho, Diné, Suquamish, Paiute, Yakama, and many other peoples; they do not see, as a clear-eyed geologist would, an evocative topography, a particular place shaped by the particular way water trickles and flows across the land; they see a wasteland overlaid with blueprints for American autobahns and one-stop megastores.

But rain follows the "big box" of commerce no more than it follows the plow, and more often than not the transformed landscape belies the developer's promise. Instead of cities that nurture connections between people and place, enriching communities and the health of the natural world, westerners are faced with the vanishing Ogallala aquifer and the concrete channels of the Los Angeles River, with architecture at odds with the western environment and urban neighborhoods reeling from the impacts of sprawl.

These crises come as no surprise when we recognize that nature and the American city have almost always been seen in opposition. As J. B. Jackson wrote, Jefferson and Thoreau each "established a distinct anti-urban tradition, still honored by many who know nothing of its origin." Jefferson's interest in developing an agrarian society grew out of his hostility toward cities, which he saw as "sores on the body politic." Thoreau's antipathy for urban life matched his regard for nature: he saw man as "an inhabitant, or part and parcel of nature, rather than as a member of society." As we've seen, Jefferson's antiurbanism yielded the grid, but virtually no ideas about urban design. Thoreau's, though he never intended it, gave us the broad lawns and isolated homes of the low-density Romantic suburb.

The desire to control nature gave us another extreme view of urban life. In 1927, when the influential Swiss architect and theorist Le Corbusier imagined the future of cities, he foresaw a new industrial aesthetic that would free urban design from the constraints of the natural world. The city, he declared, "is a human operation directed against nature," and the house is "a machine for living in." He dreamed of "one single building for all nations and climates" and developed a strictly ordered urban plan for the modern metropolis—a "Radiant City" of uniform high-rise towers separated by open space and grand expressways.

To be sure, Le Corbusier's rhetoric could be mechanistic and rarified, but it was propelled by a humanistic desire to create clean, bright, comfortable cities for all. Unfortunately, in the hands of less inspired practitioners, and sometimes even in his own, the rendering of Le Corbusier's dream in the real world tended to destroy the urban fabric. Taken to its lowest common denominator, a vision of equality and renewal became a source of dehumanizing housing projects, lifeless urban plazas, and the one-size-fits-all office building, no more native to Phoenix or Seattle than it is to Shanghai.

We can do much better than this—and we are. Alternatives to the twin problems of lifeless cities and demoralizing sprawl are already creating more fulfilling connections between city and nature, people and place. One alternative, inspired by the writings of Jane Jacobs, addresses the structure and behavior of city neighborhoods, and it is significant because it flows from a deep love for cities, not a desire to do them in.

Jacobs, perhaps the most inspired and influential champion of city life in our time, believed that American cities could be great cities, and she discovered the source of urban greatness by watching closely how cities work—on the street, day by day, block by block. Her call for urban plans that support the "close-grained diversity" of vibrant city neighborhoods changed the conventional wisdom of "urban renewal" and strongly influenced today's New Urbanist planners, such as Andrés Duany and Elizabeth Plater-Zyberk. Like Jacobs, the New Urbanists favor plans that include a mixture of dwellings, shops, civic buildings, walkable neighborhoods, a variety of building types, and dense concentrations of residents, all of which can contribute to lively, satisfying communities.

The influence of New Urbanism is strong in the West, where planners such as Peter Calthorpe are making it an option for fast-growing western cities. Calthorpe helped create the master plan for the redevelopment of Denver's former Stapleton Airport—the largest infill redevelopment project in the United States—which is designed to re-create the fabric of the city's traditional neighborhoods. Similar designs that seek to ease the social and environmental impacts of growth have been realized from Portland to Salt Lake City to San Francisco, creating an alternative for people who feel, as one Bay Area reporter wrote, "that the bland juggernaut of suburban growth has created a horrible framework for daily life."

But there are limits to New Urbanism. Its core principles have been so widely plundered that some have come to call New Urbanist developments "sprawl with a happy face." If that charge is unfair to principled practitioners, it does describe many "new town" knock-offs. And while many of today's urbanist strategies do create more livable cities— pedestrian-friendly neighborhoods, more vital street life, plentiful green space—they often don't see cities in the overarching context of the natural world and, thus, they ultimately fall short of a truly *sustaining* urbanism. Energy and transportation systems still burn fossil fuels; building materials harmful to human and environmental health are still used; precious water still runs off impermeable surfaces;

urban manufacturing remains wasteful and unsafe; and economic activity is not considered an integral part of the designer's domain.

The world needs something more. If we want beautiful, thriving, enduring cities, cities that nourish nature and culture and enhance the legacy of the cities we inherited, perhaps we first need a new way of seeing, a lens that reveals the true nature of our designs. Le Corbusier and the other early modernists could not see what our generation sees. They could not see our living biosphere. They could not see, as scientists do today, the structure of molecules and the dynamics of ecosystems. They did not see economies within ecologies— we can. And with these lenses, both telescopic and microscopic, designers can begin to reimagine the urban landscape. We can see the city as a whole—from the molecules of our materials to the ecology of our region—and develop urban plans informed by the laws that govern life itself. We can see nature as part of the city and the city as part of nature. And we can apply this life-affirming vision to all of our designs, creating buildings, communities, cities, and regional plans that enhance environmental health, economic vitality, and social well-being.

Though modernism may have missed the view, the father of American landscape architecture, Frederick Law Olmsted, understood the synergy of ecology, economy, and equity in urban design. Remembered chiefly for his 1857 design for New York's Central Park, Olmsted's legacy is much broader and far-reaching. Not only did he and his son design urban parks throughout the country—including parks, grounds, and arboretums in Tacoma, Palo Alto, Seattle, Boulder, Spokane, and San Diego—Olmsted made nature an integral, socially meaningful part of the urban landscape. Landscape architect Anne Whiston Spirn notes that Olmsted applied a deep understanding of natural processes to build aesthetically pleasing landscape *systems*. "Through the design of parks and parkways," she writes, Olmsted sought "to improve the city's climate, to alleviate air and water pollution, to mitigate floods, and to provide a naturalistic counterpoint to the city's buildings and bustling streets." On his vast Fens and Riverway project in Boston, he combined woods and wetlands, water purification and public transit, in "a new type of integrated, multifunctional, urban open space . . . a fusion of art, agriculture, engineering, and science."

Building on Olmsted's legacy, contemporary architects and planners are revitalizing western cities with designs that more fully integrate air, water, earth, and sunlight into urban life. In Davis, California, a plan for a residential neighborhood orients buildings and streets to enhance the cooling and ventilating effects of the "delta breeze," which flows through the city on summer evenings when coastal fog drives air currents inland along the Sacramento River. In Los Angeles, a resurrected regional parks plan is the centerpiece of a community development initiative that seeks to restore the Los Angeles River, making it a vibrant social gathering place, an environmentally sound catchment for storm water, and a hopeful symbol of renewal for surrounding neighborhoods. In other cities, this vital dialogue with natural processes is bringing forth a profusion of innovative solutions. We see rooftop gardens that absorb and filter rainwater, ease the heat-island effect, and offer urban residents daily interactions with soil, plants, and other living things. We see skyscrapers that harvest the energy of the sun and office buildings warmed and cooled by geothermal currents rising from underground. We see brownfields restored by trees that draw toxins from the earth and wetlands that filter the wastewater of urban communities. We see an emerging synergy between nature and the city that has the potential to create a beautiful, deeply satisfying urban realm.

In the cities of the West, a vital rapport between nature and culture can be sustained only if each strategic planning choice makes ecological, social, and economic sense, not just for the present, but well into the future. We can achieve this when urban design is based on timeless principles that serve as a reference point as a city develops holistic, integrated plans for its future.

This is not just wishful thinking. The city of Chicago recently engaged in such a planning exercise to serve Mayor Richard Daley's quest to make it "the greenest city in America." The fruits of this labor, the Chicago Principles, were characterized by one city official as "a set of guiding 'green' principles . . . that describe the city's ideals, set its course, and define its means."

The Chicago Principles embrace the commitment to sustainability set forth in the nine declarations of The Hannover Principles, the design guidelines my colleague, the German chemist Michael Braungart, and I crafted for the city of Hannover, Germany, in 1992. The Hannover Principles insist on the right of humanity and nature to coexist in a healthy, supportive, diverse, and sustainable condition. They recognize the interdependence between elements of human design and the natural world; call on designers to eliminate waste and rely on natural energy flows; and conceive of design as a powerful, regenerative force.

These principles offer a robust, comprehensive approach to urban design in stark contrast to those that seek merely to minimize human impact; they give designers the tools to create more positive effects, not just fewer negative ones. Consider the design of Gap Incorporated's office building in San Bruno, California; to enhance energy effectiveness and the qualities of the local landscape, the building was designed with an undulating roof blanketed in soil, flowers, and grasses. Echoing the local terrain, the roof reestablishes several acres of San Bruno's coastal savannah ecosystem. The living roof also effectively absorbs and filters storm water and provides thermal insulation, making the landscape an integral part of the building design. In addition, a raised-floor cooling system allows evening breezes to flush the building while concrete slabs beneath the floor store the cool air and release it during the day. The windows are operable so that the delivery of fresh air is under individual control, daylight provides natural illumination, and comfortable public gathering areas merge indoors and out.

Recognized as one of the most energy-efficient buildings in California, the Gap building demonstrates the effectiveness of ecologically intelligent systems. By tapping local energy flows and enmeshing the building in the surrounding landscape, the design outperforms the designs of buildings that set energy efficiency as their highest goal. It also enables the building and its inhabitants to *participate* in natural processes in ways that allow an ongoing celebration of the rich relationship between human creativity and the abundance of the natural world.

Imagine *this* writ large in western cities. Imagine the Seattle Principles, the Salt Lake City Principles, the Denver Principles. Imagine buildings, neighborhoods, transportation systems, factories, and parks all designed to enhance a city's economic, environmental, and social health. Imagine urban designs that reach beyond sustainability to create beautiful, diverse, culturally rich cities defined by their harmonious rapport with the landscape.

The French anthropologist Claude Levi-Strauss captured well the poetic confluence of natural and cultural forces in the city. Cities have often been likened to symphonies and poems, and the comparison seems to me a perfectly natural one. They are, in fact, objects of the same kind—the city may even be rated higher, because it stands at the point where nature and artifice meet. A city is a congestion of animals whose biological history is enclosed within its boundaries, and yet every conscious and rational act on the part of these creatures helps to shape the city's eventual character. By its form, as by the manner of its birth, the city has elements at once of biological procreation, organic evolution, and esthetic creation. It is both a natural object and a thing to be cultivated; individual and group; something lived and something dreamed.

Cities are organisms, and cities are designed—something lived and something dreamed. They have both natural and man-made metabolisms. And when the human technologies of the urban metabolism operate by the same laws that govern the natural world, our cities will approach the effectiveness of the earth's living systems. High-tech buildings, for example, can perform like trees; they can make oxygen, sequester carbon, fix nitrogen, distill water, provide habitat for thousands of species, accrue solar energy, build soil, create microclimates, and change with the seasons.

We can create buildings like trees—and cities like forests—by following three essential principles that allow designers to apply the intelligence of natural systems to human designs: waste equals food; use current solar income; celebrate diversity.

The first principle, waste equals food, invokes an age-old model. A fruit tree's blossoms fall to the ground and decompose into food for other living things. Bacteria and fungi feed on the organic waste of both the tree and the animals that eat its fruit, depositing nutrients in the soil in a form ready for the tree to take up and convert into growth. One organism's waste becomes another organism's food, and nutrients flow perpetually in regenerative, cradle-to-cradle cycles of birth, decay, and rebirth.

Waste equals food is a crucial urban principle because it allows us to conceive of regenerative, closed-loop systems on multiple scales, from the community garden to the regional economy. Applied to design, it translates first of all into safe, healthful material flows that generate no waste. Imagine a scenario in which textiles made with natural materials and safe chemicals are tossed into community gardens to nourish the soil when they wear out, becoming food for biological systems; where high-tech polymers and metals are designed for closed-loop systems that circulate valuable materials in perpetual cycles of production, recovery, and remanufacture. Safe manufacturing and cradle-to-cradle material flows not only ensure that the materials we build with are beneficial, they also provide a clean, productive economic base for healthy urban growth. By eliminating the very concept of waste, human industry becomes a regenerative thread in the urban fabric.

On the scale of building and community design, closing the loop allows us to respond to natural flows of water and energy. Closing the loop on water flows means designing a site in harmony with local topography, soil, and vegetation so that rainwater percolates slowly through the earth and follows a natural course through the watershed rather than racing down a concrete culvert. This may be the most important consideration for architects and planners in the West. Simply meeting code is not enough. We need to go beyond best practices and discover ways to honor and celebrate life-giving water in our designs. In central California, a residential neighborhood is doing just that: eschewing a conventional underground drainage system, the community created a natural system of wetlands and swales to retain and filter storm water and in the process created a cherished public space that also provides habitat for migrating birds. A study in Portland, Oregon, meanwhile, found that roof gardens on just a third of the city's downtown buildings could retain nearly seventy million gallons of water a year.

The second principle of good design recognizes the unlimited energy of the sun, which powers nature's cradle-to-cradle cycles and provides the earth's only perpetual source of energy income. Long thought to be a distant promise, the age of solar and wind power is here. Following technological advances in the past decade, the cost of a wind-generated kilowatt hour in the West is now cheaper than a kilowatt hour generated by natural gas. Work is advancing rapidly on solar technology that will make it an equally effective source of clean, renewable energy.

The open spaces of the West make the region rich in renewable energy. In Nevada, solar collection on one hundred square miles can produce enough power to meet America's energy needs. In the Big Sky country of Colorado, Texas, Wyoming, and the Dakotas, high-tech windmills dot the horizon, prompting some to call the High Plains the Saudi Arabia of Wind. In Sacramento, residents can purchase all of their electricity from supplies generated by renewable sources and the municipal power company encourages the use of solar energy by installing photovoltaic systems on private homes and public buildings.

All of these developments will influence the future of western cities. While natural light and fresh air are becoming more common elements in the energy systems of new buildings, the direct use of solar and wind power is not often seen as a viable option. This will change. Let's anticipate and encourage that change. Let's create solar-powered buildings like the Adam Joseph Lewis Center for Environmental Studies at Oberlin College, which is designed to eventually produce more energy than it consumes—no fossil fuels required. Let us imagine the immense implications of wind-powered mass transportation in western cities, a shift already underway in Calgary, where the subway is partially powered by prairie winds.

As urban residents enjoy the benefits of cleaner air, the demand for renewable power will transform wind into a new cash crop for western farmers. A dispersed system of windmills on many farms will provide more benefit to more people, and allow lands never meant for large-scale agriculture to return to their natural state. Once widely adopted, solar and wind power generation will change the region's energy infrastructure, reconnecting rural areas to cities through the cooperative exchange of energy and technology—and even end the West's reliance on hydroelectric power. Clean energy, economic development, thousands of jobs, free-flowing rivers—all by using the energy of the sun.

The third principle, celebrate diversity, recognizes that all healthy ecosystems—natural and urban—require a multiplicity of interdependent forms. In a healthy ecosystem, each organism fits exquisitely in its place, and in each system an abundance of fitting organisms thrive together. In short, evolution generates biodiversity.

Good urban designs generate diversity as well. Rather than offering Le Corbusier's "one single building for all nations and climates," we can celebrate the distinctiveness of western landscapes with buildings and streets and community plans exquisitely suited to the character of each place. Designers aiming for what "fits" attend carefully to the local landscape. They study its geology, hydrology, vegetation, and climate. They observe the lives of local flora, fauna, and grasses. They explore traces of natural and cultural history. So, too, do they study the *social* ecosystem, for the urban landscape is often common ground, and the public spaces that draw people together—street, library, market, park—generate the convivial energy that is a city's heart and soul.

In the end, good urban design is a search for fitting forms. It is a composition of the natural and cultural, an attempt to bring harmony to the urban symphony. Whether we are designing a single building or a master plan for a city block, our success depends on fluency in what Anne Whiston Spirn calls "the language of landscape," on knowing how to read the story of the place before us.

In the West, urban designers are not alone in this pursuit. There is a great tradition of western literature, from John Muir to Wallace Stegner to Terry Tempest Williams, that beautifully renders the wild landscapes of the West—what Stegner famously called the "geography of hope." The poetry of place they have created is a repository of regional knowledge that has the power to remove the scales from our eyes, allowing us to see through the static map to the lively territory. Designers informed by this tradition will understand our place in the world more clearly and will be better equipped to respond to the western land with vision and grace.

But the city, by and large, is rarely included in these fine renderings. It is time for a new tradition, a distinctly regional poetic urbanism that calls upon designers to act as place-makers. The urban West faces daunting challenges. At the same time, the future holds magnificent possibilities. Thus, we have a choice before us. We can bemoan the obstacles of outdated zoning or the seeming gridlock in city hall, or we can see every site, every building, and every block as an opportunity to create a regenerative relationship between nature and the urban world.

As place-makers we cannot help projecting ourselves onto the landscape. The human species has an image-making mind, and the city is always something of a dream. But as we dream of our ideal cities, as we conjure the human weft on the geological warp of the land, we can begin to see more clearly the lineaments of the place we inhabit, the true character of the territory, its *genius loci*. And then, as we shape the character of our cities, we will make places that celebrate both human creativity and a rich, harmonious relationship with the living earth. We will create a new geography of hope.

PART 2: EXPLORING NEW URBANISM

THE TRADITIONAL NEIGHBORHOOD
AND URBAN SPRAWL

ANDRÉS DUANY AND ELIZABETH PLATER-ZYBERK

The congested, fragmented, unsatisfying suburban sprawl and the disintegrating urban centers of today are not merely products of laissez-faire, nor are they the inevitable results of mindless greed. They are thoroughly planned to be as they are: the direct result of zoning and subdivision ordinances zealously administered by planning departments.

If the results are dismaying, it is because the model of the city being projected is dismal. These ordinances dictate three criteria for urbanism: the free and rapid flow of traffic, parking in quantity, and the rigorous separation of building use. The result of these criteria are that automobile traffic and its landscape have become the central, unavoidable experience of the public realm.

The traditional pattern of walkable, mixed-use neighborhoods has been inadvertently prohibited by current ordinances. Thus, designers find themselves in the ironic situation of being forbidden from building in the manner of our admired historic places. One cannot propose a new Annapolis, Marblehead, or Key West, without seeking substantial variances from current codes.

Thus, there are two types of urbanism available: the neighborhood, which was the model in North America from the first settlements to the Second World War; and suburban sprawl, which has been the model since then. They are similar in their initial capacity to accommodate people and their activities; the principal difference is that suburban sprawl contains environmental, social, and economic deficiencies that inevitably choke sustained growth.

The neighborhood has the following physical attributes:

• It is a comprehensive planning increment: when clustered with others, it becomes a town; when standing free in the landscape, it becomes a village. The neighborhood varies in population and density to accommodate localized conditions.

• It is limited in size so that a majority of the population is within a five-minute walking distance of its center (1/4 mile). The needs of daily life are theoretically available within this area. This center provides an excellent location for a transit stop, convenient work places, retail, community events, and leisure activities.

• The streets are laid out in a network, so that there are alternate routes to most destinations. This permits most streets to be smaller, with slower traffic, as well as have parking, trees, sidewalks, and buildings. They are equitable for both vehicles and pedestrians.

• The streets are spatially defined by a wall of buildings that front the sidewalk in a disciplined manner, uninterrupted by parking lots.

• The buildings are diverse in function, but compatible in size and in disposition on their lots. There is a mixture of houses (large and small), outbuildings, small apartment buildings, shops, restaurants, offices, and warehouses.

• Civic buildings (schools, meeting halls, theaters, churches, clubs, museums, etc.) are often placed on squares or at the termination of street vistas. By being built at important locations, these buildings serve as landmarks.

• Open space is provided in the form of specialized squares, playgrounds, and parks and, in the case of villages, greenbelts.

Suburban sprawl has quite different physical attributes:

• It is disciplined only by isolated "pods," which are dedicated to single uses such as shopping centers, office parks, and residential clusters. All of these are inaccessible from each other except by car. Housing is strictly segregated in large clusters containing units of similar cost, hindering socioeconomic diversity.

• It is limited only by the range of the automobile, which easily forms cachment areas for retail, often exceeding thirty-five miles.

• There is a high proportion of cul-de-sacs and looping streets within each pod. Through traffic is possible only by means of a few "collector" streets that, consequently, become easily congested.

• Vehicular traffic controls the scale and form of space, with streets being wide and dedicated primarily to the automobile. Parking lots typically dominate the public space.

• Buildings are often highly articulated, rotated on their lots, and greatly set back from streets. They are unable to create spatial definition or sense of place. Civic buildings do not normally receive distinguished sites.

• Open space is often provided in the form of buffers, pedestrian ways, berms, and other ill-defined residual spaces.

The neighborhood has several positive consequences:
• By bringing most of the activities of daily living into walking distance, everyone (especially the elderly and the young) gains independence of movement.
• By reducing the number and length of automobile trips, traffic congestion is minimized, the expenses of road construction are limited, and air pollution is reduced.
• By providing streets and squares of comfortable scale with defined spatial quality, neighbors, by walking, can come to know each other and to watch over their collective security.
• By providing appropriate building concentrations at easy walking distances from transit stops, public transit becomes a viable alternative to the automobile.
• By providing a full range of housing types and work places, people of various ages and economic classes are integrated and the bonds of an authentic community are formed.
• By providing suitable civic buildings and spaces, democratic initiatives are encouraged and the balanced evolution of society is facilitated.

FIG. 1 The street as automotive sewer: streamform highway geometries sever walking connections and preclude pedestrian life.

FIG. 2 The street as a complex, multipurpose social organism: a boulevard, ideal for driving, parking, walking, and sipping coffee.

Suburban sprawl has several negative consequences:

- By assuming that the people will drive to and from all activities, the need for large streets and parking lots becomes a self-fulfilling prophecy. The exhaust emissions resulting from such trips are the single greatest source of air pollution in the United States.
- By the construction of an excessively asphalted infrastructure, the natural landscape is destroyed. Each automobile not only generates roadways, but also requires a paved parking place at the dwelling, another at the work place, and yet another at the shopping center.
- By consigning the bulk of the available public budget to pay for asphalted infrastructure, the human infrastructure of good schools, post offices, fire stations, meeting halls, cultural buildings, and affordable housing is starved.

Certain classes of citizens who suffer particularly from the pattern of suburban sprawl include:

- The middle class, which is forced into multiple automobile ownership. The average yearly cost of car ownership is $9,000, which is the equivalent of a $90,000 mortgage payment. The possibility of owning one less car is the single most important subsidy that can be provided toward affordable housing. By forbidding mixed-use areas, the investment of personal time in the activity of commuting is mandatory. A person who drives two hours a day spends the equivalent of eight working weeks a year in the car.
- The young, below the legal driving age, who are dependent on adults for their social needs. They are bused to schools, to and from which they cannot walk, and isolated at home until their working parents arrive. The alternative is to relegate one parent to a career as the child's chauffeur. The single-family house with the yard is a good place for childhood only if it is structured as part of a neighborhood. Within these, the child can walk or bicycle to school, to play, to the store, to the movies, and to friends' houses.
- The elderly, who lose their self-sufficiency once they lose their drivers' licenses. Healthy senior citizens who may continue to live independently within a neighborhood are otherwise consigned to specialized retirement communities where their daily needs are met at great cost.

Suburban sprawl usually accommodates the correct balance of work places, living places, schools, and open space in what appears to be proximity. However, proximity is not enough; the detailing of the public space to accommodate the pedestrian is also necessary:

- Buildings must be aligned along streets and squares. The current fashion of staggering or rotating buildings hinders the creation of public space defined by the buildings.
- Trees along streets must also be aligned in a disciplined manner. This is particularly important to remedy spaces when overly large setbacks cannot be avoided. Picturesque planting patterns should be reserved for parks and squares, not for streets and avenues.
- Parallel parking must be provided on most streets. A layer of parked cars psychologically protects the pedestrians from traffic. Parking lots, when they are needed, should be placed to the rear of buildings to avoid the gaps that make sidewalks uninteresting to use. House lots, if less than fifty feet wide, should be provided with alleys so that garage doors do not overwhelm the street facades.
- At intersections, the radius at the curb should not exceed fifteen feet. This maintains a viable pedestrian crossing distance and reduces the speed of automobiles making the turn.
- High-capacity streets within urbanized areas should have the geometry of avenues, not of highways. Highways are unpleasant for pedestrians and deteriorate adjacent building value, while avenues are compatible with both buildings and people. Highways should be reserved for the countryside and be built without strip development.

In a neighborhood, affordable housing occurs naturally and in a highly integrated manner. This is achieved by the following means:

- The affordable housing looks like the market-rate housing, using similar exterior materials, windows, and building forms. Affordable housing is not segregated and is never clustered in large numbers. A good ratio is one affordable unit to ten market-rate units.
- Housing is provided above retail establishments. This type of dwelling can be provided for the cost of construction alone, because the cost of land can be assigned to the retail component of the building.
- Garage apartments or cottages are available in the backyards of single-family houses. These rental units, of limited size, provide extremely affordable housing that is interspersed with market-rate housing. This also allows teenagers to stay at home and the elderly to live with their families.

Current codes monitor only traffic flow, parking counts, the segregation of building use, and the safeguard of wetlands. New codes must be written that include effective provisions for the neighborhood, which is true human habitat in all its complexity.

THE URBAN NETWORK

PETER CALTHORPE

California is projected to grow by twelve million people in the next twenty years—the Los Angles Basin by seven million alone. Many other metropolitan areas, while not growing as fast, are experiencing major migrations to suburban areas. As much as we may like development to focus solely on infill and redevelopment, such efforts will only solve part of the growth problem. Even Portland, Oregon, with its Urban Growth Boundary and strong urban design policies, only satisfies 30% of its growth with infill and redevelopment. There is a critical need for a new paradigm of growth in undeveloped sites, one which complements urban infill and revitalization—a design that matches a new circulation system with the new forms of land use now emerging through New Urbanism and Smart Growth.

Our transportation network is still a suburban grid of arterials punctuated with freeways. On occasion a transit line may overlay this auto-oriented framework supporting Transit-Oriented Development and the revitalization of some historic towns and cities. But short of that, New Urbanism and Smart Growth are forced to grow within a network designed for sprawl.

The old paradigm is simple; a grid of arterials is spaced at one-mile increments with major retail centers located at the intersections and strip commercial buildings lining its inhospitable but very visible edges. Overlaying the grid in rings and radials is the freeway system. The intersection of the grid and freeway becomes fertile ground for malls and office parks. This system is rational, coherent, and true to itself, even if increasingly dysfunctional. Its land use matches the transportation system in a way that New Urbanism, when dropped into this network, cannot.

We must develop a new circulation pattern to match new land uses—one that accommodates the car as well as transit and that reinforces, rather than isolates, walkable places. Bringing daily destinations closer to home is a fundamental aspect of urbanism, but is not the complete solution to our access needs.

Unfortunately, to assert that we must build transit rather than freeways is simplistic, just as calling for infill development to the exclusion of new growth is unrealistic. This is not to say that transit and infill are trivial pursuits, but, that they are not, and never will be, the whole story.

Now more than ever, regions define our lives. Our job opportunities, cultural interests, and social networks are bigger than any neighborhood or town. Even if we double the percentage of walkable trips in a neighborhood and triple transit ridership, there still will be massive growth in auto trips—not to mention an exploding quantity of truck miles. We need a system that accommodates all modes efficiently while at the same time supporting urbanism throughout the region.

A New Transportation Network

The alternative transportation network proposed here is diverse and complex, mixing differing types of auto uses with transit, biking, and walking. It must set up a new hierarchy of arterials and boulevards that allow for through traffic without always bypassing commercial centers—a road network that reinforces access to walkable neighborhoods, urban town centers, and transit without cutting them off from local pedestrian movement. This new network must incorporate transit in a way that is affordable, appropriately placed, and inherent to the system. And finally, it should reserve freeway capacity for long trips while providing alternate means for daily work commutes and shopping trips.

Our firm developed the "Urban Network" for Chicago Metropolis 2020, a private regional planning effort of the historic Commercial Club (figure 1). The plan for new growth areas around Chicago proposes three types of major roads to replace the standard arterial grid: transit boulevards, throughways, avenues, and connectors. The transit boulevards combine semi-local auto trips with transit right-of-ways, the throughways are limited-access roads for longer trips, the avenues lead to commercial destinations, and the connectors provide for local circulation within neighborhoods.

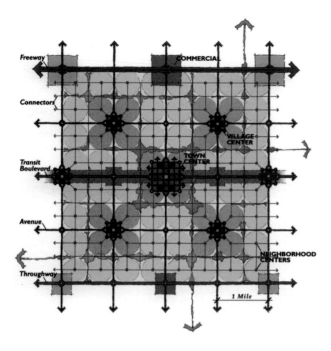

FIG. I "Urban Network" for Chicago Metropolis 2020.

These alternate street types breed a different set of intersections—roundabouts and couplets of one-way streets. They replace the slow, overly scaled intersections of our standard signalized arterials. The roundabouts are placed to expedite traffic on through streets and the couplets are placed to allow urban development adjacent to, and actually within, a major intersection.

The transit boulevards are at the heart of this new network. They are multifunctional arterials designed to match the mixed-use urban development they support. Like traditional boulevards they would have a central area for through traffic and transit, along with small-scale access roads to support local activities and pedestrian environments, at the edges. It is a place where cafes, small businesses, apartments, transit, parking, and through traffic all mingle in a simple and time-tested hierarchy.

These transit boulevards would be lined with higher-density development and run through a town center of sorts approximately every four miles. In the commercial center only, the boulevard would split into two one-way streets set a block apart, creating an urban grid of pedestrian scaled streets. No street in such a town would contain more than three (and typically two) travel lanes, allowing pedestrian continuity without diverting auto capacity. In addition, this one-way system eliminates left turn delays, actually decreasing travel time through the area.

The transit system running along the boulevards and through the towns could be light rail, streetcars, or bus rapid transit (BRT). Because of its frequency, it is important that the transit system be, to put it bluntly, cheap. When light rail is not possible, the capital and operational costs of BRT are the most affordable, and make it finan-cially viable for widespread use. New, super-efficient natural gas engines and advanced bus design would make such buses reasonable companions to the urban environment of the boulevard.

In contrast to the boulevards, the throughways are single-use roads that provide for truck and longer distance auto trips, much like our older highways do today. They are a viable alternative to congested freeways or stop-and-go arterials. Roundabouts would be placed at one-mile intervals, supplemented by infrequent right-in, right-out curb cuts in the form of roundabouts, which are particularly important to this system, as their average intersection delay is up to half that of the typical signalized arterial intersection.

The throughway would support truck- and auto-oriented land uses, such as low-density manufacturing, warehousing, and light-industrial development. In some areas these roads could have regional open space areas and greenbelts lining them. The tendency for strip development along such roads would be offset by the availability of development opportunities on the boulevards and avenues, and in village and town centers.

Avenues would intersect both the throughways and boulevards at centers set at one-mile intervals. These avenues would allow for frequent intersections, just as our existing suburban system does. However, at major intersections they would support a village center with an urban couplet of no more than two-lane streets, similar to the town centers. Between centers, these avenues could have a parkway treatment lined by alley-loaded, large-lot homes—as in the historic neighborhoods of many American cities.

Finally, a system of connector streets forms a finer grid of approximately 1/8 mile spacing (not shown in the diagram) within neighborhoods as well as diagonal routes that provide direct access to local village and town centers. These streets are more frequent than the standard collector type of street, and therefore serve to disperse the traffic in such a way as to create livable environments along them. This system also functions to relieve the avenues of local trips, thereby allowing a smaller street section at their one-mile increments.

Urban Places in the Urban Network

The Urban Network would replace the old system of so-called functional street types wherein streets serve a single function in a linear hierarchy of capacities. The new street types combine uses, capacities, and scales. The transit boulevards combine the capacity of a major arterial with the intimacy of its local frontage roads and the pedestrian orientation that comes with its transit system. The avenues are multilane facilities that transition into a couplet of main streets at the village centers. Streets, like land use, can no longer afford to be single purpose.

The Urban Network integrates new and old forms of urban development in appropriate and accessible locations. Walkable town and village centers are placed at the crossroads of the transit boulevards and avenues. Residential neighborhoods are directly accessible to these centers by local connector streets as well as the avenues. The industrial, warehouse, and other auto-oriented uses are close to the throughways.

Each urban land-use type has the appropriate scale and type of access. The town center is pedestrian friendly, as well as accessible to the boulevard's through-traffic and transit line. The villages are directly accessible by foot, bus, car, and bike from their surrounding neighborhoods, while their couplet streets bring the auto traffic needed by their retail areas. Auto- and truck-oriented uses can be located at the intersections of the throughways, away from the transit and mixed-use centers.

Making Retail Work

The retail within the village and town centers needs adequate access, visibility, and an appropriate market area. For example, it takes a minimum population of 10,000, or just under two square miles of mixed-density housing, to support a full-service grocery store.

In the Urban Network, a village center, anchored by such a grocery store, is located at major avenue intersections without being cut off from the surrounding development. Diagonal connector streets provide direct access for pedestrians, bikers, and cars from the adjacent neighborhoods while the couplet allows comfortable pedestrian movement through the center. Surrounding the village are four neighborhoods each defined by a readily walkable quarter-mile radius and a mix of uses enhanced by access to the village center.

An example of a village center organized this way is in San Elijo, located about forty miles north of San Diego. This site, originally planned around a standard intersection of two arterials, was redesigned to place a village green at the intersection of four one-way streets. In one quadrant the grocery store anchors the primary retail section, while in others housing and civic buildings line the streets. Two main streets lead up to the green, and mixed-use buildings that surround it. In two of the quadrants a school and community park complete the center.

A town center contains a much larger quantity of retail, along with higher-density housing, major office development, and a more extensive street system. Issaquah Highlands, thirty miles east of Seattle, is an example. This center is placed at the intersection of a major new arterial (projected to carry about 50,000 ADT [average daily traffic] to a new freeway interchange) and the entry to a new community of approximately 3,500 units of housing. Some 500 more units are planned in the town center, along with 900,000 square feet of retail and commercial space. The Microsoft Corporation has also acquired part of the town center for a second major campus of approximately three million square feet.

Splitting the arterials into one-way couplets allowed an urban grid to organize the site and provided for a pedestrian-scaled environment. The standard configuration had a primary intersection with a 166-foot pedestrian crossing, while the couplets had two streets, one forty feet long and the other just twenty-eight. In addition, the traffic engineers found that the auto travel time through the center was actually reduced by 11% when compared to the conventional intersection pattern. The town is now planned to contain about 500 units of housing, and 900,000 square feet of retail and commercial space in addition to the new Microsoft campus.

Another example of a large-scale application of the Urban Network is the preliminary plan for the 20,000-acre St. Andrews expansion area north of Perth. This plan shows a hierarchy of neighborhoods, villages, and towns set into an Urban Network with open-space systems buffering the coast and weaving through the community.

As with any circulation system, the spacing and configuration of the Urban Network would bend to environmental constrains and existing development. In retrofitting areas, certain existing suburban arterials could be converted into transit boulevards. Some intersections could be reconfigured into paired one-way couplets where retail redevelopment is deemed appropriate. The network would work with existing freeways, but may represent an opportunity to replace freeway extensions with a combination of transit boulevards and throughways.

Beyond the Neighborhood Scale

The Urban Network is a framework of transit and circulation corridors that supports walkable neighborhoods and urban centers. It posits a new hierarchy of streets, new intersection configurations, and a new set of land-use types. However, it employs much of the same technology and many of the same institutions that build our current suburban infrastructure. Road builders would still lay down asphalt, automakers could build buses, and developers could still build communities.

All the advantages of New Urbanism—its compact, land-saving density, its walkable mix of uses, and its integrated range of housing opportunities—would be supported and amplified by a circulation system that offers fundamentally different choices in mobility and access.

Smart Growth and New Urbanism have begun the work of redefining America's twenty-first century development paradigms—now it is time to redefine the circulation armature that supports them. It is short-sighted to think that significant changes in land use and regional structure can be realized without fundamentally reordering our circulation system. Only an integrated network of urban places and multiuse street systems can support the changes we need for the next century of growth.

NEW URBANISM
A FORUM, NOT A FORMULA

ELLEN DUNHAM-JONES

What is New Urbanism? What actually defines it? Is it a collection of projects—defined largely by Seaside and Celebration (developments in Florida) as the most published and ergo the most representative? Is it a formulaic approach to urban design that employs compactness, figural public spaces, mixed-use, mixed-income, walkability, and sometimes transit to reproduce the scale and style of traditional villages? Is it a collection of people, a cult of converted developers and designers worshipping at the altar of Andrés Duany?

I would like to propose that—although New Urbanism is associated with all of these characteristics—it is not embodied in any one project, scale, approach, or person. Rather, New Urbanism is a collective effort to transform the regulations and practices that currently reproduce urban sprawl by developing and implementing alternative tools, regulations, and practices that allow for a wider range of experiences, from urban through rural. At its most significant and most fundamental level, New Urbanism is the effort of the members of the Congress for the New Urbanism (CNU) through various task forces, chapters, and councils, to redesign the rules of the game.

Unfortunately, this project of radical change has been far less visible than the individual projects. Many architects simply see the projects, and their knee-jerk response to the neo-traditional styling is to assume that New Urbanism is inherently conservative and committed to preserving the status quo. This type of reaction to styling focuses only on a post-modern cultural reading—by now quite conventional—of what the projects represent when viewed within the trajectory of modern architecture. Regrettably, it also completely ignores the social and environmental performance of the projects and the significant transformations to the status quo resulting from changing regulations to allow for mixed-use, mixed-income areas, higher densities, and walkability. By linking land use and transportation, replacing single-use zoning codes with form-based codes, promoting transit-based development, varied housing and building types, and the creation of community-building public spaces, New Urbanists are diversifying the monocultures of suburbia.

Is this reformist activity at risk of simply replacing one formulaic template of development with another? Can alternative standards and tools raise the bar on design without also kneecapping desired innovations? If much of the distinction between urban and suburban places has to do with the degree of diversity versus predictable uniformity, how do new regulations best create a sense of place without stifling urbanity? The responses to these kinds of questions get debated at the annual congresses and on the very active New Urbanist listservs. By presenting both the new tools that CNU has evolved and some of the debates that continue to enliven sustained discussion, I argue that New Urbanism is a forum, not a formula. It is an ongoing project of reform filled with debates on an evolving body of tools and strategies—at a wider range of scales than is commonly recognized—and that can never be illustrated by any single New Urbanist project.

In part, the debates go back to the diverse interests of the founders. In 1991, when Judy Corbett received funding from the California Air Resources Board to convene a group to discuss alternatives to suburban sprawl, the six architects did not know each other well or share the same goals. Elizabeth Plater-Zyberk and Andrés Duany were focused on increasing social interaction through stronger engagement of the houses with streets designed as outdoor public rooms in what they called Traditional Neighborhood Developments (TNDs). Peter Calthorpe was more motivated by environmental concerns and their application to Transit-Oriented Developments (TODs). Dan Solomon, Stefanos Polyzoides, and Elizabeth Moule brought concerns for urban spatial sequences and regionalist architecture to the table. Although the six did not share the same primary interests, they soon realized the synergistic advantages of combining their interests and targeting their common enemy: the regulations and formulaic practices that reproduce suburban sprawl and make urbanism illegal in most of the country.

With "design matters" as their mantra, the founders made a committment to bringing physical planning and design back into the planning process. One of the foremost regulations they challenged was single-use zoning, a legacy of

FIG. 1 CNU's forum always incorporates plenty of debate, including Saturday night boxing matches at CNU XV. Hazel "Placemaker" Borys lands a point in a bout with Jim "It's All Good" Kunstler.

FIG. 2 From *Malls to Main Streets* is one of several publications, reports and resource guides authored or sponsored by CNU.

MALLS INTO MAINSTREETS
an in-depth guide to transforming dead malls into communities

FIG. 3 CNU members and local city planners collaborate on a project to code a city neighborhood during an Urban Lab at CNU XIV in Providence. The lab, Coding for Neighborhood Evolution, was organized in conjunction with the Providence Department of Planning and Development and was facilitated by SmartCode consultants. Existing urbanism was analyzed and a SmartCode template and regulating plan were customized for local character.

CIAM (Congres International d'Architecture Moderne). Having been largely educated in the footsteps of CIAM's Team X, the six wrote an alternative set of principles to guide New Urbanism, and decided to begin holding their own congresses. The first was in 1993; today, CNU attracts a diverse and multidisciplinary membership. Many get involved because of a deep commitment to the environmental benefits. Others are attracted to the engagement with social and civic issues. Still others are drawn to the predominant neotraditional design aesthetic. All learn from each other and from the interdisciplinary basis of the discussions (figure 1).

In addition to critiquing each other's projects, the early congresses and publications were focused on advancing New Urbanism through clarifying diagrams and principles. As the characteristics of TNDs and TODs were refined, numerous volunteers took on the job of collectively writing the charter of the New Urbanism.[1] A nomenclature task force, led by Duany, was specifically charged with gathering definitive descriptions of place types into the lexicon of the New Urbanism. The ongoing debate over architectural style got its start at this time. Many argued that style was secondary to planning and did not need to be discussed in the charter, let alone stir up controversy. Others, including Charles Barrett and Léon Krier, nearly derailed the charter's ratification at CNU IV because of its lack of specific language advocating traditional design. The later inclusion of the phrases "Individual buildings should be seamlessly linked to their surroundings. This issue transcends style," hardly eased the tensions. Attributed to Dan Solomon, its opening of the door to modernist interpretations of context aroused impassioned criticisms and defenses that continue today.

Gradually, as New Urbanism has gained wider acceptance, the forum's scope has enlarged. While early graphic codes focused predominantly on the interface between the building and the street, more recent form-based codes have focused on the graduated differentiation between neighborhood centers and edges. Increased discussion of Smart Growth in the mid-nineties further expanded these ideas to the scale of regional design and the graduated differentiation between centers and corridors targeted for growth and areas targeted for conservation. A task force is now working on integrating New Urbanism into comprehensive plans. Meanwhile, New Urbanist projects continue to expand across a wider range of regional locations. The early attention to greenfield projects expanded first to inner-city Hope VI projects, and later to urban and suburban brownfield and grayfield redevelopments.[2] Calthorpe integrated his TODs into his proposal for the more regionally systemic Urban Network and got into vigorous debates with Duany over the merits of urban growth boundaries versus the establishment of rural preserves.

Simultaneous with the increased attention to regional issues, New Urbanist discussions have become more operational, and the early dialectical diagrams have evolved into tools and standards. While the early CNUs were spiked with stealthy strategies for getting around the limitations of conventional regulations, the ambition now is to rewrite the regulations themselves. The mixed-income strategies of TNDs were formalized into HUD's (Housing and Urban Development) design guidelines for Hope VI public housing projects, and later into Urban Design Associates' pattern books. Duany reorganized the lexicon into the six zones of the Urban-Rural Transect. As managed by the SmartCode, the transect introduces a graduated diversity of building types, street types, lot sizes, and frontage and landscaping requirements into the layout of neighborhoods.[3] A joint task force of members of CNU, the United States Green Building Council and the Natural Resources Defense Council developed

LEED-ND (Leadership in Energy and Environmental Design-Neighborhood Design), incorporating many of the principles of TODs and Smart Growth into a new LEED certification category.[4] Similarly, the New Urbanists' early concerns for traffic calming and context-sensitive transportation design have led to the drafting of a new design manual of transect-based thoroughfare standards jointly developed by CNU, the ITE (Institute of Transportation Engineers), and the FHWA (Federal Highway Administration). If approved by ITE as a recommended practice, the manual is expected to be adopted by states and municipalities, making it much easier to build walkable, context-based streets that better accommodate pedestrians, bicyclists, and transit.[5] Nonetheless, the FHWA's continued insistence on inclusion of single-use, auto-oriented areas, only limited functional classifications, and high design speeds relative to pedestrian and bicyclist safety have stirred debates amongst New Urbanists over accepting marginal improvements.

Questions of architectural style continue to invoke impassioned debate at CNU, on the listservs, and amongst architectural critics of New Urbanism.[6] Other controversial topics include the question of certifying either people or projects as properly New Urbanist, endorsement of school vouchers, and whether the inclusion of national retail chain stores is necessary or counterproductive to the making of viable, successful mixed-use places. A lively culture of critique infuses these debates, and the discourse—if often boosterish—is generally of a high intellectual caliber, advanced by the multiple disciplines participating.[7] However, despite all of the successful alliances CNU has forged, the forum does repeatedly privilege the same voices and has been perceived as akin to an exclusive club. The organization of smaller, theme-based councils, local CNU chapters, and groups like Next Generation and the Council for European Urbanism are intended to allow more voices to advance the discussion, debate the many questions, and sustain the spirit of constructive criticism of the early, smaller CNUs.

The success of the forum is perhaps best gauged not only by its ability to vigorously debate controversial topics, but also by its ability to quickly and effectively collaborate not only on the writing of the charter's principles, but also on their implementation. This was best revealed in the Mississippi Gulf Coast charrette (officially called the Mississippi Renewal Forum), held less than two months after Hurricane Katrina in 2005.[8] Instead of wasting time debating first principles, the New Urbanists were able to get to work right away, listen to stakeholders in the devastated towns, and share redevelopment plans and strategies to strengthen their downtowns, better integrate the casinos, and replace the destroyed auto-dependent patterns with walkable communities. Divided into eleven teams for the eleven towns, as well as specialized overview teams focused on the region, transportation, social impact, retail, architecture, and flood hazards, the two hundred charrette members produced unique, site-specific proposals for each town. That they were not cookie-cutter urban designs speaks to the abilities of the teams to creatively manifest

the principles of the charter in non-formulaic responses to diverse conditions.

Finally, it is the comprehensive nature of the charter itself that resists formulaic reduction. Spanning scales from an entire region to a specific building and engaging processes from ecosystems to participatory design, the charter exceeds easy formalization—and realization. No single project can manifest all of the principles of the charter, let alone demonstrate its commitment to diverse choices within the interrelated scales. Individual projects, much like individual CNU members, can only contribute to the larger collective discourse. In this sense, the model of interconnected places, systems, and scales that the charter lays out is itself a model of the forum that New Urbanism is striving to achieve. It is an ambitious model and there is much work for future congresses yet to do. New alliances with the public health community, new strategies for allowing further evolution and affordability of New Urbanist places, and new approaches to architectural style are but a few of the upcoming agenda items that will further enrich New Urbanist discourse and projects. Meeting these and other new challenges while trying to live up to the charter's impressive goals will require that New Urbanism remain a forum, not a formula.

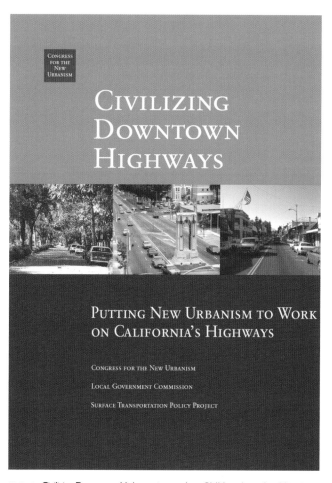

FIG. 4 *Civilizing Downtown Highways* is another CNU-authored publication aimed at helping municipalities learn from successful strategies at implementing more context-sensitive designs where state highways pass through downtowns.

MAKING CLOTH FROM THREADS

DANIEL SOLOMON

Some people just don't like what large sections of America look like, especially the parts where two thirds of the land is used for parking lots, and they don't like the way most of the food you can get along the highway tastes. Recently some have discovered something new and sinister in a ubiquitous Americana that already made them cringe. More and more they see fat, diseased, lethargic children; or they see hyperactive, restless, uncontrollable children who can't get through a school day without medication. Sometimes they hear of violent children. Something very bad seems to be going on in the land of the bacon cheeseburger, the Lincoln Navigator, and the chauffeur mom. Whatever is wrong seems to be all-of-a-piece: a way of making the world and a way of being in the world. Fat kids and crazy kids seem to be part of a much larger pattern of things, and their problems seem to be more like the symptoms of a disease, rather than the disease itself.

It does not take a great diagnostician to figure out some of what is going on. If your daily workout is the 150-foot trek from your parking lot to the elevator, you're not likely to make the cover of next month's *Planet Muscle*. If your twelve-year-old and six of her classmates test positive for type II diabetes, there is a pretty good chance they all get driven to school, and the school district has nice deals with Burger King and Pepsi. If at some point, school officials bought into the bright idea that windows are distracting in classrooms and might get broken anyway, that might explain why 20% of American second graders are on daily doses of Ritalin. Everyone goes crazy without daylight, but children go especially crazy, and neuroscientists can tell you exactly why.

Currently, the topic of physical fitness has a new currency as we have discovered that we are falling apart, and the physical world in the form we have been furiously constructing it for the last half century appears to be complicit in our demise. Fitness, or lack of it, is suddenly front-page news. The insufferable Dr. Phil hectors the mothers of fat kids to an audience of millions in prime time. Surgeon General Richard Carmona has proclaimed that our national security is in jeopardy because 50% of all young Americans are too fat to fight. Obese teenagers are not merely unhealthy, unhappy, and unattractive; they threaten our oil supplies, the very life force of democracy. Fitness has gotten to be a serious business.

Now is not the first time that politicians, planners, and others have made the connection between ordinary ways of building cities and pandemic problems of public health. Architecture and urbanism, on one hand, and public health on the other have had a long and stormy relationship. The first stirrings of what we would recognize as modernity in relation to the building of the American city, in fact, did not come from architects or urbanists—they came from social reformers, doctors, and public health activists who had little patience for the musings of most architects. It was a response to cholera and tuberculosis, not any aesthetic or cultural notions that laid the groundwork for the modern city.

In the half-century prior to World War I, however, the dominant voices in the emerging professions of architecture and city planning made a particular point of *excluding* the pathology of slums and the health crises they spawned from their domain of interest. As Daniel Burnham's "White City," part of the Chicago World's Fair of 1893, became the model for the City Beautiful movement throughout America, Charles Mulford Robinson, Burnham's contemporary and the City Beautiful's most prominent spokesman, left no doubt about the matter:

> We have first to remind ourselves, then, that our own subject is not sociology but civic art. . . . We may reasonably assert that civic art need concern itself only with the outward aspect of the houses, and therefore that for such details—sociologically pressing though they are—as sunless bedrooms, dark halls and stairs, foul cellars, dangerous employments, and an absence of bathrooms, civic art has no responsibility, however earnestly it deplores them.

With the hindsight of a hundred years it is easy for us to see how hollow these words were, because it was precisely those "sociological details" that lay to waste the civic art of the City Beautiful movement. Even the recasting of City Beautiful as the City Efficient could not save its neoclassical aestheticism from the relentless *tramp-tramp-tramp* of the modernists. The modernist hegemony is a story of people with a broad, forward-looking world view displacing people with narrow, tradition-based ones—people who could lay claim to a public health agenda, and the problems of the industrial slum displacing people who thought of that as someone else's job.

It is worth observing that after seventy years of the modernist hegemony, things have turned topsy-turvy, and it is now the modernist establishment whose aestheticism has no concern for raging public health crises. Robinson's words again have a familiar ring. His sentiments are an earlier, more primitive version of the same elitist distinction between *architecture* and *mere building* that architecture's most distinguished theorist, Kenneth Frampton, builds his life-work on. *Architecture* is a critical act, but *mere building* is a "banal, almost metabolic activity," the stuff of "animal laborians." Physical well-being is not high on the list of concerns for the critical theory crowd that now dominates the modern architectural academy.

At the end of the nineteenth century there were exceptions to the self-imposed distance that the architectural and academic establishment made for themselves from issues of public health and the American city, but they were just that—exceptions. The effective activism to reform the ways in which the normal fabric of the American industrial city was built came not from the leading architects of the day, but from public health advocates, many of them women, and from journals such as *Plumbing and Sanitary Engineer*, which sponsored the architectural competition that led to one of the great milestones in American public health and city building—New York's New Tenement Law of 1901.

Throughout that same half-century prior to World War I, during which public-health-oriented building reforms took place with scant help from the architectural establishment, there was a clearly accepted type form of what a "man of substance" was supposed to look like. The great decision makers, whether they were heads of state, generals, or architects, all conformed more or less to this ideal type form of the man of substance, here represented in the formidable personas of H. H. Richardson and Kaiser Wilhelm's Grand Admiral von Tirpitz.

After World War I, men of substance took on a different look. What Le Corbusier and his generation managed to do was to weave a new way of being, an aesthetic and an ethic out of what had been disconnected threads of avant-garde culture from the prewar world. There was nothing new about the threads, but the tapestry he and others made from them was totally new. It consisted of physical fitness (as personified by his protagonist, the boxer), germ theory (the microbes that caused disease lived in ornament, which was therefore a pestilence itself), public health (which had been responsible for all housing reform since the 1880s), cubism (which gave the movement its aesthetic), and sexual liberation (which made it all fun). Amongst the high modernists of

the 1920s and 1930s, sex was a much more popular pastime than it is in most circles today.

When Le Corbusier did wear clothes, he was as stylish as Fred Astaire (here shipboard on the way home from Rio with Josephine Baker, no less). His perky American mistress Margurite Tjader Harris and her young son Hillary were no less so.

After a particularly wild night in Chicago, Le Corbusier showed how ludicrous the ways of "men of substance" of the *ancien régime* were to him and to his generation, by donning an egg dish as his version of a Prussian-style spiked helmet, worn in all seriousness, by Kaiser Wilhelm and Feldmarshall von Moltke just a few years earlier.

The point of all this is that our own position is not so unlike that of people just before and just after World War I, who saw disparate but related cultural threads floating around that no one has quite yet woven into cloth. For us the threads are not cubism, germ theory, and sex; they are environmentalism, urbanity, physical fitness, and good food. If we are half as smart about it as Le Corbusier and the modernists were, we may have as much fun making cloth out of threads as they had, and maybe, just maybe, we may have as much impact on the making of the world that they had—maybe a better one.

Modernists of all stripes—from those who wanted to remake the city as a densely populated verdant park, to those like Frank Lloyd Wright, who wanted to abandon it altogether and live in sylvan exurban harmony with nature—all of them imagined a world remade, in which the vigor and physical health of humanity would be restored. The great paradox is that the very building conventions that came out of modernism's embrace of public health activism are responsible for much of our current public health crises. The unwalkable city is the child of modernity. It is as impossible to walk from one place to another in Le Corbusier's ideal Radiant City as it is in Frank Lloyd Wright's dream, Broadacre City. Even modern architecture's most unimpeachable social agendas—things like fire safety and universal access—have had unintended consequences that discourage physical activity. Architects struggle every day with volumes of rules that make it difficult simply to build a stair that people will use to get from here to there.

This great and ironic inversion—the rootedness of modern city planning *in* public health and the devastating consequences of modern city planning and building practices *for* public health are today most vivid in China. Currently, miserably overcrowded and unsanitary eighteenth- and nineteenth-century neighborhoods have been destroyed by tens of millions of square meters each year, replaced by dispersed, sunlit new housing estates built on the German *Zeilenbau* model from the 1920s, or Orange County sprawl from the 1970s. As this occurs, public transport and the private automobile have largely replaced the bicycle as the dominant mode of urban transport. Globalization has also brought American franchise food to China. Suddenly, and for the first time, China has massive problems of coronary artery disease, diabetes, and obesity that were unknown in the five millennia of China's past.

Our own realities take on surreal dimensions as we see them reflected in the fun-house mirror of the new China. These reflections help us to see the grotesque in our own environment, and to see that our situation is not unlike that of people who felt the stirrings of modernity before World War I. We have our own well-established version of an ancien régime, and we know that something is not right in the world where the fat kids live. The shocking statistics on the obesity and diabetes pandemic assembled by public health officials Richard Jackson and Murray Frumpkin show clearly that the parts of America that were laid out in the last half century are profoundly unhealthy.[1] Atlanta, Phoenix, and Houston are disaster zones, while New York, San Francisco, and Boston have no such problems.

As in 1910, the elements of a new synthesis are lying around, waiting to be put together. A series of isolated but related cultural movements, each with their passionate circles of enthusiasts, have not yet succeeded in coming together with the force of the modern movement in the 1920s. The food movement, New Urbanism, Green Architecture, physical fitness, which itself has two elements—exercise and diet—are among these related agendas. Something else that is important and of the same spirit is what is sometimes referred to as phenomenological architecture—buildings that reconnect us to the weather, the time of day, the cycle of the seasons, and the tactility of materials.

All of these agendas imply latent alliances that have not yet come to pass. When we wrote the charter for the New Urbanism twelve years ago, we imagined a coalition of overwhelming force that would include the greenies, foodies, fitness junkies, and very good architects who made places that were glorious to be in. This coalition would create a new canon of design that would make the aesthetics of our own ancien régime seem as ridiculous as spiked Prussian helmets and Grand Admiral von Tirpirtz's whiskers seemed to the contemporaries of Le Corbusier.

THE UNBEARABLE LIGHTNESS
OF NEW URBANISM

EMILY TALEN

New Urbanism without social complexity is dreary. In the coming decades this simple truth will compel New Urbanists to do more than create a physical shell of hoped-for diversity; it will force them to master the art of creating social mix in the same way that they have mastered the art of civic design. Out of necessity, New Urbanists will learn how to become the great integrators—experts at bridging the destructive social policy/urban design chasm that emerged out of the 1960s. The shift will occur because the alternative—"light" New Urbanism, devoid of realized social value—will become unbearable.[1]

This will require breaking with a design-centric past, however. Most New Urbanists view the current rule-driven system of land development—the one that makes it necessary to appease people who don't understand the critical importance of good design—as insufferable. Unfortunately, they have at times translated this understandable frustration into an inexcusable ambiguity about achieving social objectives. While the political burden can not be denied, New Urbanists need to reverse this, squelching in the process any attempt to equate social policy savvy with so-called big city liberalism and the failed federal policies that are so easily ridiculed.[2]

This may be the natural evolution of things, as New Urbanism emerges from its primordial phase. During the first two decades issues like street calming, parking lot location, retail mix, and the optimal dimensions of sidewalks, streets, and blocks dominated internal discourse. New Urbanist sympathizers defended these preoccupations as essential to the cause: proper built forms provided tangible models necessary for a country that had lost its ability to build good places. The task was so daunting that those of us not directly involved in the building trades threw our energies into providing whatever polemical, statistical, and scientific support we could muster.

Growing out of adolescence, New Urbanism is now forced to consider the deeper implications of its existence. This has been intensified by two events. First, the election of George W. Bush and a general shift to the right has meant that New Urbanism is now forced to accomplish its goals in an anti-planning atmosphere that heralds private property rights and limited public control above all else. Second, the tumultuous events surrounding Hurricane Katrina and its aftermath, to which New Urbanists were naturally drawn, have spotlighted New Urbanism and what it is attempting like never before. The first event abruptly severed a crucial alliance that had formed between New Urbanists and housing advocates. The second forced New Urbanists to come to terms with their own capacity to address the problem of concentrated poverty, particularly whether it would be possible to create, as a replacement, socially and economically integrated communities. Both events have forced New Urbanists to carefully consider the limitations of their design-only, politically neutral approach.

While New Urbanists were busy touting the valuable object lessons of places like Seaside, a development in Florida, the social principles of New Urbanism fell farther and farther from view. Some saw that the lack of social achievement had the potential to dismantle the moral potency of New Urbanism. While it was clear that its design principles were dictated by social equity principles—the mixing of housing types and land uses, the provision of public facilities, the elevation of civic life, an emphasis on walkable access for all—it was becoming increasingly unclear whether New Urbanist design could deliver.

If a movement becomes overconcerned with design achievements and underconcerned with social effect, it becomes a cliché of planning failure. Principled ideals that buckle under the weight of market success are a truism in United States planning history. In a society where the market is highly revered, models of social justice easily mutate into models of affluence. If left unaddressed, critics of New Urbanism will be right: social equity goals attached to design schemes are mere rhetoric. New Urbanism will have accomplished only a facade of social improvement, and the label of "yuppie infantilist fantasy" for the upper middle class will ring alarmingly true.[3]

Earlier generations of planners—from Ebenezer Howard to Clarence Stein, Benton MacKaye, and Lewis Mumford—

agonized about this. Continuously confronted with the problem that city design in a capitalist democracy merely creates better places for those who least need help, they cajoled government officials and assorted philanthropists to enlist in their cause. The question for New Urbanists is whether their commitment to social justice will lead them to do the same—to do what it takes to realize their social vision.

The problem is that what it takes is not very glamorous. It will not appeal to designers and architects who adore the clarity of figure-ground relationships, the inspiration of watercolor renderings, and the motivational form of buildings properly placed around the town square. Instead, it will require uncomfortable alliances with social activists, patience with programmatic details, cultivation of institutional connectedness, and an astute understanding of process in addition to form. New Urbanists must come to see the less sexy aspects of their endeavor as essential to giving weight and substance to their designs.

Early twentieth-century planners seemed to have had more of a stomach for such things. Ebenezer Howard worked out, in excruciating detail, the financial schemes that would keep his garden cities socially just. Members of the elite Regional Planning Association of America, a clear forerunner of the New Urbanists, were equally committed to figuring out ways to keep things affordable. Strategies ranged from the minute, such as use of particular building materials, to the profound, such as calls for the complete restructuring of the United States economy. A century later, the task before New Urbanists has not gotten any easier, but the proposals for implementation are decidedly more timid.

Socially just urban patterns are about creating complexity, and building complexity in a Western, capitalist, twenty-first-century democracy is about good design, good social policy, and good social institutions. The policy and institutional requirements make design issues—street widths, building typologies, etc.—look like a cakewalk.

Maintaining affordability is the most significant policy issue. The simple truth is that while New Urbanist neighborhoods are built for social diversity—mostly by mixing housing types—they are unlikely to stay diverse. Gentrification pressures are high. Therefore, actual achievement of the socially mixed neighborhood requires a proactive, programmatic, political response. Many New Urbanists resist this. Matters of design are palatable to a conservative constituency, while policies that either regulate the private market or call for the expenditure of public funds are not. The good news for New Urbanists is that they do not need to sign up for policy duty—there are plenty of people working this domain already, pushing for progressive strategies like housing vouchers, the Earned Income Tax Credit, and the targeting of affordable housing to low-poverty neighborhoods. But they do need to expend much more effort promoting an active dialogue among the players and constituencies involved. New Urbanists need to take it upon themselves to build the necessary bridges.

On the affordability issue, the answer is conceptually simple: what is needed is a better merger between good design and good policy. Many New Urbanists prefer political neutrality, but if that is their position, they must be prepared to forego social objectives. While it may be easier to work toward regulatory destruction—getting rid of environmental regulations, restrictions on growth, exclusionary zoning, and impact fees—proactive work in other domains will also be needed. Above all, New Urbanists must cultivate interdisciplinary thinking. Community development and affordable housing advocacy groups need to be working in tandem with designers and developers. This may be welcomed; those involved in neighborhood revitalization from the policy side have acknowledged that one reason they have not had more success is "a lack of strong, organized constituencies."[4] New Urbanism can help deliver such a constituency.

There are other connections to be nurtured. New Urbanism rests on the idea that in order to attract and sustain a diverse range of residents, neighborhoods must be well serviced and safe. There must be good parks and schools, and spaces and streets must be kept secure. Practically speaking, this means not only an adequate level of funding for public facilities, but also a healthy and active network of civic institutions. In a socially complex situation, this takes special effort, as bonds among residents are likely to come under stress exactly because of the diversity that exists.

New Urbanists cannot avoid the complications involved. As they know, wealthier residents are unlikely to want to move into an area that contains affordable housing—or even housing occupied by people with lower incomes than themselves—based on fears about property values and the quality of local services, especially schools. The repeated dismantling of this worry in terms of the effect of low-income housing on property values notwithstanding,[5] the perception that parents will have to send their children to under-performing schools and expose them to higher levels of crime and other dysfunctional behaviors is a very significant issue. In response, New Urbanists must be vigilant and pursue all angles—task forces, neighborhood meetings, mediation—whatever it takes.

Another complication stems from the fact that different kinds of people living together in one neighborhood require different kinds of services and facilities. This means that a socially complex New Urbanist community will have to work hard to match services to populations.[6] For example, public transportation and affordable daycare are likely to be much more important to poor families than wealthy ones. African Americans may have different tastes in neighborhood attributes than Caucasians. New Urbanists are going to have to involve themselves in efforts to ensure that the type and spatial location of amenities in their neighborhoods are appropriate to the needs of residents with very different kinds of needs.

Given all kinds of human resistance, New Urbanists have to find ways to emphasize the positive aspects of diversity that are immediately recognizable. They should work together with civic institutions to find ways to communicate that the multiple objectives of social diversity are mutually reinforcing: that diversity is a generator of economic health, and improved access to all kinds of services is a clear and highly beneficial outcome of diversity. Civic institutions will be needed to engage residents in ways that overcome their fear of others, help them take control of whatever public safety issues arise, and work to build social connectedness instead of isolation and exclusion. New Urbanists must find ways to connect multiple neighborhood-level interests in ways that are mutually sustaining.

All those seemingly intangible social concepts—social capital, collective efficacy, civic engagement, informal control—are the conceptual strength undergirding every New Urbanist endeavor. New Urbanists need to figure out how to make these ideas practical and real. This hasn't really happened yet. While there is an assumed understanding that New Urbanism works, even thrives, on such concepts, no one seems to know how to put them into play. As they figure this out, solutions will be born of necessity. Invigorating connections within socially heterogeneous neighborhoods will require an effort focused on increasing the capacity of different kinds of neighbors to work together; this does not mean everyone has to be friends, but it does mean that a certain level of familiarity will need to be encouraged in order to make the socially complex place work. More than ever, residents will need to be engaged and civically minded. Residents will have to feel that their voice is genuinely heard, and that whatever anxieties they have about living in a place full of complexity are addressed.

All this means that New Urbanism may need a different conceptualization of the way in which complexity, community, and neighborhood fit together. There are plenty of prominent people to enlist in this cause. Cornel West's view is that "sense of home" means being in a place that recognizes the importance of difference. Robert Putnam has explored how diversity generates "bridging" social capital, the all-important kind of capital that occurs among people of different socioeconomic groups. Scholars have hypothesized that social diversity, not homogeneity, is the basis of "active neighboring." Amitai Etzioni is proposing a "diversity within unity" platform that meshes, at least philosophically, with everything New Urbanism stands for. Others have explored the power of diversity as a tool for rebuilding social capital, documented in books like *Dry Bones Rattling: Community Building to Revitalize American Democracy.*[7] The notion that community can be diverse, whereby groups maintain separate cultural identity and homogeneity is not essential, goes against conventional views about neighborhoods in America. New Urbanism should relish it.

Some New Urbanists are already engaged—connecting to social policy groups, involving themselves in the workings of civic institutions, reaching beyond matters of pure design. There are some who are firmly open-minded about doing what it takes to achieve social justice in well-designed communities, but the connections are not fully embedded in the New Urbanist organizational establishment. Actual achievement of socially just community building is mostly optional. Builders of exclusive resort communities are welcomed into the club, even given awards. There is no accounting of social goal achievement, little understanding of what it will take to achieve equity, and little disclosure about the failure to get there so far. Politically conservative developers are welcomed with fanfare while policy activists working from the left are non-present.

New Urbanists are impatient with vague calls for social justice that aren't linked to tangible action, so let me offer five very specific actions the New Urbanists can undertake now: sponsor a conference that puts social policy advocates and urban designers in the same room; invite housing advocates to the next CNU conference and make sure they are fully engaged with New Urbanist leadership; keep track of progress in meeting social justice goals by setting quantifiable measures; fund a demonstration project that could be used to work through the ins and outs of creating a truly diverse New Urbanist community; give a special award to any New Urbanist development that meets its social diversity objectives.

The New Urbanists should be applauded for illuminating the connection between social equity and city design. Now they must move forward with it. They need only to recognize that their job is incomplete, and that there is more to urbanism than building the right container. If they do that, they will successfully create the kinds of places we really need.

THE CHALLENGES OF ACHIEVING
SOCIAL OBJECTIVES THROUGH MIXED USE

JILL GRANT

New Urbanism has become closely associated with mixed-use development as it has become more prominent in recent decades. Mixing uses promises to allow New Urbanism to achieve many of its social objectives, including affordability and diversity. The pattern of segregated uses that result from a philosophy of "everything in its place," as Constance Perin[1] put it, certainly undermined the modernist city. As long as uses remain segregated, cities seem unlikely to provide affordable housing close to work and services and to ensure the diversity of people, places, and uses vital to urban living.

The primary approach in New Urbanism advocates mixing types of uses, such as commercial and office with residential. It simultaneously encourages mixing intensities of uses, such as multiple-unit housing with single, detached-unit housing.[2] Thus the New Urbanist community might properly reflect the concentrated and fine-grain mix of uses and housing types found in European or Asian cities.

Planners have widely adopted the New Urbanist philosophy,[3] and in many communities have begun to implement its strategies in the hopes that mixing would achieve social objectives that have proven resistant to other efforts. Certainly many of its proponents want to create communities that can provide homes to meet a wide range of incomes and abilities, and which allow people to meet their daily needs without requiring access to a car (figure 1). But practice reveals the challenges in achieving these aims. First, New Urbanism has not become the dominant development paradigm. Second, even when New Urbanist projects are built, they do not necessarily produce affordability and diversity as desired.[4] In this essay I briefly consider some of the challenges of achieving social objectives like affordability and diversity through mixed use.

Affordability

New Urban approaches advocate a mix of housing types, sizes, and price points. By designing smaller lots, and including accessory dwelling units over stores and garages, planners hope to offer a range of housing products to suit most household types.[5] Increasing the supply of affordable housing would thus allow New Urban approaches to contribute to equity and diversity.[6]

New Urban practice shows some good examples of housing mix that accommodate a range of households. Poundbury, a new community in Dorset, England, includes 20% non-market housing: charitable organizations build the units for less affluent households.[7] The city of Vancouver, Canada, requires developers to provide 20% non-market units in projects in its central area (figure 2): slim towers and ground-level town houses create good examples of modernist New Urbanism.[8] Some European projects, such as Karow Nord[9] in Berlin, Germany, implement New Urban approaches on a large scale with a high proportion of affordable units.[10] Extensive use of non-profit housing associations results in a higher proportion of affordable units in European projects than is generally the case in North America.[11] Government financial support allows these urban villages to meet the needs of low-income households while maintaining high design standards.

American New Urban projects may have begun with the intent of providing affordable housing, but experience indicates that they seldom achieve it. Because of their high quality and attractive environment, many have generated a market premium of 25% or more than comparable conventional units.[12] Some New Urban developments feature very large houses on small lots.[13] Small-lot developments typically appear in inflationary housing markets that drive up land values and hence deny affordability. Although social housing in the Prince of Wales's Poundbury is affordable, the market units are expensive: "Prices for these houses vary between £230,000 and £425,000—well above the norm for this part of Dorset."[14] Houses in Seaside, a development in Florida, originally sold for modest prices,[15] but now go for millions.[16] Fine traditional homes may provide status symbols for elites who choose urban styling over conventional suburbia.[17] The prices on market-rate homes in New Urbanist projects are generally higher than comparable units in neighboring conventional projects.

New Urbanists increasingly acknowledge that their projects have become good investments, rising as much as 25% in value in a year.[18] Garde's analysis finds that New Urbanist projects have not created affordable housing in the United States.[19] Neuman describes the market barriers to integrating affordable housing into projects.[20] Although New Urbanists argue that reducing road dimensions and lot sizes can improve affordability in the long term,[21] the higher design standards and upgraded infrastructure associated with the model add to the cost in the short term.[22] Significant cost savings for residents would depend on substantially higher net densities that prove difficult to achieve in practice in many markets.

Some examples of market-driven New Urban developments have proven relatively affordable. New Urban News describes projects with smaller homes and simpler architectural detailing designed to keep costs moderate.[23] The developers of McKenzie Towne in Calgary indicated in interviews that they reduced the expensive design features of the initial offering to appeal to the starter market in the late 1990s (figure 3). Carrying extensive financing to build the infrastructure of the first phase, and facing the market pressures of

FIG. I Orenco Station lies about a fifteen-minute walk from the light rail station that links it to downtown Portland, Oregon.

FIG. 2 Vancouver, Canada, is a good example of modernist New Urbanism.

FIG. 3 A small house in McKenzie Towne in Calgary, Canada.

FIG. 4 Kentlands' main street features dentists' offices and martial arts' halls, but few pedestrians on a Saturday afternoon.

enting buyers to a remote suburban location, the developers sought strategies to sell property more quickly. Designers therefore moved to a more conventional plan and house designs that reduced construction costs to appeal to the robust starter market. Reducing costs required sacrificing some New Urbanist principles like high-quality design.

Redevelopment provides important opportunities for New Urbanism within existing urban areas. In some cases, New Urbanist projects may unintentionally undermine affordability by making areas more desirable. Projects may contribute to escalating prices and gentrification; as they encourage affluent households to move back to the inner city they displace low-income households.[24] Some New Urbanists see gentrification as good for the city.[25] Andrés Duany says, "It is the rising tide that lifts all ships. . . . What spokesmen for the poor insist on calling gentrification is actually the timeless urban cycle of a free society organically adjusting its habitat."[26] Such socioeconomic change increases tax revenues that cities crave. Marshall quotes Duany as arguing that "affordable housing is not what cities need. Because they don't pay taxes. They bankrupt cities."[27] While some New Urbanists want affordability, others see it as unimportant.

FIG. 5 The heart of the mixed-use town center in Cornell in Markham, Ontario, (a new town designed by Duany and Plater-Zyberk) sits empty after closing in 2006. Retail struggles to thrive in the New Urbanism centers.

FIG. 6 Ground floor retail awaits tenants in this Brussels, Belgium, New Urbanism project.

Although Duany and Elizabeth Plater-Zyberk suggest that New Urbanism contributes to more inclusive communities,[28] in recent writings they point to the need for government support to facilitate affordable housing.[29] Practice has convinced some New Urbanists that the market alone cannot address affordability. It also reveals conflicting objectives within the movement. New Urbanists crave market success while hoping to demonstrate social equity: the former may, unfortunately, come at the cost of the latter.

New Urbanist principles played a major role in the philosophy of community development and redeveloping American public housing in the late 1990s and early 2000s. Deitrick and Ellis noted successes in Pittsburgh,[30] and Steuteville[31] says that the HOPE VI[32] program worked wonders. Responding to New Urbanist critiques of concentrated poverty,[33] HOPE VI advocated mixed housing and mixed-use projects at a human scale.[34] The projects sought to renovate public housing and improve poor neighborhoods by adding new uses and mixing in market tenants. As implemented, HOPE VI resulted in a net loss of sixty thousand affordable units.[35] While the new mixed-income communities provide attractive living environments near city centers, Pyatok argues that, as a whole, the application

FIG. 7 The new community of Upton, just south of Northampton in the United Kingdom, employs many principles associated with New Urbanism.

of New Urbanist principles to public housing removed poor people from their neighborhoods, ignored issues of poverty, and proved socially regressive.[36] Sufficient evidence is now available to suggest that mixing housing types generally cannot solve the affordability problem without other social interventions.

Diversity

By mixing uses and housing types New Urbanist approaches attempt to create social spaces to integrate a range of household sizes, incomes, and types. Duany et al. claim, "While it is only a start, a small corner store does wonders to limit automobile trips out of the development, and does more than a social club to build the bonds of community."[37] New Urbanists argue that mixing uses avoids sprawl. Mixed use has also been a key strategy for stimulating an urban renaissance in Europe.[38] New Urbanist projects invariably plan to include residential, commercial, and usually institutional or office uses, often mixed at a fine scale (within the building or within the block).

In practice, however, achieving the level and types of mixed use desired has proven difficult.[39] For example, Kentlands has a good supply of residential and commercial uses, but office development did not meet the initial targets.[40] Kentlands' main street has mostly service uses, while the commercial uses concentrate in a regional mall, leaving the town center eerily quiet (figure 4). Store locations in New Urbanist projects visited in Canada, Belgium, and the United States often remained unoccupied, sometimes several years after construction (figures 5 and 6). The Potsdam-Kirchsteigfeld urban village in Germany projected thousands of jobs, but few materialized.[41] Designating areas for mixed use does not guarantee that the mix will work, especially in communities with commercial alternatives.

As Thompson-Fawcett notes of the urban village movement in the United Kingdom, "There is an express objective here to encourage people to meet with social difference, in order to enable an understanding of, and empathy for, heterogeneity, and thereby enhance community civility and democracy" (figure 7).[42] The New Urbanists see mixing people as socially healthy.[43] They want to create social mosaics to replace ghettos. According to New Urbanist thought, mixing creates venues for social interaction that turn *difference* (with its negative connotation) into *diversity* (with a positive connotation).

In practice, though, mixing people does not prove easy. Private developments in North America rarely include non-market housing, thus limiting the range of residents to those households able to cover rents or purchase prices. When projects do integrate market and non-market units, tensions between households in the different unit types may present issues.[44] Sociologists will not find this surprising: as Wright notes, cross-class friendships are rare.[45] The New Urbanist ideal of generating social harmony by mixing community residents often encounters resistance in everyday life where people construct social (and sometimes physical) barriers to integration.

Garde found little ethnic mixing in American New Urbanist projects.[46] The diversity quotient for Seaside, for instance, falls well below that of the state of Florida generally.[47] Frantz and Collins[48] and Ross[49] comment on the paucity of African Americans in Celebration, a development in Florida. New Urbanist projects rarely reflect the class or ethnic diversity of the wider society.

Many projects create homogeneous middle- and upper-class neighborhoods with homes priced well above the mean for their area. Falconer Al-Hindi[50] and Till[51] characterize traditional neighborhood developments as exclusive and conservative places; Veregge argues the communities exemplify a limited version of history that focuses on Anglo heritage.[52] Far from celebrating diversity, New Urbanist developments may minimize it.

Till sees a "geography of otherness" as implicit in neotraditional town planning.[53] Heritage-themed projects encourage a particular kind of cultural identification. Based on a case study, Day questions New Urbanism's ability to accommodate Latino diversity in California;[54] Mendez disagrees in principle, arguing that the compact form associated with New Urbanist approaches could suit Latino lifestyles.[55] Advocates for seniors see New Urbanist communities as meeting the need for "aging in place,"[56] but some worry about the ability of traditional styles (with elevated front porches) to facilitate accessibility for the mobility-impaired.[57]

Given the empirical evidence from practice to date, the ability to generate and accommodate diversity remains an unproven point for New Urbanism. Planners can designate areas as suitable for mixing, but market and social factors play the key roles in actually achieving social, economic, and cultural diversity.

Toward Social Mix

While New Urbanism creates beautiful places, the evidence available does not generally support claims that, through mix, it can solve problems such as a lack of affordability and diversity. New Urbanist developments enjoy no immunity from the social problems and fears of contemporary society. The movement's optimistic promise to contribute to developing more civil and authentic communities remains suspect for many observers of urban issues. The challenge of building affordable, diverse, and inclusive communities demands much more than good urban form. Mix is a necessary but not sufficient condition for achieving good community. Social integration requires concerted action to create opportunities and accommodation for all community members. These ambitions may be beyond the ability of designers to deliver through good planning.

PART 3: SUBURBIA, SPRAWL, AND URBAN DECLINE

3.1

THE SUBURBAN CITY

DOLORES HAYDEN

> It is the city trying to escape the consequences of being a city
> while still remaining a city. It is urban society trying to eat
> its cake and keep it, too.
>
> —Harlan Douglas
> *The Suburban Trend*, 1925

When Kenneth T. Jackson published his prize-winning history of suburbs, *Crabgrass Frontier*, in 1985, he concluded, optimistically, that the United States was turning away from suburbia. He suggested that "the long process of suburbanization . . . will slow over the next two decades." He predicted that rising energy and land costs would lead people back to urban centers.[1] Instead, in the last two decades, Americans have settled on the distant fringes of metropolitan regions faster than ever before, while older downtowns have lost population, jobs, and economic vitality.[2] Downtowns with offices, stores, museums, and entertainment drew Americans from the 1870s to the 1950s, but a suburban trend in the mid-1920s became a suburban tide in the 1950s. By 1970, more Americans lived in suburbs than in either central cities or rural areas. By 2000, more Americans lived in suburbs than in central cities and rural areas combined. The United States had become a predominantly suburban nation. Although inner cities still housed certain institutions important to metropolitan regions, many key economic and cultural centers such as corporate headquarters and regional theaters had relocated to suburbs.

After almost two centuries of steady growth, suburbs have overwhelmed the centers of cities, creating metropolitan regions largely formed of suburban parts. In the suburban city of the early twentieth century, all seven historic suburban landscape patterns continue to exist. Most political entities include the fragments, overlays, collisions, and erasures of more than one pattern, because suburban growth has been constant across the political boundaries of states, counties, cities, towns, and villages. Metropolitan regions reveal what critics call suburban sprawl, the lack of land use controls or environmental planning.[3] They also reflect a culture of easy obsolescence, where yesterday's picturesque enclave may be sliced by today's new highway leading to tomorrow's edge node.

There have been many efforts to rename the spread-out suburban city. "Galactic metropolis" taps a word from outer space. "Regional city" combines spread and center. So does "sprawl city." "When Suburbs Are the City," the title of a paper by historian Sam Bass Warner, Jr., captures the problem in words that everyone understands.[4]

In the spaces of the suburban city lie metropolitan complexities. American suburbia has always been physically and socially diverse. The outskirts of mid-nineteenth-century cities housed noxious industries like slaughterhouses and glue factories, social reform establishments such as poorhouses, orphanages, contagious disease hospitals, and prisons, plus temporary sites for camp meetings and traveling circuses.[5] There were suburban temperance communities as well as squatters on marginal land. Although the history of the suburbs includes countless examples of exclusion implemented through developers' deed restrictions, bankers' red-lining, realtors' steering, government lending policies, and other discriminatory practices, not all nineteenth-century suburban residential areas were white, Protestant, and elite. From about 1870 on, many working-class and lower-middle-class families were attracted to the periphery of the city, where land was cheap and houses might be constructed with sweat equity. While nineteenth-century immigrants often spent time in inner-city tenements before moving out to streetcar suburbs, today some new immigrants to the United States head straight to the suburbs to live where jobs are easier to find.

Some affluent suburban communities remain almost entirely white and Protestant, but there are also Irish American suburbs, African American, Polish American, and Chinese American ones, as well as older streetcar suburbs like Boyle Heights in Los Angeles, a place that has welcomed successive waves of new immigrants from Mexico, Russia, and Japan.

Sometimes the impact of ethnic diversity can be seen and heard in the suburban landscape: New Haven's Italian American neighborhoods reveal gardens of basil, tomatoes, and oregano, as well as yard shrines honoring the Virgin; Latino families in East Los Angeles decorate their front yards with traditional *nacimientos*; Sikhs have renamed a street in Fremont, California, for their Gurdwara Temple; Polish Americans have established talk radio in Polish from suburban Pomona, New York; Chinese Americans offer news and entertainment in Chinese out of Freeport, Long Island; and Indian immigrants broadcast from a radio station in Metuchen, New Jersey.[6]

The diversity of suburbia is evidence of assimilation and a source of conflict. Suburban residents from different ethnic backgrounds have purchased older single-family houses and yards only to use them in new ways. In Silver Spring, Maryland, planners are reexamining the term "household" to deal with perceived overcrowding by extended families from Latino backgrounds. In Fairfax County, Virginia, Vietnamese, Indians, Arabs, Pakistanis, West Africans, and East Africans have joined Latin Americans looking for affordable shelter near their suburban jobs. Many households are large, multigenerational groups, with aunts, uncles, brothers, sisters, cousins, and grandparents helping to pay the rent or make the mortgage. Their cars crowd small driveways. Dozens of these immigrant families have paved over their front lawns to make it easier to park, offending their neighbors. In June 2002, Fairfax County passed a controversial regulation forbidding homeowners to pave their front yards.[7]

If suburban space has sometimes resisted ethnic diversity, it has been even less accommodating to changes in household composition and women's roles. Men of all classes have portrayed the suburban home as a retreat from the cares of their jobs. But since the time of the borderlands, houses have been workplaces for millions of women of all classes and all ages—paid cooks, cleaning women, and nannies, as well as unpaid housewives and mothers.

Almost two centuries later, household composition has changed.[8] Married couples with children are no longer dominant in suburbs; they are outnumbered by young singles and the elderly living alone. As suburban families have become more diverse and millions of housewives have found paid work, the male-breadwinner family with stay-at-home mom and two children, in a peaceful three-bedroom colonial with a leafy yard and sociable neighbors, predominates only in reruns of old sitcoms. Still, gendered work often remains the rule. Women lug groceries, push strollers, make meals, and serve as "taxi parents." Men do yard work and maintenance. New nurturing roles are evolving in new kinds of households, including those of employed women, single parents, single people, same-sex partners, and two-worker couples, but millions of suburban women have moved into the paid labor force while retaining their "second shift" at home. Because women hold jobs in every economic category, the roads are filled with women commuters as well as taxi parents. "I drove on down the Trail of Errands," sighs the main character in *Carpool*, a novel by Mary Cahill.[9] The "Trail of Errands" is far longer than it needs to be because single-family zoning is often too rigid and the regulatory system in mortgage banking has been formed around the sale or resale of one kind of house for one kind of family—a male breadwinner, a female housewife, and their young children.

Dismissing and Rediscovering Suburbia

Suburbia conceals as well as reveals its complexity. For years, when urban historians wrote about the "city," they meant the center, the skyline, downtown. Suburbs were left out of traditional "city biographies," which emphasized economic development, population growth, and the achievements of business leaders and politicians. Everyone knew that large suburbs existed and had something to do with the process of urbanization. But most historians thought they were less significant than the city center: spatially, because they were less dense than centers; culturally, because more of their attractions involved nature than architecture; and socially, because their daytime activities involved women and children more than men.

Because of prejudices about density, high culture, and gender, suburbia resisted scrutiny. It evaded art-historical analysis, derived from the aesthetic assessment of outstanding buildings, and urban analysis, based on demographic and economic statistics. As a result, many urban historians were surprised that the consistent spatial push for residential development at the very edge of the city finally brought about the dominance of a suburban pattern in the metropolitan landscape as a whole. They were intellectually unprepared for the shift.

In the 1970s and 1980s, architects and urban theorists also largely ignored suburbs or lambasted them as banal areas of tract houses. Artists and writers tended to agree, perhaps because television, films, and advertising often represented American family life in comfortable suburban houses as a mindless consumer Utopia. Synonyms for "suburb" in the 1970s included "land of mediocrity," "middle America," and "silent majority," as well as outskirts, outposts, borderlands, and periphery.

Today there is far more interest in suburbs and less agreement about their character. Beginning in the 1980s and 1990s, architects and landscape architects started to reconsider the American suburb as a built product. Some studied the social and cultural history of vernacular building and landscapes.[11] Others argued that better design was the key to better suburbs. These "New Urbanists" designed model developments, rewrote zoning codes, and attacked highway engineers who encouraged traffic.[12]

During the same decades, a group of sociologists, geographers, and planners created New Urbanist sociology, unrelated to New Urbanist architecture.[13] They analyzed the forces driving urban growth. While suburbs and greenfield construction were not their main focus, they studied the political economy of places, researching how the built environment had been financed, planned, designed, constructed, and marketed. Harvey Molotch's 1976 essay "The City as a Growth Machine" called attention to the ways local elites dealt with land as "a market commodity providing wealth and power."[14] These social scientists attacked "planned sprawl" and wrote about "growth machines" or "sprawl machines," suggesting that pro-growth lobbies were comparable to the corrupt urban political machines that figures like Boss Tweed forged in the mid-nineteenth century.[15]

New Urbanist sociology has directly influenced community organizing. "The engine of growth is powered by the fortunes resulting from land speculation and real estate development," wrote activist Eben Fodor of Eugene, Oregon. "The primary business interests are the landowners, real estate developers, mortgage bankers, realtors, construction companies and contractors, cement and sand and gravel companies, and building suppliers."[16] In *Better Not Bigger*, Fodor concluded that professionals whose jobs depend upon growth—including planners, architects, landscape architects, surveyors, interior designers, and engineers—tend to support new development. He argued that planners and members of the design professions have often chosen not to criticize their clients for fear of losing them.[17]

Along with historians, sociologists, planners, and architects, geographers have joined suburban debates. Years before Kenneth T. Jackson defined the suburb as a community of middle-class commuters' residences, many geographers asserted that the American suburb had "evolved" beyond being a "bedroom suburb" for workers who commuted to the center for their jobs. The geographers studied jobs in the periphery. As early as the 1960s some of them claimed that they saw enough new employment at the outer edge of metropolitan areas to call the fabric that was thriving "urban." Could a booming place be suburban and urban at the same time?

Urban historian Robert Fishman said yes. In 1987 he startled readers by announcing the era of "the suburb" was over. He defined the American suburb as a place for commuters, as Jackson had, but he defined it even more narrowly as an exclusive and leafy residential enclave of male-headed upper-class and upper-middle-class families, a "bourgeois Utopia," primarily Protestant and white. For Fishman, a "classic" suburb was a Main Line Philadelphia railroad suburb between the 1920s and the 1960s.[18] What existed in the 1980s, he thought, was a "post-suburb" or a "technoburb."

The rush was on to invent new terms: outer city, shock suburb, out-town, edge city, boomburb, and exopolis. *American Quarterly* sponsored a debate about the redefinitions, "Bold New City or Built-Up 'Burb?"[19] Did scholars and planners need new words? New words often obscure old problems. Words like post-suburb, techno-burb, and exopolis suggest that ordinary citizens will not understand issues. They imply that massive new construction is inevitable, and they encourage designers and planners to develop futuristic solutions for fringe areas.

Urban growth has been a continuous economic and political process. Because federal supports for private real estate development—throughout the eras of the sitcom suburbs, the edge nodes, and the rural fringes—have consistently favored new construction, Americans have abandoned existing built environments, willingly or unwillingly. The conservation and repair of urban and suburban fabric depends on a fuller understanding of why unplanned growth has prevailed.

Arguing for the metropolitan context of suburban landscapes, this history attempts to reconnect city and suburb, showing that since the early nineteenth century suburbs have been important to the process of urbanization and economic growth, perhaps as important as the crowded centers of cities. Defining the seven historic landscapes of urban expansion can lead to more precise proposals for their reconstruction. The vernacular houses and yards of suburbia, the older suburban and small-town centers, so long overlooked by urban historians, are an essential part of American life. Their fabric could be preserved by sympathetic practitioners, skilled developers, architects, planners, and public historians, who mend and reweave landscapes while adding new housing, services, and amenities. This would demand both political insight and cultural understanding.

By 2003, when most Americans lived in suburban cities, many of the spatial conventions and social expectations of the nineteenth and early twentieth centuries remained tangled in memory and manners. Change is difficult when suburban houses and yards are infused with the pieties of Protestant, Catholic, and Jewish "family values" and also contain the purchases of a society inundated with advertising and consumer culture. Long ago, Catharine Beecher promoted the "Heaven-devised plan of the family state" with a Gothic cottage. In the 1950s Elizabeth Gordon championed "the architecture that will encourage the development of individualism" in *House Beautiful*, calling modern family houses and private gardens a bulwark against communism. Both authors saw private housing as a stage for middle-class consumption, and consumption as the route to economic prosperity, a view they shared with developers, manufacturers, and utilities. This is the "Consumers' Republic" historian Lizabeth Cohen has defined, but not the side of suburban life twenty-first-century environmentalists wish to preserve.[20]

At every stage of suburban development in the United States people created more frugal patterns, places where earning and nurturing were essential parts of daily life. Some of these patterns appeared in working-class suburbs. Some appeared in communitarian settlements, new towns, Greenbelt towns, and cooperative multifamily housing projects. All were part of suburban choices before the 1950s, and they are alternatives to remember. In most cases, designs to conserve energy and land had merit, and some, like the solar houses of the 1940s, were brilliant. Excessive private consumption was not inevitable. It was the result of sustained pressure from real estate interests and their allies in government to marginalize the alternatives to unlimited private suburban growth. As the production of built space came to dominate the economy, replacing the production of manufactured goods, the pressures increased.

Current environmental campaigns aim to increase sustainability and reduce the consumption of nonrenewable resources. These campaigns to halt unchecked growth will fail unless most Americans know the complex history of their own suburbs, and how major developers, with increasing collaboration from the federal government, have mass-marketed ever-larger private developments while neglecting to consider the environmental consequences or to build infrastructure for public life. Politicians of both major parties have supported hundreds of antisprawl initiatives across the country. The next step is to understand how, over almost two centuries, sales of model houses for the millions have overwhelmed more sustainable alternatives for housing and urban design. Seven historic patterns of suburban neighborhoods embody the material history of Americans' private dreams even as they form complex and problematic urban realms.

SPEED, SIZE, AND THE DESTRUCTION OF CITIES

DOM NOZZI

City planners are charged with the task of providing professional recommendations about how a community can protect and promote its quality of life. Yet the insidious and now overwhelming introduction of car travel into American society has created an awful dilemma for planners. By their very nature, cars create vicious cycles within which their users are increasingly dependent on using them. Cars therefore are continuously building a growing army of users demanding that conditions be improved for car travel.

In fact, nearly everything today's American city planners are asked to do is aimed at softening the detrimental effects of cars: zoning that strictly segregates residences from offices and retail; expansive storm-water basins; enormous building setbacks; regulations to protect us from the awful, gargantuan "Big Box" retailer from "Anywhere, USA" which draws seemingly endless numbers of cars; regulations for light pollution spawned by the high-intensity illumination needs of the car; regulations that cordon off auto sales and services; generous landscape buffers and berms; gigantic parking lot requirements—each of these tasks represents the effort to reduce the negative effects of the car, yet actually enables and promotes even *more* dependence on car travel, thereby closing the self-perpetuating loop. The dilemma for city planners is that they work within a society that strongly desires an improved car "habitat"—yet the habitat necessary to provide a high quality of life for *people* frequently and significantly clashes with the car habitat.

Much of what New Urbanism is about pertains to efforts to restore the timeless tradition of designing communities where people, not cars, are the design imperative. Not to eliminate cars, but to ensure that they are disciplined and obligated to respect and yield to the needs of the people's habitat.

Let us take a look at important ways in which cars have come to degrade the habitat of people—thereby harming our quality of life. These mechanisms are self-perpetuating. That is, as we travel by car, a growing number of us are compelled to become increasingly dependent on car travel, and therefore find ourselves increasingly insisting on community designs that further lock us into car dependence and a downwardly spiraling quality of life.

Fortressing

Dangerous, high-speed, reckless, inattentive driving is now of epidemic proportions in nearly every community in America. Motor vehicle collisions with bicyclists and pedestrians have remained at unacceptably high levels for several decades. The hostile, high-decibel conditions delivered by high motor vehicle speeds on American roads has led to costly, growing efforts to buffer homes and businesses from these frenzied, perilous, increasingly wide suburban highways. Fortressing efforts such as berms, masonry walls, large building setbacks, thick vegetation, and grade separations have all been tried. Those houses and commercial establishments that are unable to tolerate these increasingly roaring raceways are being abandoned or relocated to outlying, sprawling locations. Much of this abandonment contributed to the widespread decline of American main streets in the '60s, '70s, and '80s.

The quandary is vividly clear: More and more, we are frustrated to discover that high-speed motor vehicles are simply incompatible with a livable community for humans, despite all our efforts to separate ourselves from the growing speedways that are engulfing us.

Speed

High-speed roads are not only inhospitable to houses and businesses; they also create a "barrier effect" in which it is increasingly difficult to use such roads for bicycling and walking (or even transit). Consequently, per capita motor vehicle trips grow in the community. In combination with the higher speeds, fuel consumption, air pollution, and blood pressure rise significantly.

As an aside, it should be noted that perhaps the most important reason that high-speed roads discourage and endanger bicycle and pedestrian trips is the "speed differential" between motor vehicles and those bicycling or walking. When motor vehicles move at modest speeds of, say, fifteen miles per hour, the speed differential between vehicles, bicycles, and pedestrians is relatively small. Motorists have more reaction time. Bicyclists and pedestrians feel more comfortable next to slower speed cars. Collisions with cars are more rare and more likely to result in survival.

What Are the Origins of High-speed Roads?

Motor vehicles, by their nature, require an enormous amount of space. This is a growing problem—as our emergency service vehicles, passenger cars, and commercial trucks continue to grow in size—resulting, unintentionally, in the need to have overly large street and intersection dimensions. Indeed, a car takes up so much space that roads become congested with only a modest number of vehicles on them. Because congestion happens so quickly when cars are used for transportation, the advent of the car in the early twentieth century led road planners to push for wider road lanes (in some instances from eight feet wide to twelve feet wide) and an increase in the number of travel lanes (often from, two lanes to four or more).

The growth in the size of roads led to an inexorable, vicious cycle. Because an emphasis on expanding and promoting the car habitat (roads and parking lots) inevitably led to a decline in the quality of the human habitat (neighborhoods and main streets), the early twentieth century witnessed a growing desire to flee the increasingly congested, dirty, and degraded in-town locations for the "greener pastures" of suburban life in peripheral locations.

Most humans lead busy lives. They have what is known as a "travel time budget," wherein there is a desire to maintain an equilibrium in the amount of time devoted each day to regular travel (such as the commute to work). Cross-culturally and throughout history, we have learned that this travel time budget, on average, is approximately 1.1 hours per day.

The growing desire to escape cities being degraded by aggressive, high-speed motor vehicle travel meant, primarily, that there was a pressing need to widen roads to enable a growing number of cars to travel at high speeds for greater distances (in order to maintain the 1.1-hour travel time). Unfortunately, this set into motion a downwardly spiraling vicious cycle, in which high-speed motor vehicles brought us increasingly degraded cities, which pushed a growing number of us to flee to peripheral locations. The growth in peripheral residences led to a growing popular demand for bigger, faster roads.

And each time we built bigger, faster roads, we degraded that ring of city growth (by creating a congested, unpleasant car habitat), which, in turn, pushed a growing number of us to flee to an even more peripheral location in a never-ending process.

The Forgiving Street

Over the course of the past several decades, American motorists have been given the opportunity to drive primarily on what are called "forgiving streets." The forgiving street design was born in the minds of engineers who observed car collisions with trees, other cars, and bicyclists. The supposed solution seemed obvious: remove trees, parked cars, buildings, and other "obstacles" from the shoulders of the street; increase lane width; add additional travel lanes.

The theory was that such treatments would mean that incompetent, inattentive, higher-speed motorists would be forgiven if, for instance, they drove too fast or drove off the roadway, because there would be fewer obstacles to crash into.

What the engineers forgot about was human nature. Humans, by nature, tend to drive at the highest possible speed that can be driven safely. Traditionally, narrow streets with on-street parked cars and buildings and trees right along the street meant that a street could only be driven safely at about twenty miles per hour. Drivers needed to drive relatively slowly, courteously, and attentively (in other words, carefully) to safely negotiate such streets. But today, with the stubborn adherence to the theory that forgiving street design increases safety, we now find ourselves, ironically, with streets that are much *less* safe. Forgiving streets allow even inattentive, high-speed, reckless, low-skill drivers to drive "safely" at, say, forty miles per hour without crashing into the aforementioned obstacles.

The result of the forgiving street paradigm should have been predictable. Less safe, higher-speed streets increasingly filled by motorists who are chatting on cell phones or putting on lipstick as they drive. And it should come as no surprise that the forgiving street is breeding an army of incompetent drivers, because it requires less skill to drive than the traditional street.

Conventional traffic engineers and elected officials were happy to learn that forgiving streets provided an additional "benefit;" Not only did we expect them to increase safety, but they would also *speed up traffic*. So support for the forgiving street was found from not only those seeking greater roadway "safety," but also those who lived in and benefited from the construction of peripheral, sprawl housing (which is enabled by higher-speed roads).

Because nearly all of our roads have now been built to be supposedly forgiving roads, the vast majority of American drivers now have the *expectation* of being able to drive at high speeds *at all times*. As a result, it is essential that we ratchet down these high-speed expectations by incrementally calming our roads throughout the community. Having only one or a handful of calmed roads in a community does not typically work well, as most of its drivers retain the expectation of high-speed driving because only rarely, if ever, are such drivers obligated to slow down. If the expectation of high-speed driving persists, the infrequent instances of calming can result in a significant level of "road rage" (and non-compliance) by motorists who believe they are entitled to drive sixty miles per hour on community roads.

Lack of Parking?

Perhaps one of the most common suggestions for "improving" downtowns in America is to recommend that more free parking be created to address what is perceived to be a parking shortage. That supposed lack of parking is the primary cause of downtown decline.

As motorists, we quickly conclude that the recipe for a healthier downtown is to make it cheaper and easier to park. This reasoning claims that people are not going downtown because they can't find the free parking they can find in suburban shopping centers. Isn't it obvious? The clear answer is the oft-heard exhortation "We need more free parking to help downtown!"

Obvious, that is, until we discover, as so many downtowns have learned, that there are plenty of places to park, but hardly any places to go to *after* one parks. Could it be that in our rush to provide abundant downtown parking that we have replaced attractive downtown activities with highways and parking lots?

I believe that in nearly all struggling, downwardly spiraling American downtowns what is most needed to attract the suburban population is to provide more *attractions*, not places to park in order to reach them. We need to dedicate ourselves to densifying and intensifying our downtowns if they are to become healthier. Vacant lots need to be converted to buildings with active uses, and vacated buildings, likewise, need to be activated.

The already common saying, "if you build it, they will come," is apropos here. A downtown that is alive, exciting, human-scaled, walkable, and filled with activities is a downtown that most people will figure out a way to get to, regardless of any perceived lack of free parking. We're all aware of major attractions in our communities that draw enormous numbers of people, even though the available parking is thought to be insufficient: the annual arts festival; the major parade; the big sporting event. We are also well aware of walkable, exciting cities that are thriving places, drawing thousands and millions of visitors each year even though the amount of free parking in such cities is extremely limited. Visitors are so eager to visit such wonderful places that they are more than willing to put up with expensive, scarce parking. And who among us is unaware of dying downtowns that have plenty of free parking but don't have any sort of critical mass of downtown activities that would attract people?

A downtown is healthy almost exclusively because of "agglomeration economies;" that is, downtowns survive because of a concentration of government offices, residential density, services, and cultural events in a relatively small space. Indeed, agglomeration economies are the basis for why cities (and their outlying residential areas) form. Concentrating activities, buildings, and services in a small space increases efficiency and maximizes economic health—largely by drawing high numbers of people and minimizing the distance they must travel in order to interact (or spend money). These concentrated downtown entities thrive in part based on the synergistic, spillover benefits that downtown proximity to nearby activities provide. Off-street parking detracts from each of these factors—particularly density and synergy.

Per person, cars consume an *enormous* amount of space. If we add up the size of a parking space, and the space needed to maneuver to the space (aisles, shy distance, etc.), a car needs approximately three hundred square feet of space (a person sitting in a chair takes up about five square feet—a seventeenth of a car's required space). Space must be used efficiently in order for there to be a healthy downtown, where agglomeration economies mean that space should be very, very dear. The colossal consumption of space by cars, therefore, can be quite detrimental.

Regrettably, a dead or dying downtown strives to revive itself, typically, by seeking to provide *more* parking to attract people. But because there is a net loss in terms of downtown space given up per motorist, this becomes a losing proposition. Because it consumes so much space, additional parking chases away opportunities to establish or strengthen agglomeration economies—there is less downtown land available for buildings, activities, and services when more parking is provided. The result is that more parking is akin to destroying a village in order to save it. The added parking delivers relatively few people to downtown (because of how much space is needed per person), and most of those people are spending only trivial amounts of money—if any—once they arrive, thereby not compensating for the valuable downtown space they are consuming.

A modest, human scale is the design feature that enables a downtown to compete with outlying, suburban, car-oriented areas. Downtown can never out-compete the suburbs on suburban, car-based terms because the suburbs will always be able to provide more parking and wider highways more cheaply. A downtown can only compete where it can have competitive leverage—that is, where it can be compact, walkable, romantic, unique, rich in history, and human scaled.

Escaping the Downward Spiral

What can a community do to escape this downward spiral? To escape this spiraling community dispersal (driven by a declining quality of life), the path is clear: slow down motor vehicle travel and restore the tradition of using modest, human-scale dimensions for streets, building setbacks, and distances between homes, shops, parks, and jobs.

We are fortunate that, while nearly all American adults now use a car for nearly every trip, it is not at all necessary for us to strive for the impossible, undesirable objective of getting rid of all cars. The good news is that we can keep them, but we need to become more their masters, rather than their slaves. That means we need to design our communities and our roads to obligate motorists to be better behaved, primarily by driving at more modest speeds and doing so more attentively. When these things happen, we find that community quality of life can be maintained, and even improved, *despite* the presence of cars.

Another crucial aspect of "well-behaved" motor vehicles is to return to the tradition of building communities that provide many choices for travel and housing, so that folks are not required to make *all* trips by motor vehicle. Creating travel choice means a return to the tradition of establishing mixed-use, higher-density neighborhoods wherein homes are intermingled with modest shops, offices, civic buildings, and pocket parks. This sort of traditional, mixed-use neighborhood design substantially reduces trip distances, which means that walking, bicycling, and transit use become more feasible and likely. Short distances and mixed uses also mean that streets do not need to be oversized, sparing our roadways from having eleven- or twelve-foot-wide travel lanes in four- and six-lane roads.

These factors contribute to a crucial, inevitable result: slower, more attentive motor vehicle travel, which leads to safer, more livable driving—and more livable communities, in which driving is *optional* rather than *required*.

RESTRAINING SPRAWL

A COMMON INTEREST
TO ENHANCE THE QUALITY OF LIFE FOR ALL

LOUISE NYSTRÖM

Until fairy recently, Europeans have associated sprawl with the American way of life, i.e., homes on big lots, congested highways, and car dependence. European sprawl was not really recognized until the 1990s, with the development of environmental awareness and the quest for sustainable urban development—to live in such a way that natural, economic, and social resources are not deteriorated to the extent that future generations are not free to live their lives.

Urban sprawl is a process of change that implies higher per capita urban land consumption, resulting in overall lower population densities and increasing distances between urban functions such as homes, services, jobs, recreation, and education.

If planners agree on the harmfulness of sprawl, there are, of course, proponents, arguing that sprawl is simply a result of increased living standards and nothing much can really be done to prevent it.[1] Furthermore, the proponents argue that all kinds of planned development are intrusions on individual freedom: people have the right to build their homes and drive their cars wherever they please. And maybe worst of all, the proponents argue, anti-sprawl measures will only distort the economy and make sprawl worse. The sprawl advocates admit that there are social and environmental problems caused by the car but argue that these can only be solved by developing safer and smarter automobiles in combination with curbing the damage of cars by tolls, more roads, and more cars.

Certainly, sprawl does offer some gains: the house buyer can find a new big home in the periphery for less money than in the city where land is more expensive; developers can build more and bigger homes; more roads, more pipes and finally: more cars mean more jobs.

But there are also costs. Among the *environmental costs* there are increased energy consumption for transport and heating, loss of agricultural land and landscapes, pollution (air, water, ground, noise, light), and surface sealing causing greater flood risks. *Economic costs* are, for instance, more commuting time and thus less time for work and leisure, more public expenditure on infrastructure, increased retail and office space, and costs for urban transformation, such as abandoned structures and loss of local tax revenues in out-migration areas. *Social costs* include spatial segregation, difficulties for nondrivers, such as the elderly, the poor, and children; societal retreat, e.g., in gated communities; and, finally, deterioration of the inner city and its cultural heritage. Among the most famous American anti-sprawl advocates is Dolores Hayden, who has also inspired the European debate.[2]

Three Case Studies

In this section three European case studies are discussed, Vienna, Leipzig, and Stockholm. They demonstrate that sprawl is indeed a European problem as well. Further, the European sprawl is not only related to unchecked dispersal, but also occurs in planned land use and policy driven situations. It can also take place despite population decline, as seen in the Leipzig analysis.

In the 1960s and 1970s sprawl was mainly caused by housing policy, due to the need to improve housing conditions for the crowded population in the unsanitary inner city, by building new housing at the periphery, a periphery that was constantly moving further out. But at that time, it still was held back by the needs to be close to public transport, causing housing districts to remain concentrated along tram or underground lines. Later, in the 1980s and 1990s, sprawl was mainly driven by transport policy. With the increase of car ownership and the improved road network, the demand for single family houses could take place unbound by the restrictions of public transport coverage. Furthermore, improved expressways opened up new locations for industry and trade. Lorries replaced railways for regional and interstate goods transport. The transformation of retail from small shops within walking distance to large external shopping malls, resulted in consumers taking over a great deal of the distribution of groceries and other consumer goods.

However, things have shifted in the early twenty-first century, with an increase in the appeal of urban life, resulting in densification, and older, semiperipheral industrial sites being redeveloped for housing (figure 1).

Vienna

After a decline, Vienna's population started growing in the 1980s, mainly because of immigration from foreign countries, not least from the East after the fall of the iron curtain in 1989. In 2001 it was close to 1.6 Mio. The immigrants settled in the north and eastern outskirts of Vienna proper. At the same time many Viennese citizens moved to the far periphery, where many elderly turned their summerhouses into permanent residences. However, the working population settled at closer distances from the inner city. The average commuting distances almost doubled between 1971 and 1991, while the average commuting time stayed the same both for car and train commuters. Commuting by automobile increased but train commuting remained the same.

Lower real estate prices combined with good traffic access in the near periphery attracted industrial development, shopping malls, wholesale, and retail. The change of logistics from railway transport to lorries relocated the industrial sites from former railway locations to interstate junctions. The very generous policy of allowing agricultural land to change into housing or industrial uses helped the process along, and was a source of great income for the farmers.[3]

Leipzig

Urban sprawl is often linked to urban growth, as people move to the city for jobs and a better life. But after the fall of the iron curtain in 1989 the new cities in the German *Länder* experienced the combination of sprawl and population decline. When these Länder—nicknamed at that time the "Wild East"—were opened up for investors, development surged. The process was supported by local governance viewing urban development as highly desirable, as well as federal programs and tax regulations designed to attract capital into Germany's new states. Finally, a lack of public planning instruments and rules, together with an inexperienced planning bureaucracy, left a kind of vacuum for investors.[4]

From 1992 onwards Leipzig experienced a period of heavy, exponentially increasing residential sprawl, reaching its peak by the end of 1996 with a population of around 0.7 Mio in the urban region. The restoration of the inner city with its often heavily damaged old buildings was impeded by restitution claims and until the mid-1990s the region's real estate market was still dominated by a scarcity of (decent) housing. The demand for good homes was satisfied by an increasing number of suburban apartments and houses offered on the market. This happened at the same time as a dramatic drain of people to the West, caused by rapidly increasing unemployment in the former GDR (German Democratic Republic).

However, in the late 1990s, residential out-migration was no longer swelling in Leipzig. With the ongoing resolving of restitution claims and the growing supply of reconstructed dwellings in the inner city, the regional market of property and housing leveled off. The temporary federal fiscal incentives into the East German real estate market ended except for refurbishment subsidies in the inner city. Planning administrations had now caught up on their delay in planning and the land conversion restrictions became more effective. New investments into retail and leisure facilities in the inner city made the city more competitive.

Stockholm

After World War II the Stockholm region expanded to its present 1.8 Mio, with 0.8 Mio in the city of Stockholm. The biggest expansion was in the ten years around 1975 when a third of the Swedish housing stock was built.

If sprawl is associated with unplanned development, this is not the case for Stockholm, or any Swedish city for that matter. After World War II widespread growth occurred in the Stockholm area. This was primarily an outcome of controlled planning. Government norms and loans to the public housing sector have, together with the so called Municipal Planning Monopoly, ruled Stockholm's urban growth. Plenty of space, air, and green areas, as well as function and traffic separation, are well-established Swedish urban planning objectives. During the last decade, however, the prevailing vision has been that of the integrated, physically concentrated European town. The background for this is multifaceted and driven by the desire for: more effective and mixed land use, efficient public transport, as well as reduced natural resources depletion and enhanced social mix. In addition, there are aesthetic arguments in favor. Expressways, traffic barriers, and urban wastelands are in general considered to contribute to ugly and disharmonious landscapes, while the compact diverse cityscape is viewed as attractive both for residents, businesses, and tourists.

However, the Stockholm region has multiplied its built environment since World War II. This development is partly due to the topography. Stockholm is situated in a region with plenty of water, which has affected regional planning. But demography has also played a part. With the lowest household size in Europe (2 persons/household in 2000), the need for dwellings is, of course, great. Housing production is not as much a result of immigration as of household size reductions, which, in turn, is due to an aging population as well as youngsters leaving their parent's home at an early age. Furthermore, the demand for bigger homes contributes to expansion. A single or a couple now occupies the two-bedroom flat that was comfortable for a four-person family in the sixties.

The Stockholm migration flows go both into the city core and out from it. The most expensive flats are in the center of

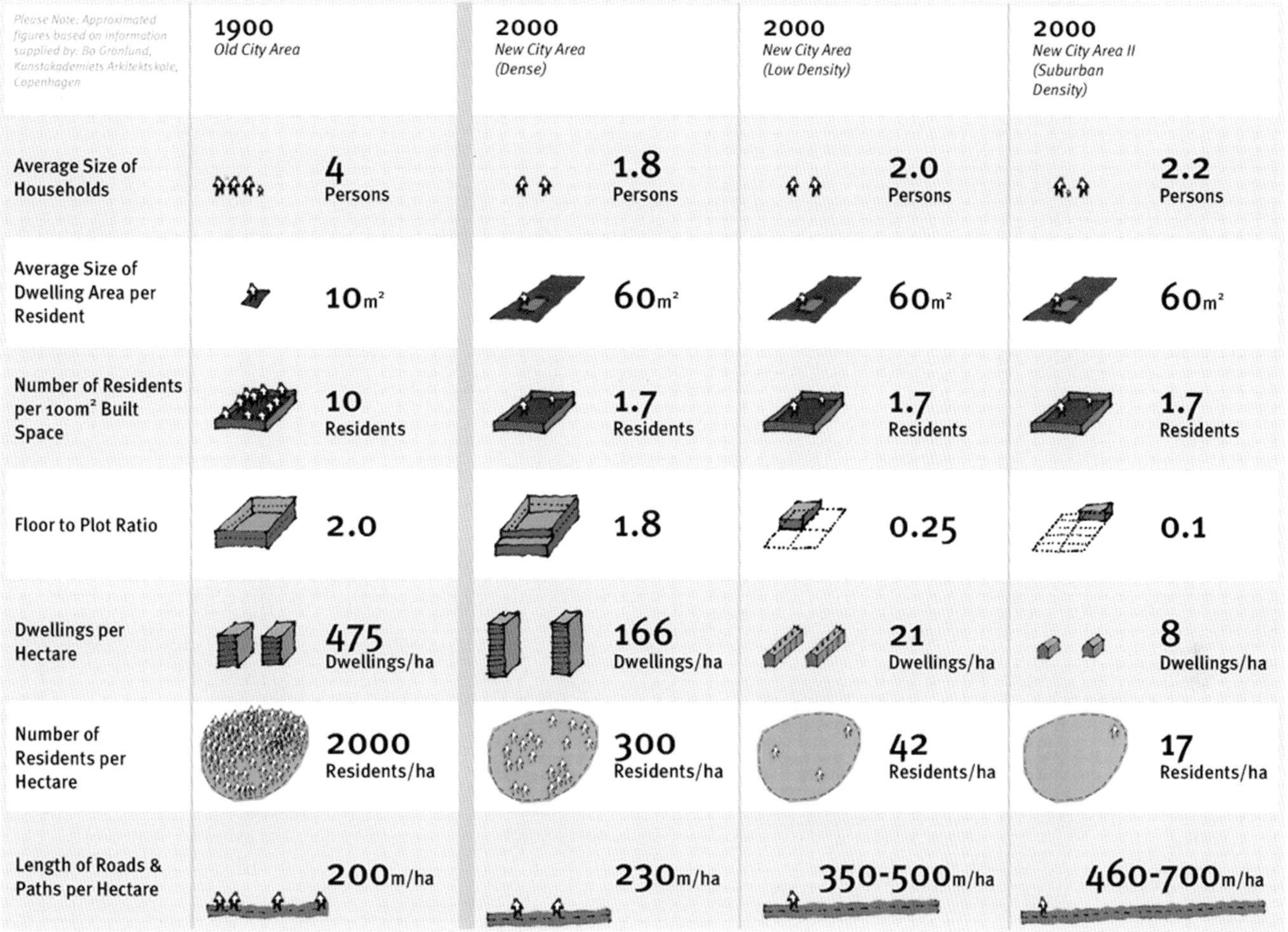

	1900 Old City Area	2000 New City Area (Dense)	2000 New City Area (Low Density)	2000 New City Area II (Suburban Density)
Please Note: Approximated figures based on information supplied by: Bo Grönlund, Kunstakademiets Arkitektskole, Copenhagen				
Average Size of Households	4 Persons	1.8 Persons	2.0 Persons	2.2 Persons
Average Size of Dwelling Area per Resident	10 m²	60 m²	60 m²	60 m²
Number of Residents per 100m² Built Space	10 Residents	1.7 Residents	1.7 Residents	1.7 Residents
Floor to Plot Ratio	2.0	1.8	0.25	0.1
Dwellings per Hectare	475 Dwellings/ha	166 Dwellings/ha	21 Dwellings/ha	8 Dwellings/ha
Number of Residents per Hectare	2000 Residents/ha	300 Residents/ha	42 Residents/ha	17 Residents/ha
Length of Roads & Paths per Hectare	200 m/ha	230 m/ha	350–500 m/ha	460–700 m/ha

FIG. I Overview of a century of sprawl development, 1900–2000.

Stockholm, unaffordable for the majority. Such flats are in renovated nineteenth-century buildings or in new developments on former industrial and harbor sites, supported by Stockholm city's infill policy: "Build the city inwards." They are inhabited by "empty nesters," having sold their suburban houses, but also by young affluent families with children. The number of Humvees has multiplied in recent years in inner Stockholm, as well as the number of baby carriages. The other stream goes far out of the city, to affordable homes, e.g., refurbished summerhouses (1,000 per year), and long commuting times. But the small, and often medieval, cities around Stockholm, like Mariefred, Enköping, and Strängnäs, also have a resident influx. On the high-speed train the Stockholm center is reached in forty-five minutes. A third kind of residence is in the multifamily rental housing semiperipheral districts built around 1970. This is where the least affluent live, the unemployed, the single mothers, and the immigrants.

Stockholm, and its region, have one of the best and most used public transport systems in the world. About 70% of the people traveling to work from the suburbs to the inner city use public transport during rush hours. However, private car traffic keeps increasing, grid-locking the streets into the center at rush hours. After a long political debate, congestion fees combined with public transport improvements were tried in 2006. The experiment was successful, reducing the vehicular traffic by 20–25% compared to the same months before the experiment. Driving time in rush hours was reduced by 30–50%. The investments were estimated to be paid off in four years. But in a consultative referendum in September 2007, voters said no to congestion charges in return for improved public transport.

Soon after, however, the new liberal government decided to make congestion charges permanent, but now, in return for new and improved peripheral motorways around Stockholm. By that, the government paved the way for further private driving in Metro-Stockholm, as well as a greater separation between the (affluent) inner-city residents and the rest of the Stockholmers.

The requirements for more space in Swedish urban areas increased dramatically between 1960 and 1990. But there were signs of a slight densification in the late 1990s, which was attributed to greater preferences for urban living and greater environmental awareness.

FIGS. 2 AND 3 Hammarby Sjöstad is a recent urban development on former industrial land in Stockholm. It is built with ecological ambitions to satisfy present-day demands for high residential quality. However, the flats are too expensive for the majority.

Twelve Arguments Against Sprawl

Returning to the more general level, the arguments against sprawl could be summed up in twelve points:

1. *Sprawl aggravates poverty.* Only 9% of the world population has access to a car. If sprawl is bearable for car drivers it makes life more difficult for non-drivers. The World Bank goes as far as arguing that poverty and sprawl work in a vicious circle.[5] Poor people cannot afford a car, limiting their access to cheap stores, jobs, and education, thus they end up in *accessibility poverty*. As a result they must spend more time getting to these places, resulting in *time poverty*. They are more exposed to traffic: *health and safety poverty*. All this commuting is tiring, and suffering from *energy poverty*, people's vigor for getting a good job or a better education is reduced, resulting in poor jobs or unemployment: *income poverty*. The circle is closed.

Sprawl requires cars also in wealthy countries, such as Sweden. But a third of the population, when one includes children above five years of age, do not have a driver's license. Fifty percent of the elderly (over sixty-five years of age) do not have access to a car, and neither do a third of the single parents. Maybe one should be glad at the fact that 86% of all men, sixteen- through sixty-five years of age, do have a car.

2. *Sprawl is a threat against equality.* Sprawl requires taking children to school and afternoon activities as well as driving an elderly parent to the dentist or the drug store. These obligations (still) are female occupations, and thus more women work part-time and fewer women can compete for the top jobs because of their family commitments.

3. *Sprawl boosts segregation.* Monofunctional land use is a feature of sprawl, with large affluent single-family areas separated from the more affordable multifamily housing districts.

4. *Sprawl is a health hazard.* Research has shown that Americans that live in areas where the car is necessary weigh more than those that live in areas where it is possible to walk and cycle.[6] Also in Sweden childhood obesity is increasing, maybe as a result of the increasing distances to schools. Seventy-five percent have farther than 400 meters to go to school, often on busy and dangerous roads. They have to be taken there by car.

5. *Sprawl reduces safety and security.* It is more dangerous to live in the suburbs than in the inner city if traffic accidents and assaults are added together.

6. *Sprawl disfavors enterprise.* In knowledge society, enterprise is dependent on the kind of face-to-face contacts, interactions, and spontaneous encounters that develop in an urban context. Whereas small shops and businesses thrive in the dense city, sprawl is for big box malls and corporations.

7. *Sprawl aggravates consumer goods distribution.* Fifty percent of adult Swedes have to go farther than 400 meters to the closest grocery store, thus they need a car to get their shopping done and they can't send their children on errands.

8. *Sprawl is costly for society at large.* Infrastructure investments, such as roads, sewage, and water pipes, are used badly. American research has found that smaller mortgages in outlying communities give the false impression that the overall cost of living in these areas is lower. But low housing costs hide the higher cost of transportation and other costs in these areas that turn up at the gas station and as increased taxes for roads, water, and sewer pipes.[7] Additonally, public transport is less economically viable because of fewer riders; elderly home aids have to use more time on traveling and less time on care, children have to be transported to schools either by parents or school buses. Garbage collection and mail delivery is less effective. And people waste time on commuting instead of on more productive activities.

9. *Sprawl is an environmental menace.* Land sealing increases flood risks. Car travel causes global warming, due to carbon dioxide emissions, and eutrophication as well as acidification of ground and water due to sulphur and nitrogen emissions. Natural resources are depleted.

10. *Sprawl deprives culture and fine arts.* The fewer people that can walk and cycle to the center, the fewer that can go to the theater, concerts, or exhibitions.

11. *Sprawl hampers new life styles.* Many want to live as singles and take part in urban public life, close to jobs, shops, and entertainment. For instance, a third of all Swedish households consist of singles. But developers aim for suburban single-family house construction and not for the construction of suitable and affordable housing types for urban singles. The result is overpricing of inner-city flats, and urban life is inaccessible for the less affluent.

12. *Sprawl congests the inner city.* The fewer people that commute comfortably by public transport, the more they have to take the car, resulting in congested streets and roads.

Conclusion

There are two basic views on sprawl: sprawl supporters say that it is a natural development, which is the result of a growing economy and it improves the lives of people. People like their suburban homes and their cars—the so-called American way of life. To force people to crowd into a dense city and crammed buses would be unfair and undemocratic. Finally, the sprawl supporters say that all measures to restrain sprawl are ineffective. The sprawl opponents say that sprawl is just a matter of a laissez-faire attitude, that many prefer urban life to cars and suburbs; that it is a menace to health, environment, and cityscape; that it is costly and unrelated to economic growth. And sprawl is indeed possible to curb, as is being done in Stockholm, for instance.

In fact, the sprawl debate is an offshoot of a century-old controversy on self-interest versus common interests. It is in this view that we have to tackle sprawl. Is the common interest to save natural resources and resist global climate changes more important to us as individuals than the unhampered right to live where we want and drive our cars where we want? Or is the development of our common interests indeed a way to improve the individual welfare of everyone?

THE EMERGENCE OF MIXED-USE TOWN CENTERS IN THE UNITED STATES

TOM MARTINEAU

Premature Headlines

The *Washington Post*'s "Outlook" section of February 6, 2005, declared, "The battle's over. For half a century, legions of planners, urbanists, environmentalists, and big city editorialists have waged war against sprawl. Now it's time to call it a day and declare a victor. The winner is, yes, sprawl."

Barely more than a year later, it appears that the *Washington Post*'s declaration of victory for sprawl in the United States was as premature as the *Chicago Daily Tribune*'s headline "Dewey Defeats Truman" on November 3, 1948.

In fact, the *Washington Post* "Outlook" article may have been totally asynchronous: in its issue of December 1, 2004, the *National Real Estate Investor* noted the following:

While the number of mixed-use developments is rising rapidly in city centers, the true wave of the future is in suburbia. Greenfield and higher-density development in suburbia are providing developers with financially profitable and socially responsible opportunities, while benefiting communities. . . . The majority of projects on the rise today integrate two uses at a minimum, and usually more. From the suburbs of Washington, D.C., to the fringes of Dallas, mixed-use developments are nestling into communities. For developers, these projects generate higher financial returns.

Mixed-use development offers several attractive benefits. Most obvious is the diversification of risk for owners, especially at a time when many commercial real estate sectors are experiencing soft fundamentals. The incorporation of multiple types of amenities into a single project is practical because people want the convenience of living, shopping, and working, all within one common area.

In the midst of some of the most egregious examples of sprawl, true mixed-use town center developments are springing up in significant and increasing numbers all over the United States. This trend in United States real estate development is acknowledged and chronicled in "The Mixed Use Issue" of the acclaimed American trade publication *Retail Traffic* of March 2006. When a publication normally devoted to the business of retail shopping within the low-density, segregated residential/commercial/office use patterns of suburbia extols the livability and profitability of true high-density-town centers with shop houses communal space, markets, and festivals, it is time to examine the possibility of a new trend. In the five major articles of "The Mixed Use Issue," the following mixed-use developments are cited:

- Zona Rosa, Kansas City, Missouri
- Sugar Land Town Square, Houston, Texas
- Southlake Town Square, Dallas-Fort Worth, Texas
- The Woodlands, Houston, Texas
- Kierland Commons, Phoenix, Arizona
- Victoria Gardens, Rancho Cucamonga, California
- The Spectrum, Falls Church, Virginia
- Westgate City Center, Glendale, Arizona
- Stapleton Community, Denver, Colorado
- San Francisco Center, San Francisco, California
- Grand Avenue Project, Los Angeles, California
- Beekman Project, New York, New York
- X Aragon Mixed Use Tower, Coral Gables, Florida
- Rockville Town Center, Rockville, Maryland
- The Brookwood, Buckhead area, Atlanta, Georgia
- The Grove, Los Angeles, California
- Greater Fells Point, Baltimore, Maryland

In addition, the following development companies and design firms are featured or mentioned:

- Steiner + Associates, Columbus, Ohio
- Continental Real Estate Companies, Miami, Orlando, Jacksonville, Florida
- Planned Community Developers, Sugar Land, Texas
- Woodbine Development Corporation, Dallas, Texas
- Cooper & Stebbins LP, Southlake, Texas
- Forest City Enterprises, Inc., Cleveland, Ohio
- Waterford Development, LLC, Reston, Virginia
- Development Design Group, Inc., Baltimore, Maryland
- Perkowitz + Ruth Architects' Studio One-Eleven, Long Beach, California

- KA Architecture, Cleveland, Ohio
- Jarmel Kizel Architects and Engineers, Livingston, New Jersey
- FRCH Design Worldwide, Cincinnati, Ohio
- Marcus & Millichap Real Estate Investment Brokerage Co., offices nationwide
- MacFarlane Partners, San Francisco, California
- RTKL, Baltimore, Maryland and offices worldwide
- Danac Corporation, Bethesda, Maryland
- Urban Realty Partners, Atlanta, Georgia
- Caruso Affiliated Holdings, Los Angeles, California
- Struever Bros. Eccles & Rouse, Baltimore, Maryland

These lists of mixed-use developments, developers, and design professionals represent only a small sample of the totality of mixed-use projects and firms involved in such real estate development. An internet search will reveal to a greater extent the size and scope of mixed-use community development in the United States.

The True Role of Urban Sprawl

At best, low-density urban sprawl has served as an interim solution in the growth and development of the United States. As future development and growth are necessarily moving in the direction of greater density, and as the limitations and flaws of residential-only sprawl are better understood, developers and designers are returning to the mixed-use town center planning principles of most successful communities in Europe and elsewhere.

Instead of declaring sprawl "the victor," a more accurate historic view of the urban sprawl phenomenon in the United States is perhaps as follows:
- Victorious American soldiers returning from World War II sought to form families and to settle down. The ensuing baby boom in the United States created an unprecedented demand for new and affordable housing;
- New, affordable housing was most easily created where large, contiguous areas of low cost land were available—in the suburbs;
- Such housing was marketed successfully by developers and builders as the "American Dream:" a single family home with its own backyard in suburbia, away from the noise and pollution of the inner city;
- Soldiers who had served honorably in the United States military were afforded low-cost Veterans' Administration mortgage loans to finance the purchase of such homes;
- This embodied the "rights of the victor:" to own an unattached house on its own land, with the freedom to do whatever one wanted in or on one's own property;
- Exclusionary zoning became the rule in most suburban communities: residential, commercial, office, education, recreation, and industrial zones were created and rarely, if ever, intermixed;
- As families settled in suburbia, large shopping malls and centers followed, causing many downtown commercial establishments to falter and close;

- Other places of work remained in the inner cities, requiring those who had moved to the suburbs to commute greater distances every workday;
- The daily commute from home to work in the city, and from work to home again, was created;
- In the 1920s, General Motors Corporation had created its own markets by initiating a covert campaign to eliminate the popular rail-based public transit systems that were ubiquitous in and around the country's bustling urban areas (at the time, only one in ten Americans owned cars, and most people traveled by trolley and streetcar);
- Within three decades General Motors—with help from Standard Oil, Firestone Tire, Mack Truck, and Phillips Petroleum—succeeded in decimating the nation's trolley systems while seeing to the creation of the federal highway system and the ensuing dominance of the automobile as America's preferred mode of transport;[1]
- Without readily accessible public transportation, suburban homeowners needed at least one car, and often two: one for a family member to commute to work, and another for the other family member to ferry the children to piano lessons, cheerleading practice, soccer practice, and perhaps even to school;
- As more services were needed for automobiles, low-density commercial sprawl developments (sometimes called "petro-slums") grew on major non-residential roads, consisting of gasoline stations; tire, muffler and other car repair facilities; automobile dealers; car washes; strip malls; restaurants; banks; pharmacies; etc.—many of which featured drive-through services;
- Those unable to drive—mostly children and the elderly—were excluded from the mobility automobiles provided, unless a person able to drive could take them to different places;
- School districts were forced increasingly to purchase and operate expensive school buses on a routine basis because even suburban elementary schools were only 5–10% walkable due to the low-density nature of the residential development;
- The freedom of the daily automobile commute was transformed into the traffic jams of the morning and evening rush hours;
- The rush hours gave way to occasional outbursts of road rage;
- The American images of the frustrated commuter, the soccer mom, and the teenage mall rat were formed;
- Obesity became an epidemic in adults and children because the automobile was the predominant mode of long-distance motion for nearly everyone;
- By the 1980s suburban life became recognized by many as a tarnished American dream because it failed to provide the density needed for true livability, and it was especially inimical to children and the elderly;
- By the 1990s alternative, higher-density community developments were conceived, where adults and children could walk short distances to shops and stores, or could take a bicycle, bus or tram when longer distances needed to be traveled;

• Suburban sprawl was the interim solution to a need for rapid growth—cheap land allowed low-density suburban development and the misguided separation of uses into residential, commercial, office, and even recreation and education;

• In the twenty-first century United States, sprawl must by definition densify as further growth and development take place;

• Mixed use is the higher-density form of evolution when compared to sprawl development;

• Suburban residential "bedroom communities" are beginning to be recognized as not being real communities at all: true communities need at least commercial, recreational, and office uses, and a way for all age groups to "own" them by being able to walk to many destinations or being able to use public transit or to bicycle in safety;

• Many aspects of current mixed use developments are still in need of better execution, but the American development and community design professionals will learn how to achieve "True Urbanism";

• Suburban sprawl is nearly unique to the United States, but isolated examples also exist in Canada and Australia; Europe has, by and large, resisted imitating the United States;

• Europe has many models of True Urbanism, with roots that are thousands of years old, and some examples even exist in the United States and Canada; see the website of the International Making Cities Livable Conferences for the principles of True Urbanism.[2]

Three Current Examples of Mixed-Use Developments

Three examples of mixed-use developments are noted briefly, and can be classified like T-shirts: small, medium, and large.

Winthrop, Brandon, Florida. This mixed-use community has three major uses on a total of 149 acres (figure 1).
• Residential
  • 184 townhomes;
  • 228 single family homes;
  • 370 apartments; and
  • 51 live work units that incorporate ground floor commercial space with upper level residential space.
• Town Center – commercial and office
  • Publix anchor store;
  • Various convenience retailers; and
  • Offices.
• Market and Community Theater
  • Covered open air market; and
  • Black-box community theater.

Winthrop's facilities are all within easy walking distance, and the Miami-based firm of Duany Plater-Zyberk & Company designed its original scheme. In the vast, low-density community of Brandon, Winthrop is the first mixed-use development (figure 2). It is a small community whose residents still suffer from the drawbacks of the surrounding urban sprawl.

FIG. I Winthrop mixed-use community.

Residents who work outside the community must still follow a traditional daily commute. Although an elementary school is within walking distance, other schools are not walkable, and require busing. Public buses are available but are cumbersome to use in reaching a variety of destinations with ease. Outside of Winthrop, the automobile is still the transportation medium of choice. As more mixed-use developments grow in the area, public transportation will become increasingly more reliable and frequent due to increased density and demand.[3]

Suwannee Town Center, Gwinnett County, Georgia. This community on over sixty-three acres consists of three-story shop houses, a paved commons with outdoor theater and fountain, row houses, and single-family homes. According to its official Web site,

This mixed-use area, anchored by a 10-acre urban-style park, embodies Suwannee's vision for "live . . . work . . . play . . . shop. It is the place that comes to mind when you think of Suwannee, offering a sense of community . . . a sense of belonging . . . a sense of home. . . . The Town Center mixed-use project includes commercial/retail space, office/professional uses, and residential units. All of these uses are designed to be functionally integrated. Street-level retail creates a walking/shopping experience. Office uses provide employment and customer activity. Residences provide homes for workers and "built-in consumers" for Town Center's other functions. The park imparts a sense of place and offers a place to relax and to gather both as families (small groups) and as a community. The Town Center development, in part a response to growing concern about urban sprawl and sustainability, demonstrates the City of Suwannee's leadership in growing carefully and responsibly in a region where small-town Georgia is rapidly disappearing.[4]

The Suwannee Town Center development is also within a virtual sea of suburban sprawl, and has similar problems to those mentioned for Winthrop. When the Atlanta subway (MARTA) was planned and constructed twenty-five years ago, Gwinnett County voters rejected a spur into their county. Gwinnett County has now upgraded its public bus system, which should allow Suwannee Town Center residents convenient access to MARTA trains in a nearby county.

Rockville Town Square, Rockville, Maryland. Although its area is about the same as for Suwannee Town Center, the density of Rockville Town Square promises to be much greater. According to its website, Phase I of the project is a fifteen-acre development consisting of

• Shops, restaurants, residences, and offices. In addition to being Montgomery County's newest address for entertainment, condominiums, and a public plaza, the new streetscape will serve as an attractive gathering place.

• Rockville Town Square, whose first buildings will open in late fall 2006, will be home to the Rockville Regional Library, the largest library in the Montgomery County system. The Rockville Cultural Arts Building will contain the Metropolitan Center for the Visual Arts at Rockville (currently Rockville Arts Place) and a new business incubator.

• The focal point of Rockville Town Square will be an open-air plaza that will serve as a meeting place and as a host to community events and concerts.

• "Windows on Rockville Town Square" will be 644 condominiums that top the shops and restaurants in Town Square. The units are selling briskly, with the cost of some surpassing the $1 million mark. The project also will include the city's required number of Moderately Priced Dwelling Units (MPDU), which will be about 96 for this project (15% of the total).[5]

• The eventual build-out of Rockville Town Square is expected to comprise sixty acres, and will include more commercial, office, and residential facilities. The Saturday Market, discontinued many decades ago, will be reinstituted. This development is in a mature public transportation zone, and will thus be instantly friendly to all age groups.

Conclusion

Mixed-use developments in the United States are on the increase, and will eventually revitalize inner cities and areas of low-density suburban sprawl. It is not taking developers and design professionals very long to realize that this is the type of community development most people seek. In addition, it has been the experience of developers that such multi-

FIG. 2 A new traditional neighborhood with a town center, located southeast of Tampa in Brandon, Florida. Master Plan by Duany Plater-Zyberk & Company.

use designs can be more profitable than the urban sprawl developments common during the past fifty-plus years. Many developers, instead of merely selling off their products, seek to remain owners, largely because they can reap greater profits over the long term.

Thus the true headline in the *Washington Post* "Outlook" section should have been "America Returns to Traditional, Livable Community Design." Yaromir Steiner, CEO of Steiner + Associates, when asked in the March 2006 issue of *Retail Traffic* if mixed use is a fad, replied: "The mixed use is a return to basic urban design principles, it is certainly not a fad. We believe instead that over the next twenty-five years, the single-use retail environments will be a disappearing product type. It is the elimination of the mixed-use urban and suburban hubs in the second half of the last century that was a misguided fad."

URBAN DESIGN AND THE METROPOLIS

ROBERT BEAUREGARD

The juxtaposition of growing suburbs and stagnant or declining central cities anchors a discourse with which most urban scholars, particularly those in the United States, are quite familiar. The discourse has been a staple of United States urban studies since at least the 1950s. And—even though the suburban periphery has been invaded by (edge) cities, inner-ring suburbs are experiencing "urban" problems, and cities that were once declining are now either resurgent[1] or becoming more like the suburbs[2]—this core theme has persisted. Like any discursive formation, however, the city/suburb debate is more than an empirical mapping of prevailing realities. It also shapes other debates, one of which involves the spatial fault lines of urban design.

For the most part urban designers gravitate to design modalities that reject the inherent nature of suburban development and thereby leave unattended vast swaths of the built environment. The suburban fringe is perceived as both foreboding and repellent.[3] Yet a healthy debate exists around the possibility of suburban design. On the one side are the New Urbanists and, on the other, their critics.[4] The former embrace the suburbs as an opportunity, while simultaneously de-emphasizing—though not neglecting—the cities. The latter privilege the city as the only site of great architecture and planning. They cast the suburbs as lacking these qualities and, worse, resistant to change. Regrettably, this debate stifles "popular" design and reproduces the city/suburb division even as it is less and less viable as a credible representation of contemporary metropolitan areas. Nevertheless, because of their shared commitment to density and mixed use, these antagonists are finding common ground.

Although the United States cannot claim to be the country where suburbs originated—England has the stronger case[5]—it was the country in which they were first mass-produced.[6] Beginning in the years after World War II, real estate developers built subdivisions of affordable, single-family detached homes in the urban periphery. These homes were small and, in part because they were produced using assembly-line techniques, affordable for young families in the expanding middle class. Numerous households fled the over-crowded housing of the central cities for a piece of land and a detached home in an environment that was decidedly newer, less congested, and more bucolic.

The flight of residents from the cities was not matched by migration into them. As a result, these cities began to shrink.[7] Manufacturing continued to decentralize after World War II and was soon joined by retailing. With households and jobs leaving, the industrial cities developed numerous social and economic problems. Their tax bases contracted and public services were cut back, property values stagnated, many neighborhoods became less desirable, and, in the worst cases, industrial areas and once-thriving waterfronts were virtually abandoned. An influx of African Americans from the South, and discrimination against them when they arrived, produced ghettos that gave additional impetus to the flight of white households.

The contrast between declining (and increasingly poor) central cities and growing (and affluent) suburbs became the dominant theme of a discourse of decline that extended from the 1950s through to the late 1970s. The discourse became less alarmist and more optimistic in the 1980s, as gentrification flourished in inner-city neighborhoods and cities began to experience reinvestment. That decade also brought a surge in the construction of downtown office buildings and shopping malls, while the 1990s followed with a rise in tourism, middle-income housing, entertainment, and high-end retailing.

At the same time, edge cities (concentrations of office and retail) began to appear in the suburban fringe, while suburbs of an earlier vintage faced a migration of minorities, rising poverty and crime, and physical obsolescence. With city life becoming more desirable and the suburbs more "urban," the earlier contrast between descending cities and ascending suburbs became less apt. Nonetheless, the city/suburb dichotomy holds firm.

Most urban designers, and particularly the critics of New Urbanism, join the discourse on the side of the cities. The models of town planning and urban design that are celebrated typically involve cities or places within them: for example, the Piazza del Popolo in Rome, the Ringstrasse of Vienna, L'Enfant's late eighteenth-century vision for Washington, D.C., and Victor Gruen's 1956 plan for downtown Fort Worth. Even the much-admired parks—Central Park in New York City and the Fenway park system in Boston—are considered urban. And, although supposedly suburban examples exist (consider Welwyn and Hampstead in England or Radburn, New Jersey and Kansas City's Country Club Plaza in Missouri), they generally exhibit one or the other (if not both) of the two qualities that attract urban designers: relatively high density and mixed uses. By contrast, Frank Lloyd Wright's Broadacre City appears in urban design textbooks as an oddity or as an example of a failed modernism, rather than a source of innovation. The "urban" bias of urban design—its affinity with the city—prevails.

At the same time, urban designers are vehement critics of suburbia. They deride its uniformity, philistine intentions, and overall banality. Nothing is right, and nothing can be learned or accomplished there. Rather than being planned to create visual excitement and emotional experiences, subdivisions are engineered to maximize the number of buildable lots and minimize infrastructure and road costs. Houses are devoid of aesthetic value, and rare are the places where people can meet or where land is left public to provide access to nature. Equally repellant is sprawl—the sins of suburban development etched into the landscape at a regional scale. In short, the suburbs are an anathema rather than an opportunity for making a creative contribution.

The suburban antagonism described above needs to be tempered by a few, significant exceptions. Numerous attempts to address the regional scale appear in the history of urban design. They range from the suggestive work of Patrick Geddes to the efforts of the Regional Plan Association in New York and the regional environmental insights of Ian McHarg. More recently, Ellen Whittemore has called for an engagement with the suburban field so as ". . . to surface its own complexities and subtleties and claim its right to be understood as the form of the contemporary city."[8] Smart Growth and Livable Communities are two such initiatives.[9] New Urbanism is another.

Instead of bemoaning the paucity of design in the suburbs—at the scale of the house, the lot, the subdivision, and the urban periphery—New Urbanists offer solutions.[10] Drawing on the social and physical qualities of the American small towns of the late nineteenth and early twentieth century, they propose novel site designs and higher design standards for suburban developments. Rather than monotonous arrays of houses along curved streets, they look to create visual and experiential variety, minimize the impact of the automobile and encourage interaction among residents, including the provision of places where people can mingle. Furthermore, New Urbanists call for mixing households with different incomes and the inclusion of shopping areas and public buildings (e.g., post offices) to serve local needs and encourage social engagement. At the core of their efforts is an attempt to foster community by mimicking the pur-

ported sense of belonging of the American small town of the late nineteenth and early twentieth century.

New Urbanists also propose an aesthetic for the new, suburban, built environment. They offer homes with porches, garages hidden along alleyways, and decorations that distinguish one building from the next. By adhering to codes and patterns, they also hope to achieve a uniformity that results in a coherent (sub)urban fabric.

Like their critics, however, the New Urbanists reject the low densities and homogeneous land uses of the mass suburbs. In fact, their developments are at higher densities than what suburban developers traditionally have produced. Moreover, they include nonresidential uses. Invoking the densities and land use patterns of small towns, the New Urbanists elaborate an earlier response to the monotony of typical tract-housing development—the planned unit development of clustered housing, open space, and varied site design.

Despite the differences between New Urbanists and their critics, they agree on transit-oriented developments.[11] The clustering of housing, retail, office activities, and even community services around mass transit stops meets the density and mixed-use requirements that both consider essential. Transit-Oriented Developments (TODs) also match their shared bias (stronger with critics than New Urbanists) against the automobile. In addition, they constitute rudimentary edge cities and thus bridge the divide between suburban and urban development patterns.

TODs provide a space in which all urban designers can meet. More importantly, they enable suburbs to be imagined as having the potential to absorb and nurture design interventions. Transit nodes are meant as an alternative to low-density subdivisions, as well as crowded and congested central cities. They constitute a middle ground. In this sense, they promise to reshape, along with edge cities, the city/suburb discourse. That TODs are premised on greater reliance on mass transit, always problematic in a society dependent on the automobile, suggests that they are most likely to be exceptions to prevailing patterns of development, thereby leaving the suburban fringe beset by sprawl.

Further to their benefit, the New Urbanists reflect on suburban and urban development at the metropolitan or regional scale, something to which their critics are much less attentive. One such proposal is the rural-urban transect. It uses a density gradient and the idea of functional hierarchies to organize the mix and spatial distribution of land uses. The idea is simple: higher-density places (for example, central cities) are best for higher-order functions (for example, corporate headquarters, organ transplant centers). This greater density, in turn, supports a concentration of transportation alternatives and engenders relatively high land values. Functions, densities, land prices, and transit options decline from the core to the periphery. By doing so, they engender different spatial opportunities and thereby compel unique design sensibilities. The rural-urban transect organizes the region and by doing so organizes intervention as well.

In this way the New Urbanists suggest how to (re)configure the metropolitan region and thereby erase both sprawl and the banality and monotony of suburban subdivisions. Their critics have few comparable ideas. Rather, distaste for the suburbs, and a corresponding city bias, leaves them dismissive of suburban design. That they de-emphasize the regional scale further stifles a positive response to sprawl and suburban uniformity.

Quite tellingly, New Urbanists also avoid the suburban fringe. In fact, they have cordoned off the suburbs so as to focus their attention on the high end of the market where cluster developments are more profitable and thus feasible. In this way, the New Urbanists join their critics in ignoring the design problems posed by mass-produced housing and sprawl. Both leave unattended the twin challenge of providing good, affordable design and creating a "workably expressive *suburban* urbanism."[12]

My argument is not, I should note, an endorsement of New Urbanism.[13] Its linking of design and community is problematic, the design palette is limited and aesthetically conservative, and, generally, New Urbanist developments do not break sufficiently from traditional tract housing or even cluster development. The whole approach is too cautious. Moreover, the rural-urban transect is excessively formal, overly rationalistic, rigid, and disengaged from the ways in which development actually occurs.

The point of my essay is to chide both New Urbanists and their critics for ceding the suburban ground to private developers. In a country where suburban development prevails, ignoring its design deficiencies is socially and professionally irresponsible. With suburbs spreading globally and one country after another adopting this form of American urbanism, the omission is of even greater concern.

In the discourse of growing (and sprawling) suburbs and stagnant or declining central cities (even resurgent ones), urban design has opted for a narrowly restricted role, one that wholly ignores dominant patterns of development. This is regrettable. Instead of bemoaning the suburbs or embracing New Urbanism, urban designers would have more of an impact—and likely be reinvigorated—by confronting the challenge of low-density development and its regional manifestation, and doing so in a way that simultaneously breaks from the city/suburb divide and "radically re-imagine(s) the suburban landscape."[14]

PART 4: STREETS, TRANSPORT, AND PUBLIC REALM

4.1   LIVELY, ATTRACTIVE, AND SAFE CITIES— BUT HOW?

JAN GEHL

A Matter of Life or Death—There is a Choice!

Lively or lifeless public spaces very much depend on the quality provided and the overall invitation to the likely users to walk, stay, sit, or otherwise enjoy these spaces. Surveys from existing city areas, as well as new towns and new city districts and developments, have shown striking differences concerning life and lifelessness. Everything points to the quality issues being of considerable importance, and the evidence likewise points to the need for a more systematic and careful treatment of the public realm in order to secure a good quality and a good level of attractiveness.

Roles of Public Life in Present-day Society

Faced with empty public spaces in many new developments, as well as the more or less abandoned mistreated existing city streets, one may well ask if access to public space as a meeting place for people is at all meaningful in the present day of electronic and privatized societies with people living farther and farther apart, using still more square meters per person, in smaller and smaller households. Would not the abandoned and deserted public realm be a logical and acceptable answer to these new challenges? Can the digital, indirect world substitute for direct contact with other people and to the surrounding society?

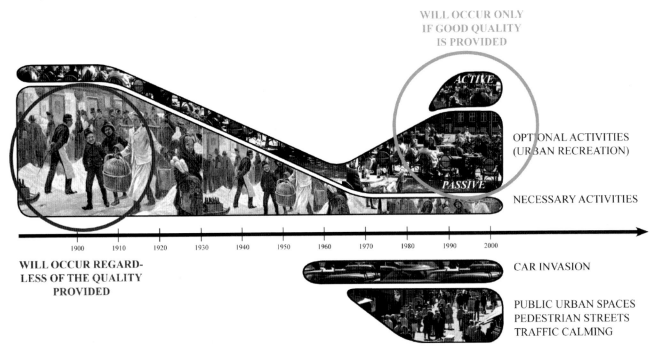

FIG. 1 The importance of public space quality.

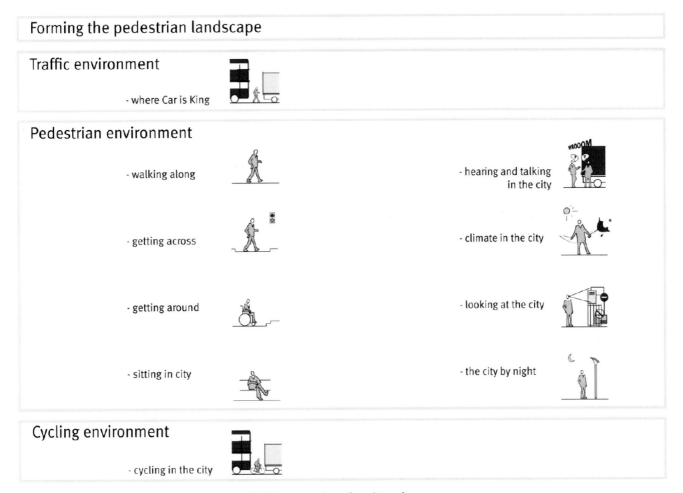

Forming the pedestrian landscape

Traffic environment

- where Car is King

Pedestrian environment

- walking along

- getting across

- getting around

- sitting in city

- hearing and talking in the city

- climate in the city

- looking at the city

- the city by night

Cycling environment

- cycling in the city

FIG. 2 From "Towards a Fine City for People—London 2004." Quality analysis of conditions for pedestrians (and bicyclists) in central London: overview of activity categories to be analyzed.

The multifaceted and intensive use of any public spaces of good quality will in themselves be an answer to these questions. The universal finding is that whenever quality is provided, people come. Access to other people, to possibilities for experience and recreation among others, are in high demand, and these opportunities have important roles for upholding or strengthening the overall policies for friendly, humane, open, democratic, and safe societies (figure 1).

The Character of Public Life in the Present Societal Situation

Comparing street scenes from the turn of the previous century with present day street scenes, an obvious change in the volume and character of public life stands out. In the bustling street scenes from around 1900, nearly all people are engaged in some type of necessary activities. People are present because they have to be, regardless of whether quality is provided or not. Use of public spaces was an important part of daily life, and the spaces were filled to overflowing with all kinds of activities. In the process, public spaces also functioned in the ever-present role as meeting places for people.

These types of streets scenes, filled with people who were forced to use the public scene, are still to be found in many countries with less developed economies.

Street scenes from our present day society show a distinctly different pattern use. Many fewer people are present because they are forced to be there. Some do need to walk or take public transport to and from work, but many others have alternative options for transport, for reaching services, and for shopping. Services can be arranged over the internet and shopping accomplished in the same way or in privatized, out-of-town shopping malls.

The overall picture of present day public spaces reveals that most of the people are present not because they have to be, but because they want to be. They have decided to come and to stay because the public spaces continue to offer valuable opportunities for people in present day society. The optional character of most public life activities in today's cities places very high demands on the quality offered by the public spaces. If the quality is failing, people will not come; they have many other interesting things to do. However, if the quality is there, if the public spaces are well placed, well designed, and inviting, evidence from all over the world points to the fact that people appreciate and use them. If the quality is right people will come! Thus, if lively attractive and safe cities with active streets, squares, and parks are to be realized in the twenty-first century, good quality pedestrian activities are vital.

Inviting Public Life into Existing City Areas

The quality offered for pedestrians in existing city districts is in many cases appalling. Obstacles, sidewalk interruptions, curbs, difficult street crossings, fences, and so on harass whoever is left on the narrow sidewalks. Places for sitting or enjoyment are scarce. A method for improvements, pioneered in Copenhagen and by now widely used (the latest example being central London), is to record systematically how people use the city, thus *making the people using the city visible*. Based on this knowledge (diagnosis) a cure for improvements can be worked out. Books such as *Public Space—Public Life* and *Towards a Fine City for People* (London 2004) describe in detail how such a method can be applied and which tools to use. Furthermore, the *Public Life—Public Space* book from Copenhagen describes the amazing increase in the use of public spaces which, following the many quality improvements, occurred in the course of the past four decades (figures 2 and 3).

P R O T E C T I O N	**1. Protection against Traffic & Accidents** - traffic accidents - fear of traffic - other accidents	**2. Protection against crime & violence (feeling of safety)** - lived in / used - streetlife - streetwatchers - overlapping functions - in space & time	**3. Protection against unpleasant sense experiences** - wind / draft - rain / snow - cold / heat - polution - dust, glare, noise
C O M F O R T	**4. Possibilities for WALKING** - room for walking - untiering layout of streets - interesting facades - no obstacles - good surfaces	**5. Possibilities for STANDING / STAYING** - attractive edges »Edgeeffect« - defined spots for staying - supports for staying	**6. Possibilities for SITTING** - zones for sitting - maximizing advantages primary and secondary sitting possibilities - benches for resting
	7. Possibilities to SEE - seeing-distances - unhindered views - interesting views - lighting (when dark)	**8. Possibilities for HEARING / TALKING** - low noise level - bench arrangements »talkscapes«	**9. Possibilities for PLAY / UNFOLDING / ACTIVITIES** - invitation to physical activities, play, unfolding & entertainment - day & night and summer & winter
E N J O Y M E N T	**10. Scale** - dimensioning of buildings & spaces in observance of the important human dimensions related to senses, movements, size & behaviour	**11. Possibilities for enjoying positive aspects of climate** - sun / shade - warmth / coolness - breeze / ventilation	**12. Aestetic quality / positive sense-experiences** - good design & good detailing - views / vistas - trees, plants, water

FIG. 3 Protection, comfort, and enjoyment—what public space should provide.

Inviting Public Life into New City Areas

Most new towns and new developments are planned with the explicitly stated proposed to create a lively, attractive, and safe city or district. Nearly all of them appear to fail in reaching anywhere near such a goal. Many factors combine to make it very difficult and complicated to achieve active public spaces in new areas; people are very spread out, densities are low, functions are segregated even where integration has been attempted, buildings frequently only house one function, and concern for active ground floors are generally absent. Add to this the haphazard creation of spaces between buildings and the general neglect of climatic considerations and disregard for existing knowledge concerning human behavior. There is no careful invitation for life and activities to be found here! People hurry through the spaces if they venture outside at all, and a general emptiness becomes almost automatic.

It must be observed that life in present day public spaces is a very fragile one. Only if conditions are right will walking and lingering be commonplace. Thus, planning of public spaces must be done extraordinarily carefully. The tools have been developed. It can be done—several outstanding examples like Aker Brygge (Oslo), Skarpnäck (Stockholm), and Almere (Holland) can be found next to the many failures.

Traditionally new developments have been planned based on the formula: first buildings, then spaces, and then—perhaps—life. This formula must, in present day planning, be turned about, and the questions should be in the order: What kind of life do we want here? What kind of spaces will be needed for this life? How can the buildings in this area be placed and formed to support these spaces and the life in this area?

In short, the formula must be: first *life*, then *spaces*, then *buildings*—and in said order, please.

GREAT STREETS AND CITY PLANNING

ALLAN JACOBS

University-based urban design studios are important! At such a studio class in the 1980s, in the Department of City and Regional Planning at the University of California, Berkeley, the subject matter was the Van Ness Avenue corridor, one of the very few north-south travel ways of San Francisco. A period of three weeks, during the studio, was given over to research of streets thought to be of possible importance to the student designers: widths and other dimensions, trees and their spacing characteristics, building relationships to the streets, spaces, and whatever might seem helpful. The literature searches were disappointing; very little was found and what there was, generally, was devoid of things like dimensions or scales, and included very little on surroundings.

One of the students was astounded—it was Michael Freedman, who has since become a highly successful and excellent designer of streets, along with his partner, Greg Tung, another ex-student—he was even angry and could not fathom why, in the 1980s, there was so little available, especially at a place like Berkeley. Wasn't this, after all, supposed to be a research university? His indignation seemed on target, to me, and so started the years of research on the physical, designable qualities of streets and their contexts. The research on multiway boulevards, with Elizabeth Macdonald and Yodan Rofé, and research on arterial streets would follow. The idea was a simple one: to collect as much information about the physical qualities of streets and their contexts as possible and make it accessible to practicing professionals, students, and academic researchers, if, God forbid, any of the latter might really be interested in physical realities, for their use. The boulevard studies had another objective as well: to determine if, as I suspected, tight multiway boulevards, like so many in Europe and some in the United States, were not the dangerous traffic hazards that United States traffic engineers made them out to be; and, indeed, to see if one of them could even be built in the United States using current street design standards, assuming that a community wanted to do so. We were to find, of course, that, no, those grand public ways were not inherently more dangerous than other arterials that carried like amounts of traffic, that good design is what makes the difference, and, no, they could not be built in the United States under today's standards and norms. Neither the grand Avenue Montaigne in Paris, nor the spectacular Ocean Parkway in Brooklyn, a designated city land-

mark, would be possible. In short, the purposes of both the street and boulevard studies were fairly straightforward, to assemble information that could be useful to professionals and researchers, to get that material accessible to them, and, if possible, along the way, to find some answers to some questions about why some streets are better than others.

Along the way, of course, one picks up all kinds of information and knowledge that was never anticipated: the square-mile maps, for example, of many different cities, the original intention of which was merely to show the urban settings of chosen streets, all done at the same scale (as were the streets) to allow easy visual comparisons. To see a square mile of Venice, which includes a very large part of that city, next to a square mile of San Francisco is to realize that these are very different urban places. Today, I see map drawings like that quite often, whenever a designer is trying to show that his proposal is appropriate, and like a city that the client knows and values positively. And, those visual comparisons start one into wonderful little exercises, like counting the numbers of intersections and blocks in one city versus another and another and another. Soon one has new measurements of urban scale. Counting pedestrians on chosen streets, too, leads to comparisons of crowding and comfort. Surveys of both ordinary citizens and design professionals helped to identify the best streets as well as to pinpoint the characteristics deemed to be most important. So much information that was never anticipated just seemed to roll in. In the end, at least regarding the streets, it was possible to determine those physical characteristics most associated with "great streets," the best, the most pleasurable on which to spend time. These are summarized in the concluding chapter of *Great Streets*, which follows this introduction.

Of the unintended consequences of the street and boulevard studies, perhaps the most unexpected have been the commissions to design new ones. That certainly was never the intent. But once the books were published (and even before), citizen activists and professionals alike came to our doors, wondering if we couldn't help them or if they could be involved in one way or another in street designs. Elizabeth Macdonald and I have been involved in the design of seven streets in recent years, to say nothing of a number of neighborhoods and specific area plans. The most exciting of these have been C.G. Road in Ahmedabad, India, designed with Bimal Patel, and the recently completed Octavia Boulevard, in San Francisco, championed by a neighborhood group and voted on by the city's electorate to replace a two-level freeway. Along the way, one continues to learn lessons, not the least of which is how difficult it is to change the minds of traffic engineers and the standards and norms that have so long been a part of their culture. But as the existence of the new streets shows, it can be done. There is a large market out there for better, more humane, multipurpose, community-making streets. People, in their communities, need help, and I do believe that the street research, started in a student design studio, has helped.

Following is a reprint of the concluding chapter of *Great Streets*. Readers might want to have a go at the whole book and, if satisfied, move on to *The Boulevard Book*.

Great Streets and City Planning[1]

The twentieth century has seen the development and widespread acceptance of two major city design manifestos; that of the new town or Garden City movement, and the Charter of Athens.[2] Both were in large measure responses to the building excesses and resultant foul living conditions of the nineteenth-century industrial city. Change was in order and dramatic changes were proposed. Both manifestos, reflections perhaps of not so different utopian ideals, concentrated on new building, and both ultimately eschewed streets as they had been known— as central and positive to urban living. Ultimately the new town- and Garden City-inspired communities became the models for the moderate- and low-density suburban development that emphasized central green areas rather than streets as the means of achieving face-to-face communication, and buildings well setback and, if possible, divorced from streets. The superblock idea, not inherently antistreet, became that way as it became part and parcel of both design movements.[3] Both, too, called for a separation of land uses, rather than a healthy integration, and both were to achieve their ends via massive public initiatives and centralized ownership and design of land.

The Charter of Athens could find realization on either new sites, like Chandigarh or Brasilia, or in the older central cities. In the latter, there would have to be clearance of large unhealthy urban environments in order to rebuild at a scale necessary to have an impact. Here, the rejection of streets as places for people and for the making and expression of community was even stronger, in favor of efficiency, technology, and speed—and, to give credit, in favor of health as well—as the prime determinants of street design.[4] Building orientation to streets was seen as a fundamental wrong. The most memorable images of what those developments might look like are perspectives taken from a viewpoint high in the air with the uniform height of tall, tall buildings as the horizon line, or drawings of two people sitting at a table somehow overlooking a large, presumably public space with no one in it. This could not be said of the early garden cities, notably in communities like Welwyn Garden City, where houses did indeed face narrow streets [. . .].

As well-intentioned and socially responsive as those manifestos were, their results, abundantly visible by the 1960s,

rarely encourage or celebrate public life. They seem to be more consistent with separation and introspection—buildings and people alone, with space on all sides—than with encountering and dealing with people regularly. They have been more consistent with vehicle movement than with people movement. Fewer things that people need or want are close at hand or within walking distance. They seem to have forgotten that communities are not made in automobiles, nor are people directly encountered.

Better models than these two were in order: ones not so dependent on central power and ownership and design; ones that saw incremental physical change and conservation as more desirable than massive clearance of what existed; ones that were based on not only an acceptance, but also a desire for and love of urban life, of encountering people in healthy environments. They were forthcoming, not least in Jane Jacobs's book of the 1960s, *The Death and Life of Great American Cities*, that challenged the city-building practices of the times.[5] Other notable critiques and alternatives have followed.[6] Kevin Lynch's *Theory of Good City Form* set out values that a good city should strive to achieve, as well as Lynch's own utopian model, with remarkably comprehensive appendixes that catalogue other theories and models.[7] In 1987, the late Donald Appleyard and I put our thoughts into writing, spurred and aided by students, in what we called "Toward a New Urban Design Manifesto."[8] Responding to social values and objectives of urban life such as comfort, identity and control, access to opportunity, imagination and joy, authenticity and meaning, community and public life, and urban self-reliance, we called, in rather general terms, for six physical qualities: livability; a minimum density; an integration of uses; buildings that defined space rather than being set in space; many rather than fewer buildings; and public streets. The present inquiry has been directed toward spelling out in greater detail what is required to achieve one of the fundamental parts of good cities; good—no, *great* streets.

There remains considerable tenuousness, iffiness, in the determination of what makes great streets, and that will continue. Places to walk, physical comfort, definition, qualities that engage the eyes, complementarity, and good maintenance are physical characteristics of all great streets, but far from all streets that have them are great. More is required: what I have been calling magic. In some respects, the problem, if it can be called that, starts with the multiple social purposes of streets. It is useful to review them.

Beyond functional purposes of permitting people to get from one place to another and to gain access to property, streets—most assuredly the best streets—can and should help to do other things: bring people together, help build community, cause people to act and interact, to achieve together what they might not alone. As such, streets should encourage socialization and participation of people in the community. They serve as locations of public expression. They should be physically comfortable and safe. The best streets create and leave strong, lasting, positive impressions; they catch the eyes and the imagination. They are joyful places to be, and, given a chance, one wants to return to them. Streets are places for activity, including relaxation. The best streets continue, are long-lived.

It may be that the purposes of streets relating to movement and access are afforded greater attention in industrial societies because they seem reasonably clear, easily objectified, and measurable. Comfort is increasingly measurable, the other objectives much less so. Participation and socialization often mean different things to different people. Imagination and joy cover many concrete possibilities. Community may be realized by directly working with others or by each person doing his or her part separately. It is not always clear why people go to one street and not to another—the reasons may change, and they may have nothing to do with physical qualities. Physical qualities of streets, it has been observed, may not be the most important contributor to making community. They can help, but their direct contributions are likely to remain murky. Nonetheless, they are important; people spend time and money on making them fine settings for their activities, and it is the physical qualities that designers design.

Considerable progress has been made in establishing operative definitions of some of the qualities that make great streets. More is measurable and definable than we once thought. We continue to know more about definition, transparency, spacing (of trees, for example), human scale, and what makes new buildings fit in with others in specific environments. Much, however, remains uncertain, and so it is not easy to know when a quality has been achieved in the best way, or when, for example, buildings are so tall as to be oppressive. In the realm of street design, it may not be all that critical to know the answers to some of these questions with precision. Understanding what the most critical factors are, and knowing what has been tried and worked—or failed—in a variety of situations may be enough. Street design, like any other creative act, always involves what I call leapmanship: a point where it is necessary to jump from the known to something else that is desired, without knowing for sure where one will land.

There is magic on great streets, and presumably in their making. It is more than putting all of the required qualities on a street, and it is more than having a few or many of the physical, desirable things that contribute to them. Sorcery and charm, imagination and inspiration are involved, and may be the most crucial ingredients. But they cannot be without social purpose. The making of great streets is not an exercise in design for design's sake, solely to satisfy someone's concept of beauty. The magic may not be all that exciting or dramatic at the time of design. To use a non-street example, it seems that Thomas Jefferson was clear in his social and educational objectives for the University of Virginia: community, teachers and students living together while respecting each other's privacy, the centrality of knowledge as expressed in the library, and the importance of land, gardens, and views as parts of a full life. He put them together in a straightforward, seemingly simple way, not without knowledge of physical models gained from study and experience. The result is, in the end, magic. One can imagine that the best streets were done that way, and will continue to be. Models,

a knowledge of what has been done in the past, can help bring the magic into being. Jefferson used and adapted models for his university. Too often, however, models aren't referenced or used. Finding them—what they look like, their dimensions, their contexts, their relationships to each other—has been difficult. That is a major purpose of this book: to offer knowledge about the best streets so that the creativeness, the magic, may come to be for new streets.

Design counts! Great streets do not just happen. Overwhelmingly, the best streets derive from a conscious act of conception and creation of the street as a whole. The hands of decision makers, sometimes of specific designers, are visible. In cases where the initial layout and properties of the street evolved, such as at Strøget or the Ramblas, there is likely to have been a major concerted design effort at some point in time to make the street what it has become. By contrast, some fine streets have evolved to what they are without planning, the Via dei Giubbonari most notably, and there seems little in the way of program or special policy to maintain it. Similarly, compelling streets in medieval cities are plentiful, and they are all of one type. The objective of design may well have been not a great street, but rather a street that simply does its job. And there are as many or more bad streets that have been designed. But the best streets, by and large, get designed and then are cared for, continuously.

Technology, some say, makes cities as we have known them unnecessary. Advances in communication and new methods of production make it less necessary for people to live in close proximity to each other. Today's cities are leftovers from methods of production and achieving security that are no longer necessary and can disappear. There is evidence as well that many people, particularly in North America, given a choice, would not prefer cities—but rather what has become known as a suburban lifestyle or a low-density, non-urban lifestyle. Nonetheless, even assuming that they were unnecessary, cities would still be desirable for many people. We can build and live in cities because we want to—not because we have to, but because they offer the prospect of a fulfilling, gregarious life. Urban streets have been and can be major contributors to that kind of life.

Continually I return to an awareness of the large proportion of urban developed land that is devoted to streets and to the understanding that the purpose of streets is much more than to get from one place to another. Streets, more than anything else, are what make the public realm. They are the property of the public or are under direct public control. The opportunity to design them in ways that meet public objectives, including the making of community itself, is as exciting as it is challenging. If we do right by our streets we can in large measure do right by the city as a whole—and, therefore and most importantly, by its inhabitants.

The best new streets need not be the same as the old, but as models the old have much to teach. Delightful, purposeful streets and cities will surely follow.

TRUE URBANISM AND THE EUROPEAN SQUARE

CATALYST FOR SOCIAL ENGAGEMENT
AND DEMOCRATIC DIALOGUE

SUZANNE CROWHURST LENNARD

The multifunctional European square is the key to true urbanism,[1] the traditional form of building cities on democratic principles that first evolved in ancient Greece and spread across Europe in the democratic revolution of the eleventh to thirteenth centuries.

Since then, multifunctional squares have been a distinguishing characteristic of European cities. Many are still important today as catalysts for public dialogue; their historic significance in the development and sustenance of civic engagement and democratic institutions cannot be overestimated.

These squares offer a *place* for communication that, in Robert Putnam's words, provides the basis for "bridging social capital,"[2] where a diversity of citizens, young and old, and from different social and economic strata, are drawn together to exercise their citizenship as members of the polis.

In current terminology, these are the places where social capital is invested and drawn on. They are places where inhabitants offer mutual assistance, cooperation, exchange information, and are engaged in a wide array of activities that demand their participation. Young people and immigrants are drawn there to learn about the society and become acculturated and accepted as members of the community.

Catalyst for Democratic Engagement

The multifunctional urban square, a uniquely European invention, was intimately connected to the development of democratic self-government. The square provided a setting for dialogue and decision making, empowering participation in the life of the community, raising mere inhabitants to the level of citizens. The investment that each Athenian made in the social life in the agora helped to create the first form of democracy in Ancient Greece.[3] As Aristotle said, "Only the constant interchange of talk unites citizens in a polis, in a community."

The marketplace was a significant factor in the intense reinvention of democratic city government in the Middle Ages. Across Europe, from Spain to Sweden and from Belgium to Hungary, hundreds of new towns were founded, each with a market square at its center. This democratic movement was so compelling that, to attract settlers, the most prominent location on the square had to be selected for the new symbol of self-government, the city hall (figures 1 and 2).

By the end of the twelfth century the communal revolution was won in Western Europe. City communes were recognized as self-governing bodies. "At the call of the bell from the town campanile, the citizens flocked to assemble [on the marketplace], and chose their municipal officers . . . the municipal assemblies were the first representative governments since Tiberius; they, rather than Magna Carta, were the chief parent of modern democracy."[4]

Social Life on the Square

Still today those squares that maintain their multifunctional character (e.g., Freiburg's Münsterplatz, Padova's Piazza delle Erbe and Piazza della Frutta, Ascoli Piceno's Piazza del Popolo, Olomouc's Horni Námesti, Salamanca's Plaza Mayor) are catalysts for conversation, discourse, and dialogue. Diverse people with varied agendas are drawn together; friends meet, pause and chat, introductions are made, news and information exchanged, issues of common concern discussed, and opinions debated. There is much to stimulate conversation on the square: the price and quality of produce at the market, civic, political and religious issues, as well as personal experiences, details about family, work, state of health, and mutual friends and acquaintances.

This "significant conversation . . . the ultimate expression of life in the city"[5] reinforces social networks and cements bonds among the community as a whole. As Wendell Berry observes, "community exists only when people know each others' stories."[6]

The presence of city hall is a constant reminder of civic issues, and ensures that elected representatives—especially candidates—are visible and accessible. Political and informational tables appear from time to time (in front of the

FIG. 1 Piazza del Popolo, Ascoli Piceno, Italy.

FIG. 2 Marienplatz, Ravensburg, Germany.

Rathaus, for example, on Munich's Marienplatz) to raise awareness of important issues; demonstrations may even take place on the square (e.g., Old Town Square and Wenceslas Square in Prague during the Czech Velvet Revolution).

The square also serves as the stage for civic celebrations and festivals involving the whole community. Siena's Palio takes place on Piazza del Campo in front of Palazzo Pubblico (city hall). Festivity and celebration are essential to human life and provide children and young people the opportunity to play valued roles, and to share with adults the delight, laughter, and joy that bind the community together.

When functioning at its best the European square fosters sociability,[7] that is, interaction for its own sake, to give pleasure to each other—not to enhance one's status or position, but to increase each other's sense of well-being. Sociability may involve gossiping, bantering, storytelling, joking, and flirtation intermixed with seriousness, concern for the other, and expressions of support, even love. For the Italian philosopher Luciano De Crescenzo, love is the motivation for all social interaction.[8]

On the multifunctional European square, more than on any other urban public place, all can hear and see each other.

Each person's appearance, their demeanor and behavior are visible to all. Accessibility is easy, even for persons in wheelchairs. The physically and mentally disabled clearly take pleasure in being there; like others, they share the basic human wish to be confirmed, acknowledged, and accepted by others. According to Martin Buber, actual humanity exists only where this mutual acknowledgement unfolds.[9] Alcoholics and others considered "undesirable" also enjoy the ambience of the square; their appearance is less troublesome when they are present among many other people.

The square offers an important learning environment, especially for children and youth.[10] By repeated observation, imitation, and practice in relating to a range of adults in multiple contexts they learn the behavior, attitudes, and social skills that transform them into competent, responsible adults capable of—and interested in—participating in the life of their community (figure 3).

On the square they learn how to relate to a broad diversity of people—older or younger, those who are handicapped or from different socioeconomic and ethnic backgrounds—and they learn how to respond to different points of view and different value systems. They can observe relationships and

FIG. 3 Münsterplatz, Freiburg, Germany.

behavior that may not be expressed in the home, expressions of tenderness, caring gestures, animated arguments quickly resolved, serious discussion, or unrestrained gaiety. In the best squares they may observe an adult caring for and taking responsibility for another human being, acts of altruism or civil courage.

The European square provides the opportunity for generations to identify with each other so that social and cultural traditions can be maintained. Those European cities that have done the best job in maintaining community life on their main square have also been able to maintain their special character, identity, and loyalty to their cultural heritage.

Essential Characteristics

The squares that still serve these democratizing functions are those that have retained their multifunctional character and are embedded in a truly urban context.[11]

Building uses around the square include a civic presence, usually city hall, reminding citizens of their civic responsibilities and keeping their representatives in close contact. People are drawn to the square by the diversity of shops serving daily needs, restaurants and cafes extending tables into the square. Apartments over shops overlook the square,

maintaining jurisdiction ("eyes on the street") especially at night, and a residential population to frequent the square during the day; a large residential population lives within close walking distance.

The square is the main crossing point of pedestrian routes through the city. The compact urban fabric on all sides provides a rich diversity of uses: residential, commercial, offices and services, health, education, and religious institutions are within walking distance; walking through the square on their way to work, school, shops, or other errands, people's paths cross, greetings and meetings take place.

The square has a welcoming sense of enclosure, with proportions like those of a large banquet hall or ballroom. Entering through a narrow entrance or beneath a dark arch one knows immediately that one has arrived at the city's heart and need go no further. Attention is focused on the life within the walls.

Successful squares are trapezoidal (Venice's Piazza San Marco), roughly triangular (the Markt in Tübingen or Trier), fan-shaped (Piazza del Campo, Siena), oval (Verona's Piazza delle Erbe), or doughnut-shaped with a building in the middle (Olomouc's Horni Námesti, and most Polish squares). They are seldom symmetrical, since this seems to demand pomp and circumstance, rather than impromptu social life (Salamanca's Plaza Mayor is an exception to this rule). Elongated street market places are more difficult to reclaim from the automobile.

The city's most significant buildings provide a beautiful backdrop to the drama of social life, and the supporting architectural "frame" is human in scale, with windows, balconies, and doors accommodating and generating a human presence. Placement of buildings around the square transforms it into an unforgettable three-dimensional composition.

The square is primarily a place for people and social life, not for vehicles: to ensure this, traffic may be banned at the most populous times of day, access may be restricted to residents and delivery vehicles, and speed may be limited to twenty kilometers per hour(about twelve miles per hour) or walking speed. Paving designs, mosaics, and emblems emphasize that those on foot are considered the primary users of the square.

To make the square hospitable for social life there are formal and informal places to sit and talk, benches angled to permit eye contact, ledges, steps, walls, and planters designed as a place to pause or rest. Shelter from climate extremes is available in the form of porticoes, umbrellas or trees; fountains, streams, flowering baskets, and bushes play a role in enhancing the square's aesthetic appeal. Playful and informative works of art that provide seating act as focal points, drawing people together and generating interaction.

Most significant in generating social life and civic engagement are the weekly (sometimes daily) farmers markets set up in the morning and removed at midday to make way for other events in the afternoon. Festivals draw the participation of community members in their organization and enactment; street entertainers, musicians, and special events draw the community as observers and generate conversation.

Threats to the Democratic Character of the European Square

Not all European squares exhibit, or have retained, this delicate balance of diverse characteristics and multiple uses necessary to generate social life and civic engagement.

The architecturally magnificent Baroque squares (e.g. Salzburg's Residenzplatz), designed to afford impressive views of bishop's palaces and as settings for the display of power are less hospitable for community social life. The monofunctional residential squares in the United Kingdom are unsuited for democratic dialogue, particularly since the gardens are often gated and locked. Grand intersections of traffic arteries (e.g. Paris's l'Étoile and Place de la Concorde) cannot be considered places for pedestrians.

A historical analysis of many European squares shows a gradual process of privatization, reducing space available for general assembly: temporary market stalls became permanent structures, and eventually rows of buildings encroached on the open space. These building accretions were removed from most German and Polish squares even before WWII.

FIG. 4 Piazza del Campo, Siena, Italy.

In marketplaces in the United Kingdom, however, the process continues to diminish possibilities for assembly or democratic dialogue.[12]

Between 1950 and 1970 most European squares became parking lots; Piazza Carlo Felice, Torino; Place des Héros, Arras; and many in the United Kingdom are still dominated by cars. Some European city centers and main squares are now dying because big-box retail is being constructed on the outskirts and residents are moving to the suburbs. A few cities go to extreme lengths to draw people back to the square.[13]

The tourist industry commandeers some of Europe's most beautiful squares (Piazza San Marco, Venice; Náměstí Svornosti, Cesky Krumlov; Römerplatz, Frankfurt): grocery stores, pharmacies, and supermarkets are transformed into souvenir shops, and historic town halls are converted into museums. Commercial interests, department stores or banks dominate other squares—Bonn's Münsterplatz, Krakow's Rynek Glowney (figure 5).

A gradual erosion of the democratic character of some squares is also caused by pressure from commercial interests (such as television networks and record companies) to stage ticketed concerts on the square; these are broadcast and provide huge profits for the companies but cause resentment in the population, who finds itself shut out.

FIG. 5 Market Square, Krakow, Poland.

Learning from
the European Square

The existence of an open space in the center of the city does not guarantee that social life will take place there, even if it is set within an appropriately built mixed-use fabric and conforms to the necessary architectural principles. City government decisions to permit use of the square as a car park, to permit privatization of the square for permanent construc-tions or for temporary profit, to zone the square and sur-rounding blocks for office development, commerce or tourism, to build sprawling suburbs, malls and big-box retail at the city's periphery—all such decisions affect how well the square can fulfill its historic mission.

However, if a will for civic engagement exists, no more perfect catalyst has ever been created than the archetypal multifunctional European square embedded in a truly urban, human-scale, mixed-use fabric.

URBANISM AND THE ARTICULATION
OF THE BOUNDARY

ALI MADANIPOUR

As a major constituent part of civil society, the public sphere is a collection of material and institutional common spaces, in which the members of society meet to share experiences, to present and exchange symbols and create meaning, and to manage their own affairs.[1] Scientific discoveries, technological development, urbanization, and globalization have all transformed the speed and scale of events, and hence the nature of cities and the relations between public and private spheres.[2] The modern city has gone through a spatial and temporal process of dispersion, creating nonconverging networks, in complete contrast to the cohesive nodal role of the public space in much of urban history. From integrated small settlements, cities have grown in size, scattered and fragmented along functional and social lines. To accommodate change, public and private spaces have both exploded and multiplied as part of this urban growth and transformation. Domestic space has moved from an integration of work, leisure, and living to ever more precarious, monofunctional, intimate, and exclusive spaces of smaller households. The public space has also lost its role in the integration of cultural, economic, and political aspects of urban life. While in ancient city-states the town square was the place for the market, socialization, and politics, the new cities have dispersed these activities, some of which do not require physical proximity anymore.[3]

Technological advances have relocated some activities and led to a fragmentation of urban space. Financial interests of nonlocal investors and large-scale developers have replaced personal and emotional attachments of local developers. In some large cities, the only emotions that local residents show toward their local public spaces are negative, resulting from the fear of crime. In urban regeneration schemes, rather than a multidimensional, open-ended part of social life, public space is being used as an instrument to achieve certain ends. Chief among these ends has been the perceived need to increase the competitiveness of a place. As cities and regions compete in the global marketplace, safe and attractive environments are essential in attracting investors, workers, and visitors. The city becomes an aesthetic display for sale, and the public spaces become an integral part of this privatization and commercialization.

These explosive processes have had both positive and negative outcomes. The tyranny of a particular social organization, of a single place and a single event, has given way to more freedom of choice and a plurality of forums for social life. At the same time, it seems any attempt to overcome the narrowly instrumental use of space and to bring the fragments together to construct meaningful places requires a huge collective effort. This is especially so when the citizens of suburbanized and polarized cities find it difficult to acknowledge the significance of public infrastructure and common space for all.

II

Public spaces of cities, almost anywhere and any time, can be described as places outside the boundaries of individual or small group control, mediating between different private spaces and used for a variety of often overlapping functional and symbolic purposes. Public spaces are multipurpose, accessible spaces distinguishable from, and mediating between, demarcated exclusive territories of households and individuals. These spaces are considered public if they have been provided and managed by public authorities, have concerned the people as a whole, are open or available to them, and are being used or shared by all members of a community.[4]

Public life is partly a performance, where symbols are presented and exchanged, and where masks are displayed, compared, and reshaped. The city becomes a stage for this performance, a theater made of these settings and appearances. When the street is not used as a stage and public life is not formed of playacting, some argue, civility declines.[5] A key task in social life, therefore, is the management of surfaces, creating a civilized social space through a balance between concealment and exposure, between public and private spheres, which is only possible through careful construction and maintenance of boundaries.[6] These surfaces are essentially appearances, gestures, and patterns of behavior, but also include buildings, facades, and all elements of the city that are displayed in its public spaces.

Public space is the institutional and material common world, the in-between space that facilitates copresence and regulates interpersonal relationships. By being present in the same place with others, shared experiences of the world become possible and a link is made with previous generations who experienced (or future generations who might experience) the same physical reality. This connecting role that bridges time endows public space with permanence. Shared experience also becomes possible by copresence with others through the same institutions, such as rituals, performances, public opinion, etc.

Public space is a place of simultaneity, a site for display and performance, a test of reality, an exploration of difference and identity, and an arena for recognition in which representation of difference can lead to an awareness of the self and others, and to an examination of the relationship between particular and general, personal and impersonal. It is a place where many-sided truths coexist, and tolerance of different opinions is practiced. It appears that the modern city prevents this, as individuals use private cars to pass through public spaces, segregate themselves from others into areas and neighborhoods, and connect to others through the medium of complex, abstract, bureaucratized institutions. It is therefore essential that public space facilitate unmediated relations among human beings, alongside mediated relations.

III

Public spaces of the city are spaces of sociability, where social encounter can and does take place. These spaces of sociability, however, are not always accessible to all. For example, the formation of distinctive neighborhoods, with a centrally located public space aimed at facilitating social interaction and integration, is one way of giving a distinctive flavor to the spaces of sociability. Neighborhoods are promoted as a unit of city building, as an environment-friendly urban form that reduces travel and energy consumption, and where impersonal urban space can be broken into interpersonal spheres of communities. Neighborhoods are used as tools with which urban space can be subdivided into manageable parts, where ever-larger developers can engage in large-scale urban development projects. They are where systems of differentiation can be formed to establish spatial differences along ethnic, cultural, and economic lines, and a refuge be created for protection from the anonymous world of the city and its constantly changing conditions and anxieties, created by entry into and out of the industrial era. The role of public space then becomes, simultaneously, a medium of promoting pedestrian movement, a location for social interaction, a tool for urban management, a showcase, a selling point for the developer, a system of signs to assert different identities. In a sense, the establishment of neighborhoods can extend the

private realm by creating a semiprivate, semipublic realm, where a smaller number of urban residents may be aware of each other and of their differences from the rest of the citizens. The public space here, then, serves a variety of purposes, all of which appear to create some distinction and interpersonal exchange in the midst of the impersonal urban world, which can only be maintained by devising tools for the exclusion of those who do not belong. By their nature, therefore, these spaces are not meant to be accessible to all, and hence, less public than those in the impersonal city centers. As elite, marginalized, or communitarian spaces, these are conditioned spaces, providing advantages for some while limiting access for others.[7]

IV

Public and private spheres are *interdependent*, and largely influence and shape each other. This is best exemplified in the relationship between the self and the other, which lies at the heart of public private relationships. The private sphere is simultaneously located in the privacy of the mind, is extended to personal space of the body, is superimposed on land in private property, and is associated with a unit of social organization—the household—in the home. The most private space of all is the space inside the mind, which can be kept hidden from others, but is shaped in a dialogue with the body, i.e., other organs and the unconscious impulses and desires, as well as with the physical and social world outside.[8] The inner private space of the body and the public space of the world are, therefore, interpenetrating and interdependent. The subjective space of consciousness, the sociopsychological personal space of the body, the institutionalized spaces of exclusive private property, and the intimate home have formed the different layers of the private space. The contents of each layer, however, are subject to pressures from inside and outside, and therefore constantly changing, with boundaries that are often ambiguous and contested. In practice, therefore, public and private spaces are a *continuum*, where many semipublic or semiprivate spaces can be identified, as the two realms meet through shades of privacy and publicity rather than clear-cut separation.

The boundary between the private inner space of the self and the public space outside is the body itself. The articulation of this boundary takes place through many forms of communicative devices, some of which have been developing for long. From body-transforming ornaments, such as piercing and painting the skin, to wearing outer layers, such as functional items of clothing and symbolic performative items of jewelry, to body gestures, patterns of behavior, and language, the boundaries between the self and others, between private and public spheres are mediated and articulated for protection and communication. In this articulation, the role of the boundary becomes ambiguous, as it is simultaneously a part of the private and public spheres. It is the area where the two meet and are kept apart, shaped by the two spheres and shaping them at the same time. The treatment of this boundary gives meaning and significance to the distinction between the public and private spheres. It is here that the first person and third person views of the world meet, where the subject's authority rooted in an empirically distinguishable private realm meets the public realms of language, space, and other institutions.

V

The significance of the boundary may be seen to be due to its materiality. Like any other social object, humans imbue it with meaning through production and use. Through mutual or collective agreement, we associate symbolic significance with the objects we use in our daily lives.[9] For example, a small wooden structure can be called and used as a chair only through such agreed symbolization. The common world of things, therefore, helps bring people together and construct meaning. The boundary between public and private spheres is one such object, which we use in a symbolic capacity to characterize particular parts of our lives. The boundary, however, has an extra significance, as it lies between two spheres, in a mediating, defining role. It reflects a system of power relations, as it is a line drawn in space to separate the world into two spheres. Through creating barriers, it has been used to shape behavior, control access, and manage different social groups.

The wall that separates two neighbors from one another, home from street, and city from countryside lies at the heart of the notions of law and society.[10] City building, therefore, is partly a boundary-setting exercise, subdividing space and creating new functions and meanings, establishing new relationships between the two sides. The way boundaries are established, articulated, and related to the private or public spheres often has a major impact on the character of each side, defining many characteristics of urbanism in general. The boundaries are simultaneously means of separation and communication. Colonnades, front porches, semipublic gateways and foyers, elaborate facades, and courtyards are some of the ways the boundary between the public and private has been articulated to allow interaction and communication between the two realms.

This dialogue between the two realms, rather than rigid walls, promotes a civilized ambivalence, which can only enrich social life. At the same time, there are pressures to separate the two clearly, such as in the conduct of public officials who should keep their public duties apart from their private interests or in the need for the protection of a person's private sphere from public gaze. It becomes the task of a multiplicity of boundaries to express and shape this coexistence of ambiguity and clarity. The boundary no doubt reflects an expression of power and, therefore, there are there are those who benefit and those who suffer from it. But the ability to regulate concealment and exposure appears to be needed for all, as so few would wish to live in an undifferentiated common space. Rather than abolishing this ability, a dialogue is needed that ensures the parties can redraw the contested boundaries through negotiation, allowing for permeability and adjustment while protecting the basic need for regulation. This means combining legal and political clarity while allowing for practical and social flexibility, with a degree of permeability that would facilitate interaction and communication.

VI

A central challenge in urbanism is to find a balance between the public and private realms. Two questions that need addressing simultaneously are: How can a realm that caters to a social individual's cultural and biological need to be protected from the intrusion of others be established? And, how can a realm that caters to the needs of all members of a society to be protected from the encroachment of individuals be established? In response, there are those who wish to expand individual freedoms at the expense of public needs, and those who promote the expansion of the public sphere by expanding the realm of the state and restricting the private sphere. Urbanism can be threatened both by those who undermine the public realm and by those who do not acknowledge the necessity of the private realm, as the two are interdependent, not mutually exclusive.

As the shape of the city and the characteristics of urban life are influenced by the way public and private distinction is made, the role of urban designers becomes ever more significant. By articulating the boundary between the two realms, a civilized relationship can be promoted, where the threat of encroachment by private interests into the public realm and the threat of public intrusion into the private sphere are both minimized and carefully managed. A porous and highly elaborate boundary that acknowledges and protects both individual and collective interests and rights is what distinguishes a sophisticated urban environment from a harsh one.

THE NEW URBANISM AND PUBLIC SPACE

GEORGE BAIRD

It is a complex matter for me to comment on the phenomenon of public space in relation to New Urbanism. I am neither a card-carrying member of the movement's Congress, nor a militant opponent of it. I am, however, keenly interested in the important question of the status of public space in our times.

To start with, I can say that I find many CNU (Congress for the New Urbanism) orthodoxies in respect to public space retrogressive. Reiterations of the historic forms of public space—especially in the suburban and exurban regions in which new New Urbanist neighborhoods are so frequently created—are clearly problematic. For example, to reinvoke today the residential square that is so familiar in history, from Bloomsbury to Gramercy Park, necessarily makes one of two worrisome presumptions: either that obsolete forms of social life can be revived; or that the forms of public space can be manipulated on a purely formal basis without any ongoing consideration of the social forms that gave rise to them. A design methodology that does so has to be seen as either historicist or formalist.

But if the nostalgia of some New Urbanists for anachronistic urban forms is problematic, this is not to say that many of the characteristic stances of opposition to the New Urbanism are not also seriously misconstrued. The dystopic fascination of the opposed urban tendency that Douglas Kelbaugh has named Post-urbanism with the scaleless systems of infrastructure that typify so much recently created regional urban form, is surely no less problematic than the misplaced nostalgia of the New Urbanists. If they are engaged in a hopeless effort to perpetuate historically superceded forms of public space, their opponents have succumbed to an equally problematic loss of confidence in the very idea of publicness in the city in our time—that is, of course, when they have not also lost confidence in the idea of the city itself. As a result of their dystopic fascination, in the worlds of architecture and urbanism we now find ourselves over and over again presented with image after apocalyptic image of highly complex urban highway interchanges (SMLXL);[1] of hugely scaled, multiple-lane highways traversing vast new urban territories (Pudong); or the characteristic forms of urban conurbation that typically result from the combination of the two (Tysons Corner).

Then, too, the tenor of the arguments the Post-urbanists use to demonstrate the putative pertinence of such images to urban design in our time itself oscillates erratically between a masochistic professional self abnegation on the one hand, and an apocalyptic eschatology on the other. According to the first version of this way of thinking, the architect, urban designer, and planner are powerless functionaries lacking any and all of the capacities of citizenship, such as those that might have a material effect on the future of the world in which they, like the rest of us, will live. Or, alternatively, these professionals are enjoined to cast off the old-fashioned garments of traditional professionalism, and to participate instead in the pleasurable, allegedly inevitable procedures of global capital at work in the urban realm. The current, highly evident professional oscillation between these stances has become so acute as to suggest that the ambiguous, febrile cultural interpretation typical of the writings of Jean Baudrillard has now been extended, in the eyes of Post-urbanism, to encompass the entire arena of invention in contemporary urban form.

For those like myself, who seek to eschew such extremes of contemporary design discourse in regard to public space—those who still believe deeply in the importance of public space as a key component of contemporary urban form—there remains, of course (for our ongoing theoretical consideration and admiration), one particular, extraordinarily robust and resilient urban form of amazing historical durability. This is, of course, the "street." The residential square may now have become a historical anachronism, "post-urbanism" may be complicit in the creation of vast expanses of urban void, but the street everywhere endures, and continues to be—and deserves to be—the primary locus of publicness in architecture and urbanism today. In his seminal text *The Fall of Public Man*, Richard Sennett observed that the quintessential definition of a city is a place "where strangers are likely to meet."[2] To this day the street remains the central locus of such urban publicness, and while the rhetoric of neither New Urbanism nor Post-urbanism has chosen to focus on it—it does, after all, lack both historic charm and apocalyptic charisma—neither has chosen to eschew it altogether, either.

For me, what distinguishes the street from the square—especially the square in its historic, residential format—is a set of key social and physical conditions: anonymity, a-focality, and interconnectedness. Anonymity because of the sheer possibility in the space of the street for "strangers to meet;" a-focality because the street, unlike the square, is not configured to focus the attention of its occupants in any particular way—indeed, it presupposes a certain Benjaminian distraction; and interconnectedness because every efficacious urban street always leads to numerous others. By contrast, the historic residential square was not really anonymous—indeed, many of the historic examples were even gated, so that only residents of the surrounding residences facing the square held keys to the gardens in their centers. By the same token, such a space is necessarily more focal, and less interconnected than the street, precisely because of this higher degree of familiarity of occupants with one another, as well as with the space of the garden in the square itself.

At the same time, the street is quintessentially distinct from the characteristic void that is the locus of Post-urbanist theoretical fascination as well. The primary reason for this lies in its primary phenomenological condition of "boundedness." Typically, the street is not spatially limitless; typically it has edges. Especially efficacious streets have edges that both contain and animate the citizenry moving about within them. It is for this reason that streets are such potent catalysts to urban assembly, and that they form such a powerful basis of the theory of retail marketing. (Even interior retail malls *pretend* to be streets for this reason.) Interestingly enough, the street is also a seedbed of politics. It is the characteristic spatial containment offered by the historic form of the street that provides the social condensation that makes for effective political protest. For this reason protest groups seeking to organize demonstrations always prefer to locate them within the system of streets close to the centers of cities. By the same token, in recent years it has become clear that police, and other administrative entities attempting to defuse such protest, have learned to seek to permit such protests only in those extensive, imprecisely "bounded" voids Ignasi de Sola-Morales taught us to call "terrain vague."

An academic colleague currently working together with me on an urban research project at the University of Toronto, Professor Robert Levit, shares a number of my predispositions with respect to efficacious contemporary urban form. Studying the typical form of existing suburbs of Toronto, Levit has found himself impelled to formulate a condition of space in the urban field that he thinks is a very desirable one. He calls it "interiority." Interiority, for him, is the characteristic condition of historical urban fabrics, wherein one finds evident significant, and perceptible modulation of spatial order. According to his line of argument, large-scale streets establish one tangible scale of inhabited spatial order for

FIG. 1 Garrison Woods, a New Urbanist project in Calgary, Alberta, Canada.

urbanites. Interconnecting with such streets are other, secondary ones that present them with a different, smaller-scaled, more intimate spatial order. Within the overall hierarchy of qualities of space within the urban fabric in question, then, this relative condition-at-a-smaller-scale, for Levit, constitutes interiority. One could illustrate his point by comparing two urban figure-ground drawings provocatively juxtaposed by Colin Rowe and Fred Koetter in their well-known urban design polemic, Collage City. The two are central Parma and the proposed city center designed by Le Corbusier for the French town of Saint-Dié. Looking at the two together, one would quickly see that central Parma embodies an urban spatial condition of interiority, while Le Corbusier's proposed plan for Saint-Dié does not. Indeed, one can state that few contemporary projects—especially those of a Post-urbanist orientation—possess little interiority at all. While working on our study, Levit found himself concluding that interiority was not discoverable in the recently built western suburbs of Toronto. Indeed—again, shades of Pudong—he even observed that Mississauga City Center made him feel as though he were in China!

This last conclusion seems especially regrettable. After all, the historical Chinese city, with its complex patterns of

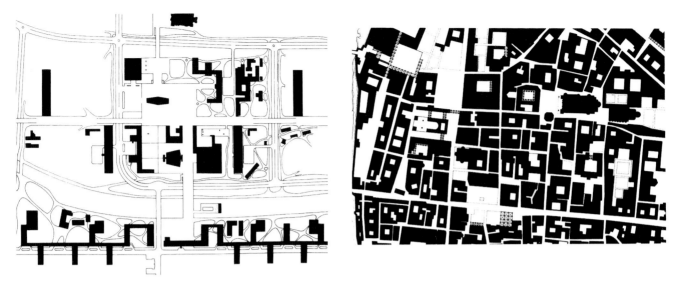

FIG. 2 A figure ground comparison between Le Corbusier's plan for St. Die and the city of Parma. Wayne Copper, from *Collage City*, by Colin Rowe and Fred Koetter, published by The MIT Press.

streets, laneways, and courtyards, is a world cultural triumph of subtle urban space modulation. Observing this strange contemporary evolution of urban form in our time, I find myself driven to conclude that Camillo Sitte was correct after all when he mounted his famous critique of the urban development of the Ringstrasse in Vienna, seeing it as lacking adequate urban spatial definition. It is as though he has been vindicated by history, despite his dismissal by the heroes of modernist urbanism, a century after his framing of his subtle "artistic principles" of urban space making.

Given these surprising recent realizations, it seems all the more odd that during the same period of time that such principles as Sitte's have been returning to the minds of some of us in the area of urban design theory, certain key figures within New Urbanism have been moving in an opposite direction. I have in mind here the revisionist position that has been elaborated by Andrés Duany since the publication of his text on the concept of the "transect." Followers of Duany's publications will recall his conclusion that a substantial group of the characteristic building types of the contemporary urban field, including shopping malls and big-box retail stores, simply cannot be integrated within the sort of desirably fine-grained urban fabric sought by New Urbanism. As a consequence, Duany has argued that any effort to modify the characteristic site plans of such facilities is a waste of designers' time, and that rather than attempt to domesticate them, wise and efficacious urbanists should simply do their best to relegate them to exurban locations, *fuori le mura* (outside the city walls), as it were.

Urbanists and urban designers in my own region of Toronto, Canada, have been puzzled by this turn of events in the New Urbanist camp. Our own recent historical experience suggests that this is an especially problematic and retrograde decision. A little local urban history is needed to explain our position. For many years now, we have found ourselves puzzled by the arguments of New Urbanism for increased gross and net residential densities. The reason for this has been that in our own region such densities (for peripheral greenfield developments) were already high and continuing to rise. Indeed, the net residential densities for ground-related family housing in the region of Toronto have now become so high that it is difficult for many of us here to see how innovative design practice can make them much higher still. Instead, many of us working in the Toronto region are now in the process of realizing that there are only two obvious further loci of realistic further potential density increases within the typical field of urban development overall—at least in our own region. One of these loci is a group of extant small urban centers in that region that are indeed capable of further densification, especially if they are served by adequate public transit. (It is understood, of course, that this densification will entail infilling with residential building forms of higher densities than those typically associated with ground-related family housing.)

The other locus of potential further urban density increase—the more relevant one for the purposes of my current argument—is that vast area of the urban field that does not comprise residential neighborhoods at all. Indeed, it comprises everything else. (In the region of greater Toronto, it is estimated that this territory comprises well over half of the total field of urbanized land.) It is made up of larger scale retail facilities (all the ones Duany is now proposing to exempt from the exigencies of New Urbanist site planning principles), employment lands, and the entire total of all forms of urban infrastructure: highways, utility corridors, transit corridors, public institutional, educational, and service uses, and so on. It seems to many of us here in the Toronto region that it is exactly this vast territory that needs to become the locus of the next threshold of urban design innovation. It is our view that this needed innovation should aim both at the more efficient utilization of urban land as well as at the reconstitution of forms of public space in the city at a scale that can actually facilitate active public life by the citizenry. But what the appropriate form will be, both of the adapted urban form of such facilities and of accompanying new forms of public space among them, remains, in substantial measure, still to be determined.

In conclusion, let me draw a comparison between two recent urban projects that together fall more-or-less within the definition of New Urbanism, but which also exhibit significant differences. I am speaking, on the one hand, of the Duany Plater-Zyberk & Company project of a few years back: Kentlands, outside of Washington, D.C.; and a recent one within the inner city of Calgary, Alberta, Canada. The Calgary project is called Garrison Woods, on account of the fact that it occupies the site of a former Canadian military base. Garrison Woods has clearly been deeply influenced by both the site planning principles and residential iconography of Kentlands. Similar street patterns, similar forms of local recreational space, and similar forms of secondary units on lots that formed part of the design for the earlier Kentlands can be found at Garrison Woods.

But Garrison Woods occupies an inner-city infill site (albeit a very large one), while Kentlands is located on a site that is almost exurban, as opposed to suburban. And this difference in regional location seems to have had a profound effect on the Garrison Woods overall site plan, generating a number of significant differences from Kentlands, despite the numerous obvious similarities. For example, along the streets which bound the site of Garrison Woods, new houses have been located facing the existing houses across the street. Thus, even though the site planning on the "new" side of the street is denser than that on the site that already existed, the completion of the street as a normally two sided one significantly contributes to the integration of the precinct as a whole, into the one that surrounds it. Then too, the retail component of Garrison Woods is also more successfully integrated into both the new neighbourhood itself, as well as the larger precinct in which it sits. Surprisingly, the implemented version of the retail component at Garrison Woods resembles some of the early versions of those planned for its model Kentlands, but which failed to make it through to implementation there. Thus one finds that at Garrison Woods, there really does exist a traditional block of street related retail stores, such as was sought for at Kentlands.

More remarkable still, one also finds a local "shopping center, the site plan for which succeeds in using ancillary pad retail facilities to bracket and contain the parking lot in the fashion also originally proposed for Kentlands, but not so tightly implemented there. Finally, the entire retail precinct is located on one edge of the Garrison Woods neighborhood, oriented both inwards to the new neighborhood, and outwards to the existing surrounding one, thereby contributing further to its integration into the larger urban fabric of the city of Calgary.

This heightened form of integration also plays a significant role in defining the character of the system of public space, both within Garrison Woods and within the larger urban fabric of its surroundings. Garrison Woods is not a gated community, and despite the fact that it offers a wider range of forms of street, residential form and open space than are found in the larger urban fabric surrounding it, its street systems are devised to facilitate continuous movement from the surrounding streets into Garrison Woods itself. Thus the system of public space is conceived as a binder of the new neighborhood to the older inner city, rather than as one divided into an inner and an outer system.

Indeed, it may be appropriate to conclude by observing how tragically the idea of the gated community undermines the idea even of the urban safety that the continuous historic urban street system has traditionally provided. After all, the whole point of the "gates" of the gated community is to keep the danger of the larger urban world outside at bay. But, of course, the very same gates that putatively keep the extant urban danger out paradoxically have the effect of slowing down any possible escape from any possible danger arising inside the compound. Ironically enough, the core idea of urban safety promulgated by Jane Jacobs all those years ago in *The Death and Life of Great American Cities*—eyes on the street—is undermined by the very idea of the gated community, on account of its reduced level of street activity, its reduced urban heterogeneity, and its self induced conditions of domestic isolation.

In retrospect, it would seem that Sennett's observation remains as true today as it was when he made it in 1977. Quintessentially, a city remains "a place where strangers are likely to meet," and this condition is a primary and essential condition of publicness in urban life.

TRANSIT-ORIENTED DEVELOPMENT IN AMERICA
STRATEGIES, ISSUES, POLICY DIRECTIONS

ROBERT CERVERO

Transit-Oriented Development (TOD) has gained currency in the United States as a tool for promoting smart growth, leveraging economic development, and catering to shifting housing market demands and lifestyle preferences. By focusing growth around transit nodes, TOD is widely viewed as an effective tool for curbing sprawl and the car dependence it spawns. By channeling public investments into struggling inner-city settings, TOD can breathe new life and vitality into areas of need. And by creating more walkable, mixed-use neighborhoods with good transit connectivity, TOD appeals to the lifestyle preferences of growing numbers of Americans, like childless couples, Generation-Xers, and empty-nesters.

TOD is as well poised as any land-use strategy for breaking the vicious cycle of sprawl and car dependency feeding off one another. By leveraging affordable housing and reducing the need for car ownership, a virtuous cycle can instead be set in motion, with increased transit usage helping to reduce traffic snarls and compact station-area development putting the brakes on sprawl—at least according to theory.

This paper reviews strategies and issues related to TOD in America. Particular focus is given to TOD's role in linking public transit, housing policies, and sustainable urbanism. Experiences are drawn mainly from the United States—the global extreme of consumerism in both private transportation and housing.

TOD in America

TODs in the United States usually feature mixed land uses configured around light or heavy rail stations, interlaced by pedestrian amenities. Not all are conducive to transit riding, however, for such reasons as the continued prevalence of free parking, thus in many instances, the term "Transit Adjacent Development" (TAD) is a more accurate descriptor.

The most prominent TODs, at least visually, are joint developments—i.e., private-sector projects built on transit agency property as a quid pro quo. Over one hundred joint developments presently exist on, above, or adjacent to United States transit-agency property (figure 1).[1] Most common are ground and air-rights leases followed by operation cost sharing. United States transit properties in continually growing metro areas like greater Washington, D.C., Atlanta, Dallas, San Diego, and the San Francisco Bay Area have been particularly aggressive in pursuing joint development. Washington's WMATA is in a league of its own, having engaged in thirty projects of varying sizes and scope since its inception in the late 1970s (including Bethesda, Maryland currently the nation's biggest joint development money-maker, earning the agency some $1.6 million in annual lease revenue); two up-and-coming joint development projects, White Flint and New Carrollton, will be the agency's biggest and most renumerative joint development ventures over the coming decade.

The TOD Housing Connection

The connectivity between affordable housing and TOD is underappreciated. A significant component of increased traffic in the United States has been the widening distance between homes and jobs, forcing workers to spend more time on the road in return for affordable housing. Most Americans opt to spend more on commuting in return for cheaper housing. A study in Portland, Oregon found that for the same size home, new home buyers could save about $2 a day in mortgage costs for every mile they moved farther out.[2] A generous estimate of the cost of driving is 50¢ a mile. So out and back, that's an extra dollar against a $2-a-day reduction in mortgage costs. While from a personal perspective this means living far away yields net savings, society at large bears the brunt of increased tailpipe emissions, time losses from traffic jams, and reduced open space.

In 2001, housing accounted for one-third of spending by United States households, twice the amount spent in 1972, which reflects higher home ownership rates and bigger and more expensive houses.[3] Together, housing and transportation costs accounted for 52% of annual consumer expenditures nationwide.

From a personal "pocketbook" perspective, smart-growth strategies like housing construction near transit stations mean higher housing costs per square foot, but because units are usually smaller, net price effects are moderated. Reduced outlays for transportation can lower the "bundled" cost of housing and transportation. Residents of affordable units in large United States cities average 25% to 35% fewer cars, travel more by transit, and need less parking. Residing in compact transit-served neighborhoods can cut these costs in half or more.

The TOD Parking Connection

One factor that unnecessarily inflates the cost of housing near transit stops is excessive, or at least inflexible, parking standards and zoning requirements. If there is any spot on the map where it makes sense to revamp parking standards, it is neighborhoods in and around transit stations. Many station-area residents buy into neighborhoods near rail stops for the very reason they want to shed one or more cars, thus freeing up money for other purposes, whether to buy a nicer house or travel more often to the Caribbean. At the Alma Place housing project in upscale Palo Alto, California, just two blocks from the Caltrain commuter rail station, peak-hour parking demand is just four-tenths of a parking space per unit, even though parking is free.[4] Nonetheless, lenders and local planners often insist upon two parking spaces per residential unit (since, in the former case, this is what their financial spreadsheets tell them is necessary, and, in the latter case, this is what time-honored parking codes say are needed).

One way to get the parking ratios "right" is to replace regulatory codes with market prices. This can most easily be done by decoupling, or unbundling, the price of housing from the price of parking spaces. Most ownership housing and apartments have parking included in the base price of a unit. Those who do not own or may not need a car must pay for a space anyway, needlessly driving up the cost of housing. Unbundling parking can thus promote affordable housing objectives while also creating a more walking-friendly environment. Below-grade parking nearly sunk the Pentagon Row mixed-use TOD in Arlington, Virginia because of cost inflation; the project continues to struggle financially despite high-occupancy levels. Arlington County planners learned their lesson, decoupling parking and housing codes for the Market Common mixed-use project at the Clarendon Station. The project's site design was changed accordingly, making extensive use of surface and curbside parking and in so doing improving the project's bottom line.

Barriers to TODs

As dense, mixed-use forms of development, many of the barriers to TOD are generic to all forms of compact growth—NIMBY (not in my backyard) resistance, higher risks and costs, institutional inertia, and so on. Still, some of the barriers to smart growth are more pronounced when it comes to TOD. One is the "congestion conundrum:" the fact that nodal development around a transit station increases spot congestion, prompting some jurisdictions to downzone. Another is the logistical dilemma of accommodating multimodal access needs, which often results in station road designs and parking layouts that

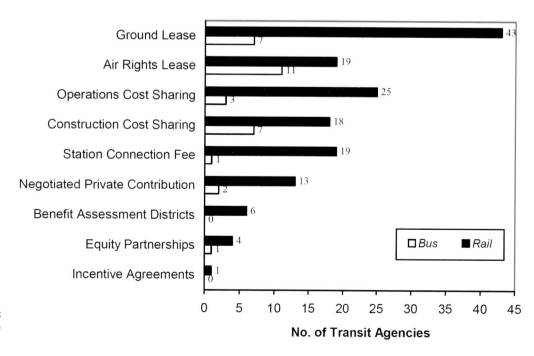

FIG. I Distribution of transit joint development projects in the United States, 2002.

detract from the quality of walking. More fundamentally, this represents a conflict between the role of a station as a functional "node" (particularly in the minds of transit managers) and a desirable "place" (particularly in the minds of urban planners). Still another stumbling block unique to TODs is the rationalization of on-site parking. Many transit officials side with the needs of car-using patrons versus the preferences of TOD tenants and pedestrians, invoking one-to-one replacement policies to ensure parking is in ample supply.

Mixed land uses, a characteristic trait of TODs, pose a host of difficulties not only in terms of design but also in lining up funding, investors, and contractors. Planners sometimes impose a design template of ground-floor retail and upper-level housing or offices—i.e., vertical mixing—on any and all development proposals within a TOD. Mixed-use projects are much trickier to design, finance, and sometimes lease than single-use ones. Finding the right formula for mixed land uses can be every bit as difficult as rationalizing parking policies. Vertical mixing is particularly problematic. Quite often, the ground-level retail component of mixed-use TODs suffer the most, in part because they are poorly laid out. Ground-floor retail, for example, is doomed to fail unless it opens onto a street with busy foot traffic and convenient car access. Mixed housing-retail projects also pose unique design challenges. Ground-floor retail needs greater floor-to-floor height (typically fifteen to eighteen feet) to be marketable, compared with the eight to ten feet between residential floors. This means the entire ground floor, including multifamily areas, must have higher ceilings, which increases project costs. Ground-floor restaurants pose problems such as where to put the exhaust shafts for kitchens. The exact size and location of restaurant space may not be known until leases are signed. Designers must thus allow exhaust shafts to be put in several potential locations, which can reduce net leasable space. And ground-floor restaurants might be unappealing to upper-level residences seeking quiet and privacy in the evening. Local governments need to be sensitive to these issues and focus more on achieving a desired land-use mix within a transit station area as opposed to individual parcels—i.e., pursue "horizontal" neighborhood-scale mixes versus "vertical" within-building mixes.

The Mobility Benefits of TOD

If there is any single aspect of TOD that all sides agree is beneficial to society as a whole, it is increased ridership. TOD is poised to relieve traffic congestion, improve air quality, cut down on tailpipe emissions, and increase pedestrian safety in transit-served neighborhoods by coaxing travelers out of their cars and into trains and buses. However, congestion relief and environmental benefits accrue to an appreciable degree only if TODs result in people who formerly drove alone now switch over to transit (as opposed to making new trips or switching from bus to rail).

I recently collaborated on a study that measured the ridership bonus of transit-oriented housing in California. For twenty-six residential projects within one mile of a California rail station that were studied, the mean share of commute trips by transit was 27%.[5] For those living between two and three miles of a station, the mean share was 7%. Thus, those living within walking distance of a rail stop were around four times as likely to rail-commute as those living within a distance more oriented to bus access (i.e., two to three miles) and nearly six times as likely as those living beyond three miles but within the same city as the housing projects under study. Ridership rates varied dramatically by circumstances. A sensitivity analysis from a binomial logic model that predicted the likelihood of station-area residents rail-commuting showed, for example, in situations where commuting times were comparable by transit and highway, the absence of flex-time privileges at the workplace and availability of free parking was associated with a 14% likelihood of taking transit to work; if parking was no longer free and flex-time was available, the probability shot up to 90% (figure 2).

Ridership gains tied to transit-based housing are significantly a product of self-selection. Those with a lifestyle predisposition for transit-oriented living conscientiously sort themselves into apartments, town homes, and single-family units within an easy walk of a transit node. That is, being near transit and being able to regularly get around via trains and buses weighs heavily in residential location choice. High ridership rates are simply a manifestation of this lifestyle preference.

TOD and Land Market Impacts

Another way to gauge the benefits of TOD is to examine impacts on the value of affected properties. To the degree that housing and commercial uses near rail stops reap accessibility benefits, these projects should sell for substantially more on the open marketplace. This, however, can work against the goal of affordable housing. Public policies, however, are available to redress unintended consequences—namely gentrification and displacement of working-class households.

The weight of evidence in areas experiencing healthy rates of growth is that development near transit stops enjoys land-value premiums and generally outperforms competitive markets. This generally holds for residential housing, especially condominiums and rental units. At Dallas's Mockingbird station TOD, for instance, residential rents in mid-2003 were going for $1.60 per square foot per month; other comparable nearby properties not served by transit were getting $1.30, or 20% less. Most tenants are thirty- to forty-five-year-old professionals who can afford to own but prefer to rent. Six top-floor penthouses at the Mockingbird project rent for up to $4,600 per month. In Englewood, Colorado, apartments rented at CityCenter—a transit-oriented village with civic uses, a cultural and performance center, and retail—were twice as expensive as comparable units elsewhere in the city.

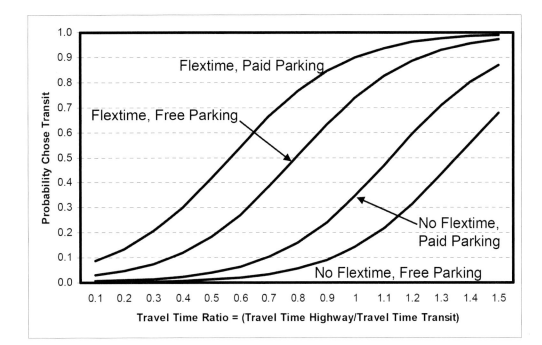

FIG. 2 Sensitivity of rail commuting to parking prices, availability of flextime work schedules, and travel time ratios via highway versus transit, based on model for predicting the likelihood of California station-area residents commuting by rail transit in 2003.

Preconditions for Premiums

Experiences show that the price premium effects of TOD are not automatic and quite often a number of preconditions must be in place. One is that there be an upswing in the economy, with plentiful demand for real estate and, importantly, worsening traffic congestion. Only then will there be market pressures to bid up land prices and a clear benefit of having good rail access as an alternative to fighting highway traffic. Also important are public policies, such as zoning bonuses, which further leverage TOD and system expansion that produces the spillover benefits of a highly integrated network. Because TODs take time to evolve, experiences also suggest land-value benefits take time to accrue.

The importance of these factors—a robust economy, supportive zoning, network expansion, and maturation—is underscored by experiences in Santa Clara County, California. During its infancy, the Santa Clara County light-rail system had no measurable effects on land values,[6] though this generally corresponded to a recessionary period; by the system's tenth anniversary, when the real estate market had revved up, traffic congestion had markedly worsened, station area densities had been upzoned, and the system's track mileage had doubled, land-value benefits were appreciable. I recently estimated a hedonic price model that netted out the effects of proximity to transit from other factors that influence land values in Santa Clara County.[7] This study found that in 1999 substantial benefits accrued to residential parcels within a quarter-mile distance of a light-rail station. Large apartments near light-rail stops, for example, commanded a premium of around $9 per square foot. Compared to parcels that were within four miles of a light-rail station, this translated into an overall land-value premium of 28%.

Which part of a region a station lies in can also have a bearing on land-market impacts. Transit needs to be in a neighborhood with a reasonably healthy real estate market and free from signs of stagnation or distress if significant premiums are to accrue. In San Diego, I found significant land-value premiums for commercial properties in the Mission Valley light-rail corridor, an area that has generally enjoyed sustained growth over the past decade, again using hedonic price modeling.[8] Pro-development policies introduced by local governments, like overlay zoning to encourage mixed land uses and targeted infrastructure investments, had a hand in bolstering commercial property values in the Mission Valley, however what mattered most was this happened to be the region's primary growth axis. This stands in marked contrast to the South Line wherein little effort has been made so far to leverage TOD, in large part because of stagnant growth, and predictably no meaningful land-use changes have occurred. For this first leg of the light-rail system, funded solely with local monies, the overriding objective was cost minimization. The South Line operates on disused freight track that abuts sagebrush and an odd mix of warehouses, factories, a military complex, and various auto-oriented uses. Moreover, the South County area has not been "where the action is." Employment has barely increased in this part of San Diego County since 1980. Accordingly, transit was not poised to induce appreciable land-use changes.

The light-rail extension to Mission Valley has been an entirely different story. The North County area was abuzz with real estate construction when the Mission Valley rail extension opened. The Mission Valley extension, moreover, represented a sea change in the thinking of the region's transit decision-makers. Rather than trying to minimize

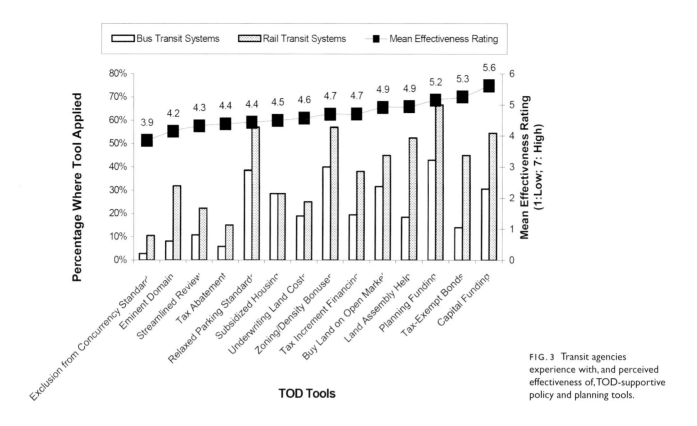

Legend: Bus Transit Systems | Rail Transit Systems | ■ Mean Effectiveness Rating

Percentage Where Tool Applied (left axis: 0% to 80%)
Mean Effectiveness Rating (1:Low; 7: High) (right axis: 0 to 6)

TOD Tools (x-axis): Exclusion from Concurrency Standards, Eminent Domain, Streamlined Review, Tax Abatement, Relaxed Parking Standards, Subsidized Housing, Underwriting Land Costs, Zoning/Density Bonuses, Tax Increment Financing, Buy Land on Open Market, Land Assembly Help, Planning Funding, Tax-Exempt Bonds, Capital Funding

Mean Effectiveness Ratings: 3.9, 4.2, 4.3, 4.4, 4.4, 4.5, 4.6, 4.7, 4.7, 4.9, 4.9, 5.2, 5.3, 5.6

FIG. 3 Transit agencies experience with, and perceived effectiveness of, TOD-supportive policy and planning tools.

costs, the mindset became one of maximizing development potential. The Mission Valley line, for example, crosses the San Diego River three times in order to site development on the flat valley floor and preserve the sensitive hillsides that define the valley. Further helping to promote station-area growth in Mission Valley was the city of San Diego's progressive TOD ordinance that created incentives for compact, infill development near light-rail stops. These efforts paid off. Between 1982 (when the light-rail extension was first proposed) and 1995, the Mission Valley saw the addition of 7,000 new housing units, 2,375 new hotel rooms, 1.6 million square feet of retail space, and some 6 million square feet of office inventory.[9] Since 1995, these figures have trended steadily upward.

Revitalizing Suburban Towns with Commuter Rail

In 1964 William Alonso advanced the trade-off theory to explain residential settlement patterns in industrialized societies. Middle-class households, Alonso theorized, tended to substitute lower-cost suburban living for higher-cost transportation. Accordingly, residential land prices taper with distance from urban centers matched by rising commuting cost curves.[10]

Due to major rail enhancements and an affordable housing crunch, Alonso's trade-off model is alive and well along the New York–Northeast New Jersey axis of the east coast. New York's position as the preeminent center on the urban hierarchy has held its own over the past several decades; as a

command and control post in the global economy and an international center of culture, arts, and entertainment, the city's, and particularly Manhattan's, economic future remains bright. This is reflected in high residential rents. Today, a two-bedroom, 1,200-square-foot, unfurnished apartment in the average price range in midtown Manhattan goes for around $3,200 per month. Manhattan workers pay a high premium in return for minimal commuting costs (both monetarily and in time investments). Alternatively, one can live across the Hudson River in a waterfront apartment in Hoboken, New Jersey, and pay under $2,000 for the same unit. Ferry-oriented housing projects, such as Port Imperial, just north of Hoboken, have been built in the past few years on former industrial brownfields to serve this very market—namely, New York City workers who would prefer to pay less for housing (or get more for their money) and are willing to take a ten-minute ferry ride to and from Manhattan each workday. Go out farther to New Jersey townships like South Orange, Rahway, and Rutherford—all within a thirty-minute rail commute of Penn Station in Midtown Manhattan—and one finds even better housing bargains. In neighborhoods surrounding recently refurbished traditional train stations in these places, the residential rent gradient falls to a typical range of $800 to $1,200 per month for similar housing. Thus, within a half-hour commuting radius from midtown Manhattan, one finds a fairly differentiated housing-transportation marketplace, enabling households to trade-off housing and commuting costs according to lifestyle preferences. With the help of good planning practice and supportive public policies, these unfolding market dynamics have given rise to rail- and ferry-oriented developments in a diversity of settings.

The Challenges of TOD Implementation in the United States

Moving from the theory to the practice of TOD can be fraught with difficulties, especially in car-dependent America. The strongest tool at the disposal of local governments in the United States to shape and control TODs is zoning, usually in the form of overlays. Most overlay zones are introduced on an interim basis to head off auto-oriented uses that might compromise a TOD and specify desired land uses as-of-right, such as housing and convenience shops. For urban TODs, densities of twenty to thirty dwelling units per residential acre and floor area ratios of 1.0 and above are not uncommon. Some of the more progressive TOD zoning districts, such as is found in Portland, Oregon, Seattle, San Diego, and Denver, also lower requirements for car parking and sometimes even for bicycles. The city of San Diego, for instance, recommends parking reductions as high as 15% for urban TODs.

Besides zoning, other tools frequently used in the United States to leverage TOD include: funding for station-area planning and ancillary capital improvements; density bonuses, sometimes used to encourage affordable housing; and relaxation of parking standards.[11] These measures, moreover, received high marks in terms of their overall effectiveness among transit professionals who responded to a national survey on TOD in America (see figure 3, which breaks down the relative frequency of use of tools by rail and bus systems). Next in the order of frequency of usage have been land-based tools, like land purchases on the open market (for land-banking and potential "deal-making") and assistance with land assemblage. For the most part, redevelopment agencies have applied these tools, meaning their role in leveraging TOD has been mainly limited to economically depressed or blighted neighborhood settings. Because of the higher risk involved, redevelopment tools have often been accompanied by other funding sources, sometimes with a dozen or more participants involved in the process.

Implementation strategies that are procedural in nature, like expediting entitlement reviews and excluding TODs from concurrency requirements, have been applied less often in practice and are also viewed by public-sector interests as less effective than other measures in jump-starting TOD. This view, however, does not square with that of many TOD developers. Interviews with thirty-five TOD developers from across the United States revealed that tools that increase certainty, reduce turnaround time, and upgrade transit services are generally preferred. Streamlining the project review process falls within this realm. However, developers also generally agree that supportive zoning, help with land assembly, funding set-asides for streetscape improvements, and other tools within the sphere of public-sector control can be a boon to TOD implementation in some circumstances.

TOD's Promising Future

America is in the midst of a sea change when it comes to linking transit and urbanism. In more and more once car-dominant settings, yesterday's design templates are being discarded in favor of TOD. Also different from the past is that it is not just public policies and interventions that are paving the way for TOD. Unfettered market forces are also having a profound impact. The less desirable features of sprawl—car dependence, congestion, excessive amounts of time behind the wheel, and a feeling of isolation from cultural offerings—are prompting more and more Americans to leave the suburban edge and head to transit-served subcity nodes and even the traditional inner city.

In America, TOD resonates with the general public and often finds support across political and ideological lines. Nearly everyone understands if there is a logical place for targeting compact mixed-use growth, it is around transit stations. In America today, transit-oriented housing stands as one of the most promising mechanisms for promoting multiple urban policy objectives—affordable housing construction, sprawl containment, and reduced car dependence. Bold new policies are beginning to surface across the country, ones that push conventional boundaries and acknowledge the unique market niches that are being served. These include market-based initiatives like Location Efficient Mortgages and unbundling of parking and housing costs, as well as government incentives such as targeted infrastructure investments and the flexing of parking standards. Standard designs, cost pro formas, and building code templates need to be challenged for each and every transit-oriented project, in large part because the TOD market is not very standard. Experiences show that new housing built near rail stops often appeals to single professionals, childless couples, and empty-nesters who value amenities as much as the amount of living space and who often own fewer cars and log fewer miles on their odometers than the typical urban household. Standards for mortgage qualifications, building designs, and parking supplies need to reflect these market realities. To the degree that market-responsive policies are introduced, shifting demographics and lifestyle preferences will reduce the need for government subsidies and regulatory interventions, save for those that aim to help the poor. Ultimately, the marketplace will drive station-area planning and designs, with policy interventions focused mainly on making neighborhoods surrounding transit nodes better places to live, recreate, shop, and do business.

RECOMBINANT URBANISM

DAVID GRAHAME SHANE

As a teenager in London in 1962, I was deeply impressed when Crick and Watson received the Nobel Prize for their genetic research. The idea that two continuous strains of genetic code arranged in a double helix, with hybrid carbon bridges between them, could account for all cell growth haunted me as I became an architect. Years later, as I completed my book in 2003, I realized that the same schema could be applied to the urban codes I was dealing with. The city and the country were two cultural poles found in all societies, and urban actors at various periods had created a variety of hybrid combinations of urban and rural relationships, ending now with our contemporary, global, network city.

Urban actors work as key agents, switching between the poles and altering the codes, timing their move to take maximum advantage of their situation. They have only a limited toolbox of forms and recombinatory devices, but their timing and sense of the capacity of the network was crucial to urban growth.

Kevin Lynch: City Theory and Design as a Recombinatory System

Recombinant Urbanism begins with Kevin Lynch because he provided a language and notational system to describe the emerging regional city based on the automobile in his *Image of the City* (1960). In his diagrams and text he highlighted the conceptual models that designers and inhabitants used in their navigation and design of cities. His last book, *A Theory of Good City Form* (1981), outlined not only a system of recombinatory urban elements, but also three "normative" city models built from these elements according to the value systems of three dominant sets of urban actors. Although he rejected these powerful, normative models in favor of a "performative" urbanism based on scientific codes, I—like many other later scholars—found them incredibly useful [Spiro Kostof also used these models in *A City Shaped* (1991)].

Lynch never articulated the recombinatory nature of his system of models and their relationship to his system of elements. In *A Theory of Good City Form* he made a basic distinction between places of stasis and spaces of flow. In his normative model of the "City of Faith" a single, static center dominated all spatial flows, referring all feedback to this single center and creating a static, hierarchical order inside an enclave, with chaos outside. In his modernist "City as a Machine" the dominant code changed to logic of the spaces of flow, breaking apart the old closed "city-forms" and opening up "city-regions" round high-speed lines of transportation and communication. Lynch did not detail his third model, the "City as an Organism," broadly hinting that it was a heuristic model based on learning, pattern recognition, and feedback loops to an informed citizenry. It was a recombinant mixture of Jane Jacobs's *Death and Life of Great American Cities* (1961) and the early green/ecological movement of Rachel Carson's *Silent Spring* (1962).

Despite his own early remedial involvement in the redesign of central Boston after the insertion of the Central Artery in the 1950s, Lynch remained opposed to urban design. He was a modern pragmatist at heart, and his own projects often involved large-scale systems redesigns. He used Christopher Alexander's recombinatory *A Pattern Language: Towns, Building, Construction* (1978) to deal with the specifics and the small-scale historical fabric of the city. His theories emphasized a bottom-up, small-scale approach, where informed citizens became major urban actors through participation and outreach programs managed by professionals to create the "Ecocity."

Lynch made a great distinction between his city modeling techniques and contemporary urban design. Following on the ecological work of Patrick Geddes and Iain McHarg (who used the layering capacity of computers to isolate different systems and ecological territories in the landscape), Lynch practiced what he termed "City Design" and "City Theory" in his large-scale, landscape-oriented work. He was a predecessor of contemporary Landscape Urbanism, as exemplified by James Corner and Field Operations. Corner easily identifies different urban systems that correspond to Lynch's normative models as layers in a complex, global and local, network city. Corner incorporates a sense of a long-duration time scale and just-in-time, flexible programming to build a performative model of how actors, the landscape, and the city might interact to form a commons—a prepared ground for the emergence of new, recombinatory city forms.

The Emergence of Urban Design as a Recombinatory Practice

As the dominant actors and conceptual model of the city change over time, the contemporary concept of design would have to change also—from the archaic city to the scientific city, and on to the relational systems of the Post-modern city. Reacting against machine-city concepts, in his *L'architettura della città* (1966), Aldo Rossi made a comprehensive argument that highlighted a past European rationalist and scientific tradition, stretching back to Cerda in Barcelona and German Rationalists like Stübben in the nineteenth century. Here designers maintained a rigid distinction between the public monument and small-scale, recombinatory fabric, as detailed by Rob Krier in his *Urban Space* (1979). But by then, Rossi had recognized the failure of this total, closed system approach in his *Analogical City* drawings (1976), which spotlighted the fragmentary nature of the Post-modern city with its collage of built forms and typologies from different ages of development.

Many authors described the collapse of the rationalist, scientific approach to planning and looked for small-scale recombinatory models. Christian Norberg-Schulz, in *Existence Space and Architecture* (1971), made a phenomenological critique of modernism as a closed system of knowledge, contrasting this with personal knowledge and shared, group, unwritten, vernacular traditions. Dalibor Veseley's urban design studios at the Architectural Association in London, in the late 1970s, with Mohsen Mostafavi, provided an example of performative and community-based design for the generation of small, public urban spaces that included memory, history, and the archeology of the site. The contemporary Cornell School of so-called Contextualist enclave design, headed by Colin Rowe and Fred Koetter, drew on this tradition, while their *Collage City* (1978) advocated the collage of urban elements such as urban enclaves and streets to form a recombinatory city.

Nineteen seventy-eight also marked the emergence of fragmentary urban design as the solution to the breakdown of city planning and the near financial bankruptcy of New York City. The new, recombinatory system found its first application in Alexander Cooper and Stanton Eckstut's winning 1978 entry for the Battery Park City enclave. The two architects recombined New York's traditional zoning codes from 1916 (with street section and facade controls) with modernist building codes for slab or tower block typologies (from the 1960s), additionally providing a splendid riverside esplanade. This simple yet undeniably recombinatory system of urban enclave coding was later developed by the New Urbanist movement into a comprehensive strategy for the design of large suburban lots in the 1980s and 1990s.

In 1978 Rem Koolhaas also published his *Delirious New York*, celebrating both the generic, large-scale, modern architecture of Wallace Harrison and the abrupt, filmic jump cuts of urban montage made possible by the skyscraper section in the dense city core. Based on Alvin Boyarsky's earlier reading of Chicago as a multilayered city, *Delirious New York* inspired the deconstruction and reinvention of the city section [in such schemes as Zaha Hadid's The Peak in Hong Kong (1981) or Bernard Tschumi's Parc de la Villette (1982)]. The Peak provided for a rhizomic system of assemblage, allowing individuals to select and recombine their paths through a network of three-dimensional spaces, sequencing their experience of the city section.

Enclaves and Armatures as Recombinatory Urban Elements

Paola Viganò, in *La citta elementare* (1999), emphasizes how any system of design that deals with the city must create a system of urban elements, and these elements will nec-

FIG. I Urban Elements: Enclave, Armature, and Heterotopia diagrams from *Recombinant Urbanism* (2005).

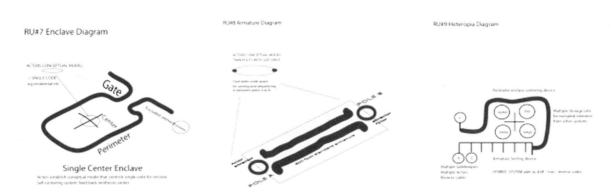

RU#7 Enclave Diagram

Single Center Enclave

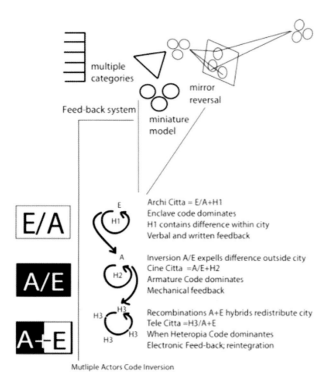

E/A

A/E

A+E

Mutliple Actors Code Inversion

multiple categories

Feed-back system

mirror reversal

miniature model

E
H1

A
H2

H3
H3
H3
H3

Archi Citta = E/A+H1
Enclave code dominates
H1 contains difference within city
Verbal and written feedback

Inversion A/E expells difference outside city
Cine Citta = A/E+H2
Armature Code dominates
Mechanical feedback

Recombinations A+E hybrids redistribute city
Tele Citta = H3/A+E
When Heteropia Code dominantes
Electronic Feed-back; reintegration

FIG. 2 Urban Elements: Heterotopia: Code change mechanisms; Using the Three "M's," mirror, multiple, and miniaturization techniques, actors shift the role of the enclave and armature in heterotopias, altering the dominant code in the city, from *Recombinant Urbanism* (2005).

essarily have to be recombined by urban actors over time. In addition, Viganò clearly identifies a third urban system, the *città diffusa* ("Diffuse City") or "Reverse City," wherein previous urban codes are broken and landscape, topography, ecology, and even agriculture enter the urban mix to form what she terms a space-body matrix in a new urban territory (linking to Landscape Urbanism). Viganò sees collage and montage as basic assembly systems for this Reverse City, where the old modernist logic is transformed by modern communications and transportation systems.

Enclaves and armatures form the basis of this transformative system. The word enclave, derived from the French word to cut off or cleave, is fundamental to land subdivision, the making and documenting of agricultural fields and culture. In Lynch's terms it is concerned with stasis and rest, while in Rowe's terms it is a place where a particular actor can flourish, creating their own fragment and culture. Safe enclaves form the basis of all urban systems, and have dominated the culture of the agricultural world, becoming stopping places in the later systems of flow, like department stores or malls, factories or warehouses, in production and consumption systems.

Armatures, on the other hand, are linear sorting devices that handle flow, with carefully calibrated resting places along their edges (like numbered storefronts along a high street or main thoroughfare). Rowe thought of armatures in terms of "Great Streets" like New York's Fifth Avenue, beside Central Park, while Lynch thought of them as well-

worn "paths" used by pedestrians in the city. Paths could be stretched in space and time to become the highway approaches to the city [as in his *A View from the Road* with Donald Appleyard (1963)]. Robert Venturi, Denise Scott-Brown and Steven Izenour provided the new notational system for observing such stretched armatures in their *Learning From Las Vegas* (1972). Armatures could also be compressed down to 600 feet inside multilevel malls as described by Barry Maitland in *Shopping Mall: Planning and Design* (1986).

Actors in different recombinatory systems used enclaves and armatures in very different ways for different purposes. In *Recombinant Urbanism* I make a distinction between enclaves and armatures in three different systems of assembly, naming enclaves as type 1, 2, or 3 depending on whether they are in the single-center, agricultural model (e1); in the twin pole, center, and edge model of the industrial system (e2); or in the hybrid, post-industrial system of the Reverse City (e3). Similarly, armatures can be categorized in this way as a1, a2, a3, with the addition of notations for stretched (<a2>) or compressed (]a2[). I then propose formulas for the three models, where h is the heterotopia, which will be discussed below. When the actors employing enclaves dominate, the City of Faith = e1/ (a1+h1). When armatures dominate, the City as Machine = a2/a2+h2. I also provide diagrams showing the shifting relationships possible between enclaves and armatures, and analyze Peter Wilson and Katarina Bolles's Munster Library (1988-93) in these terms.

Heterotopias as Places of Change and Recombination

Although both Lynch and the duo of Rowe and Koetter focused on urban actors, neither were very clear about how change could be accommodated in their cities. Lynch had special experimental enclaves where social experiments could take place, like the hippy communes of the 1960s. Koetter and Rowe had "Ambiguous and Complex Buildings" that tied together the different phases of urban development, operating on several scales in terms of the city plan. Michel Foucault, in his short radio talk "Of Other Spaces" (1964, online at http://www.Foucault.info), provided a much more convincing model of how urban actors changed cities through their control of activities in specific places with recombinant codes.

Foucault called these places heterotopias, literally the "place of the other." Heterotopias, like all enclaves, have defined boundaries that are more or less porous, and controlled entrances. Whereas normative enclaves are single-function and mono-cultural, Foucault describes heterotopias as multicellular, allowing disparate spaces, places, times, activities, and people to coexist within the larger boundary of a single cell held within the larger urban system. Heterotopias were unusual in the complexity of their structure and feedback mechanisms that enabled urban actors to coexist.

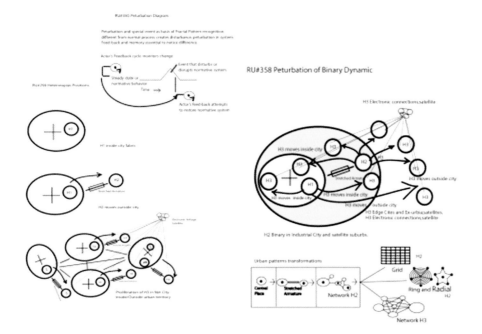

FIG. 3 Urban Elements: Urban Actors shift position of heterotopias in city as catalyst for change. H1 heterotopias hidden in city, H2 heterotopias outside the city, H3 heterotopias proliferate in and outside city, becoming mobile. "Cha-Cha-Cha" diagram showing shifting heterotopias from model to model, from *Recombinant Urbanism* (2005).

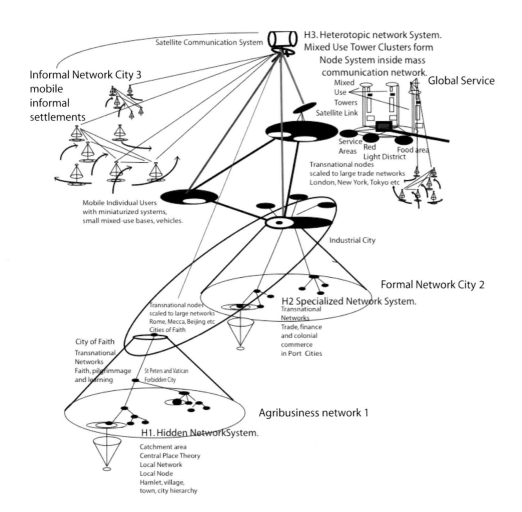

FIG. 4 Urban Elements: Layered drawing showing Archi Citta, overlaid by Cine Citta, overlaid again by Tele Citta. Tele Citta has three elements, global satellite communications system, fixed high-density service nodes, and mobile, low-density "urban fields" with mobile actors. Each system contains its own version of a heterotopia, from *Recombinant Urbanism* (2005).

Foucault described this complex system of feedback and control in terms that I call the three *m*'s. The first *m* consists of a mirror function (derived from Lacan's theories of delirious self-definition in a mirror), so that heterotopias reflect their surrounding society but reverse the dominant codes, allowing for the coexistence of forbidden mixtures. The second *m* consists of a system requiring that these places be reflexive miniatures, a city within a city, mirroring in miniature the larger surroundings of the city's structure and values. Finally, the third *m* required that these mixing places had to be multiple, that is, they contain multiple cells, perhaps in multiple layers, in which to mix different categories of people or flows of energy.

Foucault tried to create a heterotopology to describe the logic of these recombinant places. Foucault was professor of the history of the systems of thought at the Collège de France in Paris, and he clearly identified three spatial systems and three types of heterotopias. The first system was one of emplacement, the equivalent of Lynch's City of Faith, based on fixed centers. The second was a system of extension, based on Galileo's geometry, where there was a continuous space of extension through which the celestial bodies moved with a machine-like precision that could be calculated by man, revealing that old centers were merely resting points in a line of movement, the equivalent of Lynch's City as a Machine. Finally, there was the system of relations, which created fixed or mobile, flexible "sites." The examples Foucault gave of such sites in 1964 included information moving with a set pattern through a communication system, or cars that move in relationship to each other through a traffic jam.

Foucault insisted that all systems had their blind spots, their heterotopias where recombinant change took place, and that this was basic to any system of logic. In his system of emplacement there were "heterotopias of crisis," where individuals went and were hidden in the fabric of the city without disturbing the dominant order of society (my h1 category). In his system of extension there were "heterotopias of deviance," such as prisons, hospitals, asylums, cemeteries, etc., which removed those who could not conform to the dominant work ethic to specialized institutions outside the city, where they could then be reformed and helped by specialists in a rigid discipline (my h2 category). In his system of relationships there could be "heterotopias of illusion," where codes were very flexible and fast changing, the opposite of the prisons. Foucault gave as examples theaters, cinemas, museums, art galleries, the stock exchange, bordellos, and bath

temporal layering of munich

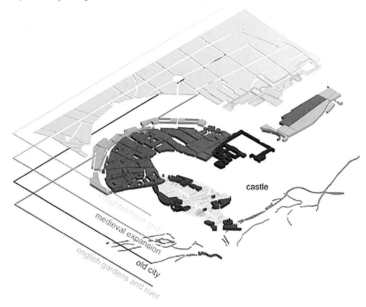

historic armature **palace and expansion** enlightenment armature

FIG. 5 The interwoven layers of the Global Meshwork City model.

houses—all places that could contain multiple actors, values, and time systems at once and could switch image systems and value systems very quickly (my h3 category).

Conclusion: Heterotopias in Network Cities

Looking back at *Recombinant Urbanism* it is clear that the double helix of Watson and Crick only works as a basis for city modeling up to a certain point. The initial opposition of city and countryside was dissolved in the city-as-machine model, where movement and stasis became the binary poles. Now we appear to operate in a world of virtual or conceptual mapping versus the physical world, where advertising and media communications can rapidly alter our perception of the network city. Whereas heterotopias as places of change were once hidden and then moved out of town, now heterotopias of illusion and pleasure have proliferated everywhere. They are in the old center as tourist attractions, in the inner city as garden-suburbs and middle-class utopias, and in the edge city as theme parks and malls. As urban designers we are still learning how to operate in this global system of heterotopias of illusion; think of Dubai, but also of vast urban slums as in Rio or Mumbai—perhaps our new heterotopias, category h4.

SPATIAL CAPITAL AND HOW TO MEASURE IT
AN OUTLINE OF AN ANALYTICAL THEORY OF URBAN FORM

LARS MARCUS

The extraordinary thing about cities is not that they are so different but that they are so alike.

—Bill Hillier

New Urbanism: Yet Another Normative Theory in Urbanism

New Urbanism has, in the last decade, established itself as maybe the most influential movement in contemporary urbanism. Like most such movements it has done so in opposition and debate with established paradigms of practice and knowledge; that is, it has been a critical and outspokenly ideological movement. New Urbanism thus fits well into Françoise Choay's description of theories in urbanism where, through a close reading of the tradition, she finds them to be, on the one hand, projects to build general theories on urbanism, but on the other, programs propagating new ideals.[1] Put simply, theories on urbanism have been inherently *normative*, telling us what cities should be, rather than *analytical*, telling us how cities work.

Bill Hillier has also discussed this aspect of theories in urbanism.[2] In short, he puts forth the quite alarming conclusion that we are rich in theoretical support for the *generation* of urban designs, but poor in well-founded support for the *prediction* of the actual performance of such designs. A conclusion well supported by the fact that so much of urban planning and design in the twentieth century has failed to deliver on its claims. What we really need then, is not yet another normative theory on urbanism—rather, we should have grown disenchanted of them—but an analytical theory on urbanism. That is, a theory that develops knowledge on the relation between *urban form* and *urban life* so that we can better predict the effects of *urban designs* when realized. That is not saying that a vivid debate on the ends of urban design is not essential, it is saying that such a debate is not of much use if we do not have the knowledge to reach the ends once we settle on them.

In general terms, what I want to address is the relationship between urban form and urban life and how these two generate a sociospatial category that we call *urbanity*. Put more distinctly, I want to address how urban form, as a result of urban design, influences urban life, that is, how it supports, hinders, and organizes it, thus creating variations of urbanity. In the following, I will propose and try to show that urban form in doing so creates something that can be called *spatial capital* and that this is possible to measure.[3]

Urbanity as Accessible Diversity

What we need as a point of departure is an apposite and powerful definition of urbanity by which we can start to discern urban forms that will be particularly influential on it. It follows that we are looking for a definition on a generic level as to not get caught up in particularities. At the same time it is important to stress that we are talking about urban form as the concept is understood and used in *architecture* and *urban design*, that is, as something that directly relates to human experience and action in urban space. This is important since it means that we are not looking for the more abstract measures typical for *urban geography*, such as density measures and gravity analyses.

The single most common concept in such definitions is the density measure just mentioned; whether *density* of population, building mass, or other things. Still, the concept of density is problematic. First, it conveys many technical problems of description constantly debated in geography.[4] Second, density in itself is far from an adequate description of urban form, especially on the experiential scale addressed here. For example, high density can be achieved both in traditional inner-city grids as well as in large modernistic housing estates, but its impact on urban life in the two cases differs dramatically. What really matters is the degree of *accessibility* to density, which is something achieved by design of the urban

FIG. 1 Urban space as structured and shaped by urban form in a city district in Stockholm (top left), and the axial map of the same area (top right).

FIG. 2 The distribution of spatial integration, correlating in this case with observed pedestrian movement by 70% (R2=0.70).

FIG. 3 Building density per plot (bottom left), and accessible building density per plot (bottom right), where the latter correlates to accessible population density by 82% (R2=0.82).

fabric of streets and buildings; that is, urban form. Furthermore, high density does not in itself necessarily tell of urbanity, even though easily accessed. Many institutional areas for example, such as hospitals, can be both dense and accessible but we do not regard them as typically urban, other than in a derived sense. Another variable needs to be added, and I propose that to be *diversity*. As a matter of fact, the two variables of accessibility and diversity often override the impact of density; for example, many small cities with low density present a high accessibility and diversity and thereby also a strong sense of urbanity.

The short generic definition of urbanity proposed here is therefore: *urbanity, both socially and spatially, is primarily constituted by high accessibility and high diversity*. Put in more concrete terms; we live in cities so that we can get close

to many different things. This is not saying that density is unimportant, and it will be returned to; it is proposing that the two concepts of accessibility and diversity are more poignant descriptions of urbanity. According to the theory of spatial capital then, *urban form generates variations in spatial accessibility and diversity, with direct effects on social accessibility and diversity, which are possible to measure, whereby, in turn, it is possible to measure variations in urbanity as a sociospatial category*.

3. Spatial Accessibility and How to Measure It

The next step is to find analytical means that can capture and measure aspects of urban form that directly relates to human action and experience, which heavily influence the degree of accessibility and diversity for urban life.

The most developed technique for such analysis when it comes to accessibility on the detailed scale we are discussing here is beyond doubt spatial *integration analysis* developed in *space syntax* research. Instrumental for such analysis is the invention of the *axial map*, which is a representation of urban space, as structured by urban form, from the point of view of an experiencing and acting human being, where each axial line in the map represents an urban space that is possible to visually overlook and physically access (figure 1). In short, such analyses measure the accessibility of each and every axial line from each and every other axial line in the map, which is called the *integration value* of each line. Such analyses have proven, in a long series of studies around the world, that there is a strong correlation between such integration values and pedestrian movement, that is, a most generic aspect of urban life (figure 2).[5]

From this fundament other studies have been able to find other correlations, where movement is the intermediary. It is, for example, not surprising to find that streets that are well integrated in the system and therefore collect a lot of movement also become prominent locations for retail. This has also been confirmed in many studies.[6] Taking one more step, it also seems likely that such streets in the long run may gather higher rents for the letting of floor space. Also this has been confirmed.[7]

The accessibility measure developed in space syntax research has been further developed into *place syntax analysis*.[8] Integration analysis, as well as space syntax research in general, deals with the analysis of urban space per se, in that what is analyzed is the accessibility to urban space in itself without any regard of the "content" of space, such as residential population, retail, or bus stops. There is an important point to this approach, since the differentiation of space as a system in itself, apart from its content, is seldom done with any consistency in urban analysis. At the same time, what we often look for in urban analysis is accessibility to particular contents in urban space such as the ones mentioned above. In *place syntax analysis*, the axial map is used as a distance measurer to such contents, loaded as place data on, for example, plots or address points. It is thereby not only possible to analyze the accessibility to other spaces, but also the accessibility to specific contents in space as well. Place syntax analysis can therefore be said to deal with *specific spatial accessibility*, such as accessibility to different attractions, while integration analysis deals with *general spatial accessibility*, that is, accessibility to urban space in itself.

Returning to the issue of density, place syntax analysis thus presents a new and in many respects more life-like mode for representing geographical data. While traditional geographic descriptions most of the time deal with representations of such data as *density within geographical units*, such as city districts, blocks, or plots; place syntax deals with representations of the *accessibility within a certain radius*, for example, walking distance, to such data (figure 3). We can then produce maps showing "accessibility to density" that bring back density to our discussion, but now seen through the lens of accessibility, so to speak. Such descriptions of accessibility to different kinds of content in space can be regarded as one mode for the analysis of spatial capital. But as earlier argued, it is easy to see how urbanity is constituted not so much by density in itself as diverse density.

Spatial Diversity and How to Measure It

For the variable of diversity, where there are no analytical techniques as sophisticated as integration analysis developed, I propose that we need to shift focus from *experientially defined space*, such as the axial line, to *legally defined space*, such as, the privately and publicly owned domains we call plots or properties (figure 4).[9] The reason for this is that the plot, through its disposer, represents the presence of an actor in urban space, and furthermore the location of the influence of that actor. Such actors normally develop particular strategies for their domains. An area with comparatively many plots then seems to have the potential to carry a higher amount of such actors and thereby a higher amount of strategies for action, where it seems likely that this, in turn, would produce a larger amount of diversity among these strategies. In the end, such an area seems to carry the potential to more easily develop a diverse content than an area with comparatively few plots and hence few actors and strategies. Obviously other things, like land-use regulations, can override the effect of this, but what I am trying to capture here is the particular influence of urban form in itself.

Here again place syntax analysis could be useful, this time not to measure the accessibility to different contents in urban space, but the accessibility to specific types of space in urban space, such as plots or address points. For example, one can measure the accessibility to plots within a radius of, for instance, three axial lines from each plot in an area, which, following the argument above, could show the distribution of potential diversity in that area. Still, the measure would be heavily influenced by the local accessibility, since the size of a radius of three axial lines varies a lot depending on the length of the lines. This effect can be normalized in either of two ways, either by dividing each such measurement with the accessible plot area within the same radius, or by setting the

FIG. 4. Experientially defined space, where each axial line represents a space that is visually and physically accessible (left), and legally defined space, where each plot represents a domain of an actor defined by legal restrictions (right).

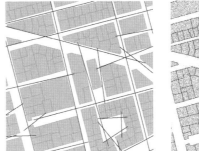

FIG. 5 The distribution of spatial capacity, measured as accessible density of plots (left), correlating with accessible density of lines of businesses by 40% (bottom left) and accessible density of age groups by 69% (bottom right).

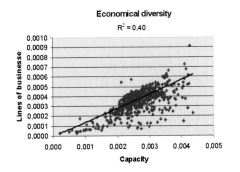

Economical diversity

$R^2 = 0,40$

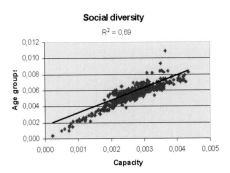

Social diversity

$R^2 = 0,69$

radius to three axial lines but not more than, for example, 500 meters. Such measurements will in the following be referred to as a measurement of *spatial capacity* (figure 5).[10]

When this technique was tested, what, in effect, was measured was the accessibility to plots from each and every plot within three axial lines, divided by the amount of accessible plot area within the same radius. These measures were then correlated to the accessibility to both economic and social indices of diversity, where the economical index in this case was lines of businesses, and the social index was age groups. It turned out that spatial capacity correlated to 40% with the economical index (R2=0.40), and to 69 % with the social index (R2=0.69),[11] implying that the higher spatial capacity within a radius from a plot, the more lines of businesses and age groups within the same radius, that is, the higher diversity.

Conclusion: Spatial Capital— a Measurement of Urbanity

We can then see how integration analysis and place syntax analysis present powerful techniques for the analysis of spatial accessibility as well as diversity, showing how urban form is most influential on generic aspects of urban life, where it furthermore follows that spatial accessibility and diversity change according to urban design.

Spatial capital, measured by spatial integration and spatial capacity, then constitute a procedure to measure urbanity that promise to be both clarifying and useful in *urban design* as well as *urban analysis*. It is important to say right a way that such a measurement does imply that the higher accessibility and diversity the higher spatial capital, but it *does* not imply that a higher spatial capital is always *better*. In urban design it is rather a measurement that is able to tell, whether certain design solutions will create greater potential for spatial accessibility and/or diversity or not, where the appropriate level for this only can be judged in relation to the design task at hand. That is, it can work as a most important *design support* but not as a *design director*.

In urban analysis it can be useful both as a straight description of the variations of spatial capital in an urban area, or as descriptions of spatial accessibility and diversity separately (figure 6). The latter case, for example presents the interesting opportunity to discern urban subcategories. There is an abundance of taxonomies and typologies used in the discourses of urbanism, the *transects* in New Urbanism being just one. There are good reasons for that, since categories and types simplify communication. The problem is that such typologies often have weak ties to urban life, which make them isolated and rather uninformative typologies of urban form per se. The theory of spatial capital on the other hand, presents the opportunity to discern such categories or types with an unusually strong analytical foundation, where urban form is tied to generic aspects of urban life, constructing genuine sociospatial subcategories of urbanity. From such a description, four fundamental urban categories can be suggested (table 1), where I want to stress that there are no implied values to the different categories. Once again returning to density, it is furthermore obvious how the table could be extended by the addition of a high- and low-density type for each category.

FOUR SUBCATEGORIES OF URBANITY AND SUGGESTIONS FOR IDEAL CASES, DISCERNED THROUGH THE THEORY OF SPATIAL CAPITAL

Urban category	Accessibility	Diversity	Ideal case
Super-urban	High	High	Manhattan, NY
Pseudo-urban	High	Low	Peachtree Center, GA
Sub-urban	Low	High	Atlanta Sprawl, GA
Anti-urban	Low	Low	IBM Headquarters, NY

Discussion: Spatial Capital as Exchange-value and Use-value

The concept of capital has in recent decades been intensely discussed and extended; according to Pierre Bourdieu for example, we, besides *economical capital* also have *cultural capital* and *social capital*.[12] The more precise meanings of the concept are often forgotten though, as discussed by the economist Hernando de Soto, at times even when it comes to economical capital. In his book *The Mystery of Capital*,[13] there is a thorough discussion on how a certain value can be translated into capital, which is of more general interest than his specific propositions in the same book on how to solve world poverty, which are clearly more debatable.[14] His main example is land and how land becomes capital. The question

is trickier than it first looks, according to de Soto. His answer is that, on the one hand, land, or rather different land parcels, need to be geographically defined and their particular social and economical values described, measured, and put into documents representing the land parcels, and, on the other hand, these documents need to be authorized and integrated in a legal system where such things as ownership and economical transactions are controlled and guaranteed.

In this context, what I have called *spatial capital* seems to be a contribution to the possibility to measure the effects of urban form on land value. We all agree that different locations in cities have different economic values, which influence such things as property prices and rents. And even though markets react on exactly such values, it is difficult to analyze the variable of location in itself, especially on the detailed scale we are referring to here. The analytical techniques above then seem most interesting as a means to develop more precise tools for such evaluations, especially when it comes to predicting how new urban projects will create new location values, as well as redistribute already present ones. Obviously there are other values at work here, such as the value of what is actually built, but the theory of spatial capital specifically aims at the evasive value of urban form.

This presents the *exchange-value* of spatial capital, suggesting how the value of urban form literally can be translated into economical capital. But just as important is the *use-value* of spatial capital, that is, the value urban form represents in a multitude of ways for every day urban life, socially, culturally, and environmentally. And even though not all needs requests high spatial capital, in general, that is exactly what cities have been answering to; the generic need for people and societies to access differences as a means for social, cultural, and economical development. In the end we see here a reason behind the perpetual movement into cities; for those without economical, social, or cultural capital, the city has always offered spatial capital.

FIG. 6 The variations of urbanity according to the definition of spatial capital as accessible diversity, where spatial diversity is measured as the amount of accessible plots within a radius of three axial lines (left), and spatial integration and capacity overlaid in one map, showing the continuous variations of spatial capital (right).

CENTRALITY AND CITIES

MULTIPLE CENTRALITY ASSESSMENT AS A TOOL
FOR URBAN ANALYSIS AND DESIGN

SERGIO PORTA AND VITO LATORA

Introduction: Centrality and Cities

If you ask a grocer where he would locate his new shop you will probably see him mumbling a little bit in search of something. He is exploring his mental map of the city or the neighborhood. Then he will come out pointing his finger on the map and saying: "yes, that's the best location." Why that? "You know—he will point out—here's where all the people pass when going to work every morning, then here, at the corner between Massave and Pearl (I am picking up an example from Boston), you are quite close to everywhere in the neighborhood, then Massave is really a spine that everyone knows in the city, for it is straight down to the river, then to the South End and downtown as well." There is a lesson here about how a real city works. It asserts the crucial importance of one factor, among many others, what we call "centrality." Everyone knows that a place which is central has some special features to offer in many ways to those who live or work in cities: it is more visible, more accessible from the immediate surroundings as well as from far away, it is more popular in terms of people walking around and attracting potential customers, it has a greater probability of developing as an urban landmark and a social catalyst or offer first level functions like theaters or office headquarters plus a larger diversity of opportunities and goods. That's why central locations are more expensive in terms of real estate values and tend to be socially selective: because such special features make them provide a reasonable trade off to larger investments than in less central spots of the same urban area.

If you look at where a city center is located, you will mostly—if not always—find that it sprouts from the intersection of two main routes, where some special configuration of the terrain or some particular shape of the river system or the waterfront makes that place compulsory to pass through. That's where cities begin. Then, departing from such central locations, they grow up in time adding buildings and activities here and there, firstly along the main routes, then filling the in-between areas, then adding

streets that provide cyclic routes and points of return, then, as the structure becomes more complex, forming new central streets and places and adding buildings around them again. It is an evolutionary process that has been driving the formation of our urban bodies, the heart of human civilization through the ages, for most of the seven millenniums of the history of cities until the dawn of modernity and the very beginning of the industrial age. Thus, we understand that centrality is not just at work at the heart of contemporary urban life, linking spatial forms and collective behaviors, but it is rather, at the heart of the evolutionary process that made our cities what they have always been, with a strong impact on how they still are today.

At this point, the reader should be aware of the idea that urban planners and designers have spent most of their time trying to understand and manage how centrality works in cities. Nothing could be less true. Despite the relevance of the issue, studies on centrality in cities have seldom been undertaken and never as a comprehensive approach to the subject. Geographers and transport planners have used centrality as a means to understand the location of uses and activities at the regional scale or the level of convenience to reach a place from all other points in an urban system[1]: in so doing, they have built their understanding on some hidden assumptions, particularly on the notion of centrality that, putting it shortly, is limited to the following: the more a place is close to all others, the more central.

Since the early eighties *space syntax*, a methodology of spatial analysis based on visibility and integration, has been open to urban designers and has offered them a whole range of opportunities to develop a deeper understanding of some structural properties of city spaces, but such opportunities have seldom been understood, often perceived as a quantitative threat to the creativity embedded in the art of city design. From a technical point of view, however, *space syntax* does not escape some of the shortcomings of regional analysis and transport planning: it is not a study of centrality in its own sake, it is mainly based on the same concept of being central as being close to all others. It does not focus on the different geographies that different ways of being central actually "shape" a city structure and how such different geographies correlate with the *dynamics* that take place in a city (like commercial location, real estate values, or information flows). However, recent developments from within the *space syntax* community seem to have acknowledged centrality and have opened to a more diversified concept of spatial configuration in relation to approaches of social psychology and cognition. In any case, *space syntax* aside, urban designers have in general simply skipped the problem: they basically deal with the aesthetics of the urban landscape and the components of urban form that embed regulatory issues like the height of buildings or the F.A.R. (floor-area ratio). More recently, urban designers have investigated a whole range of new issues that address the question of the liveability of places under the great umbrella of urban sustainability: that's where this paper actually comes from.

In this paper we present a discussion of centrality in cities and a model, named Multiple Centrality Assessment (MCA), which helps to manage centrality for urban planning and design purposes. In so doing, we summarize a research that we have undertaken for the last couple of years and is now being published in a journal of urban planning and physics.[2] In addition, we are hereby offering the first results of a new effort aimed at putting some light on how *centrality*, in its various forms, correlates to several *dynamics* of city life, research which is actually still under way over larger cases and datasets.

Representing the City

Our research on centrality in cities is based on representing *the structure* of the city (which we identify as the system of city streets and their intersections) by means of a mathematical object called a *graph*, which is a set of points, or *nodes*, linked by a set of lines, or *edges*. Graphs have been widely used for developing a deeper understanding of how complex systems of all sorts actually work. The property of a graph is, in fact, to focus on the relationships between individual components rather than the properties of such components themselves: in this sense, nodes might well represent components as different as coauthors in scientific systems (linked by coauthorships), routers in internet systems (linked by telephone cables), airports in air-communication systems (linked by air routes), or individuals in social systems (linked by prey-predator, acquaintanceship, professional or sexual relationships, contagious disease transmissions) and many, many others. In our case, we chose to represent street intersections as nodes and streets as edges between nodes: one street as such is just between two intersections, no matter the number of turns or curves it presents. Intuitive as it might appear, this format is not the only possible one: *space syntax*, for instance, is based on an opposite representation where nodes are streets and intersections are edges; moreover, in *space syntax* one street such as just between two turns, no matter the number of intersections it presents, following what geographers call a "generalization process" of geographic entities. However, the point is this: our representation (figure 1, image 1), which we call *ungeneralized primal*, is the standard format for all transport planners and geo-mapping professionals on earth: that makes our MCA model capable of taking advantage of an immense amount of information already marketed and constantly updated worldwide, i.e., the road graphs of all traffic departments of municipal or regional administration bodies.

Defining Centrality

Basically, the professionals who have addressed a specific work on centrality itself are the structural sociologists: they actually have been doing since the early fifties as a means to manage challenges coming from human, economic, or institutional organizations. Structural sociologists have examined such problems in terms of how each person (organization) is related to each other person (organization) in the reference system (the organization or the system of organizations), and they have done this in a *quantitative* way. They developed three main measures: on one hand, they counted how many edges each node has, and called this *degree centrality*, or C^D; on the other hand, they counted how close each node is to all others and called this *closeness centrality*, or C^C; finally, they measured to what extent each node is traversed by the shortest paths that link each other couple of nodes and called this *betweenness centrality*, or C^B. We have added two other indices: the first measures how much each node is critical to the system as a whole, in terms of the drop of the system's efficiency that would follow the removal of the node with all associated edges, and we have named this *information centrality* or C^I; the second measures how much the real paths that connect each node to all others diverge to the virtual straight paths, and we have named this *straightness centrality*, or C^S.

In order to deal with such indices we should agree on a definition of distance: not surprisingly, sociologists measured the distance between two nodes (persons or organizations) in terms of the number of other nodes that separate them; in fact, they studied nonspatial systems, i.e., systems where the position of nodes is not defined in space (spatial distance does not make a difference). In our case, we measured the distance in terms of the number of meters that separate two nodes (street intersections) along the connecting edge (street); in fact, we have embedded our street graphs in space rooting the whole process in a Geographic Information System (GIS) environment.

Centrality Over Planned and Self-organized Cities

The first result of our studies might not strike the audience like an intellectual bomb but it actually emerges as the foundation of many interesting practical uses especially in urban planning and design: despite the extreme fragmentation of the graph, centrality does not sprout up here and there in a scattered manner, but rather it forms legible routes and areas consistently ordered in a hierarchical spatial distribution (figure 1, images 3–6). Routes and areas of similar levels of centrality emerge over the complex urban system according to some internal rules that vary from index to index giving place to a multifaceted geography of cities. Urban places that are central in terms of closeness may not be as central in terms of betweenness (very often they are not central at all). In short: there are apparently many ways for a place to be central in a city. But there is more: The geography of centrality that emerges for a given index calculated at the global scale (i.e., relating each node with all others in the system) typically diverges a lot from that calculation, for the same index, at the local scales (i.e., relating each node to a subset of nodes located within a certain distance d from it (figure 1, images 2, 3). That means that a place may not just be different according to different *kinds* of centrality, but also to different *spatial scales of behaviors*: if you are shopping for your ordinary daily needs you use a certain city, if you need rare services (like attending a university course or a dance performance), you use a different city.

Not all cities' structures are complex in the same way and to the same extent. Planned and self-organized cities look very different: the former exhibit a geometric flavor for their streets which are very often regularly spaced and oriented so that we recognize shapes of Euclidean geometry like triangles, rectangles, or pentagons, while in the latter, i.e., medieval urban fabrics grown gradually and "spontaneously" through history without any central control, we hardly recognize anything but a mess (figure 1, image 1). But is that really a mess, chaos, or is it just that we are not capable of seeing an order of a different kind? Other biological, social, technological, economic, or cultural self-organized systems—virtually all other systems that have passed through an evolutionary process and, as such, are not the product of one single agent—have been found to exhibit some astonishingly similar properties. The basics of such a shared property is a largely heterogeneous, "scale-free" distribution of centrality among the nodes: you have very few nodes that take high centrality and a lot of nodes that take quite a bit. We have shown that the same rule actually applies to organic, historical, self-organized urban patterns while it does not to planned ones. So, even if we do not see it at first glance, historical patterns *do have an order*—though not one of a Euclidean kind: they

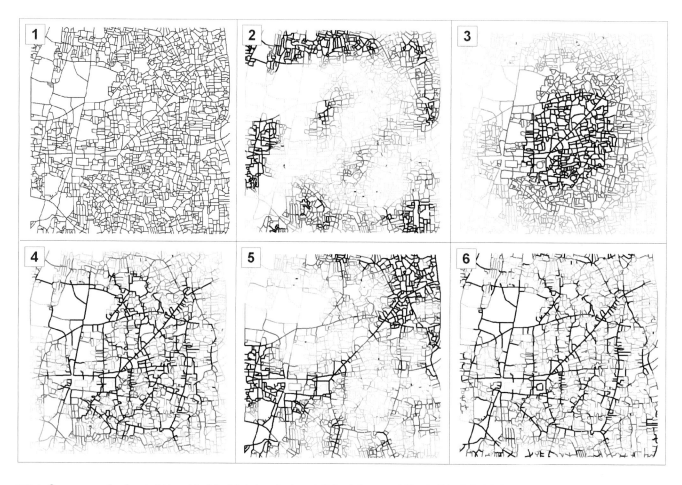

FIG. I One square mile of central Ahmedabad (India): 1. the primal graph; 2. local closeness (C^C_{400}; d=400mt); 3. global closeness (C^C_{Glob}); 4. global betweenness (C^B_{Glob}); 5. global straightness (C^S_{Glob}); 6. global information (C^I_{Glob}).

BOLOGNA

Correlation between centrality and community commerce/service locations.
From left to right: variables of Centrality Commerce/Service location dynamics;
1: extension of the bandwidth considered in KDE;
2: ratio of cells with both Centrality (C) and Dynamic (D)=0;
3: both C and D≠0;
4: C≠0 and D=0;
5: C=0 and D≠0;
6: Pearson index of linear correlation.

Rank #	Correlated Variables		KDE Bandwidth	Linear Correlation
	Centrality	Activity	Meters	Pearson Index
1	C^B_{Glob}	Comm+Serv	300	0.727
2	C^B_{Glob}	Comm	300	0.704
3	C^B_{Glob}	Comm+Serv	200	0.673
4	C^B_{Glob}	Comm	200	0.653
5	C^C_{Glob}	Comm	300	0.641
6	C^C_{800}	Comm+Serv	300	0.620
7	C^C_{Glob}	Comm+Serv	300	0.615
8	C^C_{Glob}	Comm+Serv	300	0.608
9	C^C_{Glob}	Comm+Serv	200	0.583
10	C^B_{Glob}	Comm+Serv	100	0.567
11	C^C_{800}	Comm+Serv	300	0.565
12	C^B_{Glob}	Comm	100	0.555
13	C^C_{Glob}	Comm	200	0.547
14	C^C_{Glob}	Comm+Serv	200	0.546
15	C^C_{Glob}	Comm	300	0.533

TABLE 1. Top 15 Pearson correlations between kernel densities of street centralities and commercial/service activities in Bologna

actually exhibit the same order of most other organic systems in nature, an order that ensures extraordinary performances to such systems in terms of adaptability to external threats, capability to modify and react, diffuse information efficiently, and strengthen local ties. The "small-world" property, which emerges in self-organized systems as the capacity to achieve good performances both at the local and the global level, also is detectable at the highest grade in medieval urban patterns. Here, no matter if Arabic or European, rich or poor, hot or cold, Islamic or Christian, the urban structure ensures a cost comparable to that of a tree-like structure but with an efficiency comparable to that of a completed, interconnected network. The same "small world" behavior, though at a much lower grade, is present in gridiron and mixed fabrics; con-

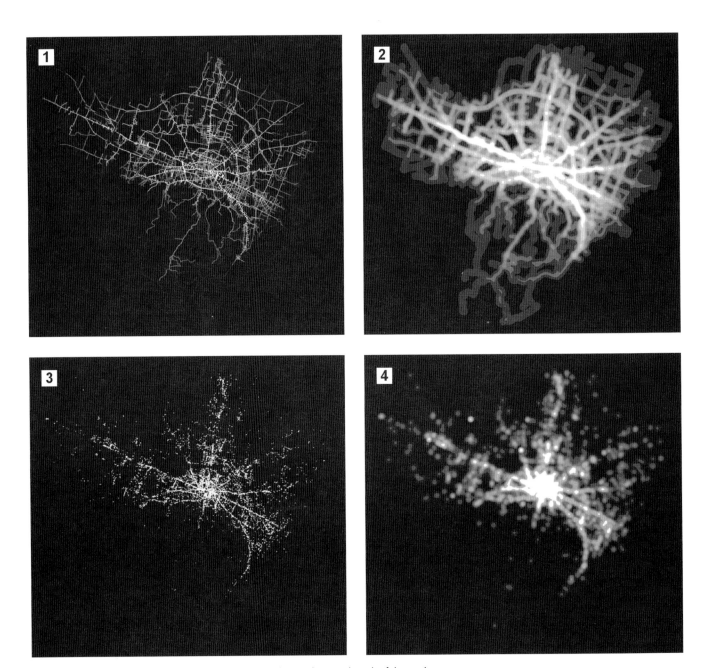

FIG. 2 Bologna (northern Italy): Global Betweenness centrality on the primal graph of the road system, one outcome of the MCA application (1); Kernel Density Evaluation (bandwidth = 200 mt) of Global Between-ness (2); community commerce and service locations (3); Kernel Density Evaluation (bandwidth = 200 mt) of commerce and service locations (2). The linear correlation between density values of panels 2 and 4 reaches the highest score (Pearson=0,673) among those mentioned in the table.

versely, modernist or suburban lollipop fabrics do not exhibit such properties as they minimize the cost of the network generating on the other side, a failure in the efficiency of the system as a whole.[3]

Centrality and the Location of Community Retail and Services

Cities have grown in history following (to a certain extent) rules of centralities that are factors of efficiency in making complex urban systems competitive in evolution. The idea is

that we can actually see some clues of this in how several dynamics of particular relevance correlate on the ground to the spatial distribution of centrality. We have worked out a first test over the city of Bologna, northern Italy. Here, we correlate the *centrality* indices of closeness, betweenness, and straightness, computed at the global and local levels, to *dynamics* inherent to daily urban life, i.e., the location of community-level commercial activities and services.

Rather than comparing centrality and commerce/service dynamics on a street-by-street basis,[4] we have explored in Bologna a different methodology based on the Kernel Den-sity Evaluation (KDE), a density function based on Euclidean distance widely used in geographic information science and spatial analysis.[5] The resulting KDC methodology presents a twofold advantage: on one hand, it nicely captures the decreasing influence that centrality shows in the urban space as the distance increases from a given location (not only shops facing a street take advantage of that street's centrality, but also those located nearby on the parallel streets, though at a lower level); on the other hand, it overcomes the problem of achieving fine cross-referenced data needed for a street-by-street correlation analysis.

In this study, after a preliminary MCA step, we "covered" the Bologna urban region with a grid of 2,771,956 square cells (edge=10m). We then calculated the Kernel Density of each cell of the study region in terms of all centrality indices (derived by MCA) and, on the other side, all commerce and service locations. Then we produced a table where, for each cell (record), Kernel density values of both kinds were associated. In the table we report some structural data of cell values and the resulting Pearson index of linear correlation for each couple of considered variables. Such index expresses how much two quantities are correlated by giving a number between −1 (most negative correlation) and 1 (most positive); however, the value of the Pearson correlation decreases as the dataset size increases due to statistical fluctuations.[6] We chose to limit the dataset to cells containing at least one non-zero value. Resulting Pearson values are positive for all couples of variables (see Table 1) varying from 0.351 to 0.727; the index reaches the highest score—extremely significant for a dataset of such magnitude—for global betweenness central-ity. Such findings suggest that centrality, especially global betweenness, are driving forces as crucial factors in the evolution of city life as the location of community retail and services, a correlation that also emerges through the simple visual comparison of spatial maps (figure 2).

Conclusion: Centrality and City Design

How can we understand where to locate shops and retail services in a proposed development? Where can we place the main hall in a company headquarter? What impact can we expect from the realizing a new bridge or road on the rest of a city system? How can we better integrate a neighborhood (like a social housing estate) in its immediate and global surroundings? These are all crucial questions in sustainable urban design processes and centrality, it turns out, is a driving force in all of this. MCA, as a tool for managing centrality in real spatial systems at all scales, can help decision makers directly and efficiently with scientific-based assistance in processing architectural and urban design.[7] The same approach is also being experimented with in more specific areas of transport planning and management: how can we improve the performance of a public-transport system by adding just a certain amount of new lines or stops? Is a proposed transport-system extension plan actually going to give the right answers to one community's needs? The application of MCA to "classic" transport planning issues is one of the main directions of development for our current research.[8]

INTEGRATED APPROACHES AND DYNAMIC PROCESSES

ARUN JAIN

The paradox of cities is that they can be both simpler and more complex than we imagine them. They can be simpler if we know where not to micromanage. They can be more complex whenever we realize what they must socially, economically, and culturally do *together* in order to be "successful" or vibrant.

The world is increasingly a smaller place. The ease of information sharing and the demands for ever quicker responses have encouraged generic planning and urban design "fixes." This trend is reflected in formula driven development strategies, urban form, function and design. Such responses weaken the competitive advantage and identity of cities. When compounded by increasing uncertainty about the future, it is clear we need to develop better understanding and more dynamic ways to ensure urban vitality.

For continued gains in urban quality, cities face a number of challenges. Urban design frameworks that not only recognize and build upon the complexity of urban networks, but also allow simpler, more naturally responsive evolution within might help.

The Complexity of Cities

The study of cities and their urban design is strewn with excellent if often forgotten concepts. In 1965, Christopher Alexander in his famous article "The City is Not a Tree" urged us to appreciate that the tree analogy was too simple and that a "semi-lattice" or interlaced series of networks was perhaps better. In 1973, Horst Rittel codified the nature of problems asserting that most city scale (i.e., planning) and urban design issues were, in fact, "wicked," meaning that such problems were not easy to define, inevitably had nondiscrete solutions, and always generated undesirable side effects. He maintained that solutions to such situations can never be true or false but only be thought of in degrees of good or bad.

The larger point here is that cities are better thought of as complex interlaced systems or networks and that their best qualities (often intangible) lie meshed inside this web. The resulting social (nonphysical) and physical urban networks that develop might be complex, but simply facilitating these networks and embracing their natural outcomes might be the most essential ingredient for uniqueness, identity, and character to thrive.

By extension, the uniqueness and appeal of a city may come not so much from its slavish adherence to "best practices," guides, and development standards, but more from drawing out the unique ways in which existing interlaced networks express themselves. The built manifestations of urban form and the ability to realize them are but an extension and likely outcome of these realities and forces.

This is not to suggest at all that the role of urban design is insignificant. To the contrary, its value (depending upon how you define it), is very much intertwined in recognizing the complex mesh of tangible (physical infrastructure, demographics, economy), intangible (prevailing zeitgeist, aesthetic norms, development economics), and tentative (environmental and social ethic, planning and political) networks unique to each urban place.

The Role of Urban Design

Talking about urban design is complicated by how we individualize our understanding and use of it in discourse. Much of this confusion can be avoided if we make our positions explicit.

Clearly, urban design can be thought of in many ways. For some it is simply the design of the urban environment. For others it means dealing with design and development issues that embrace public private partnerships and the quality of resulting spaces. Often urban design aspires to create or enhance city form that is inspiring for the average citizen and a source of shared identity. Each interpretation is not mutually exclusive and underscores the importance and role of urban design.

We know that urban design ideas and approaches alone cannot answer all of a city's concerns. Yet it's strongest impacts on the design of cities can be condensed into three broad areas.

Urban Form

Thinking of urban form and how it may define the relationships between public and private space, or be drawn upon primary business districts and corridors, or be enhanced by the strategic placement of open space and public amenities add value to cities and their life.

Urban Quality

Although each city must find its own path to achieve desired quality, leaving room for communities to grow and evolve positively are important reassurances for a citizenry to invest, own, and belong. Being deliberate about such issues better assures the long-term global, regional and local relevence, and vitality of cities. Urban design is important to ensure the right emphasis of where citizens can and should experience comfort, quality, and inspiring places.

It is no mystery that places most treasured are those that are rooted in events of deep meaning (not always happy) to their citizens or rulers. Lest we forget, architecture and urban design are regularly relied upon to respond to and provide such meaning.

Identity

In a globally competitive world, many cities now routinely evaluate their place and relevance, often carving out specific niches and strategies to remain noticed. Some like Glasgow, Scotland reorient toward youth, culture, and technology, others like Bilbao, Spain invest in highly noticable architecture, yet other American examples like Chicago and Portland continue to pursue strategies for balanced development, urban beauty, and sustainability. Urban design can help translate such desired emphases.

The Challenges Before Us

There are several shared conditions that challenge our ability to impart good urban design in cities.

Fear of Change

Despite the ever-increasing desire to prevent change, we all know cities, their life, and cultures are never static. The larger challenge before us, is thus, not how change can be stalled, but rather, how change can be comfortably accommodated. This issue is complicated by the fast pace at which change is increasingly thrust upon us. Unless giant unforeseen forces come to bear, the rate of change of technology, social structures, cultural habits, economic and resource issues, politics, religious dogma, and the environment itself will continue to increase in unpredictable ways. Traditional (usually static) methods of planning and urban design do not fit this fast dynamic well.

The Confused Role of Design

The relationship of the design fields with other aspects of city planning continues to change in interesting ways. Often design is the final manifestation of all other considerations, sometimes it is a (poor) substitute for them and yet, in other instances it is an afterthought. Rarely is design integrated into processes that might first, help jointly understand a problem and then, collectively strategize appropriate responses to it. In continuing to focus on aesthetic predispositions, the complex ("wicked") problem solving skills designers are so well qualified to address are often marginalized. Too many times we are collectively seduced into thinking that we can "design" our way out of every problem. Dogged pursuit of the "*build it and they will come*" approach also remains one of our largest collective failings.

Nostalgia and Planning Determinism

It is telling that the urban places we continue to hold in greatest esteem are often the old parts of cities where the chaos and confusion remain at odds with contemporary planning and safety standards. Where such places have managed to remain authentic (and not tourist traps or shadows of their past), social order and function seem to drive urban form. If this is to be believed, then clearly, urban form is most genuine when it reflects its inhabiting culture. The idea that the design of urban environments should be used to manipulate social behavior (i.e., induce "good" civic habits) to unwilling (or unwitting) inhabitants seems destined to result in disingenuous outcomes.

Plurality and Citizen-Driven Processes

Developed societies have evolved into an era of plurality greatly impacted by collective decision making and citizen-driven design. If this model is to continue to bear fruit, the ability to ensure good urban quality will depend on the maturity and foresight of citizens as much as the skills of urban designers and city planners to elevate bigger, long-term concerns. In every instance this will be predicated on the ability of prevailing political institutions to prompt, endorse, or encourage such thinking and action.

Unbalanced Development Standards

Understanding where development controls and standards make positive impact are subjective, but clearly an area where we can do better. If ponderous regulation and standards are burdensome, reliance on market driven forces alone are not sufficient either. When excessive, controls choke growth and creativity, loosely formulated they have little impact. When the need for development supercedes the desire for urban quality, the cost of recovering such quality becomes higher.

One has only to look to the developed world to see the great impact of inherited bad planning and rampant uncontrolled development. Rapidly urbanizing cities, notably in China and India, have great development challenges before them, but also great opportunities to leapfrog over such mistakes.

What Should We Plan For?

Never before has their been greater trepidation about what we should plan and design for. Should we seek energy effi-

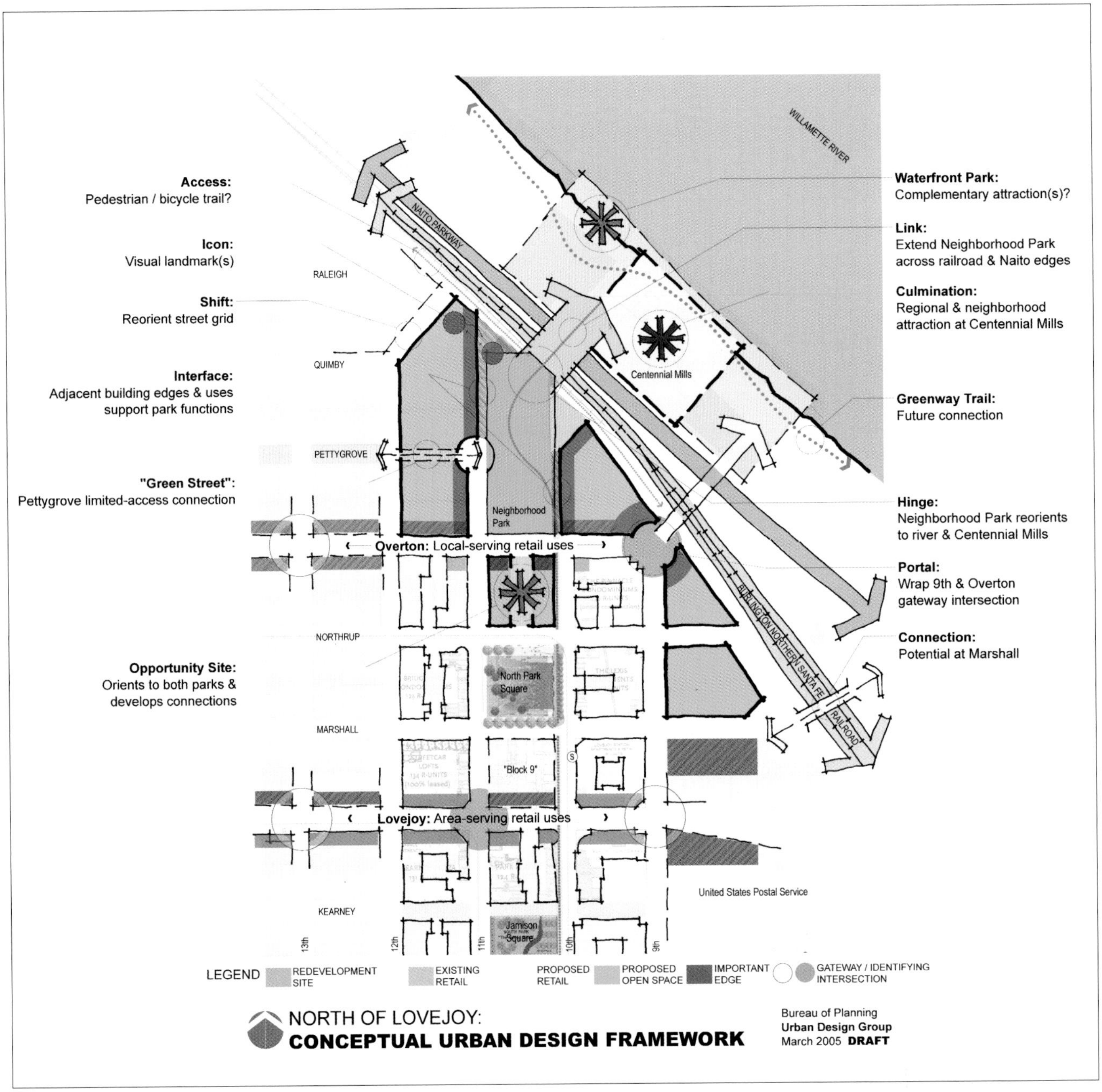

Access:
Pedestrian / bicycle trail?
Icon:
Visual landmark(s)
Shift:
Reorient street grid
Interface:
Adjacent building edges & uses support park functions
"Green Street":
Pettygrove limited-access connection
Opportunity Site:
Orients to both parks & develops connections
Waterfront Park:
Complementary attraction(s)?
Link:
Extend Neighborhood Park across railroad & Naito edges
Culmination:
Regional & neighborhood attraction at Centennial Mills
Greenway Trail:
Future connection
Hinge:
Neighborhood Park reorients to river & Centennial Mills
Portal:
Wrap 9th & Overton gateway intersection
Connection:
Potential at Marshall
WILLAMETTE RIVER
NAITO PARKWAY
BURLINGTON NORTHERN SANTA FE RAILROAD
RALEIGH
QUIMBY
PETTYGROVE
NORTHRUP
MARSHALL
KEARNEY
Centennial Mills
Neighborhood Park
Overton: Local-serving retail uses
North Park Square
"Block 9"
Lovejoy: Area-serving retail uses
Jamison Square
United States Postal Service
13th
12th
11th
10th
9th
LEGEND
REDEVELOPMENT SITE
EXISTING RETAIL
PROPOSED RETAIL
PROPOSED OPEN SPACE
IMPORTANT EDGE
GATEWAY / IDENTIFYING INTERSECTION
NORTH OF LOVEJOY:
CONCEPTUAL URBAN DESIGN FRAMEWORK
Bureau of Planning
Urban Design Group
March 2005 DRAFT

FIG. 1 Urban Design Framework for Portland, Oregon's Pearl District. Diagrams in this essay: Urban Design Group, Bureau of Planning; Portland, Oregon.

ciency, economic growth or superiority, beauty, social equity, political stability, safety, defense, compactness, or cost effectiveness? Should our city design approaches work with trends we can project or should we imagine cities that will better deal with a growing sense of uncertainty? It is much easier to respond to immediate needs and forces then address uncertain needs.

Flexible frameworks that capture desired longer-term interrelationships while easing more immediate growth and enhancement opportunities might help such dilemmas.

Shifting the Paradigm

For the forseeable future cities will remain the preferred nexus of people and settlement. Yet their ability to provide quality of life to their inhabitants is directly related to the extent to which the type (variety), complexity (richness), and density (critical mass) of their networks can remain attractive. With this in mind, the future concerns of cities might revolve around the following attributes:

INTEGRATED THINKING

Integrated approaches to community building and better links between the public good and private development initiative. Leveraging more out of individual efforts, creative public private enterprises.

ADAPTABILITY

The ability to accommodate rapidly changing and unpredicatable economic, demographic, and social trends as well as flexible infrastructure to support such changes.

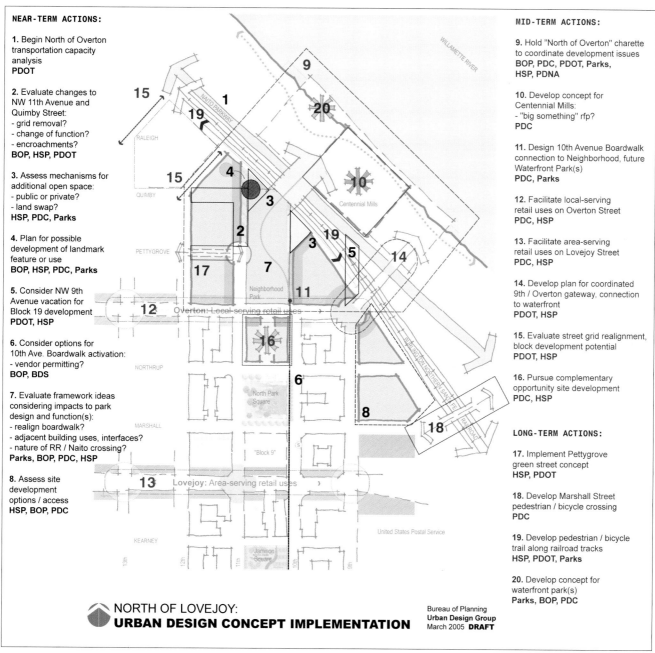

FIG. 2 Implementation Framework for Portland's Pearl District.

RESILIENCE
Encouraging robust urban structures and natural systems. Education and health networks, better links between environmental and economic health, accommodating regional shifts, diversified economy, and social infrastructure.

COHERENCE
Developing coherent local relationships with regional character and growth. Clear links between regional and local ecologies, social systems, environments, and economies.

QUALITY
Ensuring it for the natural and the built urban environment, social and cultural life, public health, and education.

DIVERSITY
Pursuing it in all desirable forms—cultural, social, ethnic, religious, economic, and aesthetic. Developing networks that support desired attitudes and the tools to attract, retain, and grow.

SUSTAINABILITY
Seeking sustainable economic, environmental, and social systems—finding better balances between energy and resource consumption and waste production, considering the critical mass necessary to sustain desired cultural, economic, and social mixes.

BALANCE
Identifying and developing strategies for balanced communities, identifying and pursuing desirable proportions of social mixes, public amenities, jobs, housing, health, education, arts, and nature.

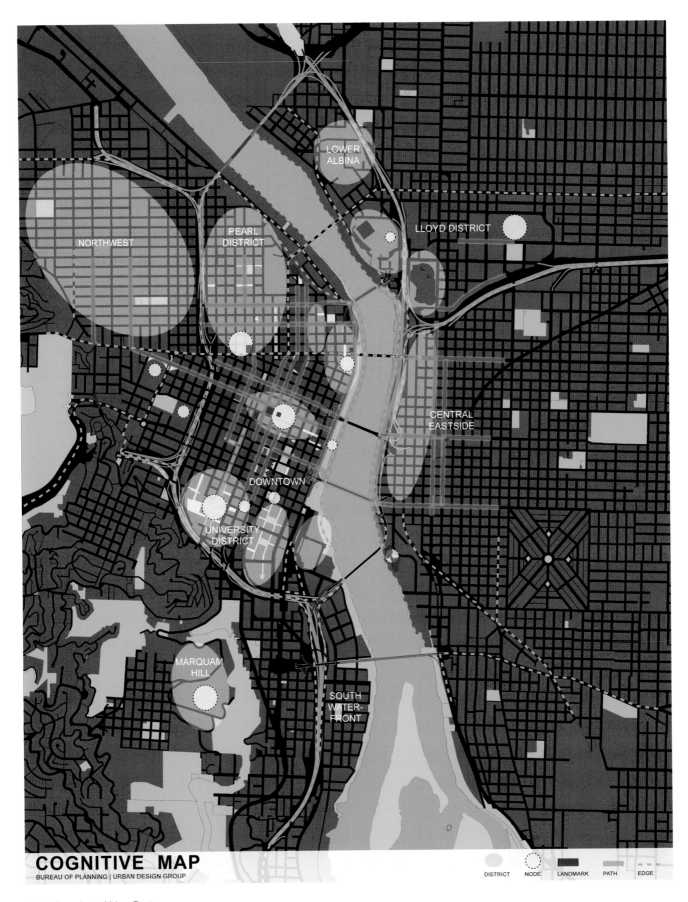

LOWER
ALBINA

LLOYD DISTRICT

NORTHWEST

PEARL
DISTRICT

CENTRAL
EASTSIDE

DOWNTOWN

UNIVERSITY
DISTRICT

MARQUAM
HILL

SOUTH
WATER-
FRONT

COGNITIVE MAP
BUREAU OF PLANNING | URBAN DESIGN GROUP

DISTRICT   NODE   LANDMARK   PATH   EDGE

FIG. 3 Speculative Urban Design
Framework for central Portland.

URBAN DESIGN DIAGRAM

BUREAU OF PLANNING | URBAN DESIGN GROUP

REINFORCED EDGES   PRIMARY CORRIDORS   VISUAL REFERENCE   HINGE   TERMINII   CONNECTIONS

FIG. 4 The Urban Design Framework for Portland, Oregon.

It is clear that urban design alone cannot adequately address all these concerns. But to the extent the above attributes can be translated into good public experiences and urban spaces, it can help articulate which parts of the urban landscape need more or less attention.

How can urban design help organize and provide such clarity? Portland, Oregon is beginning to examine how urban design frameworks can generate public debate about its priorities for the future (figures 1 and 2). Starting with its central city, these frameworks consider both the city's quantitative and qualitative attributes. Understanding the city's physical assets (built and natural) in terms of its networks identifies gaps but also future opportunities. Understanding which places are most valuable by virtue of location, purpose, or prominence helps define areas of special opportunity. Such areas can then be thought of as either catalytic, or areas that should be banked for higher and better uses (figure 3).

There are several high-value physical elements of a city that might form its essential urban framework. These might be important corridors, locations of prominence, places that create or have particular meaning, transition areas, or related community assets. Future strategies may then stitch these elements together to enhance physical and social urban networks that generate urban vitality. Together these can be imagined to be the physical "bones" of the city or armature upon which the rest of the city might rest (figure 4).

Simplicity then might come from leaving the spaces in between to resolve themselves with only the most necessary regulation, basic urban design goals and development standards. Urban quality can be largely assured if the public private interfaces remain the primary focus. Creative strategies that can link internal networks with the larger external ones will allow natural change and evolution otherwise constrained by more rigid planning systems. In Portland, rapidly developing areas are subjected to periodic and strategic urban design workshops to dynamically respond to new context. Context and scale sensitivity temper the discussions and outcomes.

The Future of Cities

If we learn how to see them, cities are the very best reflections of their cultures. The roots of all that is at one end, exhilarating or profound, or at the other, theatrical or banal, can be found in their cultural past and present. The vitality of cities comes from the pushes and pulls between these conditions.

Strategic, master and urban design plans for cities have limited shelf lives and require tremendous resources to achieve consensus. Cities must find ways to better identify, and then use their core elements with the networks that connect them. The future success of cities will ultimately lie in their ability to dynamically respond in positive ways to changes we cannot presently anticipate. Urban design can play an important part in facilitating such desired outcomes.

PLANNING FOR WALKABLE STREETS

RICK HALL

"Reengineering the Suburban DNA" documents the core issue that prevents current street design policy and manuals, specifically the *Green Book* of the American Association of Highway and Transportation Officials (AASHTO), from allowing for walkable street design. Although the *Green Book* clearly offers guidelines and not standards, many agencies, nonetheless, interpret and adopt the guidelines as standards.

The single most serious problem stems from AASHTO's defined purpose for arterial streets. Arterials serve motor vehicle mobility. No pedestrian function is specified in the primary description of this roadway's function. The entire first chapter entitled "Highway Functions" is dedicated to the two main functions of streets and highways; motor vehicle mobility and land access. Arterials serve the former and "locals" serve the latter. Pedestrians are occasionally discussed, and even supported, in the following 1,000-plus pages. However, the pedestrian mobility purpose never influences or overrides the arterial's dominant vehicle mobility function to influence design speed, lane width, or other key design elements.

If compact, walkable, urban communities are to flourish, the existing set of functionally classified facilities must be augmented to include a set of thoroughfares that have pedestrian mobility as a primary function. This function would require many design elements to be reevaluated, resized, and documented, the most significant of which is design speed. Narrower lane width, shorter curb return radii, and build-to lines along the street are key elements requiring review and adjustment.

In addition to the five functionally classified thoroughfares presented in the recommendations, six context zones are discussed. Context zones provide a descriptive system for quantifying land-use patterns by compactness, diversity, and character from most rural to most urban. In contrast to the current urban or rural breakdown of land-use patterns used in AASHTO's *Green Book*, the six context zones better reflect the true complexity of urban land development patterns. They, in turn, provide a logical zone structure for assigning specific street types. Boulevards and avenues, for example, provide walkability and vehicle mobility for urban core, town center, and neighborhood general context zones. Freeways are recommended for rural context zones only.

Primarily, areas with a future vision of high pedestrian mobility must have low design speed characteristics that insure comfort for the pedestrian experience and also satisfy the subordinate goal of vehicle mobility. Outside these pedestrian-dominant areas, current AASHTO functionally classified arterials, collectors, and locals will continue to apply.

Planning for Walkable Streets

The private automobile provides, and will continue to provide, high levels of mobility for travelers in most developed countries. Increased personal mobility has enabled a wide variety of daily experiences that were unavailable to the average nineteenth-century citizen. As auto use increased, however, only a few individuals could visualize the dramatic change in store for urban and rural landscapes. Soon after introduction of the mass-produced automobile, urban form began a dramatic transformation. Post–World War II cities, especially in the United States, began to accommodate the pervasive use of private automobiles. A growing list of negative side effects has also emerged. Within the past several decades, the negative "side effects" of the auto age on patterns of community development (primarily suburban patterns) have been analyzed and many individuals are advocating an urgent course of corrective action. Many of these corrective principles are embodied in the New Urbanism movement.

Walkability, a cherished quality of pre-World War II neighborhoods, was essentially absent from general suburban planning practice from 1940 to 1980. Without consideration of walking as a viable travel mode, development patterns became auto dominant. In his landmark book, *The Geography of Nowhere*, James Howard Kunstler succinctly defines suburbia's two greatest problems; "the extreme separation of uses and the vast distances between things." In *Suburban Nation*, authors Andrés Duany, Elizabeth Plater-Zyberk, and Jeff Speck have successfully documented negative suburban impacts resulting from a singular focus on the auto mode, including isolation, high vehicle miles of travel, diminished air quality, and a degraded sense of place.

Solutions that help redirect urban development patterns can best emerge from a clear understanding of the transportation planning history leading to post-war suburban development. Few have described the history of transportation and land use evolution (at the neighborhood level) better than Michael Southworth and Eran Ben-Joseph in their book, *Streets and the Shaping of Our Towns and Cities*. Their research discovered the following response to increased auto use:

> Design of the residential street network is based on statistical information and research that is primarily oriented to facilitating vehicle movement on large-scale streets and highways. Such standards have then been mechanically adopted and legitimized by local governments to shield themselves from any responsibility for road performance. . . . Modifications have been discouraged and because higher governmental agencies have not openhandedly allowed flexibility, lesser agencies have been reluctant to do so. . . . Lenders in turn have been hesitant to support a development outside the mainstream, particularly when it did not conform to established standards and regulations.

In response, designers from many professions have penned texts and journal articles to clarify problems and propose solutions. Discussions within the New Urbanism movement provide substantial insight and have achieved a more diverse pattern of transportation use and community form. These advances have often come after strenuous debate, analysis, and compromise regarding contemporary transportation design standards and the manuals guiding these standards.

Design Guides

Two reference guides are discussed here with respect to auto and pedestrian mobility. The *Green Book* used in the United States and *Calm Streets* published in Sweden. First, AASHTO publication, *A Policy on Geometric Design of Highways and Streets* (known informally by its color as the "Green Book"), is the primary guide for roadway design in the United States. Within AASHTO, substantial progress is being made in achieving greater design flexibility for rural and suburban roads. Historically, however, state and local officials have interpreted AASHTO strictly; they have become somewhat more relaxed since FHWA policy makers are now encouraging changes from the top. However, even with the positive "Context-Sensitive Design" emphasis, AASHTO policies in urban areas are still fundamentally in conflict with many transportation design concepts found in the New Urbanism. Pedestrian mobility, the key to New Urban walkability, is not part of the roadway's stated purpose. The pur-

pose of each functionally classified roadway is defined by the degree to which it serves motor vehicle mobility.

Basic Green Book Assumptions
The *Green Book*'s first chapter defines the function of three roadway classifications: arterial, collector, and local roadways. This introductory chapter, entitled "Highway Functions," contains within its seventeen pages the vehicle oriented functional classifications that guide the remaining one thousand pages of design discussion. All design parameters relate to these three defined functions. As stated in the *Green Book*:

> The functional concept is important to the designer. Even though many of the geometric standards could be determined without reference to the functional classification, the designer must keep in mind the overall purpose that the street or highway is intended to serve. This concept is consistent with a systematic approach to highway planning and design. The first step in the design process is to determine the function that the facility is to serve. . . . The use of functional classification as a design type should appropriately integrate the highway planning and design process.[1]

The *Green Book* establishes "principles of flow specialization and movement hierarchy" that help define this functional classification of roadways. "This classification recognizes that individual roads and streets do not serve travel independently. Rather, most travel involves movement through networks of roads and can be categorized relative to such networks in a logical and efficient manner."[2]

These factors relate directly to a roadway's dual function of providing 1) access to property and 2) vehicular travel mobility. Figure 1 describes the proportion of these two functions assigned to each roadway classification.[3] Arterials primarily serve traffic mobility and locals primarily serve land access needs. Collector roads gather traffic from the local streets and, when warranted, distribute traffic to the arterials. The conflict between providing access to land and serving through vehicle movement is the primary justifica-

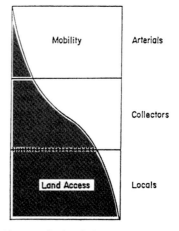

PROPORTION OF SERVICE

FIG. I Relationship of functionally classified systems in serving traffic mobility and land access.

tion for different roadway types, or classifications. Slow moving vehicles preparing to enter "terminal facilities" are incompatible with the carefully defined higher speed/mobility function of arterials. Thus, arterial access from adjacent land is heavily regulated to maintain higher vehicle mobility. This highly controversial regulatory activity has grown into the access management specialization; professionals dedicated to preserving vehicle mobility on arterial roadways in the face of constant requests for land access, primarily from the private sector.

Traffic calming, an additional specialization, creates no less controversy as its goals for vehicular travel speed *reduction* conflict with motorist's desire for increased vehicular mobility and higher "level of service" (LOS). For arterials, speed is the primary measure of LOS, which could be more accurately labeled as the "Vehicular Speed Index," except that the service level measured is in line with the AASHTO functional classification defining vehicle mobility/speed as the ultimate purpose of the arterial roadway. These definitions are the foundation of all urban street design and thus have significant implications for discussions regarding slower traffic in cities, towns, and communities attempting to design main streets and other highly walkable urban environments.

Calm Streets Assumptions
The book *Calm Streets*, written in Sweden, yields a planning process for safer, more eco-friendly, pleasant, and attractive streets in urban areas (figure 2). Speed is thoroughly discussed with numerous techniques proposed to generate pedestrian friendly environments. The fundamental definitions of street function, however, follow the arterial, collector, and local street functions described in the AASHTO *Green Book*. In *Calm Streets*, thoroughfares carry long trips to other main links, which connect to local links providing neighborhood-level mobility. All definitions are in terms of motor vehicle mobility, without reference to the pedestrian contributions to urban mobility.

Impacts on the Urban Setting
The transportation DNA for suburban places (verses urban places) resides in the functional classification "Mobility vs. Land Access" diagram (figure 3). Along with other forces influencing land use, the philosophy behind the *Green Book*'s Chapter 1 definitions and their resultant design criteria have guided most development since World War II toward *suburban* patterns. Just as DNA guides cell growth, this diagram's simple curve contains instructions guiding how roadways function and how land uses must be arranged in a "logical and efficient manner" to facilitate the movement of motor vehicles. Arterials provide vehicle mobility, local roadways access land. Transportation agencies throughout the world follow these instructions with great conviction. Figure 3 appears in every basic transportation textbook in America and has similar counterparts in many developed countries. Some of this system thinking may have evolved from the rail transportation era where rail system managers benefited greatly from a tiered system for central operations and plan-

FIG. 2 *Calm Streets*, written in Sweden, yields a planning process for safer, pleasant, and attractive streets in urban areas.

ning. The hierarchical system fails in urban settings where individuals operate each vehicle independently, without central control of schedules, routes, and modes.

Three key factors explain the conflicts between tiered, auto-oriented system definitions, such as the *Green Book* policies, and the walkable, New Urbanism design principles:
- Functional classification is based on motor vehicle mobility.
- Mobility is defined based on high vehicle speed.
- Pedestrian comfort and safety require low vehicle speed for safety.

First, the entire functional classification system was conceived during the 1950s and described in the 1960s when walking was no longer considered a viable mode of transportation. This led to dysfunctional definitions based on *vehicle* mobility only. High-speed roadways began to separate land areas, making pedestrian movement between them highly improbable. Sidewalks disappeared from development regulations and blocks attained marathon lengths. Even compatible land uses were set far apart, assuming only vehicles would be used for access. These suburban-style regulations severely constrain new efforts at urban development. Once imbedded in the "guidelines," the motor-vehicle-based theory has yielded rural and suburban patterns where no one is expected to walk.

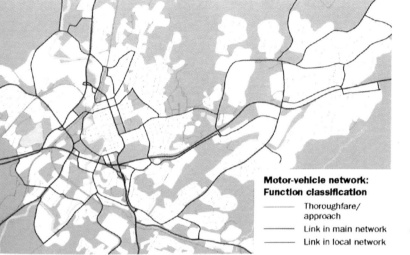

Function classification		
Type of network	**Type of link**	**Chief traffic function**
Main network	Thoroughfare or approach Other links in main network	Motor-vehicle traffic through or to an urban area Motor traffic between districts in urban area
Local network	Link in local network	Motor traffic within a neighbourhood unit
The longest distance between a start/destination point inside a neighbourhood unit and the nearest connection to the main network should not exceed 400 m.		

Motor-vehicle network:
Function classification

——— Thoroughfare/
approach
——— Link in main network
——— Link in local network

**Function classification
of the motor-vehicle
network**

The motor-vehicle
network's function
classification is
presented on a map.

FIG. 3 Mobility diagram.

Second, mobility depends on vehicle operating speed (i.e., travel time). Higher average speeds on arterials lead to better levels of service. In keeping with the functional class theory, LOS analysis only applies to the vehicle mobility (or speed) of *arterial* roadways. Collectors, and to a greater degree locals, have land access as a priority function. Thus, there is no acceptable LOS technique to evaluate collectors. The United States Highway Capacity Manual (HCM) addresses arterials with signalized intersections, not collectors or local streets.

Finally, high vehicle speed severely limits pedestrian activity. Walking along a street with auto and truck speeds above thirty miles per hour is an uncomfortable and unsafe experience. The probability of severe pedestrian injury rises dramatically the more vehicle speed exceeds twenty-five miles per hour. Placing pedestrians (and trees and buildings) further from the travel way edge to increase urban travel safety yield even higher vehicular speeds and thus reduced safety. Crossing higher speed arterials is an additional problem. Desired separation between intersections on arterials is set to maintain adequate signal progression, and thus, the highest possible vehicle mobility. This forces 1/4 mile intersection spacing for optimal signal timing. To serve even average development density, arterials with intersecting collectors must have multiple through lanes and turn lanes. Both of these features create wide

intersections at great distances apart, which further frustrate pedestrian movement.

As a result of functional classification theory, communities that desire walkability are limited to an existence within a square mile area or so, bounded by arterials and major collectors. As land use densities along arterials increase, traffic from widely spaced, side street collectors usually require four lanes. These four lane collectors further disrupt walkability deep into the neighborhood.

Due to these three conflicts, a substantial disparity exists between publications such as *Calm Streets* and the AASHTO policies on geometric design versus the transportation design parameters leading to greater walkability in mixed-use New Urbanist communities. Lower vehicular design speeds (to accommodate pedestrians) and narrow street widths (to achieve these lower speeds) are the most common design conflicts with AASHTO arterial street guidelines. The functionally classified hierarchy of roadways, performing specific functions of vehicle mobility and access, was intended to provide a logical street and highway network for American travelers. For rural places the theory performed as planned. In urban areas, however, one major unintended consequence occurred. New, urban pedestrian-scale communities, with walking as a viable mode of travel, were essentially absent until the advent of Seaside, a development in Florida, in 1980.

Recommended Solutions

Actions to minimize confusion between walkability and auto dominance should begin with steps by implementing agencies and their mentor organizations. First, leading transport agencies, such as the United States Federal Highway Administration and AASHTO, must refine the use of a single area type to define urban areas. A variety of area types would better reflect the true diversity of urban character (and associated roadway types). In its "transect" definitions, Duany and Plater-Zyberk outline "sub-urban," "general urban," "urban center," and "urban core" context zones (T3 to T6) that accurately describe different development patterns from most rural to most urban. These context zones, or area type descriptions, are recommended as a framework for specifying a broader array of roadway types.

Second, a broader array of roadway functional classifications must be defined. Each roadway's primary function should be established as either vehicle mobility or pedestrian mobility (including bike and transit). This solution is also recommended in ITE's report entitled "Traditional Neighborhood Development Street Design Guidelines." Portland, Oregon manages its mobility by designating each urban street's function by travel mode. Varying priority levels for each of the four modes (walk, bike, transit, and auto) can be designated for one street. In short, new, functionally classified thoroughfares, defined for walkable communities, should augment the existing classification system, not replace it.

The *Smart Code* by Duany and Plater-Zyberk, defines specific urban context areas as pedestrian priority zones. This also specifies the character on the surrounding area, up to several miles away from the corridor's right-of-way. Thoroughfares within these smart code urban context zones (T3 to T6 in table 1) would facilitate pedestrian movement first and then accommodate vehicles in a way that does not inhibit walkability.

In urban context zones, boulevards are defined to carry longer vehicle trips, thus they have some characteristics similar to the current urban arterial function. This new boulevard functional definition, however, replaces the arterial definition in areas deemed "walkable context zones." Boulevards would be assigned an *equal* functional priority between pedestrian and vehicle mobility (indicated by Veh/Ped in table 1). The boulevard is the ultimate urban walkable thoroughfare, emphasizing vehicle mobility in the faster moving center lanes. As such, boulevards have a higher priority placed on vehicle mobility than do streets or roads. The primary function of highways, including freeways, would still be vehicle mobility, but they would only be designed for rural zones (T1 and T2 in table 1). This recommended augmentation of the urban functional classification framework is shown in the table.

Design criteria must be established for each new functional classification. To maintain lower operating speeds required for walkable context zones, lower design speeds must be established. To help achieve this, posted speed should equal design speed in walkable context zones.

Preliminary studies in urban settings show that lane width effectively controls vehicle speed in the low ranges of 20 to 30 mph needed for walkability. However, with its current emphasis on auto mobility, AASHTO only recommends minimum design speeds of 31 mph in central business districts and intermediate areas.

Although these issues can occasionally be successfully resolved with implementing agencies, and may eventually lead to the desired development approvals, augmentation of the functional classification definitions by adding new context-specific thoroughfare classifications that support walkability is strongly recommended. These new thoroughfare definitions will correct the current over emphasis on auto mobility.

In summary, new functional classifications designed to augment existing arterial, collector, and local definitions should be adopted by agencies with jurisdiction over transportation planning and public works implementation. As a result, designers would have significantly reduced liability and local agency reviewers would have the foundation for ordinances that facilitate walkability as a valid part of the transportation system.

TABLE 1: PRIORITY OF ROADWAY FUNCTION BY CONTEXT ZONE

Functional Classification	Context Zone/Roadway Function					
	T1 Rural Preserve	T2 Rural Reserve	T3 Sub-urban	T4 General Urban	T5 Urban Center	T6 Urban Core
Boulevard	N/A	N/A	N/A	Veh/Ped	Veh/Ped	Veh/Ped
Avenue	N/A	N/A	Pedestrian	Pedestrian	Pedestrian	Pedestrian
Street	N/A	N/A	Pedestrian	Pedestrian	Pedestrian	Pedestrian
Alley	N/A	N/A	Pedestrian	Pedestrian	Pedestrian	Pedestrian
Transitway	On Freeway	On Freeway	Pedestrian	Pedestrian	Pedestrian	Pedestrian
Lane	Veh/Ped	Veh/Ped	Pedestrian	Pedestrian	N/A	N/A
Road	Vehicle	Vehicle	Pedestrian	N/A	N/A	N/A
Highway	Vehicle	Vehicle	N/A	N/A	N/A	N/A

PART 6: REAL ESTATE, CITY MARKETING, AND CULTURE

URBAN RETAIL PLANNING PRINCIPLES FOR TRADITIONAL NEIGHBORHOODS

ROBERT GIBBS

One of the primary advantages of Traditional Neighborhood Designed (TND) communities over conventional suburbs is the opportunity to walk to shopping and entertainment venues. However, few New Urbanism communities have successfully implemented retail centers. In many cases, the TND community's retail is not developed until years after the last residential phase is completed.

Often, TND retail centers fail to meet minimal sales necessary for their business owners to earn a reasonable income. The underperforming centers result in businesses that offer limited goods and poor service that cannot compete with market driven retail centers. Many TND developers are hesitant to take the risk to build the commercial phase of their community because land values are much higher for residential than retail.

Developing and managing retail centers remains one of the most risky of all real estate categories. Retailers must respond to ever changing consumer trends and demands, while constantly fending off new competition. As a result, the retail industry relies upon proven methods and techniques to minimize the risk and to earn a market rate of return on their investment. Many of the most desirable historic neighborhoods and TNDs have clusters of successful retailers.

Unlike suburban development, where various commercial land uses are well buffered, TND retail and residential communities are closely intertwined. As a result, the vitality of TND retail can directly impact the surrounding residential. In extreme cases, boarded up storefronts, and undesirable tenants—such as tattoo parlors and pawn shops—can cause the adjacent home values to nosedive. Conversely, popular and useful retailers such as coffee shops, cafes, and food markets contribute to the quality of life in the neighborhood. It's in the best interest of the community that the retailers meet or exceed industry sales standards.

Shopping Center Types

Shopping centers are divided into six primary typologies that group business types into proven supporting clusters. Each type of center appeals to distinct market segments and has specific sizes, tenants, location criteria, and site-plan standards. Centers that deviate from these industry standards and sizes are considered risky and difficult to finance or lease.

These primary shopping center types are: the corner store, convenience center, neighborhood center, community center, regional center, and the lifestyle center. The community, regional, and lifestyle centers range from 200,000 to 1 million square feet, and require minimum populations of over 50,000 to 150,000 to be supportable. In addition, each of the above shopping center types can be "supersized," (i.e., super neighborhood center, etc.) by up to 50%.

Although all shopping center types have been developed following the best practices of the New Urbanism, smaller corner stores, convenience, and neighborhood centers are the most common in TNDs.

Corner Stores

The smallest and most useful retail type, the corner store, ranges from 1,500 to 3,000 square feet. These small stores offer beverages, food, and sundries that are needed on a regular basis by most households, workers, and travelers. Beer, bread, cigarettes, prepared sandwiches, sundries, and snacks represent the bulk of their sales. These stores primarily offer convenience over selection and value (figure 1).

Corner stores are ideally located along major local roads at the busiest entry to the neighborhood. However, in densely populated TNDs, the corner store can be sustainable within the neighborhood when located along its primary street. The store also benefits if located adjacent to community buildings, parks, and schools; although, schools often dislike corner stores being near their campus because of their appeal as student hangouts.

Approximately 1,000 households are necessary to support the average corner store. This represents one corner store per each TND neighborhood, based upon a five-minute walk. However, this number can be reduced significantly if the store is located along a major road with 15,000 cars per day or more. Corner stores that also sell gasoline are supportable with virtually no adjacent homes. Sales from construction

FIG. 1 A popular corner store located in historic Charleston, South Carolina.
All photos in this essay by Robert Gibbs.

FIG. 2 The author's convenience center located in Birmingham, Michigan. The center includes a food market, dry cleaners, two banks, pharmacy, and a plumber. It was built around 1945 and located at a signalized intersection leading to a traditional prewar neighborhood. The center is surrounded by two churches, a fire station, and office building.

trades prior to the completion of an entire neighborhood can potentially support a corner store.

The average corner store will yield approximately $210.00 in sales per square foot per year, or a total of $300,000 to $600,000 per year. In gross, sales will be significantly higher if the store sells packaged liquor or gasoline. Annual rents for the average corner store will average $14.00–$16.00 per square foot. Rents and sales are significantly higher in dense urban areas. Developers will often offer the store owner a significant rental discount in order to have the amenity for its neighborhood. Rent only represents 8-10% of most retailers' total operating expenses. Such a discount is not advised, since if the store is not sustainable from the onset, the business owner will often fail or quit.

Convenience Centers

Typically between 10,000 and 30,000 square feet, these centers offer an array of goods and services geared towards the daily needs of the surrounding neighborhoods. These centers are often anchored with a small specialty food market or

pharmacy. The balance of the center usually includes five to eight small businesses ranging from 1,500 to 3,000 square feet each. Convenience center tenants offer a limited balance of food, personal services, and local offices. On average, a Convenience Center will have two carry-out foods, a hair, salon or barber shop, a bank, food market, and one to two small neighborhood businesses. Typical tenants include a bagel store, bakery, bank, coffee shop, dry cleaners, financial services, florist, food market, ice cream, laundry center, mail center, package liquor, personal services, pharmacy, real estate offices, or tailor. The author's convenience center includes a plumber, who keeps all of the old homes in working order (figure 2).

Each of these small businesses would have a difficult time if located on a stand-alone site. However, by being grouped into a walkable cluster, each business helps to generate impulse traffic and sales for the other. A homemaker stopping at the dry cleaners may stop and purchase a pizza for dinner. A worker picking up a coffee may also purchase a dozen bagels for the office. A visit to the food market for

FIG. 3 Neighborhood centers are always anchored with full-sized supermarkets and range in size from 60,000 to 80,000 square feet in total size. This is Simsbury Shopping Center, West Bloomfield, Michigan.

a gallon of milk and loaf of bread is easier (and will save time) if the trip can be combined with a visit to the bank and hair salon.

Convenience centers need about 2,000 households to be supportable, or two TND neighborhoods. These centers must be located along a major road and ideally at the primary entry to both neighborhoods. Their average trade area typically extends up to a one-mile radius. Average sales for convenience center retailers are $225.00 per square foot per year. Annual rents average $15.00, with a range of $12.00 to $18.00 per square foot, per year for the centers. Convenience centers earn their highest rents from coffee, fast food, telephone, dry cleaners, and unisex hair care stores. The lowest rents typically come from dollar stores, barber shops, bakeries, liquor/wine shops, laundry, women's hair salons, and family restaurants (ICSC Dollars and Cents of Shopping Centers, 2004).

Neighborhood Centers

Anchored with a supermarket, pharmacy, and video store, neighborhood centers offer a full depth of goods and services not available at corner stores or convenience centers (figure 3). These centers are typically visited once or twice per week by most households living within a one to two mile radius. The neighborhood center's primary anchor is a full-sized supermarket typically ranging from 45,000 to 60,000 square feet. This major anchor is the engine that supports most of the other smaller businesses; so much so, that when a supermarket closes, many of the other tenants will immediately leave the center.

Neighborhood centers generally range from 60,000 to 80,000 square feet in total size (including the supermarket) and typically require six to ten acres of property. Site planning using TND principals can potentially reduce the center's size by up to 20%. These centers have an overall blended parking ratio of 4.0 cars per 1,000 square feet of gross building area. The supermarket and restaurants will demand higher parking ratios around their business.

These neighborhood centers require 6,000 to 8,000 households to be located within their primary trade area. The typical suburban trade area is one to two miles. However, in very rural areas it is not unusual for residents to drive over fifty miles weekly to visit a neighborhood center. Dense urban centers can support a supermarket every few blocks.

These centers have, on average, ten to fifteen smaller retailers such as bagels, bakery, bank, bike shop, card shop, carry-out restaurants, coffee shop, deli, dollar store, dry cleaners, electronics, eyewear, family shoes, family restaurant, financial services, florist, food market, frame shop, hardware, home furnishings, ice cream, jewelry, laundry center, mail center, package liquor, personal services, pharmacy, tanning salon, telephone store, and video rental. Office users include: accounting, financial services, medical, and real estate. Women's apparel is becoming more common in neighborhood centers, led by Talbot's or similar retailers.

Neighborhood center sales and rents vary widely from business type. On average, the centers average $245.00 per square foot per year in sales. Rents range from $7.25 per square foot for supermarkets to up to $40.00 for coffee shops. The anchors typically only pay enough rent to cover the debt service on their building. The inline retailers, in effect, subsidize the supermarket and other key anchors. In exchange, the supermarket and anchors attract shoppers to the center with massive advertising campaigns and lower margins.

The highest paying rents in neighborhood centers come from ATMs, juice and coffee beverages, bagels, fast food (Mexican), decorative accessories, imports, and jewelry. Variety-dollar stores, hardware, supermarkets, pharmacies, and fabric shops tend to pay the lowest rents in neighborhood centers. The highest sales are earned by drugstores, coffee shops, Mexican fast foods, supermarkets, jewelry stores, restaurants with liquor, and mail packaging centers. Telephone stores, tanning salons, dollar stores, nail salons, fabric shops, video rentals, and men's wear tend to have the weakest sales volume in neighborhood centers.

Many TND developers and New Urban planners often try to limit the size of the supermarket to 20,000 to 25,000 square feet. However, small supermarkets are impractical due to the large variety of goods demanded by the average American household. Today's supermarket must carry a much greater variety of each product than it did in the 1960's when a 25,000 square foot A&P was considered "full sized."

For example, the old A&Ps only offered three to four soft drinks as compared to today's selection of dozens of brands, sizes, and varieties (i.e., Coke, Diet Coke, Caffeine-free Diet Coke, Cherry Coke, etc.), each available in three to four packages. Supermarkets also offer bakeries, delis, more produce, frozen goods, heath aids, check out lines, etc. Demanding a small grocery store is akin to restricting the variety of goods that shoppers must consume. For example, let them eat my brand of cereal instead of being able to select from among 150 brands and sizes.

This being said, our culture's excessive consumerism is not defensible or sustainable. However, should the TND be forced to develop a small grocery instead of what the market demands, then the center is vulnerable to a full-sized center opening nearby? The new supermarket would likely take a significant amount of market share away from the TND supermarket and eventually threaten the center itself. One should assume that the market will always eventually prevail and that ignoring the market is too risky.

The neighborhood center is a favorite for lending institutions and investment houses. They earn a proven income stream and it is assumed that families will always need to purchase groceries. Recently the neighborhood center has been threatened by the discount super centers, where it is estimated that they can put up to two supermarkets out of business when entering a market. In addition, the popular green grocery stores and warehouse clubs are attracting well-educated higher end consumers away from the standard supermarket. Retail development is forever reinventing itself.

Site Plan and Parking

Convenience-oriented neighborhood businesses must offer convenience in order to be competitive with major shopping centers and big-box stores. The center should be planned to allow for most of the retailers to face the primary road and neighborhood entry street. Ideally, most neighborhood residents will drive through a section of the retail to and from home. Given that the average household produces ten trips per day, a dwelling neighborhood could produce up to 10,000 daily trips along the shop fronts. Local businesses mostly rely on the impulse visit and have limited advertising budgets; this exposure is a must.

The corner store or neighborhood center should also be oriented to allow for easy pedestrian access from the surrounding neighborhoods. Surface parking lots should be hidden behind small liner retailers or orientated towards the primary highway. As much as possible, a seamless transition for residential to neighborhood should be maintained.

FIG. 4 Many urban shoppers prefer parking along the street as close as possible to the front of their shopping destination, and will avoid stopping if an on-street space is not available.

Parking remains one of the most critical issues facing any retailer. This is especially true for neighborhood retailers. As a result, easy to use parking is essential. Ample free parking near the store's entry is a must. That being said, parking should not dominate the site plan, and walkable store-lined streets should be maintained as much as possible.

Shoppers have different parking expectations for convenience neighborhood shopping visits than they do for major shopping centers. When visiting community or regional centers, shoppers tend to make multiple store visits for extended time periods. In exchange for the greater variety of stores and merchandise offered at the shopping center or big-box retailer, shoppers are willing to park further away from storefronts than they would in a main-street setting. Shopping center visitors will also perceive parking to be more convenient and closer if they can see the store (or mall) entry from their parking stalls, even if its hundreds of feet away.

In contrast, these same shoppers will demand parking directly in front of the destination store in a small town or convenience center. Should such a space not be available, the typical shopper will believe that parking is problematic and less convenient compared to the modern shopping center. As a result, this shopper will tend to avoid the location for shopping in the future.

Many neighborhood shoppers prefer to run in and out of specific businesses and are unwilling to park in remote lots. This double standard held by American consumers is not necessarily fair, but the behavior is a reality that must be addressed. The unwillingness to park in remote lots could change should the shopping district reach a critical mass of over 250,000 square feet of general merchandise businesses that would collectively offer a broad selection of desirable retailers.

Economics and human behavior will always prevail, squeezing the shopper out of the preferred parking spaces. When visiting destination main-street shops, most consumers prefer convenient parking to free parking. While attempting to visit a store, most shoppers will continue along their way if they cannot find parking. However, if a street space or surface lot is available, even for a small fee, the shopper will likely park and shop.

If located in a small town or city, most neighborhood businesses will locate on the periphery of the downtown. These businesses would have a difficult time surviving a downtown because of its lack of convenient parking. Densely populated cities with high incomes have proven to be an exception to this standard, where land prices are too steep to support surface parking.

Business Practices

A major weakness of many TND commercial centers is the lack of modern business practices and management. In some cases, retailers have been left to fend for themselves, with little or no required management participation and organization. These practices can result in low sales, high turnover, and eventually a failed center.

One of the most common mistakes with TND neighborhood retail is the lack of required minimal store hours. It's impractical for small independent retailers to maintain extended hours. However, one of the top complaints of many shoppers is the limited hours of small retailers and centers. Approximately 70% of all retail sales occur after 5:30 pm and on Sundays.

In addition, good lighting, clean walks, and well-maintained street furniture are essential for a competitive commercial center. A center that does not keep extended hours is limiting itself to one-third of the market share. Limited hours and poor maintenance convey a sense of poor service and lack of value to time-stressed families.

Please find below a summary of basic recommended guidelines for TND neighborhood center management:

- Establish a required Common Area Management (CAM) fee as a part of the tenant's base rent. This fee is to be used by the shopping center management for maintenance and marketing of the center's common area.
- Require high design standards for store fronts and signage. Adopt a 70% minimum clear-glass frontage (as measured between three to eight feet from finished walk) at the first level for all new construction. Avoid suburban shopping center-type signage and storefronts.
- All on-street retail *must* have managed on-street parking in front of the store.
- Businesses should be encouraged to differentiate themselves with signage, color, and facade alterations. Allowing them to reinforce their brand also emphasizes the downtown's wide selection of goods and services. Avoid an overemphasis on continuity of color and form.
- Reduce the front valance flap height to eight inches maximum. Only permit canvas type fabrics; plastic fabrics should be prohibited. Permit two colors for awnings. Small logos or business names on awnings should be permitted.
- Maintain minimal hours to 7 pm weekdays and to 9 pm at least one evening per week. Require 9–5 Saturday hours.
- Develop a mixed business plan that limits overlapping goods and services, while still maintaining healthy competition.
- Cross-merchandise with other downtown merchants by sharing window and interior display props.
- Highlight holidays and seasons with prominent displays located at the front and center of the store.
- Paint storefronts and interiors on a regular (one to two year) basis.
- Clean and paint front doors and windows three to four times per year. Wash store doors four to five times daily.
- Maintain control over interior store plans, merchandising, lighting, and displays.
- Require storefront window displays to be updated monthly.
- Keep all storefront lights on a central timer to remain illuminated until 10 pm.
- Large common trash cans should be located in alleys or the rear of buildings. These containers should be enclosed, if possible, kept clean, and free of pests and odors. Restaurant containers should be cooled during warm weather.
- Implement a common marketing campaign for the center and its merchants.

CONFRONTING THE QUESTION OF MARKET DEMAND FOR URBAN RESIDENTIAL DEVELOPMENT

LAURIE VOLK AND TODD ZIMMERMAN

"Demand" for housing is often an illusory concept, particularly when applied to urban neighborhoods. The depth and breadth of the potential market for urban housing, however, can be determined and is often substantial, even in cities that have seen little or no new housing produced in years.

Historically, urban areas have experienced population loss, often severe, and conventional supply/demand analyses typically project that trend to continue, with the result that forecasts of demand are often minimal, if not negative. Conventional supply/demand analyses ignore the potentially significant impact of newly introduced housing supply in urban areas on settlement patterns, particularly when that supply is specifically targeted to match the housing preferences and economic capabilities of draw-area households.

All too often, research methodology limits the scope of possible results. For example, if housing market analysis is focused only on the supply side—i.e., values and occupancies of existing dwelling units (typically adjacent neighborhoods) and values and absorption rates of new residential construction (typically in greenfield locations)—then the "demand forecast" will be limited to those housing types that are currently available. Even the most rigorously applied supply/demand methodology rarely reveals the actual scope of new housing potential. This is because most "market analysis for real estate uses general marketing theory; however, out of necessity, it must consider the geographical concerns of spatial concentrations of supply and diffused demand."[1] Rarely is this miss match adequately resolved.

Because of this miss match, demand for new housing in a specific location cannot be definitively determined through research, however rigorous. The multiple factors that enter into the housing decision cannot be statistically isolated even through the most complex empirical analysis. Thoughtful observers of residential settlement patterns know, that when it comes to housing analysis, rigorous empirical inquiry only leads to additional questions.

Although demand for urban housing cannot be quantified, the characteristics of the various types of households that represent the potential market for urban housing can be determined. An understanding of these household characteristics can guide the public and private sectors toward adopting strategies for developing and sustaining urban neighborhoods. The most difficult challenge is to marshal economic forces through proper positioning, timing, and phasing to exert a positive influence on urban settlement patterns.

The challenge is an important one. The creation, reestablishment, restoration, or enhancement of neighborhoods is the foundation of any rational initiative for sustainable regional development. Without the connections between residents and shopping, employment and recreation, infrastructure and resource efficiencies will continue at the current low levels.

Supporters of the status quo maintain that if there were a genuine market for urban housing, there would already be plenty of it. Apologists for the current leap-frogging pattern of low-density, narrowly targeted, single-use development still argue that the current pattern is simply continuing "the relentless outward expansion of cities into suburbs and beyond."[2] This thinking suggests that we are ultimately headed toward some sort of housing entropy, in which every household is equidistant from every other household, and all community and commerce is experienced in cyberspace out of necessity.

Those same supporters also cite as "empirical evidence" decades of American household movement to environments characterized by steadily decreasing densities. However, this supposed evidence is largely meaningless. In most metropolitan areas, American households buy into the current settlement patterns because they lack genuine choice.

Housing production generally follows the path of least resistance: easy-to-finance and easy-to-build units on land that is environmentally "clean," in a "good" location in a metropolitan area that is experiencing reasonable job growth, for which it is deemed appropriate zoning and approvals can be readily obtained. The builders and developers follow the well-defined and efficient delivery system of housing as "product" that is the end result of a long conspiracy of good intentions, from the Euclid zoning decision to the Americans with Disabilities Act. This usually translates into the efficient "unibox" detached houses on former agricultural land.

There is more residential development in fringe locations, then, simply because it is significantly easier to accomplish than development on urban sites: exurban tracts are larger; entitlements are less complicated; and a majority of acquisition, development, and construction lenders have a high comfort level with single-use greenfield development. It is the higher degree of difficulty that has made urban residential development a "niche product." This does not mean that urban housing can find only a niche market. Compact urban development is beginning to be embraced by too many builders, developers, financial institutions, and government agencies—from local to federal—to remain marginalized as a niche.

Conventional housing-market analysis generally does not attempt to address the specific needs or desires of the increasingly diverse pool of housing consumers. Supply/demand analysis is generally the analytical tool of choice. But the type of supply/demand analysis that often passes for new housing research is nothing more than an analysis of the market performance of currently marketed subdivisions and master-planned communities, combined with simple, often marginally related demographic data. If forecasts of household change are included, they are usually straight baseline projections, which assume that the recent pattern of change in the numbers of households will continue into the future. Analysis of supply-side data can range from rudimentary to quite sophisticated. Nevertheless, most new housing research is predicated on two very questionable premises: 1) that the change in the number of households will continue the trend of the recent past, and 2) that the only housing types that will meet with market acceptance are those that have demonstrated sales success in comparable locations.

Reliance on supply-side analysis often leads to local myopia. Builders, real estate brokers, and other real estate observers are often subject to an antiurban bias, justifying their opinions with supply-side data.

The distortion of supply-side analysis has often been aggravated in urban areas by the mismatch of existing urban housing units and the households that have the potential to move to urban neighborhoods. In some cities—for example, Baltimore or Philadelphia—the market feasibility of new housing construction was dismissed because hundreds of row houses already existing in the city did not sell despite prices that were quite low. In these instances, the issue was not the prices, but rather the sizes of the existing units. Too many were too small and too plain to be viewed as worthy of restoration or renovation through sweat equity; this is particularly true when the market consists of young singles and childless couples who are seeking convenience and location rather than lower-value units. An understanding of the characteristics of the potential market for urban housing, then, can reveal these miss matches.

The heavy reliance on competitive sales data has led the housing industry into a peculiar self-referential inward spiral, in which the houses of many builders are converging into amazingly similar units. Continued ad absurdum, this convergence means that in the future there will be just one house type built in America. A benefit of this scenario of monotony, one would assume, is that production would be very efficient.

Academicians generally dismiss these limited housing research studies; ". . . in recent years the quality of market studies in real estate has been widely criticized."[3] However, despite many decades of scholarly analysis of empirical real estate-related data, few of the scholarly research techniques have been adopted by housing developers. Only real estate portfolio analysts and acquisition managers have empirical tools on which they can rely. Just as supply/demand analysis often works quite well in describing the market for packaged goods, if carefully applied, it can also provide useful insights into performance projections of investment-grade, income-producing real estate assets.

In contrast, those seeking practical tools with which to gauge the potential for new residential initiatives—public and private sectors alike—have, as often as not, been led astray by supply/demand analysis. The emphasis often placed on unquantifiable "demand" can be misguided.

Forecasting the demand for new housing is so challenging because housing dynamics are fundamentally different than those of other consumer durable items. Unlike other purchase transactions of consumer goods (from impulse items to big-ticket items), housing is a product that is fixed in place requiring that the purchaser must move to acquire it. As Dowell Myers has pointed out, this creates the unique causal relationship between population and housing in which the arrow of causation changes direction depending upon geographic scale.[4]

The relationship between the demand for housing and the number of new households may vary significantly depending on scale. At the broadest geographic scale (metropolitan statistical area and above), housing demand—and its corollary, the number of new housing units that is required to respond to that demand—is derived primarily from projected changes in the number of households; barring wholesale demolition, fire loss, and abandonment of existing housing stock, new housing is not likely to be absorbed without a corresponding increase in households. At the local level, however, and assuming a neighborhood's housing units are at "stabilized full occupancy," there can be no increase in households if there are no new housing units built in which they can be housed.

Housing, therefore, is unique among consumer items; because it is fixed in place, supply can create its own demand, the results of which are seen in the low-density settlement pattern of the past several decades. However, this peculiar dynamic of "build it and they will come" can only occur when those new housing units are well matched to the characteristics of the households that comprise the potential market. The success of dispersed, relatively low cost per square foot detached housing has been its match with the demographic bulge of family households that is now beginning to wane as the baby boom generation—those born between 1946 and 1964—begin to move from the "full nest" to the "empty nest" life stage. (As a result, the recent remarkable increase of high-priced detached houses that match the expectations of the baby boom households in the peak earning years—the first generation in American history in which it is common to have two incomes contributing to those peak earnings—is now waning in a number of American markets.)

The critical question for urban housing, then, becomes not so much the quantities of market demand but rather the qualities of the market potential.

Because of the lack of meaningful comparables in urban locations, the methodology most often employed to determine both quantity and characteristics of the market for urban housing has been some kind of survey research. Survey research can be effective if its objectives are set with the recognition that what can be quantified is not market demand but rather market potential. The two pitfalls of survey research regarding urban housing (or any housing, or any survey for that matter) have to do with the sample—i.e., *who* one asks—and questions—i.e., *what* one asks.

A sample can be biased despite the most rigorous efforts. Projecting survey results based solely on sample demographics can be perilous. Households with virtually identical demographics can have very different attitudes. If a sample does not have the same cultural values as the population as a whole, survey results could over- or underestimate the potential market for urban housing. Some cultural values have correlated positively with a preference for compact and urban neighborhoods. For example, households that place greater value on experience than on material goods are more likely to value the diversity and cultural opportunities associated with urban living.[5]

A more serious flaw with survey research is the difficulty of conveying an appropriate image of an urban neighborhood. Questions are often vaguely worded, asking the respondent's attitude toward living "downtown" or "in the city." Often the vagueness is purposeful, to allow the most open interpretation and least bias from a population that has little familiarity with urban living. There is no single urban residential archetype; the neighborhoods of American cities vary greatly in both density and character, from the detached houses of Charleston to the apartment buildings of Manhattan. The fundamental problem is that many, if not most, Americans, lacking an urban frame of reference, are unable to conceive of an urban neighborhood as a habitable place. Many suburbanites have simply no idea what a stable urban neighborhood would look like or be like; for them, the word "urban" still conjures images of crime, congestion, and blight.

If these limitations and difficulties are recognized, well-designed survey research is probably the least complicated conventional methodology that is capable of providing approximations of both the quantity and characteristics of households that make up the potential market for urban housing.

Professionally facilitated qualitative research, including focus groups and interviews, can help distinguish the characteristics of potential urban residents and can determine individual unit and neighborhood preferences at a relatively detailed level. Even the best qualitative researchers, however, require guidance in assembling panels or prospective interviewees; they must, in effect, know who the market is in order to learn about it in detail. No qualitative research is capable of determining the depth and breadth of the market.

It is from analysis of migration trends and mobility rates that the depth and breadth of the potential market can be determined. Migration data quantifies how many households move into a market area, and from where they are moving. Mobility rates quantify those households that move within a market area.

The number of households that could potentially move to a given location in a given year describes the practical upper limit on market potential.

Migration analysis need focus only on in-migration, rather than out-migration or net migration. Net migration is of little consequence even when a local market has been stigmatized by precipitous household loss. For example, the cities of St. Louis and Detroit have both experienced, and continue to experience, dramatic out-migration; nevertheless, there is still market potential for the downtown areas of both cities, as has been demonstrated in both cities over the past five years. Thousands of households have moved within and into both cities every year; until recently, those numbers have simply been lower than the numbers of households that have moved out.

While migration and mobility analysis provide a means for determining the quantity of those households that could potentially move to an urban location, the more difficult task is determining their qualities and characteristics, and how those qualities and characteristics influence housing preferences.

Some household characteristics can be obtained through conventional research techniques, as noted above. Triggered by our work, geodemographic analysis, a methodology not previously applied to housing, has been proposed as a means of identifying which middle-income suburbanites have the potential to relocate to central cities.[6] Even without the refinements of migration and mobility analysis, target marketing was found to augment conventional data, and to have the potential to provide cities with a deeper understanding of their market advantages.

Over the past eighteen years we have used our proprietary target market methodology, which combines geodemographic data with migration and mobility analysis, to determine the depth and breadth of the potential market, and the optimum market position for new development or redevelopment based on the characteristics of that market.

It is important to emphasize that the supply-side context cannot be ignored; the supply-side context provides benchmarks of housing value. Although proposed new housing units need not be hostage to the supply-side context, neither can new construction be positioned in ignorance of supply.

Other Significant Urban Market Issues

A thorough understanding of urban residential dynamics has implications far beyond typical supply/demand concerns. Issues range from physical form to phasing:

There is no single housing formula.

Seeing urban markets as a function of market potential specific to an area means that one must accept that there is no formulaic housing mix to attract new households to urban neighborhoods. Good neighborhood revitalization must be responsive to local market dynamics—i.e., the preferences of the different household groups that make up the market for new urban housing. Household mix—the proportions of empty nesters, younger singles and couples, and families that make up the new housing market—can be very different from city to city and from neighborhood to neighborhood.

The market potential for urban housing need not be a "zero-sum game."

A corollary to the concept that housing supply can create its own demand is that, citywide, the creation of new housing in any one neighborhood need not be a "zero-sum game." This is an important issue when many city neighborhoods perceive themselves to be in competition for a limited number of households. New housing can be introduced into an urban neighborhood without cannibalizing other emerging neighborhoods. The key is neighborhood positioning. Careful positioning is second nature to the best developers of master-planned communities, but is usually ignored by municipalities and sponsors of neighborhood revitalization. Emerging neighborhoods that target the proper potential market can change housing dynamics in the entire city. When new housing options are created within a city, these new units can capture households that otherwise might have settled elsewhere. They may also retain households that, because of a life stage or economic change, might otherwise have moved out of the city.

New construction has the power to attract the potential market.

A powerful rationale for an increasing number of households to leave familiar urban neighborhoods is the desire for newly constructed housing. In the same regard, introducing newly constructed housing into an existing neighborhood usually presents an attractive alternative to former residents of the area who have previously moved out of the city. The expense and aggravation of continued repairs to older housing stock can overwhelm many households; new construction—with new appliances in kitchens and baths, floor plans that match modern lifestyles, and ample closet space in the bedrooms—becomes increasingly attractive.

Phasing can influence the market.

To attract the potential market, new urban housing construction must be seen not only in spatial terms—i.e., where and in what form housing should be built—but also in temporal terms—i.e., when each housing type should be introduced to the market. Just as with any suburban development, the first phase can make or break the development. What is at stake is more than the obvious efficiency of infrastructure and a careful matching of expenses with revenues. The first phase can have an impact on the potential market as well.

The first phase must consider the image that is presented to the community at large. The type of housing built at the property's most visible edge must be very carefully targeted; it will convey most powerfully the character of the neighborhood to the potential market.

Finally, the tenure mix of early phases can be critical. Despite the widespread objective of bringing home ownership into the city, rental housing can be an excellent first phase for neighborhood revitalization. Rentals can quickly transform neighborhoods, particularly those that have non-residential elements. Rental units are leased at a much faster pace than for-sale units are sold. Renters typically spend more time in the public realm because they are generally younger and their units are generally smaller than those of homeowners.

The public realm should be matched to the market.

Just as it is important to provide a range of housing matched to the potential market, it is equally important to provide a public realm that meets the cultural and leisure interests of that market. The commerce and culture of urban locations usually attracts young singles and childless couples, both young and older.

Family households may also appreciate these attributes, but schools and security issues frequently deter households from remaining once children appear. Cities can retain families if they provide the three significant community elements that are required to establish or sustain urban residential neighborhoods—safe and secure streets, sufficient green space, and good schools.

The urge to suburbanize should be avoided.

Knowledge of the characteristics of households that have the potential to populate urban neighborhoods provides a final important insight: They will be attracted to appropriate urban design, not to an urban reinterpretation of low-density suburban forms. Good urban design places as much emphasis on creating quality streets and public places as on creating quality buildings.

Design should not signal socioeconomics.

For urban neighborhoods to attract and sustain a diverse mix of households, a neutral socioeconomic design is required. The affluent will live in mixed-income neighborhoods if the occupants' income levels or tenure is not discernible from the street. This can be achieved through consistent construction quality and the mixing of rental and for-sale buildings and units throughout the community.

THE NEED FOR PATIENT EQUITY IN CREATING GREAT PLACES

CHRISTOPHER B. LEINBERGER

Over the past decade, much has been learned from the urban designers and developers from before the 1930s, our grandfathers' generation and before, such as J. C. Nichols (Country Club Plaza in Kansas City), George Merrick (Coral Gables, Florida), and the Rockefeller family's development of Rockefeller Center. They have become role models to be emulated in recently revived downtowns, suburban town centers, New Urbanism projects, transit-oriented developments, and lifestyle centers. While nearly all of the attention today has been on the *urban design* lessons of our grandfathers, there are *financing* lessons they can teach us as well.

The most important financing lesson to be learned from our grandfathers is to recognize that since the beginnings of urban civilization, real estate has always been a long-term asset class. The Internal Revenue Service in the United States dictates that structures are depreciated over thirty-nine years. The United States National Park Service, the agency that designates historic tax credits, considers buildings historic if they are over fifty years old. Owners of well-built buildings generally reach a decision point of whether to redevelop the major systems, common areas, and facade every forty years or so. One of the reasons downtowns are reviving so quickly over the past few years is the positive market response to rehabilitation of historic structures, buildings that we could generally not match in construction quality today. However, real estate has changed over the past half century. Today, most real estate projects have a seven- to ten-year life span as a "class A" property; this is the result of a reduction in the construction quality of our projects and encouragement of the building of commoditized, single purpose, conventional products.

To build great projects like Country Club Plaza or Rockefeller Center, mixed-use projects built in a walkable environment, our grandfathers undoubtedly employed something in very short supply today; patient equity. To many this is an oxymoronic phrase, as equity is the most expensive and therefore most impatient of all capital. Patient equity was generally employed in the past because it was a requirement if one wanted to move the project forward, but also because of the developers' pride in building something of which J. C. Nichols called "enduring value."

Most developers of similar walkable, mixed-use projects today are probably not aware that they are already investing considerable patient equity. They end up investing it without upfront planning as the project unfolds, in the form of the unanticipated time needed to obtain public approvals, the need for better construction finishes, and countless other reasons discussed below. However, there is probably a need for even more patient equity than they are currently unconsciously investing to insure three things: the success of the project; the strength of the mid- and long-term cash flow of the project; and a guarantee that the developer maintains control of the project so as to be the beneficiary of this cash flow. As is well known, proper financial structuring in the early stages of a real estate project's life is essential for success, which entails lining up the required equity and debt. Not planning for an essential source of equity could potentially result in minimizing the financial performance of the project, or even be a financial disaster. If patient equity is a requirement, not providing enough can jeopardize the project and the developer's financial future. If one is going to develop a special project, built for the ages, why only go part way regarding the financial structure of the project?

Two Forms of Real Estate Development

It is important to make a distinction between the two forms of real estate development. Revitalizing a downtown, developing New Urbanism, or creating a mixed-use lifestyle center, similar to the older projects mentioned above, involves the creation of *walkable urbanism*. A walkable place is where most—and possibly all—of life's daily needs (shopping, recreation, school, restaurants, employment, etc.) are reachable on foot or by transit. The preconditions for walkable urbanity include:

• Having significant residential buildings within walking distance of local-serving retail and a park,

• Having the entire walk be continuously pedestrian friendly and safe,

• An average net residential density of at least eight dwelling units to the acre to support the local-serving retail and transit (planned or currently available),

• Being within walking distance of work for at least one member of the household or within walking distance of transit that links the household to employment.

While car use is a given in any form of development in contemporary society, the purpose of developing walkable urbanism is to allow for walking to be the *preferred* method for the majority of trips from a residence. The resulting density where walkable urbanism is achieved is when the net floor-area ratio (FAR)[2] is over 0.8 in a suburban town center or New Urbanism suburban project, 3.0 to 4.0 in a midsized downtown, and much higher in more intense downtowns like Manhattan, London, or Shanghai, possibly going as high as 40.0.

The only other alternative to walkable urbanism is drivable suburban development, which is the modular, car-based transportation form of metropolitan development—sprawl. Drivable suburban development does not allow for transportation options other than automobiles. Due to its low-density nature, this form of development does not support transit and there are generally no destinations that are walkable on a day-to-day basis. Drivable suburban development has been the basis of real estate finance over the past three generations. The FAR of conventional development is between 0.05 and 0.30.

The "Double Whammy" of Increased Costs and Risks of Walkable Urbanity

Walkable urban places generally cost more to develop and have higher financial risks than drivable suburban development. The primary reasons for the higher costs of walkable urban development include higher construction costs, building an urban product people are walking next to (as opposed to rapidly driving past), increased land costs, and the possible need for modified zoning. The increased risk for developers translates into higher financing costs. There are a number of reasons for this, some structural and some temporary, including not as much experience by investors in walkable urban projects, prices that may be higher than comparables in the market, need for a critical mass of mixed-use product to insure success which might not be in place yet, number of units or square footage delivered per phase may be larger than drivable suburban development, intensified NIMBY, not in my backyard, opposition and increased entitlement risk.

The net result of higher cost construction and perceived increased risk is that it is significantly more difficult to finance walkable urbanism. This is the ultimate double whammy; higher construction costs and higher financing costs to deliver what the market is demanding.

The Role of Patient Equity

Patient equity pays the increased costs and mitigates the risks of walkable urbanism. Patient capital is additive; it is layered on top of a conventional development budget, as shown in the example below.

	CONVENTIONAL PROJECT		WALKABLE URBAN PROJECT	
Conventional Equity	$200,000	20%	$200,000	16.6%
Debt	$800,000	80%	$800,000	66.7%
Patient Equity	$0	0%	$200,000	16.6%
Total	$1,000,000	100%	$1,200,000	100%

A development budget is comprised of equity and debt. The conventional equity expects a 20-30% IRR, has ownership of the project, provides the construction guarantee,[3] and generally is 20% plus or minus of the total development budget. When patient equity is added to the mix, the conventional equity takes a different role with a different return. When patient equity is provided, the conventional equity is referred to as "first-tranche" equity or mezzanine debt. In exchange for having additional equity in the project (the patient equity), which is behind the first-tranche equity in cash flow priority, and no financial guarantees of the construction loan (which the patient equity provides), it will receive a lower rate of return and no ownership. Instead, the first-tranche equity or mezzanine debt will receive 100% of the after-debt service cash flow until both the negotiated cumulative or noncumulative rate of return is achieved and the principle is returned. Currently first-tranche equity or mezzanine debt receives between 10% to 15% priority return.

With the retirement of the first-tranche equity, 100% of the after-debt service cash flow of the project is available for the patient equity providers. It can be expected that first-tranche equity is retired between years three and seven of the project's life, so the patient equity providers have to wait until then for financial returns.

The conventional debt provided for the project with patient equity will probably stay about the same in absolute dollar terms, but will be a proportionally smaller piece of the total development budget, as shown above. This could result in a potentially major benefit. If the debt to value ratio drops from the conventional 80% to, say, 66% as shown in the example, there is the possibility that the bank will not require as much of a construction loan guarantee or any at all—i.e., it becomes a non-recourse loan. This is due to there being significant equity (patient equity plus first-tranche equity or mezzanine debt) in front of the debt on the project. While there is no established market for pricing the value of providing a construction guarantee, it is certainly worth at least 25% of the ownership in the project, and sometimes more. This is a considerable financial return to the developer if a construction guarantee is not required or even if the guarantee required can be negotiated to "burn off" faster than normal.

Return on Patient Equity

So why would a patient equity provider trade off the lower risk short-term return for a higher risk mid- to long-term return? Because there could be significantly higher cash flows as the project matures. Unlike drivable suburban development, where the cash flows have been hybridized to be front-end loaded, the result of lower construction costs and building simple commoditized conventional product types, it appears that cash flows from various forms of walkable urbanism get better over time. There is an *upward spiral* of value creation as the critical mass of the walkable place is achieved and enhanced. The reason this happens in walkable urban places is that *more is better*. As more development takes place within walking distance, there are more people on the street, rents and sales prices go up, resulting in land and building values to go up, resulting in tax revenues and cash

flow to go up, thus creating this upward spiral. Another term for this upward spiral in a reviving district, viewed either positively or negatively depending on who is using it, is gentrification. However, it generally takes time to achieve the critical mass or expand the walkable district, hence the time lag in cash flow generation.

There is anecdotal information that might point to the financial viability of walkable urban projects.

Reston Town Center

In the late 1980s, Mobil Land, the real estate subsidiary of Mobil Oil, owned the master-planned community of Reston, located in the state of Virginia on the Dulles Tollway in the Washington, D.C. metropolitan area (figure 2). At the intersection of Reston Parkway and the Dulles Tollway, a 200-plus or minus-acre (81 plus or minus hectares) greenfield site had always been planned for a town center for the master-planned community growing rapidly around it. The form that the town center took was unlike anything developed in the post-war era of the United States up until then. It is comprised of a main street with sidewalks and parallel parking on both sides of the street, the buildings coming right up to the sidewalks and

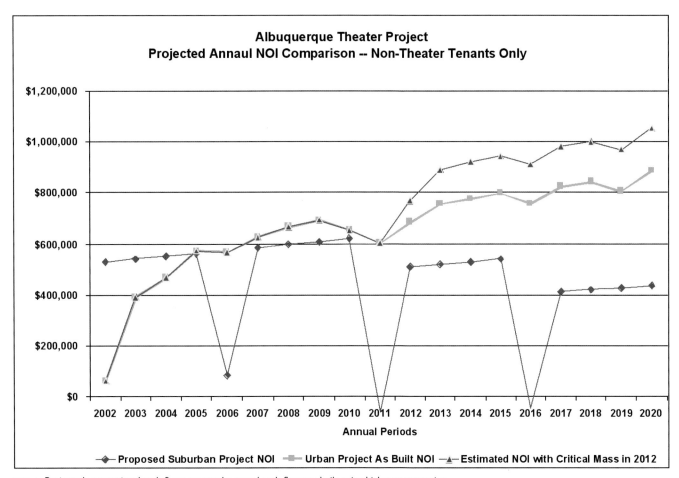

FIG. I Projected conventional cash flows versus the actual cash flows as built, using higher construction costs for nontheater portion of the Century Theatres Block, Albuquerque, New Mexico.

hidden, decked parking supporting the 770,000 square feet of office, hotel, and retail space developed in the first phase. When it opened in 1992, it immediately became a "place," achieving critical mass of walkable urbanism, such that it became a favorite destination for western Fairfax County residents as well as tenants. The second phase of 900,000 square feet of office space added in 1997 increased the walkability of the place. However, it was with the addition of thousands of condominiums and rental apartments, as well as additional office and retail space, in the late 1990s and early part of the 2000s, that confirmed Reston Town Center's role as a major regional-serving walkable urban place; what the current owner refers to as "a downtown for the twenty-first century."

An analysis of the entire investment over the life of the development has not been undertaken, due to multiple ownerships of Reston Town Center and the only recent recogni-

tion that Reston Town Center was the country's first lifestyle center and worthy of analysis. However, the current rental rates and sales prices demonstrate the premium that walkable urbanism commands.

Reston Town Center is the only walkable urban place in the market. The general Reston area and the Dulles Corridor require a car for all transportation needs, and are comprised of single-purpose product. Taking the midpoints of these rental and sales price ranges, they show a nearly 50% price premium for Reston Town Center over the rest of the market.

Century Theatres Block

The Historic District Improvement Company (HDIC) developed the Century Theatres Block in Albuquerque as the catalytic project starting the revitalization of the downtown area when it opened in November of 2001. The project consists of a 47,000 square foot, fourteen-screen movie theater, 25,000 square feet of retail, and 25,000 square feet of office space in a mixed-use, walkable form. Initially HDIC proposed a joint venture of the project with a major international development firm and financial projections were produced by that firm. These projections assumed conventional suburban construction quality and tenant improvements as well as suburban rental rates.

	OFFICE		CONDO-MINIUM	RETAIL
	Rents/SF	Vacancy	Rents/SF	Rents/SF
Reston Town Center	$40–45 (gross)	0%	$550–575	$50–60 (triple net)
General Reston Area	Mid $30s	3%	$340–475	$35–40
Dulles Corridor	High $20s	12%	No product	Mid $30s

FIG. 2 Market Street, Reston Town Center, Virginia.

FIG. 3 Cahill Park, Avalon, San Jose, California.

It became obvious to HDIC that the construction quality of the joint venture development as proposed would not be sufficient for the project to catalyze the revitalization of downtown. The conclusion was reached that conventional suburban quality development would not be appropriate, and the joint venture was dissolved in a friendly manner. HDIC became the sole developer and built a project that had a 40% higher construction and tenant improvement budget than the conventional budget. This required additional equity; patient equity. The development budget became 5% conventional equity, 67% debt, and 27% patient equity. The patient equity included HDIC cash, land, structured parking, and developer fees. It achieved developer nirvana; the construction loan was nonrecourse due to the high proportion of equity.

The resulting comparative cash flows between the conventional joint venture development and the actual results are shown in a chart (figure 1). Only the nontheater cash flows are shown, because the theater construction costs and lease were the same under both scenarios.

As can be seen, the early actual returns were in fact lower than the conventional projections. However, the cash flows have recently surpassed the conventional projections, and seem set to significantly surpass the conventional projections in the future. The primary reason for this is that the achieved rents were much higher than were conventionally projected, pointing to the pent-up demand for a higher quality, walkable product. However, the short-term returns were lower because the development budget was so much higher.

In addition, most of these early cash flows were dedicated to the repayment of the principle and interest of the conventional equity providers. The conventional equity providers should be completely paid off by 2007 and nearly 100% of the cash flow will then accrue to HDIC. The control and ownership of the project is firmly held by HDIC so it will see the mid- to long-term cash flow the project is forecasting.

AvalonBay Communities, Inc.

Going public as a REIT (Real Estate Investment Trust) in 1993 as a spin-off of Trammel Crow Residential, Avalon-Bay has always concentrated on building and owning rental apartment projects in markets with "high barriers to entry." Many times that has taken the form of developing and owning in walkable urban districts, such as downtown Stamford, Connecticut and San Francisco, or transit-oriented Ballston on a metro line in the Washington, D.C. area. As a result, over half of the portfolio is in walkable urban locations. Combined with an acknowledged outstanding management team, the walkable urban portfolio has resulted in AvalonBay being one of the highest regarded rental apartment REITs in the United States. It has consistently been the most profitable apartment REIT as well as providing the highest shareholder return for apartment REITs. As a leading investment analyst said, "AvalonBay is my favorite pick in the apartment sector." AvalonBay achieved this superior long-term financial performance while also having to satisfy the short-term returns that same investment analyst was constantly demanding, which was quite a feat (figure 3).

Sources and Providers of Patient Equity

There are many sources of patient equity. These sources include land/buildings, developer fees, parking improvements, off-site improvements, professional fees, and (always preferred) cash. The providers of patient equity are broad-based. They include land/building owners, the project's developer, investment allocated to venture capital by institutions, REITs with strong current cash flow, individual investors, nonprofits (especially if long-term oriented investment might fit the mission of the nonprofit), and state and local governments.

The percentage of patient equity that should be invested in a project, as a percent of the total development budget, will naturally vary from project to project. However, experience seems to indicate that somewhere in the 10–30% of the total development budget should be patient. The increased patient equity in a walkable urban project is used to increase construction quality, pay for the increased time to obtain entitlements, and for the other reasons walkable urban development costs more than drivable suburban development. The patient equity lowers the inherent risk of developing walkable, mixed-use projects and places. Having the project less leveraged may result in less of a need or no need for a construction loan guarantee, allowing the patient equity providers to own more of the project and sleep better at night. The developer of a project with patient equity has a much better opportunity to maintain ownership, not having to sell the project to cash out the conventional equity provider, as is often the case.

Most walkable urban projects probably employ more patient equity today than their developers recognize upfront, since it seems to be a requirement for mixed-use, walkable projects. However, investing patient equity was not what most developers set out to do; the project just required it, so it was put into the deal incrementally. It is time to recognize that patient equity is a necessity and should be planned for upfront. The need for patient equity to create special walkable places the market is demanding also creates cash flow potential for years to come. We might just see real estate become a long-term asset class once again.

A CHANGED FOCUS ON RETAIL AND ITS IMPLICATIONS ON PLANNING

ANDERS ALMÉR

A street with shops on the ground floor and a mix of apartments and workplaces above is the ideal city core setting for many planners, not only those who call themselves New Urbanists. The planners like the attraction of retail, making the city scene lively. As much as they like small shops in the center they dislike the big-box retail units on the outskirts of town, though the boxes are accepted as openers to new development areas. In this dispute you seldom hear why the retail industry has changed and why it looks like it does today. A better understanding of the driving forces of retail industry could make future development areas, including retail, both flexible and financially sound.

Retail planning and city planning were once more or less the same. Cities were formed around marketplaces. Today retail planning is ahead of city planning, and it is now more difficult to encompass it in an urban structure. New driving forces have changed the retail landscape over the years, at an ever-increasing tempo. Some of the inventions behind the change are the bar code, information technology in general, the internet, brand retailing, and new financial instruments.

These driving forces are the prerequisite for planning and construction of large retail buildings, which often result in the same cloned and boring environment. It is, however, possible to implement a planning foresight that could create flexibility for future use and also be sound investment logic.

Disruptive Changes

The history of modern retailing has seen some changes that have altered the fundamental economics of the industry, causing changes that C. M. Christensen and Richard Tedlow call disruptive.[1] The first was the emergence of the department store, the second was the mail-order catalogue, and the third was discount department stores.

They all changed the relation between the margins stores can earn and the frequency with which they can turn their inventory over. The fourth, upcoming disruptive change will probably be internet retailing. Still, all these disruptive changes occurred within the industry itself, adding to its productivity.

The emergence of so-called big-box retailing has changed our perspective of what retailing is, and we instinctively feel we have to protect the small shop operator against this threat. It is therefore perhaps difficult to acknowledge that these big formats are one of the reasons for the productivity gain in the whole economy. In an article in the *Financial Times*, Cris Giles claims that in the past decade, the productivity in the United States economy has moved ahead of Europe. This is due to the development in just three industries; retail, wholesale, and finance. In retail the United States's advantage is almost entirely due to the building of new shops and the closure of existing stores that had become uncompetitive. "The Wal-Mart effect, in other words, transformed the United States economy as much as it transformed the United States landscape."[2]

According to a study from the Swedish Institute for Growth Policy Studies, the development in the retail sector is in many ways conditional on the introduction and the large-scale dissemination of information technology. Information technology has increased quality and productivity in all stages of the distribution chain.[3] Gross investment in the retail industry was 60% higher in 2001 compared to 1994, which made this industry much more capital-intensive. The investigation also concludes that the increased productivity in Swedish retail is not as high as in the United States, but is significantly higher than the European Union. Contrary to what has happened in Europe and the United States, retail employment has not increased in Sweden.

Big-box retail thus plays an important role for general productivity gains. One reason why so many feel an antipathy toward this form of retail is perhaps the role especially planners and architects assign to retail—its assumed role of creating lively streets or places. The scenarios presented are often illustrated with images depicting the life in boulevards in nineteenth-century cities. This is not the true face of retail today, not even in the cities where most illustrations arise.

The Retail Format's Life Span Gets Shorter

The life span of the retail format has become shorter. To anticipate that is of great importance to the owner of the property, who very often is not the retail operator. An analysis of large, single format retailers showed that between 1986–1990 the earnings growth rate was much higher in the first years, but after that decreased sharply compared to what happened twenty years before.[4] The reason behind this development has been discussed, and the most likely is the claim that it is an effect of brands competition. The important thing is, however, that the shorter life span makes retail property investment a more risky business, and therefore demands more flexibility.

The Financial Focus

The most well-known shopping center developer in the United States after Victor Gruen was perhaps James Rouse. James Rouse was behind centers like Fanueil Hall Market in Boston and South Street Seaport in New York, but also Columbia, Maryland. Columbia was an attempt to build a city with inspiration from European, and especially Scandinavian, cities. But Rouse also understood that money could come as easily from managing shopping centers, even more so than it could from selling goods [5]

Today new financial instruments and information technology makes that process even easier. The focus has shifted to finance. Saskia Sassen has described that process:

> Financial services firms have invented instruments that liquefy real estate, thereby facilitating investments and circulation of these instruments in global markets. Yet part of what constitutes real estate remains very physical. At the same time, however, that which remains physical has been transformed by the fact that it is represented by highly liquid instruments that can circulate in global markets. It may look the same, it may involve the same brick and mortar, it may be new or old, but it is a transformed entity.[6]

Retail property is attractive because of the cash flow it generates, as well as its openness to change and possibilities to improvement if necessary. The tenants are often multistore brands, and often they are publicly noted on the stock market. The investors are big financial institutions and pension funds, who like the transparency, with the same tenants in all centers, and many centers constructed in much the same way. The investment is seldom long-sighted, and lasts, on average, five to seven years.

If we look at the life span of mass department stores we see that it was much shorter than the buildings they were using. Many city cores are still left with abandoned department stores, desperately turned into some *galleria*-inspired format. In the United States, and to an increasing degree in Europe, the shopping centers of the 1970s are too inflexible to meet the demands of the tenants. The traditional shopping center, or mall, became a commodity sometime in the 1980s in Europe.

The financial focus of big investors still causes the construction of obsolete retail structures: the imagined control and the size of the total investment can result in premature obsolescence—but by then investors may have found their exit.

Consumers

Consumers are revolting against the widespread sameness. Trust in big brands is at an all-time low, and consumers are less likely to buy mass-produced and distributed merchandise. They are attracted to new innovative ways of communication, often with the involvement of artists and skilled designers. Future brand retail needs to be far more organic process. Due to online retailing speeding up the process of basic purchasing, consumers now have more available time. With the emphasis placed on the physical experience, providing the desire for a customer to have a grand interaction has become an art form in itself. New consumer behavior is increasing the complexity of retail center management, which in turn demands a more flexible structure of the centers.

Brands

What James Rouse created with his Festival Centers (Fanueil Hall) was an urban environment in the center. Fanueil Hall is situated near the Charles River in downtown Boston. This might have been done due to his ambitions as a city builder. What he created was something well in line with what modern brand retailing wants. The setting has become much more important, primarily due to the emergence of strong brands. This kind of retail is taking over certain social relations and, in a smaller scale, creates communities. The brand is not a direct tool to sell a product: rather, it provides an environment, an ambience, which anticipates and programs the agency of consumers.

Adam Andersson, at the University of Copenhagen, writes with regard to brands that "today the value of brands. . . builds only in part on the qualities of products. To a great extent it is also based on values, commitments, and forms of community sustained by consumers. This way, brands are mechanisms that enable a direct valorization of people's ability to create trust, affect, and shared meanings: their ability to create something in common."[7]

The brands make it possible to create environments of different kinds. To the consumers the constructed environments fill the same needs as the real cities. Graham and Marwin call it instrumental urbanism.[8]

The Cloning Effect

The tenants in the malls tend to become the same all over the world. They are ranked and measured, and are regarded as a quantified risk of a certain degree. A local store is a higher risk as a tenant, as they do not have a record. Based on these

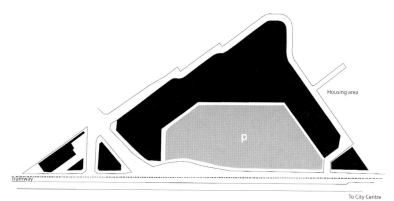

FIG. 1 This master plan for a major city in Poland focuses on a big-box retail store and parking.

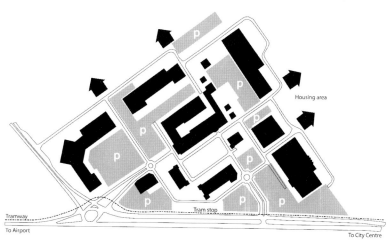

FIG. 2 An alternative plan for the same site in Poland divides the site into smaller parcels with a grid structure. A tram line connects a smaller town with the center of the major city.

assumptions, it is logical to assemble the well-known tenants in an enclosed building with total control of the shopping environment. The center then theoretically becomes an investment vehicle that can be monitored from far away.

The physical reality of the center will, however, create substantial problems when retail format life spans change. If the encapsulated operations of the tenants cannot just be replaced by other operations, then the whole building becomes obsolete. This is where the retail-park format can offer a better solution, because it is better suited to integrate with the local market.

Retail Parks

After the fall of the Berlin Wall an invasion led by the big retailers and their investors took place in Eastern Europe. The big-box concept was carried out in an unprecedented way, and few regulations made a hindrance to the process. The result is the same neglect to encompass the boxes within the city structure that surrounded them. Still, the boxes are today's version of retail—one that we have to live with until the internet offers a different option.

The boxes in a retail-park format can, however, be a point of origin for place building in the suburbs, if that it is what is planned from the beginning. The following example, from a major city in Poland, shows the first master plan (figure 1). The triangular shape of the site allows for building 90,000 square meters (approximately 900,000 square feet)

in one banana-shaped building. In front of it you have room for 7,000 parking places.

A small team made an alternative plan (figure 2). The site was divided in smaller places with a grid structure. Along the baseline there is a tram line connecting an important small town with the center of the major city. The tram was considered important from the beginning. Today there is an European Union-financed project to make it a light–rail line. From the tram station a pedestrian walkway through the retail park was planned. The grid structure also foresees future development outside the plot where internal roads can connect. The structure of the center gives it a flexibility to change the content of the buildings much more easily than it would have been if it were in more or less one big building. Maybe in the future some of the buildings could be turned into housing, considering the connections by the tram line. For the investor, which in this case is a long-term investor, such flexibility is of the utmost importance.

One of the basic ideas behind the New Urbanism movement is that planning should support the possibilities for entrepreneurs and small shops to help people to create jobs for themselves and others. The idea described above opens the retail park to its surrounding areas, where the traffic generated can benefit smaller ventures. The illusory control the investors ask for by making big malls with walls closed to the surroundings is most certainly outweighed by the flexibility offered in this model: a flexibility that should appeal not only to investors, but also to city planners.

THE ROLE OF CULTURE
IN URBAN DEVELOPMENT

GÖRAN CARS

1. Structural Change and Urban Development

Structural changes in society have led to an increased competition between cities and regions. Because of this competition, new and different assets are necessary for gaining a competitive advantage.[1] During the Fordist era the places individuals chose to live and frequent were, to a large extent, based on accessibility to work opportunities. Today these decisions are often based on other conditions, such as the image of a particular area and what it can offer in terms of quality of life. Factors contributing to quality of life are, for example, the standard of public services, the housing market, local governance capacity, access to nature, historical heritage, educational and cultural institutions, etc. As law states, cities are today forced to become more entrepreneurial than in previous decades.[2] Local governments today face greater pressure to develop strategies to make their cities more attractive and competitive.[3] Leisure and tourism have become increasingly important, both as replacements for activities in decline and as assets in strategies to raise a city's profile and create a positive image.[4] Of course, some cities have initial advantages in this respect. Others, as stated by Jewson and MacGregor[5] and King,[6] "have to be more creative in inventing, or re-presenting their charms."

In the processes of establishing or developing a positive image, both winners and losers can be identified. Many factors can contribute to explaining success or failure. One observation made in Sweden, which coincides with observations made in other European countries, is that culture plays a significant role in this respect. In many cities that have experienced growth and development, explicit cultural policies have been recognized as vital ingredients in the urban development strategy. Urban development is often connected to cultural institutions, arts, leisure, and consumer activities.[7]

The aim of this essay is to illuminate and discuss the role of culture in urban development. Special attention is paid to the impact of these cultural activities and institutions regarding economic aspects, city image, and social, economic, and image aspects on areas/districts adjacent to the cultural attraction.

2. Culture and Urban Development

New Actors Shaping the Cultural Sector

Parallel to the growing understanding of the important role of culture in urban and regional development, there has been a change in the financing and management of cultural institutions and activities in most developed countries. During the last few decades, policies that restrict spending in this arena have become common. The public budget for supporting or initiating cultural activities has shrunk. Cultural activities and institutions are expected to bear their own costs to a much greater extent than previously, and private actors have gained an important role in the financing and running of cultural institutions. Simultaneously, public institutions have often developed a more entrepreneurial approach towards culture and tourism activities in order to increase the financial contribution of tourism to government income. Thus, local governments are increasingly involved in promoting and marketing their cities as destinations to attract visitors. It is also more common that this development of attractions is created in conjunction with the private sector.

This is a tendency that can be recognized in many policy areas and issues related to urban development, and is often labeled as a shift from government to governance.[8] In the following sections the potential impacts of culture on urban development are discussed.

Economic Impact

The observations made concerning the potential positive impact of culture on urban development have paved the way for raising expectations that cultural activities and institutions might bring about positive economic impact for a city. Research and experience certainly exists that confirms the positive economic effects of culture. It is often stated that cultural activities and institutions generate income, employment, and economic growth by attracting visitors and tourists to a city or a region. Besides visiting cultural attractions, which often were the main objective for visiting the city, visitors can generate economic activity in other ways, such as travel, shopping, lodging, and food and drink. Today,

FIG. 1 Recent housing project in Stockholm. Housing is not only a roof over your head. Cultural and esthetic qualities are important for residents' well-being.

tourism is often considered one of the world's most important economic sectors, showing a high growth rate.[9] One way in which cultural activities might lead to positive economic effects is by creating jobs in the cultural sector. In Europe a well-known study examined the role of the cultural sector in the German region of North Rhine Westphalia. The study revealed that cultural industries employed about 5% of the labor force, and were growing faster than other industries.[10] However, the cultural sector's impact on employment extends far beyond straightforward employment within the cultural sector. Cultural activities often influence other sectors of the economy; for instance, visitors to a music festival will likely spend money on travel, accommodation, food, and shopping. All these activities are directly linked to the cultural activity, as they would not have happened if the cultural event did not exist. As will be shown below, these widespread effects are of economically considerable size.

However, uncertainties remain concerning these positive effects of culture. Do they always exist? Are they direct or indirect? Do they depend on the kind of cultural activity, or the specific urban context? One can question if the positive effect is a total effect of economic growth or a matter of redis-

tribution between different sectors in the urban economy. In other words, the general conditions concerning the impact of culture on economic growth are not satisfactorily elucidated. Bianchini emphasizes that the *direct* economic effects of cultural investments are often limited. His research on culture in Western Europe points instead at the important *indirect* effects of cultural activities and cultural investments, not least by improving the image of a certain city or region—something that, in turn, might imply better chances of attracting residents, businesses, and visitors.[11]

Thus, the notion that cultural activities and institutions have a positive impact, be it direct or indirect, on the economic growth of a city and a region seem to be quite common. During the last decades, so-called urban tourism has evolved into an important growth and development strategy for cities. Applying this strategy, cities are increasingly moving from the simple idea of advertising a few attractions to mobilizing a comprehensive approach of the city as a product. An important aspect when "selling the city" is to find the unique selling point—the features that stimulate the desire for people to travel and visit the city.[12] It is, however, difficult to plan the tourism industry because of its

FIG. 2 Hornsgatan in Stockholm. Culture in various forms plays a vital role in neighborhood regeneration.

fragmented nature. It is difficult to determine which resources the local residents use and which are used by tourists. Also, the proportional importance that tourists have on different markets varies from activity to activity. This may have an impact on how willing actors are to enter in a partnership around this issue.[13]

Also worth noting is that a rapid growth of tourism does not per se lead to investments in cultural and other activities which attract visitors. A problem lies in the difference between the investments necessary and the revenues generated. This dilemma is illustrated by a study of Venice, where tourists spend 2% of their money on culture, while the bulk (66%) is spent on accommodation and shopping.[14] The question is, of course, how many tourists would come to Venice if the cultural heritage of the city did not exist. The dilemma of matching investments and revenues will be discussed in the concluding section of this paper.

2.3 City Image, Civic Pride, and Identity
In our globalized world, characterized by fast change and international trends, local identity has become a key concern.

When new housing schemes, shopping malls, and hotels look the same whether they are located in Stockholm, Teheran, or Buenos Aires, culture gets to play an important role in safeguarding local culture. However, the balance between local culture and global trend is often hard to establish. As tourists we look for what is genuine—a monument, activity, or environment that is unique. However, while many tourists seek the genuine and the unique, they often appreciate familiarity, such as having coffee at Starbucks, dinner in a Chinese restaurant, or Carlsberg beer in a British pub-style bar. This relationship between local and global, traditional and new, can also cause tension. Urban planning targeted at meeting the needs of both residents and visitors is faced with the challenging task of balancing local identity and international trends.

Thus, besides the economic impact of culture, it has been demonstrated that cultural activities and institutions can contribute to improving the city's image and strengthening civic pride and identity and thereby—as a consequence—improve the city's attractiveness for business investment, residents, and visitors.[15]

FIG. 3 Cafés, restaurants, and other meeting places provides space for social interaction, creativity, and urban development.

Appreciation of the image of a city varies from person to person, depending on many factors, including age, cultural background, and interests. Nevertheless, in general terms, some cities are associated with more positive attributes than others because they offer specific attractions such as good museums, fine-art galleries, or a nicely preserved historic heritage. But cities may enjoy a positive image despite lacking such outstanding and unique features. A good image may be based on the city offering a variety of attributes and attractions, which promotes the idea that the city offers a joint product. However, cities can also be associated with a negative image, such as industrial, ugly, crime ridden, and unsafe. Thus, images of cities vary. Equally relevant is that any such image is relative and fickle. Many cities constantly make efforts to improve their image by testing a variety of approaches ranging from pure marketing to spectacular events and substantial investments in traffic and other infrastructure systems. However, two approaches have been identified as more relevant than others in changing a city's image: special events, and the construction of landmark buildings[16]; both are directly related to culture and tourism.

Efforts to improve the city's image might involve conflicts. Potential conflict concerns the relationship between values held by residents versus the values held by visitors and tourists. For example, investments made to attract tourists can coincide with preferences held by residents. The investment that can contribute to local pride, identity, and self-esteem is strengthened as a result that more people are interested in and want to visit the city. However, the reverse may be the case, i.e., the preferences held by residents and visitors/tourists are contradictory, such as when residents assess tourist investments as threats to the quality of their space. Another possible conflict concerns local traditions being used for economic objectives. They can be oversimplified by being transformed to commodities where the local people regard themselves as products.[17]

3. Swedish Experiences and Concluding Remarks

Within the Department of Urban Studies at the Royal Institute three substantive case studies have been carried out con-

FIG. 4 No to mono-function. The Globe District in Stockholm mixes housing and work places with experiences, sports, and culture.

cerning the impact of culture on urban development.[18] The results provide clear indications that these cultural attractions have obvious consequences for the development of Stockholm. Our research has found evidence that illustrates the importance of attractions for attracting tourists to Stockholm, for establishing and further developing the image of the city; and for attracting visitors, residents, and businesses; and in other ways contributing to the social and economic development in specific areas or districts. The case studies provide convincing evidence that cultural attractions contribute significantly to urban development. Our research cannot, however, be used to make specific conclusions about the impact of culture on urban development. A cultural attraction

is likely to generate economic impact and have consequences for the development of the image of the city and of the specific area where the attraction is located. Most cultural attractions will also probably trigger other social consequences. But the size and the terms of all these impacts vary from case to case, and depend on both the specific urban context and on other preconditions for the cultural attraction in question.

In Sweden, as in many other countries, cultural issues are managed as a specific sector, separate from other urban development issues in public policy and planning. One general conclusion that can be drawn from the results of the three case studies is that this no longer can be seen as a rational and reasonable way of managing cultural issues in the urban context.

Cultural issues are of strategic importance for urban development, and should be dealt with as such. In conclusion, it could be stated that *it is a crucial task for every city to develop a well-thought-out cultural strategy*. There is a need for a more strategic response to realize the potential of culture in urban development. What is argued corresponds to the writings of Bianchini[19] and the Council of Europe.[20]

Thus, arguments could be raised in favor of the formulation of a strategy of *cultural planning*. Bianchini[21] presents this concept as one way to take into account culture in policy making. According to him, the cultural planning approach should adopt a territorial remit instead of the more traditional sectoral focus of cultural policies. By doing so, he wants to see "how the pool of cultural resources can contribute to the integrated development of a place."[22] He argues that cultural resources should be placed centrally on the policy-making table, and emphasizes that the cultural planning approach should be seen as a cultural approach to urban planning and policy, rather than a "planning of culture." In other words, the cultural planning approach is not about giving a central role only to cultural issues in planning and policy-making processes; it is rather about focusing questions on urban development. But since cultural issues have proven to be of such importance for urban development, they should reasonably be given a central position in this process.

Thus, our research provides arguments for forming coalitions between public and private actors, e.g., in some sort of partnership or cultural community with the joint task of developing a coherent strategy for cultural development. A flagship investment can in itself be an investment, which significantly impacts the city's image and attraction. However, far from all flagships are successful, and the market for flagships is limited. In our case studies much of the positive impacts of cultural investments can be related to a synergetic interplay between public and private actors, and between the investment as such and its surroundings. Our research also indicates that cultural investments per se are not profitable. There is no guarantee that they will have the positive impact that was hoped for when the investment was made. The degree of success or failure can to large extent be related to how well public and private actors manage to establish arenas for collaboration and strategy formulation. In this interplay the role of the public sector is to safeguard public, city, and long-term interests. These responsibilities include providing a framework within which development can take place, e.g., through zoning regulations and policies aimed at enabling incentives for private investment, improvements of the infrastructure systems and public space, and public investment in cultural activities supplementary to investments from the public sector.

Such a cultural planning approach could also involve specific considerations of which cultural institutions and activities should be supported by public resources. It should also include strategic concern aimed at promoting local economic development, taking into account the potential positive impacts that may or may not occur as a consequence of cultural investments. Strategies must also address issues concerning the social impact of investments in culture. It is important to analyze how cultural investments will impact the city district and adjacent city districts. According to Bianchini and his concept of *soft infrastructure*, which refers to the social and cultural networks and dynamics of a place,[23] culture has to be seen as a part of a society's soft infrastructure—the types of infrastructure that are crucial for any successful policy implementation. Following Bianchini, it should be emphasized that it is not only a matter of making instrumental use of cultural resources to reach noncultural goals; but it is also, crucial for local planners and policy makers to deepen their knowledge of the soft infrastructure that makes up the local culture. Such knowledge is fundamental for successful policy formulation and planning for urban development.

HERITAGE MANAGEMENT IN URBAN DEVELOPMENT PLANNING

KRISTER OLSSON

Introduction

The face of urban development and planning has changed significantly in the last few decades. In short, economic and cultural globalization, a growing competition between cities for investment, visitors and new inhabitants, and a transition in policy and decision making and implementation from government to governance, have altered the conditions for urban management and development. Furthermore, current societal development is challenging local identity and the sense of place. Consequently, the conditions for the management of cultural built heritage have also changed. Thus, traditional concepts of cultural heritage and their management are challenged by a new urban order. The issue raised in this article is how to take cultural built heritage into consideration in urban development planning under the new conditions that are at hand.

Urban Planning, New Urbanism, and Heritage

In contemporary urban development planning there is a strong focus on spatial re-creation of the existing urban landscape. Spatial activities include redevelopment of derelict industrial sites, refurbishment of suburbs, and city center makeovers. Central components of these undertakings are often the construction of flagship development projects, entertainment and cultural amenities (e.g., concert halls, museums, and sports arenas), and exclusive housing developments (e.g., waterfront housing). The cultural built heritage is often regarded as a set of monuments and historical areas, and is foremost, included in development planning as a resource for attracting tourists. In sum, spatial activities are often carried out with reference to specific consumer groups and their private consumption, rather than in the local common interest.

New Urbanism, as a trend in contemporary urban design, can be regarded as a spatial activity in many local development strategies. The basis for New Urbanism can be found in traditional premodern planning and building, and, moreover, it can encompass a conservation ambition. According to Kelbaugh, "any development that is faithful to the principles of the New Urbanism recognizes and celebrates what is unique about a place's history, culture, climate, and architecture."[1] Nevertheless, contemporary urban development planning is, in general, not occupied with the past and the existing urban landscape as a heritage, but is foremost concerned with new developments and reforming urban built structures.

Furthermore, it can be noted that urban development and planning, through international trends, results in architectural and commercial uniformity of many cities.[2] Likewise, the principles behind New Urbanism make it a fairly non-local movement. Consequently, localities as the basis for many urban development projects are uncertain. A direction towards sameness of places is further stressed by a strong conjunction between development planning and real estate development, which increasingly is in the hands of national and international developers rather than being local initiatives.

In sum, urban development planning is concerned with space rather than with place. In other words, localities and identity in a given urban context are under scrutiny for change rather than a prerequisite for planning and development. The specific cultural built heritage—the existing urban landscape and its local meanings—is then not an obvious concern or consideration as a resource for urban development planning. The role of cultural built heritage and heritage management in contemporary urban development and planning is quite uncertain.

New Perspectives on Cultural Built Heritage

In order to integrate the cultural built heritage as a resource in urban development planning, not only for attracting external markets (i.e., new inhabitants, investments, and visitors), but also for the benefit of internal markets (i.e., local populations), new perspectives in heritage management are necessary. Heritage management has by tradition been seen as an expert and public sector responsibility, and mainly as an issue for archaeologists, art historians, and architects. In general, the heritage management sector emphasizes the future existence of especially important objects and areas with historical and scientific value. Thus, it is organized, and includes a way of working, that primarily applies to the management of specific objects and well-defined areas. Heritage management has traditionally focused on legal regulation and economic incentives as a means of control and, hence, been based on an assumption of strong local governments and monolithic and rational public planning.[3]

However, due to societal development, the traditional concepts of cultural built heritage and heritage management are challenged. It has widely been recognized that various interests and perspectives include conflicting directions regarding the management of the urban environment, and the management of the cultural built heritage is no exception. Furthermore, the notion of development planning as an instrumental rational activity is more questioned than ever, acknowledging the turn from government to governance in planning, and an increasingly important role of private interests for implementation.[4]

Hence, how local cultural built heritage should be defined and valued, are not only questions for heritage and planning experts, but also important questions for local citizens. In particular, tangible and intangible values in the urban landscape are important for local citizens as carriers of meaning and identity. As Hayden pointed out, "Urban landscapes are storehouses for these social memories, because natural features such as hills and harbors, as well as streets, buildings, and patterns of settlement, frame the lives of many people and often outlast many lifetimes."[5]

Cultural Built Heritage As an Infrastructure

Normally, the development of the urban landscape is a slow and incremental process. Buildings and other built structures are constructed, and eventually rebuilt to fit new purposes or demolished and replaced. As time has passed, some buildings or defined structures in the urban landscape have come to qualify as monuments, and, hence, been chosen for conservation activities. However, a clear majority of the structures in the urban environment have not qualified as monuments and can be referred to as the general urban landscape. This general urban landscape includes a diverse set of artifacts that are spatially and/or socially linked together. From this point of departure, the issue for heritage management is to consider the urban landscape as a whole, not only monuments, but also modest buildings and the urban landscape, as such, as a cultural built heritage.

The urban landscape, seen as a cultural built heritage, is a complex system of buildings and other built structures. Consequently, a certain object within the system is to a substantial part defined and characterized by the environmental context. Each object has an external impact on the surround-

ings. This external effect can be negative or positive, and will indirectly impact the understanding and valuation of adjacent objects. In this way the surroundings, neighborhood, district, or city, add and compound the value of each object.

This system perspective gives a foundation in which to define the built environment, and the cultural built heritage, as an infrastructure. Apart from the system or network function, the built environment is characterized as an infrastructure by general use over time and multiple functions. General use over time means that it is possible to alter the function of the built environment over time. Multiple functions means that everyone close to a building or an area is able to use it, directly or indirectly, one way or another.[6]

In the above meaning, the cultural built heritage is defined as a public good. Hence, the consumption of the heritage by one individual does not prevent and exclude other individuals from the benefits of consumption. In this economic reasoning, the view on the cultural built heritage held by experts should not have more weight than the view of the average person.[7]

Heritage Management in Planning Practice

The above reasoning signifies that knowledge about individual preferences is critical for the definition and valuation of the urban landscape as a cultural built heritage, and for understanding its public-good characteristics. However, the cultural built heritage seen as a public good is in most planning activities, in practice, not fully acknowledged and understood. In practice, urban planning is still performed as an expert and instrumental rational activity, rather than based on communicative action as suggested by many contemporary planning theorists.[8]

In Olsson, an illustrative case is discussed.[9] In this case, from the Swedish city Umeå, three high-rise apartment buildings were considered for construction by the river within close distance from the city center. One argument for the project was to put the city on the map, as well as promote Umeå as a dynamic and future-oriented city. The planning and decision-making process saw opposition from a number of citizens who expected high-rise buildings to affect an adjacent nineteenth-century brewery and the city skyline in a negative way. However, a significantly larger group of citizens announced their interest in buying apartments in the planned high-rise buildings.

During the decision-making process a survey, directed to a random selection of 1,000 inhabitants in Umeå, was carried out for research reasons. The results were unambiguous and a strong majority of the respondents objected to high-rise buildings in this particular location. However, eventually the city council permitted the project, with direct reference to the consumer group who had announced their interest in buying the apartments (figure 1). In that sense, the decision makers reduced the urban environment to a private good, rather than seeing it as a resource for a wide group of local citizens, i.e., as a public good, as the survey indicated.

FIG. I High-rise apartment buildings by the river in Umeå, Sweden.

An important finding in the survey was that a specific built environment can have meaning for a much larger group of people than those who normally are invited or actually participate in the planning and decision-making process, i.e., neighbors and those directly affected. Hence, this indicates that the process, as it is currently performed, does not reflect and include citizens' views in a proper way. Consequently, the private-good characteristics of cultural built heritage are stressed in planning—not only by private actors, but also by public planners and decision makers.

It can be discussed whether a wide group of citizens can be expected to participate in a direct way in urban development planning. Citizen participation in a broad sense, by definition, is only a consideration when it comes to the public good. However, the problem, of course, is that there are no incentives for individuals to provide for public good. The paradox is that, the larger the group of people concerned, the fewer will act in order to provide the public good in question. Consequently, there is an expectation that the provision shall be organized within public planning. The question, then, is how to take the values held by local citizens into account in the planning practice? Hence, the issue is to capture the cultural built heritage as a public good.

A plan shows results from a survey in the Swedish city of Ystad, directed to a random selection of 1,000 inhabitants. In the questionnaire the respondents were asked to mark on maps, among other things, one area in the city where they would prefer to live (figure 2). The representation in the plan shows a pattern that is made up by overlapping individual answers, whereas single answers, not overlapping ones, are excluded since they can be regarded as accidental. The darker the representation on the map, the more overlapping answers. Consequently, the patterns in the plan represent areas in the urban landscape in Ystad with a strong common interest among the local population.

As far as understanding the public good in cultural built heritage, it is necessary to acknowledge that the whole is more than the sum of the parts. In that sense, the patterns visible in figure 2 represent certain aspects of the urban landscape as a public good, whereas individual answers, which together make up the patterns, merely represent the private interest of the individual.

Hence, this reasoning suggests that the identification of public-good characteristics in the urban landscape demand quantitative analysis. It is not enough to study a limited group of people, using qualitative methods (e.g., focus groups), in order to capture the public good, or in the case of development planning practice only to invite neighbors and other directly affected interests. Even though qualitative methods complement quantitative analysis in order to understand the specific meanings that are ascribed to different parts of the city, they do not, however, contribute to a systematic mapping of public-good characteristics of the urban landscape.

Concluding Remarks

The reasoning in this article points out that, in general, the public-good characteristics of the urban landscape and the cultural built heritage do not automatically emerge in urban development planning. The task for public planning, foremost in comprehensive planning, is to guard the public good in the cultural built heritage in a much better way than what is done today. In return, it means that in order to use the cultural built heritage as a resource in urban development, not only for attracting external markets, but also for the benefit of local populations, it is essential to develop new concepts of cultural built heritage and methods in heritage management. Hence, it is a question of considering qualities of place in the urban landscape and seeing the landscape as an infrastructure, comparable to other infrastructures. Furthermore, it is also part of the task to involve a wide group of local citizens, who demand a communicative response from heritage management acknowledging the public good characteristics of the urban landscape as a cultural built heritage.

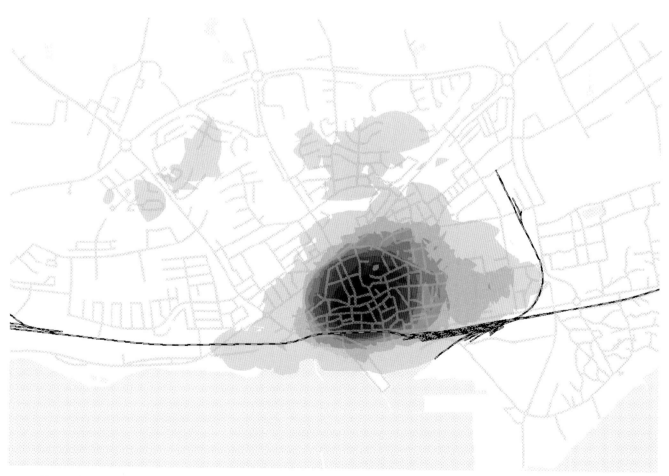

FIG. 2 Most preferred living areas in the city of Ystad, Sweden.

PART 7: SUSTAINABILITY, TECHNOLOGY, AND THE ENVIRONMENT

DOES NEW URBANISM REALLY OVERCOME AUTOMOBILE DEPENDENCE?

PETER NEWMAN

The rhetoric of New Urbanism is to build in a way that reduces automobile usage. This contribution evaluates Australian suburbs to show that while permeable street systems do indeed reduce car use the most significant impact will be on providing adequate density (at least thirty-five people and jobs per hectare) and adequate public transport (service at least every fifteen minutes, with evening and weekend services). The most powerful way to reduce car use is to build closer to the city center. If New Urbanism can help achieve these factors then it will help overcome automobile dependence, but if permeability alone is used there will be a growing integrity gap on car travel associated with such developments.

New Urbanism trumpets its credentials at reducing the dominance of automobiles in urban development. Such an aim is worthwhile in itself, but unless it can demonstrate that it works with its design criteria there will be credibility issues to address; Lee and Perl call this the "integrity gap."[1] This book seeks to push New Urbanism into greater integrity through taking what works and revising what doesn't; my contribution tries to push the transport agenda in New Urbanism.

Since we first defined automobile dependence in the 1980s, our work has been to collect data on cities, comparing their transport, land use, and infrastructure.[2] Recent data collection on Sydney and Melbourne has extended this approach so that we can now examine the same parameters at a local government or suburb level.[3] This is the scale at which New Urbanist developments focus, and hence it is possible to examine those areas that demonstrate New Urbanist ideals about permeability, density, mixed use, and transit, and compare them with those areas that don't display these characteristics as well. This will enable comparisons to be statistically significant, as there are not enough new New Urbanist developments yet to make quantitative comparisons.

My contribution will therefore examine small area data (local government scale in Sydney and Melbourne) for residential transport patterns, converted to transport energy and greenhouse gas per capita so that one overall parameter can be used to represent the transport impact of residents in a development. The parameters that are compared to this are:

- Permeability (the number of street intersections per hectare);
- Density of residents (population per hectare);
- Density of jobs (jobs per hectare, which is a way of measuring mixed use);
- A combination of these two called "activity intensity" (number of people and jobs per hectare);
- Distance from the central business district (CBD) (in kilometers); and
- Transit activity (a measure of how much of a local government/suburb has public transport services that are at least every fifteen minutes and where evening and weekend services exist).

The results show the following:

1. *Distance to the CBD is the dominant factor above all others (it explains 70% of the variance in Sydney, and 76% in Melbourne).* This means that a policy of building closer to the city will be the most important thing that can be done to respond to the problem of car dependence and its climate change/oil consumption outcomes. Of course the distance to the CBD contains within it a number of other parameters, but it offers a simple way to look at the first cut on the issue. Indeed, it is possible to make an easy calculation based only on where a development is located to predict its per capita greenhouse gases from transport. The formula is $y = x/10 + 3$, where y is the transport greenhouse gas in kilograms of CO_2 per person per day, and x is the kilometers from the CBD. It demonstrates very clearly that no matter what income levels people have in Australian cities it is where they live which will mostly determine their transport fuel use. Exurban peripheral areas have extremely high levels of transport where the highest users are similar in consumption of transport energy to some of the United States cities. The exurban areas, like Blue Mountains and Morn-

FIG. I Traditional centers based around walking are a minimum of a hundred people and jobs per hectare as in Copenhagen.

ington, therefore come out much higher than their distance alone would predict, probably as they have so few services.

2. *Activity intensity (population and jobs per ha) explains 56% of Melbourne's variance, and 71% in Sydney.* The central areas of the cities of Sydney and Melbourne, with their activity intensities of 100 and 330 per hectare, have very low fuel use; the city of Sydney has less transport fuel use than in Hong Kong (the lowest in our global sample of developed cities) as it is a dense, walking city. Inner suburbs like in the cities of Leichardt and Port Phillip, with activity intensities of 71 and 74 per hectare, have transport fuel use similar to European cities, as they are compact transit cities where most urban services are close by. Outer suburbs are similar in activity intensity (from 10 to 20 per hectare) and demonstrate high travel such as in car-dependent suburbs anywhere; they are in the range of United States cities. Exurban areas across Australian cities with densities around 5 to 7 per hectare demonstrate between two and ten times higher per capita travel than the rest of the urban areas. We have examined a range of these transport versus activity intensity graphs, and a common trait is that there seems to be a threshold of around thirty-five people and jobs per hectare, below which car dependence seems to be in-built. This is found to apply universally and is explored in terms of the travel time budget and access to services.[4]

3. *Transit activity is just as important in explaining travel patterns, with 61% in Melbourne and 58% in Sydney.* The areas of Melbourne with quality public transport (defined as not requiring a timetable, i.e., service at least once every fifteen minutes, and having evening and weekend services) follow the train and tram lines and some new bus lines. Those who live in such areas are fortunate to have options that most others across the city do not. That this can be seen to explain the broad sweep of travel, shows how important it is to provide more people with this option of service if the mold of car dependence is to be broken. The link is obviously close between the activity intensity and the public transport access parameters—the more people are able to live in areas with good transit, the more it will be used, and the more that it is used, the better the chance is of having a good service level.

4. *Permeability is also able to explain some of the variation, but it is a lesser factor, explaining 44% in Melbourne and 46% in Sydney.* Permeable street systems that enable people to move more directly through an area are likely to have less car use associated with them. The shorter distances are likely to mean that some walking trips become more viable, and also more transit services become possible. However, the data suggest that other factors by themselves are likely to be more important in reducing car use and facilitating other modes.

FIG. 2 Subcenters are a minimum of 35 people and jobs per hectare or else they are dominated by parking lots as in this Canberra shopping center.

These four urban design and planning parameters therefore emerge as the fundamental context for reducing automobile dependence. They mean that we must:

- Concentrate on redevelopment;
- Build densely in focused transit-oriented centers;
- Ensure transit is adequate for an increasing proportion of the city;
- Ensure permeable street systems through designing short blocks with many intersections.

If a New Urbanist development is being rationalized in a planning system on the basis of all these factors it is likely to be able to demonstrate a clear reduction in car use compared to any other kind of development. If they are well located then, these developments can be two to three times less car intensive as conventional developments on the fringe. The rhetoric of New Urbanism can therefore play a valuable role in helping a city find ways of reducing its ecological footprint while improving its liveability.[5]

If, however, developments are on new greenfield sites on the urban fringe, then it is going to be much harder to ensure real savings in car use occurances. These developments must ensure that all the factors of density, transit services, and permeability are provided otherwise it may not do much to reduce car use. Permeable street systems by themselves have sometimes been the only New Urbanist characteristic to survive a planning process in parts of Australia and the United States. These are likely to show less than 10% reductions in car use for the development, whereas if density and transit services can be adequately provided as well, then 30–40% reductions are possible.

GREEN URBANISM

A MANIFESTO FOR RE-EARTHING CITIES

TIMOTHY BEATLEY

Cities have historically been seen as opposed to or antithetical to nature and the natural environment. Cities and nature are, it is often believed, polar opposites, and modern cities popularly viewed as destructive of nature, gray and *natureless*, distinct and separate from natural systems. Green Urbanism rejects these historical perceptions, and argues that cities can be environmentally beneficial and restorative, full of nature, and are inherently embedded in complex natural systems.

What, more precisely, is meant by Green Urbanism, and what are its implications for urban design and planning? Green Urbanism is about city building in harmony with nature. It strives to minimize the ecological footprint of population and development and seeks to live lightly on the planet, incorporating green and ecological features as central design elements, while at the same time creating just and healthy places with a high quality of life. Green Urbanism is but one of a set of terms commonly used in describing such places. Others include: ecological cities, green cities, and sustainable cities, and there are increasing numbers of voices around the world arguing in favor of the vision I espouse here.[1]

Green Urbanism argues that cities can and must be *green*, both in the sense of making nature present (parks, forests, green rooftops) and in the broader ecological or resource-conserving sense (e.g., using small amounts of energy, reducing emissions of CO_2). The combining of the terms "green" and "urban" also makes the important statement that green design ideas, practices, and technologies can be applied very effectively within cities. Indeed, Green Urbanism calls for readjusting the agenda of environmentalism, to explicitly acknowledge the already considerable environmental benefits of city life (figure 1).

Green Urbanism envisions cities that function organically and embrace natural principles. Green architect William McDonough uses the metaphor of a tree to describe how ecological buildings should be designed and function. Green urban places, or green cities, by extension should be seen to function as forests do—powered by the sun, recycling the earth's nutrients and materials (there is nothing wasted in nature), cleansing air and water, and restorative (not destructive) of natural systems. And, like forests, cities provide beautiful shelter and habitat for humans and other species.[2]

While there is no complete consensus about what Green Urbanism looks like or entails, or what an ecological city is, the following are consistently cited qualities:

FIG. I The creative work of urban water-designer Herbert Drieseitl. The steps of the town hall in Hattersheim, Germany, have been converted into a gurgling flow-form, returning the sounds and rythmes of moving water to this town center. This urban water feature meanders through the town plaza and eventually becomes a more natural stream at the town's edge.

FIG. 2 Few pedestrian centers are as attractive or as green as this one in Kaunas, Lithuania. This pedestrian promenade extends for almost three kilometers and contains five hundred trees, an urban forest that is a significant part of the draw of this delightful pedestrian space.

Compact, Walkable Cities

Green Urbanism seeks a compact, land-efficient urban form, highly walkable and where activities and uses are mixed to a large degree (figure 2). A major goal of Green Urbanism is to overcome the wastefulness and environmental damage associated with urban sprawl. Compactness not only conserves precious land, but it also makes possible many of the other technologies and living strategies that allow cities to be more sustainable, such as public transit and district heating.[3] And at a time when the long-term health and social consequences of sedentary and car-dependent lifestyles are becoming ever clearer, walkable green cities offer a hopeful antidote. Restoring a walking culture, moreover, will be an essential ingredient in achieving many of the other green urban goals espoused here—restoring deeper connections to place, reconnecting us to nature and natural environments, for instance—all of which are nearly impossible in living environments that require even more time in cars.

Green, Organic Urban Environments

Green Urbanism seeks to bring nature into cities, and to restore, nurture, and celebrate urban ecology. Important green-urban strategies include creating parks, forests, and green spaces throughout the city (and region). Significant greening can also occur at the level of the neighborhood, block, and individual buildings, together creating an interconnected urban ecological network. Green urban neighborhoods include such things as trees, community gardens, restored streams, buildings with rooftop gardens or eco-roofs, vegetated walls and facades, and other natural features. Such green neighborhood features serve many functions at once: they provide bird and wildlife habitat, sequester carbon and reduce energy consumption, cool the urban environment (respond to urban heat island effect), contain and treat storm water, and add immense beauty to cities, among other benefits (figure 3).

In the United States the growing interest in green or ecological rooftops is an encouraging trend. Chicago mayor Richard Daley led the way by retrofitting his city hall roof with a 20,000-square-foot green rooftop, creating a marvelous urban habitat and amenity, and stimulating interest in green rooftops that has seen more than 250 ones installed, or in progress in that city in a relatively short period of time. The fourth annual Green Roofs for Healthy Cities national

FIG. 3 The Eilenriede Forest in the very center of Hannover, Germany, is part of an extensive network of large green spaces that provide beauty and respite to residents and also provide many ecological services to the region.

FIG. 4 Ecological rooftops, like this one in central Amsterdam, provide many benefits: they retain storm water, insulate and reduce energy consumption, provide habitat, sequester carbon, and add beauty to cities.

FIG. 5 In cities like Chicago, institutional rooftops (libraries, museums, etc.) are increasingly viewed as opportunities to generate power. Here, the rooftop of the Chicago Center for Green Technology, supports an extensive array of photovoltaics.

conference was recently held in Boston, and the green urban idea is on its way to becoming mainstream design and development (figure 4).

There are, of course, many outstanding examples of integrating green elements into dense urban environments. The green bridge in London connects two parks with mature trees and greenery. In Stockholm's new Hammarby Sjöstad, two eco-ducts cover roads and provide green connections. The recent daylighting (bringing back to the surface) of a portion of Ravenna Creek in Seattle, and many other cities, is another example. Much of the agenda is about ecological repair, and about rethinking urban infrastructure. Green streets, where some amount of automobiles and roadway space is given over to urban forests, community food production, and rain gardens, have been planned and built in a number of cities as an alternative form of infrastructure.[4]

Biophilic Urbanism

Green Urbanism also argues for a kind of biophilic urbanism that acknowledges the profound need for connections with nature and other forms of life—a key and important finding of the work of Harvard biologist E. O. Wilson, who coined the term *biophilia*.[5] We are hardwired as a species to need these connections, and cities can and should be increasingly

designed to facilitate them. The research has now compellingly demonstrated the value and need for exposure to nature in everyday life, and the need to design-in opportunities for daily interaction and exposure.[6] In the United States, Richard Louv's recent book, *Last Child in the Woods*, has set off an extensive (and, I believe, useful) national debate about the increasingly "de-natured" ways in which kids are growing up today, a phenomenon Louv describes as "nature-deficit disorder."[7] Little outside play and declining access, for a variety of reasons, to the forests, fields, and urban streams that were the playgrounds for many of us growing up, represent a diminished and troubling developmental path for kids today, one that does not bode well for the future care and stewardship of our communities and landscapes.

Cities Powered By the Sun

Cities must lead the way to a world profoundly less dependent on fossil fuels, and Green Urbanism argues for a sharply different model of energy production. Cities, and the buildings, homes, and facilities that comprise them, must be designed to dramatically reduce the energy they need, and to produce the remaining energy required through solar and other renewable technologies (figure 5). In an important way this is another strategy for re-earthing. This will begin

FIG. 6 At the Beddington Zero-Energy Development, or BedZED, in London, living spaces are south-facing and require little energy. Natural ventilation, thermal mass, and photovaltaics are utilized, as well as locally-sourced wood and building materials.

by using passive solar design and incorporating full spectrum natural daylight into every structure (especially buildings like schools). The economic and health benefits alone are undeniable. Furthermore, cities can become the location for the production of energy from renewable sources—wind, solar, biomass—integrated into the urban fabric. The western harbor district in Malmö, Sweden, Vastra Hamnen, is a positive example. Here energy needs are provided locally through renewable means, including the use of facade-mounted solar hot water heating panels, feeding into a district heating system. All future urban development and growth should strive to be energy balanced—that is, producing at least as much energy as it needs—and carbon neutral.

Cities and urban leadership are beginning to understand this need to tackle fossil fuel dependence and climate change. In June, 2006, the United States Conference of Mayors adopted the so-called "2030 Challenge;" this represents a commitment to reduce the greenhouse gas emissions from all new city building immediately by 50%, and by 2030 to ensure that all new buildings are carbon neutral.

Circular Metabolism
Ecological cities are cities that recognize a complex flow of inputs (food, energy) and outputs (waste, pollution) associated with urban life; they aim for a balanced system of eco-cycles, or a circular metabolism, in which the flow of inputs and outputs is minimized and wherein the outputs (wastes) become productive inputs to something else. Part of the paradigm change needed is simply an adjustment of our mental model of cities, but there are of course many things that can be done to put circular metabolism into practice. Good examples already exist. Hammarby Sjöstad, in Stockholm, takes an orientation based explicitly eco-cycles, for instance. Here, for example, biogas is extracted from household waste-water and returned to the neighborhood as cooking fuel. At a city level, more than thirty buses in Stockholm run on bio-gas similarly extracted from waste.

Cities of Abundance: the Bounty of Cities
Green Urbanism recognizes the importance of reducing the influx and long transport of many goods and materials that are needed and desired by urban residents. Cities are not just black holes, sucking in and consuming countless resources and materials from around the globe—they are, rather, places inherently capable of producing much of what urban life requires.

Few cities can be truly self-sufficient, but an important goal of a green city is to produce as many of its necessities

FIG. 7 In the car-free center of the GLW-Terrein project in Amsterdam, there are some three hundred garden plots available to residents interested in growing flowers and vegetables.

locally or regionally. Consumption is kept close to production, minimizing the environmental costs of transporting and transmitting, and encouraging more responsible, less environmentally damaging forms of production. Recent ecological projects like BedZED—the Beddington Zero Energy Development—in London, offer positive examples (figure 6). Here, about half of the building materials for this new neighborhood were derived from within a thirty-five-mile radius, including wood from local council forests and street trimmings, and brick from a local brick factory.

Cities, moreover, can be producing much more of the food they need (figure 7). New ecological districts, like Viikki in Helsinki, show how community food production can be designed in from the beginning (in the form of lovely green fingers between blocks of flats). The Mole Hill urban revitalization project in Vancouver is another example. Here, an urban alley has been creatively converted into a traffic-calmed community space, with edible bushes and landscaping throughout, and raised-bed community gardens where car parking spaces were formerly located. Urban agriculture holds much promise—from intensive commercial food production on vacant lots in downtown Chicago, to rice paddies on high-rise buildings in Tokyo—for profoundly reducing the miles traveled by food (now on average more than 1,500 miles from producer to consumer).

Sustainable and Green Mobility

Green urban places put priority on less environmentally damaging forms of mobility, with emphasis on good public transit, bicycles, and walking.[8] Land use and development decisions in these cities are coordinated with transit investments so that new residents have viable, affordable alternatives to the automobile. Green cities are bicycle-friendly cities, incorporating bicycles into the design of new housing areas, for instance, and generally working to make it easier and safer to ride a bicycle (with infrastructure such as bike lanes, bikeways, and protected bicycle parking facilities). Great bicycle-friendly cities like Copenhagen show the way. There, almost 40% (and rising) of home-to-work trips are made on bicycles, the result of explicit urban policy and considerable public investment. Its newest initiative is the establishment of a network of green cycle routes, where bicyclists commute along green corridors that provide direct connections away from car traffic.

Green cities permit and encourage walking through the creation of pedestrian-only areas, mixing of land uses, traffic-calming design, and emphasis on proximity over mobility. A trend in European green cities is the design and building of car-free (or car-limited) housing districts where new residents are prohibited or economically discouraged from owning a car.[9] Green urban places seek to adjust subsidies and incentives so as to level the economic playing field between auto and nonauto transport (e.g., reducing cost of transit while increasing charges for car parking).

Ecological Economies

Green Urbanism also supports more ecologically restorative forms of industry and commerce. This can take many forms, but includes locally-owned and managed green businesses, industries and commerce that are resource efficient and that minimize waste and pollution (and where industrial symbiosis is possible; that is, where the wastes from one industry can be used as productive inputs to another); and industries and commercial activities that utilize sustainably harvested and managed resources, and that substitute local goods for imports (e.g., food, material, and energy imported from far away). Green Urbanism embraces a variety of sustainable economic development strategies, including eco-industrial parks, green business's incubators, micro-credit programs, and programs to provide technical support for, and public recognition, of green businesses (e.g., Portland, Oregon's program Businesses for a Sustainable Tomorrow).

Ecological Governance

Green Urbanism calls for new ways of governing and managing cities. The condition and status of urban ecosystems, and the environmental impact of decisions made by city governments, become primary considerations in local decision making. Green cities take stock of their local environment, and the impact of local actions on the global environment, through a variety of tools, including state-of-environment reports, sustainability indicators, and ecological accounts. Ecological governance implies consideration in every decision or policy of their local and global impact, on the environment, the democratic involvement of citizens and neighborhoods in decision-making and governance, and an active program for educating the public about environmental issues and concerns. While many green urban decisions are best made at the local or municipal level, Green Urbanism also recognizes the need for governance structures at higher geographical levels, especially at the regional or bioregional level.

New Connections to Place and Environment

At the heart of many of these design and planning elements, from green streets to community gardens, is a sense of the need to reconnect to the places, environments, and landscapes in which we live, and in the process, to each other. Green Urbanism and the re-earthing of cities agenda is about reawakening our interest in the broader "home" in which we live, activating a sense of wonder about and interest in our environment, and nurturing an ethic of caring for these places. This is partly about physical design—reconnecting to our environment is difficult if it has been paved over or made invisible, or if it is difficult or impossible to visit or access. But the agenda is also broader, and involves the ways in which residents are living in these physical spaces, and their levels of knowledge, attitude, and interest they

bring to them. Re-earthing requires more, I believe, and demands an effort to educate and activate the latent biophilic virtues and impulses people hold. This can happen in many creative ways. One idea that I have been advocating is the notion of an "ecological owner's manual" that would be given to every new homeowner or apartment resident. Such a guidebook might serve to inform them about the specific kinds of native flora and fauna in the neighborhood, and provide information about the watershed and bioregion in which the building sits. It might provide information about where and how household waste and wastewater is treated, and perhaps places for purchasing locally grown food, among other things. Accompanying it might be a (formatted) nature journal, in which residents are encouraged to join in the ancient practice of phenology—watching and recording seasonal changes—and, in this way, connecting to place and picking up on the native nuances of weather, ecology, and the nature around them.

FIG. 8 The new ecological redevelopment of the Western Harbor (Västra Hamnen) in Malmö, Sweden, set and achieved some ambitious green goals, including the goal of providing 100% of the power needed for the district from locally generated renewable energy. They reached this goal utilizing a range of energy ideas and technologies including these facade-mounted solar hot water panels that feed hot water into a district heating system.

Overcoming the Obstacles to Green Urbanism

There are many obstacles, to be sure, in a shift to a Green Urban paradigm in cities. Viewing cities as places that can be profoundly full of nature, seeing them embedded in complex ecosystems, and as a rich network of eco-cycle flow, will require a considerable shift in mentality on the part of elected officials and urban residents (figure 8). Some of the specific agenda items—be it green buildings, stream daylighting, or renewable energy technologies such as photovoltaics—will be objected to based on cost. Changing pricing structures, and leveling financial playing fields, will be necessary to counter some of these objections. Recognizing the artificially low cost of oil and fossil fuels generally (i.e., the price does not take into account the global climate change and other impacts on the environment), adopting carbon taxes, and a host of other equalizing incentives and subsidies will be needed. Many of the cities that have made the most progress in the direction of Green Urbanism have acknowledged the importance of investing in these longer term public infrastructures—public transit, renewable energy, and local farms and food production. Political leadership is a hallmark in cities that have advanced a green urban agenda, and will be increasingly needed, as well as efforts to overcome an often apathetic general public. New partnerships can and will form in green urban cities, recognizing the positive symbiotic connections between, for example, poverty reduction and local food production, solar and renewable energy and local economic development, and walkable communities and neighborhoods and public health, among others.

ECO-TECH URBANISM

TOWARD THE GREEN AND SMART CITY

DUSHKO BOGUNOVICH

The Issues of Separation and Scale

This is a plea for an ecologically sound urbanism based on combining the so-called green design and smart design paradigms into one. There is a need for this line of advocacy for two reasons. One is that, while the two ideas as separate concepts have been around for a few decades, the combining of the two in one project is still relatively rare. The other is that the existing examples of the "green and smart" tend to be in industrial and architectural design, and very seldom in the domains of landscape architecture, urban design, and town planning.

The first concern—the observation that there is a lot of green design and a lot of smart design but not much green *and* smart design—could be described as the case of having great ends but poor means (green design) and the case of having great means but poor ends (smart design). In other words, how is it that—in an era marked by an abundance of sophisticated and affordable information technology (IT) and the rising concerns about the global environmental crisis—we are witnessing two parallel and mutually indifferent lines of production? One is environmentally friendly but technologically primitive, and the other technologically sophisticated but environmentally neutral, or even detrimental. Would it not be far more sensible to employ the full power of our advanced information and communication technology (ICT) in all sorts of green applications, as part of a mass attempt to preempt the global ecological disaster?

The second concern has to do with the scale of our designs. As long as the global environmental crisis can be deemed a design crisis—putting aside the deeper cultural, economic, and political causes—the scale of designed objects is of major significance. Surely the design of a chair, building, or even a mass-produced car has less influence on the environment than the design of an entire city park, suburb, or whole new town. So, at the global scale of our environmental problems, the size of a design project matters. But while we seem to be getting a steadily growing number of green and smart solutions in industrial and architectural design, in the realms of landscape architecture, urban design, and town planning we are only beginning to explore such solutions. These urban design professions, together with civil and environmental engineering, are the design disciplines that will determine the outcome of the global struggle for ecologically sustainable development.

In this epic project—the conversion of thousands and thousands of cities and towns around the world to the clean and green mode of operation—the idea of green and smart design will be of crucial importance. Just green will not be enough; the power of ICT will be needed to amplify what we know about the green functions of the city.

The implementation of the green and smart design principle will not be easy. The idea is perhaps obvious and easy to imagine, manufacture, and operate at the level of a window, a roof, or even a whole building. It is less easy to grasp what it implies at the level of an entire urban infrastructure network (motorways, power lines, water mains), or whole new subdivision or new town. At the scale of an entire city it tends to sound like a theoretical abstraction, rather than anything buildable. This is the challenge we must take on.

The only practicable idea of a sustainable city in the twenty-first century must go beyond the green solutions and include feedback loops and the concept of artificial and distributed intelligence. The sustainable city of the future is the so-called Eco-Tech City.

Cities and Their Design: The Need for a Double Paradigm Shift

Cities are the main aggregate cause of global climate change and other global environmental threats. Therefore, the most important action humanity can do to prevent, or at least slow down the predicted environmental catastrophe, is to change the way cities are built and operated.

Toward this end two paradigms need to shift: the paradigm of the city itself; and the design paradigm (both the

Pergola Fotovoltaica, the World Forum of Cultures waterfront in Barcelona, Spain. Source/Photos by: Relja Ferusic.

design paradigm in general, and the urban design paradigm in particular). Let us consider them one by one.

The idea of the city is not faulty in itself. We need cities. They have served us well for at least seven thousand years. Their spectacular success in cultural, economic, and demographic terms is well documented and universally recognized. But growing internal (e.g., sanitation) and external (impact on the global ecosystem) environmental problems have emerged. We know very well how problems of public health, sanitation, and security can be solved where there is both the political will and the economic means. We also know cities could be designed differently, so that they reduce their burden on the planet. What is more, we realize that, with six billion people on the planet, and with the prospect of adding another three or four in the next few decades, cities are our best chance of containing the majority of our voracious species within a relatively small territory and limiting the damage to the dry-land habitat on the planet.

Thus we need to stick to cities as the dominant model of human habitation on the planet despite their current disastrous effect on it. Rather than entertaining unrealistic fantasies of different forms and locations of settlement (on the sea, under the sea, back to villages, on to other planets, etc.), we would be better off changing our perception of cities. They are more than large agglomerations of physical structures, administrative units, or markets of goods, services, labor, and ideas. They are even more than simple human communities or "quasi-organisms;" they are ecosystems—artificial ecosystems, but ecosystems nonetheless.

Seeing cities as ecosystems when considering how to achieve their ecological sustainability allows for the planning and designing of them in ways that respect the laws of nature, particularly the laws of thermodynamics and ecology.

As physical structures, and to some extent as management systems, contemporary cities are largely based on the mechanistic engineering paradigms of the nineteenth and twentieth centuries. This is why the urban unsustainability crisis the world faces is fundamentally a design crisis—a crisis of obsolete design principles and outdated technologies.

We cannot maintain the delusion of our contemporary cities—particularly in developed countries—as templates of supposed modernization, technological progress, and cultural sophistication. The reality of the looming global environmental disaster tells us a different story. Because their design ignores the immutable laws of ecology and thermodynamics, our cities are fundamentally flawed. They are factories of entropy.

Putting aside the deeper issues of ideology, politics, and the dominant mode of economic relations, from a design point of view, the reasons for our cities being so woefully obsolete is the way they have been planned and designed. When we talk about fundamental flaws (or fundamental rules) in design, we talk about design paradigms (basic models, patterns, templates—sets of key rules to follow when solving a large family of design problems).

The fact that our cities are pushing the earth's ecosystem to the brink is surely sufficient reason to question the ruling urban design paradigm(s). At the risk of oversimplifying, we could say that, over the last two or three decades, urban design and planning theory and practice have been dominated by two design paradigms:

1. The (neo)traditionalists
2. The (neo)modernists

The traditionalist can be traced back to Camillo Sitte and Jane Jacobs, and, more recently, linked to the Krier brothers and the New Urbanism movement. Their defining characteristic is the focus on the visual beauty of the space between buildings. Their design is about the firm edges created by architecture.

The modernists, while commonly linked to Le Corbusier and his immediate predecessors Garnier and Sant' Elia, are often traced back to the grand nineteenth-century "modernizers," Cerda (in Barcelona) and Haussmann (in Paris). More recently, they include a diverse bunch of theorists and practitioners, including Koolhaas, Tschumi, and Hillier. Their focus is on the functional efficiency of transport and land use; their designs are about flows, large open spaces, and connections with the landscape.

Most contemporary urban designers and planners operate in one of the above paradigms, or a combination of the two. Only very recently have some of them started recognizing, and even openly acknowledging, the environmental agenda. Even then, they still tend to view urban ecological sustainability as either a marginal or a specialist issue.

If we want to see radical changes in the way our cities are developed, redeveloped, and operated, we must initiate a fundamental change in the way urban designers, planners, and engineers see cities. They must adopt the idea that cities are artificial ecosystems; manmade creations, but nevertheless able to mimic natural systems and organisms. Their metabolism—the throughput of matter and energy—is largely linear instead of circular, and its overall volume (or rate) is oversized (or too fast).

Design-wise, the crucial point of this Urban Ecology 101 lesson is that mimicking natural ecosystems implies not only performing natural processes (energy, water, nutrients, and other biophysical and biochemical cycles and regimes) the way nature does, but also enabling feedback loops. This ensures that the urban system is not only reintegrated with the surrounding ecosystem, but also efficient and resilient in the long term.

The "Eco-tech" Design Paradigm

The idea of joint green *and* smart design is simple. It is about combining environmental design solutions with information and communication technologies so that whatever the environmental function (e.g., energy conservation), its effectiveness and/or efficiency are significantly enhanced due to some form of regulation provided by some form of IT.

Green design then, is about achieving some ecological objective, typically in connection with energy, water, waste, materials, or habitat. Classic examples are: in architecture, louvers on a building; in landscape architecture, storm-water ponds; and in environmental engineering, effluent-treatment reed beds. It rarely includes any form of high technology; in fact, it is commonly seen as the low-tech and/or passive approach.

Smart design is not necessarily about environmental outcomes. It can be about any functional outcome, as long as it uses computer technology to provide an amplified or more adaptable version of that outcome. For example, it can be an indoor temperature regulator, which ensures that thermal comfort is maintained at all times in response to all sorts of changes (e.g., weather, number of people in the room) and not necessarily with any effort to conserve energy. Some form of feedback loop is typical, and the degree to which the solution is preprogrammed (e.g., based on a clock or calendar), programmable (e.g., can be manipulated in accord with the desires of the occupants), or "intelligent" (automatically responding to all sorts of regular and irregular stimuli according to some task optimization) is independent of environmental considerations.

Clearly, there is no reason why the principle of smart design should not be used to optimize the environmental performance of a building, a designed landscape, or an entire urban project. Equally, smart design can be used for the parallel agendas of human comfort, security, and performance efficiency, and of environmental or resource efficiency.

The point is, ICT can amplify the ability of any component of the urban fabric—buildings, open spaces, infrastructures—to use resources in a more environmentally efficient or conserving way. This is what in nature, plants, animals, and entire ecosystems do all the time. It is that particular form of natural intelligence that enables life to thrive on this planet. Now that humans have created an artificial world of an imposing scale it seems only appropriate to give it some degree of artificial (eco)intelligence, so that it can perform a degree of resource efficiency commensurate with the natural world around it.

Green intelligence is, then, what is missing in contemporary urban design. The technologies we use to run our cities are oblivious to the principles of natural ecology. At the same time, whatever patches of nature remain in the city (creeks, bush remnants, wildlife corridors, etc.) they have nothing to do with technology. If they did, the combined effect would be "neg-entropic" (life-giving).

The two worlds of ecology and technology exist side by side in our cities without any attempt to combine or support each other. Ecological principles and processes should be the template for our technologies of urban infrastructure, open spaces, and buildings. Technology (ICT primarily) could be used to monitor, regulate, and guard the remnants of ecology in the city. Ecology should inspire technology. Technology should support ecology. The way to do it is through a new design philosophy—the new design philosophy called Eco-Tech Design.

Conclusion: Eco-Tech or Landscape Urbanism?

Urban designers generally come from four backgrounds: planning, architecture, landscape architecture, and engineering. They typically take different angles on urban problems, and use different design methods. But they have a lot in common, too. At this moment in history, what seems to bring

Pergola Fotovoltaica, the World Forum of Cultures waterfront in Barcelona, Spain. Source/Photos by: Relja Ferusic.

them together more than anything else is the enormous task of radically transforming our cities so that they stop destroying the planetary ecosystem.

In this urgent enterprise, the four types of urban design professionals will have to learn to respect their various perspectives on design, while at the same time build solid common ground. That common ground should be twofold: first, the paradigm of the city as an ecosystem; and second, the green and smart—or eco-tech—design paradigm.

The eco-tech design paradigm—the principle that a designed urban object is resource efficient with the help of ICT—sounds a bit too much like an engineering-dominated view of design, and in a certain sense it is. What is paradigmatic (showing/telling) about it is the idea of a rational, scientifically informed approach to urban design. It is clearly geared to ensuring our cities get in harmony with the carrying capacity of this planet before it gets rid of us, using ICT. It might, indeed, sound like a project in which engineers would dominate!

This raises the concern about the subtler humanistic, and ultimately aesthetic aspects of urban design. Would they be lost under the stern focus of the city-as-an-ecosystem (rather than city-as-a-work-of-art) approach? Would beauty, character, and atmosphere become things of the past under design envisioned as the smart and green (rather then the design-as-an-art) approach?

Not necessarily. The green *and* smart design paradigm needs to be seen as part of a larger body of an emerging urban design and planning theory. This theory is not necessarily an Eco-Tech Urbanism theory; it might be more appropriate to call it Landscape Urbanism (as many already have).

Landscape Urbanism, while allowing for the idea of a city as an ecosystem (and embracing some form of measurable, and technologically-assisted, urban environmental sustainability as absolutely imperative in the twenty-first century), also contains the notion that an ecosystem is also a landscape of sorts, which means a visual phenomenon, readily subjected to aesthetic judgment and imaginative resolutions.

However, the Landscape Urbanism theory is not yet our guarantee that creative imagination will survive in the era of sustainability-directed urban design. It is an unfinished theory, and currently the subject of a number of different interpretations. But the fact that it is a project in the making should be seen as an invitation to take part. Participation will ensure that the emerging "post-neotraditionalist" and "post-neomodernist" theories of urbanism include both our need for survival as biological beings and our subtler needs as spiritual beings. That cities must become sustainable by no means precludes them from inspiring us with their meaning and beauty, as they have for thousands of years.

ON COMMUNITY
(FROM ZOON POLITIKON TO MULTITUDE)

LARS LERUP

The suburban city is held in place not only by geography, morphology, and metabolism, but also by increasingly important jurisdictional confines: cities, counties, school districts, water districts (that often stretch far beyond the city limits), flood control districts, toll road authorities, air control districts, and oft-shifting voting districts. In addition, software technologies are encroaching on the physical domains of Neighborhood and Community, which in turn are losing their presence and becoming increasingly vague, both in concept and extent—particularly the ancient sociopolitical community centered on the public space, Hannah Arendt's agora, the culture of the City. The demise of this culture's public places is closely related to the progressive expansion of individualism and independence—or to mobility. Tracing the movements of any of the highly mobile suburbanites may suggest both pattern and domain, but there is no reason to believe that such consistency reveals either Neighborhood or Community— only large samples of dwellers with roughly coinciding habits would. Yet progressive city builders speak and write excitedly about "place," neighborhood, and community—about their importance and their relevance. In this light, the relentless privatization of property and behavior in the suburban city has left a huge historical lacuna, a loss that the ever-moving suburbanites may not have noticed because they have been busy instead constructing "community without propinquity"—a self-created community, facilitated by easy lines of new communication and transportation, which is not dominated by space. Thus, it is not clear that the suburbanites see the lack of public domain as a loss. However, it is clear, from the academic point of view, that suburbanites have lost out, not only on public space but, more significantly, on the public domain—which, in turn, allows developers and their cohorts of city officials free rein, while the citizenry remain in a kind of urban adolescence. This is an adolescence that in some parts of the country can overnight grow into a sophisticated form of NIMBY-ism (not in my backyard-ism)—yet developers encountering such wrath don't see this as anything but utterly adult behavior. This confusing mixture of apparent lack, purported loss, and strident citizen action suggests that the "miss-ing public domain" may rather be a sign of a dramatic change taking place right under our eyes now, as a reflection of "life after the city."

Replacement Therapy

If, for a moment, we operate under the premise that the absence of a public domain is a loss, it is clear that many compensatory systems can provide communion for those seeking it—the most virulent form being BANANAs (Build Absolutely Nothing ANywhere at All). I refer to these systems as *replacement therapies*, elements in themselves satisfying the need for community while simultaneously demonstrating the lacuna. It is also clear that some of these therapies are so effective that they may forever obscure the actual need for a public domain. The Lakewood Church in Houston is a case in point. Its website proclaims the following:

> Jesus brought the gospel into the market place, the village square—everywhere people gathered, and The Lakewood International Center will become the "village square" of Houston. With more than 2 million people currently attending events each year, there is hardly a more visible or familiar landmark in the city. Its location alone will allow us to present a message of hope to more people than any outreach in the history of Houston. . . . Today, it is a sports and concert arena. At the Compaq Center, millions of people have watched the most gifted sports figures and entertainers in America. Its history has been one of excellence, crowning champions in the world of sports. . . . And continuing in that great and awesome tradition, The Lakewood International Center will become a place that will crown "Champions of Life."[1]

Lakewood Church inaugurated its 16,000-seat auditorium on July 16, 2005. The number of visitors to the church each year makes it the largest church in the country. This is an example of the progressive replacement of social and political man with a multitude of private agents, all on their own errands. The total mobility of today's social and technical environment, with its arsenal of television sets, cell phones, and internet connections, has displaced the city and its plazas as political space more completely than any previous social or technical revolution. No longer undertaken for purposes of political gathering, the design for *urbanität* or *stim* (as in stimulation) has become a purely nostalgic and quaint exercise—a quest for a particular appearance: "Oh yes, we have a village square, but, truth be told, we only go there to fly kites." In other cases, the design is a mercantile attempt to generate retail frenzy—recreating urbanity in the shopping mall. Both are a form of replacement therapy that disguise an empty village square with the projected potential for a will to gather.

Lakewood Church may be the most sophisticated expression of these attitudes. On its website, by making direct reference to the ancient "village square" of the Holy Land, Lakewood equates the traditional community life of the public domain, once shared by all citizens, with the supposed village square inside its own church, although here only the messenger (Pastor Joel Osteen) and his flock have entry. Gone are the Romans, the moneylenders, the hawkers, the kibitzers, and Peter Sloterdijk's Diogenes, the street philosopher—contrarian whose antics reveal the true cynicism of the city—gone, in short, are the citizens. All have been replaced by the *flock*, which variously includes psychiatric counselors, childcare workers, disaster assistants, and the spiritual leader. This subtle sleight of hand has transformed the *public* into the *semiprivate*, populating the space with "Champions of Life." Likewise, in the suburban metropolis, the city cops of the village square have been replaced by "security," and public land has become private space. The ubiquitous nongovernmental organization (NGO) has taken over for the city. As Alain Touraine says provocatively, "City and Society no longer exist." Beyond Lakewood's spiritual square and an assortment of other pseudosquares lies only the *system*: the streets, the parking lots, the runoff technologies, and the endless freeways. We have clearly arrived in the Post-City.

The Public Domain

If these replacement therapies are truly reflections of a loss, however obscure to those replacing it, what are we missing? And what do we have to change to achieve it? Or, to put it more philosophically, what do we have to do to reach *true mobility*? (This is an idea that has been expanded upon at length in my book, but for now let me say that true mobility is a measured mobility that takes into account all the costs of mobility to reach a sustainable level.)

In the progressive's estimation, such a change or action must center on citizenship and the public domain. Although the immense suburban project is clearly a success from many points of view, ranging from economics to lifestyle, it is also clear that the current model of development (a process entirely in the hands of the property market as tweaked by developers and city officials) will soon reach saturation, at which point the side effects will begin to threaten the initial achievements. If this threat is collectively perceived as a cri-

sis, pragmatics will kick in and rule the solution. Two distinct trajectories then emerge: one that leads to the "social construction" of a public domain, and one that is led by an "incentivized market" under the guidance of an enlightened public sector—or, according to the English political scientist David Marquand, Gladstone versus Schumpeter. However the problem is understood, the suburban city has to reorient its obsession with growth and total mobility towards the wider and loftier goal of the public good. Supposedly, either of these methods would implement the necessary physical repairs that will "induce" citizens to perform their duties of citizenship. Neither of these, to me, entirely satisfy the philosophical question just raised—but there may be a third way.

Community on Demand

Supposedly, all we need do is to constitute a new public realm or hand it over to the market! But is it enough to simply point a finger at this lack, or is the construction process much more complicated, particularly in light of new suburban conditions? For instance, is the picture dramatically different in the eerie glow of millions of TV screens, the buzz of cell phones, and the whir of e-mail culture—in the emerging *netocracy*? This is a world in which new formats for community emerge every day—where the ancient agora has become a network, rather than a place. Does this change the answer to the progressive's concern? Have we simply shifted from the hardware of the street to a network with a greatly expanded menu of components enhanced by a panoply of software?

A third proposition for this cultural shift would go as follows: *Accept that the ancient agora, with its zoon politikon, is but a nostalgia that has been under continuous and radical renewal. This renewal today is visible in the emergence of a multitude of willed communities—Communities on Demand.*

In the Netherlands, as has been shown by Bas Princen, willed, seemingly spontaneous, extremely temporary communities (formed around bird-watching, four by four off-road adventures, trail biking, surf casting, parasailing, radio-controlled airplane meets, paramilitary war games, and kite flying, often orchestrated via cell phones or internet websites) utilize dormant space (both private and public) all across a highly suburbanized and constructed landscape—what I refer to as "lite hunting." In cities like London, New York, and Tokyo, a more explicit hunting for companionship is taking place with the help of cell phones. For example, Dodgeball, a new software program, allows young barhoppers to use text messaging to build ever-expanding social networks along friendship patterns—a willful expansion of the six degrees of separation. In the United States, particularly in areas of dense suburban development, by using phones and the internet, spontaneous communities have emerged overnight to fight change, sometimes resulting in growth boundaries and other forms of redlining.

Now, is the formation of these so-called interest groups, lite hunters, mobs, or possess replacement therapy for the supposed loss of community? Or is it an indication of a resurrection, from the bottom up, of new public realms—revealing a new expediency, a new agility? Smart Communities. as grass-roots democracy today, operate on the collective understanding that the ancient City formula of policed public space is defunct, and that any reconstruction of a new public domain must be worked on from within the very kernel of community: *the willed collective—however temporary*. In effect, we may be seeing the emergence of a new sociopolitical nanotechnology.

Conclusion

The modern concept of community populated by an ideal political subject has always had a downside. Hannah Arendt's *zoon politikon* held an elite position based on exclusion. Her "speech and action," in all its purported freedom and openness, was privileged speech, much farther away from what we think of as democracy and representative speech (the type of political speech we hear on C-SPAN when broadcasting from Congress). With apologies to the "community urbanists," history seems laden with idealized tales about communities past and the apocryphal lament for the demise and corruption of the public domain. Yet such a lament is not unfounded. In a city like Houston, we clearly have zero degree of political space. Public space has been reduced to shared jogging space. Political speech here has been collapsed into the right to vote, or into the meandering and mind-numbing meetings broadcast on local television.

Yet the emergent communities on demand somehow find their space, or at least their momentary foothold, before the community dissolves. The obvious question is: Should suburban designers acknowledge and provide space for these spontaneous communities? For now, we can safely say that community and public space is today a virtual proposition—by hook or by crook in the making.

For the lite hunters, the nostalgia for the ancient city, with its comforting public places, has either outlived its utility or never appeared in their consciousness. They seem to want untainted space with abundant room for their solipsistic, ever-creative activities. Urbanists and city builders alike must acknowledge that *community on demand* cannot be designed (although it may be possible to design *for* such communities). Instead it emerges in the hands and minds of the communitarians themselves. Socially constructed, always changing, community's future is thus unknowable, in both form and content! (Besides, tax dollars are better spent on energy issues than on fantasies of how people should live communally.

The realization that mobility has loosened the ancient bond between place and behavior is hard for us to adjust to. In the past, urban designers could build community space that was used as such because there was a captive audience in the form of "the people"—now the source of the illusion of community. No longer captive, no longer "a people," the new audience of a not-yet-conceived physical space must be

seen as a multitude (Negri and Hardt), free to roam. In the end, this may be what is meant by the modern version of the "Open City." Behind the images of the so-called new towns, constructed under the rubric of a return to urbanism, a restless suburban populace is "housed"—a populace which has clearly shown that, with wheels, "we are free to go," nomads again in the seemingly endless search for true mobility.

In summation: In current suburban design (Toll, KB, etc.), material evidence seems to suggest that there is a lack of public space for this more evasive, emergent, and *dispersed social network*. In symmetrical opposition are the valiant attempts by progressive community designers to return to a public domain predicated on *dense social networks* (de Landa) that no longer seem to exist in suburban cities. The challenge and opportunity to design anew for a public world in the global suburban city of the twenty-first century remains.

Coda

Below the many unsettling questions about community lie an even more fundamental instability, one embedded in the relation between sovereignty and human life, as revealed in the work of Michel Foucault and, lately, the Italian philosopher Giorgio Agamben. The latter's intense and complex exploration of Foucault's biopolitics suggests that the very basis for community is unsettled because of ongoing societal transformations, culminating in the total disregard for the sanctity of life in the Nazi death camps. It is on these "nameless terrains and zones of indistinction" that a new politics has to take form, and he suggests that Aristotle recognized the true fundament of such conditions when, in *Politics*, he wrote:

> Among living beings, only man has language. The voice is the sign of pain and pleasure, and this is why it belongs to other living beings (since their nature has developed to the point of having the sensations of pain and pleasure). But language is for manifesting the fitting and the unfitting and the just and the unjust. To have the sensation of the good and the bad, of the just and the unjust, is what is proper to men as opposed to other living beings, and the community of these things makes dwelling and the city.

The construction of a new community may have to go back this far, while taking into account our modern understanding of biopolitics, political techniques, and the technologies of the self, as well as Agamben's deep searches for sacred man and Bruno Latour's insistence on the inclusion of non-humans in a new political language in which all voices are heard. Agamben warns:

> A third thesis, finally, throws a sinister light on the models by which social sciences, sociology, urban studies, and architecture are trying to conceive and organize public space of the world's cities without any clear awareness that at their very center lies the same bare life that defined the biopolitics of the great totalitarian states of the twentieth century.[2]

PETROCOLLAPSE AND THE LONG EMERGENCY

JAMES HOWARD KUNSTLER

In the waning months of 2005, our failure to face the problems before us as a society is a wondrous thing to behold. Never before in American history have the public and its leaders shown such a lack of resolve, or even interest, in circumstances that will change forever how we live.

Even the greatest convulsion in our national experience, the Civil War, was preceded by years of talk, if not action. But in 2005, we barely have talked about what is happening enough to add up to a public conversation. We're too busy following Paris Hilton and Michael Jackson, or the NASCAR rankings, or the exploits of Donald Trump. We're immersed in a national personality freak show soap opera, with a side order of sports 24/7.

Our failure to pay attention to what is important is unprecedented, even supernatural. This is true even at the supposedly highest level. The news section of last Sunday's *New York Times* did not contain one story about oil or gas—a week after Hurricane Rita destroyed or damaged hundreds of drilling rigs and production platforms in the Gulf of Mexico, which any thinking person can see leading directly to a winter of hardship for many Americans who can barely afford to heat their homes—and the information about the damage around the Gulf was still then just coming in.

What is important? We've entered a permanent worldwide energy crisis. The implications are enormous. It could put us out of business as a cohesive society.

We face a crisis in finance, which will be a consequence of the energy predicament as well as a broad and deep lapse in our standards, values, and behavior in financial affairs.

We face a crisis in practical living arrangements as the infrastructure of suburbia becomes hopelessly unaffordable to run. How will we fill our gas tanks to make those long commutes? How will we heat the 3,500-square-foot homes that people are already in? How will we run the yellow school bus fleets? How will we heat the schools?

What will happen to the economy connected with the easy-motoring utopia—the building of ever more McMansions, Wal-Marts, office parks, and Pizza Huts? Over the past thirty days, with gasoline prices ratcheting up above three dollars a gallon, individuals all over America are deciding not to buy that new house in Partridge Acres, thirty-four miles from Dallas (or Minneapolis, or Denver, or Boston). Those individual choices will soon add up, and an economy addicted to that activity will be in trouble.

The housing bubble has virtually become our economy. Subtract it from everything else and there's not much left besides haircutting, fried chicken, and open-heart surgery.

And, of course, as the housing bubble deflates, the magical mortgage machinery spinning off a fabulous stream of hallucinated credit to be repackaged as tradable debt, will also stop flowing into the finance sector.

We face a series of ramifying, self-reinforcing, terrifying breaks from business-as-usual, and we are not prepared. We are not talking about it in the traditional forums—only in the wilderness of the internet.

Mostly, we face a crisis of clear thinking, which will lead to further crises of authority and legitimacy—of who can be trusted to hold this project of civilization together.

Americans were once a brave and forward-looking people, willing to face the facts, willing to work hard, willing to acknowledge the common good and contribute to it, willing to make difficult choices. We've become a nation of overfed clowns and crybabies, afraid of the truth, indifferent to the common good, hardly even a common culture, selfish, belligerent, narcissistic whiners seeking every means possible to live outside a reality-based community.

These are the consequences of a value system that puts comfort, convenience, and leisure above all other considerations. These are not enough to hold a civilization together. We've signed off on all other values since the end of World War II. Our great victory over manifest evil half a century ago was such a triumph that we have effectively, and incrementally, excused ourselves from all other duties, obligations, and responsibilities—which is exactly why we have come to refer to ourselves as consumers. That's what we call ourselves on TV, in the newspapers, in the legislatures. Consumers. What a degrading label for people who used to be citizens.

Consumers have no duties, obligations, or responsibilities to anything besides their own desire to eat more Cheez Doodles and drink more beer. Think about yourself that way for twenty or thirty years and it will affect the collective spirit—and behavior— very negatively. The biggest losers, of course, end up being the generations of human beings who will follow us, because in the course of mutating into consumers, preoccupied with our Cheez Doodle consumption, we gave up on the common good, which means that we gave up on the future, and the people who will dwell in it.

There are a few other impediments to our collective thinking that obstruct a coherent public discussion of the events facing us, which I call the "Long Emergency." They can be described with precision.

Because the creation of suburbia was the greatest misallocation of resources in the history of the world, it has entailed a powerful psychology of previous investment—meaning, we have put so much of our collective wealth into a particular infrastructure for daily life that we can't imagine changing it, reforming it, or letting it go. The psychology of previous investment is exactly what makes this way of life nonnegotiable.

Another obstacle to clear thinking I refer to as the "Las Vegas-i-zation of the American mind." The ethos of gambling is based on a particular idea: the belief that it is possible to get something for nothing—the psychology of unearned riches. This idea has now insidiously crept out of the casinos and spread far and wide and lodged itself in every corner of our lives. It's there in the interest-only, no-down-payment, quarter-million-dollar mortgages given to people with no record of ever paying back a loan. It's there in the grade inflation of the Ivy League colleges where everybody gets As and Bs regardless of performance. It's in the rap videos of young men flashing $10,000 watches acquired by making up nursery rhymes about gangster life—and in the taboos that prevent us from even talking about that. It's in the suburbanite's sense of entitlement to a supposedly non-negotiable easy motoring existence.

The idea that it's possible to get something for nothing is alive and rampant among those who think we can run the interstate highway system and Walt Disney World on biodiesel or solar power.

People who believe that it is possible to get something for nothing have trouble living in a reality-based community. This is even true of the well-intentioned lady in my neighborhood who drives a Ford Expedition with the "War Is Not the Answer" bumper sticker on it. The truth, for her, is that war IS the answer. She needs to get down with that. She needs to prepare to send her children to be blown up in Asia.

The Las Vegas-i-zation of the American mind is a pernicious idea in itself, but it is compounded by another mental problem, which I call the "Jiminy Cricket syndrome." Jiminy Cricket was Pinocchio's little sidekick in the Walt Disney cartoon feature. The idea is that "when you wish upon a star, your dreams come true." It's a nice sentiment for children, perhaps, but not really suited to adults who have to live in a reality-based communities, especially in difficult times.

The idea that "when you wish upon a star, your dreams come true" obviously comes from the immersive environment of advertising and the movies, which is to say, an immersive environment of make-believe, of pretend. Trouble is, the worldwide energy crisis is not make-believe, and we can't pretend our way through it, and those of us who are adults cannot afford to think like children, no matter how comforting it is.

Combine "when you wish upon a star, your dreams come true" with the belief that it is possible to get something for nothing, stir in the psychology of previous investment, and you get a powerful recipe for mass delusional thinking. As our society comes under increasing stress, we're liable to see increased delusional thinking, as worried people retreat further into make-believe and pretend.

The desperate defense of our supposedly nonnegotiable way of life may lead to delusional politics that we have never seen before in this land. An angry and grievance-filled public may turn to political maniacs to preserve their entitlements to the easy-motoring utopia—even while reality negotiates things for us.

I maintain that we may see leaders far more dangerous in our future than George W. Bush. The last thing that this group needs is to get sidetracked in paranoid conspiracy politics such as the idea that Dick Cheney orchestrated the World Trade Center attacks, which I regard as just another form of make-believe. This is what we have to overcome to face the reality-based challenges of our time.

At the bottom of the Peak Oil issue is the fear that we're not going to make it. The Long Emergency looming before us is going to produce a lot of losers. Economic losers; people who will lose jobs, vocations, incomes, possessions, assets—and never get them back. Social losers; people who will lose position, power, advantage. And just plain losers;people who will lose their health and their lives.

There are no magic remedies for what we face, but there are intelligent responses that we can marshal individually and collectively. We will have to do what circumstances require of us.

We are faced with the necessity to downscale, rescale, right size, and reorganize all the fundamental activities of daily life: the way we grow food; the way we conduct everyday commerce and the manufacture of things that we need; the way we school our children; the size, shape, and scale of our towns and cities.

I'm not optimistic about most of our big cities. They are going to have to contract severely. They achieved their current scale during the most exuberant years of the cheap-oil fiesta, and they will have enormous problems remaining viable afterward. Any megastructure, whether it is a skyscraper or a *landscraper*—buildings that depend on huge amounts of natural gas and electricity—may not be usable a decade or two into the future.

All indications are that American life will have to be reconstituted along the lines of traditional towns, villages, and cities much reduced in their current scale. These will be the most successful places once we are gripped by the profound challenge of a permanently reduced energy supply.

The land development industry as we have known it is going to vanish in the years ahead: the production home builders, as they like to call themselves; the strip mall developers; the fried food shack developers—say goodbye to all that.

We are entering a period of economic hardship and declining incomes. The increment of new development will be very small, probably the individual building lot. The suburbs as are going to tank spectacularly. We are going to see an unprecedented loss of equity value and, of course, basic usefulness. We are going to see an amazing distress sale of properties, with few buyers. We're going to see a fight over the table scraps of the twentieth century. We'll be lucky if the immense failure of suburbia doesn't result in an extreme political orgy of grievance and scapegoating.

The New Urbanism movement has been broadly misunderstood over the past decade, especially by some of the major morons in the mainstream media, such as David Brooks and John Tierney of the *New York Times*, who repeatedly make the fatuous argument that suburbia must be okay because Americans overwhelmingly choose to live in it. Well, that's nice. The trouble is that suburbia is coming off the menu. In a world of oil, seventy-dollars and upward per barrel, suburbia is a dish that can no longer be served up in America's economic kitchen. Someone should inform the waiters.

The New Urbanists are the only group I know of who offer a comprehensive set of intelligent responses to the awful challenges we face in a looming megacrisis of the environment. Assuming that the human race wants to carry on, and do so under civilized conditions, we are going to need collective dwelling places, civic habitations. It has yet to be determined what scale will be possible, and exactly what kind of energy will be available to us for running them. But the signs so far indicate that the scale will have to be much more modest than what we are currently used to, and the quality will have to be much higher.

The New Urbanists performed an extremely valuable service to this society over the past decade. They dove back into the dumpster of history and retrieved the knowledge needed for the design and assembly of real civic environments—knowledge that had been thrown away gleefully by the traffic engineers and municipal Babbitts in the delirious years of building the easy-motoring utopia.

One day soon, America will wake up from its infotainment-fueled sleepwalk and start desperately looking for answers to the predicament it finds itself in. A lot of that will revolve around the basic question of where we live, and how things in it are arranged. When that wake up occurs, the New Urbanists will be ready, reliable, confident, and congenial as always—something like our country used to be.

The action in the years ahead will be in renovating existing towns and villages, and connecting them with regions of productive agriculture. Where the big cities are concerned, there is simply no historical precedent for the downscaling they will require. The possibilities for social and political distress ought to be obvious, though. The process is liable to be painful and disorderly.

The postcheap oil future will be much more about staying where you are than about being mobile. And, unless we rebuild a United States passenger railroad network, a lot of people will not be going anywhere. Today, we have a passenger railroad system that the Bulgarians would be ashamed of.

Don't make too many plans to design parking structures. The postcheap oil world is not going to be about parking, either.

But it will be about the design and assembly and reconstituting of places that are worth caring about and worth being in. When you have to stay where you are and live locally, you will pay a lot more attention to the quality of your surroundings, especially if you are not moving through the landscape at fifty miles per hour.

We are going to have to reorganize everyday commerce in this nation from the ground up. The whole system of continental-scale big-box discount and chain store shopping is headed for extinction, and sooner than you might think. It will go down fast and hard. Americans will be astonished when it happens.

Operations like Wal-Mart have enjoyed economies of scale that were attained because of very special and anomalous historical circumstances: a half century of relative peace between great powers; and cheap oil—absolutely reliable supplies of it, since the OPEC disruptions of the 1970s.

Wal-Mart and its imitators will not survive the oil market disruptions to come, not even for a little while. Wal-Mart will not survive when its merchandise supply chains to Asia are interrupted by military contests over oil or internal conflict in the nations that have been supplying us with ultracheap manufactured goods. Wal-Mart's "warehouse on wheels" will not be able to operate in a noncheap oil economy.

It will only take mild to moderate disruptions in the supply and price of gas to put Wal-Mart and all operations like it out of business. And it will happen. As that occurs, America will have to make other arrangements for the distribution and sale of ordinary products.

It will have to reorganize at the regional and the local scale. It will have to move merchandise shorter distances at multiple increments and probably by multiple modes of transport. It is almost certain to result in higher costs for the things we buy, and fewer choices of things. We are not going to rebuild the cheap-oil manufacturing facilities of the twentieth century.

We will have to re-create the lost infrastructures of local and regional commerce, and they will have to be multilayered. These were the people that Wal-Mart systematically put out of business over the last thirty years: the wholesalers, the jobbers, the small retailers. They were economic participants in their communities; they made decisions that had to take the needs of their communities into account. They were employers who employed their neighbors. They were a substantial part of the middle class of every community in America, and all of them together played civic roles in our communities as the caretakers of institutions—the people who sat on the library boards, and the hospital boards, and bought the balls and bats and uniforms for the Little League teams.

We got rid of them in order to save nine bucks on a hair dryer. We threw away uncountable millions of dollars worth of civic amenity in order to shop at the big-box discount stores. That was some bargain.

This will all change. The future is telling us to prepare to do business locally again. It will not be a hyperturbo consumer economy. That will be over with. But we will still make things, and buy and sell things.

A lot of the knowledge needed to do local retail has been lost, because in the past the ownership of local retail businesses was often by families. The knowledge and skills for doing it were transmitted from one generation to the next. It will not be so easy to get that back, but we have to do it.

Change is coming whether we like it or not, whether we are prepared for it or not. If we don't begin right away to make better choices, then we will face political, social, and economic disorders that will shake this nation to its foundation.

These are huge tasks. How can we bring a reality-based spirit to them? I have a suggestion. Let's start with one down-to-earth project that we can take on with confidence, something we have a reasonable shot at accomplishing, and fairly quickly—something that will address our energy problems directly and will make a difference for the better. Let's get started rebuilding the passenger railroad system in our country.

Nothing else we might do would make such a substantial impact on our outlandish oil consumption.

Any person or any group who finds itself in trouble has to begin somewhere. It has to take a step that will prove to itself that it is not helpless, that it is capable of accomplishing something, and accomplishing that first thing will build the confidence to move on to the next step.

That's how people will save themselves, how they will reconnect with reality-based virtue.

We were once such a people. We were brave, resourceful, generous, and earnest. The last thing we believed was the idea that it was possible to get something for nothing, that we were entitled to a particular outcome in life, apart from the choices we made and how we acted. We can recover those forsaken elements of our collective character. We can be guided, as Abraham Lincoln said, by the better angels of our nature.

We lived in a beautiful country with vibrant towns and cities, and a gorgeous, productive rural landscape, and we were sufficiently rewarded by them, such that we did not always feel driven to seek refuge in make-believe all the live-long day. When we wanted to accomplish something we set out to do it, to make it happen, not merely to wish for it. We knew the difference between wishing and doing—which is probably the most important thing that adult human beings can know.

I hope we can get back to being that kind of people. This effort here today is a good start.

PART 8: URBAN DIGITAL SPACES AND CYBER CITIES

8.1 ## CONNECTIVITY AND URBAN SPACE

WILLIAM MITCHELL

From ancient times, buildings and cities have not only provided shelter for their inhabitants, but they have also produced spatial subdivisions of human activity. At urban scale, this is a consequence of zoning and land-use decisions. At building scale, architects subdivide interiors into specialized spaces assigned to particular activities.

In addition to differentiating activities in this way, urban designers and architects organize them into clusters. Generally, for the sake of efficiency, they attempt to locate highly interconnected activities in close proximity to one another. As a consequence, since proximity is a scarce resource, activities with fewer interconnections become more widely separated. Furthermore, spatial separation is often employed to minimize conflicts between incompatible activities—noisy ones and those requiring quiet, for example.

Here I shall argue that ubiquitous digital networking challenges long-established conventions and practices of spatial subdivision and clustering. This isn't a simple matter of substituting telecommunication for transportation, and thereby eliminating proximity requirements and dissolving traditional activity clusters, as many have thought. The logic is subtler, and when properly understood it opens up opportunities to create new spatial patterns, with positive social and cultural properties, at urban, neighborhood, and building scales. In particular, it suggests a new take on New Urbanism.

The Role of the Program

Essentially, an architectural program consists of an exhaustive list of the spaces to be accommodated in a building, together with their floor areas, environmental requirements, and adjacency and proximity requirements among them. Programs are often prepared, by programming specialists, before architects are engaged, and they are conceived of as specifications of client requirements. In the early stages of design, architects transform programs into diagrammatic floor plan layouts and massing concepts that satisfy these

requirements as closely as possible. Through the stages of schematic design and design development, architects take care to retain consistency with these early space allocation diagrams. Finally, the program is used to check that the architect actually met the client's needs, and as a starting point for occupancy planning and facility management. It is a crucial control device.

All this seems eminently reasonable, but it depends upon some underlying assumptions that are increasingly questionable in an era of digital interconnectivity. Today, increasingly significant architectural and economic benefits can be realized by critically departing from these assumptions, and exploiting the new design opportunities that this departure enables. It no longer suffices merely to network traditionally programmed buildings and fill them with electronic devices.

Contingent Versus Stable Space Use

The most fundamental assumption of the traditional architectural program is that of *stable space use*. A program only makes sense if it is assumed that spaces have much the same uses over time, and should therefore be optimized for those uses. Private office spaces, for example, are different from meeting rooms or social spaces—with different area, environmental, and adjacency requirements—and are designed in response to those differences.

Furthermore, under traditional assumptions, *high move and conversion costs* exert an additional stabilizing effect. If you have many books and paper files, moving from one office to another is time consuming, costly, and disruptive; you don't do it lightly. And conversion of, say, conference rooms into offices in response to changed space demands is slow and expensive, and removes the space from the useable inventory while the conversion takes place.

Under these conditions, circulation efficiency within a building tends to degrade over time—a process much like that of fragmentation of disk space. The initial layout may be carefully organized to minimize unnecessary circulation, but patterns of demand gradually change, and some of the initially programmed uses change, so that the assumptions on which they were based no longer hold. However, because of move and conversion costs, it is not realistic to keep adjusting the layout to maintain efficiency as this happens. There is no equivalent to running a utility to clean up your disk space.

But, where work is supported by ubiquitous connectivity and portable and mobile devices, space use can become much more fluid. Anywhere that you can sit down with a laptop and get a network connection, or use your cellphone, becomes a potential work space, recreation space, or place to go shopping online. Where work materials and tools are stored in portable memory, or delivered via the network, move costs reduce almost to zero; to change offices, you simply pick up your laptop and go. And, with ad-hoc space occupancy and negligible move costs, readjustment of proximities is quick, easy, and continual; if you need to be adjacent to someone, you just walk over and sit down for a while.

Overall, I propose, buildings for the mobile, networked era need a few, very broad categories of space defined by basic human needs rather than many, highly differentiated categories. And, like locations in computer memory, locations within them are assigned uses as needed and then immediately freed up for other uses when the need no longer exists.

The consequences of this, if it is effectively managed, are higher duty cycles for spaces, more efficient utilization of available spaces, and better operating efficiency. Spaces that would otherwise be assigned as private offices don't have to be vacant while their occupants are in meeting spaces, for example, and inefficient layouts don't have to be maintained because they are too slow, difficult, and costly to change.

Multiplexing Space

A second—and now questionable—assumption of traditional space programming is that users spend fairly lengthy chunks of time in particular activities at particular locations (individual work in offices, meeting in conference rooms, eating in cafeterias, shopping in retail space, and so on), and circulate from space to space as activities change. The motivation for this coarse-grained allocation of time, in traditional work environments, is obvious. If building users switched activities too frequently and sliced their time too finely, they would continually be running from space to space, and they would never get anything done.

A related factor is the traditional incompatibility of certain activities. Quiet work and noisy music are incompatible, and a traditional architectural response is to locate them in separate spaces. It is the same with eating and drinking and consulting library books; librarians, concerned about book preservation, don't like to see them in the same space.

One effect of networking and mobile electronics is to eliminate many of these incompatibilities, and consequently the need for spatial separation. In the age of the iPod, you can have music and quiet work in adjacent seats. And, in the age

of electronic delivery of text to laptop screens, you can consult a book at a cafeteria table without worrying about getting ketchup on the pages.

A second effect is the possibility of electronically switching among activities, at a rapid pace, without physically moving. Switching from doing your e-mail to attending a meeting to recreation no longer necessarily mean going from your office cubicle to a conference room and then a recreation space. You can simply go, on your computer screen, from an e-mail browser to videoconferencing and then a music player. The transition costs are now negligible, so you can slice time as finely as you want. This can be difficult for managers who want to keep close track of what you are doing, or if you need to fill out time sheets for charging purposes, but it removes rigidities in time allocation and eliminates the wastage of time in movement.

Fine time slicing shades imperceptibly into multitasking. If you keep several windows open on your computer screen at once, you can fluidly rotate your attention among them, and you can keep an eye on several at once—an impossible strategy if even minimal movement from space to space intervenes.

Probably the most important effect, though, is the creation of new synergies among activities. In traditional work spaces, for example, group meetings and consulting technical references in the library have been separate activities, conducted in separate spaces at different times. But, where participants in a meeting have wireless laptops, they can instantly Google a topic when it comes up in discussion, and then inject the results back into the discourse. This creates a new, flexible, and powerful way of pursuing and debating ideas.

There is a useful analogy, here, with telecommunications. Old-fashioned buildings allocated particular spaces to particular uses, and users had to switch spaces. This was unavoidably wasteful. Similarly, old-fashioned telecommunications systems allocated channels to fixed uses. But, in both cases now, we can use clever multiplexing techniques to overlay multiple uses and efficiently utilize available capacity.

Technologically Humanized Versus Technologically Dominated Space

It is often assumed that advanced, electronically serviced space—as suggested by these examples—must look and feel high-tech. In fact, precisely the opposite is true; *really* advanced technology tends to disappear into your pocket or into the woodwork, and to make few demands on the architecture. Instead of responding to technological imperatives, it can respond to basic human needs for light, air, view, and sociability.

In the recent past, for example, telephones were part of the architecture—attached to walls or desks. Now, of course, they have become extensions of our mobile bodies. Within some pretty broad limits, technological imperatives no longer determine where you can conduct the activity of telephoning. At the same time, though, there is even greater need for environments that provide the socially desirable options of speech privacy and freedom from auditory disturbance wherever you may need it—for example, the addition of "silent cars" to trains.

Even more recently, audiovisual presentations were always conducted in darkened rooms, with the secondary consequence that presentation spaces were often located in the interiors of buildings where there wasn't any natural light anywhere. This was for the simple technological reason that available displays were dim. But today's high-powered video projectors and large, flat-screen monitors can operate effectively in rooms with quite high levels of natural light. So these rooms can now be designed—in a far more humane way—in response to the basic human desire for light, air, and view rather than the requirement, due to technological limitations, for darkness.

In the early computer era, the machines were delicate devices that required precise climate control. Environments dominated by these machine requirements were inhospitable to human beings, but there was no other option. Today's laptops, though, are extremely robust. You can use them safely in far less controlled environments that are designed around the needs and desires of people. You can even take them outside, under a tree, to work on a beautiful spring day.

Varied Versus Repetitive Environments

In addition to being rigidly programmed, the large-scale buildings of the industrial era—and, ironically, those of Silicon Valley and Route 128 are no exception to this rule—were modular and repetitive. This was because, in order to meet pressing budget and schedule requirements, architects invariably had to trade off complexity for scale—to pursue the economies of scale that resulted from one-size-fits-all strategies. But, through the use of three-dimensional digital modeling in design, combined with digital fabrication and mass-customization strategies in building production, it is now possible to radically readjust the parameters of this tradeoff. It is now feasible, on reasonable timeframes and budgets, to create large-scale buildings that are nonrepetitive and sensitively responsive to their contexts and to the basic human desire for varied and interesting environments.

Paradoxically, the best buildings of the twenty-first century will incorporate their advanced technology very unobtrusively, and they will have more in common with preindustrial buildings than their industrial-era predecessors: they will be highly varied; they will be permeable to light, air, and view rather than tightly sealed off; and they will provide ecosystems of spaces that can be fluidly and dynamically occupied rather than rigid realizations of old-fashioned space programs.

Realtime Space Markets

Under conditions of fluid, dynamic, ad-hoc space occupancy in a building, a space market begins to operate. The building's managers are space providers, the occupants are space consumers, and the task is to effectively match supply to demand on a minute-by-minute basis. This is a potentially demanding task. It is easy to imagine coming into work in a large building, and wandering around—increasingly frustrated—looking for a place to sit down and get to work. It would be much like searching for a space in a crowded airport parking structure.

Mobile connectivity is the key. A simple system, for example, might employ sensor technology to keep track of currently unoccupied desks and, via mobile devices, direct new arrivals to them. More sophisticated systems might perform complex tasks like arranging meeting spaces at the nearest available locations to the current centroids of scattered groups of employees, conducting eBay-style auctions for highly desirable spaces, or implementing congestion pricing for space in the most popular locations. These markets could take advantage of the distributed intelligence and self-interest of building users, and create powerful incentives to use their space effectively and efficiently.

Traditional real estate markets have relatively few transactions, and operate with time constants of months or years, so real-time, mobile information usually isn't crucial. Hotel room markets have many more transactions, with time constants of days, and it is sometimes useful to have real-time availability information. Space markets for street parking have a great many transactions, time constants of hours or minutes, and often entail onerous searches, so real-time availability information would be great if you could get it. Future workspaces will probably operate as highly dynamic space markets, with transactions conducted at a very rapid pace, and mobile, networked devices playing an essential role in connecting users to available spaces that best meet their current needs.

How Connectivity Adds Value

Commercial and industrial real estate development is largely a game of adding value to land by intensifying its use. New technologies have always played a crucial role in this. Technologies of high-rise construction—particularly the steel frame, curtain wall, and elevator—enabled the skyscraper development of the Chicago Loop, Manhattan, and other urban cores. Electric light enabled much more effective use of buildings after dark. Air-conditioning opened up sites in hot climates to more intensive development. And, as described above, digital networking has an additional intensifying effect. Few systematic studies of this have been carried out so far (and they are sorely needed), but it seems clear that effectively managed networked work space should achieve higher densities of occupants per unit floor area, and higher duty cycles for spaces.

For building managers, higher densities and duty cycles should translate into reduced space inventories and greater capacity to respond to organizational growth and change without inventory expansion. Since rising energy costs produce rising space costs, economizing on square footage is even more important than it has been in the past.

More crucially still, well-managed networked space should reduce traditional rigidities in spatial organization and barriers to effective intercommunication and collaboration. Space that is fluidly occupied, and allows effective multitasking, is more able to respond effectively to rapidly changing needs and conditions, and to generate benefits from synergistic groupings and overlays of activities. And space that is humanized through reduced dependence on old-fashioned technology should provide higher levels of user satisfaction.

For developers, these benefits potentially translate into higher rents. But it is not automatic. It is necessary to make the design and management moves that are required to realize the potential benefits, to rethink traditional metrics—for example, calculations of net-to-gross ratios and rentable areas—for the new conditions, and to effectively make the justifying arguments to potential renters.

On the cost side, the cost of integrating networking with new construction is generally marginal, so it makes no sense not to do it. It can, however, be surprisingly difficult and expensive to retrofit older buildings with wiring closets and vertical and horizontal wiring distribution space, and this must be factored into decisions about the future of older building stock. On the other hand, adding good networking can be a crucial factor in the successful adaptive reuse of historic structures; it is unobtrusive, but it opens up new use possibilities.

In general, compelling economic logic can be expected to drive the transition to highly networked space and related new patterns of space use. Under most circumstances, the benefits (from the perspectives of both real estate developers and building occupants and managers) are high and the costs low.

A New Take on New Urbanism

These conditions suggest a new take on New Urbanism. At its best, New Urbanism has provided a powerful critique of orthodox modernist practices of spatial subdivision and clustering of activities. In particular, it has identified the disadvantages of coarse-grained land-use patterns and the kinds of activity clustering that result from reliance upon automobile transportation, and it has reminded us of the advantages of fine-grained mixed-use configurations at building and neighborhood scales. At their least convincing, New Urbanists have marketed the nostalgic return to preindustrial patterns (accompanied by sentimentally historicist architectural imagery) as the remedy for modernist ills. But it is misleading, and obscures emerging possibilities, to frame the argument as one between modernism and neotraditionalism.

Instead, we should recognize that characteristic technologies of the post-industrial, ubiquitously networked twenty-first century are creating new architectural and urban opportunities by breaking down old prescriptions and rigidities—shifting the emphasis from stable to contingent space use, from single-use spaces to multiplexed spaces, and from slow-paced to real-time space markets. They are robust and flexible—reducing the need for spaces and clusters organized around the rigid requirements of machines and technological systems, and making it technically and economically realistic to organize varied, humane spatial patterns around fundamental human needs. They challenge traditional distinctions among work, residential, retail, and recreational spaces, and the building types and urban patterns derived from these. As we begin to explore and understand their spatial implications they will, I suggest, provide the foundation for a new New Urbanism.

URBAN NETWORK ARCHITECTURES AND THE STRUCTURING OF FUTURE CITIES

STEPHEN GRAHAM

Currently a whole swathe of new media technologies are being unevenly assimilated into urban places in what amounts, in effect, to a third industrial revolution based on speed-of-light digital exchanges. What are the relationships between this process of technological development and diffusion and our urbanizing world?

One starting point is a powerful set of debates that emerged, particularly in the Anglo-Saxon world, in the 1980s and continued through the mid-1990s. Arguing that these technologies were about the collapse of distance and the "end" of geography, a wide variety of media and popular commentators, from Alvin Toffler to Nicholas Negroponte, implied that the fully digital world would make cities essentially unnecessary. The assumption here was that, with this collapse of distance, due to electronic technology, face-to-face meetings based on the copresence of people and their bodies located in time and space—the very stuff that has always driven cities to grow—would somehow become irrelevant. Why put 250 people in the same conference room, if the qualities of the technology, the qualities of the new media, mean that we can distribute, decentralize, and all access the equivalent experience through virtual travel, based on the speed-of-light flows of bits, rather than the much more problematic and costly flows of physical atoms—our bodies—in, out, and around cities? In a world of digitally immersed simulations of buildings, spaces, experiences, and senses, surely everything will soon be "one click away," and anything will be possible anywhere, anytime? Surely we could then profitably reverse the congestion and centralization that has actually provided the raison d'être for urban settlements and develop an effectively posturban civilization that is more socially and environmentally sustainable?

Many influential commentators adopted such a perspective between the 1960s and the 1980s. Marshall McLuhan argued that "The city will fade like a fading shot in a movie." Paul Virillo, the influential French architectural philosopher, suggested that with the intensity of the new technologies, cities might actually emerge as "paradoxical agglomerations," in which relationships to faraway places were as strong as the local relationships. And Alvin Toffler suggested that we might all decentralize from the Londons and Copenhagens of this world, and actually live as "prosumers"—hybrid producers and consumers—in individualized "electronic cottages."

The reality of contemporary urban and technological change, however, is a great deal more complex than such simplistic ideologies suggesting the total substitution of the place-based material and corporeal world by ever-advancing digital technologies. Yes, we are seeing an explosion of digitally mediated, economic, social, and cultural activities. And yes, these sometimes allow face-to-face transactions, and the transport flows that they sustain, to be totally replaced by digital flows (as with phone or 'net banking). But essentially what we are seeing is the subtle weaving in of these technological practices into a world that is not becoming less urban, but is, in fact, becoming *more* urban. So it is not a case of new technology somehow displacing, or being at war with, the city. As always in the last six thousand years of history, it is a case of the complex combination of technologically mediated and face-to-face interactions combining to usher in change in urban landscapes.

Even in Europe the statistics demonstrate that larger and larger proportions of the population are living in urban areas. Yet people are not simply concentrating in traditional urban settlements with single dominant centers and people commuting in and out on rather rhythmic daily patterns. Rather, "multiplex" urban regions are emerging with multiple centers, multiple flows, and, most importantly, highly dispersed and fragmented temporal and spatial structures. The sprawl of urban regions has been most commonly discussed in the United States, North America, and Australia. But in Europe, too, we also see a sprawl beyond the traditional core of the city and the rapid growth of peripheral retail, office, mobility, transaction, and logistics spaces based on the combined use of automobile, logistics, and informational and technological systems.

The juxtaposition of centralization and decentralization, via information and transport systems, is a key feature of contemporary economic change. This is usefully captured by Anne Markusen's recent work. She argues that, on the one hand, a range of "sticky spaces" are maintaining and even strengthening, their strategic roles as high-value-added centers of control, research, and innovation within our globalizing world. On the other hand, she argues that we are seeing a striking decentralization of other lower-value-added activities away from major strategic central cities—activities that go on behind the call center, behind the internet—in to what she calls the "slippery spaces" of routinized decentralization based on cutting costs and information technology (IT) mediation.

At all scales we see this tension between concentration and decentralization embedded in the relationships between urban and network architectures. Processes of centralization are juxtaposed with processes of decentralization within national and international urban systems. As a result, the urban periphery can be the center, the center can be the margin. And a much more fluid, and fractured urban form results. Importantly—despite many predictions that growing IT use will reduce transport flows—trends right across the world are toward more and more physical mobility. So again we are not seeing an overall reduction in the physical movements of commodities, freight, or human bodies in and around our cities. Evidence from France shows clearly that, over the past two hundred years, physical and electronic communications have grown exponentially and in parallel. Thus, cities and urban life today are characterized by more and more physical mobility combined closely with more and more electronic mobility (mobile phones, electronic transactions, e-mail, electronic transport and logistics systems, etc.). Subtle and complex sets of relationships between the two define how they work together in our lives, in our institutions, and in our cities.

Understanding Contemporary Urbanism: Parallel Architectures of Urban Space and Network Space

So how can we make sense of these new multiplex urban landscapes with their multiple flows and mobilities, their complex and decentered structures, and their contradictory juxtapositions? How can we understand our urbanizing planet, which is at the same time a world of intensifying technological mobilities? One way of addressing these questions is to explore paradigmatic urban spaces. Drawing from my recent book with Simon Marvin, *Splintering Urbanism*, this is my aim in what follows. Here I deploy a "sociotechnical" perspective that brings architecture and urbanism together with issues surrounding the social and technical makeup of mobility systems like the internet and transport systems. For too long urbanists have left such issues to be the province of the civil engineer. But to understand this new world, it is necessary to develop a parallel perspective that looks at the architecture of urban space and the architectures of, what we could call, network space, together. This requires an interdisciplinary perspective drawing on sociology, planning, geog-

raphy, and urbanism, as well as the sociology of technology. In what follows, by way of example, I seek to analyze the parallel urban and network architectures of seven paradigmatic spaces of the contemporary city.

Global Finance Spaces: Sticky Spaces of "Glocal" Control and Coordination

The first set of exemplar spaces that need to be understood are global financial spaces. In such sticky spaces we are seeing the intense centralization of strategic activities. Here in the global finance centers—Lower Manhattan, Central London, and Tokyo being the three pivotal "global" cities—we have the strategic spaces for orchestrating global capitalism. We see the connective power of these cities when we look at the global airline and optic fiber networks that connect them. For example, a whole range of new electronic highways that are being laid along the bottom of the oceans directly interconnect the centers of these global cities. Such networks don't go from national frontier to national frontier—as the old telegraph and telephone networks did. They go from desk to desk. This is a classic example of what you might call a "glocal"—meaning global and local—network. Such glocal desk-to-desk electronic networks help illustrate the debate in the new urban literature about how geographical scale is being remade, about how global and local are so intimately bound up, that we can no longer separate them.

Thus dozens of new optic fiber networks are being designed to carefully concentrate on the oceanic corridors between London and Manhattan. When we look at the city scale, we see their urban equivalents. London, New York, and the other global centers have seven or eight private, optic fiber systems threaded through every little centimeter of the space that underpins them. We tend to ignore these crucial electronic infrastructures because they are invisible. What is interesting about these systems is that they don't cover whole cities. They don't cover whole nations in the way that infrastructure is assumed to. Rather, they are based on principles of cherry-picking the best markets and the best spaces within liberalized conditions. In central London, for example, the COLT fiber system only covers the financial district, with a little loop out to the Docklands and the West End. Even the edge of London is marginalized by this network.

City agencies are now expending enormous efforts on selling themselves not just as physical transport hubs, but also as electronic communication hubs. And there is an enormous effort to demonstrate the connectivity, the effectiveness, and the electronic power of city centers as glocal spaces of extraordinary digital connectivity. This is vital because in global finance everything you do shifts around the world in zeroes and ones within milliseconds. Such networks' architectures are therefore of extraordinary importance.

Thus on the one hand, global finance centers are reaching out to be interconnected intimately together. On the other hand, in this post–9/11 world, we are going to see a more and more thorough rethink in terms of the relationships between the global financial cores and the wider cities within which they are based. There is going to be a massive intensification of surveillance and scrutiny of boundaries. One existing example that is likely to be copied is the so-called Ring-of-Steel around the central city of London. It is a system for restricting and monitoring car entry put in after a couple of terrorist attacks by the IRA in the early 1990s. Cars entering in and out of the city of London are digitally photographed. The Ring can reveal automatically whether the car is stolen within four seconds through linkage to databases.

Such systems are already moving towards face-recognition capability. In the medium term known terrorists going through American airports will actually be sparking off silent alarms through the massive improvement in facial-recognition technologies. So what we are essentially seeing is a paradoxical process. At the same time as global city spaces are reaching out to each other through the most amazing physical and electronic mobilities ever seen, there is a much more provisional relationship with the local level. Again this problematizes the idea of the open city and of the free mobilities of people.

Technopoles: Sticky Spaces for Technological Innovation

A second example of sticky space is the technopole. Technopoles are, as Manuel Castells and Peter Hall argue, the foundries of the information age. They are the spaces of continuous innovation, which, like financial cores, require highly concentrated face-to-face contacts that sustain complex technological innovation. Many cities have invested heavily in labeling themselves as technopoles in efforts to proclaim themselves as the new innovation spaces where the dense co-presence of leading corporate players in leading edge sectors meet. Technopoles are usually centered on suburban campus-like spaces on the edge of leading global city spaces.

An enormous investment is going on in the planning world to try and create technopoles. The benefits for those cities that do manage to develop the advantages to bring in IT and biotech innovation are clearly enormous. At last count, there were around 150 cities around the world, that were using the word "silicon" in their marketing campaigns—the "silicon," "cyber," or "techno" prefix brings with it a whole new language for the very old art form of selling a place, of selling a city (see http://www.tbtf.com/siliconia.html).

Most ambitious of all such technopole strategies is the so-called multimedia supercorridor (or MSC)—a brand new fifty-kilometer (thirty mile) linear city built south of Kuala Lumpur in Malaysia. It is anchored by a giant new international airport. There is a new national capital. There are new special development spaces for the software and IT companies that the Malaysian state is trying to bring in along with investors in what is essentially a manufacturing economy at the moment. There are even new laws put into place for maintaining the intellectual property rights of corporations

and for allowing the totally free migration of so-called knowledge workers.

But, as with global financial cores, we have to ask the question of how these spaces relate to the wider city. And there are a lot of commentators, not the least of which are within Malaysia itself, who criticize the enormous public investment in these high-quality, highly luxurious technological city spaces. For example, in 1999 a Malaysian newspaper, the *Star*, used a satirical cartoon to portray the new city. It emphasized the high cost of entry: residents of the MSC entered the hermetically sealed, clean, green space of the MSC in limousines. Notices emphasized the privatized, clean air of the MSC and contrasted it to the sense of chaos and pollution in the old core of Kuala Lumpur. Essentially, then, the territorial politics of technopoles often amount to a socially regressive, state-funded secession of technological elites from the conflicts and contestations of older city spaces.

Cyber Districts: "Homes" of the Internet

A third type of highly clustered, highly concentrated sticky space that is emerging is what you might call urban internet space. Such places drive content creation for the internet, and digital industries more generally. The assumption that the internet is actually a nongeographical medium, because its accessibility spreads to most places, is simply not true. If one maps the hosts of internet content, as Matt Zook has, the pattern is very concentrated. In the example of the United States, it is concentrated in cities like New York and San Francisco, cities that have the traditional advantages in terms of venture capital, publishing, education; and art, culture, and design. It is possible to map these concentrations at the level of the city, too. The dot-coms in central Boston, for example, show a predictable concentration on the downtown financial core, the highly gentrified Back Bay area, and around MIT and Harvard. But the largely African American neighborhood of Roxbury is virtually devoid of an internet-based economy. So the digital divide is being etched into the spaces of our cities in quite powerful ways, which researchers are now starting to understand.

High value-added internet activities are clustering into chic, trendy, up-and-coming urban neighborhoods where dot-com entrepreneurs most want to locate. These spaces are emerging all over Europe, as well as in the United States. And a new type of architecture is emerging along with them. Disused office spaces are being converted into live/work spaces for web entrepreneurs, digital design companies, digital architecture companies, and the games and virtual reality industries.

We are also seeing a new set of infrastructures being developed for these clusters of internet activities. One IT network in London—Sohonet—very much follows the logic of the fiber networks that serve the global city financial district. Sohonet delivers very good optical fiber capacity connections to digital media companies in the central London media cluster. It offers the ability to download the digital production takes of the day from Los Angeles film studios overnight so that the postproduction work on the films can be done in London when Los Angeles is off work or asleep. So, once again, we have a classic glocal infrastructure that allows a very sophisticated use of the world's time zones. This, in turn, supports the precise management of the relations between concentrations in place and connectivities across space.

The dot-com-driven development of selected inner cities amounts to the latest type of gentrification of cities. In cities like San Francisco such processes are driving the diversity—socially, economically, and culturally—out of the city as selected urban neighborhoods become gentrified as spaces for high-tech elites.[1] A major resistance campaign against the moving in of dot-coms into certain districts of downtown San Francisco is now emerging based on the argument that the internet has, in effect, undermined the cultural mix of the city. There have been massive explosions of house prices and rental prices, as well as a large number of evictions of the broad and bohemian range of counter cultures that previously located in places like South of Market and the Mission districts. So again, these internet technologies, far from being some disembodied cyberspace, are supporting radical urban changes in very real places.

Slippery Spaces of Decentralization: Call-Center Cities

Far away from the places of contested concentration, the reverse side of our story emphasizes the use of new technological networks to support the decentralization and distancing of routine transactions and flows from major urban regions. In the new logic of globalized place competition, the spaces that become home to such routinized transactions—which Markusen labels slippery spaces—are thrown together in a ruthless game of interarea competition based on the use of cheap labor, low costs, and public subsidies to attract profoundly mobile corporate investment. As organizations reorganize and restructure themselves to take advantage of the powers of IT, we are seeing a massive growth of call centers based on industrial systems for processing millions of calls a day. Such work-flow systems are still about urbanization, even though they are about removing activities from the core of the major high-cost global cities as well. We are seeing call centers grow in low-cost, more peripheral cities with relatively large amounts of labor but not with the service infrastructure and labor that these companies need. Only very rarely are these activities going into rural locations.

Such call-center geographies are now taking on a truly global dimension and some call centers are now moving to India. Certain users in the United Kingdom, for example, when they ring to ask about their electricity bill, the calls are being answered in Delhi. The Indian workforce in such call centers watch soap operas from British TV so that they can understand British regional accents. They have local temperature readings of what the weather is like in Manchester to try and provide empathy with the user, the customer, when the call comes in. In essence, then, unlike

global finance, R and D, and internet-content industries that fuel the construction of sticky spaces, such activities are globally mobile. They don't need a high concentration to support continuous innovation. These are the slippery space activities that are counterpoised to the financial, media, technopoles discussed above.

There is currently a global scramble to be a center for these decentralizing investments. A global competition is developing between peripheral cities and regions within the global north, and emerging newly industrialized spaces in the global south. Developments like the Jamaica Digiport, for example, are enclaves in the developing world which are selling themselves as digitally connected slippery spaces, as new urban spaces to electronically project services to wherever is necessary at very low cost. Initially Jamaica was servicing the American market, but with the massive collapse of global communications costs, these sorts of divisions of labor and competition are starting to emerge on a truly global scale.

Machine Spaces: Slippery Space and the Scramble to Host Internet Hardware

In addition to the human side of this call-center revolution, there is a whole new type of urban landscape emerging for basing the actual machines of the internet. We generally think of the internet as a nonmaterial phenomenon. But actually it is based on millions and millions of computer, telecommunication, service, and electricity systems that have to be based somewhere. Again there is a scramble to be that base. This is leading to some very odd transformations and spaces. For example, Sealand, an unused antiaircraft fort six kilometers (approximately four miles) off the coast of Essex in the United Kingdom—has been taken over by a group of web entrepreneurs, and offered as a nonregulated space for hosting web services. The owners are basically saying to corporations that they can come to Sealand and host anything they like on the web—they are completely free of national and European Union regulations. No questions are asked as long as they are paying for the service. In a similar vein, whole parts of the Caribbean are emerging as locations for the all-night gambling and porn industries.

A final range of technological hardware and data storage spaces that are emerging are spaces that are attractive because they are *not* on the internet. This is an attempt to avoid computer hacking, viruses, and the risk of cyber terrorism. The United States government, for example, has now agreed to create an entirely separate internet for its own use that will not have any connection whatsoever with the rest of the internet. In addition, a range of former missile launching silos in Washington State are being reorganized as ultrasecure, earthquake-proof, terrorist-proof data storage systems.

Such data-secure enclaves are likely to proliferate. In the wake of the World Trade Center collapse many companies are unlikely to recover. This is not only because of the tragic loss of key personnel; it is also because they have lost data, the most important resource after their staff. In the next decade there is thus going to be an enormous emphasis—and this is already starting—on the development and management of highly secure, fairly anonymous, and highly decentralized spaces in which data is securely input on a continuous basis.

Mobility Spaces and "Economies of Conjunction"

A penultimate set of exemplar urban spaces that we need to discuss are the mobility spaces of our emerging urban landscapes. There is a major trend currently for those spaces that exhibit what economists call *economies of conjunction* to become enormous growth poles. Economies of conjunction are simply those economies that arise from a combination of excellent access to road and rail systems, IT systems, and good airport and port links. Such spaces become critical strategic nodes because today's economies are based on the minute, "just in time" organization of flows using computers. Those spaces where the flows can be coordinated and organized, thus, become critical to the city.

The airport is perhaps the most strategic conjunction space of all, and a very strong emphasis in urban planning currently is to intensify the connection between the airport and the city—particularly through dedicated high-quality rail links as we see in Oslo and London's Heathrow airport. This idea of the city as an airport—the idea that a seamless flow of people and freight can be organized between the city and the airport—is now a central emphasis because of the critical strategic importance of airport spaces.

But, once again, such debates do not assume an equivalent flow or mobility for all. Rather, we are seeing a growing emphasis on the use of the techniques of electronic surveillance to improve the mobility of selected, privileged people while reducing it for others. For example, INSPASS—a system developed by the Biometric Consortium—is now operating between the United States and about twenty other countries around the world. It is a system through which highly mobile, frequent travelers use a smart card with a handprint scanned into it to bypass immigration controls in airports. While technology is used to enhance the mobility of INSPASS users, however, the mobility of others—especially "illegal" immigrants—is undermined by similar technological systems (face scanning, CCTV, etc.).

The strategic mobility spaces of cities articulate closely with flows of freight, too. Fifty percent of the world's trade, by value, now goes by air. By weight this would probably only be 0.001%. The high-value materials of our technological civilization are thus being coordinated through air flights and through special spaces for transshipment. An example is the Global TransPark in North Carolina. What it offers is a city-sized system for freight exchange. Aircraft can come in and load, and they have direct links to major highway, port, and railway systems, in addition to all the usual tax and customs incentives of a free port. TransPark is a classic example of how economies of conjunction, in terms of freight exchange, are being carefully designed into strategic urban spaces.

Network Architectures, Surveillance, and Urban Consumption Spaces

Turning to our final set of exemplar city spaces, it is also very important to consider the ways in which cities as consumption spaces are being repackaged, redeveloped, and managed in new ways based on technological flows, practices, and mobilities. The last fifty years have seen the widespread privatization of public space through the construction of malls and theme parks across cities. But the techniques of privately managed public space are now being adopted by the managers of older consumption spaces in city and town cores. In the United Kingdom, for example, town and city centers are increasingly trying to compete with large out-of-center malls that have invested in CCTV systems. They are also investing in new CCTV technologies. Importantly, such CCTV systems are now being digitized and are merging with computer databases of human faces. Once this computerization process is complete, and the limits to the technology are worked on, we will start to see real facial tracking systems straddling cities, nations, and perhaps continents. This is already being tested in the eastern London suburb of Newham, where 150 known young offenders are being tracked in their movements around the district on a daily, round-the-clock basis.

Conclusions

What can we conclude from such a wide-ranging discussion? We know a range of processes is clearly at work that bring renewed centrality to selected cities in our world of dynamic flows and complex technological mobilities. Through such processes, technology is being used to concentrate the financial activities of the global city, to concentrate research and development, and to concentrate the activities of the internet within privileged, so-called sticky places. These groups of activities will be the motors of the growth of the future city because they force the need for people to be copresent, to be in one place, and to experience the richness of face-to-face interaction. These sorts of things are not going to be substituted by IT; they are going to be complemented by IT. For cities that manage to sustain growth in these key industries, new centrality and new economic development is going to be forthcoming.

However, this story of renewed technological centrality is not going to be every city's future. A much more problematic future faces those cities that are unable to reach critical mass in these new centralizing activities, where the institutional, social, and cultural advantages just do not exist to realize the status of sticky space. Such slippery spaces are likely to include peripheral cities, old industrial cities, and many cities in the developing world. In such places a scramble for mobile investment dominates the way in which city agencies are trying to plan themselves. The worry with the strategy of bringing in call centers and mobile manufacturing, however, is that it is basically very vulnerable. It is vulnerable if the call center uproots because of a decision in a head office ten thousand miles away in India; it is very vulnerable if the call centers are replaced by automated computer software.

Our first conclusion, then, is that the emerging technological landscape has a very uneven geography. There seems to be a growing sense of winner-takes-all, a sense of the big cities, the metropolitan cities with the assets to concentrate growth in these new sectors, totally dominating. Inevitably, this creates a sense of fracture between those cities and the surrounding hinterlands—both near and far. As a result, we need to rethink the whole question of the relationship between so-called global cities and the traditional idea of the hinterland. On the one hand, highly privileged nodes are being brought together globally via the best technological connections available. On the other, as we saw with central London, there is more and more a sense of fracture in the relationships between these nodes and the surrounding cities and hinterlands.

My second conclusion is that more and more of our urban relationships are now being organized and mediated through software. To really understand the digital divide, for example—the relationship between the information-haves and the information-have-nots—we need to understand the ways in which software is mediating our social relationships. Software mediates and conditions people's access and entry to an exploding world of services. Systems like facial recognition, CCTV, smart cards, and smart call-center systems, use software to subtly provide very different experiences for different users. Utilities in the United Kingdom, for example—often based in the sorts of call centers that I have just been discussing—actually have a mechanism that knows who is calling instantly. This is because they can read the phone number of the caller. This call liner identification (CLI) is linked to computerized databases that automatically queue people who pay their bills more quickly than people who do not pay their bills. This is about social exclusion through software, but neither group necessarily knows it is happening. So, again, it is a question of software sifting the population, splintering what used to be a rather homogenous mass, and treating people differently.

Take a second example. The internet was designed to be nuclear war proof. What that essentially meant was that every packet of data that flew around the internet was given equal priority. So if it were busy, everyone faced problems, no one could get to the internet servers they wanted. But as the internet has become more commercialized, the architecture of it is being changed. More private companies are laying special types of internet architecture which can prioritize the packets that are flying around, so that people who are paying a premium service, those with broadband, the metropolitan elite, will literally bypass congestion and experience seamless internet service. However, people who use dial-up with old modems or whatever are not going to receive such premium services. So software becomes a means of differentiating users in very profound and important ways and, again, neither group is likely to be aware of the wider picture.

It is very clear from this discussion that our understanding of our urbanizing world requires a parallel perspective. We need to think about how cities and city spaces are changing at the same time as looking at the architecture of the technological systems that connect and mediate our urban spaces and lives. One without the other provides less than half the story. If we have a totally integrated view, we might begin to understand the whole story of how place, space, power, and technology interweave to shape the contemporary urban condition.

LOCATIVE MEDIA URBANISM

MALCOLM McCULLOUGH

Being Here Now

Must "media" mean remoteness? Whether the word indicates global communications, passive entertainments, distributed organizations, disembodied processes, or the attention economy of all of these, it implies trouble for urban space as we have known it. You don't have to be standing on a sidewalk full of people yakking into thin air on their hands-free phones to share this concern.

Fortunately, a fresh branch of the media arts is taking on problems of place. What happens when information technology moves out beyond the desktop and into the sites and situations of everyday urban life? What happens when media become embodied in access, spatial in operations, and place based in content? What cultural roles emerge for technologies of positioning, tagging, sensing, and ad hoc networking?

"Locative media" deliver information about places to those very places. Furthermore, they filter it, interlink it, and personalize it. Vigorous cultural production already surrounds these media. For example, in California, in the season when this book has gone to press, web elite assembled for *Where 2.0* and artists exhibited ninety-nine projects on the "interactive city" at *ISEA06*.[1]

Beyond these early adopters, and as with any such technocentric movement, a larger society benefits more when people with a longer and less IT-centered view take part in formative work. Thus, locative media may now interest urbanists; and good urbanism may direct these new media practices into worthwhile genres.

Transition: Five Trends

"Ubiquitous computing" may not be as profound a wave as the World Wide Web or the personal computer in the two previous decades respectively, but it is at least the biggest echo in the present. It may also be far the most social. This has largely been a consequence of mobility. No longer just business machines, no longer just for an educated elite, and no longer so overtly driven by Americans, these newest media may do more than their predecessors to shape urban experience. Or at least they may upset it. The chaotic, swarming, information-streaming realities of a rapidly urbanizing world recast the challenge of urban design.

Popular adjectives include *tangible, mobile, pervasive, invisible, embedded, physical, environmental, everyware,* and *ambient*. Although this is not the moment to debate how ubiquitous computing became the prevailing technical future, it is appropriate to challenge the "anytime/anywhere" universalist tendencies of this technological model with a healthy emphasis on locality. Since these are the usual implications of *ubiquitous*, please choose any other word.

A young Berliner takes out her "handy" to photograph some street market wares, stream them to her photo sharing service, and tag them according to her own cultural categories. To her, this is apparently more interesting than shopping per se. Perhaps she has found away to resist the commercialization, or at least to make the theming of the city at least partly her own. Presumably she hopes that her tags will link with those of her friends, and that this information will be shared not at home, but out in the very places that it describes. She may be less aware, but we should note here, that such locally situated communication fits well within the longer history of the city as a stage for public discourse, in which commerce is a means and not the end. More to the point, this simple act of "urban markup" represents several aspects of transformation in recent information media. Of these, consider five:

1. From Virtual to Embodied

Dematerialization had been the standard fare of the cybercity doomsayers, but it turns out that dematerialization has its limits.[2] For, instead of one great disembodied "cyberspace" that you enter through the looking glass of a desktop computer screen,[3] this newer web, the "geospatial web," or "internet of things," brings media experience back to the messy multiplicity of street level. This happens enough to make the word *cyberspace* sound dated. What has changed is the belief that the way to find and use networked information is overly solitary, sedentary, or virtual. Also changed is the fact that there is less physical space (as when even media moguls get stuck in traffic), and more of a return to physical space as recreation. Even former virtual communitarian Howard Rheingold had his epiphany about smart mobs in a real (or perhaps hyperreal) space: Japanese teenagers in lit-up Shibuya.[4] Activities that engage space and place willingly thus become more interesting and unusual as subject matter for design. Embodied computing (that word fits well here) particularly concerns those sorts of activities that despite being information intensive have failed to dematerialize.[5] It is of interest how many of these are urban.

2. From Macro to Micro
Up to now, studies in media urbanism have most often focused at the macro scale.[6] This is understandable in an era of information infrastructure building. Economic geographies have dominated studies of networked cities, especially from the standpoint of technology as agent of organizational change. It is commonly observed how media writ large tend to concentrate production and reorganization in a few select cities, and then to create long-distance tunnel effects among them.

So much emphasis on the far away produces cultural anomie, however. You know these laments. The throughput of global capital markets now dwarfs the sum of nations' gross domestic product. Out there in the space of flows, places have become mere operands in the fiscal abstractions of global capital. Big disinterested money obliterates local value at almost every turn. So, must any stewardship of place appear to be against capitalism, against technology (except, say, your dishwasher), and essentially an act of nostalgia? And are citizens turned consumers consigned to drift in the placeless spaces that result, and to act out their social detachment by plugging into as many technical media distractions as they can, streaming from all over the planet, preferably all at once?

If to dwell any further on such laments seems futile, consider a different perspective: What if, under a media world built on the fast-and-far, the real frontiers are in the close-and-slow?

Locative media pursue exactly this. Although built on many of these macro phenomena, the tech world now turns its focus to the micro scale instead. While study of universalizing global infrastructures may remain necessary, even central, to media urbanism, henceforth it is no longer sufficient.

3. From Universal to Situated
Despite recent temptation to be connected to all things always, most of us proceed better when our communications are shaped by physical contexts, social protocols, and cultural institutions—otherwise there would be no sense of disruption when people talk thoughtlessly on their mobile phones. Although most of these situational cues are complex socializations, such as an ethnographer might study, more and more of them have become mediated technologically, and so have become the subject matter of interaction design.

Consider one simple irony faced by technologists: the more practical and affordable the engineering performance and feature count of a medium becomes, the less likely it is to remain key to its social success. In other words, appropriateness surpasses performance as the essential factor. Appropriateness may be organizational or personal, casual or practiced, and functionally ergonomic or just conceptually aesthetic, yet it is almost always a matter of context. (Persistent contexts, appropriately configured, are, incidentally, sometimes referred to as architecture.)

Technology applied without awareness of context tends to behave obnoxiously: music comes out of restroom ceilings; a computer interrupts someone's presentation to offer software upgrades. Much as cars come with unintended side effects like creating air pollution (which so far has not been enough to discourage use), so with pervasive computing comes information pollution, autonomous annoyances, and loss of privacy. (Surveillance may be less by any Orwellian "big brother," however, than by ten thousand commercializing "little brothers;" this, too, must lie outside the scope of this essay.)

In any case, outright refusal to engage new technology rarely leads toward better cultural outcomes. One corollary in the law of unintended consequences is that happy results are the product of active appropriation. It is important to try things out. Amid times of portentous technological change, there may be as much to be lost by denial as by uncritical acceptance. Right now the best countermove to universal computing is situated computing.

4. From Behavior to Intent
Consider some fundamentals. Note that in the psychological fundamentals of interactivity, context is not so much the setting of an activity as it is one's *engagement* with it.[7] Environment is not an *Other*, or an empty container, but a perception of persistent possibilities for action. As people learn cumulatively from repeated engagements, they come to associate settings with particular states of intent. This includes not only the spaces, but also all other aspects of the embodiment, such as the objects, labels, and props of an activity. Through these, engagement comes to be "about" something.[8] For example, this is why meditation teachers insist that a particular spot in the house be set aside for no other purpose.

Traditionally the main reason for putting up with technological annoyances has been work. The embodiment of the most complex technologies has been the workplace. The activity being studied by the process designer was almost always a production task, and the worldview in which the designer had been trained was most often mechanistic. But even in workplaces, it became clear that postindustrial knowledge work required less procedure and more participation.

Thus began a general shift in the ethnographic focus from behavior to intent. Sociological staples as presentation of self; acting out tacit cultural geographies; strategic creativity; and goal sharing as the basis for community have increasingly informed technologists as they move computing toward its escape from the desktop and into urban space.

Indeed, twenty years have now passed since Lucy Suchman's influential *Plans and Situated Actions*.[9] How experts play situations has become important subject matter for media design. Conversely, how situations cue intentions has become a central concern in activity theory. So when ethnographers now bring their methods to the street-level experience of mobile computing, such as Mimi Ito has done with the pedestrian social navigation in Tokyo,[10] the work has deeper roots than may first appear. People use locative media to decide what to do together.

5. From Pushing to Posting

"What if content is something you do, not something you are given?"[11] John Thackara's "Articles of Association Between Design, Technology, and the People Formerly Known as Users"[12] declared the design challenge of pervasive computing as a need to depart from the passive mentality of mass media. Active authorship is what makes the web a web.

Chris Anderson's coinage of the "long tail" perhaps summarizes this mood best recently.[13] This theory explains the impact of large numbers of items with low numbers of instances. Worldwide, the integral sum of bottom-up street transactions—flea markets, food carts, pick-up games, meet-up points, etc.[14]—outnumber those that have been top-down formulated, branded, and pushed by corporations. Like the valuation of apparent chaos by Jane Jacobs's urbanism, but infinitely more diverse and interlinked, the long tail implies a participatory urbanism that resists the sterilizing effects of big organizations inevitable preference for predictability.

"Doing" the long-tailed city often takes the form of markup. Would-be *flâneurs* are now streaming their *dérives*. The popularity of the photo sharing service Flickr has allowed people to share their sequences of urban experience by posting images so frequently that those are experienced as streams. (Here is rich social experience of the city that does not require so much brand-induced consumption.) The markup comes with what Thomas Vander Wal has called "folksonomies:" bottom-up taxonomies in social software.[15] Online sharing of tagged information about physical things has advanced considerably.

What gives urban markup relevance to architect urbanists is the intrinsic preference for density. For example, in the friend-awareness service Dodgeball, members navigate socially by sending their location and receiving identities of others within a ten-block radius. Press on Dodgeball observes: "As the technology increasingly allows us to satisfy more eclectic needs, any time those needs require a physical presence . . . the logic of the long tail will favor urban environments over less densely populated ones. . . ."[16]

These are rudimentary examples of street-level practice in what for most is still a universalizing broadcast media society, but they are early applications of what has become quite normative, namely the use of handheld communications media for self-organizing social purposes, in particular, urban contexts.

Objective: Media of the Close and Slow

Digital media and New Urbanism have too often been caricatured at opposite ends of some political spectrum: the one for techno-libertarian futurism, the other for neoconservative nostalgia. Yet each of these movements has vigor, and each apparently offers something sensible for the cultural multiplicities and political centers that exist beyond their own supposedly dogmatic ranks. Now the two have been brought together by a shared concern for locality. Urbanism helps with the cultural problems raised by mobile media; locative media enrich any approach to place-making. Because place and culture are intertwined, it follows that more place-centered interaction design becomes a more culturally valuable endeavor.

In a complementary manner, these fields may help one another overcome any reflex toward totalizing models. For mobile and embedded computing to be culturally healthy, they cannot remain universal and always on, which are some usual implications of "ubiquitous." Under the many transformations described above, an active engagement with context produces a different experience than passively consuming worldwide media.

As the embodiment, personalization, and bottom-up economies of mobile and embedded computing kick in, the older top-down cultural models of urban experience are not enough. Besides the infrastructure itself, there is urbanism in how people obtain, layer, and manage their connections. Like attention itself, any belonging to community or place is made partial and multiple by this mediation.

For New Urbanism to endure in a manner at all appealing to a world so connected, it must open itself to emergence, appropriation, and bottom-up unpredictability. (These are the very traits that distinguish its more admirable origins in Jacobs from its less admirable origins in Disney.) Place becomes less a branded location, and more a relative state of mind that one gets into by playing one's boundaries and networks.[17] To imagine an urbanism not primarily driven by either shopping or spectacle would be a healthy departure from much recent development—locative media attempt just this.

WHAT IS THE INTERNET DOING TO COMMUNITY —AND VICE VERSA?

BARRY WELLMAN

A three-year-old New York girl reports meeting her imaginary friend when they sporadically "bump" into each other on the street. If they "miss each other," they leave messages on their imaginary voicemails. Nowadays, even a three-year old can no longer count on having an imaginary friend readily available at home. But she thinks that she can count on voice mail.

That even three-year-olds have such fantasies suggests how computer-mediated communication has come to pervade everyday life. That the *New Yorker* magazine published the girl's fantasy suggests how surprised people are about how computer-mediated communications have become routinely incorporated into people's fantasies—and lives. This article analyzes the interplay between the internet and community.[1]

Heavenly Utopia

As recently as the early to mid-1990s, utopians and dystopians fantasized like three-year-olds about the internet. All things seemed possible. Discussions about the impact of the internet often were unsullied by evidence and informed by conjecture and anecdote. Travelers' tales from internet *incognita* focused on the exotic and treated the unusual as routine. The bulk of media reporting described a parallel world of role-playing, gender-bending, and erotic pursuits, much like sixteenth-century European accounts portrayed America as filled with beasts, Amazons, and centaurs. More sober discussions had their own fantasies: they extolled the internet as egalitarian and globe-spanning, rarely considering how differences in such things as power and status might affect interactions online. For many pundits, the internet was seen as a magical device that was going to transform community, with everyone supposedly connected to everyone, without boundaries of time and space.[2]

Hellish Dystopia

Yet some early accounts were dystopian, fearing the internet as the hellish destroyer of identity and community. Lurid accounts were widely circulated of dangerous Pied Pipers harassing women and children online.[3] A major concern was the supposed inauthenticity of internet contact. Critics wondered if relationships between people who never see, smell, touch, or hear each other could be the basis for true community. Texas-based broadcaster Jim Hightower sounded the alarm on ABC radio:

> While all this razzle-dazzle connects us electronically, it disconnects us from each other, having us "interfacing" more with computers and TV screens than looking in the face of our fellow human beings.[4]

A decade later, similar concerns abound. In a moral panic, politicians and newspapers worry that the allegedly sixty million denizens of "MySpace"—a website where many teens put up self-descriptions and connect with each other—will lure teens away from authentic community into harassment and degradation.[5] Continuing a state tradition, Texas Attorney General Greg Abbott warned on July 11, 2006: "children simply cannot be safe with the current landscape of cyberspace chat rooms and social networking sites."[6] This continues the longtime tradition of pastoralist nostalgia for what supposedly were the good old days a generation ago.[7]

From Technological Determinism to Social Affordances

Those who see the internet as utopian heaven or dystopian hell have four things in common:

1. Their debates rest largely on supposition and anecdote rather than on systematic ethnographic observation, surveys of what people actually did, or laboratory experiments.

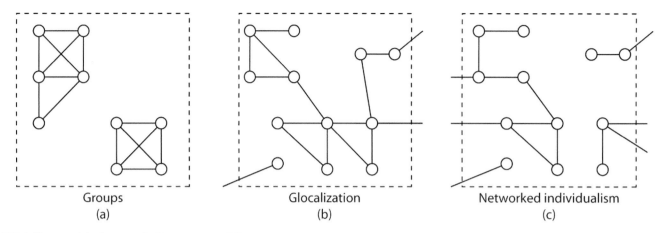

FIG. I **Three models of community.** © Wellman Associates 2005.

Groups	Glocalization	Networked individualism
(a)	(b)	(c)

2. They are technological determinists: they believe that the sheer introduction of a technology inevitably changes social relations and social structure. Their technological determinism is both presentist—thinking that the world had started anew with the internet—and parochial—assuming that only things that happen on the internet are relevant to understanding the Internet. Yet, spatially-dispersed, long-distance communities flourished well before the internet,[8] and a multitude of social, economic, and psychological phenomena are relevant for understanding who uses the internet, why, and for what purpose.[9] The medium is not the message, despite Marshall McLuhan's aphorism.[10] Rather than determining behavior, the nature of the technologies creates "social affordances:" possibilities, opportunities, and constraints for interpersonal relationships and social structures.[11] While the internet makes it possible for people to communicate quickly and cheaply across continents and oceans, it does not force people to do this and it does not force them to stop neighboring.

3. They assume the internet has a unique, immersive power to draw people into online communities and away from other pursuits. Paradoxically, while denouncing the internet as inauthentic, dystopians have highlighted its attractiveness, describing an internet so magnetic that people are in danger of being trapped in its clutches. Once caught in the web, would people be able to escape into traditional forms of community: chatting at cafés, pubs, and front yards, or visiting relatives and friends?

4. They mistakenly assume that those who communicate online, communicate *only* online. They see the internet as a separate social system rather than as a part of people's lives.

The Internet in Everyday Life

From Hope and Hype to Scholarship

From being a fantasy object in the 1990s, the widespread expansion of the internet to encompass a majority of people in the developed world made the light that had dazzled in the firmament become grounded and embedded in everyday things. The growing usability of the web, e-mail, blogs, and

their kindred transformed the internet from a world of wizards to something as routine as telephone calls had become. As cyber dreams have faded, the internet has become more important as it has become routinized and institutionalized, used by more people in more countries and in more different ways. Analysts now relate involvement in the internet to other ways in which people connect with each other, off-line as well as online such as Facebook. In some cases, they are designing social software to connect friends, workmates, and strangers.

How Important Are Online-Only Worlds?

Although the online-only world of virtual community seized attention in the early days of the internet, it turns out to play only a small role in the larger scheme of things. A high percentage of internet users also see each other in person or talk on the telephone.[12] By contrast, only a small percentage engages in online-only activities: virtual communities, role-playing games, multiplayer gaming and gambling, and cybersex. And, even in these cases, there may well be prefatory or subsequent in-person contact.

Although online-only worlds are statistically small, they can be important niches for communities, and personally important for individuals. For example, religiously orthodox Muslim women are often socially isolated in North America. Many have joined an online discussion group in which they can socialize, assuage loneliness, exchange social support and advice about how to deal with North American societies.[13] Yet, even this spatially-dispersed discussion group is not an online-only world. Members often travel to see each other, either on purpose or because they happen to be in the same city. In similar ways, people who work together online often find ways to meet in person at conferences, personal trips, or organizational get-togethers.

How Does the Internet Affect Community?

The utopian/dystopian debate continues, but it now accompanied by evidence that online communication rarely stands alone, rather, it is part of an ensemble of in-person meetings and phone calls. Evidence that the internet is weakening community was the first to be widely reported. The "Homenet" study[14] showed that some new users ("newbies" in internet slang) initially became a bit more alienated and less sociable with household and community members. However, the evidence now suggests that the internet does not isolate people from community, but may well enhance community. For example, further study of the same Homenet people has shown that alienation and the loss of sociability disappears over time as newbies become more used to the internet, with extroverts especially active users.[15]

What About Local Community?

Has the internet fostered the transformation of community into a McLuhanesque "global village,"[16] and in so doing, weakened local community? After all, people can communicate almost instantly by e-mail 24/7/365. Despite the internet's ability to leap across continents at a single bound, it does not appear to have destroyed local community. For example, Keith Hampton and Barry Wellman's study[17] of "Netville," a Toronto suburb, shows how the internet can sustain local community. "Wired" residents who had access to a high-speed internet service and an accompanying discus-

sion group neighbored more than their nonwired counterparts. Wired residents know the names of three times as many neighbors, talked with twice as many, and had been invited into the homes of 1.5 as many as their nonwired neighbors. E-mail and an online discussion groups gave wired residents opportunities to identify residents who shared common characteristics and whom they might want to know better. Thus, the internet intensified the scope and amount of overall neighborly contact, online and off-line.

If the internet neither isolates people nor weakens local community, does it affect community at all? A variety of evidence suggests that communication over the internet with friends and relatives adds on to in-person and telephonic communication. Community is "glocalized" (figure 1), combining local and spatially dispersed interaction.[18] The more frequent contact via the internet—e-mail, chats, instant messaging, interactive blogs, and the like—is associated with frequent contact on the phone and in person. In our "Connected Lives" study of the Toronto area of East York, those who use e-mail daily talk in person and by phone at about the same rate as those who use e-mail less frequently.[19] But the internet users add on e-mailing, chating and instant messaging to phone and in-person contact.

FIG. 2 **A three-computer household in Toronto, Canada.** © Wellman Associates 2005.

Is the Rest of the World Coming to Look Like America Online?

Experience shows that different societies use the internet in different ways. For example, many people in Europe and East Asia use advanced mobile phones to communicate online: surfing the web, and exchanging e-mails, and short text messages.[20]

Catalonia offers another contrast. Catalans are extensive users of web searches to find out things and of web services to book theater and travel tickets. But they do not exchange many e-mails,[21] perhaps because many Catalans live near each other and prefer to meet in cafés at night: hugging, smoking, chatting, and gesturing. Mobile phones sit beside them, ready to incorporate other close friends and relatives into conversations via e-mails and short text messages.

In the third world, people often use public-access points, such as internet cafés or schools. This creates simultaneously the possibility of individually connecting to the internet while having community members sitting nearby in person.

What is the Internet Doing to Community?

The internet is not a self-contained world. Rather than operating at the expense of the "real" world of in-person contact, the internet is a part of the real world, with people using all means of communication to connect with friends and relatives. It has not dragged people away from their households, friends, relatives, and neighbors, nor has it led most people to become heavily immersed in online pursuits with soul mates around the world. Indeed, the home has become the most important base of internet use for many, mundanely integrated into daily life (figure 2).[22] It is also becoming more difficult to distinguish "the internet" as a special medium as a variety of computer-mediated communication proliferates—from e-mail to chats, instant messaging, short text messages, and videoconferencing—as pictures, music, and videos become attached to e-mail messages, and as telephone calls make use of the internet's facilities.

Yet, as the internet has become incorporated into everyday life, it has fostered subtle changes in community. In the old days, before the 1990s, it was *places* that were largely connected: households and workplaces linked by telephone, cars, planes, and railroads. Now, it is individual *people* that are connected. Where before each household had a telephone number, now each person has a unique internet address and carries a personal mobile phone. It is striking that the 2006 debate about "social isolation in America"[23] focused on the decline in the number of people available to discuss important matters in personal networks—wherever these discussion partners might be. This is in marked contrast to the 1960s' focus on neighborhoods as the locus of the supposed decline of community.[24]

In effect, the internet and other new communication technologies are helping people to personalize their own communities. Although the evolution of "*networked individualism*"[25] started before the internet, the developing personalization, portability, and ubiquitous connectivity of the internet are accelerating the turn toward individual connectivity (figure 1). And, as portability develops from laptops to handheld computerized communication devices, people's whereabouts increasingly become less important for networking. Each person becomes a switchboard, between ties and networks. They remain connected, but as individuals available for contact anywhere and at anytime. They are no longer rooted in the home bases of home, café, and workplace. This is neither a dystopian loss of community nor a utopian gain, but rather the transformation of community from groups to networks.

THE SANTA FE–ING OF
THE URBAN AND URBANE

JOEL GARREAU

Human settlements are always shaped by whatever is the state-of-the-art transportation device of the time; shoe leather and donkeys enabled the Jerusalem known by Jesus. Sixteen centuries later, when critical transportation had become horse-drawn wagons and ocean-going sailboats, you got places like Boston. Railroads yielded Chicago—both the area around the "El" (intraurban rail) and the area that processed wealth from the hinterlands (the stockyards). The automobile resulted in places with multiple urban cores like Los Angeles. The jet passenger plane allowed more contact with such "edge cities" to rise in such hitherto inconvenient locations as Dallas, Houston, Seattle, and Atlanta, and now Sydney, Lagos, Cairo, Bangkok, Djakarta, and Kuala Lumpur. (Not to mention today's Stockholm, London, Amsterdam, Paris, Toronto, and Milan.)

The dominant forms of transportation today are the automobile, the jet plane, and the networked computer. What does adding the networked computer get you? I think the answer is "the Santa Fe–ing of the world" (figure 1). This means the rise of places, the entire point of which is face-to-face contact. These places are concentrated and walkable, like villages. Some are embedded in the old downtowns—such as Adams Morgan in Washington, D.C., or the Left Bank of Paris, or the charming portions of what in London is referred to, somewhat narcissistically, as "The City." Some are part of what have traditionally been regarded as suburbs or edge cities, such as Reston, Virginia, or Emeryville/Berkeley, California (figure 2).

Many, however, erupt far beyond our current understanding of metropolitan areas, wherever people find it nice to congregate. Santa Fe, New Mexico, is a remarkable example of this trend. It is the home of a world-renowned opera, charming architecture, distinguished restaurants, great places to buy used boots, quirky bookstores, sensational desert and mountain vistas, and major diversity, while being little more than a village of 62,000 inhabitants, far from the nearest major metropolis. This "Santa Fe–ing" means urbane well beyond the current definition of urban (figures 3, 4, and 5). It means aggregation *and* dispersal. As with all innovation, its impact is first seen among people with enough money to have choices. But as the cost of enabling technology drops precipitously, this effect is already transforming the built environment worldwide—including, in such unlikely places as Croatia and Ecuador. I have a hunch this transformation is spreading even more rapidly than was the case with the automobile or the jet plane, because it involves putting an increasingly high value on whatever is valuable about a place that *cannot* be digitized.

The logic of this hypothesis starts with the question: "In the twenty-first century, is there any future for cities of any kind?" After all, some would have us believe that with enough bandwidth, each of us can wind up on his or her own personal mountaintop in Montana, being lured down into the flatlands only to breed (figure 6).

That's a preposterous view of human nature, of course. There's a reason solitary confinement is a punishment—we are social animals—but the question makes a serious point; many of the historic reasons for human concentration are gone. It's been a century since you've had to live within walking distance of your factory. Today, you often don't even need to be within driving distance of your office—as anyone with a cell phone knows. (I'm not advocating this arrangement, I'm reporting it.) You certainly don't need a metropolis to acquire anything a dot-com is willing to sell—which is a very great deal, and growing exponentially.

Absent a cataclysm of biblical proportions, like the collapse of globalization as a result of disease, I think this means the one and only reason for congregation in the near future is face-to-face contact. Period. Full stop. The places that are good at providing this will thrive—think Oxford, England. The ones that are not will die. Cities are not forever. You have not heard much lately from the Babylon Chamber of Commerce.

(Among the cataclysms much ballyhooed at this writing is the run-up of oil prices. Perhaps I'm wrong not to be tremendously worried by this, but allow me to note that there is not a petroleum geologist on earth who thinks we are running out of oil. They observe that we are running out of

cheap oil, which is not the same thing. The Stone Age did not end because we ran out of stones. Similarly, the history of technology suggests to me that the "Petroleum Age" likely will end because of superior alternatives finally becoming economical as the price of oil increases. The internal combustion engine is a technological problem likely to be addressed by technological responses.)

There are nearly one hundred classes of real estate out of which you build cities, according to William J. Mitchell, the former head of the architecture and planning department at MIT. They are all being transfigured. The classic example is bookstores. If all you want to do is exchange money for a commodity, the path with least friction is often Amazon.com. In backwaters where, just ten years ago, buying or even borrowing a non-best seller was a chore that took weeks, hundreds of thousands of titles are now within one click. Does this mean bookstores have disappeared? Of course not. The half of them that have survived and even grown since the 1990s, however, have morphed. The critical elements are no longer the shelves. They are the couches, cappuccino machines, and cafes. Bookstores have become places to loiter, face-to-face, among like-minded people.

What about grocery stores? Do they have a future? What happens when it becomes cheaper for the supermarket to deliver your toilet paper to you than it is to heat, light, and pay rent and taxes on the store? Under what circumstances would you ever again get in your car to drive to a market again? For me, the answer is that I want to have face-to-face contact with my tomatoes—or anything else you might find in a social setting like a farmers' mar-

ket. I'm not sure I'd trust the kid at the dot-com to pick out my spare ribs—although if the emporium were called The-FrenchMarket.com, I might. If the grocer wants to ship me my barbecue sauce, however, I won't mind. Ninety-five percent of everything one finds in a supermarket is flash frozen, shrink-wrapped, and nationally advertised. We are in the midst of a burgeoning freight revolution, in which the stuff is coming to us, rather than us going to the stuff—as anybody who has Christmas shopped lately may have noted. When the grocers enter this realm, that will be fine by me. In fact, I can't think of anything in an entire Wal-Mart that I would regret having delivered in a big brown van. Visiting a Wal-Mart doesn't give me enough of a psychic boost to justify a drive now. Of course, if big-box retail migrates into the digital ether tomorrow, we'll have an enormous challenge figuring out the adaptive reuse of their buildings. What will we make of them? Roller skating rinks? Greenhouses? Nondenominational evangelical churches? Artists' lofts? Whatever the answer, I doubt their passing will be mourned.

What about college campuses, is there any future for those? After all, the University of Phoenix, the online learning establishment, became one of the hottest growth stocks of the early twenty-first century. Internet MBAs abound from some of the world's most distinguished schools. Why bother ever getting out of your pajamas to learn?

Again, I think the answer is face-to-face contact. After all, distance learning is nothing new. Benjamin Franklin engaged in correspondence classes. The United States military is awash in senior officers with advanced degrees from the

FIG. 2 Culpeper, Virginia.

University of Maryland, which has pioneered its outreach programs to people in remote locations.

However, I think distance learning will always be everyone's second choice. It works best for people who do not have the time or money for the conventional academic experience. The first choice remains the traditional universities. Getting into them has become insanely competitive and expensive. Why are they so desirable? Because sitting in class, absorbing information from a lecturer, is only a tiny part of the college experience. College is where many people meet their first spouse. It's where they develop a network of friends that they'll likely maintain for life. It's an entertainment center and an athletic center. Oh, and as for learning—most of the stuff that has stuck with me came out of dorm sessions at one in the morning, engaging in face-to-face contact with smart people.

As we shall see, the impact of face-to-face contact on urban calculations includes office space, and even home locations. But why is this transformation occurring now?

It all starts with Moore's Law. On July 18, 1968, Gordon E. Moore transformed the world when he and Robert Noyce founded a company called Intel. They would usher in a new age. The desks of the whole world would wind up featuring strange new appliances, these dun-colored boxes with "Intel inside." Moore and his early compatriots would become billionaires many times over.

But it was back in 1965 that Moore made the observation that may truly secure his place in history, for it may have the most consequence for the future of human kind. What he noted, in an article for the thirty-fifth anniversary issue of

Electronics magazine, was that the complexity of "minimum-cost semiconductor components" available for a dollar had been doubling once a year, every year, since the first prototype microchip had been produced six years before. Then came the breathtaking prediction. He claimed this doubling would continue every year for the next ten years. Carver Mead, a professor at Caltech, would come to christen this claim "Moore's Law."

Moore's Law has sprouted many variations over time. As the core faith of the entire global computer industry, however, it has come to be stated this way: the power of a dollar's worth of information technology will double every eighteen months, for as far as the eye can see. Sure enough, in 2002, with a billion transistor chip, the twenty-seventh doubling occurred right on schedule. A doubling is an amazing thing. It means the next step is as tall as all the previous steps put together. The thirty consecutive doublings of anything man-made that we have achieved at this writing—an increase of well over five hundred million times in so short a time—is unprecedented in human history. This is exponential change. It's a curve that goes straight up.

Such continuity is new—take the time before the American Civil War. The number of miles of railroad track in the United States doubled nearly seven times in the ten years between 1830 and 1840, from twenty three miles to 2,808. That was impressive. It was a curve that would be as steep and world altering as was the chip's in the 1960s.

Nonetheless, in the beginning, most people viewed the railroads as a curiosity for the elite. They still traveled by water, on horseback, or on foot. Most people didn't use computers in the 1960s, either.

FIG. 3 Canal in Amsterdam.

Here's the difference: for railroads, the pace of growth was not sustainable. You needed more and more land and steel and coal to expand the system. Those are finite resources. So the curve began to level off. It took forty more years, until 1880, to get the next five doublings, to almost 100,000 miles. It took another thirty-six years, to 1916, for the United States's railroads to make their final doubling plus a bit, reaching their peak of over 254,037 miles.

Make no mistake: the railroads changed everything they touched. They transformed Europe. North America was converted from being a struggling, backward, rural civilization mostly hugging the east coast into a continent-spanning, world-challenging, urban behemoth. New York went from a collection of villages to a world capital. Chicago went from a frontier outpost to a brawny goliath. The trip to San Francisco went from four months to six days. The West became a huge vacuum, sucking record numbers of immigrants across the Atlantic. Distance was marked in minutes. Suddenly, every farm boy needed a pocket watch. For many of them, catching the train meant riding the crest of a new era that was mobile and national. A voyage to a new life cost twenty-five cents.

Of course, as railroad expansion ran out of critical fuel—including money and demand for their services—things leveled off, and society tried to adjust to the astounding changes it had seen during the rise of this curve. Historically, adapting to this sort of upheaval has been like shooting the rapids. We start in the calm waters to which we are accustomed, bump and scream and flail through the unprecedented waters, then emerge around the bend into a very different patch of calm water, where we catch our breath and assess what we've done. The last transcontinental railroad completed in the United States was the Milwaukee Road in 1909. In part, that was because of the rise of a new transformative technology: the millionth Model-T rolled off the assembly line in 1915.

Moore's Law would have been revolutionary enough if chip power had leveled off in the 1980s after fourteen doublings—comparable to that of the railroads over eighty-five years. Our world today, marked by ubiquitous personal computers, would have ensured that. But the curve did not stop. The computer industry still regularly beats its clockwork-like eighteen-month schedule for price-performance doubling.

Another way of expressing Moore's Law is far more recognizable to many people: the price of any given piece of silicon can be expected to drop by half every eighteen months. Who hasn't eyed a whiz-bang $2,000 computer as a Christmas present, only to see an equivalent machine drop in price to $1,300 by the next holiday? Before ten Christmases pass, the gift becomes a ghost. It has been cast aside. Not because it doesn't work—it chugs along just fine. But we have changed. It now seems so clunky. The power that could have only been bought with $2,000 ten years before can be expected to be available for $31.25, according to Moore's Law. By then the power is so unremarkable that you can get it for free with a subscription to the *Economist*. Of course it no longer sits on a desktop. It has disappeared into watches, cell phones, jewelry, and even refrigerator magnets with more power than was available to the entire North American Air Defense Command when Moore first prophesied in 1965. In some cases that power seems to dissolve into pocket lint—so unremarkable you don't even register that it's there.

It essentially disappears. Take smart cards—you may have some and not even know it. They frequently look like credit cards. But they have chips in them, so they have significant powers. They allow you to enter especially secure buildings or store your medical records or pay your subway fare. Passports come equipped with them.

Full-blown versions are tiny computers without a keyboard or a screen: by 2002 these smart cards matched the processing power of a 1980 Apple II computer; by 2006 they matched the power of a 386-class PC, circa 1990; before 2010 they will have Pentium-class power—all for less than $5 apiece. Think about that—a $4 Pentium. Retail items such as disposable razors increasingly come with radio frequency identification chips, smaller than a grain of rice, which deter shoplifting. Those chips have the power of the state-of-the-art commercial computers of the 1970s. They cost pennies. They are designed to be thrown away.

The effect of Moore's Law on the built environment is profound. For example, will we ever need offices outside our homes? After all, haven't we all heard plenty about telecommuting?

Sure, but how many of us have discovered with some chagrin that the most productive five minutes of our work day has occurred around the shared printer? Somebody asks what we're working on. Conversations ensue. "Oh really? Did you know that Jane was working on something like that?" "There's this guy you've *got* to talk to; I'll send you his phone number as soon as I get back to my desk." "I was just reading about that very subject; I'll e-mail you the name of the book."

This kind of casual face-to-face contact is irreplaceable, no matter how cheap or immersive video technology gets. Humans always default to the highest available bandwidth that does the job, and face-to-face is the gold standard. Some tasks require maximum connection to all senses. I don't know whether we trade pheromones or viruses, or whether it simply allows us to read the other person's expressions and body language with the greatest precision. But when you're trying to build trust, or engage in high-stress, high-value negotiation, or determine intent, or fall in love, or even have fun, face-to-face is hard to beat.

This would seem to argue that some old patterns endure, and that's true. But think of the twists this new premium on human basics suggests. Suppose you decided that you could get all the face-to-face you needed two days a week. Would that influence where you lived? Would the mountains or the shore start looking good to you? Suppose you decided that you could get all the face-to-face you needed three days a month. Would the Caribbean start looking good to you?

Residential real estate is being transformed for these reasons. In the United States, the explosive growth is in places far beyond any metropolitan area, like the Big Sky Country of Montana, the Gold Country of the California Sierras, the Piedmont of Virginia, and the mountains and coasts of New England. For eons, when we've visited a nice place on vacation, we've asked ourselves, "Why am I going back?" Now, however, we have a new question: "Why *am* I going back?"

Santa Fe is more than eight hundred miles from Los Angeles, yet it is only semi-jokingly referred to as Los Angeles's easternmost suburb. To find out why, check out the airport any Monday morning.

If we accept that many rich people are going to find attractive this scenario of dramatically different settlement patterns that feature new aggregation—widely dispersed—the question then becomes whether information technology will ever become a global influence on the built environment, shaping the way the middle class and even the working class live, the way railroads, jets, and automobiles did.

I would argue that the answer is yes. "Jet set" used to refer to the wealthy. Horseless carriages were once a luxury. But none of this is any longer true. If it were, planners would not be so upset at the vision of a China full of automobiles.

In fact, this "Santa Fe–ing" pattern of dispersion plus aggregation looks a lot like the behavior of corporations over the last half century. The only difference is that now, due to Moore's Law's continuing precipitous drop in the price of information technology, the benefits have become affordable to a burgeoning number of individuals.

For half a century, corporations have put each piece of their puzzle wherever they find comparative advantage. They figured out that with enough mainframes and toll-free telephone lines, they could put their headquarters one place, their research and development a second place, their factories a third

FIG. 4 The West End neighborhood of Dallas, Texas.

FIG. 5 Hvar, Croatia.

place, their back shop paper shuffling a fourth place, their call centers a fifth place, and their salesmen all over the place. This IT-driven dispersion contributed hugely to the rise of aggregations we see in the edge cities of places like the Route 128 corridor around Boston, the birthplace of high technology.

Talk to corporate location specialists and they will happily tell you that of the top one hundred things their clients look for, the first ninety nine are all really one thing: a qualified workforce. If the facility in question is a sneaker factory, that means people who will work for pennies an hour, and the answer may be Malaysia. If this means advanced innovation, the answer is places where smart people are willing to cluster, like Silicon Valley—and Bangalore, India.

The core premise of the Santa Fe–ing hypothesis is that this sort of choice is now available to millions, and soon billions. In 2008, it is expected that a momentous moment will arrive, when the majority of all humans on earth will be networked via cell phones. Because of the ability of Moore's Law to bring technology to the masses at an accelerating rate, similar choices are now available to individuals, who can look to live, work, play, pray, shop, and die wherever they see comparable advantage. They are no longer inextricably tethered to huge, centrally located organizations.

At the time of the American Revolution, in the Agrarian Age, more than ninety-five percent of all people lived outside what then passed for cities, because wresting profit from the land through farming, trapping, forestry, and the like was how wealth was created. Today, however, technology has allowed a tiny number of people to farm thousands of acres, and the number of people in these occupations in the United States has dropped to less than two percent.

Similarly, half a century ago, at the height of the Industrial

Age, the majority of all Americans were in blue-collar manufacturing jobs. Today it's nineteen percent and dropping, while the number of people in "service occupations" exceeds seventy-eight percent. This is not all about a decline in industrial competitiveness. The United States's steel industry is the most productive in the world. That's because it has lowered the number of man-hours per ton of steel to very low rates, by the increasing use of information age cleverness to make its product. Even automobile manufacturing has used information technology to redraw the map of where it builds cars. Who, a generation ago, would have expected Mercedes to locate its United States assembly plant in Alabama?

There's no reason to think the rest of the developing world is not following this pattern (figure 8). There are already thirty African nations with more cell phones than landlines. If you look at the billboards in a megalopolis like Lagos, you will be convinced that the three biggest industries in Nigeria are evangelical churches, health food supplements, and cell phones. At this writing, it's already been five years since Filipinos ousted a tyrant for the first time using cell phone text messaging to mobilize hundreds of thousands of people for street demonstrations in under an hour. In developing countries the proportion of people with access to a phone grew an astonishing twenty-five percent in the 1990s, according to the Worldwatch Institute, an organization devoted to "an environmentally sustainable and socially just society." One in five of the world's population had used a mobile phone by 2002—up from 1 in 237 in 1992. This remarkable pattern fueled connections to the 'net. In 1992, just 1 in 7,788 of the world's population had used the internet. In 2002, 1 in 10 had.

To be sure, these patterns are not distributed uniformly. In places capable of great technological sophistication, such as China and Russia, governments who fear their own dissidents—and thus try to control information—have attempted to intentionally slow the revolution, the RAND Corporation has noted. Some Middle Eastern societies recoil at dissemination of Western ideas in general, and pornography in particular. Latin America is hampered by low literacy rates. There are some failed places on earth marked by such outrageous politics, pathetic infrastructure, abysmal annual incomes, and few cities that it's hard to imagine how they will achieve any significant development any time soon. Singapore researchers examining internet uptake in Asia pointed to a familiar list of failed suspects—Bangladesh, Cambodia, Kazakhstan, Laos, and Myanmar, for example.

Nonetheless, the gap between the haves and have-nots has hardly proven to be hopelessly rigid, as the migration of software-writing jobs to India has demonstrated. The International Telecommunication Union, tallying broad measures of connectedness worldwide, including affordability, found Slovenia tied with France. Korea, Hong Kong, and Taiwan were ahead of the United States. In the Caribbean basin, access for the Bahamas, Saint Kitts and Nevis, Antigua and Barbuda, Barbados, Dominica, Trinidad and Tobago, Jamaica, Costa Rica, Saint Lucia, and Grenada were ahead of Russia. The Eastern European nations of Estonia, the Czech Republic, Hungary, Poland, the Slovak Republic, Croatia, Lithuania, Latvia, Bulgaria, Belarus, and Romania were ahead of China. The Singapore researchers found that a lack of English-speakers did not necessarily correlate with poor technology pickup. In a post-literate world—in which the internet increasingly becomes something you watch and listen to, rather than read—low literacy rates were less a barrier than one might expect, at least in Asia. The digital divide seems to be narrowing, a University of Toronto study says. The demographic lag between those who use the internet in developing countries and those who use it in the United States was about five years, the Canadian researchers reported. This technology is getting to the masses a lot faster than did electricity, radio, washing machines, refrigerators, television, air conditioners, and automobiles.

The big difference between information technologies and others separating the haves from the have-nots is price. Because the curve rules, costs drop dramatically. The transformative stuff quickly becomes affordable and ubiquitous, even in developing countries. How can this not have consequences for our material world?

Every urban African I've ever talked to would prefer to be living in his or her village. They say they came to the city for economic opportunity, not out of preference. They return to their villages every chance they get. If, as the price of information technology approaches zero—transforming everything from transportation to markets—at the same time that the problems of megalopolises become more and more intractable, the value of being someplace that is great for reasons that can't be digitized will broaden.

If this puts a cap on the growth of megalopolises by spreading the benefits of urbanity more broadly—the way the automobile drained immigrant ghettos like the Lower East Side of Manhattan into the former cow pastures and potato farms of New Jersey and Long Island during the middle of the twentieth century—I'm not sure that's so bad.

What started in Santa Fe could transform the world.

FIG. 6 A market in Marrakesh, Morocco.

PART 9: SOCIAL CAPITAL AND MUTUAL BENEFIT

9.1

CREATING COMMON SPACES

URBAN PLANNING, LOCAL MEDIA, AND TECHNOLOGY

ROBERT PUTNAM AND LEWIS FELDSTEIN

Again and again, we find that one key to creating social capital is to build-in redundancy of contact. A single pitch is not enough, whether you are pitching unionization or Christian salvation. Common spaces for commonplace encounters are prerequisites for common conversations and common debate. Furthermore, networks that intersect and circles that overlap reinforce a sense of reciprocal obligation and extend the boundaries or empathy.

Sociologists refer to this aspect of social networks as "multistrandedness:" how many different layers of connection do they unite? When you frequently encounter the same person at the market and the ball field and a political rally, your ties with her are multistranded. Particular practices can facilitate the forging of multistranded ties. Thus, Saddleback's lawn flags make visible the overlap among networks of religious community, neighborhood residence, and national identity. Like the "Are You Reading *Mockingbird*?" buttons in Chicago, they allow participants to recognize affiliations they share with folks they see every day, opening the door to the conversations that can turn shared interests or common membership into personal connection.

Urban planning, architecture, and technology can each foster redundancy and multistrandedness by creating opportunities for encounters that knit together existing ties. Because local arrays of built space and communications technology act as "background structural factors" in most of our cases, their true importance is not always manifest. But in certain of our cases, activists have made crafting spatial infrastructure a conscious priority. The Chicago library system altered its fundamental mission (and changed its physical planning) precisely because leaders recognized the importance of shared space for building community.

Experience Corps organizers create places and occasions for their volunteers to meet up—mailboxes in the school office, a classroom with coffee and doughnuts to start the day—and human support networks flourish within them. "If this room wasn't here," says one volunteer, "we'd be in bad shape."

Urban design can facilitate the same dynamics on a larger scale. Tom McCall Waterfront Park was an important victory for social capitalists in Portland precisely because it replaced a superhighway (designed to speed commuters out of the city) with a public park (designed to foster common conversations and repeated encounters). Dudley Street activists struggled six years for a community center that could bring their weight lifting benches, computer lab, and after-school programs under a single roof. Local post offices around the country used to provide sites for redundant, multistranded encounters, but that role as a site for social-capital creation was not part of the intended purpose of the United States Postal Service. Saving "inefficient" local post offices would have made more sense if their contribution to community building had been part of the cost-benefit equation.

Local newspapers that provide a forum for exchange among editors, reporters, readers, and residents (categories that themselves overlap) play a comparable role. In their pages, interviewers and interviewees explain innovations, rally support, display successes, tell personal stories that crystallize collective aims, and hold local leaders and organizations accountable to the community. Above all, they provide a common space for common arguments. It is no coincidence that Portland and Tupelo—the two cases in which social-capital building seems to have become fully embedded in the public life and governance processes of an entire city—both have unusually active and enduring local newspapers.

As we searched out case studies of social-capital formation for this book, we found new communications technologies to be most important as support and stimulus for long-standing forms of community, rather than as instigators of radically new "virtual communities" (despite the expectations of some optimistic pundits and despite our best efforts to find examples of the latter). The "Do Something" website turned out to be one of the least dynamic parts of the project, much to the founders' surprise. Yet in the same years the need to access resources available only online was drawing Chicagoans back into libraries, providing the public demand that has helped turn the new local libraries into crossroads and clearinghouses for the neighborhoods that surround them.

Craigslist, too, is both a crossroads and a clearinghouse for a physical community: the greater Bay Area. As is the case with the Chicago libraries, individuals turn to craigslist with a specific query. Again like the libraries, the richness of craigslist as a social site is the way disparate resources and myriad social networks overlap in a single space, so that one query leads to multiple encounters, which can deepen into ongoing relationships. In this sense craigslist is the very opposite of a narrowband listserv, where the only thing that links participants is their interest in one topic (be it 1964 T-birds or Italian politics) and the ties created online never overlap with participants' off-line social worlds. Renting apartments and finding backgammon companions for trips to the laundromat are not normally handled on the same channel. That they are in craigslist is the reason the website has become a true connective tissue for Bay Area lives.

Of course, it is still early in the life cycle of the internet as a social force; the future may hold important innovations. We venture to suggest that those innovations that allow us to link virtual to other kinds of connections will be the most powerful in their effects. Computer-based technology matters not because it can create some new and separate form of virtual community, but because it can broaden and deepen and strengthen our physical communities. Just as an alloy is a mixture of several metals that has different and more advantageous properties than those of any of its constituents, so we should be aiming to craft alloys of electronic and face-to-face networks that are more powerful and useful than either kind alone.

Like plazas and parks, local newspapers, and neighborhood libraries, internet technology could create social spaces within which we see how our numerous networks of interest and interaction overlap and intersect. In constructing any such spaces, we have a vital collective stake in fostering local input and ensuring public access. Claims about the economic benefits of privatization or consolidation in all these realms (urban spaces, municipal services, media, and communications) need to be evaluated in the light of social-capital "externalities," or we risk signing away vital community resources before we fully recognize their worth.

Over the past generation, America's communities have undergone profound social and cultural changes, which meant that as the new millennium dawned, we were no longer building the dense webs of encounter and participation so vital to the health of ourselves, our families, and our polities. These changes included the privatization of leisure time that accompanied the explosion of electronic entertainment; the labor market changes that drew ever greater numbers of adults out of home-based unpaid work and into long hours of paid employment; and the suburban sprawl that bifurcates our communities of residence from our communities of work. Reweaving social webs will depend in part on the efforts of dedicated local leaders who choose to pursue their goals (whether teaching phonics, unionizing workers, or reducing on-the-job injuries) through the sometimes slow, frequently fractious, and profoundly transformative route of social-capital building. But reweaving will also depend on our ability to create new spaces for recognition, reconnection, conversation, and debate. Creating these spaces will require innovative uses of technology, creative urban and regional planning, and political will.

THE THIRD PLACE

A BELATED CONCEPT

RAY OLDENBURG

In his book, *Growing Up Absurd*, Paul Goodman declared that a man has only one life to live, and if during it he has no great environment, no community, he has been irreparably robbed of a human right. Most Americans were robbed of that right following World War II, largely because we failed at urban development. While downtown areas suffered the disruptions of urban renewal and the several programs which followed, the multitudes adopted Henry Ford's solution, that of abandoning the city altogether. Suburban sprawl thus became our primary urban feature everywhere controlled by restrictive zoning and construction codes. Prefaced with assurances that the good of the community was uppermost, those codes effectively destroyed community. The planning that followed focused on the needs of automobiles, not people.

Inevitably, the privatization of life and the accompanying desiccation of the public sphere produced enough stress, alienation, and loneliness to bring urban planning under harsh scrutiny. Urban sprawl had substituted hectic commuting for the free time workers once enjoyed after work and before the dinner hour. Everywhere couples were encouraged to buy into housing they could not easily afford for the home was no longer part of a supportive community, but a replacement for it. Stay-at-home mothers were starved for adult company, while working mothers were often exhausted by the dual responsibilities of wage earning and homemaking. Daily opportunities to relax with friends and neighbors had all but disappeared.

The growing body of literature on the subject was replete with the perplexing phrase "sense of community," as though the realization of actual community were an illusive, mystical, and seemingly unattainable possibility. To this observer, community exists when and where those who share a locality and its concerns freely and frequently associate with one another, and the cardinal sin of post–World War II urban planning was that it denied them the places to do so.

In earlier times, and in addition to home and the workplace, there were "third places," where people met to relax, converse, and enjoy one another's company. A variety of them existed within walking distance of people's homes, and they included soda fountains, beauty parlors, bait shops, diners, coffee counters, taverns, candy stores, barber shops, town squares, produce markets, post offices, and cafes. The lack of a generic term for the variety of establishments in which people were able to mix with those of other interests and occupations has proved unfortunate. Neither their collective fate nor their common virtues were well understood or even valued as they should have been.

To the contrary, the importance of third places and the socializing they host has often been viewed negatively. There are powerful interests, manifest in the corporate regard for the general population, that want people to work hard, earn as much as they can, and spend it quickly. Simple pleasures, a relaxed pace of life, inexpensive leisure, and ample time reserved for friends and family are anathema to a culture which places far more emphasis on the consumer role than on citizenship. Additionally, there is a residual Puritanism in America that admonishes against "wasting time," particularly in public places.

The Need for Third Places

An accounting of the virtues or beneficial functions of third places therefore seems very much in order. These follow in no necessary order, and are not claimed to be definitive, but the sum of them should convince even the skeptic that the loss of third places has had a deleterious effect on our society.

We may initially note that democratic societies require active and open involvement of people with one another. John Dewey put it well when he opined, "the heart and final guarantee of democracy is in the free gatherings of neighbors on the street corners to discuss back and forth and converse freely with one another." Third places are superior venues in this regard, because they are more inclusive than other forms of association. More occupations, more life styles, more points of view come into contact in third places than in narrow interest groups which tend to nourish meager personalities.

All research on the subject demonstrates the positive relationship between having friends and living a longer and happier life, and the more friends the better. But there can be a problem, as some have observed—friends are nice, but one needs protection from them. One needs a good measure of control lest friends "get in your hair" when you don't want them around. It appears that the only way one can have a good many friends and meet them often is to have a third place that they also frequent. Given the casual informality of third places, one may visit when one wishes, stay as long as one wishes, and leave when one wishes.

When and where third places exist in residential areas, they serve as "ports of entry" where newcomers may gain a quick orientation on the locale and what it offers. Third places also serve to unify the neighborhood such that, for the most part, everybody knows everybody else. That most residential areas are now devoid of such places seems strange indeed, for Americans change residence more often than in the past, and have no easy way to meet those who live close by and whose company might be enjoyed. Developers may market their subdivisions as communities, but community is what the home buyer is protected from when there are no gathering places where local residents can easily associate with one another.

To the extent that the accumulation of social capital is beneficial to local economies, third places play an obvious role in fostering it. Social capital is generated when the people living in an area come to know one another's interests, resources, and skills and trust develops between them. In the course of informal socializing prospective partners, investors, managers, operators, and employees form relationships that result in business ventures contributing to the economic growth of the area.

Third places often serve as both sorting and staging sites for a neighborhood. People become known for their temperament, interests, skills, weaknesses, hobbies, etc. Out of the larger mix, smaller associations may be formed including close friendships. When natural disasters occur, the able-bodied assemble and do collectively that which can't be done individually and can't await bureaucratic intervention. In the aftermath of hurricane Andrew which devastated South Florida in 1992 some of the men ventured out wanting to help those in need, but there was no place for them to go to meet with others of like-minded concern. Situations like this reveal residents total dependency upon state and local agencies because their inability to help one another has been sacrificed for the excessive privacy imposed upon postwar residential areas.

To be regularly involved in a third place is to enjoy the benefits of a support group. Beyond the emotional support and the spiritual tonic that camaraderie bestows, there is a good deal of practical help. As one listens to the conversational banter in third places, one gets the impression that there is no agenda of topics—but there is. Needs are always attended to, be they for information, advice, the loan of a tool, or a helping hand. The regard third-place habitués have for one another is evident in the concern expressed when one

of "the gang" is absent. Two sequential absences and someone will be sure to check on the absent person's welfare.

Third places serve as informal political forums, as the common man's intellectual forum, and as places wherein people provide their own entertainment. Laughter is far more often heard in this company than in any other round of daily life, and laughter, we are informed, is good for one's health. Third places allow retired people to keep in touch with those still working, and they encourage people to retire where they've spent most of their lives rather than making a final migration to Sun City. Finally, third places are magnets that draw people who have moved away to return to visit. Old acquaintances are renewed in settings fondly remembered.

Changing Third Places

The general stores where second generation westward-moving immigrants gathered are gone as are the candy stores, grist mills, gambling saloons, millinery shops, and other kinds of establishments at which earlier generations congregated. Not yet extinct but close to it is the soda fountain, the "bar without booze," of which well over 100,000 once served everyone in their respective neighborhoods. Taverns have declined as the nation has entered its third prohibition movement. Chicago, which once had over 10,000 of them, has fewer than 2,000 today. The post office, once a daily meeting place for many, serves a miniscule proportion of the population compared to what it did in earlier times.

The decline in informal gathering places has occurred not only because they are now prohibited in most residential areas, but also because they are being replaced in commercially zoned areas by chain operations which operate on an impersonal, high volume, fast turnover basis. The chains thrive by killing off local independent establishments over which they have major advantages in adverting, in visibility to newcomers, and in being able to purchase consumables in volume at substantially reduced prices. As cloned establishments replace unique ones, the nation as a whole loses the variety of choices and experiences it once afforded its citizens. The corporate colonization of the public realm, coupled with unifunctional zoning codes that facilitate it, will make it difficult to replace the local-owned independent third places that were the best of them.

With the decline of the tavern, the coffeehouse has finally come into its own in the United States. In the sixties, a wave of them began to appear in our larger cities. Most were rather sleazy places, appealing mainly to young adults still living at home but wanting to get out of the house and relax amid friends in places they could afford. Equipped with cable spools as tables and paperback books rescued from the trash, they operated on a shoestring, but they rekindled the desire for a more livable urban habitat.

Meager as they were, these coffeehouses often began the cycle of renewal in dilapidated urban neighborhoods. They would attract young artists and display their sketches and paintings and that, in turn, would attract experience-seeking yuppies and before long rents would begin to rise and the neighborhood would be well on its way to restoration.

Urban planners neither planned these modest ventures nor acknowledged their debt to them revealing, once again, their distance from the real needs of the people.

More recently, coffeehouse chains, especially Starbucks, have become dominant. Whether or not one considers them third places seems to depend upon one's previous experiences. Those who've known the unifying camaraderie of a well-run neighborhood tavern or coffee shop discount them while those who've known no better tend to embrace them.

Coffee has also become an important ingredient in the promotion of both churches and libraries as third places. Urban sprawl and a high rate of residential migration have combined to separate churches from the communities they once served. When people walked to it, the church was a community center and to make it that again, it must become a place visited more than once a week and for more than just traditional church services. Many churches are adding multiuse facilities including gymnasiums, locker rooms, meeting rooms, etc., with a coffee shop at the core. For churches that respond in this fashion, bad urban planning has been beneficial. Many get involved with the church in no small part because it offers connection to community otherwise unavailable.

Libraries are also capitalizing on the disappearance of informal public gathering places. As they now must compete with electronic information systems, libraries find that they can offer what Google cannot—a third-place ambience. The old prohibitions against talking and beverage consumption are going by the way and coffee served in more pleasant, comfortable, less austere surroundings adds new appeal to this old institution.

Third-place libraries are special in two important ways. First, like the soda fountains of earlier times, they mix the generations which most third places do not do. When one considers all the grief, immature behavior, and alienation attending the segregation of age groups in our society, this is no small matter. Second, libraries encourage life-long learning and self-improvement, which is no small matter either, given the failings of public education in America today.

One of the fastest growing kinds of third places in the United States may not be recognized as such. Since the mid-nineties, the number of dog parks has grown exponentially. With over forty million households with dogs but not the space to provide adequate exercise for them, coupled with the willingness of many municipalities to provide that space, there has been a veritable explosion in the number of dog parks, to say nothing of the more than two hundred dog beaches already in existence.

Several factors combine to make dog parks, people parks as well. Dogs need daily exercise, ensuring that visitation will be regular and frequent. The presence of the dogs and mutual fondness for them facilitates easy introductions with much talk about each other's pets. The owners' daily schedules will find the same people running into one another over and over again at the same time of day. The owners, along with their dogs, usually find these outings in natural surroundings refreshing, even recuperative. A scant two decades ago, the fortunate few found a vacant lot to walk their dogs after work. Now dogs are bringing their owners together much as children have always brought adults together.

Another possibility of experiencing a third place can be found in museums. For most museums to sustain themselves they must attract repeat visitors, and simply changing the exhibits a few times a year does not pay the bills. Nor does the addition of a gift shop suffice, even though many visitors get no farther. There must be novelty and comfort and, ironically, occasional escapes from art—anyone who has walked the wing of the Louvre Museum in Paris in which the Mona Lisa is displayed may know the feeling. So much art to be viewed in so short a time dulls appreciation. Little desire remains to view the rest of the four hundred thousand items on display.

On any Thursday evening, weather cooperating, the Walker Art Center in Minneapolis will play host to a thousand or more visitors. An upscale restaurant, an artificial intelligence program that interacts with visitors, an invitation to the book club, dabbling in the art lab, movie screenings, and lectures combine to add entertainment and excitement to the visit. The Walker exemplifies the trend in museum evolution.

Whether museums will eventually evolve into third places remains to be seen. The point here is that many of them are trying to be regularly-visited gathering places, more for the local population than for out-of-town visitors.

Yet another third place experience worth monitoring is called *herfing*. Herfing refers to the practice of smoking cigars in the company of fellow aficionados. Cigar smoking is quite unlike cigarette smoking; only one is smoked during a session, it is not inhaled, and it is a bona-fide gourmet experience with the minimum price per cigar usually set at three dollars. Herfs, as these sessions are called, involve comfortable chairs, conversation, and all-male company in its least active state short of sleep. It has become fashionable to deride "good ole boy" networks and smoking in any form, thus the enjoyment derived may eventually be confined to private homes. Cigar parlors reached their peak of popularity in 1996, after which many yuppies gave up on them.

Herfing is worth monitoring because it represents one of the last bastions of all-male association, and mixed company is a powerful form of censorship. Just as women have needed protection from the "rough" world of men, so too, do men need protection from the "soft" world of women, but this argument seems to have few supporters at present.

Two pretenders to third-place status also deserve attention because they offer easy availability and false promise. Many today argue in favor of "virtual" third places. . . finding community in the computer as it were. However, if one accepts the virtues of third places as identified above, the notion is untenable. On the contrary, the computer, like television, is yet another aid to isolation. Unfortunately, many among the younger generations are ill at ease in face-to-face meetings with strangers, and much more comfortable communicating via computers in the safety of their homes. The need, in a democratic society, to interact with people who think and feel differently than we do and who have different interests, seems lost on the proponents of "virtual community."

Another false step toward reclaiming third places is in the notion that the workplace can supply it. We have already seen, thanks to the privatization of life inherent in urban planning, that the family cannot replace community. The workplace has even more limitations: it excludes all other members of the family; it offers no social support to those who lose their jobs; it lacks sufficient connection to the wider community; it holds to no higher values than shareholders' earnings; it assumes that everybody likes their job; and it discourages association off the work lot. For some people, admittedly, the workplace serves as their third place, but upon retirement they lose their support group when they need it most. Many a wife has suffered the "lost soul continually underfoot," the retired husband with nowhere to go and nothing to do.

Prospects

Third places will never again appear in the number or variety that Americans once enjoyed, nor will we be able to walk to them as we once did. Sprawl continues to be the major mode of urban development. The highway lobby seems unstoppable as more and wider roads are funded to lead to even bigger big-box stores. There seems no successful way to retrofit residential subdivisions, even if codes were amended to permit it.

President Lyndon Johnson observed that "greed and stupidity" shaped our cities after World War II. Greed remains, but we are less stupid, as evidenced by the rash of writings documenting the evils of urban sprawl. American ingenuity, fueled by the human need for community, is called upon to effect improvements. Urban infill is a promising development as those returning from the suburbs discover how much easier life is when one can walk to several necessary or desired destinations.

The emerging "cafe society" movement is also promising, for it leads away from entertaining in domestic privacy and toward engaging new friends and old in public venues. The movement, if successful, will be a boon to our democratic society, for cafe society is far more inclusive than home-based entertaining. Those who have neither the space nor the means to entertain at home can at least afford a glass of wine or a few beers in the pleasant atmosphere of a cafe located along a lively street.

My title suggests that the third place concept is belated. It is predicated on the belief that if we had understood the similarities between coffee counters, taverns, soda fountains, barber shops, and other informal gathering places, and if we had recognized their essential contributions to human community, the evils of restrictive zoning and urban sprawl might have been avoided. That may not be true; it may be that vested interests well understood that isolated, alienated people become voracious consumers who cling to the belief that the way to happiness and contentment is material acquisition, and then lobbied successfully to create the conditions that maximize consumption.

DEMOCRACY AND "NEIGHBORLY COMMUNITIES"

SOME THEORETICAL CONSIDERATIONS ON THE BUILT ENVIRONMENT

KEVIN LEYDEN AND PHILIP MICHELBACH

Most social scientists who study neighborhoods are familiar with the work of Jane Jacobs.[1] According to Jacobs, spontaneous contacts between neighbors lead to social trust. As she notes:

> The trust of a city street is formed over time from many, many little public sidewalk contacts. It grows out of people stopping by at the bar for a beer, getting advice from the grocer and giving advice to the newsstand man, comparing opinions with other customers at the bakery and nodding hello. . . . Most of it is ostensibly utterly trivial but the sum is not trivial at all. The sum is such casual, public contact at a local level—most of it fortuitous, most of it associated with errands, all of it metered by the person concerned not thrust upon him by anyone—is a feeling for the public identity of people, a web of public respect and trust, and a resource in time of personal or neighborhood need.[2]

Jacobs argued emphatically that pedestrian-oriented, mixed-use neighborhoods, those with locally owned shops, stores, restaurants, bars, and other accidental gathering places, are essential for the health of a community. These places provide opportunities for social interaction and discourse without formal pressure to get to know neighbors. This sort of environment enables residents to maintain their privacy and be social simultaneously. Jacobs stressed the linkage between the built environment and social trust, which she argued is important for a successful community.

In this piece we want to build on Jacobs's view of people embedded in neighborhoods and examine the theoretical basis for arguing that neighborhoods help to foster democratic citizenship. There is solid empirical evidence that citizens are clearly affected in their decisions to participate politically by the skills they learn or the contacts they make at school, work, and church, and within community groups.[3] In addition, scholars of social capital—defined as the social networks and the norms of reciprocity and trustworthiness that arise from them—stress the interplay between community involvement, sociability, trust, and engagement in political affairs.[4]

But beyond this recognition that social environments matter, only a handful of scholars have examined whether the built environment might also affect political participation or other aspects of the way democracy functions.[5] Few attempt to actually measure community or recognize that that community comes in different physical forms. Putnam[6] provides some evidence suggesting the need to commute (associated with car-dependent suburban living) explains some of the decline in social capital in the United States. And, examining the impact of community design—indirectly—Oliver[7] concludes that it is the lack of conflict in communities rather than the lack of social interaction that explains low political participation rates in modern homogeneous suburbs. Leyden,[8] however, came to a very different conclusion after examining data directly collected at the neighborhood level. He asked whether the way we design our communities has implications for the proper functioning of democracy. More specifically, he examined whether individuals living in mixed-use, pedestrian-oriented neighborhoods are more likely to participate politically (or have higher levels of social capital more generally) than individuals living in modern auto-dependent suburban subdivisions. His findings strongly suggest that a neighborhood's design—and the social relations that design either encourages or discourages—plays an important role for democratic citizenship. Neighborhoods that are pedestrian-oriented and mixed-use appear to enable people to interact informally, which in turn enhance their willingness to be politically active.

Ignoring the City: The Political Theory of Neighborhoods

One might expect that the theoretical basis of this argument would be well elaborated. After all, one of the earliest truly social scientific studies examined how a sense of community affects individuals.[9] Nevertheless, we find that this question's theoretical background is under-studied. Political theory has been largely—and strangely—silent

FIG. 1 A Chicago neighborhood within walking distance to shops, restaurants, schools, and public transportation.

about how community design may affect democracy.[10] This is unusual because political theory as an enterprise has been deeply interested in how the construction of communities interacts with the development of conceptions of citizenship. For instance, classical Greek political theory, which most political theorists treat as the beginning of a conversation about politics stretching over more than two millenia, was explicit about the importance of the built environment for politics. Aristotle's *Politics* is a telling example precisely because it sits as the theoretical center to an empirical project—the collecting and analyzing of all known constitutions by Aristotle and his students. Aristotle famously makes the claim that, "man is by nature a political animal."[11] The argument about the appropriateness of one specific political arrangement—the Greek *polis*—to human flourishing is necessarily downplayed in most discussions of Aristotle because it makes him unapproachable to us: virtually no one is interested in reviving small city-states in which a very few adult male citizens are afforded the leisure to participate in politics through the exploitation of slaves and women. But Aristotle's argument is a kind of accusation against those who would argue that community design is unimportant for governance—for him, the only politics worthy of the name takes place in a highly specific built environment. That

FIG. 2 Convenience shopping with a lot of it catering to the maintenance of cars.

239

environment is even more relevant for us because the polis was small in scale (no more than forty thousand male citizens) but also because of the centrality of face-to-face interaction among this small group of citizens on an ongoing basis and on foot in the *agora* (marketplace). The agora was the most important location for social interaction, as citizens took much of their pleasure in walking and talking together.[12]

The silence of contemporary political theory on this issue is striking, but it is perhaps not accidental. The twentieth-century urbanist Norton E. Long once issued a friendly challenge to the political theorist Leo Strauss: Long would write a piece on Aristitotle if Strauss authored one on urban politics. Long published "Aristotle and the Study of Local Government,"[13] but Strauss never chose to write on concrete cities. Long was reacting to the then-recent (and to him disturbing) turn of political theorists away from their traditional engagement with the rest of the discipline.[14] Indeed, until the mid-twentieth century, mainstream political theorists were interested in practical—one could even say pragmatic—questions.

John Dewey, Democracy, and the Importance of "Neighborly Communities"

The connection afforded by face-to-face interaction was decisive for classical Greek theory: Socrates spent his days in the agora interrogating and inciting his fellow Athenians.[15] Although the argument emphasizing this social context—the importance of the built environment and its implications for democracy—has been largely ignored by contemporary scholars, this was not always the case. As recently as the mid-twentieth century the American philosopher and education reformer John Dewey emphasized the social environment in explaining human behavior and even human nature itself: "Everything which is distinctly human is learned . . . to learn to be human is to develop through the give-and-take of communication an effective sense of being an individually distinctive member of a community."[16]

Dewey saw himself concerned with the solution to a practical political problem. To him, there was an undeniable mismatch between the hopes for democracy and its actual functioning. Liberal institutions including constitutional

FIG. 3 Suburban desert with "drive-thru" charity receptacle.

FIG. 4 Eyre Square, Galway City, Ireland. Public places are important for encouraging social interaction.

rights, universal suffrage, and frequent elections—although essential to democracy—did not seem to enable the public to voice their true concerns and wishes, and actually play a role in the governing process. To Dewey, the question was not how does the public govern but how to *enable* the public to govern: "By what means shall [the public's] inchoate and amorphous estate be organized into effective political action relevant to present social needs and opportunities?"[17] The goal, Dewey emphasized, should be to figure out or "discover the means by which a scattered, mobile, and manifold public may so recognize itself as to define and express its interests."

Dewey, like most contemporary political philosophers and scientists, did not believe that most individual citizens could simply or naturally understand politics. He is, after all, perhaps the profoundest modern thinker on democratic education. And his writing has a populist cast which runs counter both to his reputation and to the progressive era ideal of scientific governance.[18] He did not believe in an "omni-competent individual."[19] Human beings have a limited capacity to judge what is before them and are thus likely to take many mental and emotional shortcuts based upon custom and habit. However, Dewey concluded that the potential

political intelligence of ordinary people should not be underestimated: "Until secrecy, prejudice, bias, misrepresentation, and propaganda as well as sheer ignorance are replaced with inquiry and publicity, we have no way of telling how apt for judgment of social policies the existing intelligence of the masses may be."[20]

For Dewey the key to this problem was to educate and to always seek ways to improve political education and sources of information so that citizens might be able to make sense of their world and its politics. It is of decisive importance then, that for him this education required promoting and encouraging *neighborly communities*. Dewey believed that democracy *required* face-to-face interactions in neighborhoods and local associations. "In its deepest and richest sense a community must always remain a matter of face-to-face intercourse."[21] Indeed, Dewey considered the neighborhood on par with the family in importance. "Family and neighborhood with all their deficiencies have always been the chief agencies of nurture, the means by which dispositions are stably formed and ideas acquired which laid hold on the roots of character . . . vital and thorough attachments are bred only in the intimacy of an intercourse, which is of necessity restricted in range."[22] "Democracy,"

FIG. 5 Pedestrian streets of Galway City, Ireland.

he reports, "must begin at home, and its home is the neighborly community."[23]

Dewey's faith in "a close neighborhood experience"[24] was based neither on naiveté nor sentimentality. He was not trying to re-create some sort of merely imagined idyllic notion of community. He recognized that modernity was affecting and dislocating local communities. And he acknowledged many existing neighborhoods were far from ideal when it came to face-to-face interaction. However, he argued that personal engagement at the neighborhood level was essential to democracy and thus should be encouraged: interactions and discussions tend to ground reality and help citizens to make sense of their world. Through 'face-to-face' "conversation," "dialogue," and "relationships" ideas and symbols are shared, challenged, and understood. Dewey suggests that this social testing of ideas as they "circulate by word of mouth from one to another in the communications of the local community" give rise to a superior form of social intelligence that surpasses that held by one individual. It is these communications, as they "pass from mouth to mouth" "that only gives reality to public opinion."[25] This is not an argument for isolation within neighborhoods, but rather he believed the best way to remain connected and test reality was to be engaged in face-to-face interactions with our neighbors in local communities.

Neighborhoods and the Eclipse of the American Res Publica

However persuasive Dewey's arguments, there is reason to be somewhat suspicious of this claim that walkable neighborhoods are a kind of education to democracy. After all, any number of authoritarian regimes has neighborhoods. However, in historical terms, the centrality of a "bourgeoisie" in explaining demand for Western democracy makes clear the importance of their physical location.[26] "Neighborly communities" or public places where face-to-face interactions can occur may serve to strengthen or enhance democratic citizenry where and when basic democratic institutions are in place already. Dewey is an American thinker and perhaps his theory ought to be considered primarily in this light.[27] We want to use Dewey's thought as a kind of case in American intellectual history in order to explain why he voices the convictions he has, why political theorists typically no longer consider such arguments, and how understanding Dewey helps give us traction in understanding the connection of the built environment to democracy.

We have already suggested that Dewey was writing before a change in the academic subdiscipline of political theory: pragmatism, which stressed political engagement, receded alongside changes in the concerns and orientation of academic political theory in the mid-twentieth century.[28] If Dewey's thoughts were the victim of a change in fad, this would account for his somewhat lonely position. But there is reason to believe that his thought is part of a tradition in American political thought that both goes back to the earliest founding and continues to this day. It is noteworthy, therefore, that in *The Public and Its Problems* Dewey seems obsessed with the loss of town hall democracy.

The public deliberation that began in Puritan New England towns was predicated on an architectural design: houses were close together in a neighborhood, with agricultural land spreading out from this town center.[29] Although the town population was homogeneous in terms of a sense of mission to begin with, the town model reinforced the sense of community and necessitated the kind of discussion absent from nondeliberative democracy. By the time the Constitution was adopted, attachment to small-scale democracy had waned, at least among the Federalists. But the "anti-Federalist" commitment to democracy and the republic as a community of communities remained a part of American politics and political theory even as the Federalists denigrated rule by the rabble, or what was then termed "the democracy."[30]

The idea that democracy requires, and in a sense is defined by, interaction in local communities is present as well in Thomas Jefferson's thought.

> Jefferson . . . had at least a foreboding of how dangerous it might be to allow the people a share in public power without providing them at the same time with more public space than the ballot box and with more opportunity to make their voices heard than election day. What he perceived to be the mortal danger to the republic was that the Constitution had given all power to the citizens without giving them the opportunity of *being* republicans and of *acting* as citizens. In other words, the danger was that all the power had been given to the people in their private capacity and that there was no space established for them in their capacity of being citizens.[31]

This, in turn, is strikingly similar to the view of New Urbanist critics of sprawl:

> In the absence of walkable public places—streets, squares, and parks, the *public realm*—people of diverse ages, races, and beliefs are unlikely to meet and talk. . . .In the suburbs, time normally spent in the physical public realm is now spent in the automobile, which is a private space as well as a potentially sociopathic device. The average American, when placed behind the wheel of a car, ceases to be a citizen and becomes instead a *motorist*.[32]

According to this view, car-oriented, suburban community designs contribute to the decline of democracy because they emphasize the privatization of space and minimize public space and social interaction. While not all suburbs are the same of course, many do attempt to intentionally minimize face-to-face interactions by doing away with sidewalks, parks, and by zoning shops, restaurants, and even schools and places of worship out of the neighborhood. Casual interactions, conversations or chance meetings along the lines envisioned by Jacobs or Dewey become highly improbable. Such suburban designs eliminate public space by alienating people from their neighborhoods. The result does not even strengthen the "home," but rather orients each individual in the home to structures of power outside it through work, school, and media.[33] Radical Euclidian zoning not only separates uses, it functions to separate all aspects of life. Housing is separate from work, from school, from recreation, from shopping, and so on. Worst of all, one is often required to drive by automobile to each aspect of one's life or what was formally thought of as one's community. This is mirrored in the idea for political division of labor in modern representation that Dewey connected to a lack of possibility for democratic action: we no longer directly participate, but rather outsource our politics to practical and theoretical professionals.

Conclusion

Our major purpose in this chapter was to consider some of the existing theory on the relationship between the way we design and interact in our communities and democracy. Although we definitely find scholars who have explored this important relationship (or simply assumed it was important), we do not find a clear or mature theoretical tradition. We hope for this theory's rapid further development.

FIG. 6 Architectural weeds: Can democracy flourish here?

SPRAWLING CITIES

KARL OLOV ARNSTBERG

I'm going to start at the end of the eighteenth century. London had long since driven out Paris as Europe's largest and most powerful city; in the year 1800, its metropolitan area already had a population of 1.1 million inhabitants. London was not only a very big, but also a very dense city. Home and work were inseparable, and there were no neighborhoods exclusively given over to commercial, office, or residential functions. Production took place in the small shops of artisans, and public buildings, hotels, churches, warehouses, shops, and homes were interspersed, often located in the same structure. The density was so high that it took only a couple of hours to walk from the very edges to the center. This meant that the growing middle class had to live in the extremely congested urban core. Even for the wealthy urban elite everyday life was, with reference to certain qualities, pretty much the same as for the urban poor—crowded, dirty, noisy, and unhealthy. The city became economically more and more important, but at the same time more and more difficult to live in. The bourgeoisie both hated and feared city life. No wonder they developed two strong withdrawals, still highly relevant today. One was *domesticity*, the other was the *suburb*.

In 1864 the British art historian and author John Ruskin delivered a series of lectures in Manchester. They concerned domesticity, and to him the ideal Victorian suburban wife was a kind of manager at home. Also, the church gave the women the role of guardians of the Christian home. In their opinion a decent woman's only task outside the home was charity work among the local poor. Her responsibilities at home could be specified, not unlike the male responsibilities in the outer world. It was her duty to supervise the servants, educate her children, and manage the household accounts. She had important *work* to do in order to secure the home's tidiness, comfort, and loveliness. According to Ruskin:

> This is the true nature of home—it is the abode of peace; the protection not only against damage but also against terror, doubt, and division. If it does not work that way it is not a home. When the anxiety of the outer world penetrates into it, when an incoherent, uncharitable, and hostile world is al-

lowed to cross the threshold by a husband or a wife, it ceases to be a home. It becomes just a part of the outer world, with a roof over it and a fireplace. But as long as it is a sacred place, an exalted temple, a temple of the heart . . . it is a home.[1]

This new and emotional type of family motivated the middle class to create the suburban lifestyle. The aim, as Ruskin also pointed out, was to protect the individual against external threats, against what is "out there" in the world inhabited by strangers. One may talk about a division between the three functions of a home: to work in, to live in, and to sell or exchange the fruits of one's production from. Only the living remained in the home.

Characteristic for this new type of living was that it was private—which meant that it was exceptionally difficult to build an organic and well-functioning society around it. The home turned into a symbolic conspiracy for the family in general and for the nuclear family in particular.

The nuclear family was a nineteenth-century invention. In his famous book *The Family, Sex, and Marriage in England, 1500–1800*, Lawrence Stone describes the domesticated nuclear family as a handful of individuals bound to each other by warm affective ties. The older nuclear family was "open," in the sense that influences from neighbors and kin usually were more important than the ties between father, mother, and children. It was also fragile and often very short lived. Stone writes that it was neither very durable, nor emotionally or sexually very demanding.[2]

The American sociologist Richard Sennett claims that what happened was that a wall was built between our subjective experiences—those we have in our consciousness—and our outer, physical environment. Our cities look the way they do because we are afraid to reveal our inner thoughts. The cause behind this is that city-dwellers are forced to share their everyday existence with others who are, and remain, strangers. Strangers cannot be expected to be benevolent. If outer life were just a simple reflection of inner life, we would all be exposed to each other. Therefore, we have to create a contrast between an inner life and the outer life, which do not correspond with one another, to the extent that the former is under our power, the latter is not.

The city is on the outside, home on the inside. The family is its own kingdom and, until double work "liberates" them, it binds the women in what Sennett calls both a secular *purdah* and an *émigration intérieure*. He writes: "Stated baldly, 'home' became the secular version of spiritual refuge; the geography of safety shifted from a sanctuary in an urban center to the domestic interior."[3]

This is the background leading up to the period of the eighteenth century when the wealthy merchant elite of London started to acquire weekend villas, where they went by private carriage each Saturday afternoon, and returned to the city the following Monday morning. One could say that the suburban life started with the wife and children remaining in the weekend house, while the male breadwinner commuted. The historian Robert Fishman writes that the weekend houses were the ready-made materials from which the bourgeoisie created suburbia.[4]

To give just one example, Clapham was one of the favorite sites for wealthy Londoners in the eighteenth century. There they raised the new domestic suburban architecture, with detached country houses. There they could escape from the urban poor and the messiness of the city. They created a new kind of community for like-minded Evangelical people, worshipping family life and with direct contact with nature. The functions of the home gradually become differentiated. The children get their own room, the parents get one room in which to receive guests and represent the family, another in which to sleep and make love (quietly, so the children could not hear). A separate eating room is also required, in which a specific behavior ("table manners") is produced. The social graces were directed inward, toward the mutual education and moral betterment of the nuclear family itself. With this ideal kind of home they unintentionally shaped a new urban quality; the urban landscape, with houses in private gardens; the first version of suburban sprawl.

The Transformation of Suburbia

Before the suburban process started in towns like London and Manchester, the suburbs were just the urban outskirts. In *The Structures of Everyday Life*, French historian Fernand Braudel writes:

> Every town in the world, beginning with the West, has its suburbs. Just as a strong tree is never without shoots at its foot, so towns are never without suburbs. They are the manifestations of its strength, even if they are wretched fringes. Shoddy suburbs are better than none at all. Suburbs housed the poor, artisans, watermen, noisy malodorous trades, cheap inns, posting-houses, stables for post horses, porters' lodgings. Bremen had a face-lift in the seventeenth century; its houses were constructed in brick, roofed with tiles, its streets paved, a few wide avenues built. But in the suburbs around it the houses still had straw roofs. To reach the suburbs was always to take a step downwards, in Bremen, London, and elsewhere.[5]

Since the fourteenth century, and for more than three hundred years after, the suburb was an inferior place. In Chaucer's *Canterbury Tales* the suburbs are described as "corners and blind alleys where robbers and thieves instinctively huddle secretly and fearfully together." In Shakespeare's London a whore could be called "a suburb sinner," because of the many brothels on the urban fringe. To call a man a "suburbanite" was a serious insult.[6]

These overwhelmingly negative connotations had to change when wealthy Londoners started to move out to their weekend houses. The emergence of suburbia needed a complete transformation of urban values, since the modern suburb had no precedents in the preindustrial city. Suburbia was a contradiction of the older principle that said that the core was the only proper place for the elite to live. It also contradicted the nobility's definition of land as *productive*. In the emerging suburbia land was organized for *consumption*. Nevertheless, this new and exemplary version of suburbia was the result of improvisation, not a design idea, like Ebenezer Howard's Garden City. Maybe Mumford gave the best explanation of the change when he wrote that suburbia is "a collective effort to live a private life."[7] With the suburban detached house situated in a wholly residential area, the bourgeois family could escape both from the industrial estates and the working poor, with their horrible dwellings. It really was a flight from the industrial world they themselves were creating. But more than that, suburbia could well be seen as the birth of the class-segregated society, the end of the mixed society, as planners of today often romanticize.

Friedrich Engels's 1844 description of what had happened to Manchester is famous.[8]

> The town had an elegant business district with principal buildings in Gothic and Venetian styles; warehouses, banks, counting-rooms, offices, commission houses, and agencies. Visitors met for the first time ever an urban core that was quiet and empty after business hours, since nobody lived there. This business district was surrounded by a factory zone, densely packed with workmen's dwellings, chimneys, and the factory buildings with their steam-driven machines. Beyond the region of smoke, in the suburbs, the bourgeoisie had their villas. An observer, Thomas Parkinson, believed that there was no town in the world where the distance between the rich and the poor was greater. There was far less personal communication between the master cotton-spinner and his workmen than between the Duke of Wellington and the humblest laborer on his estate.[9]

The Americans were not far behind. Frederick Law Olmsted, the famous landscape architect and planner who had his greatest success with Central Park in New York, laid out sixteen suburbs together with his partner, Calvert Vaux. He was convinced that no great city any longer could exist without great suburbs.[10] To summarize, the origin of suburbia is truly Anglo-American.

When Olmsted believed that no great city could exist without suburbs for the affluent citizens, he was wrong. Not completely, of course; in the same way that some wealthy Englishmen insisted on staying in the city core, there were some new suburban villas in France—but they were considered quite eccentric.

The French bourgeoisie favored the city core which the English saw as more or less unliveable, and rejected suburbia. The French ideal was an apartment in a large building located on a busy boulevard near the center of the city. How come? The story goes like this: During the 1840s successful French merchants created a new urban district, Chaussée d'Antin, where they could practice the same principles as the English did in the suburbs: domesticity, privacy, and class segregation. In stark difference from the house plans in London, in these elegant French houses work space and family space were kept apart. The apartments often occupied a whole floor with elegant suites of rooms. The shops with their large windows did not have any connection with the residences. Servants and tradesmen had to use back doors and back stairs. Only the residents and their guests used the main stairways. To make a difference between the servant's and the family's space was important. The latter was decorated with parquet floors, elaborate plastering, marble fireplaces, and gold-framed mirrors. The servant's space consisted of the kitchen and the rooms facing the courtyard. Thus, within the city, the French elite acquired the domestic isolation that the English had achieved by fleeing to suburbia.

These apartment houses of Chaussée d´Antin served as models for a future middle-class housing in the same way as the suburban villas did in London and Manchester. Instead of combining domestic values with a countryside lifestyle, the French elite preferred to combine privacy with urban pleasures, such as theaters, balls, cafes, and restaurants.

When the English suburb was developed, no major concentration of money was needed. But for Paris the situation was different; Napoleon III wished to transform the chaotic and still medieval Paris, with its dwindling and narrow streets, into a grand imperial capital. A large city could not be modernized piecemeal. In order to accomplish this, he gave almost dictatorial powers to the prefect of Paris, Baron Haussmann. To summarize a revolutionary change with a few words, Haussmann transformed Paris into an elegant modern city with boulevards and prestigious apartment houses, symbolizing the adherence to the Napoleonic regime.

> The poor, who received none of the largess that Haussmann bestowed on the favored bourgeoisie, found their neighborhoods demolished and were forced by government policy to move to the outskirts. Industry too was forced to the periphery and a working-class industrial belt was formed in precisely those picturesque areas which might have attracted middle-class villas.[11]

In a period of two decades Paris achieved its classic form and inspired many other European cities, from Lyon and Marseilles to Berlin and Stockholm. Especially Vienna and Prague used Paris as a model and developed urban cores with monumental apartment houses. This urban design soon spread through central and eastern Europe. No wonder Paris is seen as the cultural capital of the nineteenth century. However, it should also be said that the Parisian model was by far more class-bound than the Anglo-American one. The great Parisian boulevard was possible to accomplish in the nineteenth century, but could hardly be repeated in the Western world of today.

The urban architecture of the nineteenth century is the architecture of a society with an uninterrupted bourgeois power, a society where the workers—as long as there had been workers—were the underdogs. The twentieth century, with the labor movement and the new political ideologies, changed this situation. In Europe we can follow how the French bourgeoisie ideal for city building, with boulevards and high stone houses in closed block formations, from the 1920s was criticized and rejected. The representative function and the classical aestheticism were despised, as they were said to belong to the old class society, and thus responded poorly to the people's everyday needs. The early modern style, with its social conscience, is primarily to be understood as a reaction against the 1900's industrial, urban societies disregard for the workers material and social conditions.

Modern style became a strong symbol for a happier future. It worshipped sunlight and health, it advocated good, but cheap and mass-produced houses. It proposed loose and function-oriented urban housing as a desirable ideal. The architects of the 1930s, the first broad architectural generation, perceived planning as a cure for the slum and social destitution. Inspiration was picked up from industry and the society should be organized according to the principles of Taylorism, to become successful.

Planning and building were also guided by an increasingly more powerful social science. The newborn paradigm had talented and energetic advocates, not the least among which were architects. They did not consider modernism as a style comparable to, for example, new classicism. It was rather conceptualized as an unavoidable and logical consequence of the period's intellectual, social, and technical circumstances.

The new hegemonic power and the new architecture, hegemonic as well, should together shape a totally different society, a society where the architecture in itself was supposed to result in another, a liberated and more democratic society, a society denying traditions and with its interest facing future. As the Norwegian sociologist Dag Österberg noticed, there was—despite the Great Depression and the Second World War—a relieving joy during the thirties and forties—"Swing it, teacher!" as Alice Babs sang.[12]

Housing was soon to become one of the major questions, and if we use Sweden as an example, from the forties onwards the state and the municipalities took full responsibility for citizens housing. A subsidiary system was developed, as well as a detailed framework of regulations, meant to provide the whole population with affordable, sound, spacious, and well-equipped homes. Different from many other countries with their private enterprises and a more ore less supplemental social housing policy, housing in Sweden was organized as a national interest. Subsequently the public housing sector was, and still is, much bigger in Sweden than in most other nonsocialist countries.

Architecture, quantitative social sciences, and domestic policies during the period from 1930 to 1975 were synchronized with each other and welded together into one of the hardest knowledge constructions ever in Sweden. Through building regulations, physical planning, subsidizing systems, norm collections, and God knows what else, it ruled and designed the physical shape of Sweden. Its success was, as is well known, complete, and the most visible result was the suburban residential area. Even if the planning and building enterprise seemed commonsensed and a little extreme, the underlying conception was particularly utopian: that it was possible through physical planning and architecture to reach the equal and classless society, an Eden producing an everlasting happiness among its citizens.

Well, as we all know, it didn't work. The twentieth century has seen two architectonic planning paradigms implode. The first was that of Baron Haussmann's, the dense European town with its parks, boulevards, and bound-block formations. The architects of the 1920s and 1930s turned away in disgust. The old aestheticism appeared to be mere fraudulent proceedings in the new light of what "the masses" really needed. But the modern style has also been emptied from within.

Today, public space in the cores of European towns and cities are as crowded as they were in London two hundred years ago, but there are some differences that make life much more attractive in the city cores of today. First, the physical quality: the infrastructures work; clean water and pollution are kept under control. Yes, transportation is still a problem, but we do not have to walk halfway up to our knees in mud. In short, city centers are nice places. Second, the stranger is not as threatening anymore. We have beggars, criminals, drug addicts, madmen, and homeless people in what seem to be a growing number—also in European cities, of course, but not much of a slum in the city cores—compared to many cities in the United States. The typical situation is one of well-dressed strangers, sometimes displaying different values but basically *consumers* like myself. They come from many different places, but with the same intention: to use the city core and its facilities as a public living room. Some work there, some live there, some are guests. They shop, eat, and drink. They go to the cinemas and theaters. And because of all these present strangers, the city can function. As happy consumers the strangers are welcome, indeed. Two hundred years ago they made large cities more or less unlivable for the affluent citizens. Today the situation is the opposite. They make the city cores attractive. In Stockholm as in Manchester and in London, the inner-city apartments are the most expensive, more expensive than suburban villas. Urban citizens have finally accepted the stranger. It is possible to share the public room with them. And you can withdraw without being noticed. Living or being among strangers gives you the possibility of being private.

So we have reached a situation where we desire more of what we had and once despised. The billion-dollar question is: can we accomplish this once again? Can we return to the city of the nineteenth century, the dense, mixed, walkable, and beautiful European city, more inspired by Paris than by London? The New Urbanists say yes, we can do it again. If this is what we like, we can indeed accomplish it. And when I listen to them, especially when I listened to Peter Calthorphe two days ago, I was really convinced. Certainly this must be possible!

Let me be crystal clear on this: I like New Urbanism. The more I understand it, the more I like it. I think *yes, yes, yes— this is so good!*

But then, as a researcher, I have to ask, is this where the urban developments around the world are heading? Are Portland, Seaside, and Prince Charles's Poundbury the future? Well they already are, in some chosen places. But will New Urbanism ever become hegemonic, or as successful as it deserves to be? But then again, I'm not much of a believer anymore. I will end my lecture with some comments on this.

My first objection concerns the sheer number of people. Peter Calthorpe told us that Los Angeles was growing— very much and very fast. This population growth mainly consisted of poor people. Los Angeles is not the glamorous version Hollywood presents, but it is more and more like a third-world metropolis.

Well, Los Angeles has got company. There are more than twenty *megacities*—that means more than ten million inhabitants—in the world today. Take São Paulo in Brazil as an example. It is said to be the fourth largest city in the world, with around eighteen million citizens and still growing. In 1960 roughly 20% lived outside the central city. In 1990, this number had increased to over 40%, which indicates a severe sprawl. Or take Lagos in Nigeria. Today it has around fourteen million inhabitants, but in twenty years it might well be the biggest city in the world, if we are to believe the United Nations. Tokyo, with suburbs, seems to have around thirty five million inhabitants. Major cities dominate in Northern Europe as well. The biggest city, Saint Petersburg, has an official population of five million; the real number could well be eight million. The World Bank estimates that in year 2025, 88% of the worlds total population growth will take place in urban areas. And 90% of this urban growth will occur in very poor cities like Dhaka, Cairo, Tiajin, Hyderabad, and Lahore. This means that growth, which traditionally is seen as the key to social and economic progress, will go totally out of control. Indeed this also means sprawl, but of a much more desperate kind than we usually discuss, when we keep to our more handy European conditions.

Furthermore, it means that the suburbs will dominate— it is there that most people live and work. Emerging business and commerce happens more in the suburbs than in central cities. Sometimes the city even becomes a suburb to the suburbs! So far the world has not seen an end to the centrifugal dynamic, where urban areas get larger and larger, more and more spread out.

My second objection is that the English invention of suburbia, Haussmanns's brutal cleansing of Paris, and the modern style that spread all over the world were all, in their own time, very convincing solutions to major societal problems. Answers to questions on the urban destiny of Europe—nothing more, nothing less. Today, urbanism is not something happening to Europe alone, it is global, and as a solution New Urbanism has neither the right magnitude nor the right price tag. New Urbanism is a reaction—yes, a clever one, but to me it seems like the ant sitting on the elephant's neck, pulling the animal's ear and shouting, "now we go in that direction." Sorry to say, but I suspect the elephant will not obey.

The spread out and monofunctional urban landscape is king. Even declining European cities like Liverpool and Leipzig are sprawling. Or take Budapest, a very beautiful and great European city, it is nice and fun to visit, but to live there? The living standard is still low, compared to the West, and if the raise is as fast as the Hungarians hope for, Budapest will have a severe sprawl in the next decade. Not because of necessity, but because many of the inhabitants dream of a house of their own. The middle class leave and the urban poor stay, the picture is quite familiar. Next step is that some of the affluent intellectuals and professionals will wish to move back. Well, then we have gentrification as the next problem. Gentrification and New Urbanism might, to the eye, be quite similar, but socially and economically they are not. Gentrification is one of the pieces in the segregation puzzle.

My third objection concerns segregation. A lot of researchers, architect, and politicians have noticed segregation as a major problem, even, *the* most serious problem of our age. We have all read about gated communities in the United States, and we know what happened in Stockholm and elsewhere in cities and towns all over the world. Segregation, once a planning ideology in the form of zoning, has today turned into a major urban process, gentrifying inner cities and dumping weak undesirable groups and citizens in areas and places considered downright ugly or just hopeless.

Let me make a very definite statement: the affluent people, the urban winners in this world of ours, have never had any desire for sharing the reality of urban poor, homeless people, low lifestyles, or displaced immigrants and ethnic minorities. Segregation is a major threat against Western lifestyles, but as planners and researchers we have to face it. If sprawl is the king, segregation is the queen.

My fourth objection is that New Urbanism seems not to be very good in handling growth. I might be wrong here, but my impression of what has happened to Portland is that it looks strong as a program, but still the achievement has been rather modest. Around 90% of transport is still done by car, and due to the roads not being developed, traffic congestion is more frequent and worse than in comparable United States cities. People living in an "anticar urban surrounding" still require a car to go about their daily routines. Furthermore, the inner-city apartments cannot really compete with suburban single houses. Today there is a lack of suburban houses, which forces the prices up. One of the reasons is that Oregon is dominated by white middle-class people, who do not feel inclined to share their neighborhood with less successful people. It is also a paradox that after the creation of the city boundary and with the smart growth program, Portland acquired a good reputation for environmental qualities and for being an anticar town. Subsequently, it has had a significant influx of migration, particularly from California. Many moved to Portland, and the population density since the program started has increased by 53%. Four months ago the city of Portland increased its urban-growth boundary to the boundary previously planned for 2040. To me it seems as though Portland is ending up in precisely what should be avoided: traffic jams, air pollution, and high costs of living.

My fifth objection concerns *placelessness*. Urban winners are not stuck to specific places anymore. Not even factories matter, the most place bound of everything during industrialism. Today the brand is the most cherished asset and production could be moved around surprisingly freely in the world. And at the same time as the stinkin' rich get even richer and have more and more lovely living places to choose from, the stinkin' poor get poorer and increasingly stuck in places the rich are very successful at avoiding.

My sixth and last comment concerns the market: as long as the market determines the agenda, there will not be much of a mixture. A developer in housing will not produce public squares, for example—they cost money, and who is going to buy them? What is more, developers *specialize*. One is in office buildings, nothing else; another makes exclusive apartments and does not have the competence to make cheap ones. Neither one is interested in projects outside his own realm.

If we wish to have a mixed society, we have to make use of public invention. We have to take land out of the market for reallocation through a "command" for social housing, schools, hospitals, etc. Such interventions are quite common in Europe, but in the long run the property market appears to return, "underperforming" land and buildings, to their proper place in the market hierarchy. For example, many high-value flats for rent in central Stockholm have been transferred to the market. The tenants have made housing cooperatives and bought their own apartments. I have done this twice, and this way I earned a lot of money I didn't really deserve.

I could say even more, and it is indeed a dark, pessimistic picture, I realize that. But to me it seems as though the urban world isn't playing the game the New Urbanists propose. There are other games going on—much more powerful ones.

BEYOND THE NEIGHBORHOOD

NEW URBANISM AS CIVIC RENEWAL

DAVID BRAIN

Common representations in the mass media have continued to encourage the perception that the New Urbanism is a movement focused merely on a nostalgic simulation of idealized small towns.[1] Although it is true that New Urbanists have consistently emphasized the importance of design, their understanding of traditional urbanism is more than nostalgia for front porches and nineteenth-century architecture. At the core of the movement, there is an urban ideal that is very much a response to contemporary challenges, even as it draws on traditional architecture and urbanism. Close study of traditional urban forms is only part of the emerging practice of urban design as an integrative discipline that promises to bring new coherence to the complex work of place making. At the core of the movement, one finds a growing body of theory, practice, and technique intended to cut through bureaucratic procedure and technical specialization, in order to achieve the making of places that are lively, coherent, walkable, beautiful, conducive to healthy community life, and responsive to substantive needs and human experiences.

In order to reconstruct the civic art of building neighborhoods and towns, the New Urbanists have found it necessary to change not only their own practices as professionals, but also the regulatory apparatus of local governments, significant areas of public policy, the practices of lending institutions and real estate investment interests, the habits and routines of developers, the assumptions of real estate market analysts, and the expectations of home buyers. In other words, the New Urbanism has become an effort to re-form the entire institutional matrix of the contemporary development regime, and to construct the practical basis for an urban ideal in the face of particular challenges posed by the institutional forces that have shaped urban and suburban landscapes since around 1960.

It has turned out that pursuit of an urban ideal requires social and political innovation with broad ramifications, as well as fundamental innovations of technique.[2] In this regard, I have identified three transformative tendencies, each with profound implications: 1. a reversal of the patterns of techni-

cal specialization and an integration of the rationalized but fragmented problem-solving techniques typically applied by specialists within the relative isolation of their professional disciplines; 2. a reconfiguration of the practical interface between technical expertise and democratic politics in planning; 3. formation of a new discipline of urban design, as an integrative practice connected to a normative ideal of urbanism.

In order to understand the significance of the New Urbanism, firstly one needs to understand the implications of an urban ideal that is not simply a communitarian fantasy of neighborliness and face-to-face familiarity, but a practical conception (and manifestation in material culture) of civic renewal. Secondly, this transformation of design and planning practice is dependent upon a revival of a public culture of place making that goes beyond the professionalized disciplines with a stake in the process. Finally, the idea of an urban/rural transect manifests a practical sensibility that can be appropriately described as "civic," establishing the basis for translating a new urban ideal across professions and across levels of scale from neighborhood to region. It also addresses a series of sociological and political problems posed by this new urban ideal.

In contrast with evidence regarding the decline of social capital, Sirianni and Friedland have traced a countertrend characterized by what they call "civic innovation."[3] This broad movement for civic renewal encompasses efforts to re-frame the connection of citizens to public life by challenging the dominance of both political and professional elites. Innovative solutions to community and environmental problems rely on the extensive cooperation of partners who might otherwise have found themselves caught up in an adversarial politics: citizen groups, professional experts, officials representing public administrative and regulatory bureaucracies, nonprofit organizations, business, and industry. The new modes of cooperation found in case studies of civic innovation are not simply pluralist coalitions of groups acting primarily in defense of their own interests, but they are a matter of collaboration oriented to a substantive common purpose—the essence of a civic sensibility.

Against the background of this broader wave of civic renewal, one can see important political implications of the New Urbanist introduction of substantive interests, geared to the quality of human life and experience, into the practice of planning and the politics of land-use decisions, both of which have become dominated by procedural and technical rationality.[4] The transect-based approach (to be explained below) exemplifies the effort to turn community vision into practical strategies for managing change, without too much being lost in the translation into expert interventions and bureaucratic routines. To the extent that the cumulative effects of architecture and urban design can be rendered as a self-conscious and purposeful focus of effective participatory democracy, this might be seen as a key component of the reconstitution of a comprehensive civic capacity, across even the most diverse and contentious interests.

The Conventional Development Regime

In popular parlance, the problem is "sprawl," but this language captures only the land-consuming spread of development across the landscape, not the underlying logic of a pattern of development that affects redevelopment in the inner cities as much as it affects new greenfield development on the metropolitan fringe. The consumption of land that many regard as its key characteristic is actually a side effect of the way the development industry turns land into real estate commodities.

There are four components of the development regime that comprise the technology of what the New Urbanists refer to as conventional suburban development:

• *Capital*: The protocols of lending institutions, the standards tied to federal guarantees, the secondary mortgage markets, real estate investment trusts, and other financial instruments for constituting investment in real estate separate from the social investment in place.

• *Bureaucratic administration*: The regulatory apparatus, including comprehensive planning cycles, zoning, land development codes, subdivision regulations, health and safety regulations, administrative requirements, and requirements for public hearings.

• *Professional expertise*: The division of labor between expert disciplines, each with its distinctive techniques and standards of professional competence and achievement.

• *Politics*: The so-called public process has become a set of structured and often legally mandated opportunities for "public input" at the interface of technical expertise and interest group politics.

These four components form an interlocking system, a technology of place making that is dominated by procedural rules rather than substantive rationality, decision making oriented to specialized concerns without an overarching vision, abstracted quantitative measures rather than particular qualities of place. In each area, conventional practice revolves around techniques for reducing the particularities

and contingencies of place to conventional types that can be rendered in quantitative terms. This institutional matrix has had profound implications for the politics of land use and environmental responsibility, and generally for the erosion of civic capital in recent decades.

In the complicated business of real estate, the avoidance of risk involves avoiding projects that don't fit the standardized protocols in an interlocking system of financing formulas, measures of market feasibility, standardized building types, zoning categories, and routinized design and planning practices.[5] Conventional zoning provides a clear example of the logic of the regulatory apparatus under this regime. Once single-use zones have been mapped, it becomes easier to write rules that can be consistently applied in a way that is responsive to the demands for procedural fairness crucial to a regulatory system oriented to maintaining both property rights and real estate value. Conventional zoning ordinances carefully limit the intervention of regulatory authority to a minimal condition for maintaining predictability of exchange value. As variances and zoning changes are negotiated over time, the rational mapping of uses becomes a confusion of ad hoc adjustments in which the organization of uses reflects the contingencies of land availability, market dynamics, and political bargaining, largely without regard to the local ecology of uses in a place. The resulting geography reflects the play of economic interests and institutional forces that are ageographic and that disrupt the orderliness and legibility of spatial forms.[6]

Since the 1960s, there has been an expansion of opportunities and expectations for public participation in the planning process, especially in those places where growth pressures have produced dramatic changes over the last two decades. With expanding requirements for both staff and public review of each proposal, the system of technical and administrative rules increasingly carries the burden of channeling the mobilized political energy of popular reaction. Vocal popular interest has helped to drive a proliferation of regulations oriented to a widening range of specific environmental, economic, and social concerns. The decision-making bodies (planning commissions, city and county commissioners, etc.) find themselves operating in an intensified political atmosphere, under constant public scrutiny and subject to dramatic public criticism. When decision makers respond with painstaking attention to the rules and procedures in order to avoid being seen to respond to special interests, they inadvertently encourage the perception that government is unresponsive and subject to behind-the-scenes influence by powerful interests. Popular mobilization latches onto the same legal and procedural technicalities as the only tactic available to put the brakes on a development process that appears driven only by profit and self-interest.

The introduction of environmental regulation into this process has exacerbated the tendency for the process set up to primarily meet expectations of technical and administrative rationality to become the institutional frame for the popular politics. There has been a "quiet revolution" in land-use regulation since the 1960s, largely in response to the perception of environmental degradation associated with the acceleration of suburbanization into open land.[7] The primary focus of this revolution has been an effort to protect ecological systems in remaining undeveloped areas by protecting wetlands, hillsides, sensitive habitats, and endangered species. It has also focused on requiring each project to mitigate or internalize its own impacts, with a proliferation of regulations that reflect parcel-by-parcel solutions to the problem of reducing the environmental impact of growth. This aspect of the regulatory process offers crucial leverage for citizens and citizen groups interested in obstructing the development of any given parcel of land, for whatever reason. Sincere and reasonable concern for environmental impact of development is mixed with both specific "not in my backyard" reactions, and a generalized fear of "out of control" development. The political burden on the process is tremendously amplified by the combination of legal recourse and moral positioning afforded by environmental regulation.

Each development proposal, each parcel of land, each tree becomes a front-line skirmish in what often ends up being framed as a desperate battle to save the planet from greed and irresponsibility. The totalizing character of the rhetoric of environmentalism, combined with a rhetoric of community values, turns land-use decisions into moral battles that allow little room for the habits of compromise and civility necessary for successful democracy. An embattled planning staff, with limited personnel, resources, and a narrowly defined technical expertise, often finds itself caught between the moral passions of citizens, the arguments of land-use attorneys, and dueling experts representing both sides.

As a result of the uneasy intersection of popular mobilization with a technical and legal process, conventional planning practice produces a system of regulations as lists of prohibitions and incentives. The process undermines trust as it inadvertently encourages developers to do whatever is necessary to meet the permitting requirements, and their opponents to do whatever is necessary to obstruct the process. Conflicts often produce a downward spiral in the quality of the development proposals, as well-intentioned developers are replaced by more aggressive and unscrupulous ones, and as the developers are driven to meet the absolute letter of regulations that are often uncoordinated or even contradictory, in order to avoid the undesirable eventuality of being compelled, as they say, to "meet the neighbors" in a public hearing.

The public process becomes an awkward hybrid of technical expertise, legal argument, and public reaction, an opportunity for public reaction rather than as a formative process of deliberation, opinion formation, or participatory decision making. In the name of procedural fairness and democratic process, we have created a process that is unreliable from the standpoint of all parties. The participatory mechanisms that have been instituted since the 1960s tend to produce or reinforce frustration, disillusionment, and cynicism with respect to the public process, encouraging political discourse and practice that is persistently adversarial, hostile to negotiation and compromise, and frequently a fundamental obstacle to good planning decisions and effective implementation of

plans once adopted.[8] In spite of being fueled by popular reaction against the status quo, the result is ultimately a reinforcing of the "business as usual" patterns of development, and the likely obstruction of any proposal that does not slide easily through the routines and standardized protocols. Ironically, the resulting frustration has both fueled an interest in the New Urbanist alternatives, and made such alternatives more difficult to achieve as a result of the inability of a pluralist politics to overcome the inertia of conventional practice and a politically charged regulatory system.

Regime Change: The New Urbanism

Although the New Urbanist movement encompasses considerable diversity of opinion and practice, there are a few core ideas that capture the logic of its reforming of planning practice: the neighborhood, the *charrette*, the practice of form-based coding, and the urban/rural transect. Not everyone in the movement regards these things in the same way, but they exemplify central tendencies and illuminate key changes in the program of action associated with planning and design.

The Urbanity of the Neighborhood
In contrast with emphasis on the separation of uses, the neighborhood appears as the fundamental unit for the combination of uses into a "balanced mix" at a human scale relevant to daily life. Where conventional real estate focuses on the discrete commodity, the neighborhood unit provides a commonsense example of a place where diverse real estate products are assembled into a mutually supportive whole. Where a conventional subdivision is composed of houses, a traditional neighborhood development assembles houses into streets and blocks in a manner that adds value by giving coherent form and identity to the place. Where the conventional subdivision is a more or less homogenized mass of comparable products, perhaps packaged with some common amenities, a traditional neighborhood development assembles a mix of uses and housing types into an organic whole that is more than the aggregation of its parts. Where a subdivision can be built out, a neighborhood can be complete (and still continue to change). Where a conventional subdivision ages and goes out of fashion, a neighborhood can mature.

The underlying importance of the neighborhood unit is that it evokes a commonsense experience of what the New Urbanists define as urbanism: the extent to which each house, each building, each public-works project, contributes to the completion of a neighborhood or town, to the achievement of emergent possibilities, to a history that gives the place depth and meaning, and to the richness, variety, amenity, functionality, and pleasure of the public realm.

The Charrette as Urbanism in the Making
There is considerable variability in the use and details of the charrette process among practitioners, but the key idea is that

it combines efficient collaboration among the designers and technical experts with facilitated opportunities for engagement with both the general public and specific stakeholder groups. The charrette requires specialists to acquire sufficient general understanding of the project to be able to discuss issues with other specialists. Alterations in the professional division of labor happen both immediately and in the longer term as new categories of consultants with this kind of collaborative capability emerge.[9]

In many conventional forms of participation in planning, citizens become data points, as if the ideal were a kind of mechanical aggregation of particular perspectives and interests. The process is set up with the expectation that citizens will be opponents or supporters of proposals, on the basis of preexisting interests and unaffected by understanding or opinion formation that might emerge in and through the process itself. In a charrette, in contrast, citizens ideally become collaborators rather than data, forming opinions and contributing to the formation of design solutions alongside the designers and planners.

The charrette process is emblematic of the effort of New Urbanist practitioners to break down the obstacles to change that result from technical specialization, and to reconfigure the interface between technical expertise and politics. It also exemplifies a pragmatic approach to testing ideas with short feedback loops, in contrast with the usual effort to reduce decision making to questions answered by plugging data into abstract models. Because the design team works in close collaboration with stakeholders, formulating and testing specific proposals in a series of "pin-ups" and public workshops, it promises to be a form of civic education comparable to Alexis de Tocqueville's conception of the role of the jury in American political education. It is an opportunity for citizens to wield power, but under the tutelage of a particularly educated elite (judges and lawyers, in Tocqueville's case) that bring discipline, responsibility, and an understanding of precedent. Most importantly, the goal is not negotiation of a pluralist compromise, but an emergent substantive vision that can, in turn, provide a principled justification for any necessary compromises between conflicting interests.

Coding for Urbanism

Every neighborhood in areas characterized by rapid growth in the United States has had the experience of a disastrous project that had been approved as meeting every requirement of the zoning code and land development regulations. In some cases, neighborhood opposition even forces compliance in ways that make the project ultimately more damaging to the neighborhood than it might otherwise have been. Conventional zoning, enforcing compatibility by imposing similarity, provides little grip on the likelihood of any new development to contribute positively to the neighborhood. For this reason, New Urbanists have focused on developing form-based codes.

A form-based code typically includes two kinds of considerations: the urban code, relating to the scale and massing of a building, typological treatments of frontage (yard, stoop,

shop window, arcade, etc.), and the way the building sits in relation to the street; and the architectural code, which specifies (to whatever degree desired by a community, tightly or loosely) the patterns of architectural expression. The urban code is the grammar and syntax of urbanism, and the architecture is the vocabulary.[10] The underlying point is to establish the rules according to which diverse pieces can contribute cumulatively to the quality of the whole or to the achievement of an overarching vision.

Why code rather than simply dictate by design? In the New Urbanist conception, urbanism is distinguished from a large-scale architectural project by the fact that it is the work of many hands, accomplished over time. Urbanism, in this conception, refers to the fact that the forms of human settlement are ways of realizing certain collective values, including both the economic value of real estate and the use values that are realized in and through the common construction of place. Urbanism implies a public realm construed as a particular kind of emergent social accomplishment, a common landscape with qualities and resources that are the product of the way human settlement is organized in space and given built form. It is not just a matter of an aggregation of buildings, but the form and character of that aggregation, the particular balance struck between orderliness and accident, conservation and change as individuals pursue their own interests and projects over time. In particular, urbanity is associated with an articulation of public and private that varies across different segments of the landscapes occupied by humans. The practice of coding is a way to create a framework for the minimal collaboration necessary for the quality of urbanism desired, elevating common practice to a consistent level while not constraining excellence in design.

The Urban/Rural Transect

In order to link coding to community values and the particularities of place, it is necessary to articulate a framework of normative principles that can operate across scales and between professional specialties. The urban/rural transect provides the basis for such a framework.

In general, a transect is simply a cross section, a line traced across different ecological zones. In ecology and environmental science, one draws a line along some gradient—wetland to upland, deep water to the shallows of the coral reef, valley floor to mountain top—and then takes samples at regular intervals as a way of analyzing the kinds of life that inhabit different areas in the ecosystem. It is a technique that allows the scientist to make sense of the norms and patterns that make each ecological zone distinguishable from the others, but also to understand the way different parts of the ecological system vary together as you move between distinctive zones. An analysis that moves along a transect between definable ecological zones provides an opportunity to capture both the associations that produce distinctive attributes within zones, and the distributions of certain plants and animals across zones.

As a planning tool, the transect is a technique for creating a system of classification of human habitats based on a conceptual continuum from the most rural to the most urban conditions.[11] This system makes it possible to specify the characteristics of typical elements—streets, buildings, landscaping—in a way that defines different kinds of places along this continuum. The gradient from rural to urban encompasses variations in the relationship between human settlement and natural conditions, in the articulations of public and private, and in spatial morphology and building typologies associated with interconnected variation in managing relations of humans with each other and with nature. Finally, it is a system that ties the most local conditions of lot, building, block, and street to the distributions that make up the ecology of places that constitute cities and regions.

Aside from its technical merits for planners, the transect framework offers the possibility of specifying an array of choices in a way that helps to clarify their interconnections and consequences, illuminating the way choices at different scales can concatenate to produce valued outcomes, or the way they might be juggled in a series of necessary trade-offs.[12] A transect-oriented system allows us to understand each choice as embodying both a value and an allocation tied not just to the individual utility, but also to the emergent character of places. We can sensibly ask: Does it or does it not contribute to creating distinct places that offer a variety of neighborhood types, and the sense of "choicefulness" that Brower has found associated with neighborhood satisfaction?[13] Whereas conventional coding organizes choices by constraint, transect-based coding organizes choices internally, as normative principles that enable and generate meaningful patterns of difference.

Along with its comprehensive perspective, transect theory brings analytical precision and empirical techniques derived from environmental science to the task of describing the variety of human and natural environments that make up a regional system. In this way, it becomes a principled but also empirically supportable framework for contextually sensitive urban design that allows us to envision a full palette of good neighborhoods, and serving as a basis for writing codes that can resolve complicated issues at the level of the neighborhood, town, city, or region. In the context of the politics of planning, the discursive framing of individual choices as allocations within a larger ecology of places, and as contributions to cumulative effects at different levels of scale (block, street, neighborhood, district, city, and region), allows individuals to see their place in a common world for which they bear some responsibility. This combination of choice and recognition of the context of choice can be understood as the basis for civic capacity, since each choice is represented in terms that clarify its relationship to maintaining the value and viability of the whole.[14]

Conclusion

The routines, practices, and institutional protocols of conventional development are characterized by business models, investment strategies, design and planning approaches, and a regulatory culture that encourage the manufacturing of "location" rather than places, driven by institutionalized abstractions that lack meaningful connection to social context. In contrast, New Urbanists have worked to revive the ability to build neighborhoods and towns—with identities, histories, and traditions embedded in communities—instead of subdivisions and "lifestyle centers" characterized only by superficial theming, product mix, and price points. What this means, essentially, is that one establishes a normative framework in which each building project can be understood as contributing to the form as well as the functions of a place. Ideally, this is to be achieved not by the hand of a single designer emulating historic cities or working scenographic effects by fiat, but as the cumulative effect of genuinely individual architectural statements—as an open conversation and not simply a scripted dialogue. The transect is a theory and technique for reconstituting a sense of context, enabling urban design to serve as the integrative discipline in a context-oriented practice of place making.

New Urbanists have tried to jump-start the culture of place making by reviving an understanding of the medium of the built form. This ambition on the part of New Urbanist designers and developers is simultaneously an effort to restore the authority of the design and planning professions with an interest in the city, and an effort to articulate a discipline that knows its limits, that knows how to let go and allow history to take over. The best of the New Urbanist projects are not places that simulate historical towns, but places that use the emulation of traditional precedents to create the ability to have a history, to develop and change over time. I suggest that the transect-based framework, as a theory of urbanism with a set of associated techniques and practices that cut across professional specialties, has rapidly gained currency precisely because of its ability to frame this balancing act of professional authority, market dynamics, democratic aspirations, and a process ideally subject to historical contingencies.[15] In connection with the charrette process and form-based coding, transect-oriented planning offers precise and defensible regulations of urban form, an ability to relate specific decisions to an integrative vision, an ability to encompass the diversity necessary for a sustainable urbanism, and the techniques for managing change that might otherwise undermine the quality of places.

New Urbanism has typically not been explicitly connected to the broader movement to build civic capacity—neither in principle nor in practice. The most common interpretations of New Urbanism would not find this particularly surprising. New Urbanism has been variously mischaracterized as a naïve communitarianism, a manifestation of postmodern theming, a justification for gentrification, and a reflection of the withdrawal of the upper middle class into nostalgic enclaves.[16] Much of the confusion regarding the political implications of the New Urbanism is rooted in the shortcomings of contemporary political discourse, with its lack of clear alternatives to welfare-state liberalism, free-market conservatism, and the paralysis of pluralist politics.

Underlying the emphasis on physical design, the thrust of the New Urbanist effort is toward the mutual recognition of responsibility for producing a common world that reflects the formative aspirations of a community.[17] In the context of urbanism, physical design becomes a manifestation of a kind of social capital, a manifestation of trust and reciprocity in the pursuit of private interest and the improvement of private property, understood as part and parcel of a larger whole on which those interests depend.

The vivid and effective articulation of a civic sensibility in the form of neighborhood and town, the combination of positive effects on health, economic vitality, social equity, and quality of life articulated as goals if not promises within this framing of the civic challenge, the very concreteness of the issues and their ability to appeal across class and race—it is a project that calls out for civic innovation in much the same way as the watershed restoration projects and other environmental issues. Even so, the problem remains of articulating a connected political discourse that begins to explicate and resolve the tension between the ideal of creating a "sense of community" and a public-spirited political life, a public sphere capable of both encompassing and transcending differences.

URBAN DESIGN AND DEVELOPMENT IN THE SWEDISH TRADITION

KNUT STRÖMBERG

The traditional, so-called rational approach to urban planning, with its sectoral organizations and procedures, demonstrates weaknesses when it has to deal with what are often large-scale and complex urban regeneration processes that have to integrate and mediate between a broad variety of interests. There are no single departments or decision-making bodies that have the sole knowledge and competence to handle decisions in such complex issues. The new way of working is based on a variety of formal and informal design dialogues and negotiations among formal stakeholders, public agencies, financiers, citizens, NGOs, and lobbying groups. The crucial moments concern the linking of the informal dialogues with the formal political processes for decision making and conflict resolution.[1]

Swedish urban planning and development is currently in a transition from formal, hierarchical, sectoral government to more lateral, network-based forms of cooperation in design processes where public agencies are just one of many parts. This transition is not unique to Sweden—we see the same tendencies in many European countries. In Sweden the Building and Planning Act dates back to the postwar period, and it has been revised incrementally thereafter. In laws and regulations, the public Swedish planning system was provided with strong means for planning, and the municipalities were to provide housing and good urban facilities and environments. The main tools were *public housing financing systems, semipublic housing corporations,* and *rent control* based on *user value.* A detailed, regulated system for the design of flats, playgrounds, streets, and everything else that could be financed by public loans guaranteed quality standards. The housing financing system was loan based, with low, subsidized rents, which implied large transfers of tax money to stimulate a very high consumption of housing. The subsidies were not directed to special low-income groups, but instead were based on the *general welfare system* provided for all.

During the 1980s, it was foreseen that these large transfers would result in ever-higher tax burdens, and the loan system might eventually explode. The national government had to change the system, and subsequently deconstructed it. The public sector lost its strong means for development con-

trol, and there was also a risk of losing public faith in professional competence.

Over the last twenty years public planning departments have been less proactive, and a continuously larger number of issues are dealt with as *reactive responses to market-based initiatives.* Many public departments have not yet adapted to the new situation.

New Approaches to Urban Development

Processes of urban growth and change are driven by many different powers. Most are not meant to directly result in urban changes, but do so through complex chains of human decisions. Causes are often out of human control: floods, deaths, an industry closing. People make decisions in their everyday life: having children, moving to a job in another city, buying a car, etc. . . . Such processes are increasingly induced by decisions made at great distances—in political assemblies, in the boardrooms of multinational firms, and in research laboratories—including factors such as oil prices, tax and discount rates, new medical technologies, etc.

These urban change processes are also driven by *competition among cities and regions* to attract business, visitors, and new inhabitants. The competition is often carried out through large investments in high-prestige urban redevelopment projects, support of cultural events, and research facilities. Some projects are of such size that they dramatically influence urban life and landscape at large, for both good and bad.

The changes that affect such urban life processes are framed by *institutional settings*: legal and administrative rules, economic conditions, existing urban artifacts, and natural conditions. The public sector's traditional role in urban development and design has diminished in Sweden, as in most European countries, over the last twenty years. Planning departments are often relegated to development control, and have to rely on outside expertise and consultants for the creative input for projects' development. The new situation is often described as a transition from *government*, i.e., formal and bureaucratic ways of planning and design, to more open and collaborative forms of *governance*.[2] This takes on many forms of cooperation between public and nonpublic organizations, as well as different forms of public/private partnerships. Such transitions are by no means simple to influence or control. The transitions are criticized for failing to promote democratic control over planning, and for inadequately providing satisfactory mechanisms for managing it.

Planning democracy is a prestigious expression in most countries, but there is no one single democratic formula. Policy formation and decision making for urban development are based on ideas of democracy dating back to ancient philosophers—ideas that stressed the importance of public discourse and debate for the development of society. The approach to governing urban planning in Sweden is based on ideals of *representative democratic government* with formal procedures for planning, public examination, decision making, appellation, and implementation. The procedures are based on supporting sectoral expert planning and other professional departments and organizations. The formal possibility for a citizen to influence decisions occurs during the public examination, or in the election of politicians. The public examination includes exhibitions, widespread notification, and often superficial consultations. This model has been criticized for its purported exclusion of citizens from a position of real influence.

Deliberative democracy is built on talk as a democratic tool. The idea is that all concerned parties should take part in the discussion during early stages of decision processes. This requires the establishment of forums for discussions among citizens and other stakeholders aimed at formulating actual problems, setting the agenda for public issues, proposing alternative solutions, analyzing those alternatives, and accompanying them with arguments and reasons before finally making choices, for which alternatives should also be recommended. A special form of public participation that has become popular during the last few years is the charrette, which is a consensus-building process carried out by a focused, intense series of meetings between interested people, stakeholders, planners, and architects, often resulting in a clear alternative plan or building proposal.

Different forms of *direct democratic planning* processes take into account all various parties' interests and desires to participate and let their voices be heard in actual projects during the planning process. The risk with this form of participative democracy is that influential people and strong groups can take the lead and bias the discussion toward their own interests. Who will vote for the long-term public interests, on behalf of the members of the future society? Who will speak up for the people living downstream?

The problems of participation and influence have long been on the agenda for different theoretical planning discourses[3] often inspired by Jürgen Habermas's ideas on communicative action and ideal dialogue. Current normative planning theories put collaboration, participation, and dialogue center stage in knowledge development, with the goal of building social and political capital among participants. They focus communication

in public arenas, how participants exchange ideas and sort out what is valid, work out what is important, and assess proposed courses of action. Public agencies are just one group of many local actors involved in a process of collaborative planning. Other theorists instead refer to Michel Foucault's concepts on power in society as a fundamental aspect for understanding planning practice.[4] Policies and strategies are being developed in contexts where complex power struggles form the background for decision making, leading to fragmented analysis and valuation, bargaining, negotiations, and incremental decision making. The communicative problem appears not only in collaboration between citizens and their political representatives; large communicative problems also exist within planning organizations, between planners, various experts, and politicians. Different models have their pros and cons, and can be argued as being either more or less democratic, or more or less efficient.

Management of Uncertainties and Power in Design Processes

Despite the growing knowledge and understanding of urban planning issues and design problems, the processes are often messy and contain high degrees of uncertainty. Frequently there are limited resources—in terms of time, money, and manpower—to investigate, analyze, synthesize, and evaluate possible alternatives. Can urban experience-based, professional and lay know-how be integrated and used for urban design and better management of these processes? Can research findings and planning theories be used in the planning and design of social settings, procedures, methodologies, and techniques for collaborative planning?[5]

The standard model for *rational planning* and decision making puts different stages of development in a logical sequence, one after the other, each one having a beginning and an end. This can be seen as an effective way to manage planning and design processes, but creative processes are at the same time analytical and synthetic—seldom linear. The risk we run with a linear process is that it can be blocked by a question not foreseen by the standard operating procedures, resulting in an issue being moved from one desk to another.[6] Another risk is that a question cannot be solved by a chain of stepwise decisions, as it requires that a whole lot of decision makers reach an agreement at the same time; you can get locked into a catch-22.

Sketching is the traditional tool for architects and planners to create images of future urban situations. With this approach it is possible to search for the best way forward in an iterative way, by going from detail to whole and back again. By formulating and testing assumptions on a preliminary level, switching from analysis to synthesis, and going forwards and backwards, it is possible to make decisions in a selective and incremental way that leads the process ahead. The framing of the situation becomes clearer during the iteration between analysis and synthesis. These kinds of processes are dealt with in *design theory* when focusing the development of artifacts in architecture or in industrial design. In planning and policy analysis this incremental way of solving problems was coined as *the science of muddling through*,[7] as opposed to *blueprint* or *synoptic* planning for so-called grand solutions.

Sketching can also be used as a tool for stimulating communication among stakeholders and interested parties in a planning process. Forrester describes a complex, multiparty planning process for the waterfront of Oslo.[8] The basis for development of methods for problem solving is to understand how professionals and laymen really work when they are tackling complex problems. Donald Schön came up with the notion of "reflection-in-action" to describe the conscious reflective way of working used by the "reflective practitioner."[9] He demonstrates how uncertainties and controversies are realities that have to be handled and the ways that professional practitioners use to frame their roles when they work, such as in the interplay between an architect and a planner. *Single-loop learning* implies performing a task in a given context with given premises. *Double-loop learning* and *frame reflection* imply learning about the premises, and thereby the possibilities of changing the conditions and frames under which the tasks are performed. Group discussion processes can reset parameters for subsequent action, and be used in setting the frame for action.[10] Different facilitation methodologies and techniques can assist such group dialogues. There are several approaches for tackling complex problems. Rosenhead gives an overview of problem-structuring approaches for management of complexity, uncertainty, and conflict.[11]

Drawing on the results of the research, a practical methodology to assist and facilitate complex decision-making processes was developed.[12] The approach sets out to articulate the kinds of dilemmas that experienced decision makers repeatedly face in the course of their work, and the often intuitive judgments they make in choosing how to respond. The approach helps users make incremental progress toward decisions by focusing their attention on alternative ways of managing uncertainty. Planning is viewed as a continuous process of moving forward strategically. The focus is on the *connectedness of decisions* with one another, rather than on the relative importance attached to each decision.

There are four main modes of activities in decision-making processes, which often have to solve several interconnected problems. One stage of decision making is, therefore, to find out possible connections between problems, a *shaping mode*. Another mode is concerned with *designing* possible courses of action to solve those problems.

There is a need for *comparison* of these alternatives and evaluation of their consequences in order to create possibilities for *choosing*. For each mode of a planning process there are different *tools*—sketching, calculation of costs, etc.—as integrated parts of specific practices used by diverse participants in the planning process. As long as these tools enrich the process, it is also possible to use them as support for learning and decision development; thus, they become tools for interaction, to support the exchange of knowledge and arguments across disciplinary and professional borders. In

the *strategic choice approach*[13] a toolbox with simple graphic techniques for the structuring and management of complexity, the handling of evaluations, and management of different categories of uncertainty is provided. This approach views the conducting of any nonroutine decision process as being governed by perceptions of the relative importance attached to three broad categories of uncertainty:

- Uncertainties about *factual conditions* such as the distribution of population, costs for public transport, etc., can be handled by research, surveys, investigations, estimations, forecasting, etc., and can often be dealt with, provided sufficient resources are allocated.

- Uncertainties about *value issues* such as the distribution of public spending between investments in public or private means of transport, etc., can be dealt with by setting the priorities or by direct involvement of decision makers.

- Uncertainties about *related issues* concern decisions in other contexts that are not on the current agenda. They may, for example, be future decisions not yet dealt with within the organization itself, or possible reactions to decisions made by people outside the domain of the organization. These uncertainties may be dealt with by extending the current decision agenda, or by collaboration and negotiation with other participants.

Balancing power relations among participants is a continuously present problem for leaders in multiparty processes and dialogues. The relations can be open, and understandable differences in power relationships can arise, such as positions in formal hierarchies, access to financial resources, etc., but it can also be *hidden power plays* among groups or individuals within an organization due to local professional cultures or personal competition concerning internal hierarchies and other forms of complex human relations. Such hidden agendas are not discussed openly— nevertheless, they are always present, and undeniably influence development. For the purpose of further understanding and handling of decision support processes, a fourth dimension of uncertainty—for the description and analysis of power games—was introduced: *intraorganizational uncertainty*.[14] Later analyses of public planning processes have shown how often these kinds of internal power plays severely influence the outcome of design processes.[15]

The *process* of working with the SCA has striking similarities with architects and other designers sketching-in, which gives them the freedom to move forward and backward between detail and whole, between analysis and synthesis, in search of feasible solutions. While the designer often creates as an individual, the basic idea of the SCA is to facilitate the *sharing of ideas, mutual learning, and the exploration of complex issues by groups of people where no one person alone can claim full understanding*. Many uncertainties will, of course, remain; the management of uncertainty does not imply that all uncertainties have to be dissolved, rather that they will be openly and deliberately handled in a way that is dependent on their impact on the situation, available resources, and urgency.

PART 10: COMPLEXITY SCIENCE AND NEW URBAN FORMS

10.1   HIERARCHY, SCALE, AND COMPLEXITY IN URBAN DESIGN

MICHAEL BATTY

In the last twenty years our understanding of cities and their design has changed radically, from a perspective based on top-down organization to one based on the self-organization of the most basic urban forms built from the bottom up. There has been a gradual realization that well-adapted cities evolve organically, and that good design must understand and adapt to such processes. In this chapter, we sketch how this paradigm, which is loosely referred to as "complexity science," is developing into an effective science of cities, which has profound implications for their design and planning. We illustrate how ideas about hierarchy and scale come together to suggest ways in which urban morphologies reveal themselves as signatures of processes built around the most elemental units of development, at the level of the building and the site. Such processes scale up as cities grow, revealing fractal geometries and emergent urban forms. For some years now such ideas have provided the hallmarks of how nature works, and the development of these ideas for cities suggests ways in which we might develop more effective and sensitive strategies for urban design.

The New Paradigm of Complexity

Fifty years ago cities were thought of as machines, and insofar as they could be scientifically managed, it was assumed that their planning came from the top down. This systems view, popular in the 1950s and 1960s, assumed that our understanding of cities could be developed in analogy to the way physical systems were constructed. Interventions to solve the problems of the city were organized through direct and often blunt instruments operated in much the same way as machines might be controlled and managed. As we know, such designs have had extremely mixed impacts and in many, if not most cases, their repercussions on other parts of the city have been unexpected and problematic. Cities have turned out to be much more complex systems than could ever have been anticipated at the time.

The reaction to this limited understanding began over thirty years ago as it was gradually realized that cities evolve from the bottom up, as the product of millions of local decisions. In a wider context, the disillusionment with central planning and the articulation of bottom-up individual responses to centralized control were quite consistent with the notion that the best and most robust designs were generated at the local level, in a much more decentralized fashion. At the vanguard of this change were people like Jane Jacobs,[1] who argued vociferously for local action and a theory of planning commensurate with such representation, and Christopher Alexander,[2] whose deeply perceptive analysis of what constitutes good architecture provided an argument for methods of design that were sensitive to what might be built from the bottom up.

This movement gathered momentum, and from many disciplines came a revolution that turned systems theory on its head. The emergence of the "sciences of complexity," as they are being called, took their cue from nature—from biology, not from physics as the earlier generation had done. The notion that many systems in many fields are best considered as evolving from the local to the global, as growing rather than being designed from the top down, came to characterize many new theories of how systems are organized, and this has profound repercussions as to how we might intervene to solve the problems that such systems invariably manifest. Alexander summarizes this rather well when he says:

> People used to say that just as the twentieth century had been the century of physics, the twenty-first century would be the century of biology. . . . We would gradually move into a world whose prevailing paradigm was one of complexity, and whose techniques sought the co-adapted harmony of hundreds or thousands of variables. . . . This would, inevitably, involve new technique, new vision, new models of thought, and new models of action. I believe that such a transformation is starting to occur . . . we must set our sights on such a future.[3]

We will proceed by demonstrating that a key structure of complexity is the concept of hierarchy, and that urban forms that emerge from the bottom up can be described by highly regular scaling across such hierarchies.[4] A theory of urban scaling, of urban allometry and the fractal city, is fast emerging based on ideas around fractal geometry, and to demonstrate this point we will provide some suggestive examples as a prelude to this new approach to urban design.

Hierarchy as the Architecture of Complexity

Long ago, Herbert Simon argued that complex systems must be built from the bottom up if they were to withstand the inevitable shocks that take place almost continuously within their environment.[5] He told the tale of two Swiss watchmakers, Hora and Tempus, who assembled watches each made from a thousand pieces. Tempus simply built each watch adding one piece at a time whereas Hora built subassemblies of ten pieces and then put these clusters together into bigger units, proceeding in this fashion until the watch was complete. When demand for watches was low, each watchmaker took much the same time to complete a watch. But as demand increased—and in this world orders were only taken by telephone—when Tempus put down a semicompleted watch, it dropped to pieces, whereas Hora simply lost the subassembly he was working on. As more and more phone calls came in, Tempus found it increasingly difficult to complete a watch. What ultimately happened, of course, was that Tempus went out of business while Hora prospered, and the watches that emerged were all built around a hierarchy of parts.

The moral of this story is that efficient and feasible design is design built from parts, notwithstanding the key conundrum that the whole is greater than the sum of its parts. Alexander's thesis was that good problem solving proceeded in this way, by making sure fitness for purpose was established at every level from the ground up. The standard way of representing such structure is in terms of a hierarchy, a tree-like or dendritic structure, which shows the order and organization of the system from the top down or the bottom up.[6] Cities and their components such as transport systems, retail centers, and community neighborhoods are all organized in this fashion; indeed they grow in this way, elaborating and differentiating their functions according to such hierarchies. Perhaps the hierarchy is too idealized a structure, and variety often comes from a more complicated form of nesting, in which subsystems and subassemblies overlap in the manner of a semilattice. But the notion that city systems are organized spatially as hierarchies is well established in ideas as diverse as central-place theory through to modular schemes for arranging housing layouts, such as that pioneered at Radburn in the 1920s.

We illustrate this idea in a diagram (figure 1), where we visualize a city or regional space partitioned into successive levels represented by a strict hierarchy. If we project this hierarchy onto the flat map, then we produce a network of connections that indicates the manner in which the spaces are connected to one another when focused on some central place. Many cities are organized like this as they grow outward from their centers. The network that emerges serves to link the spaces hierarchically, acting as a way of delivering resources to each of the subspaces. In the simplest city, where all movement is to the center, the resources diffuse quite regularly as they are delivered from the center to the periphery. In like fashion, but in the reverse direction, they accumulate as activities at the periphery are moved toward the center. The analogy with the heart delivering blood through the arteries to all parts of the body has been heavily exploited in thinking of cities in this way, as we also imply in figure 1, which consists of a series of images illustrating the way these kinds of hierarchical branching patterns "fill space," delivering resources in an efficient and parsimonious way. A one-dimensional network can thus support two-dimensional space in patterns that are self-similar at every level. These are called "fractals," whose geometry is the essential organizational pattern characterizing the form of cities.[7]

Scaling and Urban Allometry

If we count the number of elements at each level of the hierarchy in figure 1, from the smallest in area to the largest, we generate a series which, over many orders of magnitude, gives numbers $p_1, p_2, p_3, \ldots p_k, \ldots$ where p_k is the population of each element k in the hierarchy. This frequency is composed of five elements at each level of the hierarchy, and increases from 1 to 5 to 25 to 125 and so on as 5_k, while the size of each element decreases from one large unit to 1/3 to 1/9 to 1/81 and so on as 3^{-k}. It is easy to see that as the number of units increases, their size drops, but in a regular progression that is scaling where the relationship is the same, whatever the level of the hierarchy. This is the hallmark of self-organization in which systems are built from the bottom up, in modules, which are the replicators—the building blocks of life or (in this case) cities—and which are assem-

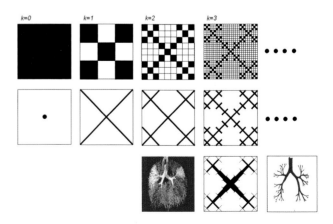

FIG. 1 Hierarchical space-filling structures: idealized models of how resources are distributed within a space.

259

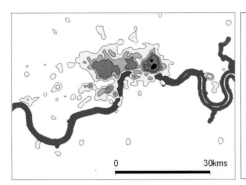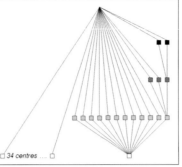

FIG. 2 The retail hierarchy in London as a lattice of overlapping centers.

bled at ever-higher levels of the hierarchy as the system grows. In this case, the scaling relationship is $f(p_k) = p^{-?k}$ where $? = -\log 5 / \log 3$.

There are many such relationships that link the numbers of elements to their properties such as density, area, the degree to which they fill their space in terms of their hinterlands or neighborhoods, and so on, and these form the essence of scaling. One of the most pervasive is the rank-size rule for cities, which in its purest form suggests that the size of any city P_r is inversely proportional to its rank r in the hierarchy, that is $P_r = r^{-1}$. This was first popularized by Zipf,[8] and remains one of the most enduring of all scaling laws. More recently, a much more coherent theory of how scaling (or allometry, as it is called in biology) in animal and human populations has been developed by West, Brown, and Enquist.[9] They base their theory on the fact that the branching patterns delivering resources to the area served at the finest scale are independent of the overall size of the biological unit, that the work required to deliver resources such as food or money to the outermost periphery of the structure is minimized, and the most efficient form of branching is tree-like, self-similar, hence fractal (figure 2).

This is a remarkable theory, in that it suggests that any kind of life—from the mouse to the elephant—has the same morphology, which scales from one size to another. If we were to scale the structures in figure 1 over many more orders of magnitude, the resources required would increase in self-similar fashion with the area served. The simplest allometry in the scaling implied in figure 1 relates the area of the growing fractal to its mass, that is, the occupied cells P_k to total cells A_k as $P_k = A_k^?$. The power $? = \log 5 / \log 9 ? 0.732$, which shows that area scales more slowly than mass, and it is tempting to think that this power is close to 3/4, although this depends entirely upon the way the branching pattern fills its space. A consequence of all of this, but one that we do not have time to explore here, is that the metabolic rates at which small structures function is far higher than that at which large structures function, but that the amount of resources expended in a "lifetime" is stable; for animals and human populations this is around a million heartbeats. Our

speculation is that the equivalent of the "metabolic rate" for cities, which stands at one end of this spectrum of human and animal populations, scales in a similar way to rates at the lower end of the spectrum—at the cellular level. This is a theory that is bound be elaborated in the coming years as the new science of cities gathers pace.

What has all this to do with urban design? Well, if we can establish that there are iron laws of geometry essential in producing optimal and efficient ways of growing cities, and if these structures emerge naturally from the bottom up, then this should affect how we design and plan. We should not try to go against this grain, but design cities so that we are cognizant of how our plans complement and merge into built environments, which continue to be mainly the product of unselfconscious design decisions produced by individuals and small groups. In this way, we might temper the somewhat blunt and disruptive top-down planning that still characterizes the modern city, and fashion new forms of urban design that are sensitive to local conditions and aspirations.

Urban Morphologies

So far our examples of hierarchies and power laws that describe allometry and scaling have been somewhat abstract, and thus it is time to put some flesh on the skeleton. The way city systems and their neighborhoods reveal their self-organization is through their form—their morphology—which is the characteristic signature of a complexity formed by growth from the bottom up. In figure 2, we show the organization of retail land uses in inner London, where the intensity of retailing in terms of its density is plotted as a contour map and where it is quite clear how varying levels can be used to show the extent of the various retail centers and their relative position in the hierarchy. Our picture is a good deal more intricate than the rather basic hierarchies developed over seventy years ago by Christaller, which formed the basis of central-place theory, but such organization still represents the cornerstone of the way cities are structured in spatial terms.[10]

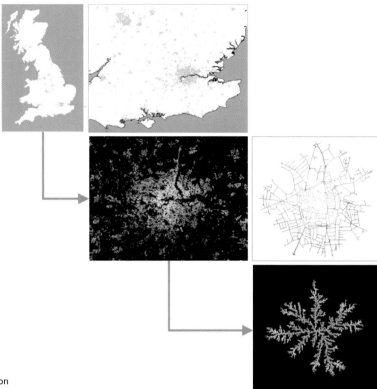

FIG. 3 The scaling of cities: urban form from country to region to city to small town and then to models of fractal growth.

If we were to link development to the network structures in figure 1, then the resulting form also mirrors the hierarchy. In fact, the network provides connections between space-filling activities—land uses—which sustain the city. The flesh on the skeleton is the pattern of population (figure 3), which repeats itself from country through city, region, and metropolis, down to small town and even beyond, to the very structure of movement at the most local level in buildings and neighborhoods. Although the pattern of branching that sustains the city is most redundant at the local level, with many cross-links, it is still the key to the way resources are delivered through movement, notwithstanding various electronic connections that are complementing and adding to the array of possible movements that underpin the rationale for the city.

Principles for urban design that are consistent with treating cities as complex systems built from the bottom up are only just beginning to be developed. Historically, rules of thumb used to structure the layout of city centers, housing estates, and factory towns tended to ignore traditional overlapping hierarchies in the quest to impose a rigorous order on development. Variety comes from the interposition and interweaving of multiple hierarchies reflecting social, economic, and cognitive networks, and good design should seek first to identify these. It should then enable the best features of such systems to be exploited, going with the flow, developing, in Mies van der Rohe's terms, "less rather than more," providing opportunities for those closest to the problem to generate their own designs, thus enabling slow and careful adaptations that steer the system toward realistic and sustainable goals.

GROWING SUSTAINABLE SUBURBS

AN INCREMENTAL STRATEGY FOR RECONSTRUCTING MODERN SPRAWL

LUCIEN STEIL, NIKOS A. SALINGAROS, AND MICHAEL MEHAFFY

A new way of understanding the growth of urban form leads to practical suggestions for reconstructing a more sustainable suburbia. Combining theoretical results with pragmatic experience—and combining "top-down" controls with "bottom-up" processes—we offer guidelines for implementing small-scale changes that eventually lead to large-scale improvements. The goal is a reintegration of the urban realm, resulting in a more humane and sustainable environment. Importantly, this can be achieved by a minimum of new investment applied all at once. Changes need to be implemented over time, and subsequent interventions will respond to the success of the preceding ones.

Introduction

Although attention tends to focus exclusively on the particular modern phenomenon called *sprawl*, we must recognize that suburban expansion has existed since the beginning of cities. A city, whether planned or haphazard in its initial form, tends to grow organically as its population increases. Legal measures that check the possible overgrowth of the central urban fabric, diverting new growth to the urban periphery, go back to the beginnings of civilization. In its earliest form, a relatively sympathetic exurbia maintained strong organic and structural ties to the city. Outer growth often completed some of the insufficient functional and spatial requirements of the tightly delimited historic city areas enclosed by natural or man-made barriers. Military and religious uses, for example, needed large open and flexible development spaces. Markets and business activities often found the ancient cities too restrictive for their activities.

These various activities and uses attracted a variety of other heterogeneous activities serving and supporting monasteries, cattle markets and fairs, military barracks, stores, travelers' inns and hostels, and—later—manufacturing and industrial installations. Houses, shops, restaurants, bars, and various services contributed to create suburbs with qualities similar to those one could find in the central cities. These benign suburbs, conceived and built as minicities, most often respected the scale, connectivity, hierarchies, and proportions found in the best urban centers, and they had a symbiotic complementarity with the cities they gathered around or grew out from. They respected pedestrian-scale principles, with the result that they were walkable urban extensions characterized by relatively flexible, organic and vital urban structure. In today's terms, they were sustainable urban morphologies.

The first historic suburban explosion happened with the arrival of urban train and transit facilities, which allowed commuters to escape daily from the crowded city, and, for the first time, to combine living in a relatively rural landscape with working in the city. Of course, this solution was totally unsustainable. The rural character did not stay that way for very long, as successive waves of commuters leapfrogged one another to move farther out to more peaceful environments. Beginning in Europe in the late nineteenth century and the United States in the early twentieth, the periphery of large cities began to rapidly expand farther and farther away from the earlier city edges following the expansion of the railway's patterns. This autocatalytic dynamic started to produce an enormous new suburban zone, with endless rows of houses and discontinuous urban sprawl along transit lines.

The second historic suburban expansion came about when the automobile became the engine of urban planning, helping to make mobility the principal and compulsive activity of individuals. It was not so much the formidable invention of the automobile itself—and its corollary, the historically exceptional age of fossil fuels—but rather the acceptance of automobile transportation as the essential and virtually exclusive connector of the various human needs. These now became dispersed by monofunctional zoning over larger territories and distances: so separated that an individual could no longer walk reasonably through this system. Automotive traffic became the indispensable tool needed to organize the connective system for the whole spectrum of human needs, from the daily domestic needs of the *res privata*, to the more refined and equally indispensable needs of the *res publica*.

Along with both of these historic waves—and in some cases accelerating them—has grown a body of political theory justifying and even celebrating the new development patterns. The Garden Cities movement, for example, sought to rationalize the new separated city, which meant the segregation of its functions within a low-density suburban hierarchy. Le Corbusier's Radiant City glorified the new car-dominated suburbs, and made them a fashionable cornerstone of modernist planning and design. His vision was the basis for Norman Bel Geddes' 1938 World's Fair diorama exhibit, "Futurama," which in turn inspired a massive wave of freeway-based suburban expansion two decades later. Le Corbusier's wildly exuberant vision of a suburban utopia seems somewhat chilling in today's era of ecological and resource challenges.

Since that time, suburbia has variously been associated with ideas of liberation, freedom of choice, autonomy, connection to nature, space and health, priority of family over society, individual emancipation over collective regimentation, private integrity over public alienation, and many more worthy goals. On closer examination, however, the connections are more imagined than real. In any case, the appeal of modern suburbia is undeniably strong. Hardly anyone has been really obliged to move to the suburbs, but clearly many

millions have elected to do so, for these and perhaps other reasons (notably economic factors, particularly land prices).

Trade-offs in the Contemporary Suburb

There are many negative trade-offs that come with the evident benefits of suburban structure as it exists today. The future, it seems, will bring many more if we continue to misunderstand basic forces behind urban growth. Debate has raged about whether the contemporary suburb is a sustainable urban typology; whether it can survive coming ecological and resource challenges—particularly the increasing diseconomies of "peak oil"—or whether its weaknesses will become so compounded over time that it will have to be drastically modified. In any case, there is little disagreement about the following negative trade-offs that already exist in today's ubiquitous suburb:

1. *Severely restricted transport alternatives.* To the extent that travel is exclusively dependent upon the automobile, those who can't drive (children, the elderly, the infirm, the poor) are at a severe disadvantage in travel to daily activities and access to needs. Those who can drive (e.g., mothers) must often act as taxi drivers for others, and sacrifice significant time and expense of their own. Walking is severely

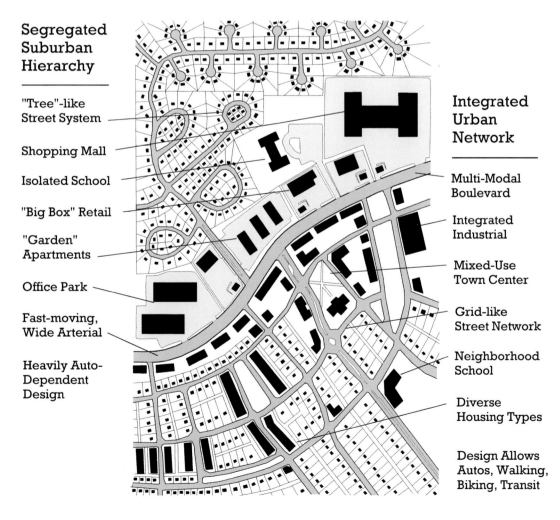

Segregated Suburban Hierarchy

- "Tree"-like Street System
- Shopping Mall
- Isolated School
- "Big Box" Retail
- "Garden" Apartments
- Office Park
- Fast-moving, Wide Arterial
- Heavily Auto-Dependent Design

Integrated Urban Network

- Multi-Modal Boulevard
- Integrated Industrial
- Mixed-Use Town Center
- Grid-like Street Network
- Neighborhood School
- Diverse Housing Types
- Design Allows Autos, Walking, Biking, Transit

FIG. I Conventional sprawl development follows a segregated hierarchical pattern, like the branches and twigs of a tree. The limited interconnectivity means residents are almost exclusively dependent on extensive automobile use, and longer average trips. By comparison, the more grid-like form of sustainable neighborhoods creates an urban network that is conducive to many more modes of travel, and shorter trips. There are other key benefits as well. Diagram: The authors.

restricted, negating its demonstrated benefits to physical, mental, and social health.

2. *Congestion-promoting geometry.* The hub-hierarchical system of roads characteristic of modern suburbs, and the compounded dispersal of destinations (more roads to get to more things requiring them to be ever farther apart) creates increasing traffic congestion over time. This wastes resources and decreases work productivity, air quality, and respiratory health, while increasing fuel consumption, expense, noise, stress, and dependence on nonrenewable and imported resources.

3. *Higher infrastructure burden.* The inefficient land-use pattern (segregated uses, hub-hierarchical roads, low density) tends to place an undue burden on the maintenance of a huge infrastructure. The tax collected per dwelling necessary to maintain aging suburban infrastructure increases over time. Increasing property taxes undermine efforts at densification, because they drive people ever farther out beyond the suburban limits, which must then grow a new and vast infrastructure.

4. *Weak public realm.* Public spaces have become dispersed, poorly populated, and expensive to manage. This is due to a failure to understand the human forces defining public space, and is responsible for a general decline of the public realm.[2] This, in turn, has been shown to result in a decline of civic interactions. There is a growing trend toward private commercial spaces and gated enclaves, thus essentially privatizing the public realm and limiting its role as social and economic catalyst.

5. *Decline of an authentic sense of place.* Contemporary suburbs pose perhaps, an even more intractable set of challenges for reform, because they lack the identity of place.

Phony names like "Stafford Pointe" and a fountain on the feeder road don't connect residents with their nonneighborhood. These suburbs have scarce civic activities; they lack adaptable historic architecture; they have a highly dispersed, poorly connected urban pattern. All these are absent as a result of the peculiar and pathological suburban geometry of postwar suburban growth. There is no *civitas* in suburbia.

6. *Degradation of livability over time.* These negative urban trends increasingly destroy the very qualities that suburbanites sought in the first place. Cars take over the roads and curbs just as much as in the city core, as individual garages eventually become filled with consumer junk, forcing cars to park outside. The only alternative is to leapfrog to a new suburban site before it, too, destroys these qualities with its own self-induced pattern of growth. This leapfrogging mechanism is the essence of a self-destroying, unsustainable pattern.

Most of the myths upon which suburbia has built its seductiveness have been exposed as false. Beyond its initial, impressive economies of scale, its increasing structural and functional failures are plainly evident. Legislation—and the special interests that it favors—helps to keep the current unsustainable model locked in, preventing any competing model from implementation. There exists a built-in momentum of doing things a certain way, following unsustainable postwar typologies from the car-dependent landscape. The market already often rewards higher-density, walkable "neo-traditional" urban developments—but only where they are not made illegal by current suburban zoning! Meanwhile, residents find themselves having to pay increasingly for the growing social, cultural, economic, energy, and ecological costs of the modern suburb.

FIG. 2 A comparison of two neighborhoods in Atlanta, Georgia. Credit: Satellite Images courtesy NASA.

FIG. 3 A comparison of the suburban infill project of Orenco Station, Oregon, with an older conventional suburb, illustrating the mixed-use grid structure of the infill project. The older suburb is a residential "monoculture," laid out in a hierarchical "spaghetti" pattern with limited connectivity. Photos by the Authors.

A Plan for Action

In the current urban and political environment, one must ask what is the most effective and realistic strategy (or series of strategies) to address the evident shortcomings of existing suburbs. These include their inefficient, hub-hierarchical, dispersed structure, the resulting over dependence on the automobile, and other problems. To be effective and realistic means that such a strategy must not rely upon utopian conditions, astronomical sums of scarce taxpayer money, or radical opportunities to reengineer or rebuild. It means, very simply, a largely incremental approach driven by typical urban forces: redirecting the same forces that created today's unsustainable sprawl.

There is no need to restructure billions of acres of suburbia comprehensively and simultaneously—even if such a massive undertaking were feasible. The steps and priorities that we discuss here can be implemented on some vital parts within any suburban system. Developing such crucial focal points using our suggestions, we can then incrementally fix the networking and add missing links to the urban fabric. This will generate healing processes and self-regenerating dynamics that can eventually spread to a wider region of the urban fabric. For example, we can intervene just on the scale of a piazza design or new public building, or a building with mixed use in the right location.

We insist that there are possible short-term economic techniques to start the process of suburban reconstruction with neither political revolutions nor high capital investments—in short, with an incremental, transformative approach. We believe the project of suburban reconstruction will be closely related to the emergence of a "New Economy," with better accounting for sustainable features, and with more justified and more equitable resulting wealth. Its immediate social and economic benefits will include sustainable local job creation, and support for new professional skills. These will be developed and offered as an opportunity for rewarding careers in real estate and building trades.

Our proposals depend on a radical new conception of what a city is, and how it functions. We base our working assumptions on the latest scientific understandings in complexity theory, which invalidate most postwar planning models. Rules accepted as valid by well-meaning government planners and academics generated sprawl and degraded city centers to the point of almost total social collapse. A living city has to be both heterogeneous and coherent: composed of distinct types of regions and functions, all working closely together. This implies simultaneous competition and cooperation between urban forces and functions. For example, commercial nodes are needed in the center of a suburban bedroom community to tie it together coherently. Such nodes need to connect both on the short (pedestrian) scale, and on the long (vehicular) scale, leading to a conflict that must be resolved by a very careful compromise in design. Once a commercial center becomes successful, legislation has to guarantee that it will not displace adjoining residences because of rising property values. As in a successful ecosystem, all competing forces must be kept in a dynamic (not static) equilibrium.

This requires a different way of thinking about the relationship between conscious choices (like political decisions) and emergent trends (like aggregate economic processes), a combination of which has produced the modern suburb. These two extremes can be thought of as top-down and bottom-up processes. It is not a question of elevating one or the other, but of how they can be integrated, and managed more shrewdly. (In fact, the relationship between the two is very complex: for example, top-down political choices also have cumulative bottom-up effects, and cumulative economic trends also have top-down individual choices at their heart.) The radical conception of "the kind of problem a city is" (to use Jane Jacobs's apt phrase) must be joined by a radical new conception of how to manage such a complex structure more successfully for maximum human benefit.

United States Urbanism and Beyond

Despite the unsustainability of the suburban model and the "tyranny of the private realm" it constitutes, the challenge cannot be dealt with without acknowledging the original purposes and ideals of suburban life. We are ready to evaluate positively some of the operational typologies and patterns developed in suburban city building. Everyone can agree that the most extreme form of scaleless and amorphous urban sprawl has contributed very little value to urban culture. Yet, the history of suburban settlements cannot be reduced to its most caricatured examples. We take into account relatively successful examples like the early Garden Cities, *Siedlungen* in Germany, and early suburban developments in the United States. A strong case can be made, we believe, that such examples offer much more functional alternatives for a living urban tradition.

Although we utilize thinking and typologies from sprawl in the United States, our method is meant to apply universally. The degeneration of urban fabric in the United States is a special case, but it is neither isolated nor exclusive. The same forces that produced it are crossing geographical and social distance into other cultures, and are influencing local neighborhoods the world over. This process is driven not only by the passion to copy all things American (even by the United States's political and ideological enemies), but also simply by the globalization of economic models that produced what they did in the United States. If nothing is done to actively counteract these trends, then the American variety of suburban sprawl is destined to become a global phenomenon.

Europe has its own particular suburbia, exhibiting far more national and local differentiations. For example, its urban landscape includes the terrifying, violence-ridden French "Cités;" the Eastern European prefabricated satellite towns; the residential middle-class, low-density areas in many European countries; the English New Towns; decaying residential zones adjoining now dead industrial zones, etc. Despite the superficially distinct morphological character of these urban typologies, the European bureaucracy is ready to unleash its destructive potential throughout European territory, using the United States's sprawl model as a template.

The reason behind this potentially disastrous mistake is that the sprawl typology is plugged into most European countries' mentality and corporate/government aspirations. Those

FIG. 4 A comparison of two neighborhoods in the Atlanta, Georgia area. Left: the traditional urban neighborhood of Adair Park, southwest of downtown, built on a grid structure with an internal distribution of neighborhood retail and other mixed uses. Right: The exurb community of Floyd, showing the classic hierarchical pattern of conventional sprawl development. Credit: Satellite Images Courtesy NASA.

FIG. 5 An illustration of how the Floyd area might be reconstructed over time, following the incremental strategy outlined here. In descending order, A: Definition of centers and boundaries—in this case, the center is a new "town center" designated in an existing mall area, and the boundary is drawn within a walkable radius. B: Beginning at the Town Center, new streets and other infrastructure form a gridded network. C: Additional streets and paths begin to connect isolated cul de sac streets, forming a more interconnected grid structure. D: The arterial is rebuilt as a boulevard supporting transit, with additional monumental structures, vistas, and "liner" infill buildings. Credit: Satellite Images Courtesy NASA.

entities are only waiting for their chance to act, having long ago decided that traditional European urbanism must be erased in the name of progress. In doing so, they betray a fundamental misunderstanding of the evolutionary nature of human environments, and the highly pertinent aggregated information in these older urban places. Planners put far too great a faith on a naive conception of the enduring "modernity" of relatively primitive industrial technology. Thus they exclude large areas of highly pertinent solution space, for no other reason than the outmoded dictates of fashion.

Five Priorities for Sustainable Suburbs

Many authors have proposed reasonable and incremental changes for urban and suburban morphology, but implementation has been haphazard and largely unsuccessful. The reason is that urban morphology is the result of deeper generative processes, which must also be changed. The configuration of buildings is driven by the physical communications network—the street pattern and infrastructure such as the networks for sewage utilities that are normally buried underground. The networks determine to a large extent how the visible, aboveground built structure is configured, and that is not going to change until the geometry of the network changes. The network, in turn, is determined by current social, political, and industrial practices in transportation and energy use and availability. Building a subway to connect low-density sprawl makes little economic sense if the transportation patterns generating sprawl remain in place; such a high-capacity, heavy rail system should be reserved for a medium- to high-density city.

Dynamic processes drive a city to function as a network, and it is essential to grasp them. A new understanding comes as a result of the recent application of scientific methods to urban structure, which are not generally known to the majority of practitioners. We have drawn on morphogenesis, as developed in biology, and on the science of networks. Christopher Alexander has shown how complex form is coherent or not, depending upon the process by which it evolves, and this relies on the sequence of steps that are allowed.[3] Healthy urban evolution can thus be guided by a relatively simple set of codes. Conversely, the wrong codes will grow a monster, regardless of the measures taken later to impose a particular form. Such changes, we believe, can be made in piecemeal fashion, much as living organisms grow new blood vessels to organs as those develop. This will

require a different management approach, and a radically different urban strategy.

Below, we outline a five-part incremental strategy, combining elements of bottom-up and top-down processes. This strategy relies upon conscious interventions and choices at three levels simultaneously: at the democratic level, wherein the shared public realm is collectively managed; at the professional level, wherein scientifically informed judgments are responsibly applied; and at the level of market exchange, wherein complex processes achieve emergent results. In any effective strategy, these three realms must be seen as elements of a complex morphogenetic process, and managed accordingly.

Step 1
A suburban area will be examined with particular attention paid to its overall size, geometry, connective network structure, and existing physical boundaries. If it meets the maximal pedestrian catchment size of being walkable in its longest dimension in thirty minutes, then we can proceed to step 2. If either its largest dimension or its area is too large, then the region needs to be subdivided into one or more pedestrian catchment regions. This is achieved by a variety of means, helping to physically enhance and articulate clearly identifiable limits. Such geographical solutions include boundaries, divisions, and a semipermeable system of neighborhood

FIG. 6 Orenco Station, Oregon.

enclosures. It is essential to provide an encompassing and unambiguous understanding of the neighborhood edge. Articulations can be features of natural landscape like canals, lakes, parks, gardens, forest, or hedges, often developed from existing site potentials, or created from scratch in derelict or neutral urban edges. Otherwise, they can be urban constructs, like planted avenues and boulevards, urban service strips, and complex thresholds of new public spaces alternating with sophisticated park strips and parkway systems. Boundaries can eventually be accentuated with the building of a substantial but permeable wall that will separate the catchment regions. This wall does not have to be a literal and uniform continuous wall construction, but should consist of a series of connected buildings articulating public spaces; enclosed courtyards and gardens; and sections of walls, gates, and monuments. This edge will create an enclosing complex sequence of architectural and urban events supporting the concept of neighborhood boundary.

Step 2

Houses that adjoin the outer boundary (whether physical boundary patterns or wall system patterns) will define the outer, lowest-density region of the suburb. This outer region (envisioned more as a ribbon than a disk) is going to be no more than a few houses in width, and will partially encircle the rest of the suburban region. As American suburbs use a block size of two houses' width, this means that the outer region will contain at most several blocks (i.e., it should not continue outward indefinitely). The vehicular roads should reinforce the encircling geometry as much as possible. The outer region will follow a zoning that is similar to the Duany Plater-Zyberk & Co. Smart Code for Zone T3.[4] While the density here looks the same as the typical suburb, the connectivity is drastically increased, and the traffic patterns become pedestrian friendly.

Step 3

The regional center will be the approximate geographical center of the pedestrian catchment region. New zoning codes will permit mixed-use buildings up to a maximum of three to five stories high, depending on the situation. We could have a commercial ground floor, a possible mezzanine with commercial or office space, and the rest of the building devoted to housing. Present setback and closeness restrictions will be immediately abandoned, and new zoning for an urban center will be adopted. The central region will be limited to roughly 20% of the total suburban region or less, and its outer edge will be strictly marked and maintained. Some such limitation is necessary to prevent the regional center from taking over the intermediate-density portion of the catchment region (because of higher commercial value), and this also follows because traditional, good, and efficient cities are organized this way.

Step 4

The intermediate ring—a region between the outer low-density region and the regional center—will be opened up to mixed use, and zoning will be changed to allow, but not require, closely built two- and three-story buildings. This region will follow a specific zoning code intermediate between the outer region and the urban center (similar to the Duany Plater-Zyberk & Co. Smart Code for region T4). This is meant to grow into a separate entity that has its own unique characteristics—neither low density nor central region, but a relaxed, mixed-use urban fabric reminiscent of traditional small towns. We suggest that a wider typological variety be encouraged, allowing for diverse budget categories of inhabitants. The necessary inclusion of public housing (spread carefully, and in a small percentage mix) distributed throughout the whole area can prevent the ghetto-like apartment blocks or segregated regions that mark our cities today. Streets can be narrowed, and setback restrictions abandoned, to allow for a denser urban fabric.

Step 5

The only major restructuring that is necessarily carried out directly by government agencies will be on the road structure; everything else can be left to commercial forces. The outer region will mostly be left alone. The intermediate ring will have to be connected with the central region via radial roads; no more than two of them need be introduced, if not already there. Incremental steps will then begin to reconfigure the connections. At present, vehicular roads are straight and wide, opening up to substantial and broad parking lots. Pedestrian paths, if they exist at all, are narrow, torturous, and fragmented. These characteristics must be reversed. New direct pedestrian paths will link open pedestrian plazas (some taken over from existing parking lots) in a continuous network. New vehicular roads will guarantee car access to many smaller and narrower parking lots, connected in a roundabout manner.[5] Most suburbs don't have this geometry, so the city must decide to open several narrow roads and close some wide roads around the regional center. These are distinct from the feeder road that now connects to the exterior of the suburb itself. Internal roads need not be as wide as the excessively broad streets in existing suburbs, so they can be built between houses, or by combining empty lots. Access for emergency vehicles will be guaranteed by pedestrian paths that can handle an occasional ambulance or fire truck.

A word on our choice of terminology: the intermediate "ring" could have any overall geometry. All we mean is that it roughly encloses a regional center with distinct characteristics, and is itself enclosed by a loosely surrounding outer region. We have no intention of imposing a definite, simplistic geometry on the urban fabric. A fixation with pure geometry has been the downfall of urbanism of the past several decades. A particular, complex geometrical network will evolve as the fabric becomes alive with human activity, and that involves internal connectivity, not overall shapes. Our aim is strictly to remake a region that is now homogeneous and disconnected on the short scale into a strongly connected, heterogeneous and complex system.

FIG. 7 Orenco Station Farmers' Market, Oregon.

The Small-Scale Approach

We need to acknowledge the sheer size of suburban real estate and recognize that to reform its shortcomings is a massive task. This vast structure, accommodating over half of all urban dwellers in the United States and Europe, was not created overnight—and its repair will not occur overnight. Rather than seeking massive top-down reconstruction projects (which have so often failed in the past anyway), we suggest that a more powerful and more effective strategy is to make piecemeal changes. These are to be effected both in physical projects and in what may be called the suburban "operating system"—i.e., the system of codes, regulations, and economic incentives. It is this legislated code structure that produced suburban morphology in the first place. We must provide tools that exploit small points of incremental change, which serve to reconnect the present fragmented structure into a more coherent, more functional urban system. Like gardeners planting seeds, and pruning or weeding a bit here and there, we must seek to induce organic processes of regeneration and reconstruction.

Following is a more detailed proposal of how to achieve such an incremental process of transformation. All of these suggestions need to be initiated by an immediate change in the zoning and construction codes, so our first task is a leg-islative one, not an architectural or urban one. Cognizant of the immense difficulties of changing codes, we have devoted the final section of this paper to this problem. These necessary changes are not necessarily in order of implementation, as a number of these changes must be done in tandem, or in a back-and-forth iteration.

Priority One: Define new neighborhood structures of centers and boundaries.

We need to redirect the existing suburban systems towards a networked pattern of neighborhoods with public centers and boundaries. Often these are emergent or latent structures already in place, perhaps around an existing civic or retail amenity. A town center will be defined as the geographical center of a roughly bounded urban region. Every neighborhood needs a clearly defined public space, well connected to the neighborhood street network and enclosed by both mixed-use and public buildings. These urban typologies have been avoided in postwar urbanism as being reminiscent of the past, but their need has been picked up by the commercial sector, which has reconstructed them (to great profit) in private shopping areas.

Here it is necessary to reverse the misguided ideology of placing the region's heart on the geographical edge, in an attempt to draw in car traffic to commercial nodes from as far away as possible. That measure only served to disconnect a commercial node from its immediate neighbors, leaving an urban region without a heart, and encouraging the proliferation of disconnected commercial strips all over the landscape. This dead geometry was the price paid for giving parking an exaggerated visibility, and sacrificing everything else to this absolute priority. There was never any need for such a drastic and ultimately disastrous geometrical reorganization. Rehabilitation can easily work now, with parking carefully thought out so that it is convenient, sufficient, and unobtrusive.

Healthy urban fabric is supported by many permeable boundaries. These were either eliminated or replaced with impermeable boundaries—both are antiurban measures. The neighborhood needs to have a clearly understandable boundary, which can be an avenue, a planted alley, a natural feature, or a landscaped system. This is a distinct idea from an isolating, impermeable boundary, such as a wall around a gated community. We are referring to the need for a psychological boundary, which enables the network geometry to take place, more than a restrictive physical boundary that cuts connections.

Typically, the regional center will offer opportunities for more elaborate, denser typologies, whereas the edge of the neighborhood can offer larger lots and different functional activities like light industry, larger institutional buildings, and suburban villa typologies with larger gardens. In this way, many of the choices of a low-density lifestyle that motivated suburban growth in the first instance can be maintained, but within a system that preserves walkability and integration. The key is to break up the present homogenous low-density geometry into regions of distinct density. Homogeneous sprawl is weighed down by its size, and becomes unwieldy and eventually dysfunctional, whereas heterogeneous adjacent regions can be made to support each other.

Priority Two: Network the existing infrastructure.
The transport infrastructure of suburbia lacks several efficient levels of network connectivity. The existing hub-hierarchy network kills local connections, and must be reversed by connecting on the same small scale. Healthy urban fabric requires better networking, nodes, and pedestrian pathways. More pathways and pedestrian routes, as well as connecting residential alleys and streets, need to be created to irrigate the suburban areas. An easy step is to switch the roles of road and alley: direct car traffic into the alley, and protect part of the main road as a continuation of the pedestrian network. Since active paths form only between complementary urban nodes, however, a prerequisite for suburban connectivity is the introduction of mixed use. This means an immediate legislative opening of commercial use within existing suburban subdivisions. Concerns of noise and pollution (part of the original reason for functional segregation) can be maintained by restricting what can be allowed into formerly purely residential zones—for example, nothing that requires vast parking needs, or that generates excessive noise and pollution.

With that in mind, suburbs need to create short, walkable new streets as an opportunity of progressively densifying, thereby beginning the process of importing new mixed-use typologies. We should create new pedestrian and bicycle connections on existing streets, with additional short paths and lanes. This implies a radically new connective geometry (although one to be achieved with very modest means). We will also develop a fully connective pedestrian and mixed-mode vehicular network. Dangerous, isolated, or unpleasant segments (where pedestrians feel threatened by vehicles) will be identified and repaired.

We need to liberalize road standards to allow skinny streets, irregular geometries, the incursion of storefront activities, boulevard layouts, and other more pedestrian-friendly street and path patterns. The principle of the walking citizen is an indispensable measure as a tool for all of these additional connections. Through a reasonable number of phases, new connections should cut through all the scales of the street armature, as well as the dimension of both distances between the intersections and nodes, and simultaneously reduce the size of suburban blocks and lots.

Priority Three: Insert monumental connections, screens, and vistas.
Once the smaller pathways and streets have been increased and the connections multiplied and enriched, stronger interventions are required at a larger scale in order to create connections between main centers, monumental structures, and social and cultural attractors. Key elements of this can be done quickly, as Baron Haussmann did so successfully with the boulevards of Paris in the mid-nineteenth century. In any case, the elements should be identified, and a plan for their progressive implementation should be adopted. Opening radial connections will have to sacrifice some built structures (as occurred in Paris), and this is an essential step to increasing connectivity. Massive rebuilding is not necessary, nor is it necessary to do everything at once.

We need to identify and build monumental connection points and terminating vistas. These don't exist in today's homogeneous sprawl, and will have to be built anew. Commerce entering a dormitory suburb will be encouraged to build so as to create a visual landmark (and be severely penalized if it tries to continue the present alienating practice of isolating itself with vast parking lots). The goal is to identify and reinforce a network of larger avenues, boulevards, parkways, and planted alleys, forming a monumental network with a comfortable section integrating bike and pedestrian lanes, transit lines, and reasonably efficient automobile traffic. Along these avenues, alleys, and boulevards, the codes will encourage the construction of a coherent street-wall frontage with mixed-use urban typologies between a minimum of two and a maximum of five floors, with progressive setbacks for upper stories (see priority five for more on this).

The perspective intersections and street terminations should be reserved for public buildings, monuments, sculptural elements, or larger landscape arrangements.

FIG. 8 Orenco Station Pavilion, Oregon.

The underlying planning principle is to use pedestrian visual feedback to anchor the urban spaces, rather than prioritizing vehicular traffic from looking at a plan, as is done nowadays (in a process that totally ignores the pedestrian experience).

Priority Four: Divide oversized blocks into urban blocks (the scissors technique).

This technique, developed by Léon Krier, rationally reorganizes larger megastructures into their organic components, divided by a pattern of convivial public urban spaces.[6] In many cities, postwar planning merged small urban blocks to create superblocks, and this mistake was copied as a template for the suburbs. We now have to do the opposite. The process begins by cutting pathways and streets into larger urbanized blocks. Their excessive present size opposes natural pedestrian connections and forces purely automobile transportation.

Our proposed outer suburban region should not be misunderstood as being composed of vast narrow housing or commercial blocks, as is often the case today with sprawl. We mean for every region to be crosscut with roads, paths, and connections, otherwise it becomes an antiurban typology. Whenever an overall urban geometry is impermeable, both pedestrian and vehicular traffic are diverted to the region's edge, so that internal connectivity suffers. The connectivity should become multiple (i.e., composed of overlapping networks), so that it is not exclusively dictated by vehicular roads.

We need to continue the pattern of connectivity at smaller scales, with passageways, internal courtyards and gardens, covered passages, and galleries, etc. Any sacrifice of private property will be compensated with the creation of new urbanizable land and potentially valuable real estate on new public spaces. Note that connectivity need not apply simultaneously for all transport modes: where a new road does not fit, a bike trail and footpath improve the situation. Healthy urban fabric requires the superposition of distinct connective networks, consisting of footpaths, bicycle paths, mixed pedestrian/car roads, and regular streets for traffic. The one-size-fits-all approach to traffic, mistakenly applied in the postwar years, has left us with a dismal overall urban connectivity.

Priority Five: Change the "operating system" of suburbia to facilitate further incremental reform.

We need to reform the zoning for any new development and for incremental infill. New zoning codes must allow the construction of mixed-use new towns with dense centers—well integrated into the transport system, having coherent, pedestrian-friendly street geometries, and having environmentally low-impact qualities. We need to end the coded bias toward monofunctional, monosocial, homogeneous, and mono-typological patterns of development.

Disincentives should be created against urban expansion into new (virgin or agricultural) areas, including a shifted burden onto permit applicants to demonstrate that market demand cannot be met within existing suburbs, and cannot be developed by infill, densification, and reconstruction of derelict areas. The way to achieve this is to charge steep development-impact fees for those projects that do not meet this burden. The market will eventually take care of this, once a major subsidy in food production is phased out. Increased energy prices will make close by farmland extremely valuable, as the low transportation costs that currently subsidize long-distance agricultural production will cease.

Legislation will create incentives for high-density new development (focusing on filling in the central core region), and disincentives for maintaining low density throughout within existing suburbs. Our model sets forth a specific notion of heterogeneous urban fabric, in which low density has its place, but cannot spread throughout a region. We need to encourage densification of existing low-density building with financial and tax incentives structured to generate regions of decreasing density around a central core. Restrictive setbacks and onerous use restrictions will be liberalized. Building low density on larger lots outside a well-defined outer ribbon will be discouraged.

We need to work to reform other sprawl-promoting practices such as (in the United States) mortgage redlining, federal highway incentives, FNMA ("Fannie Mae") mortgage restrictions on mixed use, and the like. Banks will play an increasingly decisive role, by refusing to lend money for an obviously urban-destroying project. Growing public awareness of the new connective geometry of sustainable urban fabric puts lending institutions in the spotlight as principal players in this urban game.

Putting It All Together Into the Fractal City

We have summarized our working methods as a blueprint for suburban reconstruction. The main idea is to use existing suburbs with as little intervention as necessary, but with a change in zoning and planning codes as promptly as possible, to encourage sustainable urban growth from this time onwards. Bottom-up commercial forces, in concert with shrewd top-down adjustments, will then take care of the reconstruction. We indicate the direction for reconstruction by providing codes, and exploit normal urban forces to take care of the process at their own pace. We are also optimistic that, with the correct legislation in place, the commercial sector will fund a significant portion of the reconstruction—not out of any ideological desire for a better urbanism, but simply as a smart process to do better business.

Under the right conditions, the initially homogeneous urban fabric will transform into regions of different density and mixtures of uses, a process we denote as "fractalizing the suburb." This geometric appearance will have nothing to do with basic geometric shapes (rectangles, circles, hexagons) that urbanists have traditionally imposed on a plan. The new

urban geometry instead refers to network connectivity, a much more advanced scientific concept. Living urban fabric will grow to resemble an electronic circuit board or microchip, where every node is connected and any simplistic geometrical regularity has been sacrificed to establishing network connectivity. True urban geometry is far removed from the shapes that were thought to define urban morphology over the past several decades.[7]

Because in many cases suburban geometry consists of amorphous blobs and ribbons (superficially copying the plans of picturesque traditional settlements), it was thought that this would permit a liveliness denied by a rectangular grid. That is a misunderstanding. Amorphous suburban geometry is presently disconnected, and is totally rigid. Both a blob-and-ribbon geometry (found in high-income suburbs and in the poorest favelas) and a rectangular plan (found in rigidly planned urbanism) can evolve into living urban fabric by the reconnective processes we describe. They must be allowed to do so by the codes in place. Neither initial geometry is better, nor does either geometry guarantee a living urban fabric. During its evolution into living urban fabric, a rectangular geometry will deform and become more complex on the small scale, whereas an amorphous geometry will straighten out on the large scale (a very successful top-down example of the latter being the straightening out of medieval Paris by Haussmann).

The whole suburban region is encouraged to evolve into distinct urban regions in an approximate sequence of connected pieces. Forces that act on different scale hierarchies will not be suppressed to maintain the homogeneous or segregated geometry, as is done nowadays, but will be guided to grow the network. The evolution of the network determines the urban morphology, not vice versa, and the overall coherent geometry must be supported by the road grid. If existing roads contradict or impede the evolution of urban fabric toward a circuit-board geometry, then some roads will need to be changed before that particular region can be regenerated. In most cases, the vehicular road grid itself can survive mostly unchanged, although road widths and curb radii will probably have to be adjusted.

A circuit board has to handle many connections of entirely different character, some needing the shortest path, others accommodated by less direct couplings. Healthy urban fabric establishes fragile pedestrian connections (which require straight paths, and reinforcement by surrounding built structures), and also the much more elastic vehicular connections. Cars and trucks can drive on a looped path without any problem, as long as the roads are easy to navigate. Also, cars and trucks need not drive fast within a moderately complex urban fabric. The key to connectivity and movement is access, not speed, thus reversing the priorities of several generations of planners. It is necessary to accommodate two distinct networks having mutually exclusive characteristics: pedestrian paths connecting urban spaces, on the one hand; and vehicular roads connecting parking lots, on the other. These two networks must interface, cross each other, and occasionally run parallel. The second must not be allowed to erase the first. Most important, we must not confuse the totally distinct characteristics of these two networks and apply them to the wrong one.

Legislation Prevents or Encourages Reconstruction

There are presently in place neighborhood review boards, homeowners' associations, etc., that have some influence on new building and the rebuilding of the urban fabric. These oversight entities should begin to use our prescriptions for the regeneration of that suburb or region (abandoning their present guidelines, most of which lead away from a sustainable urban fabric). This concept should work no less in any conventional suburb than in a downtown, where the process of approval is now taken for granted. The idea is to implement all these proposed guidelines in practical form.

We certainly take the view that urbanists should not get mired in endless legal wrangling, possibly getting "shot down" by some hierarchical authority. But often it is impossible to make the kinds of design changes needed without at least suspending the present requirements. That may be a particularly bad problem in the United States, where Le Corbusier-style segregated zoning and unbelievably large building setbacks, wide roads, low densities, etc., have such a stranglehold because they are legislated into codes. Unfortunately, this postwar planning model is still being embraced by other countries who seek to achieve United States-style prosperity, and who are not yet aware of the model's growing disadvantages. But here, too, we need an incremental strategy. Our recommendation is that urbanists take whatever steps they can based on the local conditions and the local political will, and not waste time tilting at windmills.

In the above section entitled "The Small-Scale Approach," we prioritize coding and legal action. Regarding previous arguments about top-down and bottom-up strategies, immediate short-term interventions (as well as the possibility to impact the larger context with smaller economic interventions, etc.), there exists a definite dilemma here. Political work and legal strategies are often tedious, long, and depend upon triggering top-down effects. Also, the relationship between legal action, coding, and their implementation is an enormously time-consuming process, involving a lot of lobbying and long-term strategies. That's the reason why we do not insist on a definite sequence for the stages of urban action. Sometimes, the coding could be a priority; for example, the coding could be a limited project that depends on coding only. At other times, there could be a larger coding effort on the regional scale like the Traditional Neighborhood Codes developed by Duany Plater-Zyberk & Co.[8]

Physical urban and architectural changes can even happen without necessarily introducing new codes, or they can take advantage of legal ambiguities. Interestingly, most projects need to be accompanied by a written document including legal and code aspects, but one wouldn't say that the coding was the most essential—it is rather the integration of didactic physical design and subtle, integrated coding that empowers the project. We definitely agree with the incredible emergency and need for a full and comprehensive legal revision and recoding strategy. In the context of this paper, however, we clearly stress feasible, short-term, tangible policies and actions. We balance these goals within a larger context of more thorough political and legal objectives to be aimed at. We are more supportive of efforts on an intermediate time frame. It will be the combined actions at various scales and levels that will constitute an overwhelming challenge to the obsoleteness of legal planning inertia, and will finally accelerate massive and drastic overhaul.

Sometimes it is not even the local zoning that prevents suburban reconstruction. We and our associates have recently experienced enormous problems in Mississippi (following the devastation by hurricane Katrina) from onerous regulations. For example, the Department of Transportation refuses to budge on their wide-road protocols, including enormous building setbacks. The only way out of this impasse was achieved by New Urbanists marshalling the governor and other forces to come in and neutralize the stranglehold of the Department of Transportation. The United States Federal Emergency Management Agency (FEMA) has also required draconian building forms in order to get flood insurance: no street-level activities; everything up on stilts; all garages below, etc. If so much as *one* resident in a community builds their house in a nonconforming way, the *entire* community gets denied flood insurance. This effectively means that they get denied mortgages!

Conclusion

The evidence already shows that the modern suburb in its current, disintegrated form (sprawl) is not a sustainable form of development, and needs to be reformed. This problem is particularly important as the developing world looks to the developed world for leadership in its own new, unavoidable suburban development. But this reform need not take away the characteristics that drove suburban expansion in the first place: a greener and more rural, livable environment, access to larger homes on larger properties, use of the automobile as an option (and not a necessity), and so on. Instead, reform needs to be aimed at creating a richer, more connected structure, allowing alternative modes of transport, greater ranges and locations for activities, and greater coverage of property. In this sense, the reforms presented here are less about limiting choice and more about expanding choice and diversity.

COMPLEX SYSTEMS THINKING
AND NEW URBANISM

T. IRENE SANDERS

This essay explores two questions: first, what have scientists learned about the structure, behavior, and ongoing development of complex systems that might be useful to architects, city planners, engineers, community leaders, and others working to revitalize fading urban areas, reenvision existing cityscapes, and cultivate the ongoing evolution of dynamic communities? Second, what can complexity science tell us about the characteristics, underlying dynamics, and patterns of interaction that encourage the emergence of beautiful vibrant cities that are alive with the qualities we recognize as community?

In exploring these questions, this essay responds to the strategic imperative of the New Urbanism to foster communities that are alive with the qualities that connect and nurture people and place. It provides an overview of complexity science; contrasts traditional planning, design, and engineering methods with the characteristics of complex adaptive systems; describes a new planning paradigm; and offers five food-for-thought observations for New Urbanists.

What Is Complexity?

The challenges we face today, and those we'll confront in the future, require new ways of thinking about and understanding the complex, interconnected, and rapidly changing world in which we live and work. Complexity science provides a new theory-driven framework for thinking about, understanding, and influencing the dynamics of complex systems, issues, and emerging situations.[1] Insights from complex systems research also provide an exciting new lens for exploring the development and ongoing evolution of cities and neighborhoods, as well as their interactions with the larger environment or context of which they are a part.[2]

From the moment of the big bang to the present the universe has grown increasingly more complex; from a primordial soup of particles, we now have stars, solar systems, ecosystems, and human societies. In the last twenty-five years, rapid advances in high-speed computing and computer graphics have created a revolution in the scientific understanding of complex systems. The same technologies that have given us instant access to news and information from around the world—allowing us to think and act as one vast interconnected system—have made it possible for scientists to study the nonlinear dynamics of systems that were once either hopelessly inaccessible or took years to understand.[3]

As a result, we now have the ability to move beyond the old reductionist paradigm; to look at whole systems, to study the interactions of many interdependent variables, and to explore the underlying principles, structure, and dynamics of change in complex physical, biological, and social systems. From health care to city planning and international politics, the new science of complex systems is laying the foundation for a fundamental shift in how we view the world, and with it the need for a shift in how we think about, organize, plan for, and lead twenty-first-century organizations and communities.[4]

Simply stated, complexity arises in situations where "an increasing number of independent variables begin interacting in interdependent and unpredictable ways."[5] Traffic, the weather, the stock market, and the United Nations are examples of complex systems.

Complexity science represents a growing body of interdisciplinary knowledge about the structure, behavior, and dynamics of change in a specific category of complex systems known as *complex adaptive systems* (CAS). Most of the world is comprised of complex adaptive systems—open evolutionary systems such as a rain forest, a business, a society, our immune systems, the World Wide Web, or the rapidly globalizing world economy—where the components are strongly interrelated, self-organizing, and dynamic.[6]

In recent years, scientists have identified many of the basic characteristics and principles by which complex adaptive systems organize, operate, and evolve, leading to important insights and research implications in almost every field. As a result, we are witnessing the integration of knowledge across disciplines and the emergence of new concepts, tools, and a new vocabulary of complex systems thinking.[7]

Across the frontiers of science, this new, more complete, whole-systems approach is replacing the old reductionist paradigm, where scientists traditionally tried to understand and describe the dynamics of systems by studying and describing their component parts. Complexity science is moving us away from a linear, mechanistic view of the world, to one based on nonlinear dynamics, evolutionary development, and systems thinking.[8] It represents a dramatic new way of looking at things—not merely looking at more things at once.

Extending our understanding about the dynamics of complex systems into the domain of human systems is the new frontier. When understood and used as a sense-making framework, insights from complex systems research provide powerful new concepts, tools, and a set of questions that can be used to understand and influence *complex sociopolitical human systems*.[9]

Of the many insights arising from complex systems research, none was more surprising or useful to researchers than the finding that complex adaptive systems across the board—whether physical, biological, or social—share a significant number of the following characteristics.[10] When used together they provide a set of insights and questions that form the framework of a new planning paradigm—a complex adaptive systems approach to twenty-first-century urban design.

I think the next century will be the century of complexity.
—Stephen Hawking, January 2000

Complex Adaptive Systems Characteristics (CASC 1–10)

1. Diversity among the components; heterogeneous parts or "agents;" sources of novelty in the system. Includes some sort of natural selection processes within agent groups that ensure ongoing evolution, regeneration, and adaptation.

2. Nonlinear interactions; widespread information flow and feedback loops.

3. Self-organization; results from attractors in the system, and from adaptation to changes in the larger environment and other agents.

4. Local information processing; local interactions among autonomous agents. Typically agents "see" only their part of the system and act locally; no global control.

5. Emergence; exhibits unpredictable global behavior or patterns; spontaneous order emerges from local system interactions.

6. Adaptation; open and responsive to changes to the larger environment or context and to other agents in the system; continuously processing, learning, and incorporating new information; making boundaries hard to define.

7. Organization across multiple scales; agents in the system organized into groups or hierarchies of some sort, which influence how the system evolves over time.

8. Sensitivity to changes in initial conditions; small changes can create big results at some point in the future.

9. Non-equilibrium; most interesting behavior/creativity found at the "edge of chaos;" healthy systems operate in a dynamic state somewhere between the extremes of order and disorder, making it easier for them to adapt to changing conditions.

10. Best understood by observing the behavior—activities, processes, adaptation—of the whole system over time; qualitative descriptions and understanding versus quantitative descriptions alone.

Cities as Complex Adaptive Systems

Complex systems research has given us a promising new way to describe and explain how societies form, adapt, and evolve in response to changing conditions.[11] The characteristics of complex adaptive systems (CASC 1–10) identified above provide a new lens through which to see and make sense of the underlying dynamics and patterns of interaction that create the emergent phenomena we call cities and neighborhoods.

Through the lens of complexity we see that cities and communities are not linear cause-and-effect systems, but rather dynamic systems where the variables (people, businesses, governments, etc.) are constantly interacting and changing—for better or worse—in response to each other, creating nonlinear feedback loops that either promote or deplete the life energy upon which their futures depend. As complex adaptive systems, communities are organized, coherent entities in which physical conditions, decisions, perceptions, and the social order are constantly changing.[12]

Complexity: Framework for a New Planning Paradigm

Thinking of cities as complex adaptive systems challenges us to review and revise our current planning, engineering, and design methodologies, which in most cases reflect a more linear, Newtonian worldview. In undertaking such a review we need to ask ourselves: first, which methods recognize the properties of complex adaptive systems? Second, what kind of knowledge about the system is provided by the method?[13]

As an example, figure 1 reexamines *futures research methodologies* through the lens of complexity in an attempt to answer these two questions for those focused on the future and others concerned with developing better foresight methodologies, as opposed to traditional forecasting methods, which are based primarily on linear extrapolations. It attempts to describe a landscape where futures research methods are used.[14] The underlying matrix is divided into four quadrants each representing a different system paradigm, including a view about how the future is created.

Differences in the basic assumptions between these four approaches can be described in the following way: the vertical dimension looks at the nature of our possible understanding of the system, and the horizontal at our

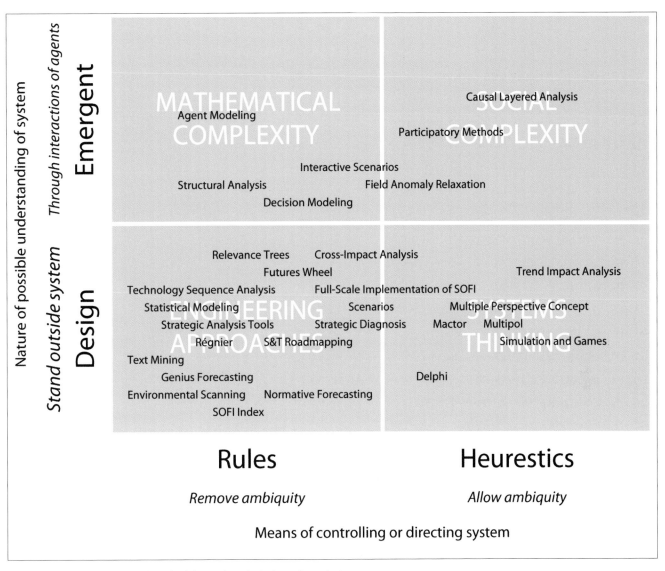

means of controlling, directing, or managing the system. In the vertical dimension design is contrasted with emergence. Engineering approaches and systems thinking represent design, and mathematical and social complexity represent more emergent processes. Vertically, the matrix represents an ontological view about the nature of things defined in terms of causality, and horizontally in terms of epistemology, i.e., what kind of knowledge can be achieved by which methods.[15]

Most methods designed to understand systems (and the future development of those systems) originated and are clustered in the engineering quadrant. Figure 1 helps us understand why we have difficulty using those methods to understand more complex, ambiguous, and emergent systems. It illustrates the point that most of the approaches we use today are inappropriate and ineffective in a complex and rapidly changing world, and it provides a template for rethinking and revising current methodologies.

Summary:
Food-for-Thought Observations for New Urbanists

These five complexity-based observations about cities and urban environments are offered as food-for-thought to those engaged in designing the communities of the future.

1. *Local interactions create self-organizing global patterns of community*. Emergence is one of the key insights from complex systems research. It refers to properties or a higher level of pattern created by the interactions of local agents in the system. What emerges does so naturally, and is not directed by a central commander or imposed by some outside source.[16]

The behavior of the whole cannot be predicted from one's knowledge of the parts of the system. In other words, the whole is greater than the sum of the parts. Complex systems often surprise us, and emergence is the process through which a system displays its creative and novel

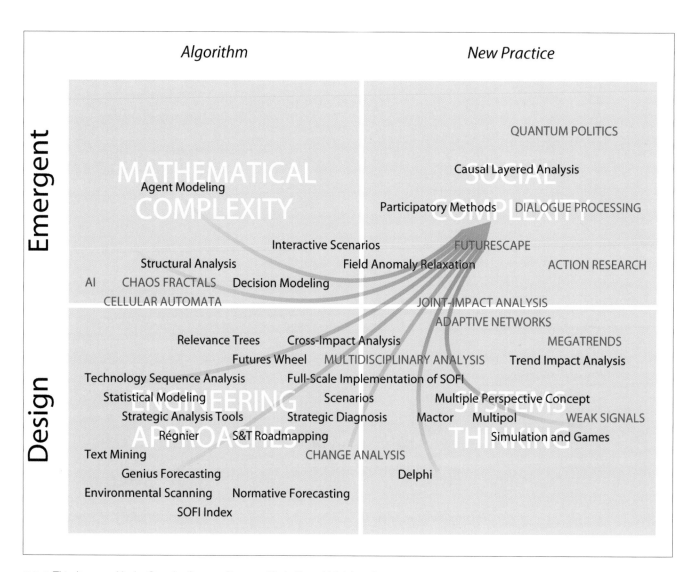

Algorithm | New Practice

Emergent

Design

MATHEMATICAL COMPLEXITY

Agent Modeling

Interactive Scenarios

Structural Analysis

AI   CHAOS FRACTALS   Decision Modeling

CELLULAR AUTOMATA

Relevance Trees   Cross-Impact Analysis

Futures Wheel   MULTIDISCIPLINARY ANALYSIS

Technology Sequence Analysis   Full-Scale Implementation of SOFI

Statistical Modeling   Scenarios

ENGINEERING   Strategic Analysis Tools   Strategic Diagnosis

APPROACHES   Régnier   S&T Roadmapping

Text Mining   CHANGE ANALYSIS

Genius Forecasting   Delphi

Environmental Scanning   Normative Forecasting

SOFI Index

QUANTUM POLITICS

Causal Layered Analysis

SOCIAL COMPLEXITY

Participatory Methods   DIALOGUE PROCESSING

FUTURESCAPE

Field Anomaly Relaxation   ACTION RESEARCH

JOINT-IMPACT ANALYSIS

ADAPTIVE NETWORKS

MEGATRENDS

Trend Impact Analysis

Multiple Perspective Concept

Mactor   Multipol   WEAK SIGNALS

SYSTEMS THINKING   Simulation and Games

FIG. 2 This diagram adds the Complex Systems Concepts–Tools Map, which is based on a complex adaptive systems view of the world. It provides an alternative, complementary causal view of systems and how things emerge (Aaltonen and Sanders 2006). Every discipline that adopts a complex systems view of the world needs to undertake this type of review.

behavior.[17] As an example, a computer program developed by Craig Reynolds in 1986 and known as "Boids" simulates the flocking behavior of birds by programming agents, or *boids*, to follow three simple rules: 1) maintain a minimum distance from other boids; 2) match the velocity of nearby boids; and 3) move toward the perceived center of nearby boids.

What appears to be very complex emergent behavior actually arises from a set of fairly simple underlying dynamics or rules. No central boid directs this process; the boids, acting only on local information gathered from their immediate neighbors and their environment, create the dynamic, elegant flocking patterns that are entirely unexpected; they cannot be predicted by just knowing the local rules defining what each boid does.[18]

Local, simple rules, motivations, and goals create complex self-organizing global behavior. Emergence helps us understand how community emerges from the local interactions of

neighbors and neighborhoods with each other and with the larger environment of which they are a part.

How could positive interactions at all levels of a system be encouraged? When negative patterns emerge, how could the interactions be influenced in a more positive direction? What are the underlying rules and dynamics that encourage interactions and positive adaptation to changes in the larger environment or context?

2. *The vitality of living cities emerges from the interactions created by multiple, connected, diverse centers of activity.* As complex adaptive systems, cities are unique, in that they usually self-organize or form around some relatively stable attractor such as a geographic or climatic feature (river, mountains, seasonal temperature variations, etc.). Soon man-made structures or attractors (churches, schools, hospitals, farms, factories, etc.) add another layer of complexity as they create new patterns of interaction in an emerging community. These

relatively stable geographic and man-made attractors serve as hubs of local activity, from which the emergent behavior or pattern of community arises.

The concepts of attractor and attraction are important to understand. Think about a tornado, for example. No external container or funnel gives a tornado its unique form. This dynamic, coherent, and focused system with a recognizable shape is formed by the interactions of the variables or attractors creating the tornado—moisture, heat, and wind rotation. A living city has many diverse and connected hubs or tornadoes of activity that give it its unique shape and personality.

What attractors can you identify in the old European cities we all love to visit? Most are characterized by multiple diverse centers of activity—cultural, commercial, educational, residential, and religious—connected by walkways, bridges, and most likely a central plaza where people spontaneously gather, celebrate, and protest.

Contrast these with the many lifeless urban renewal projects and downtown neighborhood developments where the concept of community includes Starbucks, Old Navy, a multiplex theater, a skateboard park, and restaurants surrounded by loft apartments and condos built in the midst of urban traffic and an uninviting cityscape. What's missing, and how could you encourage real interaction, connection, and vitality?

3. *Aesthetic coherence is created by recognizing and incorporating the fractal qualities of people, place, and environment.* The term fractal was coined in 1975 by mathematician Benoit Mandlebrot to describe a new concept in geometry. The word is derived from the Latin word *fractus*, meaning fragmented or irregular. *Fractal* geometry recognizes an order found within the irregular aspects of nature. It's an order that in the past we had not seen, because in a sense we didn't know how to see it—it doesn't fit the classical linear definition of order. The fractal concept helps us appreciate the orderly yet constantly changing world in which we live.[19]

There are two general characteristics that help us recognize this new type of order. First, *fractal forms are self-similar.*[20] Like ferns in a forest, bark on a tree, or the lines on our faces, patterns and shapes are repeated. Something in each new impression is familiar, a reflection of previous patterns and shapes.[21]

Second, *fractal forms are self-similar across scales.*[22] Patterns and shapes are repeated in finer and finer detail. The concept of self-similarity across scales has given us new ways to appreciate the special appeal of art and architecture. Patterns and shapes that are repeated in finer and finer detail add depth, texture, and a rich coherence to paintings and structures. The old European cathedrals are wonderful examples of self-similarity across scales, as are the paintings of Claude Monet and Vincent Van Gogh.[23]

There is an aesthetically pleasing quality to fractal forms in nature as they come together to create a beautiful whole. We respond positively to scenes where the buildings and landscape share a fractal quality. Frank Lloyd Wright had an intuitive feel for this concept, as do others who work to integrate their designs with nature. On the other hand, each of us could identify many buildings where the fractal quality is missing. These buildings jolt our senses and look like narcissistic, grotesque misfits in an otherwise richly textured city-or landscape.[24]

4. *A living city frames our interactions with subtle visual connections among people, place, and environment.* Every interaction takes place within a landscape that is captured in our unconscious mind, if not consciously recognized. If you put a picture frame around a quick conversation with a friend as you wait for the light to change at a busy crosswalk, what's in that picture frame around your interaction? Is it a park, a beautiful downtown cityscape, or buildings so high that you can't see the sky? Again, think about the cities you enjoy visiting or living in. What's in the picture? Living cities frame our interactions with views that invigorate our spirit and make us glad we're alive, too.

5. *A living city evolves within a larger context where emerging, new initial conditions will influence and shape its ongoing development.* As complex adaptive systems, cities are influenced and shaped by the larger context in which they operate. They must adapt to changes in the larger environment be they new traffic patterns, new hubs of activity, or the ups and downs of economic conditions.

The key to developing foresight about the future is to see and understand the dynamics of the big-picture context in which your decisions and designs are being made. What new initial or "perking" conditions are just over the horizon or under the radar that could dramatically influence the future of the cities you're working with? What local, regional, national, or international changes could go through your city like a bolt of lightning, rearranging its future overnight? How could you apply your thinking and planning resources now, so as to positively influence the future?[25]

Conclusion

Cities are unique complex adaptive systems. New Urbanists need to know as much as possible about complex adaptive systems theory and research, and look for ways to apply the insights and thinking to their everyday work—our future depends on it.

Note

The European Union report, "Business Knowledge Management: A Study on Market Prospects, Business Needs, and Technological Trends,"[26] uses the same model to assess organizational knowledge management in Europe, and to present a new initiative—Knowledge Management Made in Europe (KMME)—where the emerging opportunities for the European Union are seen to take place in the upper right quadrant—the field of social complexity.

NEW SCIENCE, NEW ARCHITECTURE ...
NEW URBANISM?

MICHAEL MEHAFFY

Just now an acrimonious debate has surfaced in the international press over the prominence of New Urbanist firms in post–Hurricane Katrina reconstruction. Leading proponents of avant-garde architecture savagely attack the "insipid nostalgia" of traditional revival styles that often accompany New Urbanist projects. The leaders of New Urbanism, for their part, attack an increasingly self-absorbed, neomodernist project, overly obsessed with making industrial neoplasms of the sort described recently by the critic Kenneth Frampton as "neo-avant-gardist kitsch (quasi radical in form but nihilist in content)." As Andrés Duany put it (witheringly), they "have nothing to offer real people in real life."

Duany and others believe architecture has abdicated its professional duty to lead the larger building culture—and thereby to ensure that cities meet broader human needs as much as specific artistic goals. They are on a reform mission to reclaim this professional role, on whatever strategic terms are necessary. So the debate—in its comparatively intelligent form, at any rate—is over whether those tactical concessions have gone so far as to corrupt the project, creating "simulacra" that serve the needs of particular economic interests to the exclusion of those of wider human populations. It's a fair discussion.

But clouding the debate, and fueling its acrimony, are deeper contemporary confusions about modernity and tradition, and the lingering modernist supposition that the "traditional" must somehow always be in artistic opposition to the "modern." There is not much appreciation of Jorge Luis Borges's observation that "between the traditional and the new, or between order and adventure, there is no real opposition; and what we call tradition today is a knit work of centuries of adventure."

The dualist fallacy is readily observed in the historically exceptional notion that it is *ipso facto* "wrong" to revive previously successful traditions—that by definition this *must always* be an offensive form of pastiche. But on closer inspection, this seems a curiously antievolutionary stance: for the most successful and beloved places in history have almost always been brilliant revivals and readaptations of older systems of architecture (e.g., Washington revived London revived the Renaissance revived the Romans revived the Greeks revived the Egyptians . . . and similar evolutionary patterns can be seen across cultures). In architecture, as in nature, refinement over time has the edge.

So, too, there is an odd contradiction in the argument that modern technology demands a restricted class of aesthetic and cultural response—one based on industrial minimalism and abstract expressionism—but at the same time the versatility of modern technology has liberated the constraints on architecture to an unprecedented degree. Which is it? Does modern technology really constrain us to decide that the New Orleans revival of a 1930's porch house is somehow less authentic than the revival (and importation) of a 1920's German industrial building?

It seems we are the unquestioning heirs of a residual modernist theory of history, which goes something like this: such evolutionary architectural systems—with all their complex local adaptations—are to be understood as mere "styles," with attributed expressive and political intent. A particular style is only appropriate to a particular sociopolitical context. The modern era demands a "modernist" style—an ambiguous term that is at least clear in its exclusion of anything recognizable from previous traditions or styles.

Thus is architecture reduced to what Jane Jacobs called a "thing theory"—not a complex, evolutionary environment, but merely a collection of notable artistic objects with attributes, expressions—styles. And in a weak-minded version of the genetic fallacy, these styles are to be interpreted as inseparable from the political contexts in which they may be found: Fascists liked classicism, therefore all of classicism must be Fascist. (Therefore Jefferson was a Fascist?)

The antirevivalism is notably inconsistent, too, because modernism—which as a movement does share a remarkable number of human ideals in common with New Urbanism, including decent quality of life for ordinary people—does have its own kind of revived tradition today. But at the outset modernism hitched its fortunes in large measure to an overconfident, antitraditional stance: aimed at ending the

FIG. 1 New Urbanists set about trying to regenerate the urban pattern with "Katrina Cottages," such as this modular design by Eric Moser. The building is adapted by local trades to the context and the local identity of New Orleans.

"irrational" dominance of backward-looking, oppressive, traditional culture and stepping into an eternal dawn of liberation and enlightenment. No doubt there was a lot of bathwater to be thrown out, as there surely is in any healthy self-critical culture; but the evidence cannot be denied that the naïve ideal resulted in more than a few babies being tossed out along the way.

Along with that ideal came a nearly unbridled faith in the rationalizing powers of an earlier science and technology—faith that has since been cruelly rewarded with the colossal disappointments that fell, blow by blow, in the intervening century. Today there is little left of the modernist enterprise, beyond a nihilist corpse of artistic expression for its own sake. *Pace* Derrida, there is nothing outside the art.

Meanwhile, the human business of tradition has revealed itself to be a much more sophisticated, self-organizing phenomenon than we had thought: an evolutionary repository of "collective intelligence," of useful information about how to solve various regularly occurring kinds of human problems. That intelligence seems to exist quite apart from the various repressive political regimes in which it may occur.

Such systems have an intriguing relationship to evolutionary and self-organizing systems today, including so-called "open-source," "wiki," and related collective systems. They have their counterpart in the latest trends in technology, toward more adaptive, more evolutionary kinds of processes. They are far from chaotic free-for-alls, and we now know they produce remarkable kinds of bottom-up order. They follow strict logic, but do so in a step-wise, cumulative, and ultimately powerful way. (The New Urbanists seek to tap into something similar when they talk about "swarm" behavior and the effect of "many hands" on the emergent urban design.)

Thus the basis for another kind of optimism has, ah, "emerged," and left a promising avenue for the large-scale development of useful new approaches, using biological kinds of processes. (See, for example, the discussion of generative codes earlier in this volume.)

Moreover, it has begun to transform the landscape of thought around these issues in ways that we—all of us—have scarcely begun to come to terms with. It transforms our understanding of the kinds of professional and civic problems we face, from narrow problems of "design" (and "style" and "product packaging") to interconnected sociological, economic, political, and cultural problems. And it clearly demands of us something different—different methods, different tools, different approaches—than we are able to deliver at present. It suggests that, in comparison to what is possible and necessary in a critical age, we are all still fiddling while Rome burns. And it is on this score that the New Urbanists, whatever their critique-worthy weaknesses, are about the only game in town leading the way forward. If you can't beat 'em, improve 'em.

There is a marvelous final chapter in Jane Jacobs's 1961 classic *The Death and Life of Great American Cities*, in which she describes the then-young revolution in the biological sciences of "organized complexity." Everyone in the field should be acquainted with it—not least because its gateway insights still have not been meaningfully incorporated into modern practice, in spite of a lot of lip service, almost a half-century later. Her recent death (in April of 2006) marks a professionally shameful milestone in that unconscionable delay.

Jacobs reminds us that our understanding of "the kind of problem a city is" has undergone an incomplete transformation, in parallel with the more complete transformation in our scientific understanding of the world in the last century. She presents a lucid and perspicacious account of the history of scientific thought and the way it has shaped human action, and, in particular, the way it has shaped how we think about and act upon cities.

She describes how modern science really took off, around the time of Newton, when it mastered so-called two-variable problems—like linking how many stores you can support to how many houses are in its catchment. In physics the laws of motion, for example, are also two-variable problems.

But in the early twentieth century something interesting had begun to happen: through statistics and probability we learned to manage very large numbers, where you had myriad variables interacting. The interesting thing that we found was that you could manage those phenomena as statistical averages without knowing much about the actual interactions.

This statistical science translated into the phenomenal technological power of the industrial revolution of that period. Much of our industry, and the prodigious output of twentieth-century modernity, was rooted in these powerful new statistical methods. And indeed, Jacobs points out that the early ideas of Le Corbusier and others, and the later ideas of planners—often to this day—rely upon this understanding of large statistical populations.

So, just as there has been a progression in science, there has been a progression from, say, the rigidly formal, "rational" plans of, say, Haussmann's top-down interventions in Paris, or of Ebenezer Howard and his neatly segregated Garden City plans, through to the more statistically informed plans of Le Corbusier, implemented around the world by the likes of Robert Moses and others.

In each case the problem of cities was seen as one of devising reductive engineering schemes, seeking to isolate smoothly functioning mechanical parts in place of "messy" organic conditions. This was seen as advancement and modernization. But in the earlier case it was two-variable engineering, and in the more recent case the problem of cities was also seen as one of statistical mechanics operating on large numbers. The newer science was added to the old.

Meanwhile, the biological sciences had reached a dead end with the statistical science of so-called disorganized complexity, and had to come to terms with the emergent phenomenon called organized complexity—the area in the middle, between simple two-variable problems and vast numbers of variables. Biologically speaking, that's where the phenomenon of life occurs.

It was clear even then that the problems of the human environment were in many respects emergent problems of "organized complexity." But Jacobs pointed out how the planning and architecture professions were still at that time—1960, mind you—mired in the old scientific world-view:

Today's plans show little if any perceptible progress in comparison with plans devised a generation ago. In transportation, either regional or local, nothing is offered which was not already offered and popularized in 1938 in the General Motors diorama at the New York World's Fair, and before that by Le Corbusier. In some respects, there is outright retrogression. . . .

In the near half century between then and now, it is fair to say that the "new sciences" of organized complexity have indeed triggered a revolution. We live in a world of networks, ecosystems, interactivity, and nonlinear processes. Great progress has been made in understanding the emergent

FIG. 2 New Orleans's Lower Ninth Ward has regionally well-adapted housing stock ready for renovation—but regrowth has been thwarted by a cumbersome top-heavy process. Stephanie Bruno leads the Preservation Resource Center's Operation Comeback, a more catalytic effort aimed at rebuilding and reselling abandoned or heavily damaged homes at affordable prices.

FIG. 3 New Orleans's organic pattern is an excellent example of Jane Jacobs's "organized complexity"—and its reconstruction has painfully revealed the failures of contemporary planning systems.

behavior of small, rule-based iterations, or algorithms—cellular automata and the like, and the so-called "emergent" patterns that they create.

Astonishing progress has been made in understanding one such system: the DNA code of life itself, made from just four molecules—but through a morphogenetic process adapting over time, through an astounding process of protein geometry that we are only now beginning to understand, it manages to iteratively code the astonishingly varied patterns and intricate wonders of life itself.

But there remains the embarrassing question of whether or not we in the planning and architecture professions have taken up even the merest real implications of these insights. Indeed, in the early stages of the twenty-first century, where stewardship of the built environment has not been abdicated altogether—in the sprawling suburbs, say—there remains a lot of Jacobs's "outright regression," in the superblock plans and mega projects that had their thematic and programmatic origins in the fantasies of early twentieth-century futurists. It seems that, beyond the bits of pleasing sculptural adventure, the fashionable avant-garde is achieving not much more than its own destructive brand of *de siecle* nostalgia.

But to be sure, a number of commentators have made the connection between new architecture and the new sciences—most famously, perhaps, the theorist Charles Jencks, who has proclaimed a "new paradigm" in architecture. Yet how far has Jencks's new architecture penetrated into the *real*

processes of complexity—and how much has it merely employed the *imagery* of complexity, as just another source material for poetic expression? Not that there is anything wrong with this in itself, so long as we are clear that this is our more limited project. The problem comes when it becomes a kind of simulacrum of modernity, an imaginative veneer over the old mechanical forms.

Thus do we quarrel with one another over our mutual forgeries. Jencks himself offers an instructive example of the distinction. His Edinburgh Garden is inspired by the diagram of a "strange attractor," that curious mathematical cloud of possibilities that tends to form an unpredictable, yet oddly constrained pattern in solution space. But he is not actually employing any of the insights of how strange attractors actually work. Instead, he is employing a *diagram* of a strange attractor, as a rather arbitrary (at least for noncognoscenti) shape generator for an abstract piece of art. And it is an interesting and, to this viewer, lovely idea *about* new science: but in actual morphogenesis or methodology, it is not a genuine expression of new science—any more than a house built out of *blueprints* of, say, Renaissance style buildings, is itself an expression of Renaissance architecture.

In identifying such work as *examples* of the new science, there is a telling confusion between the represented and the representation—culminating in a retreat into a kind of self-representational hall of mirrors. Perhaps the revolution that awaits is in the one where these insights are truly applied, in Jacobsian fashion, to the *process* of creating form that interacts dynamically in a civic—that is to say, urban—context. But that will be a very different kind of game.

Jencks might say (and indeed, elsewhere, has said) that any such work will be constrained by the social and political realities of modern global capitalist society, and that it is dangerously romantic to suppose that one can transcend them. The most one can do is to give an honest accounting of the new scientific cosmology, in which we recognize and begin to come to terms with our limited place in the scheme of things. Our art can't change the world, but it can deconstruct its hidden truths; and that is a kind of liberation, too.

As it happens, Jencks professes not to be a deconstructivist, or a poststructuralist (the underlying philosophy of that architectural style); but, in arguments like this, one detects the unmistakable logic of poststructuralist thinking, by any other name.

The story of poststructuralism is a fascinating one, though not altogether happy (hence Jencks's and others' denial of affiliation). To put it simply (and at risk of oversimplifying) this was an apparently sensible project to move past the weaknesses of structuralism, with its necessary reliance on a deep structure of meaning. But in so doing, poststructuralism found itself in crisis with respect to the status of reliable truth about the world. For, in this scheme of things, "truth" itself cannot really be ascertained as anything more than a cultural narrative constructed by an elite and imposed on others. Ye shall know the truth, and the truth is that there is no truth, apart from the narrative of someone in power. . . .

This philosophical position turned out to pose several serious problems, not just politically, but logically. For one thing, if the dominant truth is, as alleged, the narrative of global capitalism, which commodifies everything in sight, then one's own work of architecture cannot possibly escape being just another trivialized commodity. About all one can do is make an entertaining deconstructed spectacle of the logical contradictions inherent in such a meaningless exercise—which architects like Rem Koolhaas have become adept at doing. Shallow is the new deep.

But there is another, even more serious weakness: the epistemological position of poststructuralism is at its core self-extinguishing. If everything is a narrative text entirely dependent upon context, then so is your assertion to that effect; and I am just as able to reinterpret its meaning to fit

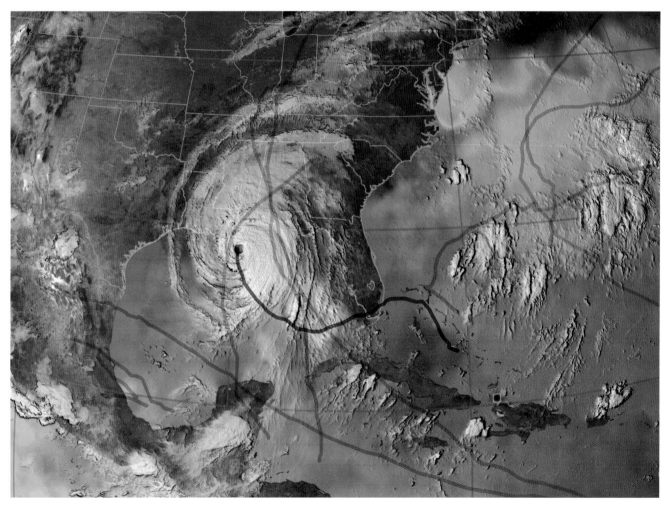

FIG. 4 **Hurricane Katrina tracking shot.** Credit: NASA Goddard Space Flight Center; Scientific Visualization Studio.

my context as I see fit. Thus, there is no possibility of establishing the most self-evident standards for collecting reliable truths about the world. Indeed, under this regime, there is not even the possibility of acknowledging such a reliable truth.

Of course there is a venerable human institution—in fact, on which a logically traditional structure—dedicated to precisely the discovery of reliable truth about the world: it is called science. So, it is not surprising that scientists were not particularly persuaded by a philosophical notion that extinguishes the possibility of epistemological integrity in their life's work. One reaction was a brilliant, if somewhat cruel parody of poststructuralism as absurdist physics, in a famous hoax paper by the real physicist Alan Sokol some years back. The paper, full of deliberately ludicrous nonsense, was published unquestioningly by a leading poststructuralist journal.

Well, science as a whole, like the theories within it, should be open to challenge and critical discourse—but with the necessary presumption that some reliable conclusions might ultimately be drawn in what would otherwise seem a pointless exercise.

True, in an age of "big science" and big business, the very word *science* has been debased of much of its original meaning. At its heart, let us remember, it is nothing more than the weeding out (from the Latin *scindere*, to separate) of what is reliably real from what is not real, what works from what does not work. This knowledge, of course, extends beyond human affairs to what works in nature, too: and indeed, through the age of great artist-scientists like Leonardo da Vinci and up until the nineteenth century, the field was known simply as "natural philosophy."

The temporary historic distraction of poststructuralism did perhaps make a useful contribution to science, reminding us that systems of knowledge do indeed have a systemic character, peculiar to the cultural system involved; but one need not dispense with the notion of reliable truth altogether to understand this. Indeed, a clear understanding of the distinction between the reference and the referent, between the symmetry and the symmetrical structure, is logically essential in any self-consistent semiotic scheme: one mountain, many views, and all that. No matter what we do with our language, an organism that is dead is certainly and sadly dead. No amount of narrative construction or deconstruction will change that reliable truth.

So, too, for a city: Jacobs's great hopeful insight is that one can make reliable conclusions about the life of a place, and about what is causing its death, and what must be done to revive it. This business is not, as the complexity pioneer Warren Weaver put it, "in some dark and foreboding way, irrational." And a powerful lesson coming home today is that this settlement business is not too disconnected from the life of the rest of the planet. Sprawl kills.

So the understanding of the human environment as a kind of biological system, complex but comprehensible, is slowly but inexorably returning to prominence. This is the real import of the New Urbanist project, however imperfect it may be. In this view, the failures of the early modernists, or the 1960's experiments in a science of human environments, were not terminal. They were rather educational, failed experiments along the way to a wiser understanding of our survivable place in the world. But we do need to gather up the lessons, and treat them as reliable truths—not merely narratives offered up by one group or another.

There are some interesting implications in all this. One favors the avant-garde artists: dynamic, occasionally radical change is indeed a part of nature—what Jencks calls "the jumping universe." Nothing is frozen in time. We must beware—particularly in a commodifying business civilization—of the tendency to create simulacra, mere derivative images of what existed before.

But another consequence of this cuts in an even more uncomfortable way for the avant-gardists. It goes something like this: along with the occasional asteroid impacts, we do still have crocodiles. That is, the jumping universe is also a universe of evolutionary continuity and endless revival. Nature loves to copy. Forms rarely break from their own evolutionary past, and when they do, it is—as often as not—disagreeable for the critters involved. In any case, it is something that comes with the territory of evolutionary process, and need hardly be contrived.

This is the uncomfortable scientific truth, like a hidden family shame within the end-stage modernist project: the slow, stable evolutionary forms of traditional architecture do, in fact, have a counterpart in nature. Revival, it seems, is a way of life. The dolphin does not mind reviving the shark's dorsal fin merely because it is "out of fashion" by 250 million years. Animals are constantly reviving and reincorporating traits that originated in the dim past. If it works, nature reuses it, and cares not a whit for the quickly dated fashions of artistic novelty.

But this hardly justifies Disney-style commodified simulacra: indeed, it points the way to their transcendence. Revival is not resuscitation. And there is indeed a necessary place for human intentionality in human culture, which, after all, is an essential dimension of art. So it is certainly possible to become stuck in the world of simulacra, to become ossified and out of place.

The New Urbanists may indeed be unfairly discounting the value of radical artistic exploration and the adventure of ideas. But although architecture is a form of action on the environment, as well as a work of artistic expression, the avant-gardists seem intent on recognizing only their work's status as an act of soaring imagination, and denying—or worse, excusing—its responsible place within an evolving human and natural environment. A burning Rome can ill afford too many Nero-modernists.

Thus, both miss a crucial point about evolutionary, adaptive *process*—and about the deeper relations between reference and subject—in a genuine and healthy culture.

To take our larger environmental responsibility seriously is to ask much deeper questions about the *process* of creating form contextually—not only as an act of imagination, but

FIG. 5 **Hurricane from space.** Credit: SeaWiFS sensor on OrbView-2 satellite, August 2000. Sea WiFS Project, NASA/GSFC and GeoEye.

FIG. 6 **Hurricane Katrina reminds us that Rome burns.** It's past time to get serious about reforming the chaotic and wasteful land-use patterns of the late twentieth century. New Urbanists might not have the right answers, but—let's be fair—they might just have the right questions.

Data from NOAA GOES satellite. Images produced by Hal Pierce, Laboratory for Atmospheres, NASA Goddard Space Flight Center.

as an act of environmental transformation, of collaboration and refinement over time . . . which is to say, of tradition. This transcends the gallery realm of art, and the processes of commmodification, and it insists—amply supported by reliable scientific knowledge—that acts of citizenship, and of genuine culture outside of commerce, are still possible. But it demands work, and intelligence.

A handful of people are beginning to ask deep questions about what this means for our methodologies, and the form of our collaborations and engagements—notable among them, our colleague Christopher Alexander. A number of other authors represented in this volume are doing the same. (This author has been privileged to join with them and others in an interdisciplinary research collaborative called the "Environmental Structure Research Group.") Many New Urbanists are, in fact, exploring ways to collaborate, in spite of lively disagreements, and to engage the economic and social realities, however imperfectly—precisely why they have been invited into post–Katrina Louisiana and Mississippi, and why they alone have been able to muster a united, if imperfect, response. They are onto something.

Thus another kind of future for architecture is starting to come into view, and if the New Urbanists don't yet have all the right answers—and surely, like any learning enterprise, they will have some wrong ones—they just might have posed many of the right questions. After an interlude of poststructuralist antithesis, the smart evolutionary synthesis will necessarily be to actually *apply* Jacobs's insights from almost a half century ago, in a serious and thorough-going way—engaging and transforming the political and economic realities along the way. Let us *apply* the insights of the new sciences, and, following Alexander, the powerful morphogenetic processes of life itself. Let us aim to create new kinds of "seeds," ones which generate the beauty and richness and sustainability of life beyond any one artist's imagination.

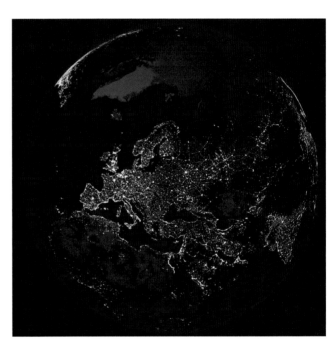

FIG. 7 The beautiful pattern of night lights in Europe reveals the complex evolutionary pattern of urban settlement on the face of the earth—and the looming challenges of growth yet to be faced by humans. Courtesy NASA. The specific image info is as follows: DMSP satellites. Data collected 1994–95. ASA/GSFC/Visualization Analysis Laboratory.

In this sense, a transformed architecture is indeed poised to regain its role as an integrating leader of the building culture, if it so chooses. It will remain a fine art, but simultaneously something much more connected to other human fields, and much more relevant to human welfare. It will return to its early modernist ideals, but combined now with a new respect for evolutionary process and organic connectivity. This will be a real professional revolution—and, rest assured, it will accommodate all manner of creative appetites.

QUANTUM URBANISM

URBAN DESIGN IN THE POST-CARTESIAN PARADIGM

AYSSAR ARIDA

Archaic thinking still moves most of urban design theory, which seems to have hit a brick wall. By taking a small detour in the history of scientific ideas, we find a burgeoning umbrella movement we call Quantum Urbanism promising to resynchronize practice with the contemporary worldview.

Missing the Turning Point

By clinging to a formal, deterministic paradigm, most postmodern urban design movements and theories, including New Urbanism, will never be able to seriously address the complex issues that challenge twenty-first-century cities.

Beyond the facile criticisms levelled at New Urbanism (reactionary nostalgia, stylistic fixation, commercialism, hypocrisy, gentrification, "geriatrication," etc.), two main sins—or limitations—of this movement are caused by its relationship to context.

On the one hand, its social and geographical realms seem to be limited to American townscapes (where it was born) and Western European—specifically Anglo-Saxon—contexts. Its models are impossible to export to second- and third-world contexts, where the largest challenges (and perhaps the greatest lessons in urbanity) are to be found. This automatically places it outside the global discussion on the fate of cities.

On the other hand, its historical and cultural outlooks are simply archaic. Although fixated on traditional urban form and values, it fails to take into consideration one crucial historical constant: that humanity has always built cities as a physical expression of its worldview.

It seems we need to take one small step back before we can go forward into the future with our thoughts.

Worldview and the City

A civilization's worldview is the collection of beliefs that shape its culture, the background metaphor resulting from the vulgarization of knowledge. From Ancient Egyptians, to Greco-Roman politicians, to medieval Christians, to modernist planners, the source of that knowledge has been superstition, philosophy, religion, and science. It has inevitably transformed each civilization's habitat, be it a giant city for the dead, the city of God, or a Ville Radieuse.

The scientific revolution of the seventeenth century triggered extraordinary advances in knowledge, leading to the industrial revolution and the boom in urbanization. But its initial caveat that science should only deal with quantifiable, objective matters has eventually caused a deep-seated malaise. Isaac Newton's Laws of Nature forged a mechanical worldview describing our universe as a giant clockwork, its parts easily divided and analyzed, with every event in a predictable, causal relationship to its future.

Over the next three hundred years, as this worldview trickled into other areas of thought, Western culture began subdividing its knowledge into ever-smaller expert disciplines, each with its own hermetic culture and language. Yet each of these new disciplines—from sociology to psychology to urban planning—stuck to a mechanical, deterministic paradigm. It was the age of utopias: build the perfect city, and a perfect society will follow.

The paradigm based on positivism and objectivism has been called the mechanical, the classical, or the Cartesian worldview.

The Seventy-Year Itch

There is a consistent lag of around seventy years between the first appearance of a major paradigm-shifting idea and its palpable effect on the physical world; it is the time needed for a whole generation to grow up taking that paradigm for granted, reach positions of power and responsibility, and finally affect architecture and the city.

Seventy years after the first breakthroughs in electricity, the spread of steamships, the railway boom, and the 1850 World's Fair extolling industrial design, Le Corbusier explicitly proposed the "house as a machine" and then "the city as a machine" vision. The modern movement of the 1920s to 1940s epitomized the mechanical worldview; it atomized our lives and our cities, and that is one of the reasons of its failure on the urban scale. Functionalism was a typical result of the industrial reductionist project, itself the direct descendant of the Newtonian/Cartesian approaches.

Coinciding with the failure of modernism's social agenda, the highly symbolic destruction of the Pruitt-Igoe housing project in 1972 signaled the beginning of a postmodern period largely imbued with formal and intellectual relativism. Remarkably, this was seventy years after Einstein first proposed his Theory of Relativity, debunking classical science's absolute vision of space and time. As a vulgar misinterpretation of Einstein's revolutionary notions, relativism and poststructuralism remained reactionary, formal movements. They gave architects and philosophers plenty to play with, but the excessive intellectualizing of every creative act proved too contrived to ensure long-term solutions to the city.

The neotraditionalist reactions that followed (including New Urbanism) were more popular with the end users, probably because they represented simple, easy-to-grasp ideas. Yet it is precisely this dumbing down of citiness that is so dangerous, as it acts as a momentary headache pill and fails to properly diagnose the complex issues at hand. This risks long term exacerbation of the problems.

Lost in Translation:
The Need for a New Conceptual Language

The city cannot be reduced to purely its functions, as the modernists did, nor to its ideas, as poststructuralists did, nor to its stones, as neotraditionalists did. Its physicality cannot be reduced to its objective form, nor can its subjectivity be reduced to melancholy or nostalgia.

The city is an immensely complex system of interactions and relationships, spaces and cultures, places and emotions, friendships and rivalries, narratives and symbols, and meanings. It is a mixture of real, imagined, and hyperreal environments; its networks distribute equally real commodities, be they goods, people, or information packets. Made by and around ever-growing numbers of unpredictable individuals and communities that now transcend geographical boundaries, the city is an emergent, self-regulating organism that is much more than the sum of its parts.

The conceptual and technical language that the establishment still addresses the city with is as unfortunate as Newspeak, the dictatorial language Orwell imagined in 1984, which would stifle any revolutionary thought. It is born in positivism, and still imagines a world of objective, measurable, and deterministic variables that can be set from the top down. Even with the best intentions in the world, with such a language we could never express the complex realities that arise with density and diversity—let alone comprehend and solve their problems.

Patchwork solutions cannot dent the unpredictable issues that will emerge as global urbanization attains a new critical mass. We need a complete rethinking of urbanism from the ground up.

What is required for such a task is a new conceptual language. The new language should be able to address the city as a complex living system. In fact, it should even force our thought patterns to embrace the complexity, rather than dumbing it down. It would allow the crossing of disciplinary and national boundaries; it would permit true cross-cultural pollination. When architecture and planning, art and philosophy, history, sociology, psychology, neuroscience, robotics, information technology, and vernacular intuition can talk together, we would learn as much from Paris as from Las Vegas, New Delhi, or Beirut. . . .

In an almost Hegelian twist of fate, today, seventy years after the discovery of quantum mechanics, the theory that describes the subatomic world, such a language is at hand.

The World According to Quark

According to quantum theory, the subatomic world is made up of possibilities and tendencies, not of physical certainties. Neither simply particles nor simply waves, the building blocks of our universe can only be described as hybrid particle waves that operate in potentiality fields whose processes are dynamically ruled by principles of uncertainty and of complementarity.

Quantum particles randomly break the boundaries of space-time. They are not fixed, dead matter, but responsive units that only "decide" which aspect to show us at the instant we look at them, and that happily break all notions of cause and effect. Quantum theory describes a deeply interconnected world, and recombines objectivity and subjectivity, mind and matter, into a unique model of reality.

These world-changing notions revolutionized the world of science, both philosophically and practically. In spite of all its "weirdness," quantum theory is considered to be our most accurate theory ever, and its practical applications (lasers, television, computers, the internet, etc.) form the very basis of our current civilization.

The metaphysical and technological doors that it opened led to the "discovery" of even more extraordinary notions: DNA, complexity theory, the world of fractals, information theory, the science of emergence, and so on. Over the last few decades, these ideas have been steadily transforming our relationship with each other and with the rest of the universe—in short, our whole worldview.

The City is Quantum

As an homage to that catalyzing theory, let's call this hybrid worldview the "Quantum Paradigm," and the associated way of looking at the city "Quantum Urbanism."

Unlike the mechanical, Cartesian paradigm of the previous era, this is a world of complementary dualities, of both/and values, of uncertainty, of choices at all scales, of interactive relationships, emergent qualities, and of sustainable, vibrant ecologies. With it comes a language that eloquently describes the chaos, uncertainty, complexity, heterogeneity, and subjectivity of urban life, and the complex artifact that is the city itself: the *urbs* and the *civitas*, the stones and the emotions. . . .

At a time when the disciplines of the city seem at a loss for words in dealing with the complexities of the new millennium, here is a powerful language (successfully tried by scientists for decades) that describes how the universe itself is shaped. Surely, the universe is a far more complex conundrum than a mere city!

A New Lingua Franca?

In his fascinating book *The Search for the Perfect Language*, Umberto Eco tells us the story of a mythical protolanguage that "perfectly and unambiguously expressed the essence of all possible things and concepts." That quest has greatly influenced Western thought, culture, and history. The intuitive search for a common lingua franca is, therefore, very much part of human tradition, and so adapting the language of the quantum paradigm across disciplines should be worth trying.

Yet we need not take that language literally; that could force us back into deterministic thought patterns and formal expressions that Quantum Urbanism urges us to go beyond. In fact, the new language is at its best when used to think of generic metaphors that can trigger the imagination into different directions. Let us consider some basic examples from the book *Quantum City*.

Particle-Wave Dualities, Events, Event Horizons

In quantum theory, every little primordial element that makes up the universe has two aspects: a particlelike aspect, that we can measure physically as having finite size and shape and position in space at a particular moment in time; and a wavelike aspect, that permeates space and time. One aspect is quantifiable, the other is more like a vibrational field that we can only describe qualitatively, in terms of intensity at a particular point.

Imagine a pebble (particle) thrown into a pond, where it creates a propagating ripple (wave), or think of a sound speaker (particle), producing sound (wave). In both cases, the pebble or the speaker have a very specific shape and size, but their wave is variable: the angle and force of the throw, the viscosity of the water, will mean bigger or higher ripples; the speaker could play speech or song or music, rock or classical, with different volume, treble, or bass settings. . . .

Quantum Urbanism sees the whole city as being made up of such particle-wave dualities, and it calls them events (figure 1). Each event is defined by its "particle" (wave source), its different "waves," and each wave's "event horizon," which is the boundary of the event's actual effect. In the case of the pebble ripple, it is the edge of the pond, for example; in the case of the speaker sound, it is the soundproof walls of the room . . . *In the city, the simplest example of a duality is a building.* Any building is particlelike, and has a physical shape that we

FIG. I **A generic duality: event and event horizon.** All images by Ayssar Arida, from the 2002 book *Quantum City*.

can measure and pinpoint geographically. We can even describe its height, materials, etc.—all architects do that, and all urban designers work with that aspect.

But most buildings also have wavelike aspects that are more qualitative than quantitative: they have a function—a house, a parliament building, a school, a church. They have subjective meaning: my girlfriend's house, the seat of authority, my first kiss, that scary priest; that meaning is different for each individual, so what to someone is "just a house," to me is "home;" and so on.

Interactions between events happen when their event horizons overlap and effects similar to interference start to appear (figure 2). Add more sound speakers, and their soundwaves will fill the room and interfere together, so that in certain points they give the impression of stereo or surround sound.

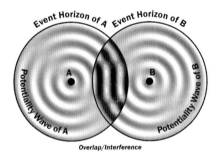

FIG. 2 Overlapping event horizons and interference.

Events also interact together to form new, higher-level particle-wave events. Clusters of buildings form a neighborhood: it is particlelike, but it also has its own wavelike layers of meaning: "my 'hood," "the red-light district," "Chinatown," etc. Neighborhoods interact together to create a city—particlelike. But it is associated with many wavelike qualities: "the Capital," "where the jobs are," "most romantic city on earth;" cities together form a country—particlelike. Its waves: "Anglo-Saxon culture," "Francophonie," "Old Europe," and so on.

Each time, thanks to the wavelike aspects, it is clear that the whole is greater than the sum of its parts, and that beyond the collection of particles is a larger picture with emergent qualities that do not exist if we cut it down to pieces and forget the waves.

The Russian nesting doll examples are never ending, but what is more exciting is that those waves are almost always linked to us as humans recognizing them: we are the actuators of the meaning of the environment (figure 3). It is a very

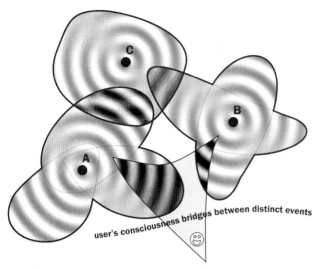

FIG. 3 Humans carry the effect of otherwise independent events in their memory and consciousness.

relevant notion in the quantum paradigm, where the observer and the observed are in a dialectic relationship very different from the absolute, objective relationship prevalent in the classical worldview.

Aren't we, after all, the perfect example of particle-wave dualities: body-soul, mind-matter, flesh-memory, individual-group, solo-team, friend-friendship, etc.?

The Society-Space-Time Continuum

By looking at the human user as another duality, another "event" in the city, urbanists can take on issues of meaning and memory, issues of gender and race and cultures, and make them part of the realm of study. Quantum Urbanism, in fact, defines three general classes of dualities: the human (people and the nonphysical events they create); the artificial (any physical creation); and the natural (landscape, fauna, and flora).

These oscillating construction blocks interact within a new multidimensional construct called the "Society-Space-Time Continuum" that integrates social, spatial, and historical contexts into a unified, organic realm. The ultimate goal of Quantum Urbanism is to make better urban space by changing the way we think and express our relationship to it.

Diventity

Quantum Urbanism steers clear of the complicated yet simplistic "qualities" and "principles" checklists of other contemporary theories, and limits itself to one deceivingly simple caveat, that "Good urban space optimizes diventity." Diventity is a powerful concept that we first introduced in Quantum City *(2002) and further developed over the last couple of years; it links diversity, density, and identity, and is defined as such: "Diventity allows identity to recursively emerge from the density of diversity, when that density reaches a critical mass."*

It is beyond the scope of this piece to delve into the details of this definition, but suffice to say that because the concepts of identity, density, and diversity are themselves generic and scalable, *diventity* itself is scalable enough to allow comparing otherwise unrelated systems (e.g., the ethnic composition of London City versus the ethnic composition of Cheltenham), and generic enough to address a wide range of indicators (e.g., environment, geography, demographics, events, aesthetics, socioeconomic class, ethnicity, volume, patterns, sensorial stimuli, functions, landscape, morphology, meaning, typology, texture, choice, and so on).

An Intuitive, Relational Language

How can we address all these notions if our very language is limited to a visual language that only knows how to describe shape and form? A visual language like the one we use everyday is by definition independent from time, because it sees only the particle aspect of things.

In *Blackfoot Physics*, an American Indian tells physicist F. David Peat that when he has to speak English instead of his native language, he feels that "he is being forced to interact with a world of objects, things, rigid boundaries, and categories in place of a more familiar world of flows, processes, activities, transformations, and energies."

A language that could also "see" the flows and waves would be a relational language, similar to the aural languages of native peoples based on the sounds of their environment, and on the belief in language as a living energy that binds them to each other and to nature.

When we start to look at the city as a collection of particle-wave dualities that include humans themselves; when we introduce in our very technical language notions that allow us to talk and discuss and develop this way of seeing the world, beyond just art; when this language spreads and permeates our different disciplines—then new thought patterns could emerge, breaking the cultural straitjacket that Western scientism has placed on our creations.

With new thought patterns we would find new solutions by tapping into the power of *informed* intuition, which will lead to new theories and new models of urbanism, which will in turn, only be relevant to each project's context. Such models are already being tested both in academia and in practice, and have already received awards and recognition in the most practical of commercial environments.[1]

We humans have, just like any evolved species, hard-wired instincts that include the knowledge of how to build our home in the most effective and magical of ways. The new language of Quantum Urbanism can help us realize that our cultures and our technologies are just as "natural" as any of our creations; when we can access our intuition with the same natural ease that a bird builds a nest or an ant its colony, only then, perhaps, will we rediscover the lost art of building organic, sensual cities deep into the twenty-first century.

PART 11: BEYOND URBANISM AND THE FUTURE OF CITIES

ANOTHER NEW URBANISM

EDWARD SOJA

For those in the city-building professions and practically everyone else in the United States, 1956 was a year of extraordinary confidence and optimism. The Fordist boom was reaching its peak, economists and policy makers were proclaiming the American economy's creative conquest of recessionary business cycles, and demand-driven mass suburbanization and spreading homeownership were expanding the middle class and its aspirations to unprecedented levels. Everything seemed possible, making the moment especially ripe for bold thinking about the remaining problems of the modern metropolis, such as the need to tame voracious and often ugly suburban sprawl and spark a renaissance in the poorer areas of the inner city.

It is only against this background that one can understand the enthusiastic and ambitious mood of the meeting of urban minds that took place at Harvard's Graduate School of Design fifty years ago. A remarkably eclectic bunch of architects and landscape architects, city and regional planners, policy makers, and developers gathered to create a pragmatic Americanized version and vision of city building under the evocative rubric of *urban design*. José Luis Sert set the ecumenical tone, specifically defining revitalized urban design as a branch of city planning, but one with a deep architectural heritage and perspective. Lewis Mumford's presence also signaled a relevant regional perspective on urban development, and a young Jane Jacobs brought to the meeting an awareness of the creative sparks induced by urban density. Through the stimulus of disciplinary convergence around a commitment to socially responsible practice, urban design was confidently positioned to become the cutting edge in the creative reshaping of the American city.

Twenty years later, however, nearly all the hopes and plans for the future had crumbled in the wake of unexpected events. The economic boom abruptly ended in the 1960s. Cities around the world exploded with demands for radical change and, by the early 1970s, the world economy had plunged into the deepest recession since the interwar years, triggering a frantic search for alternative ways to rekindle robust economic growth and control growing social unrest.

Optimism was replaced by urgent necessity, as all that once was so solid and taken for granted about metropolitan modernity, including the hopes and dreams of the new urban design, seemed to be melting into the air.

Over the next three decades, new urbanization processes would dramatically reshape the American city, but along very different lines from those imagined by the participants in the Harvard conference. By the end of the twentieth century, the modern metropolis had become virtually unrecognizable, as crisis-generated restructuring processes carried American urbanism into an almost entirely unanticipated era. So great were the changes that they made superfluous any critique of the lack of vision present among the participants in 1956. No one then could have predicted what actually happened.

In the wake of this profound reconfiguration of the modern metropolis, urban design was itself transformed. No longer at the center stage, it drifted away (in the United States, at least) from its earlier ecumenical ambitions and interdisciplinary desires to become a relatively isolated subfield of architecture. In its new position, urban design theory and practice became increasingly cut off from the mainstreams of city and regional planning, as well as the social, political, and aesthetic ambitions of European traditions of urbanism, both so vividly present in 1956.

As a professional and academic specialization, urban design seemed to wrap itself around a concept of the physical form of the city that had little to do with the rapidly changing urban landscapes it was meant to address. Comprehensive visions of metropolitan modernity were reduced in scope to narrowly defined and pragmatically feasible projects, as the urban (small u) became increasingly subordinated to Design (big D). This further isolated the subfield—not just from planning, but also from the emerging literature in geography and the social sciences—that was trying to make theoretical and practical sense of the new urbanization processes.

The great exception to these developments would appear to be the extraordinary flowering of the professional cult and culture of New Urbanism and its less ambitiously named, but perhaps more aptly descriptive British version, Neo-Traditional Town Planning. To the outsider—and probably many insiders as well—New Urbanism has been the most successful attempt to recapture, or at least simulate, the ecumenical spirit and far-reaching vision of urban design emanating from the Harvard conference. Moreover, it has proven to be remarkably successful in its applications, bringing widespread attention and lucrative projects to its practitioners and their particular and literally paradoxical "neotraditional" (*new-old*?) concept of urban design.

For all its faults, and there are many, New Urbanism has almost certainly produced better designed projects than would have occurred had normal market practices prevailed. The main argument I wish to make here, however, is that New Urbanism, for all its successes and failures, has had little effect on the isolation and detachment of urban design from a more comprehensive, multidisciplinary approach to contemporary urbanism. Indeed, I suggest, New Urbanism has deflected attention away from an effective understanding of the actual new urbanism that has been taking shape since the crisis-torn 1960s.

The startling metamorphosis of the modern metropolis over the past thirty years caught the city-building professions and the broader academic field of urban studies by surprise. Even well into the 1980s, traditional theories and practices of urban development persisted despite their growing disconnection to what was happening to cities worldwide. When the new urban worlds were recognized, their incomprehensibility, at least when seen from older ways of looking at the city, led many to proclaim the end of urbanism. New terms multiplied to mourn the death of the city as we knew it: *Transurbanism, City lite, Chaos city, Posturbanism.* It is from this theoretical vacuum and professional confusion that New Urbanism boldly consolidated its support and appeal, offering the world a way out of the incomprehensible chaos of the present through a comforting retreat to an idealized past.

Others studying the changing city, however, began to focus their attention on making practical and theoretical sense of the new urbanization processes that have been reshaping the modern metropolis. This has generated a rich and increasingly insightful literature concentrating specifically on what is significantly new and different in cities today. In *Postmetropolis: Critical Studies of Cities and Regions* (2000), I attempted to summarize and synthesize these writings on what I call the postmetropolitan transition, the still ongoing reconfiguration of the modern metropolis into a new form and functioning. From this perspective, a very different view of the actual new urbanism (without its capital letters) emerges.

Three interrelated processes have been the primary forces driving the transformation of the modern metropolis: the intensified globalization of capital, labor, and culture; the formation of a "new economy," described by such terms as flexible, post–Fordist, information-intensive, and global; and,

reinforcing and facilitating both, the spread of new information and communications technologies. Each of the three has developed distinctive discourses aimed at explaining the causes of urban transformation and what is new and different about contemporary urbanism.

The transformation of the modern metropolis and the emergence of a new urbanism are nowhere more vividly demonstrated or more comprehensively analyzed than in the urbanized region of Los Angeles. In 1956, Los Angeles was the least dense and probably the most sprawling major American metropolis. Its media-enhanced suburbia, with its auto-driven and ex-centric lifestyles, stoked such descriptions as "sixty suburbs in search of a city" and the "nonplace urban realm." Los Angeles was, back then—and for many continues to be today—a provocative and often fearsome model of the suburbanized city of the future.

Over the following fifty years, however, one of the greatest, least anticipated, and still poorly understood urban transformations experienced anywhere took place. Against all its images and suburban stereotypes, the vast urbanized area of Los Angeles surpassed the even larger urbanized area of Greater New York as *the densest in the United States*. A few census tracts in Manhattan still exceed all others in population density, but across the remaining 99% of tracts Los Angeles's density is unsurpassed. This radical reversal was not the product of clever planning efforts to control sprawl and induce sustainability and smart growth through densification, nor was it simply the result of the multiplication of edge cities or the efforts of New Urbanists and others to create swarms of "urban villages." What has been happening in Los Angeles and, to varying degrees, is also happening in many other cities around the world, is best described as a *regional urbanization process*.

Mass regional urbanization, with its combination of both decentralization (the migration of jobs and people from the old inner city) and recentralization (in new "suburban cities," as well as some old downtowns), has been replacing the mass suburbanization processes that dominated postwar urban development in most of the world's cities. These processes have expanded the size and scope of how we view the metropolitan region, and placed increasing importance on specifically regional perspectives in urban planning, governance, and public policy.

One significant effect of regional urbanization has been an "unbounding" of the modern metropolis. At a macrospatial level, it has broken open traditional urban hinterlands to extend the reach of the metropolis to a global scale, while at the same time bringing globalization deeper into the city. Accompanied by intensified transnational flows of capital, labor, and information, this has led to the formation of the most culturally and economically heterogeneous cities the world has ever known, with Los Angeles and New York leading the way.

Such terms as *world city* and *global city* have been widely used to describe the globalization of the modern metropolis, but I suggest that a more appropriate term is *global city-region*. Even without the global prefix, such terms as city-region, region-city, regional city, and regional metropolis today signify something substantially different from traditional notions of metropolitan urbanism. For a start, there has been an enormous expansion in population size and territorial scope of urbanized regions, well beyond the old commuter confines of the modern metropolis. The polycentric and increasingly networked megacity-regions of the Pearl River Delta, greater Shanghai, and southern Honshu, for example, each contain at least fifty million people, many times more than the largest metropolis in 1956. Even more stunning, nearly half of the world's population—and an even greater concentration of economic wealth and political power—are now contained in just 450 global city-regions of more than one million inhabitants.

The unbounding of the modern metropolis has also been taking place within the city-region, especially with respect to the once fairly clear border between city and suburb. What dominated the urban visions in 1956 and continues to the present for many urban observers is a view of the modern metropolis as consisting of two distinct worlds. A singular central city represented urbanism as a way of life, filled with excitement, heterogeneity, culture and entertainment, skyscrapers, and industry, as well as crime, grittiness, drugs, and poverty. In contrast, there was suburbia, with its uniformity, open spaces, detached homes, automobile-based lifestyles, relative boredom, soccer moms, commuting breadwinners, cul-de-sacs, and such political and cultural power as to define the United States (pace Duany) as a "suburban nation." Over the past half century, however, there has been an extraordinary intermixture of these two worlds, creating a growing recognition that traditional definitions of the city and urban-suburban life need a major rethinking.

Reflecting other seemingly paradoxical processes such as decentralization-recentralization, and deindustrialization-reindustrialization has been the expanding *urbanization of suburbia*, the transformation of dormitory suburbs into new outer cities, filled with (almost) everything traditionally associated with old central cities, including more jobs than bedrooms. Again, Los Angeles provides a clear example. Today, three or four of these outer cities surround the city of Los Angeles, with the largest and perhaps the oldest (along with Northern California's Silicon Valley) in Orange County, where nearly three million people live in an amorphous cluster of more than twenty municipalities of significant size. Nowhere in this cluster of "postsuburban" cities can one find what looks very much like a traditional downtown nucleus, but in almost every other way these dense clusters are cities or city-regions, and must be treated as such.

Remaining attached to older definitions of city and suburb can lead to some odd conclusions regarding these outer-city developments. For example, if densification and compactness are seen as the primary tools in controlling suburban sprawl, as is often the case, then one might conclude that Los Angeles is today the least sprawling, most compact metropolis in the United States, a rather startling possibility and a true strain on anyone's imagination. Sprawl in itself, however, is no longer what it used to be, whether referring to the urban designers of 1956, who considered it to be espe-cially insidious, or to the New Urbanists of today, with their commitment to promoting densification and compact cities. Again, some radical rethinking is in order.

A more serious problem than sprawl today is the increasingly out-of-whack geographical distribution of jobs, affordable housing, and transit facilities being created by uncontrolled (and often unrecognized) regional densification and the creation of polycentric city-regions. The new urbanization processes are creating a growing number of "spatial mismatches" that are aggravating old problems—such as access to jobs for the inner-city poor as employment opportunities decentralize to peripheral centers—as well as new kinds of postsuburban degeneration, as in spanking new boom towns built on unmet promises of job growth. In some cases, as many as 15-20% of residents must travel more than two hours each way to work, creating severe social pathologies, with increasing rates of divorce, suicide, spousal and child abuse, and teenage delinquency. These worsening urban-suburban problems cannot be addressed through local urban design or planning alone; they are fundamentally regional problems, and demand regional solutions.

To complete the picture of regional urbanization, it is necessary to look at what has been happening to the inner city. Many inner cities around the world have been experiencing a reduction in density, or what some have called a "hollowing out," tempting a few to couple the urbanization of suburbia with an equally oxymoronic suburbanization of the central city. But here the urban dynamics are much more complex. Nearly every inner city or metropolitan core in the United States has been experiencing, to varying degrees of intensity, the pair of countervailing trends mentioned earlier: deindustrialization-reindustrialization and decentralization-recentralization. This has produced many different trajectories for inner cities.

In some cases, like many of the old Fordist industrial hubs of the American manufacturing belt, deindustrialization emptied the old urban core of an often astonishing number of people and jobs, as in Detroit. In Los Angeles, too, more than a million long-term residents moved out of the inner city, along with many thousands of manufacturing jobs, virtually eliminating the automobile assembly, consumer durables, and related industries from what was the largest Fordist industrial center west of the Mississippi. But at the same time, the development of other industrial sectors—ranging from high-technology electronics to fashion-sensitive garment manufacturing to what are now called the culture or creative industries (reindustrialization), and the concentration of these expanding activities in both new and already established industrial spaces (recentralization)—brought about a stunning economic and demographic reconfiguration.

Over the past thirty years, reindustrialization and recentralization in the urban core of Los Angeles have created what may be the world's largest agglomeration of the immigrant working poor, a term developed first in Los Angeles to describe workers and households with multiple jobs yet unable to rise much above the poverty level. Almost five million foreign nationals moved into the broadly defined inner city, raising urban densities to Manhattan levels and creating, given the relatively meager changes in the low-rise residential built environment, what is arguably the worst low-income housing and homelessness crisis in any American city today.

During the same period, a highly visible downtown developed, with a growing cluster of skyscraping office buildings, a booming apparel industry, an expanding FIRE (finance, insurance, real estate) sector, and the largest concentration of government (federal, state, county, city) employment in the United States outside of Washington, D.C. Not very far away, Hollywood and other specialized clusters in the entertainment and broadly defined culture or creative industries have expanded significantly. Added to the high-technology concentrations in the outer cities, this has helped maintain Los Angeles as the largest industrial metropolis in the country, in terms of manufacturing employment, for most of the past fifty years.

The reconstitution of the urban core of Los Angeles is perhaps an extreme case of what has been happening to major cities around the world, as flows of immigrant workers replace domestic populations, often creating new frictions that cross older racial, class, and gender boundaries and cleavages. Along with the still uneven urbanization of suburbia and the growing mismatches in the distribution of jobs, housing, and public transit, almost everywhere the new urbanization processes have been generating increasing problems of social and economic polarization. Today, the income gap between the superrich 1% and the poorest 40% of the United States population is the greatest it has ever been, making it the most economically polarized among all industrialized countries. And these disparities peak in Los Angeles and New York, providing another dramatic contrast with conditions fifty years ago, when the booming expansion of the American middle class was reaching levels unparalleled anywhere in the world, and income inequalities were significantly declining.

Two straightforward conclusions can be made to this discussion of metropolitan transformations since 1956. If the city-building professions, and urban design in particular, are to respond effectively to the urban challenges of our times, they must address the actual new urbanism, rather than some well-meaning simulacrum of it. What is also clear is the urgent need for effective regional approaches to the growing problems of contemporary urbanism.

NEW URBANISM
IN THE AGE OF RE-URBANISM

ROBERT FISHMAN

Reform movements are inevitably molded by the crisis they were created to combat; for New Urbanism, this was the American urban and regional crisis of the second half of the twentieth century. When the first Congress for the New Urbanism convened in Alexandria, Virginia, in 1993, the central cities of the Northeast and Midwest had already experienced three decades of depopulation, deindustrialization, and abandonment. The 1980s had been especially marked by an unprecedented concentration of poverty—especially black poverty—in inner-city ghettos.[1] As population fled the worst urban "badlands," the adjoining first-ring suburbs were also threatened, leading to a chain reaction of abandonment and flight that accelerated sprawl at the region's edge. Thus in 1995, when the Charter of the New Urbanism called for "the restoration of existing urban centers and towns," this modest wish for "restoration" appeared to be an almost utopian hope. Even the best-established examples of downtown revitalization and gentrification seemed, in the words of the geographer Brian J. L. Berry, "islands of renewal in seas of decay."[2] The 1992 riots in South Central Los Angeles, by some measures the worst in the nation's history, seemed to promise that the grim cycle of urban decay and abandonment would extend far into the future.[3]

By contrast, the Charter's other principal goal—"the reconfiguration of sprawling suburbs into communities of real neighborhoods and diverse districts"—seemed a far more plausible aim in the context of a perpetual urban crisis. Not only was regional periphery the site where the vast bulk of new building would inevitably take place; these greenfield sites were also the tabula rasa where new patterns of compact development could be tested and then applied widely to form and reshape an edge for the whole region. Thus, the two defining images for proto–New Urbanism—Andrés Duany and Elizabeth Plater-Zyberk's neotraditional neighborhoods at Seaside (Florida), and Peter Calthorpe's "pedestrian pocket"—were both envisioned as radical reconfigurations of conventional peripheral suburban development on greenfield sites.

New Urbanism was certainly not wrong about the power of conventional suburbanization. What almost no one foresaw was the surprising resurgence of the central cities in the 1990s and beyond. From Brooklyn to Oakland, from South Boston to South Chicago to South Central Los Angeles, districts that seemed beyond saving rebounded to become precisely the walkable, diverse, mixed-use, mixed-income districts that the Charter had called for.[4] Many members of the Congress played key roles in this recovery; more broadly, the resurgence of urbanism—what I call Re-Urbanism—was a striking vindication of the larger philosophy of the movement. But Re-Urbanism has also created a very different regional context, especially for New Urbanist peripheral greenfield projects. For those seeking compact, pedestrian-friendly, transit-oriented neighborhoods, there now emerged a wonderful new abundance of opportunities *within the central cities*.

No newly built suburban project can hope to reproduce the social dynamism of these reurbanized neighborhoods. By contrast, the few genuine examples of "reconfigured" New Urbanist suburbia—whether "neotraditional" in the Duany Plater-Zyberk mold, or "Transit-Oriented Development" (TOD) in the Calthorpe mold—are almost necessarily a compromise: too dense to satisfy those households still craving the American dream house in all its large-lot glory; and yet not dense or diverse enough to match the more authentic urbanism of the reviving urban neighborhoods. New Urbanism as the "reconfiguration of sprawling suburbs" finds itself in the strange position of having to compete with the newly resurgent "Old Urbanism."

Indeed, it is tempting to assert that New Urbanism as a movement ought to "declare victory and go home." In other words, the real estate market, working from projected demand and operating through a multitude of small-scale renovation and infill projects, is now poised to produce, over the next few decades, an abundant supply of housing units in dense, transit-oriented, pedestrian-friendly "reurbanized" neighborhoods in older central cities and first-ring suburbs.

By contrast, housing economists universally project an over-supply of large-lot, automobile-dependent houses at the region's edge and a consequent drastic fall in their production.[5] Already such diverse metropolitan regions as New York and Houston are reporting that, for the first time since the 1950s, housing starts at the region's core exceed those at its edge.[6] Perhaps Re-Urbanism is all the urbanism we need.

Nevertheless, while the market will undoubtedly reinforce some of New Urbanism's aims in the coming decades, the market alone is unable to produce the region-wide transformation that the Charter calls for—especially after a half century of sprawl-dominated development. There is still plenty of steady work for an organization with New Urbanism's goals, but these goals must be reinterpreted to fit a changing demographic and economic context within the region. In part, this reinterpretation simply highlights the movement's "shift to the urban core," which has already occurred, in fact, if not in the common perception of the movement. New Urbanism has been central to perhaps the most important government housing policy promoting Re-Urbanism in the inner city: HOPE VI, the demolition of failed public housing projects and their replacement by mixed-income developments that restore the human scale of the neighborhoods that had existed on those sites.[7] As I argue below, this "urban core" aspect of New Urbanism can and must be broadened beyond housing to address issues of inner-city economic development and ecology.

More problematic, in my view, is New Urbanism's role at the exurban periphery that had initially been the key to its identity. The hope was that much-publicized projects like Kentlands, Celebration, and the Portland (Oregon) TODs would soon be succeeded by many others whose collective influence would significantly transform conventional suburban development. But, for reasons I attempt to outline below, exurban development has proved surprisingly resistant to transformation, even as its fundamental underpinnings shift. Here, I believe, New Urbanism can accomplish more by attempting less. As exurban growth necessarily slows overall, the case for fundamental change becomes both less plausible and less urgent.

To understand the possible role of New Urbanism in metropolitan regions experiencing Re-Urbanism, one must first understand how Re-Urbanism differs from the gentrification that had occurred from the 1970s to the 1990s. By definition, gentrification was narrowly based, both geographically and demographically. Affluent whites, often "single-person households" or childless couples, transformed favored districts while neighboring districts continued to decay. But, just as the urban crisis had represented the unexpected joining of many negative trends, so Re-Urbanism brought together a diverse group of urban positives that produced a critical mass for a far broader transformation. The global economy concentrated unprecedented resources in the downtowns of our favored "global cities" at the same time that these cities were again experiencing a surge of immigration and a dynamic immigrant economy. A black urban-oriented middle class finally emerged from the trauma of the Great Migration, while a largely white "creative class" (as Richard Florida has dubbed it) made the cities their environment of choice. The result was what Jane Jacobs had prophesied in the early 1960s under the title of "unslumming:" the large-scale recovery of the decayed urban fabric through small-scale, house-by-house, block-by-block renovation.[8]

With the Community Reinvestment Act and other credit reforms, many of the older residents possessed the means to buy and rehab their dwellings, thus, both profiting from the neighborhood improvement and maintaining neighborhood diversity. Built in the age of walkability, these areas usually already possessed good transit access and public spaces. And, at their best, these reurbanized neighborhoods have avoided the deep ethnic and racial divisions that had disfigured almost all previous urban neighborhoods of the "good old days," creating (at least temporarily) the most diverse districts that the American city has ever seen.[9]

If, however, Re-Urbanism has a weakness, it is the continuing dependence of the new urban immigrant and black economies on satisfying the luxury demand generated by a globalized downtown core. Because this high-end economy tends to produce jobs either at the very top or the very bottom of the salary scale, there is a real danger that neighborhoods that are presently economically diverse will resegregate into rich and poor. What is needed is a revival of an inner-city economy that produces that missing middle range of good jobs.

This need has been best addressed in Urban Design Associates's remarkable East Baltimore Plan, winner of a congress for the New Urbanism Charter Award in 2003.[10] Sponsored by Baltimore City and the Johns Hopkins University Medical Center, the plan reenvisions the now-isolated medical center (nicknamed "Fort Hopkins") as an economic driver for a broad-based revival of the East Baltimore economy. Rebab and infill housing are here complemented by plans for mixed-use loft space that would feature ground-floor retail, lab and office space, and residential units. The old network of neighborhood open spaces would be enhanced and connected into a set of green corridors. Above all, the plan foresees the economic revival of East Baltimore based on the medical center's status as a world-class facility. Instead of medical research largely conducted in suburban office parks at the edge of the Baltimore region, the neighborhood around the medical center would emerge as a high-tech research incubator, with a full range of job opportunities.

The East Baltimore Plan highlights the hidden assets that so many inner cities still possess; a similar line of New Urbanist thinking identifies and capitalizes on the assets of struggling first-ring suburbs. Briefly put, the first-ring suburbs, however defined, represent a point of transition within the region, between the pedestrian and transit-oriented development that occurred before 1930 and the extreme low-density suburbanization that occurred after the recession and energy crisis of the 1970s. Through the 1980s and 1990s, the first-ring suburbs struggled in vain to identify themselves with the automobile-dominated newer development; now, in the age of Re-Urbanism, it is their "backward-looking" features that can be reemphasized and "retrofitted" to emphasize their kinship with transit, public space, and walkability. "Retrofitting Suburbia," a collection of outstanding articles edited by Ellen Dunham-Jones and June Williamson that appeared in the Summer 2005 issue of *Places*, represents the "best guide to New Urbanism in the first-ring suburbs.[11]

In both the inner cities and first-ring suburbs, New Urbanism unexpectedly finds itself on the positive side of long-term market trends. When one moves to the edge of the region, New Urbanism's role becomes more problematic. As the movement has learned (often to its dismay), a small-scale "New Urbanist subdivision" inserted into the fragmented sprawl of a peripheral greenfield site is a contradiction in terms. If walkability, for example, is to mean anything more than a walk to the nearest collector street, there must be enough coordinated, well-planned, well-integrated, high-density development to create the critical mass for even the most modest pedestrian-oriented town center. And this requires somehow gaining control over thousands of acres over a period of decades—a virtual impossibility in the fragmented world of exurban development.

New Urbanism has thus fallen victim to much the same difficulties that the New Town movement had encountered in the United States from the 1920s to the 1960s. As Lewis Mumford and other early New Town advocates understood, capitalist real estate development thrives on the capacity to realize returns quickly; hence developers build subdivisions, shopping areas, etc., rather than *communities*.[12] But organizations capable of building whole communities take shape in such rare circumstances that widespread emulation becomes virtually impossible. From Radburn in the 1920s to the New Deal Greenbelt Towns to Columbia, Maryland, Reston, Virginia, and Irvine, California in the 1960s, the New Town experience became a history of supposedly exemplary models that no one was able to follow.[13]

New Urbanism has already compiled its own litany of exemplars, from Seaside to Kentlands to Celebration to Stapleton to the Portland TODs—with the same limited impact on the larger built environment. New Urbanism at this scale has come to depend on a "savior" developer with very deep pockets and a long time frame, or perhaps an enlightened regional government with not only the resources to fund a region-wide transit system, but the wisdom and firmness to limit development over decades to areas around the transit stops. Such saviors are rare.[14]

As I have suggested, in the age of Re-Urbanism they are perhaps not even necessary, for the market alone will surely slow exurban development. Rather than aiming for a radical change in exurban building practices, New Urbanism might accomplish more by aiming at interventions that are either modest in scale or directed more toward land-use policy than

new exurban typologies. Knitting together the often surprisingly dense and diverse "suburban clusters," as Anne Vernez Moudon and Paul Mitchell Hess call them, of self-isolated garden apartments and strip developments into an instant version of a walkable town center is one possibly fruitful strategy.[15] Another is the splitting of suburban arterials that Peter Calthorpe has proposed to create small walkable districts.[16] Most important of all are the policy interventions to support local governments aiming to preserve their rural character, and hence to preserve a green edge for the region; equally crucial are interventions against affluent suburbs whose propensity to "zone out" diversity through large-lot zoning and other requirements that limit communities to the affluent not only segregates the exurbs but pushes all but the most wealthy to seek cheaper land at the edge.[17]

Such small-scale realism will, of course, do little to remedy the long-term consequences of the last thirty years of extreme low-density development, which will be a drain on our whole society as the energy crisis inevitably assumes an ever-sharper form. At the individual level, many of those who eagerly bought large-lot dream houses at the developing edge of a region will eventually see their isolated, automobile-dependent, energy-devouring McMansions sell for less (when they can be sold at all) than a small condo in a reurbanized core neighborhood. The market, sadly, operates through its victims as well as its winners. If the victims of the postwar urban crisis had been those who, through choice or necessity, stuck with the central cities through their agonizing decline, the "victims" of Re-Urbanism will be a more affluent group who chose to pursue the logic of peripheral expansion after that logic had ceased to operate.

By contrast, New Urbanism, at least in the core areas of the region, can look forward to gaining strength from the strongest market trends that will be shaping the American built environment. In the age of Re-Urbanism, density, diversity, walkability, even transit—all these have begun to *pay*. But the market can be as dangerous when it favors a movement as when it goes against it. The coming decades could see both the painful decline of much of our recent low-density development, but also the return of the urban overcrowding that once gave high density a bad name. As planners since the nineteenth century understood, neighborhoods can be wholly walkable, lively, and dynamic, but also inhumanly crowded, viciously segregated, and designed only to maximize profit for the few. Already our most dynamic cities are seeing a precipitous decline in housing that is affordable for families with children, as well as a renewed trend toward economic segregation.[18] In this new market-driven context, New Urbanism as a critical design and social philosophy has a continuing and vital role—perhaps above all as an advocate not simply for density but for the *right kind of density*. New or old, urbanism is always about balance and diversity—which will always be the two most elusive goals for American cities and American culture.

THE NEW URBANISM
IN THE TWENTY-FIRST CENTURY

PROGRESS OR PROBLEM?

EDWARD ROBBINS

Any discussion about design and the city in the last two decades would be incomplete if it did not include the New Urbanism. As one of the most discussed architectural responses to the plight of our cities, it has generated an often acrimonious debate. On one side, it has received uncritical praise (Kelbaugh, Norquist) and, on the other, fervent criticism (MacCannell, Robbins). This debate has yet, however, to address the relevance of the New Urbanism for the new challenges urbanism will face as the twenty-first century unfolds.

The New Urbanism, Then and Now

The New Urbanism, its supporters aver, proffers a number of important responses to the challenges of contemporary urbanism. For some proponents, the New Urbanists are significant agents of resistance to continued urban sprawl and fragmentation.[1] New Urbanism also provides a voice for those who see an inner city in decline, social alienation produced by conventional suburbs, and a world dominated by the automobile. The New Urbanists' call for community, a sense of regional order, and less dependence on the car, suggests that they have an important anodyne for these urban ills.[2]

Developers find in the New Urbanism not so much an answer to sprawl and reliance on the automobile as an opportunity to establish development codes that provide for greater permissible densities than conventional planning.

For others, it offers security by establishing a set of limits that serves to guarantee the value of the homeowner's investment. Codes and other restrictions imply that the community will not change its physical form and appearance. New Urbanism sells a vision of community, rooted in our nostalgia for small town life and community; its emphasis on traditional house types and urban aesthetics suggests that this world can be resurrected and sustained. New Urbanists also set out to make us feel safe through designs that foster eyes on the street; familiarity with our neighbors; and bounded, if not gated, neighborhoods. In essence the New Urbanism provides the assurances at the expense of broad freedom of choice, in a world that appears increasingly threatening. As the architect Robert Stern put it:

> In a free-wheeling capitalist society you need controls—you can't have community without them. . . . I'm convinced these controls are actually liberating to people. It makes them feel their investment is safe. Regimentation can release you.[3]

Critics[4] argue that: 1. it is doubtful whether the New Urbanism can realize its claims; 2. it is questionable whether the New Urbanism will generate some fundamental and universal urban "good;" and, 3. even as New Urbanists reject the modernistic project, they replicate the error of its unbounded hubris and essentialism. It is the last point that may present the greatest hurdle, indeed even danger, to the New Urbanists as they confront the future.

Few projects—if any—built by the New Urbanists provide all that they promise. In one of the most publicized, Kentlands, the village relies on a conventional mall, which is based on regional automotive traffic for its economic survival, and to which the residents of the Kentlands go to shop. Seaside, New Urbanism's iconic project, took years to realize its commercial center; but it is dependent on automobile-based tourism. Seaside and Kentlands, like many other New Urbanist projects also located in areas dependent on regional malls and the automobile, illustrate that the New Urbanists have not as yet been able to deliver their promised regional plans. They have yet to integrate the proliferation of small pedestrian-based places in a way that does not also produce sprawl, fragmentation, and the domination of the automobile.

The failure of New Urbanist projects to "concentrate commercial activities, including shopping and working, in town centers"[5] is not an accident. Such commercial centers are not viable; pedestrian communities of five to ten thousand people cannot support economically feasible town centers that will adequately serve the shopping needs of its populace. At best, they might provide centers for the sale of convenience goods and personal services.[6] In a similar way, developing places where people would walk to work is just as problematic. Even in neighborhoods and cities with the densities to support a jobs/housing balance, it is unlikely that people would work where they live. Robert Cervero has illustrated that even where counties develop a job/housing balance, two-thirds of those people who live in those counties work elsewhere. Finally, the emphasis on pedestrian villages would create and increase sprawl, not diminish it. As an example, a region of one million people would have 200 neighborhoods of 5,000 people each or 100 villages of 10,000 people each; a region of five million would have 1,000 or 500 such communities. Whatever the densities, the need for schools, hospitals, shopping, recreation, churches, and other civic places spread over these villages or concentrated in nodal centers would create a web of roads and a continual growth of automobile traffic.

Even if the New Urbanists do not meet all their goals, they might still succeed at, as Vincent Scully argues, "in creating an image of community," overcoming the social dissolution that he and other New Urbanists claim is plaguing society? At the core of New Urbanism is:

> The presumption . . . that neighborhoods are in some sense "intrinsic," and that the proper form of cities is some "structure of neighborhoods," that neighborhood is equivalent to "community," and "community" is what most Americans want and need.[7]

It is a presumption that is open to serious question. Many Americans love living in the anonymous suburbs as well as in urban towers. Effective community can be and has been created by people who live in different neighborhoods, and even different cities, through mutually shared interests. Moreover, as Thomas Bender points out, trying to recapture community by imputing it to locality-based social activity regardless of the quality of human relationships is misleading. And, "if community is defined as a colonial New England town" or as some other nostalgic vision of small town America, as the New Urbanists define it, "then the prospect for community today is indeed dim."[8] It trivializes the complex and sensitive mix of social cultural practices and attitudes that go into making a community, and it assumes that community should be or must be place based.

Even where community is created, it may not always be the cure for urban problems. It might be useful in a time of urban transnationalism, and increasing fragmentation and conflict, to ask whether creating small, well-designed places built around their own commercial and social center is the best way to deal with our urban condition. This is especially important as ever more community groups are beginning to reach out for citywide and regional strategic planning, rather than mere community-based development. In a world in which bigness at the corporate and political level is growing, the need for ties between communities is also growing.

To remedy a number of the criticisms directed at the emphasis on the village, New Urbanists have moved away from a reliance on its original emphasis to a concern for regional development, which they call the "Transect."[9] The Transect is a method with which to describe the urban region and provide a model of land use. It sets out a gradient of habitats, from wilderness to urban core. As we move from one gradient to another, differences in design, based on different ecologies and social structures, become apparent and necessary. When those differences are systematized into land-use code, the Transect becomes a comprehensive alternative to conventional zoning. Through a series of various codes it becomes what then is labeled "Smart Growth;" a formulation for the urban region that moves from the densely urbanized core to the greenfields of the rural surrounds. It is, though, reminiscent of all of the New Urbanist work in its love of strict codes and rules that must be used to guide regional development.

Whatever the New Urbanists have claimed about their contributions to sustainable urban growth— a claim hotly disputed[10] on the grounds that sprawl is not a problem, and, if it were, the New Urbanists provide no real remedies—it is at best questionable whether the nostrums of the New Urbanism hold any relevance for the urbanism of the future.

New Urbanism in the Future

It is the reliance on codes, formal structures, and on an effectively essentialist instrumentalism that may be at the heart of the problems that have plagued the New Urbanism in the past, and which will limit its utility as it attempts to face the challenges of the future. The world today is faced with a rapidly urbanized future; according to the United Nations, "The year 2007 marks a turning point in history. One out of every two people will be living in a city." What is most humbling is that "*cities of the developing world will account for 95% of urban expansion in the next two decades and by 2030 will be home to 80% of the world's urban population (4 billion people).*"[11]

Of this expansion, over 1.4 billion people in the developing world will reside in slums, some with as many as a million people living in megaslum settlements, with extremely high densities, without adequate infrastructure, and, as a result, high levels of pollution, disease, and violence. Moreover, there are hundreds of thousands, even millions, of people forced—as a result of war and natural disaster—to live in urban slums or squatter settlements in perilous circumstances. These are the most serious urban problems that now confront us—problems that will only grow in size and intensity if not remedied (figures 1 and 2).

North America and Europe, though, are not immune to such problems. As the United Nations points out, refugees from African slums seeking a better life in Europe find that Paris offers little relief from the insecurity and destitution they experienced at home. Officials estimate that more than 200,000 people are homeless or living in temporary shelter in Paris. In New York City over 200,000 low-cost units have been lost in the last three years, making it almost impossible for households with an income of under $35,000 to find shelter in the city. And need we be reminded of the failures to find adequate shelter for those low-income residents affected by Katrina, and those low-income residents affected by the earthquake in Kobe who have waited over eight years for shelter?

FIG. 1 By 2030 over 1.4 billion people will live in slums, such as this urban slum in India.

FIG. 2 Pollution, disease, and violence plague slums.

Where is the New Urbanism in all this? While it might be unfair to ask architects to solve such major problems, they do have an important role to play in finding new ways to house and to design cities to help meet the challenges that the future holds. And the New Urbanists do claim that they have answers, and insist their ways are best, be it disaster or sprawl. But are they? In post–Katrina Mississippi, when asked to design a response, New Urbanists may have provided some help to elements of the middle classes, but they have mostly ignored the problems of the poor. The notion so often put forward by the New Urbanists that they design for all income levels is belied by their practice and their notion that they can provide a low-cost house for about $150,000,[12] thereby eliminating almost half of all United States households, and much more in the developing world, from access to affordable New Urbanist homes.

More critically, the strict codes associated with Smart Growth and the discussion surrounding the Transect, with its hardened ideas of what goes where, are not only irrelevant to the challenges faced by cities in the developing world, they may well be downright detrimental. For one example, many cities in the developing world are provided with supplies of affordable food because of urban agriculture, an

agriculture that can be found in city centers and suburbs of places like Kampala and Dar es Salaam, among others. The Transect and its codes would make such urban forms problematic at best, prohibited at worst. For another example, issues of the automobile and lack of densities are not problems in the slums; it is rather the opposite, as densities and the lack of transport create islands of significant despair. But slums cannot be addressed through strict codes and a firm lexicon of types. Such an approach runs counter to the need for multiple, and often even spontaneous solutions to the almost intractable problems of the slums and the challenges posed by cities in the developing world. Slums may be viewed as a type, but they are found in many different cultures with different social practices and sociospatial contexts, which also need to be addressed. Thus the one-size-fits-all approach of the New Urbanism, like modernism before it, is destined to fail if applied to these many and other, different contexts.

If for developers and upper-middle classes in the wealthier, more developed sections of the developing world the New Urbanism still resonates, for the rest of the urban world it would appear not only to be irrelevant, but also potentially detrimental. This is a shame because at its heart the New Urbanism has tried, at times successfully, to turn architecture away from its often antisocial concern with aesthetics and form alone. But its desire to create a one-size-fits-all ideology—an ideology and approach that suggested the New Urbanism had the answers to all that ails our cities, answers that derive from the concerns of only a segment of the urban populous[13]—has prevented the New Urbanists from reaching out and examining ideas whose assumptions are incongruent with their own. It is a shame because the New Urbanists' energy, good will, and desire for a better urbanism would be of immeasurable help if harnessed in a less essentialist and ideologically fettered way to the challenges that face our urban future. Thus, as I have argued previously,

> (The) opportunity [to address urban challenges] opened by the New Urbanists should not force all those concerned with the future of urbanism to get on their bandwagon. It should generate a critical debate about new solutions for what have been and still are seemingly intractable and complex problems. Designers should learn from their past that there are no singular solutions to our urban problems, and that no single one-dimensional approach to urban design can nor should shoulder such a monumental and intractable task. Rather the hubris of the New Urbanists, like the hubris of the modernists, should teach designers to approach the problems of our cities open to a range of ideas and approaches to urban problems, which will provide the basis for flexible, creative and appropriate responses to the urban condition.[14]

It was fitting when applied to the New Urbanism of the recent past; it is even more apposite as we enter the next decades of the twenty-first century.

MAKING PUBLIC INTERVENTIONS
IN TODAY'S MASSIVE CITIES

SASKIA SASSEN

The enormity of the urban experience, the overwhelming presence of massive architectures and dense infrastructures, the irresistible utility logics that organize much of the investments in today's cities, all have produced displacement and estrangement among many individuals and whole communities. Such conditions unsettle older notions and experiences of the city generally and public space in particular. The monumentalized public spaces of European cities remain vibrant sites for rituals and routines, for demonstrations and festivals. But increasingly the overall sense is of a shift from civic to politicized urban space, with fragmentations along multiple differences.

At the same time, these cities contain a diversity of under-used spaces, often characterized more by memory than current meaning. These spaces are part of the interiority of a city, yet lie outside of its organizing utility-driven logics and spatial frames. They are *terrains vagues* that allow many residents to connect to the rapidly transforming cities in which they live, and to bypass subjectively the massive infrastructures that have come to dominate more and more spaces in their cities. Jumping at these terrains vagues in order to maximize real estate development would be a mistake. Keeping some of this openness might, further, make sense in terms of factoring in future options at a time when utility logics change so quickly and often violently—the excess of high-rise office buildings being one of the great examples.

This opens up a salient dilemma about the current urban condition, and it does so in ways that go beyond the more familiar notions of high-tech architecture, simulacra, and the theming of urban spaces. All of the latter capture aspects of today's urban condition, but they are fragments of an incomplete puzzle.

There is a type of urban condition that dwells between the reality of massive structures and the reality of semiabandoned places. I think it is central to the experience of the urban, and to what I like to think of as "citiness." It makes legible transitions and unsettlements of specific spatiotemporal configurations. In this context, architecture and urban design can function as critical artistic practices that allow us

to capture something more elusive than what is represented by notions such as the theme-parking of cities.

Here I examine these questions through the lens of the actual *making* of public space and through the shifting meaning of the urban condition for those who live in cities.

Public Making Against the Privatizing and Weaponizing of Urban Space

The making and siting of public space is one pathway into these questions. We are living through a particular type of crisis in public space due to the growing commercialization, theme-parking, and privatizing of public space. The grand monumentalized public spaces of the state and the crown, especially in former imperial capitals, still tend to dominate our experience of public space. Users do render them public through their practices. But what about the actual making of public space in these complex cities, both through architectural interventions and through the practices of people?

Dwelling between megabuildings and *terrain vagues*[1] has long been part of the urban experience. In the past as today, this oscilating makes legible transitions and unsettlements. [2]It can also reinsert the possibility of *making*—poesis—citiness in ways that massive projects by themselves do not. The "makng" that concerns me here is of modest public spaces, constituted through the practices of people and critical architectural interventions that are on small- or medium-level scales. My concern here is not with monumentalized public spaces, or ready-made public spaces that are actually better described as public access, rather than public per se. The making of public space opens up questions about the current urban condition in ways that the grand spaces of the crown and the state—or the new kinds of overdesigned public-*access* spaces—do not.

The work of capturing this elusive quality that cities produce and make legible, and the work of making public space in this in-between zone, is not easily executed. Utility logics won't do. I can't help but think that the making of art is part of the answer, whether ephemeral public performances and

FIG. I **Urban debor-derings.** Hilary Koob-Sassen, The Paraculture (Video Still). Courtesy T+2 Gallery, London.

installations or more lasting types of public sculpture, whether site specific, community-based art, or nomadic sculptures that circulate among localities.[3] Further, the new network technologies open up this type of making—a making in modest spaces and through the practices of people. One question that might serve to capture critical features of this project of bringing in the new network technologies is: how do we *urbanize* open source?

Architectural practices are central to this project of making citiness, specifically those practices which can take place in problematic or unusual spaces. This takes architects able to navigate several forms of knowledge, so as to introduce the possibility of architecture in spaces where the naked eye or the engineer's imagination sees no shape, no possibility of form, pure infrastructure and utility.[4] The types of space I have in mind are, for instance, intersections of multiple transport and communication networks, the roofs of recycling plants or water purification systems, small and awkward unused spaces that have been forgotten or do not fit the needs of utility-driven plans, and so on. Another instance is a space that requires the work of detecting possible architectures where there now is merely a formal silence, a non-existence, such as a modest and genuinely undistinguished terrain vague—not a grand terrain vague that becomes magnificent through the scale of its decay, as might be an old unused industrial harbor or steel factory.[5]

The possibility of this type of making, detecting, and intervening has assumed new meanings over the last two decades, a period marked by the ascendance of private authority/power over spaces once considered public and by the increasingly direct control of urban space by the powerful and rich. Furthermore, over the last five years especially, the state has sought to weaponize urban space and to make it an object for surveillance. At the same time, the increasing visibility of restrictions, surveillance, and displacements is politicizing urban space. Most familiar, perhaps, is the impact of high-income residential and commercial gentrification, which generates a displacement that can feed the making of a political subjectivity centered in contestation rather than a sense of the civic on either side of the conflict. The physical displacement of low-income households, non-profit uses, and low-profit neighborhood firms makes visible a power relationship—direct control by one side over the other as expressed directly in evictions or indirectly through the market.

This visible politicizing of urban space is also evident in the proliferation of physical barriers in erstwhile public spaces, a medieval touch in an electronic era. This is perhaps most pronounced in United States cities, and most visible since the attacks of September 11, 2001. United States embassies worldwide increasingly resemble fortresses piling up barriers made of heavy concrete. In this context, public-access space can emerge as an enormous resource for projects oriented towards citiness rather than control. But let us not confuse public-access space with public space. The latter requires making—through the practices and the subjectivities of people. Through their practices, users of the space wind up making diverse kinds of publicness.[6]

In brief, several trends are coming together enabling practices and imaginings about making, rather than merely accessing, public space. One trend concerns some of the conditions discussed above. Specifically, the fact itself of today's wider unsettling of older notions of public space. These unsettlements arise from the limits of making publicness in monumentalized spaces, as well as from the shifts towards politicizing urban space and weakening civic experiences in cities. Both conditions produce openings to the experience—and the option—of making.[7]

A second trend is the making of modest public spaces, which may well be critical for recovering the possibility of making spaces public. This type of making was historically significant in cities worldwide. As a project, it diverges from the making of grand monumentalized spaces: it entailed making in the interstices of the spaces of power. Today this type of making is geared to the interstices of private and public power, and adds a novel dimension: the repositioning of the notion and the experience of locality, and thereby of modest public spaces, in potentially global networks comprising multiple such localities.

A third trend is the delicate negotiation between the renewed valuing of diversity, as illustrated in multiculturalism, and the renewed challenges this poses to notions and experiences of the public.

The next sections examine some of these issues.

FIG 2. **Reassembling the urban.** Hilary Koob-Sassen, The Paraculture (Video Still). Courtesy T+2 Gallery, London.

Cities as Frontier Zones: Making Informal Politics

The other side of the large complex city, especially if a global city, is that it is a sort of new frontier zone where an enormous mix of people converge. Those who lack power, those who are disadvantaged, outsiders, discriminated minorities, can gain *presence* in such cities, presence vis-à-vis power and presence vis-à-vis each other. This signals, for me, the possibility of a new type of politics centered in new types of political actors. It is not simply a matter of having or not having power. There are new hybrid bases from which to act. By using the term presence I try to capture some of this.

The space of the city is a far more concrete space for politics than that of the nation.[8] It is a place where nonformal political actors can be part of the political scene in a way that is much more difficult at the national level. Nationally, politics needs to run through existing formal systems: whether the electoral political system or the judiciary (taking state agencies to court). Nonformal political actors are rendered invisible in the space of national politics. The space of the city accommodates a broad range of political activities—squatting; demonstrations against police brutality; fighting for the rights of immigrants and the homeless; the politics of culture and identity; and gay, lesbian, and queer politics. Much of this becomes visible on the street. Much of urban politics is concrete, enacted by people rather than dependent on massive media technologies. Street-level politics makes possible the formation of new types of political subjects that are not confined to functioning through the formal political system.

Furthermore, through the new network technology's local initiatives become part of a global network of activism without losing the focus on specific local struggles. It enables a new type of cross-border political activism, one centered in multiple localities yet intensely connected digitally. This is in my view one of the key forms of critical politics that the internet and other networks can make possible: a politics of the local with a big difference—these are localities that are connected with each other across a region, a country, or the world.[9] This configuration also makes legible the fact that even if a network is global it does not mean that the practices that constitute it have to happen at the global level. Digital networks are contributing to the production of new kinds of interconnections; often these interconnections underlie what appear as fragmented topographies, whether at the global or at the local level. Political activists can use digital networks for global or nonlocal transactions *and* they can use them for strengthening local communications and transactions inside a city or rural community.

The large city of today, especially the global city, emerges as a strategic site for these new types of operations. It is a strategic site for global corporate capital. But it is also one of the sites where the formation of new claims by informal political actors materializes and assumes concrete forms.

Rethinking the Notion of Locality

It will not be long before many urban residents begin to experience the "local" as a type of microenvironment with global span. Much of what we keep representing and experiencing as something local—a building, an urban place, a household, an activist organization right there in our neighborhood—is actually located not only in the concrete places where we can see them, but also on digital networks that span the globe. They are connected with other such localized buildings, organizations, households, possibly at the other side of the world. They may indeed be more oriented to those other areas than to their immediate surrounding. Think of the financial center in a global city, or the human rights or environmental activists' home or office—their orientation is not towards what surrounds them but to a global process. These are the types of local entities I think of as microenvironments with global span.[10]

There are two issues I want to pursue briefly here. One is what it means for "the city" to contain a proliferation of these globally oriented yet very localized offices, households, organizations. In this context the city becomes a strategic amalgamation of multiple global circuits that loop through it. As cities and urban regions are increasingly traversed by nonlocal, including notably global circuits, much of what we experience as the local because locally sited, is actually a transformed condition in that it is imbricated with nonlocal dynamics or is a localization of global processes. One way of thinking about this is in terms of spatializations of various projects—economic, political, cultural. This produces a specific set of interactions in a city's relation to its topography. The new urban spatiality thus produced is partial in a double sense: it accounts for only part of what happens in cities and what cities are about, and it inhabits only part of what we might think of as the space of the city, whether this be understood in terms as diverse as those of a city's administrative boundaries or in the sense of the multiple public imaginaries that may be present in different sectors of a city's people. If we consider urban space as productive, as enabling new configurations, then these developments signal multiple possibilities.

The second issue, one coming out of this proliferation of digital networks traversing cities, concerns the future of cities in an increasingly digitized and globalized world. Here the bundle of conditions and dynamics that marks the model of the global city might be a helpful way of distilling the ongoing centrality of urban space in complex cities. Just to single out one key dynamic: the more globalized and digitized the operations of firms and markets, the more their central management and coordination functions (and the requisite material structures) become strategic. It is precisely because of digitization that simultaneous worldwide dispersal of operations (whether factories, offices, or service outlets) and system integration (the formation of a global firm) can be achieved. And it is precisely this combination that raises the importance of central functions, especially top-level headquarter functions. Global cities are strategic sites for the

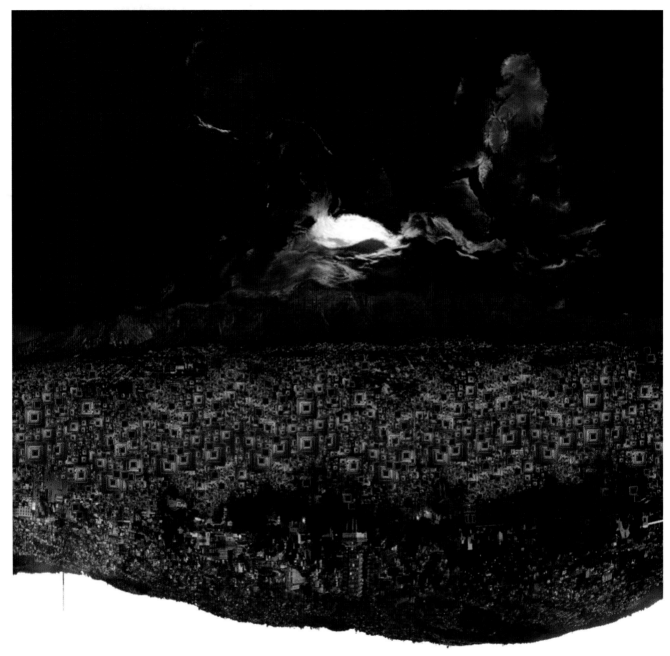

FIG. 3 **No-end urbanism.** Hilary Koob-Sassen, The Paraculture (Video Still). Courtesy T+2 Gallery, London.

combination of resources necessary for the production of these central functions.[11]

Thus, much of what is liquefied and circulates in digital networks and is marked by hypermobility, actually remains physical. And hence it remains possibly urban, at least in some of its components. At the same time, however, that which remains physical has been transformed by the fact that it is represented by highly liquid instruments that can circulate in global markets. It may look the same, it may involve the same bricks and mortar, it may be new or old, but it is a transformed entity. Take, for example, the case of real estate. Financial services firms have invented instruments that liquefy real estate, thereby facilitating investment and circu-

lation of these instruments in global markets. But even though part of what constitutes real estate remains very physical, the building that is represented by financial instruments circulating globally is not the same entity as a building that is not thus represented.

We have difficulty capturing this multivalence of the new digital technologies through our conventional categories. Typically the notion is that if it is physical, it *is* physical; and if it is liquid, it *is* liquid. In fact, the partial representation of real estate through liquid financial instruments produces a complex imbrication of the material and the digitized moments of that which we continue to call real estate. And the need of global electronic financial markets for multiple material conditions in global cities produces yet another type of complex imbrication that shows precisely those sectors that are most globalized and digitized continue to have a very strong and strategic urban dimension.[12]

Hypermobility and digitization are usually seen as mere functions of the new technologies. This understanding erases the fact that it takes multiple material conditions to achieve this outcome. Once we recognize that the hypermobility of a financial instrument, or the dematerialization of the actual piece of real estate, has to be *produced*, we make legible the imbrication of the material and the nonmaterial. Producing capital mobility takes state-of-the-art built environments, conventional infrastructure—from highways to airports and railways—and well-housed talent. These are all partly place-bound conditions, even though the nature of their place boundedness is going to be different from what it was a hundred years ago, when place boundedness might have indeed been a form of immobility. Today it is a place boundedness that is inflected, inscribed, by the hypermobility of some of its components/products/outcomes. Both capital fixity and mobility are located in a temporal frame where speed is ascendant and consequential. This type of capital fixity cannot be fully captured in a description of its material and locational features, i.e., in a topographical reading.

Conceptualizing digitization and globalization along these lines creates operational and rhetorical openings for recognizing the ongoing importance of the material world even in the case of some of the most dematerialized activities.

Digital Media and the Making of Presence

A number of new media artists using computer-centered network technologies are enacting political as well as artistic projects in cities worldwide. What I want to capture here is a very specific feature: the possibility of constructing forms of globality that are neither part of global corporate media or consumer firms, nor part of elite universalisms or "high culture." It is the possibility of giving presence to multiple local actors, projects, and imaginaries in ways that may constitute alternative and counterglobalities.

These interventions entail diverse uses of technology—ranging from political to ludic uses—that can subvert corporate globalization. We are seeing the formation of alternative networks, projects, and spaces. Emblematic is, perhaps, that the metaphor of "hacking" has been dislodged from its specialized technical discourse and become part of everyday life. In the face of a predatory regime of intellectual property rights we see the ongoing influence of the free software movement.[13] Modest "indymedia" efforts gain terrain even as global media conglomerates dominate just about all mainstream mediums.[14] The formation of new geographies of power that bring together elites from the global south and north find their obverse in the work of such collectives as Raqs Media or Palestine's Ramallah Architecture Biennale, which destabilize the center/periphery divide.[15]

Such alternative globalities are to be distinguished from the common assumption that if "it" is global, it is also cosmopolitan. The types of global forms that concern me here are what I like to refer to, partly as a provocation, as noncosmopolitan forms of globality. When local initiatives and projects can become part of a global network without losing the focus on the specifics of the local, a new type of globality takes shape.[16] For instance, groups or individuals concerned with a variety of environmental questions—from solar energy design to appropriate materials for architecture—can become part of global networks without having to leave behind the specifics that concern them.

In an effort to synthesize this diversity of subversive interventions into the space of global capitalism, I use the notion of countergeographies of globalization: these interventions are deeply imbricated with some of the major dynamics constitutive of corporate globalization yet are not part of the formal apparatus or of the objectives of this apparatus (such as the formation of global markets and global firms). These countergeographies thrive on the intensifying of transnational and translocal networks, the development of communication technologies that easily escape conventional surveillance practices, and so on. Furthermore, the strengthening and, in some of these cases, the formation of new global circuits are ironically embedded or made possible by the existence of that same global economic system that they contest. These countergeographies are dynamic and changing in their locational features.[17]

The acts of narrating, giving shape, and making present involved in digitized environments assumes very particular meanings when mobilized to represent/enact local specificities in a global context. Beyond the kinds of on-the-ground work involved in these struggles, new media artists and activists—the latter often artists—have been key actors in these developments, whether it is through tactical media, indy media, or such entities as the original incarnation of Digital City Amsterdam[18] and the Berlin-based Transmediale.[19] But new media artists have also focused on issues other than the world of technology. Not surprisingly perhaps, a key focus has been the increasingly restrictive regime for migrants and refugees in a global world where capital gets to flow wherever it wants. For instance, organizations such as Nobody is Illegal,[20] the Mongrel web project,[21] Mute Magazine,[22] the Manchester-based Futuresonic,[23] and the Bonn/Cologne-based *Theater der Welt*,[24] have all done projects focused on immigration.

In conclusion, the work of making the public and making the political in urban space become critical at a time of growing velocities, the ascendance of process and flow over artifacts and permanence, massive structures, and branding as the basic mediation between individuals and markets. Much design work produces narratives that add to the value of existing contexts, and at its narrowest, to the utility logics of the economic corporate world. But there is also a kind of public-making work that can produce disruptive narratives that can make legible the local and the silenced.

THE WORLD IS SPIKY

GLOBALIZATION HAS CHANGED THE ECONOMIC PLAYING FIELD, BUT HASN'T LEVELED IT

RICHARD FLORIDA

The world, according to the title of the *New York Times* columnist Thomas Friedman's book, is flat. Thanks to advances in technology, the global playing field has been leveled, the prizes are there for the taking, and everyone's a player—no matter where on the surface of the earth he or she may reside. "In a flat world," Friedman writes, "you can innovate without having to emigrate."

Friedman is not alone in this belief: for the better part of the past century economists have been writing about the leveling effects of technology. From the invention of the telephone, the automobile, and the airplane to the rise of the personal computer and the internet, technological progress has steadily eroded the economic importance of geographic place—or so the argument goes.

But in partnership with colleagues at George Mason University and the geographer Tim Gulden, of the Center for International and Security Studies, at the University of Maryland, I've begun to chart a very different economic topography. By almost any measure the international economic landscape is not at all flat. On the contrary, our world is amazingly "spiky." In terms of both sheer economic horsepower and cutting-edge innovation, the most obvious challenge to the flat-world hypothesis is the explosive growth of cities worldwide. More and more people are clustering in urban areas—the world's demographic mountain ranges, so to speak. The share of the world's population living in urban areas, just 3% in 1800, was nearly 30% by 1950. Today it stands at about 50%; in advanced countries three out of four people live in urban areas. The latest data show the uneven distribution of the world's population. Figure 1 shows the uneven distribution of the world's population. Five megacities currently have more than 20 million inhabitants each. Twenty-four cities have more than 10 million inhabitants, sixty more than 5 million, and 150 more than 2.5 million. Population density is, of course, a crude indicator of human and economic activity. But it does suggest that at least some of the tectonic forces of economics are concentrating people and resources, and pushing up some places more than others.

Still, differences in population density vastly understate the spikiness of the global economy; the continuing dominance of the world's most productive urban areas is astounding. When it comes to actual economic output, the ten largest United States metropolitan areas combined are behind only the United States as a whole and Japan. New York's economy alone is about the size of Russia's or Brazil's, and Chicago's is on a par with Sweden's. Together New York, Los Angeles, Chicago, and Boston have a bigger economy than all of China. If United States metropolitan areas were countries, they'd make up forty-seven of the biggest one hundred economies in the world.

Unfortunately, no single, comprehensive information source exists for the economic production of all the world's cities. A rough proxy is available. Figure 2 shows a variation on the widely circulated view of the world at night, with higher concentrations of light—indicating higher energy use and, presumably, stronger economic production—appearing in greater relief. United States regions appear almost Himalayan. From their summits one might look out on a smaller mountain range stretching across Europe, some isolated peaks in Asia, and a few scattered hills throughout the rest of the world.

Population and economic activity are both spiky, but it's innovation—the engine of economic growth—that is most concentrated. The World Intellectual Property Organization recorded about 300,000 patents from resident inventors in more than a hundred nations in 2002 (the most recent year for which statistics are available). Nearly two thirds of them went to American and Japanese inventors. Eighty-five percent went to the residents of just five countries (Japan, the United States, South Korea, Germany, and Russia).

Worldwide patent statistics can be somewhat misleading, since different countries follow different standards for granting patents. But patents granted in the United States—which receives patent applications for nearly all major innovations worldwide, and holds them to the same strict standards—tell a similar story. Nearly 90,000 of the

170,000 patents granted in the United States in 2002 went to Americans. Some 35,000 went to Japanese inventors, and 11,000 to Germans. The next ten most innovative countries—including the usual suspects in Europe plus Taiwan, South Korea, Israel, and Canada—produced roughly 25,000 more. The rest of the broad, flat world accounted for just 5% of all innovations patented in the United States. In 2003, India generated 341 United States patents and China 297. The University of California alone generated more than either country. IBM accounted for five times as many as the two combined.

This is not to say that Indians and Chinese are not innovative. On the contrary, Anna Lee Saxenian, of the University of California at Berkeley, has shown that Indian and Chinese entrepreneurs founded or cofounded roughly 30% of all Silicon Valley start-ups in the late 1990s. But these fundamentally creative people had to travel to Silicon Valley and be absorbed into its innovative ecosystem before their ideas became economically viable. Such ecosystems matter, and there aren't many of them.

Figure 3—which makes use of data from both the World Intellectual Property Organization and the United States Patent and Trademark Office—shows a world composed of innovation peaks and valleys. Tokyo, Seoul, New York, and San Francisco remain the front-runners in the patenting competition. Boston, Seattle, Austin, Toronto, Vancouver, Berlin, Stockholm, Helsinki, London, Osaka, Taipei, and Sydney also stand out. Figure 4 shows the residence of the 1,200 most heavily cited scientists in leading fields. Scientific advance is even more concentrated than patent production. Most occur not just in a handful of countries, but in a handful of cities—primarily in the United States and Europe. Chinese and Indian cities do not even register. As far as global innovation is concerned, perhaps a few dozen places worldwide really compete at the cutting edge.

Concentrations of creative and talented people are particularly important for innovation, according to the Nobel Prize–winning economist Robert Lucas. Ideas flow more freely, are honed more sharply, and can be put into practice more quickly when large numbers of innovators, implementers, and financial backers are in constant contact with one another, both in and out of the office. Creative people cluster not simply because they like to be around one another or they prefer cosmopolitan centers with lots of amenities, though both those things count. They and their companies also cluster because of the powerful productivity advantages, economies of scale, and knowledge spillovers such density brings.

So although one might not *have* to emigrate to innovate, it certainly appears that innovation, economic growth, and prosperity occur in those places that attract a critical mass of top creative talent. Because globalization has increased the returns to innovation, by allowing innovative products and services to quickly reach consumers worldwide, it has strengthened the lure that innovation centers hold for our planet's best and brightest, reinforcing the spikiness of wealth and economic production.

The main difference between now and even a couple of decades ago is not that the world has become flatter but that the world's peaks have become slightly more dispersed—and that the world's hills, the industrial and service centers that produce mature products and support innovation centers, have proliferated and shifted. For the better part of the twentieth century the United States claimed the lion's share of the global economy's innovation peaks, leaving a few outposts in Europe and Japan. But America has since lost some of those peaks, as such industrial-age powerhouses as Pittsburgh, Saint Louis, and Cleveland have eroded. At the same time, a number of regions in Europe, Scandinavia, Canada, and the Pacific Rim have moved up.

The world today looks flat to some because the economic and social distances between peaks worldwide have gotten smaller. Connection between peaks has been strengthened by the easy mobility of the global creative class—about 150 million people worldwide. They participate in a global technology system and a global labor market that allow them to migrate freely among the world's leading cities. In a Brookings Institution study the demographer Robert Lang and the world-cities expert Peter Taylor identify a relatively small group of leading city-regions—London, New York, Paris, Tokyo, Hong Kong, Singapore, Chicago, Los Angeles, and San Francisco among them—that are strongly connected to one another.

But Lang and Taylor also identify a much larger group of city-regions that are far more locally oriented. People in spiky places are often more connected to one another, even from half a world away, than they are to people and places in their veritable back yards.

The flat-world theory is not completely misguided. It is a welcome supplement to the widely accepted view (illustrated by the Live 8 concerts and Bono's forays into Africa, by the writings of Jeffrey Sachs and the United Nations Millennium project) that the growing divide between rich and poor countries is the fundamental feature of the world economy. Friedman's theory more accurately depicts a developing world with capabilities that translate into economic development. In his view, for example, the emerging economies of India and China combine cost advantages, high-tech skills, and entrepreneurial energy, enabling those countries to compete effectively for industries and jobs. The tensions set in motion as the playing field is leveled affect mainly the advanced countries, which see not only manufacturing work but also higher-end jobs, in fields such as software development and financial services, increasingly threatened by offshoring.

But the flat-world theory blinds us to far more insidious tensions among the world's growing peaks, sinking valleys, and shifting hills. The innovative, talent-attracting "have" regions seem increasingly remote from the talent-exporting "have-not" regions. Second-tier cities, from Detroit and Wolfsburg to Nagoya and Mexico City, are entering an escalating and potentially devastating competition for jobs, talent, and investment. And inequality is growing across the world and within countries.

FIGS. I AND 2 PEAKS, HILLS, AND VALLEY

When looked at through the lens of economic production, many cities with large populations are diminished and some nearly vanish. Three sorts of places make up the modern economic landscape. First are the cities that generate innovations. These are the tallest peaks; they have the capacity to attract global talent and create new products and industries. They are few in number, and difficult to topple. Second are the economic hills—places that manufacture the world's established goods, take its calls, and support its innovation engines. These hills can rise and fall quickly; they are prosperous but insecure. Some, like Dublin and Seoul, are growing into innovative, wealthy peaks; others are declining, eroded by high labor costs and a lack of enduring competitive advantage. Finally there are the vast valleys—places with little connection to the global economy and few immediate prospects.

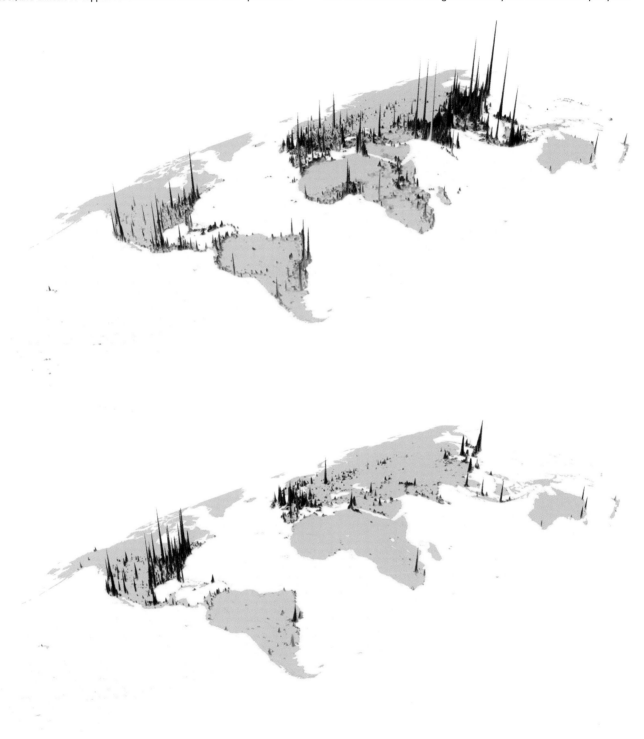

FIG. 2 LIGHT EMISSIONS

Economic activity—roughly estimated here using light-emissions data—is remarkably concentrated. Many cities, despite their large populations, barely register.

Commercial innovation and scientific advance are both highly concentrated—but not always in the same places. Several cities in East Asia—particularly in Japan—are home to prolific business innovation but still depend disproportionately on scientific breakthroughs made elsewhere. Likewise, some cities excel in scientific research but not in commercial adaptation. The few places that do both well are very strongly positioned in the global economy. These regions have little to fear, and much to gain, from continuing globalization.

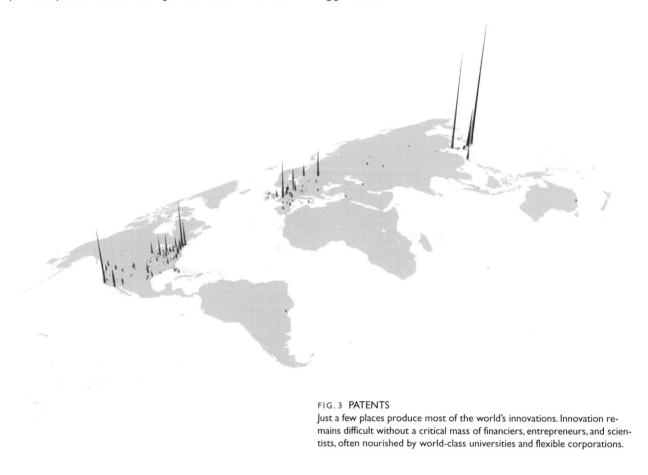

FIG. 3 PATENTS
Just a few places produce most of the world's innovations. Innovation remains difficult without a critical mass of financiers, entrepreneurs, and scientists, often nourished by world-class universities and flexible corporations.

FIG. 4 SCIENTIFIC CITATIONS
The world's most prolific and influential scientific researchers overwhelmingly reside in United States and European cities.

This is far more harrowing than the flat world Friedman describes, and a good deal more treacherous than the old rich/poor divide. We see its effects in the political backlash against globalization in the advanced world. The recent rejection of the European Union's constitution by the French, for example, resulted in large part from high rates of "no" votes in suburban and rural quarters, which understandably fear globalization and integration.

But spiky globalization also wreaks havoc on poorer places. China is seeing enormous concentrations of talent and innovation in centers such as Shanghai, Shenzhen, and Beijing, all of which are a world apart from its vast, impoverished rural areas. According to detailed polling by Richard Burkholder, of Gallup, average household incomes in urban China are now triple those in rural regions, and they've grown more than three times as fast since 1999; perhaps as a result, urban and rural Chinese now have very different, often conflicting political and lifestyle values. India is growing even more divided, as Bangalore, Hyderabad, and parts of New Delhi and Bombay pull away from the rest of that enormous country, creating destabilizing political tensions. Economic and demographic forces are sorting people around the world into geographically clustered "tribes" so different (and often mutually antagonistic) as to create a somewhat Hobbesian vision.

We are thus confronted with a difficult predicament. Economic progress requires that the peaks grow stronger and taller. But such growth will exacerbate economic and social disparities, fomenting political reactions that could threaten further innovation and economic progress. Managing the disparities between peaks and valleys worldwide—raising the valleys without shearing off the peaks—will be among the top political challenges of the coming decades.

SPACE OF FLOWS, SPACE OF PLACES

MATERIALS FOR A THEORY OF URBANISM
IN THE INFORMATION AGE

MANUEL CASTELLS

We have entered a new age, the Information Age. Spatial transformation is a fundamental dimension of the overall process of structural change. We need a new theory of spatial forms and processes, adapted to the new social, technological, and spatial context where we live. I will attempt here to propose some elements of this theory, a theory of urbanism in the Information Age. I will not develop the analysis of the meaning of the Information Age, taking the liberty to refer the reader to my trilogy on the matter (Castells 1996–2000). I will not build theory from other theories, but from the observation of social and spatial trends in the world at large. Thus, I will start with a summary characterization of the main spatial trends at the onset of the twenty-first century. Then I will propose a tentative theoretical interpretation of observed spatial trends. Subsequently I will highlight the main issues arising in cities in the information age, with particular emphasis on the crisis of the city as a sociospatial system of cultural communication. I will conclude by drawing some of the implications of my analysis for planning, architecture, and urban design.

The Transformation of Urban Space
in the Early Twenty-first Century

• Spatial transformation must be understood in the broader context of social transformation: space does not reflect society, it expresses it, it is a fundamental dimension of society, inseparable from the overall process of social organization and social change. Thus, the new urban world arises from within the process of formation of a new society, the network society, characteristic of the Information Age. The key developments in spatial patterns and urban processes associated with these macrostructural changes can be summarized under the following headings (Scott 2001):

• Because commercial agriculture has been, by and large, automated, and a global economy has integrated productive networks throughout the planet, the majority of the world's population is already living in urban areas, and this will be increasingly the case: we are heading towards a largely urbanized world, which will comprise between 2/3 and 3/4 of the total population by the middle of the century (Freire and Stren 2001);

• This process of urbanization is concentrated disproportionately in metropolitan areas of a new kind: urban constellations scattered throughout huge territorial expanses, functionally integrated and socially differentiated, around a multicentered structure. I call these new spatial forms metropolitan regions (Garreau 1991; Hall 2001; Nel.Lo 2001; Dunham-Jones 2000);

• Advanced telecommunications; internet; and fast, computerized transportation systems allow for simultaneous spatial concentration and decentralization, ushering in a new geography of networks and urban nodes throughout the world, throughout countries, between and within metropolitan areas (Wheeler et al. 2000);

• Social relationships are characterized simultaneously by individuation and communalism, both processes using, at the same time, spatial patterning and online communication. Virtual communities and physical communities develop in close interaction, and both processes of aggregation are challenged by increasing individualization of work, social relationships, and residential habits (Russell 2000; Wellman 1999; Putnam 2000);

• The crisis of the patriarchal family, with different manifestations depending on cultures and levels of economic development, gradually shifts sociability from family units to networks of individualized units (most often, women and their children, but also individualized cohabiting partnerships), with considerable consequences in the uses and forms of housing, neighborhoods, public space, and transportation systems;

• The emergence of the network enterprise as a new form of economic activity, with its highly decentralized, yet coordinated, form of work and management, tends to blur the functional distinction between spaces of work and spaces of residence. The work/live arrangements characteristic of the early periods of industrial craft work are back, often taking over the old industrial spaces, and transforming them into informational production spaces. This is not just New York's Silicon Alley or San Francisco's Multimedia Gulch, but a phenomenon that also characterizes London, Tokyo, Beijing, Taipei, Paris, and Barcelona, among many other cities. Transformation of productive uses becomes more important than residential succession to explain the new dynamics of urban space (Mitchell 1999; Horan 2001);

• Urban areas around the world are increasingly multiethnic, and multicultural. An old theme of the Chicago School, now amplified in terms of its extremely diverse racial composition (Waldinger 2001);

• The global criminal economy is solidly rooted in the urban fabric, providing jobs, income, and social organization to a criminal culture, which deeply affects the lives of low-income communities, and of the city at large. It follows rising violence and/or widespread paranoia of urban violence, with the corollary of defensive residential patterns;

• Breakdowns of communication patterns between individuals and between cultures, and the emergence of defensive spaces, leads to the formation of sharply segregated areas: gated communities for the rich, territorial turfs for the poor (Blakely and Snyder 1997; Massey 1996);

• In a reaction against trends of suburban sprawl and the individualization of residential patterns, urban centers and public space become critical expressions of local life, benchmarking the vitality of any given city (Hall 1998; Borja 2001). Yet, commercial pressures and artificial attempts at mimicking urban life often transform public spaces into theme parks where symbols rather than experience create a life-size, urban virtual reality, ultimately destined to mimic the real virtuality projected in the media. It follows increasing individualization, as urban places become consumption items to be individually appropriated (Fernandez-Galiano 2000);

• Overall, the new urban world seems to be dominated by the double movement of inclusion into transterritorial networks, and exclusion by the spatial separation of places. The higher the value of people and places, the more they are connected into interactive networks. The lower their value, the lower their connection. In the limit, some places are switched off, and bypassed by the new geography of networks, as is the case with depressed rural areas and urban shantytowns around the world. Splintering urbanism operates on the basis of segregated networks of infrastructure, as empirically demonstrated by Graham and Marvin (2001);

• The constitution of megametropolitan regions, without a name, without a culture, and without institutions, weakens the mechanism of political accountability, of citizen participation, and of effective administration (Sassen 2001). On the other hand, in the age of globalization, local governments emerge as flexible institutional actors, able to relate at the same time to local citizens and to global flows of power and money (Borja and Castells 1997). Not because they are powerful, but because most levels of government, including the nation-states, are equally weakened in their capacity for command and control if they operate in isolation. Thus, a new form of state emerges, the network state, integrating supranational institutions made up of national governments, nation-states, regional governments, local governments, and even nongovernmental organizations. Local governments become a node of the chain of institutional representation and management, able to input the overall process, yet with added value in terms of their capacity to represent citizens at a closer range. Indeed in most countries, opinion polls show the higher degree of trust people have in their local governments, relative to other levels of government. However, institutions of metropolitan governance are rare and when they exist they are highly centralized, with little citizen participation. There is an increasing gap between the actual unit of work and living, the metropolitan region, and the mechanisms of political representation and public administration. Local governments compensate for this lack by cooperating and competing. Yet, by defining their interests as specific subsets of the metropolitan region, they (often unwillingly) contribute to further fragmentation of the spatial framing of social life;

• Urban social movements have not disappeared, by any means. But they have mutated. In an extremely schematic representation they develop along two main lines. The first is the defense of the local community, affirming the right to live in a particular place, and to benefit from adequate housing and urban services in their place. The second is the environmental movement, acting on the quality of cities within the broader goal of achieving quality of life: not only a better life but a different life. Often, the broader goals of environmental mobilizations become translated into defensive reactions to protect one specific community, thus merging the two trends. Yet, it is only by reaching out to the cultural transformation of urban life as proposed by ecological thinkers and activists that urban social movements can transcend their limits of localism. Indeed, enclosing themselves in their communities, urban social movements may contribute to further spatial fragmentation, ultimately leading to the breakdown of society.

It is against the background of these major trends of urban social change that we can understand new spatial forms and processes, thus rethinking architecture, urban design, and planning in the twenty-first century.

A Theoretical Approach to Spatial Transformation

To make the transition from the observation of urban trends to the new theorization of cities, we need to grasp, at a more analytical level, the key elements of sociospatial change. I think the transformation of cities in the information age can be organized around three bipolar axes. The first relates to function, the second to meaning, the third to form.

Function
Functionally speaking the network society is organized around the opposition between the global and the local.

Dominant processes in the economy, technology, media, and institutionalized authority are organized in global networks. But day-to-day work, private life, cultural identity, political participation, are essentially local. Cities, as communication systems, are supposed to link up to the local and the global, but this is exactly where the problems start since these are two conflicting logics that tear cities from the inside when they try to respond to both, simultaneously.

Meaning

In terms of meaning, our society is characterized by the opposing development of individuation and communalism. By individuation I understand the enclosure of meaning in the projects, interests, and representations of the individual, that is a biologically embodied personality system (or, if you want, translating from French structuralism, a person). By communalism I refer to the enclosure of meaning in a shared identity, based on a system of values and beliefs to which all other sources of identity are subordinated. Society, of course, exists only in between, in the interface between individuals and identities mediated by institutions, at the source of the constitution of civil society which, as Gramsci argued, does not exist against the state but in articulation with the state, forming a shared public sphere, à la Habermas.

Trends I observe in the formative stage of the network society indicate the increasing tension and distance between personality and culture, between individuals and communes. Because cities are large aggregates of individuals, forced to coexist, and communes are located in the metropolitan space, the split between personality and commonality brings extraordinary stress upon the social system of cities as communicative and institutionalizing devices. The problematique of social integration becomes again paramount, albeit under new circumstances and in terms radically different from those of early industrial cities. This is mainly because of the role played in urban transformation by a third, major axis of opposing trends, this one concerning spatial forms.

Forms

There is a growing tension and articulation between the space of flows and the space of places.

The space of flows links up electronically separate locations in an interactive network that connects activities and people in distinct geographical contexts. The space of places organizes experience and activity around the confines of locality. Cities are structured, and destructured simultaneously by the competing logics of the space of flows and the space of places. Cities do not disappear in the virtual networks. But they are transformed by the interface between electronic communication and physical interaction, by the combination of networks and places. As William Mitchell (1999), from an urbanist perspective, and Barry Wellman (1999), from a sociologist perspective, have argued, the informational city is built around this double system of communication. Our cities are made up, at the same time, of flows and places, and of their relationships. Two examples will help to make sense of this statement,

one from the point of view of the urban structure, another in terms of the urban experience.

Turning to urban structure, the notion of global cities was popularized in the 1990s. Although most people assimilate the term to some dominant urban centers, such as London, New York, and Tokyo, the concept of global city does not refer to any particular city, but to the global articulation of segments of many cities into an electronically linked network of functional domination throughout the planet. The global city is a spatial form rather than a title of distinction for certain cities, although some cities have a greater share of these global networks than others. In a sense, most areas in all cities, including New York and London, are local, not global. And many cities are sites of areas, small and large, which are included in these global networks, at different levels. This conception of global city as a spatial form resulting from the process of globalization is in closer to the pioneering analysis by Saskia Sassen (1991) than to its popularized version by city marketing agencies. Thus, from the structural point of view, the role of cities in the global economy depends on their connectivity in transportation and telecommunication networks, and on the ability of cities to mobilize effectively human resources in this process of global competition. As a consequence of this trend, nodal areas of the city, connecting to the global economy, will receive the highest priority in terms of investment and management, as they are the sources of value creation from which an urban node and its surrounding area will make their livelihood. Thus, the fate of metropolitan economies depends on their ability to subordinate urban functions and forms to the dynamics of certain places that ensure their competitive articulation in the global space of flows.

From the point of view of the urban experience, we are entering a built environment that is increasingly incorporating electronic communication devices everywhere. Our urban life fabric, as Mitchell (1999) has pointed out, becomes an *e-topia*, a new urban form in which we constantly interact, deliberately or automatically, with online information systems, increasingly in the wireless mode. Materially speaking the space of flows is folded into the space of places. Yet, their logics are distinct: online experience and face-to-face experience remain specific, and the key question then is to assure their articulation in compatible terms.

These remarks may help in the reconfiguration of the theory of urbanism in response to the challenges of the network society, and in accordance to the emergence of new spatial forms and processes.

The Urban Themes of the Information Age

The issue of social integration comes again at the forefront of the theory of urbanism, as was the case during the process of urbanization in the industrial era. Indeed, it is the very existence of cities as communication artifacts that is called into question, in spite of the fact that we live in a predominantly urban world. But what is at stake is a very different kind of integration. In the early twentieth century the quest was for assimilation of urban subcultures into the urban culture. In the early twenty-first century the challenge is the sharing of the city by irreversibly distinct cultures and identities. There is no more dominant culture, because only global media have the power to send dominant messages, and the media have in fact adapted to their market, constructing a kaleidoscope of variable content depending on demand, thus reproducing cultural and personal diversity rather than overimposing a common set of values. The spread of horizontal communication via the internet accelerates the process of fragmentation and individualization of symbolic interaction. Thus, the fragmented metropolis and the individualization of communication reinforce each other to produce an endless constellation of cultural subsets. The nostalgia of the public domain will not be able to countervail the structural trends toward diversity, specification, and individualization of life, work, space and communication, both face-to-face and electronic (Russell 2000; Putnam 2000). On the other hand, communalism adds collective fragmentation to individual segmentation. Thus, in the absence of a unifying culture, and therefore of a unifying code the key question is not the sharing of a dominant culture but the communicability of multiple codes.

The notion of communication protocols is central here. Protocols may be physical, social, and electronic, with additional protocols being necessary to relate these three different planes of our multidimensional experience.

Physically, the establishment of meaning in these nameless urban constellations relates to the emergence of new forms of symbolic nodality, which will identify places, even through conflictive appropriation of their meaning by different groups and individuals (Dunn-Jones 2000).

The second level of urban interaction refers to social communication patterns. Here, the diversity of expressions of local life, and their relationship to media culture, must be integrated into the theory of communication by doing rather than by saying. In other words, how messages are transmitted from one social group to another, from one meaning to another in the metropolitan region requires a redefinition of the notion of public sphere moving from institutions to the public place, away from Habermas and towards Kevin Lynch. Public places, as sites of spontaneous social interaction, are the communicative devices of our society, while formal, political institutions have become a specialized domain that hardly affect the private lives of people, that is what most people value most. Thus, it is not that politics, or local politics, does not matter. It is that its relevance is confined to the world of instrumentality, while expressiveness, and thus communication, refers to social practice, outside institutional boundaries. Therefore, in the practice of the city, its public spaces, including the social exchangers (or communication nodes) of its transportation networks, become the communicative devices of city life (Borja 2001; Mitchell 1999). How people are, or are not, able to express themselves, and communicate with each other, outside their homes and off their electronic circuits, that is, in public places, is an essential area of study for urbanism. I call it the sociability of public places in the individualized metropolis.

The third level of communication refers to the prevalence of electronic communication as a new form of sociability. Studies by Wellman, by Jones, and by a growing legion of social researchers have shown the density and intensity of electronic networks of communication, providing evidence to sustain the notion that virtual communities are often communities, albeit of a different kind than face to face communities (Wellman and Haythornthwaite 2002; Jones 1998). Here again, the critical matter is the understanding of the communication codes between various electronic networks, built around specific interests or values, and between these networks and physical interaction. There is no established theory yet on these communication processes, as the internet as a widespread social practice is still in its infancy. But we do know that online sociability is specified, not downgraded, and that physical location does contribute, often in unsuspected ways, to the configuration of electronic communication networks. Virtual communities as networks of individuals are transforming the patterns of sociability in the new metropolitan life, without escaping into the world of electronic fantasy (Castells 2001).

Fourth, the analysis of code sharing in the new urban world requires also the study of the interface between physical layouts, social organization, and electronic networks. It is this interface that Mitchell considers to be at the heart of the new urban form, what he calls e-topia. In a similar vein, but from a different perspective, Graham and Marvin's (2001) analysis of urban infrastructure as splintered networks, reconfigured by the new electronic pipes of urban civilization, opens up the perspective of understanding cities not only as communication systems, but as machines of deliberate segmentation. In other words, we must understand at the same time the process of communication and that of incommunication.

The contradictory and/or complementary relationships between new metropolitan centrality, the practice of public space, and new communication patterns emerging from virtual communities, could lay the foundations for a new theory of urbanism—the theory of cyborg cities or hybrid cities made up by the intertwining of flows and places.

Let us go farther in this exploration of the new themes for urban theory. We know that telecommuting—meaning people working full time online from their home—is another myth of futurology (Gillespie and Richardson 2000, reading 29). Many people, including you and me, work online from home part of the time, but we continue to go to work in places, as well as moving around (the city or the world) while we keep working, with mobile connectivity to our network of professional partners, suppliers, and clients. The latter is the truly new spatial dimension of work. This is a new work experience, and indeed a new life experience. Moving physically while keeping the networking connection to everything we do is a new realm of the human adventure, on which we know little (Kopomaa 2000, see readings 17 and

39). The analysis of networked spatial mobility is another frontier for the new theory of urbanism. To explore it in terms that would not be solely descriptive we need new concepts. The connection between networks and places has to be understood in a variable geometry of these connections. The places of the space of flows, that is, the corridors and halls that connect places around the world, will have to be understood as exchangers and social refuges, as homes on the run, as much as offices on the run. The personal and cultural identification with these places, their functionality, their symbolism, are essential matters that do not concern only the cosmopolitan elite. Worldwide mass tourism, international migration, transient work, are experiences that relate to the new huddled masses of the world. How we relate to airports, to train and bus stations, to freeways, to customs buildings, are part of the new urban experience of hundreds of millions. We can build on an ethnographic tradition that addressed these issues in the mature industrial society. But here again, the speed, complexity, and planetary reach of the transportation system have changed the scale and meaning of the issues. Furthermore, the key reminder is that we move physically while staying put in our electronic connection. We carry flows and move across places.

Urban life in the twenty-first century is also being transformed by the crisis of patriarchalism. This is not a consequence of technological change, but I have argued in my book *The Power of Identity* (Castells 1997) that it is an essential feature of the Information Age. To be sure, patriarchalism is not historically dead. Yet, it is contested enough, and overcome enough so that everyday life for a large segment of city dwellers has already been redefined vis-à-vis the traditional pattern of an industrial society based on a relatively stable patriarchal nuclear family. Under conditions of gender equality, and under the stress suffered by traditional arrangements of household formation, the forms and rhythms of urban life are dramatically altered. Patterns of residence, transportation, shopping, education, and recreation evolve to adjust to the multidirectionality of individual needs that have to share household needs. This transformation is mediated by variable configurations of state policies. For instance, how child care is handled by government, by firms, by the market, or by individual networking largely conditions the time and space of daily lives, particularly for children.

We have documented how women are discriminated against in the patriarchal city. We can empirically argue that women's work makes possible the functioning of cities—an obvious fact rarely acknowledged in the urban studies literature (Borja and Castells 1997; Susser 1996). Yet, we need to move forward, from denunciation to the analysis of specific urban contradictions resulting from the growing dissonance between the degendering of society and historical crystallization of patriarchalism in the patterns of home and urban structure. How do these contradictions manifest themselves as people develop strategies to overcome the constraints of a gendered built environment? How do women, in particular, reinvent urban life, and contribute to redesign

the city of women, in contrast to the millennial heritage of the city of men (Castells and Servon 1996)? These are the questions to be researched, rather than stated, by a truly postpatriarchal urban theory.

Grass-roots movements continue to shape cities, as well as societies at large. They come in all kind of formats and ideologies, and one should keep an open mind on this matter, not deciding in advance which ones are progressive, and which ones are regressive, but taking all of them as symptoms of society in the making. We should also keep in mind the most fundamental rule in the study of social movements. They are what they say they are. They are their own consciousness. We can study their origins, establish their rules of engagement, explore the reasons for their victories and defeats, link their outcomes to overall social transformation, but not to interpret them, not to explain to them what they really mean by what they say. Because, after all, social movements are nothing else than their own symbols and stated goals, which ultimately means their words.

Based on the observation of social movements in the early stage of the network society, two kinds of issues appear to require privileged attention from urban social scientists. The first one is what I called some time ago the grass-rooting of the space of flows, that is the use of the internet for networking in social mobilization and social challenges (Castells 2000). This is not simply a technological issue, because it concerns the organization, reach, and process of formation of social movements. Most often these online social movements connect to locally based movements, and they converge, physically, in a given place at a given time. A good example was the mobilization against the World Trade Organization meeting in Seattle in December 1999, and against subsequent meetings of globalizing institutions, which, arguably, set a new trend of grass-roots opposition to uncontrolled globalization, and redefined the terms of the debate on the goals and procedures of the new economy. The other major issue in the area of social movements is the exploration of the environmental movement, and of an ecological view of social organization, as urban areas become the connecting point between the global issues posed by environmentalism and the local experience through which people at large assess their quality of life. To redefine cities as ecosystems, and to explore the connection between local ecosystems and the global ecosystem lays the ground for the overcoming of localism by grass-roots movements.

On the other hand, the connection cannot be operated only in terms of ecological knowledge. Implicit in the environmental movement, and clearly articulated in the deep ecology theory, as reformulated by Fritjof Capra (1996), is the notion of cultural transformation. A new civilization, and not simply a new technological paradigm, requires a new culture. This culture in the making is being fought over by various sets of interests and cultural projects. Environmentalism is the code word for this cultural battle, and ecological issues in the urban areas constitute the critical battleground for such struggle.

Besides tackling new issues, we still have to reckon in the twenty-first century with the lingering questions of urban poverty, racial and social discrimination, and social exclusion. In fact, recent studies show an increase of urban marginality and inequality in the network society (HDR 2001). Furthermore, old issues in a new context, become, in fact, new. Thus, Ida Susser (1996) has shown the networking logic underlying the spread of AIDS among New York's poor along networks of destitution, stigma, and discrimination. Eric Klinenberg (2000), in his social anatomy of the devastating effects of the 1995 heat wave in Chicago, shows why dying alone in the city, the fate of hundreds of seniors in a few days, was rooted in the new forms of social isolation emerging from peoples exclusion from networks of work, family, information, and sociability. The dialectics between inclusion and exclusion in the network society redefines the field of study of urban poverty, and forces us to consider alternative forms of inclusion (e.g., social solidarity or else, the criminal economy), as well as new mechanisms of exclusion in the technological apartheid of the internet era.

The final frontier for a new theory of urbanism, indeed for social sciences in general, is the study of new relationships between time and space in the Information Age. In my analysis of the new relationships of time and space I propose the hypothesis that in the network society, space structures time, in contrast to the time-dominated constitution of the industrial society, in which urbanization, and industrialization were considered to be part of the march of universal progress, erasing place-rooted traditions and cultures. In our society, the network society, where you live determines your time frame of reference. If you are an inhabitant of the space of flows, or if you live in a locality that is in the dominant networks, timeless time (epitomized by the frantic race to beat the clock) will be your time as on Wall Street or in Silicon Valley. If you are in a Pearl River Delta factory town, chronological time will be imposed upon you as in the best days of Taylorism in Detroit. And if you live in a village in Mamiraua, in Amazonia, biological time, usually a much shorter life span, will still rule your life. Against this spatial determination of time, environmental movements assert the notion of slow-motion time, the time of the long now, in the words of Stewart Brand, by broadening the spatial dimension to its planetary scale in the whole complexity of its interactions thus including our grand grandchildren in our temporal frame of reference (Brand, 1999).

Now, what is the meaning of this multidimensional transformation for planning, architecture, and urban design?

Planning, Architecture, and Urban Design In the Reconstruction of the City

The great urban paradox of the twenty-first century is that we could be living in a predominantly urban world without cities—that is, without spatially based systems of cultural communication and sharing of meaning, even conflictive sharing. Signs of the social, symbolic, and functional disin-

tegration of the urban fabric multiply around the world. So do the warnings from analysts and observers from a variety of perspectives (Kuntsler 1993; Ascher 1995; Davis 1992; Sorkin 1997; Russell 2000).

But societies are produced, and spaces are built, by conscious human action. There is no structural determinism. So, together with the emphasis on the economic competitiveness of cities, on metropolitan mobility, on privatization of space, on surveillance and security, there is also a growing valuation of urbanity, street life, civic culture, and meaningful spatial forms in the metropolitan areas around the world The process of reconstruction of the city is under way. And the emphasis of the most advanced urban projects in the world is on communication, in its multidimensional sense: restoring functional communication by metropolitan planning; providing spatial meaning by a new symbolic nodality created by innovative architectural projects; and reinstating the city in its urban form by the practice of urban design focused on the preservation, restoration, and construction of public space as the epitome of urban life.

However, the defining factor in the preservation of cities as cultural forms in the new spatial context will be the capacity of integration between planning, architecture, and urban design. This integration can only proceed through urban policy influenced by urban politics. Ultimately, the management of metropolitan regions is a political process, made of interests, values, conflicts, debates, and options that shape the interaction between space and society. Cities are made by citizens, and governed on their behalf. Only when democracy is lost can technology and the economy determine the way we live. Only when the market overwhelms culture and when bureaucracies ignore citizens can spatial conurbations supersede cities as living systems of multidimensional communication.

Planning

The key endeavor of planning in the metropolitan regions of the information age is to ensure their connectivity, both intrametropolitan and intermetropolitan. Planning has to deal with the ability of the region to operate within the space of flows. The prosperity of the region and of its dwellers will greatly depend on their ability to compete and cooperate in the global networks of generation/appropriation of knowledge, wealth, and power. At the same time planning must ensure the connectivity of these metropolitan nodes to the space of places contained in the metropolitan region. In other words, in a world of spatial networks, the proper connection between these different networks is essential to link up the global and the local without opposing the two planes of operation.

This means that planning should be able to act on a metropolitan scale, ensuring effective transportation, accepting multinodality, fighting spatial segregation by acting against exclusionary zoning, providing affordable housing, and desegregating schools. Ethnic and social diversity is a feature of the metropolitan region, and ought to be protected. Planning should seek the integration of open space and natural areas in the metropolitan space, going beyond the traditional scheme of the greenbelt. The new metropolitan region embraces a vast territorial expanse, where large areas of agricultural land and natural land should be preserved as a key component of a balanced metropolitan territory. The new metropolitan space is characterized by its multifunctionality, and this is a richness that supersedes the functional specialization and segregation of modernist urbanism. New planning practice induces a simultaneous process of decentering and recentering of population and activities, leading to the creation of multiple subcenters in the region.

The social and functional diversity of the metropolitan region requires a multimodal approach to transportation, by mixing the private automobile/highway system with public metropolitan transportation (railways, subways, buses, taxis), and with local transportation (bicycles, pedestrian paths, specialized shuttle services). Furthermore, in a post-patriarchal world, childcare becomes a critical urban service, and therefore must be integrated in the schemes of metropolitan planning. In the same way that some cities require additional housing and transportation investment per each new job created in certain areas, child care provision should be included in these planning standards.

Overall, most metropolitan planning nowadays is geared towards the adaptation of the space of places of the metropolitan region to the space of flows that conditions the economic competitiveness of the region. The challenge would be to use planning, instead, to structure the space of places as a living space, and to ensure the connection and complementarity between the economy of the metropolitan region and the quality of life of its dwellers.

Architecture

Restoring symbolic meaning is a most fundamental task in a metropolitan world in a crisis of communication. This is the role that architecture has traditionally assumed. It is more important than ever. Architecture, of all kinds, must be called to the rescue in order to re-create symbolic meaning in the metropolitan region, marking places in the space of flows. In recent years, we have observed a substantial revival of architectural meaningfulness that in some cases has had a direct impact in revitalizing cities and regions, not only culturally but economically as well. To be sure, architecture per se cannot change the function, or even the meaning, of a whole metropolitan area. Symbolic meaning has to be inserted in the whole fabric of the city, and this is, as I will argue below, the key role of urban design. But we still need meaningful forms, resulting from architectural intervention, to stir a cultural debate that makes space a living form. Recent trends in architecture signal its transformation from an intervention on the space of places to an intervention on the space of flows, the dominant space of the Information Age by acting on spaces dedicated to museums, convention centers, and transportation nodes. These are spaces of cultural archives, and of functional communication that become transformed into forms of cultural expression and meaningful exchange by the act of architecture.

The most spectacular example is Frank Gehry's Guggenheim Museum in Bilbao, which symbolized the will of life of a city immersed in a serious economic crisis and a dramatic political conflict. Calatrava's bridges (Seville, Bilbao), telecommunication towers (Barcelona), airports (Bilbao) or convention centers (Valencia) mark the space of flows with sculpted engineering. Bofill's Barcelona airport, Moneo's AVE railway station in Madrid and Kursaal Convention Center in San Sebastian, Meier's Modern Art Museum in Barcelona, or Koolhaas's Lille Grand Palais, are all examples of these new cathedrals of the Information Age, where the pilgrims gather to search for the meaning of their wandering. Critics point at the disconnection between many of these symbolic buildings and the city at large. The lack of integration of this architecture of the space of flows into the public space would be tantamount to juxtapose symbolic punctuation and spatial meaninglessness. This is why it is essential to link up architecture with urban design, and with planning. Yet, architectural creation has its own language, its own project that cannot be reduced to function or to form. Spatial meaning is still culturally created. But their final meaning will depend on its interaction with the practice of the city organized around public space.

Urban Design

The major challenge for urbanism in the Information Age is to restore the culture of cities. This requires a sociospatial treatment of urban forms, a process that we know as urban design. But it must be an urban design able of connecting local life, individuals, communes, and instrumental global flows through the sharing of public places. Public space is the key connector of experience, opposed to private shopping centers as the spaces of sociability.

Jordi Borja (2001), in a remarkable book supported with case studies of several countries, has shown the essential role of public space in the city. Indeed it is public space that makes cities as creators of culture, organizers of sociability, systems of communication, and seeds of democracy, by the practice of citizenship. This is in opposition to the urban crisis characterized by the dissolution, fragmentation, and privatization of cities. Borja documents, on a comparative basis, the projects of reconstruction of cities and of the culture of cities around the (re)construction of public space: the synthesis between places and flows is realized in the public space, the place of social cohesion and social exchanges (Borja 2001, 35).

This is, in fact, a long tradition in urban design, associated with the thinking and practice of Kevin Lynch, and best represented nowadays by Allan Jacobs. Jacobs' work on streets, and, with Elizabeth McDonald, on boulevards as urban forms able to integrate transportation mobility and social meaning in the city, shows that there is an alternative to the edge city, beyond the defensive battles of suburbanism with a human face (Jacobs, 1993). The success of the Barcelona model of urban design is based on the ability to plan public squares, even minisquares in the old city, that bring together social life, meaningful architectural forms (not always of the best taste, but is does not matter), and the provision of open space for people's use. That is, not just open space, but marked open space, and street life induced by activities, such as the tolerance of informal trade, street musicians, etc.

The reconquest of public space operates throughout the entire metropolitan region, highlighting particularly the working-class peripheries, those that need the most attention at socio spatial reconstruction. Sometimes the public space is a square, sometimes a park, sometimes a boulevard, sometimes a few square meters around a fountain, or in front of a library or a museum, or an outdoor café colonizing the sidewalk. In all instances what matters is the spontaneity of uses, the density of the interaction, the freedom of expression, the multifunctionality of space, and the multiculturalism of the street life. This is not the nostalgic reproduction of the medieval town. In fact, examples of public space (old, new, and renewed) dot the whole planet, as Borja has illustrated in his book. It is the dissolution of public space under the combined pressures of privatization of the city and the rise of the space of flows that is a historical oddity. Thus, it is not the past versus the future, but two forms of present that fight each other in the battleground of the emerging metropolitan regions. And the fight, and its outcome, is of course, political, in the etymological sense: it is the struggle of the polis to create the city as a meaningful place.

The Government of Cities in the Information Age

The dynamic articulation between metropolitan planning, architecture, and urban design is the domain of urban policy. Urban policy starts with a strategic vision of the desirable evolution of the metropolitan space in its double relationship to the global space of flows and to the local space of places. This vision, to be a guiding tool, must result from the dynamic compromise between the contradictory expression of values and interests from the plurality of urban actors. Effective urban policy is always a synthesis between the interests of these actors and their specific projects. But this synthesis must be given technical coherence and formal expression, so that the city evolves in its form without submitting the local society to the imperatives of economic constraints or technological determinism.

The constant adjustment between various structural factors and conflictive social processes is implemented by the government of cities. This is why good planning or innovative architecture cannot do much to save the culture of cities unless there are effective city governments, based on citizen participation and the practice of local democracy. Too much to ask for? Well, in fact, the planet is dotted with examples of good city government that make cities livable by harnessing market forces and taming interest groups on behalf of the public good. Portland, Toronto, Barcelona, Birmingham, Bologna, Tampere, Curitiba, among many other cities, are instances of the efforts of innovative urban policy to manage the current metropolitan transformation (Borja and Castells 1997; Verwijnen and Lehtovuori 1999; Scott 2001). However, innovative urban policy does not result from great urbanists (although they are indeed needed), but from courageous urban politicians able to mobilize citizens around the meaning of their environment.

Conclusion

The new culture of cities is not the culture of the end of history. Restoring communication may open the way to restore meaningful conflict. Currently, social injustice and personal isolation combine to induce alienated violence. So, the new culture of urban integration is not the culture of assimilation into the values of a single dominant culture, but the culture of communication between an irreversibly diverse local society connected/disconnected to global flows of wealth, power, and information.

Architecture and urban design are sources of spatiocultural meaning in an urban world in dramatic need of communication protocols and artifacts of sharing. It is commendable that architects and urban designers find inspiration in social theory, and feel as concerned citizens of their society. But first of all, they must do their job as providers of meaning by the cultural shaping of spatial forms. Their traditional function in society is more critical than ever in the Information Age, an age marked by the growing gap between splintering networks of instrumentality and segregated places of singular meaning. Architecture and design may bridge technology and culture by creating shared symbolic meaning and reconstructing public space in the new metropolitan context. But they will only be able to do so with the help of innovative urban policy supported by democratic urban politics.

TIGRAN HAAS

Introduction

1. The most common logical fallacies that we come across in critical attacks on New Urbanism are accusations such as straw man, *ignoratio elenchi* (arguing beside the point), equivocation, *petitio principii* (begging the question), false assumptions, and the *argumentum ad populum* (popular appeal). It should be pointed out that fallacious reasoning can often be quite persuasive, at times more so than sound reasoning—this is where the great danger lies. Usually the aim of such reasoning is to dodge sound reasoning by appealing to the emotions of the audience.

PART I. THEORIES OF URBAN FORM

I.I. CHRISTOPHER ALEXANDER

Generative Codes: The Path to Building Welcoming, Beautiful, Sustainable Neighborhoods

1. This approach to building is based on morphogenesis, which has been the basis of Alexander's work throughout his career as architect, planner, educator, theorist, and builder. The theory, connections to other fields of science, and hundreds of examples of putting this theory into action are covered in *The Nature of Order*, Alexander's recently completed four-volume work: Book 1, *The Phenomenon of Life*; Book 2, *The Process of Creating Life*; Book 3, *A Vision of a Living World*; and Book 4, *The Luminous Ground* (Berkeley, CA: Center for Environmental Structure Publishing, 2001, 2002, 2005, and 2004, respectively).

2. For example, Brian Goodwin's extensive work on morphogenesis, e.g., Gerry Webster and Brian Goodwin, *Form and Transformation: Generative and Relational Principles in Biology* (New York: Cambridge University Press, 1996).

3. *The Nature of Order*, Book 2, throughout.

4. See the Wikipedia entry for zoning law: http://en.wikipedia.org/wiki/Zoning.

5. See discussion of structure-preserving transformations in *The Nature of Order*, Book 2, chapters 3–4.

6. The word "procurement," though in common use, does not have a single established meaning. In this essay, we define procurement to mean the sum total of institutions, processes, and actions that together contribute everything required as a part of the design, planning, and building process. It spans, in short, a project's conception to its final stages of occupation and beyond, including maintenance and refurbishment.

7. Commentary in the professional literature has openly acknowledged this aim of ours, and given us credit for some success in that direction. See, for example, Thomas Fisher and Ziva Freiman, "The Real Meaning of Architecture," *Progressive Architecture*, July 1991, 100–112.

8. Duany himself has generously said this on numerous occasions: "If I had to go to a desert island for the rest of my life with only one book, that [book] would be *A Pattern Language*" (from www.katarxis3.com), and "We know that the patterns have supplied us with the right content; now we must plug this content into the power grid of modern society and its implementation process, to make the environment succeed on a wide scale. . . ."

9. It is important to emphasize that both evaluations (of columns 12 and 13) are assessments we have made ourselves. It could be argued, rightly, that this is not sufficiently objective to be relied upon as evidence for a finding. However, we have done our best to be objective about the evaluations, as far as it is in our power to be so, and it must be said that the correlation itself, even as a hypothesis, is of such importance that it virtually demands to be published. In the absence of more purely objective data, these data are at least very much better than no data at all. We would encourage performance of a comparable, more carefully controlled, longitudinal study of construction projects in which the same variables may be tested further.

10. A community mental health center for outpatients and outpatient care built in Stanislaus County, California. For a description, see *The Timeless Way of Building* (Oxford: Oxford University Press, 1979, 432–54).

11. A small group of houses and community buildings built by families themselves with the help of students from the Universidad Autonoma of Mexico and a team of builders from the Center for Environmental Structure. For a full description, see Alexander, Davis, Martinez, and Corner, *The Production of Houses* (New York: Oxford University Press, 1985). See also *The Nature of Order*, Book 2, 236–41; Book 3, 34–36, 446, 464, 479, 493–98, 551–55; Book 4, 277–9.

12. A master plan for the University of Oregon, Eugene, which gave primacy to the use of pattern languages and user design in the continuous process of development of the campus. See Alexander, et al., *The Oregon Experiment* (Oxford: Oxford University Press, 1975).

13. A settlement in the Galilee region, planned and organized by immigrants to Israel. See brief description in *The Nature of Order*, Book 3, 349–51; and Alexander, Gitai, Portugali, Anninou, and Nastou, *Master Plan and House Layout Process for Segev H* (Berkeley, CA: Center for Environmental Structure, 1982).

14. Two connected houses built for the Sala family in Berkeley, California; see *The Nature of Order*, Book 3, 249, 471, 528–29, 533–37.

15. See the users' manual and report, process for layout of neighborhoods, layout of houses by families, and management of construction sections of Alexander, Neis, Anninou, *Master Plan for Guasare New Town, Maracaibo, Venezuela* (Berkeley, CA: Center for Environmental Structure, 1983). See also *The Nature of Order*, Book 3, 340–47.

16. A farmer's market we built in Fresno, California, serving growers and farmers within a wide radius. The market has been so successful that a few years ago a book was written to record its story and the source of community that the building and market have generated: *Abundant Harvest: Scenes and Stories from Fresno's Vineyard Farmers Market*, by Sharon Young. The book celebrates the twenty-year continued existence of this market, as a human and social phenomenon created by the strong bonds of feeling between the developer, Richard Erganian, and the farmers he works with; his habit of caring; and traits of responsibility and genuine, folksy warmth. See also *The Nature of Order*, Book 3, 462–63, 504–5, 537–39.

17. A high school and college campus built outside Tokyo between 1983 to 1987. It accommodates some 2,000 students, occupies about twenty-two acres of land (some nine city blocks), and includes thirty academic buildings, playing fields, public space, and pedestrian space. This

campus has been written about on numerous occasions in the Japanese, English, German, and American press, and is also the subject of two forthcoming books: *Battle*, by Alexander, Neis, et al., and *The Human Aspect of the Eishin Campus*, by Hisae Hosoi. Many aspects of the place, people, and process that created it are described in *The Nature of Order*: Book 2, 378–96, 422–30; Book 3, 77–81, 102–111, 173–81, 187–9, 199–210, 231–36, 252–55, 269–73, 482–83, 506–9, 541–43; Book 4, 250–59.

18. See "Multifamily Zoning Ordinance for the City of Pasadena, 1987," by Alexander, Anninou, and Solomon, described at length in *The Nature of Order*, Book 2, 306–17.

19. Whidbey island, house and offices.

20. A five-story apartment building in the Komagome district of downtown Tokyo; see *The Nature of Order*, Book 3, 166–73.

21. The Julian Street Inn is a 100-bed shelter for the homeless built in San Jose, California. See an extensive account in *The Nature of Order*: Book 2, 283–98; Book 3, 120–31, 211–23.

22. A community of seventy families in Santa Rosa de Cabal, Colombia. We handled the process so that the streets were designed by the community, and each house was designed by the family. See *The Nature of Order*, Book 3, 336–38, 398–408. Described in Alexander, Tsotropoulou, Wachtel, Fefferman, and Radcliffe, Lawrence, *Layout Process for Colombian Housing* (Berkeley, CA: Center for Environmental Structure, 1991) . Also summarized with photographs in *The Nature of Order*, Book 3, 336–38, 398–408.

23. The Upham house in Berkeley, CA. For one of the most complete written descriptions of the process and steps in a large single family house, see *The Nature of Order*: Book 2, 572–632; Book 3, 459, 503.

24. Agate and Amazon, neighborhoods of student housing for the University of Oregon; see *The Nature of Order*, Book 3, 182–86.

25. Back of the Moon neighborhood, Texas, with individual houses and public common land. See *The Nature of Order*, Book 3, 82–5, 365–81, 467, 499–500.

26. West Dean Visitor's Center for the public with surrounding grounds and gardens in West Sussex. See *The Nature of Order*: Book 3, 16–17, 238–41, 244–46, 460, 466, 470, 472, 486–89; Book 4, 118–29, 286–91.

27. Complete redesign anf reconstruction of a large Berkeley, CA, house undertaken over a period of years. See *The Nature of Order*, Book 3, 412, 472, 501–2.

28. Two houses and estate. See *The Nature of Order*, Book 2, 211–13.

29. Calculation of Spearman's rho is defined in most textbooks on rank-order correlation. In our case we used the calculation method published by Professor Richard Lowry, Vassar College, which may be found at http://faculty.vassar.edu/lowry/corr_rank.html.

30. For fuller discussion of morphogenesis see Christopher Alexander, "Sustainability and Morphogenesis," Schumacher Lecture given October 30, 2004, and various references throughout Books 2 and 3 of *The Nature of Order*.

31. Deputy Prime Minister Prescott's entire initiative for creation of new housing was oriented to the developer's desire to build housing, not on a demonstrated need by buyers. The Pathfinder program, which was the culmination of his efforts, very explicitly stated that the nation and the housing supply would be served best by the commercial developers' ability to make profit.

I.2. BILL HILLIER
The New Science of Space and the Art of Place:
Toward a Space-led Paradigm for Researching and Designing the City

1. Sitte, 1889.
2. Hillier and Hanson, 1984.
3. www.spacesyntax.com.
4. Hillier and Iida, 2005.
5. Hillier and Iida, 2005.
6. Peponis, et al., 1990.
7. Hillier, 1996.
8. Described more fully in Hillier, 1999, 2002.
9. Siksna, 199x; Hillier 1999.
10. See, for example, www.spacesyntax.com.

SOURCES
Hillier, B., *Space Is the Machine* (New York: Cambridge University Press, 1996).

Hillier, B. and J. Hanson, *The Social Logic of Space* (New York: Cambridge University Press, 1984).

Hillier, B. and S. Iida, "Network and Psychological Effects in Urban Movement," in Cohn, A. G. and D. M. Mark (eds.), *Proceedings of Spatial Information Theory: International Conference*. (Ellicottsville, : COSIT, 2005).

Peponis, J., C. Zimring, Y. K. Choi, "Finding the building in wayfinding," *Environment and Behavior*, 22(5), 1990, 555-90.

Sitte, C., *Der Stadtebau nach seinen kunstlerischen Grundsetzen*; originally published in 1889, translated as *City Planning According to Artistic Principles*. (New York: Random House, 1965).

Turner, A., A. Penn, and B. Hillier, "An Algorithmic Definition of the Axial Map," *Environment and Planning B: Planning and Design*: 32:3, 2005, 425–444.

I.3. DOUGLAS KELBAUGH
Three Urbanisms: New, Everyday, and Post

1. Kaliski, John, et al., *Everyday Urbanism* (New York: Monacelli Press, 1999).
2. Leinberger, Chris, in *Places*, Summer 2005.
3. Dunham-Jones, Ellen, in personal correspondence.
4. Crawford, Margaret, et al., *Michigan Debates on Urbanism*, vol. 1 (Ann Arbor: University of Michigan Press, 2005), cover image.

I.4. PETER HALL
Urban Renaissance, Urban Villages, Smart Growth: Find the Differences

1. Bernick, M., and R. Cervero, *Transit Villages in the 21st Century* (New York: McGraw Hill, 1997); Calthorpe, P., *The Next American Metropolis: Ecology, Community, and the American Dream.* (New York: Princeton Architectural Press, 1993); Cervero, R., *The Transit Metropolis: A Global Inquiry* (Washington, DC: Island Press, 1998).
2. Jones, P., D. Hillier, and D. Comfort, "New Environments to fight Retail Fatigue," in *Town and Country Planning*, 75: 81–83; Langdon, P. "The Not-so-Secret Code: Across the U. S., Form-Based Codes Are Putting New Urbanist Ideas into Practice," in *Planning*, 72/1, 2006, 24–29.
3. Hayden, D., *Building Suburbia: Green Fields and Urban Growth*, 1820-2000 (New York: Pantheon, 2003).

I.6. WILLIAM McDONOUGH
Something Lived, Something Dreamed: Principles and Poetics in Urban Design
SOURCES

Beatley, Timothy, *Green Urbanism* (Washington, DC: Island Press, 2000).

Jackson, J. B., *Landscapes* (Amherst: University of Massachusetts Press, 1970).

Jacobs, Jane, *The Death and Life of Great American Cities* (New York: Vintage, 1992).

Levi-Strauss, Claude, *Tristes Tropiques*, translated by John and Doreen Weightman (New York: Penguin, 1973).

McDonough, William, and Michael Braungart, *Cradle to Cradle: Remaking the Way We Make Things* (New York: North Point Press, 2002).

——— *The Hannover Principles: Design for Sustainability* (New York: William McDonough Architects, 1992).

McPhee, John, *Basin and Range* (New York: Farrar, Straus and Giroux, 1981).

Reisner, Marc, *Cadillac Desert: The American West and Its Disappearing Water* (New York: Penguin, 1993).

Spirn, Anne Whiston, *The Granite Garden: Urban Nature and Human Design* (New York: Basic Books, 1984).

——— *The Language of Landscape* (New Haven: Yale University Press, 1998).

PART 2. EXPLORING NEW URBANISM

2.3. ELLEN DUNHAM-JONES
New Urbanism: A Forum, Not a Formula

1. The Charter is available at www.cnu.org. Its principles are elaborated with descriptive chapters in Michael Leccese and Kathleen McCormick, eds., *The Charter of the New Urbanism* (New York: McGraw Hill, 2000).
2. For instance, see Lee S. Sobel, Steve Bodzin, Ellen Greenberg, and Jonathan Miller, *Greyfields into Goldfields: Dead Malls Become Living Neighborhoods* (Chicago: Congress for the New Urbanism, 2002).
3. The SmartCode continues to be updated. The spring 2005 version, including discussion of the Urban-Rural Transect, can be downloaded from www.tndtownpaper.com/images/SmartCode6.5.pdf.
4. The LEED-ND Rating System Preliminary Draft Document can be downloaded from www.usgbc.org. In 2007 the system will be open for public comment before balloting and launch in 2008.
5. Like LEED-ND, the path to approval of the CNU-ITE design manual will take several years, with pilot projects and public comment expected. The 255-page manual can be downloaded from http://ite.org/bookstore.

6. Reed Kroloff, dean of the Architecture School at Tulane University and former editor of *Architecture* magazine, has been particularly vocal in the press about his criticism of New Urbanism's nostalgia, often facing off with Duany. At CNU XIV in 2006, alongside popular sessions on pattern books and traditional architectural detailing, the presentation titled "Can New Urbanism Capture the Market for Modernism?" attracted an overflow audience, and Dan Solomon's plenary talk, "What Happened to Modernity?," received a standing ovation.

7. Unfortunately, much of the discourse has not been archived and is not easily accessible. There is discussion of starting a peer-reviewed journal on New Urbanism, but for the time being the best sources for published information are CNU's various publications: *New Urban News*, various Council Reports, Rob Steuteville's *New Urbanism: Comprehensive & Best Practices Guide*, and the occasional theme issues of *Places, Harvard Design Magazine, JAPA*, or the *Journal of Urban Design*.

8. Invited by the governor and organized through Duany and CNU, 110 New Urbanists and 100 local architects and planners developed reconstruction proposals for eleven towns over one week. Plans are continuing to be developed and several of the towns have adopted the SmartCode. For more details, go to www.mississippirenewal.com.

2.4. DANIEL SOLOMON
Making Cloth from Threads

1. Jackson, R., M. Frumpkin, and L. Frank, *Urban Sprawl and Public Health: Designing, Planning, and Building for Healthy Communities* (Washington, DC: Island Press, 2004).

2.5. EMILY TALEN
The Unbearable Lightness of New Urbanism

1. In reference to Milan Kundera's novel *The Unbearable Lightness of Being*.

2. See, for example, the partisan account in Fred Siegel, *The Future Once Happened Here* (New York: Free Press, 1997).

3. Risen, Clay, "Op-Ed: Wrong Way Home," *The Morning News*, 2005 (www.themorningnews.com/archives/oped/wrong_way_home.php).

4. Blackwell, Angela Glover, and Judith Bell, "Equitable Development for a Stronger Nation: Lessons from the Field," in *The Geography of Opportunity: Race and Housing Choice in Metropolitan America*, Xavier de Souza Briggs, ed. (Washington, DC: Brookings Institution Press, 2005), 289–309.

5. Galster, et al., *Why Not in My Backyard? Neighborhood Impacts of Deconcentrating Assisted Housing* (New Brunswick: Center for Urban Policy Research, 2003).

6. Goetz, Edward G., *Clearing the Way: Deconcentrating the Poor in Urban America* (Washington, DC: Urban Institute Press, 1996). See also Bayer, Patrick, "Tiebout Sorting and Discrete Choices: A New Explanation for Socioeconomic Differences in the Consumption of School Quality," 2000. Working paper available online at http://aida.econ.yale.edu /~pjb37/papers.htm.

7. West, Cornel. "Diverse New World," in Democratic Left 19.4, 1991. Reprinted in Signs of Life in the USA: *Readings on Popular Culture for Writers*, Sonia Maasik and Jack Solomon, eds. (Boston: Bedford Books, 1997), 557–562. See also Putnam, Robert. *Social Capital Community Benchmark Survey* (Cambridge: Saguaro Seminar of the John F. Kennedy School of Government, Harvard University, 2000); Greenbaum, Susan, and Paul Greenbaum, "The Ecology of Social Networks in Four Urban Neighborhoods," in *Social Networks* 7, 1985, 47-76; and Warren, Mark R., *Dry Bones Rattling: Community Building to Revitalize American Democracy* (Princeton: Princeton University Press, 2001).

2.6. JILL GRANT
The Challenges of Achieving Social Objectives through Mixed Use

1. Perin, 1977
2. Grant, 2002
3. Grant, 2003
4. Grant, 2006
5. Lennertz, 1991
6. Talen, 2002
7. Hardy, 2003; Thompson-Fawcett, 2003
8. Beasley, 2004; Langdon, 2003
9. Although the CNU web site (CNU 2004) lists Karow Nord as a New Urbanist project, Bodenschatz, 2003, says that Germans call it a condensed suburb. CNU describes it as an infill development, but Gause, 2002, says it is a greenfield project. Sears, 2006, finds that Karow Nord has not met its targets for market units, nor for public transportation use.
10. Sears, 2006

11. Johnson, 2004
12. Eppli and Tu, 1999; Gause, 2002; Tu and Eppli, 1999
13. Brown and Cropper, 2001
14. Quote from Redwood, 2004, online. The problem of affordability applies in New Urbanism projects in other parts of the world as well. Homes in an urban village in East Perth, Australia, sold for AU$500,000, despite a plan to generate socioeconomic mix (CSIRO, 1999). A premium has also been confirmed in Israeli New Urbanist projects (Plaut and Boarnet, 2003).
15. Mohney and Easterling, 1991
16. Davis Properties, 2004
17. Baxandall and Ewen, 2000; Douglas and Isherwood, 1996
18. Katz, 2002; *New Urban News*, 2003
19. Garde, 2004
20. Neuman, 2003
21. *New Urban News*, 2001
22. CMHC, 1996; Munro, 2004
23. *New Urban News*, 2001
24. Berton 2004; Smith, 2002; Zukin, 1989
25. Dowell, 2004
26. Duany, 2000, online
27. Duany, quoted by Marshall, 1995, online
28. Duany and Plater-Zyberk, 1992
29. Duany, et al., 2000
30. Deitrick and Ellis, 2004
31. Steuteville, 2004b
32. In the 1990s, the Housing and Urban Development department of the United States government developed Housing Opportunities for People Everywhere (HOPE VI) to renovate and redevelop public housing projects.
33. Lennertz, 1991
34. Bohl, 2000
35. Goetz, 2001; Popkin, et al., 2004
36. Pyatok, 2002, 2000
37. Duany, et al., 2000: 187
38. Stead and Hoppenbrower, 2004
39. Carter, 2004; Grant, 2002; Thompson-Fawcett, 2000
40. Krieger, 1991
41. Wiegandt, 2004
42. Thompson-Fawcett, 2000: 277
43. Kelbaugh, 1997
44. Brophy and Smith, 1997; Thompson-Fawcett, 2003
45. Wright, 1997
46. Garde, 2004
47. Falconer Al-Hindi and Staddon, 1997
48. Frantz and Collins, 1999
49. Ross, 1999
50. Falconer Al-Hindi, 2001
51. Till, 1993
52. Veregge, 1997
53. Till, 1993
54. Day, 2003
55. Mendez, 2005
56. Mehak, 2004
57. Langdon, 2002

SOURCES

Baxandall, R. and E. Ewen, *Picture Windows: How the Suburbs Happened* (New York: Basic Books, 2000).

Beasley, L., "Working with the modernist legacy: new urbanism Vancouver style" (address to the Congress for the New Urbanism, Chicago, June 2004). Available online at www.cnu.org.

Berton, B. "Cultured Pearl," *Urban Land* 63, 2004, 6:47-52.

Bodenschatz, H., "New Urbanism and the European Perspective: Presumption, Rivalry or Challenge?" in Rob Krier, *Town Spaces: Contemporary Interpretations in Traditional Urbanism*. (Basel: Birkhäuser Verlag, 2003), 266–79.

Bohl, C., *Place Making: Developing Town Centers, Main Streets, and Urban Villages* (Washington, DC: Urban Land Institute, 2002).

Brophy, P. C. and R. N. Smith, "Mixed-income Housing: Factors for Success," *CityScape: A Journal of Policy Development and Research*, 3,2, 1997: 3–31.

Brown, B. and V. Cropper, 2001. "New urban and standard suburban subdivisions: evaluating psychological and social goals," *Journal of the American Planning Association* 67,4, 2001, 402–19.

Carter, D. K., "New Urbanist Tenets," *Urban Land*, 63,5, 2004, 62–4.

CMHC (Canada Mortgage and Housing Corporation), "Infrastructure

Costs Associated with Conventional and Alternative Development Patterns," *Research and Development Highlights* 26 (Socioeconomic series, 1996).

CSIRO (Australia's Commonwealth Scientific and Industrial Research Organisation), "Top Honours to Western Australian Urban Village," *Building Innovation and Construction Technology* 8, August 1999.

Davis Properties. *Seaside* (Davis Properties of Northwest Florida, Inc., 2004). (Developer's promotional material: see www.davisprop.com/ and www.seasidefl.com/.)

Day, K., "New Urbanism and the Challenges of Designing for Diversity," *Journal of Planning and Education Research* 23, 2003, 83–95.

Deitrick, S. and C. Ellis, "New Urbanism in the Inner City: A Case Study of Pittsburgh," *Journal of the American Planning Association* 70,4, 2004, 426–42.

Douglas, M. and B. Isherwood, *The World of Goods: Towards an Anthropology of Consumption* (London: Routledge, 1996).

Dowell, P., "Gentrification Okay Here," *Planning* 70,9, 2004, 43.

Duany, A., "Gentrification and the Paradox of Affordable Housing," Pro-Urb listserv, 31, October 2000.

Duany, A. and E. Plater-Zyberk, "The Second Coming of the American Small Town," *Wilson Quarterly* 16, 1992, 19–50.

Duany, A., E. Plater-Zyberk, and J. Speck, *Suburban Nation: The rise of Sprawl and the Decline of the American Dream* (New York: North Point Press, 2000).

Eppli, M. J. and C. C. Tu, *Valuing the New Urbanism: Impact of the New Urbanism on Prices of Single-Family Homes* (Washington, DC: Urban Land Institute, 1999).

Falconer Al-Hindi, K., "The New Urbanism: Where and For Whom? Investigation of a New Paradigm. *Urban Geography* 22,3, 2001, 202–19.

Falconer Al-Hindi, K. and C. Staddon, "The Hidden Histories and Geographies of Neotraditional Town Planning: The Case of Seaside, Florida," *Environment and Planning D: Society and Space* 15, 1997, 349–72.

Frantz, D. and C. Collins, *Celebration, U.S.A.: Living in Disney's Brave New Town* (New York: Henry Holt, 1999).

Garde, A., "New Urbanism as Sustainable Growth? A Supply Side Story and its Implications for Public Policy," *Journal of Planning Education and Research* 24, 2004, 154–70.

Gause, J. Allen, *Great Planned Communities* (Washington, DC: Urban Land Institute, 2002).

Goetz, E. G., *Clearing the Way: Deconcentrating the Poor in Urban America* (Washington, DC: Urban Institute Press, 2003).

Grant, J. (2002) "Mixed Use in Theory and Practice: Canadian Experience with Implementing a Planning Principle," *Journal of the American Planning Association* 68,1, 2002, 71–84.

——————, "Exploring the Influence of New Urbanism." *Journal of Architectural and Planning Research* 20,3, 2003, 234–53.

——————, *Planning the Good Community: New Urbanism in Theory and Practice*, RTPI Series (London: Routledge, 2006).

Hardy, D., "Poundbury—Planning by Royal Appointment," *Town and Country Planning*, June 2003, 155–7.

Johnson, H. L., "Affordable Housing in Europe," *Urban Land* 63,3, 2004, 14–5.

Katz, P., "Individual Investors Can Profit from New Urbanism," *New Urban News* 7,6, 2002, 12–4.

Kelbaugh, D., *Common Places: Toward Neighborhood and Regional Design* (Seattle: University of Washington Press, 1997).

Krieger, A., Andres Duany and Elizabeth Plater-Zyberk, *Towns and Town-making Principles* (New York: Rizzoli and Harvard University Graduate School of Design, 1991).

Langdon, P., "In Central Vancouver, Modernism and New Urbanism Mesh," *New Urban News* 8,8, 2003, 8–10.

——————, "The Visitability Challenge," *New Urban News* 7,6:1, 2002, 4–6.

Lennertz, W., "Town-making Fundamentals," in A. Krieger, ed., *Andres Duany and Elizabeth Plater-Zyberk: Towns and Town-making Principles*.

Marshall, A. (1995b), "When the New Urbanism Meets an Old Neighborhood." *Metropolis*, May 1995. Available online at www.alexmarshall.org.

Mehak, M. C., "New Urbanism and Aging in Place," *Plan Canada* 42,1, 2002, 21–3.

Mendez, M., "Latino New Urbanism: Building on Cultural Preferences," *Opolis* 1,1, 2005, 33–48. Available online at www.mi.vt.edu/uploads/opolis/Mendez.pdf.

Mohney, D. and K. Easterling, *Seaside: Making a Town in America* (New York: Princeton Architectural Press, 1991).

Munro, K., "Does It Pay to Maintain New Urbanist Infrastructure? A

Fiscal Comparison of Alternative Community Forms," *Plan Canada* 44,1, 2005, 25–8.

Neuman, J., "Building in affordability," *Urban Land* 62,5, 2003, 64–5.

New Urban News (collective author), *New Urbanism: Comprehensive Report & Best Practices Guide*, second edition (Ithaca, NY: New Urban Publications, 2001).

"New Urbanism Adds to Housing Value, Study Says," *New Urban News*, December 2003.

Perin, C., *Everything in Its Place: Social Order and Land Use in America* (Princeton: Princeton University Press, 1977).

Plaut, P. O. and M. Boarnet, "New Urbanism and the Value of Neighborhood Design," *Journal of Architectural and Planning Research* 20,3, 2003, 254–65.

Popkin, S., B. Katz, M. K. Cunningham, K. Brown, J. Gustafson, and M. Austin Turner, *A Decade of HOPE VI: Research Findings and Policy Challenges* (Washington, DC: The Urban Institute, 2004). Available at www.urban.org.

Pyatok, M., "Comment on C. C. Bohl's 'New Urbanism and the City.' The Politics of Design: The New Urbanists vs. the Grass Roots," *Housing Policy Debate* 11,4, 2000, 803–14.

——————"The narrow base of the new urbanists," *Planners Network* 151:1, 2002, 4–5.

Redwood, F., "Charles's Vision Expands," Timesonline, 2004. Available online at http://property.timesonline.co.uk/article/0.14051_-1316507,00.html (Accessed January 24, 2005).

Ross, A., *The Celebration Chronicles: Life, Liberty, and the Pursuit of Property Value in Disney's New Town* (New York: Ballantine Books, 1999).

Sears, T., "Karow Nord: Rebuilding the German Village," in J. Grant, *Planning the Good Community: New Urbanism in Theory and Practice* (London: Routledge, 2006).

Smith, J., "HOPE VI and the New Urbanism: Eliminating Low-Income Housing to Make Mixed-Income Communities," *Planners Network* 151, 2002, 22–25.

Stead, D. and E. Hoppenbrouwer, "Promoting an Urban Renaissance in England and the Netherlands," *Cities* 21,2, 2004, 119–36.

Steuteville, R., "Numbers Don't Lie: HOPE VI Has Worked Wonders," *New Urban News* 9,4, 2004, 2.

Talen, E., "The Social Goals of New Urbanism," *Housing Policy Debate* 13,1, 2002, 165–88.

Thompson-Fawcett, M., "The Contribution of Urban Villages to Sustainable Development," in K. Williams, E. Burton, and M. Jenks, eds., *Achieving Sustainable Urban Form* (London: E&FN Spon, 2000).

——————, "'Urbanist' Lived Experience: Resident Observations on Life in Poundbury," *Urban Design International* 8, 2003, 67–84.

Till, K., "Neotraditional Towns and Urban Villages: The Cultural Production of a Geography of 'Otherness,'" *Environment and Planning D: Society and Space* 11, 1993, 709–32.

Tu, C. C. and M. J. Eppli, "Valuing New Urbanism: The Case of Kentlands," *Real Estate Economics* 27,3, 1999, 425–51.

Veregge, N., "Traditional Environments and the New Urbanism: A Regional and Historical Critique." *TDSR* VIII,II, 1997, 49–62.

Wiegandt, C.-C., "Mixed Land Use in Germany: Chances, Benefits and Constraints. Paper Prepared for the Invitational Workshop, 'The Role of States and Nation States in Smart Growth Planning'" (Annapolis, MD: National Center for Smart Growth Research and Education, 2004). Available online at www.smartgrowth.umd.edu/InternationalConference/ConferencePapers/.

Wright, E. O., *Class Counts: Comparative Studies In Class Analysis* (New York: Cambridge University Press, 1997).

Zukin, S., *Loft Living: Culture and Capital in Urban Change* (Rutgers: Rutgers University Press, 1989).

PART 3. SUBURBIA, SPRAWL AND URBAN DECLINE

3.1. DOLORES HAYDEN
The Suburban City

1. Jackson, Kenneth T., *Crabgrass Frontier: The Suburbanization of the United States* (New York: Oxford University Press, 1985), 297–304.

2. Fogelson, Robert M., *Downtown: Its Rise and Fall, 1880–1950* (New Haven: Yale University Press, 2001).

3. For example, Adam Rome, *The Bulldozer in the Countryside: Suburban Sprawl and the Rise of American Environmentalism* (New York: Cambridge University Press, 2001); Oliver Gillham, *The Limitless City: A Primer on the Urban Sprawl Debate* (Washington, DC: Island Press,

2002). Also see Tom Daniels, *When City and Country Collide: Managing Growth in the Metropolitan Fringe* (Washington, DC: Island Press, 1999).

4. Lewis, Pierce, "The Galactic Metropolis," in *Beyond the Urban Fringe: Land Use Issues in Nonmetropolitan America*, Rutherford H. Platt and George Macinko, eds. (Minneapolis: University of Minnesota Press, 1983), 23–49; Calthorpe, Peter, and William Fulton, *The Regional City: Planning for the End of Sprawl* (Washington, DC: Island Press, 2001); Warner, Sam Bass Jr., "When Suburbs Are the City," in *Suburbia Re-Examined*, Barbara M. Kelly, ed. (New York: Greenwood Press, 1989), 1–10.

5. Schwartz, Joel, "The Evolution of the Suburbs," in *Suburbia: The American Dream and Dilemma*, Philip C. Dolce, ed. (Garden City, NY: Anchor Books, 1976), 6–8. He mentions early suburban working-class temperance communities, including Morrisania in the Bronx and Temperanceville outside of Pittsburgh. Other scholars who explore class extensively include Bennett Berger, in *Working-Class Suburb: A Study of Auto Workers in Suburbia* (Berkeley, CA: University of California Press, 1960); Carol O'Connor, in "Sorting Out the Suburbs," *American Quarterly* 37, September 1985, 382–94; and Richard Harris, in *Unplanned Suburbs: Toronto's American Tragedy, 1900–1950* (Baltimore, MD: Johns Hopkins University Press, 1996), 286.

6. Chen, David W., "All Languages, All the Time, and All Over the Suburban Dial," *New York Times*, July 17, 2001; Rourke, Mary, "All That's Holy, and Then Some," *Los Angeles Times*, January 6, 2002; Brown, Patricia Leigh, "With an Asian Influx, Suburb Finds Itself Transformed," *New York Times*, May 25, 2001.

7. Becker, Jo, "Suburban Crowding Arouses Tension," *Washington Post*, May 3, 2002; Plotz, David, "A Suburb All Grown Up and Paved Over," *New York Times*, June 19, 2002.

8. The subject of gender and suburbs now has a very large literature of its own, much of it discussed by Dolores Hayden in *Redesigning the American Dream*, rev. ed. (New York: Norton, 2002). In the mid-nineteenth century, affluent suburban women were the wives of homeowners who supervised hardworking female servants, or who did the necessary work of raising families themselves. In that era, working-class married women tended to take in boarders or find other ways to augment the family's income from the suburban house, while unmarried daughters might have paid jobs. By the late twentieth century, women of all classes became more likely to co-own their suburban residences or to own them as heads of households, although others continued to work as domestic servants. As women entered paid employment outside the home in increasing numbers in the late twentieth century, they commuted to urban and suburban jobs while continuing to care for spouses and children. The miles they drive have increased dramatically but their locational choices (for home and paid work) are still not well understood.

9. Cahill, Mary, *Carpool* (New York: Fawcett Crest, 1991), 15.

10. *Roget's International Thesaurus*, 4th ed. (New York: Harper and Row, 1977), 183, 680.

11. Works on suburban housing patterns by architects, landscape architects, and planners include: David P. Handlin, *The American Home: Architecture and Society*, 1815–1915 (Boston: Little, Brown, 1979); Gwendolyn Wright, *Moralism and the Model Home: Domestic Architecture and Cultural Conflict in Chicago, 1873–1913* (Chicago: University of Chicago Press, 1980); Dolores Hayden, *The Grand Domestic Revolution: A History of Feminist Designs for American Homes, Neighborhoods, and Cities* (Cambridge: MIT Press, 1981); Gwendolyn Wright, *Building the Dream: A Social History of Housing in America* (New York: Pantheon, 1981); Robert A. M. Stern with John Massengale, eds., *The Anglo-American Suburb* (London: Special issue of Architectural Design, 1981); Dolores Hayden, *Redesigning the American Dream: Gender, Housing, and Family Life*, rev. ed. (New York: Norton, 2002); Peter Rowe, *Making a Middle Landscape* (Cambridge: MIT Press, 1991); Cynthia L. Girling and Kenneth I. Helphand, *Yard-Street-Park: The Design of Suburban Open Space* (New York: Wiley, 1994). Handlin, Wright, Helphand, and I were all students of John Brinckerhoff Jackson, the editor of *Landscape* magazine.

12. Among these are Andres Duany and Elizabeth Plater-Zyberk, "The Second Coming of the American Small Town," *Wilson Quarterly* 16, Winter 1992, 19–50; Peter Calthorpe, *The Next American Metropolis: Ecology, Community, and the American Dream* (New York: Princeton Architectural Press, 1993); Andres Duany, Elizabeth Plater-Zyberk, and Jeff Speck, *Suburban Nation: The Rise of Sprawl and the Decline of the American Dream* (New York: North Point Press, 2000).

13. Gottdiener, Mark, and Joe R. Feagin, "The Paradigm Shift in Urban Sociology," *Urban Affairs Quarterly* 24, December 1988, 163-87 (special issue devoted to this topic).

14. Molotch, Harvey, "The City as a Growth Machine: Toward a Political Economy of Place," *American Journal of Sociology* 82, September 1976, 309–32.

15. Gottdiener, Mark, *Planned Sprawl: Private and Public Interests in Suburbia* (Beverly Hills, CA: Sage, 1977); Logan, John R., and Harvey L. Molotch, *Urban Fortunes: The Political Economy of Place* (Berkeley, CA: University of California Press, 1987); Logan, John R., Rachel Bridges Whaley, and Kyle Crowder, "The Character and Consequences of Growth Regimes: An Assessment of Twenty Years of Research," *Urban Affairs Review* 32, May 1997, 603–31; Jonas, Andrew E. G., and David Wilson, eds., *The Urban Growth Machine: Critical Perspectives, Two Decades Later* (Albany, NY: State University of New York Press, 1999); Rusk, David, "The Sprawl Machine," in *Inside Game Outside Game: Winning Strategies for Saving Urban America* (Washington, DC: Brookings Institution, 1999), 82–100.

16. Fodor, Eben, *Better Not Bigger: How to Take Control of Urban Growth and Improve Your Community* (Gabriola Island, BC: New Society Publishers, 1999), 30.

17. For example, policy analyst Anthony Downs has written: "Unlimited low-density development has dominated nearly all American policies affecting metropolitan area growth for more than four decades." The authors of a recent book quote him approvingly but state they are "concerned with the results rather than the causes of current development patterns." Anthony Downs, *New Visions for Metropolitan America* (Washington, DC: Brookings Institution and Lincoln Institute of Land Policy, 1994), 5, quoted in F. Kaid Benfield, Matthew D. Raimi, and Donald D. T. Chen, *Once There Were Green Fields: How Urban Sprawl Is Undermining America's Environment, Economy, and Social Fabric* (Washington, DC: Natural Resources Defense Council, 1999), 28, 24.

18. Fishman, Robert, *Bourgeois Utopias: The Rise and Fall of Suburbia* (New York: Basic Books, 1987). For more general discussion see J. John Palen, *The Suburbs* (New York: McGraw-Hill, 1995); David Schuyler, *The New Urban Landscape: The Redefinition of Form in Nineteenth-Century America* (Baltimore, MD: Johns Hopkins University Press, 1986); Margaret Marsh, *Suburban Lives* (New Brunswick, NJ: Rutgers University Press, 1990); Alan Gowans, *The Comfortable House: North American Suburban Architecture 1890–1930* (Cambridge: MIT Press, 1986); Andrew Wiese, "The Other Suburbanites: African American Sub-urbanization in the North before 1950," *Journal of American History* 85, March 1999, 1495–1524; Gail Radford, *Modern Housing in America: Policy Struggles in the New Deal Era* (Chicago: University of Chicago Press, 1996); Rosalyn Baxandall and Elizabeth Ewen, *Picture Windows: How the Suburbs Happened* (New York: Basic Books, 2000); Barbara M. Kelly, *Expanding the American Dream: Building and Rebuilding Levittown* (Albany, NY: State University of New York Press, 1993).

19. The literature is vast. "Bold New City or Built-Up 'Burb? Redefining Contemporary Suburbia," by William Sharpe and Leonard Wallock, in *American Quarterly* 46, March 1994, 1–30, is a review essay with responses.

20. Beecher, Catharine E., "How to Redeem Woman's Profession from Dishonor," *Harper's New Monthly Magazine* 31, November 1865: 71; Harris, Dianne, "Making Your Private World: Modern Landscape Architecture and House Beautiful, 1945–1965," in *The Architecture of Landscape, 1940–1960*, Marc Treib, ed. (Philadelphia: University of Pennsylvania Press, 2002), 182; Cohen, Lizabeth, *A Consumers' Republic: The Politics of Mass Consumption in Postwar America* (New York: Knopf, 2003).

3.3. LOUISE NYSTRÖM

Restraining Sprawl: A Common Interest to Enhance the Quality of Life for All

SOURCES

Bray, Riina, Catherine Vakil, and David Elliott, *Report on Public Health and Urban Sprawl in Ontario. A Review of the Pertinent Literature* (Ontario: College of Family Physicians, Environmental Health Committee, 2005).

Burchell, Robert W., Anthony Downs, Barbara McCann, and Sahan Mukherji, *Sprawl Costs, Economic Impacts of Unchecked Development.* (Washington, DC: Island Press, 2005).

Bruegmann, Robert, *Sprawl: A Compact History.* University of Chicago Press, 2005

Dangschat, Jens, "Case Study Vienna," in Urbs Pandens *Project Summary Paper*, 2004. www.pik-potsdam.de/urbs/projekt.

Hayden, Dolores, *Redesigning the American Dream: Gender, Housing and Family Life* (New York: W.W. Norton, 2002).

Hayden, Dolores, *A Field Guide to Sprawl* (New York: W.W. Norton, 2004).

Rink, Dieter, "Case Study Leipzig," in Urbs Pandens *Project Summary Paper*, 2004. www.pik-potsdam.de/urbs/projekt.

3.4. TOM MARTINEAU
The Emergence of Mixed-Use Town Centers in the United States
1. See http://environment.about.com/od/fossilfuels/a/streetcars.htm.
2. See www.livablecities.org/index.htm.
3. See www.sptimes.com/2002/12/20/news_pf/Citytimes/Winthrop_homes_are_go.shtml.
4. www.suwanee.com/businessgrowth.towncenter.php
5. www.rockvillemd.gov/towncenter/index.html

3.5. ROBERT BEAUREGARD
Urban Design and the Metropolis
Thanks to Andrea Kahn and Zuhal Ulusoy for helpful comments on an earlier draft of this essay.
1. Beauregard, Robert A., "Are cities resurgent?" *City* 8,3, 2004, 421–427.
2. Goldberger, Paul. "The malling of Manhattan," *Metropolis* 20,7, 2001, 135–139, 179.
3. Dunham-Jones, Ellen. "Seventy-five percent: the next big architectural project," *Harvard Design Magazine* 12, 2000, 5–12.
4. Duany, Andres. "Our urbanism," *Architecture* 87,12, 1998, 37–40; Krieger, Alex, "Whose urbanism?" *Architecture* 87,11, 1998, 73–77.
5. Fishman, Robert, *Bourgeois Utopias: The Rise and Fall of Suburbia* (New York: Basic Books, 1987).
6. Jackson, Kenneth T., *Crabgrass Frontier: The Suburbanization of the United States* (New York: Oxford University Press, 1985).
7. Beauregard, Robert A. *Voices of Decline: The Postwar Fate of U.S. Cities*, second edition (New York: Routledge, 2003).
8. Whittemore, Ellen, "Field Cartography: Representing the Suburban Condition," *Harvard Architectural Review* 10, 1998, 82.
9. Dunham-Jones, Ellen, "Seventy-five percent"; Kiefer, Matthew J., "Suburbia and its discontents." *Harvard Design Magazine* 19, 2003/2004, 56–60.
10. Talen, Emily. "New Urbanism and the Culture of Criticism," *Urban Geography* 21,4, 2000, 318–341.

PART 4. STREETS, TRANSPORT AND PUBLIC REALM

4.1. JAN GEHL
Lively, Attractive, and Safe Cities—but how?
SOURCES
Gehl, Jan, *Life Between Buildings*, fifth edition (Copenhagen: Danish Architectural Press, 1996, 2001, 2003). See also www.arkfo.dk
Gehl, J. and Gemzøe, L., *New City Spaces*, (Copenhagen: Danish Architectural Press, 1996, 2004). See also www.arkfo.dk
———, *Public Spaces—Public Life* (Copenhagen: Danish Architectural Press, 1996, 2004). See also www.arkfo.dk
GEHL-Architects, *Towards a Fine City for People—Public Spaces, Public Life, London 2004* (London: Transport for London & Central London Partnership, 2004).
See also www.gehlarchitects.dk

4.2. ALLAN JACOBS
Great Streets and City Planning
1. Reprinted from *Great Streets* by Allan Jacobs, MIT Press. Copyright © 1993 Massachusetts Institute of Technology. Reprinted with permission of MIT Press.
2. Howard, Ebenezer, *Garden Cities of Tomorrow* (London: Faber and Faber, 1946; first published 1898); Le Corbusier, *The Athens Charter*, trans. Anthony Eardley (New York: Grossman, 1973; first published 1943, from a conference of 1933).
3. Stein, Clarence, *Toward New Towns for America* (Liverpool: University Press of Liverpool, 1951). See particularly Sunnyside Gardens as compared to later designs, such as for Radburn, New Jersey, and Greenbelt, Maryland.
4. See, for example, the chapter "Traffic" in *The Athens Charter*.
4. Jacobs, Jane, *The Death and Life of Great American Cities* (New York: Random House, 1961).
5. For example, see Sennett, Richard, *The Fall of Public Man* (New York: Knopf, 1974).
6. Lynch, Kevin, *A Theory of Good City Form* (Cambridge: MIT Press, 1981).
7. Appleyard and Jacobs, "Toward a New Urban Design Manifesto," *Journal of the American Planning Association*, 1987.

4.3. SUZANNE CROWHURST LENNARD
True Urbanism and the European Square: Catalyst for Social Engagement and Democratic Dialogue
1. Crowhurst Lennard, Suzanne, and Henry L. Lennard, "Principles of True Urbanism," brochure published for the fortieth International Making Cities Livable Conference, London, June 2004. See www.Livable Cities.org. See also Crowhurst Lennard, "What Constitutes True Urbanism?," 106–111.
2. Putnam, Robert, *Bowling Alone* (New York: Simon & Schuster, 2000).
3. The agora was, as Wycherley says, "the constant resort of all citizens, and it did not spring to life on special occasions but was the daily scene of social life, business and politics. . . . Here the people could assemble to be harangued; . . . Religious assemblies at the festivals could use the same place. . . . A very simple 'change of scene' was needed to turn the primitive agora, or a part of it, into a market; temporary booths could be set up for the purpose." Wycherley, R. E., *How the Greeks Built Cities*, 55–56.
4. Durant, Will, *The Age of Faith*, 643.
5. Mumford, Lewis, *The City in History*.
6. Berry, Wendell, *What Are People For?*, 157.
7. Georg Simmel defined sociability in "Die Geselligkeit," in *Grundfragen der Soziologie*.
8. "Love… is the feeling that impels us to seek the companionship of our fellows, and the actions of love are all the things we do in the attempt to share our joys and griefs with others." Luciano De Crescenzo, *Thus Spake Bellavista*, 80.
9. Buber, Martin, "Distance & Relation," 104.
10. Lennard, Henry L., and Suzanne Crowhurst Lennard, *The Forgotten Child: Cities for the Well-Being of Children*, 51–62.
11. For a more detailed analysis of essential characteristics, see "Public Space Design," in Crowhurst Lennard, Suzanne, and Henry L. Lennard, *Livable Cities Observed*.
12. In Bury Saint Edmunds, the huge medieval marketplace is now almost completely filled with three rows of substantial buildings; Norwich is currently replacing wooden stalls that fill the marketplace with concrete and glass structures.
13. Over the summer, Saint-Quentin, France, imports hundreds of tons of sand, palm trees, deck chairs, a swimming pool, paddling pool, volley ball court, etc., to transform their square into a beach.

SOURCES
Andrä, Klaus, ed., *Marktplätze* (Berlin: Stapp Verlag, 1990).
Berry, Wendell. *What Are People For?* (San Francisco: North Point Press, 1990).
Buber, Martin, "Distance & Relation," in *Psychiatry*, vol. 20, May 1957.
Cambridge Medieval History, vols. V, VI, and VIII (Cambridge: Cambridge University Press, 1964).
Coubier, Heinz, *Europäische Stadt-Plätze: Genius und Geschichte* (Cologne: DuMont Buchverlag, 1985).
Crowhurst Lennard, Suzanne, *Genius of the European Square* (forthcoming).
Crowhurst Lennard, Suzanne, "What Constitutes True Urbanism?" *Urban Land*, Journal of the Urban Land Institute, March 2006, 106–111.
Crowhurst Lennard, Suzanne, "The European Square," in *Encyclopedia of the City* (Abingdon: Routledge, Taylor & Francis, 2005).
Crowhurst Lennard, Suzanne, "Making a Case for Public Squares," *Planning, Journal of the American Planning Association*, August 2000, 7.
Crowhurst Lennard, Suzanne, "Why Cities Need Squares," *Urban Land*, Journal of the Urban Land Institute, February 2000, 66–7.
Crowhurst Lennard, Suzanne, and Henry L. Lennard, *Livable Cities Observed: A Source Book of Ideas and Images for City Officials, Planners, Architects & Community Leaders* (with H. L. Lennard) (Carmel, CA: Gondolier Press, International Making Cities Livable Council, 1994).
Crowhurst Lennard, Suzanne, "Urban Space Design and Social Life," in *Companion to Contemporary Architectural Thought*, Ben Farmer, Hentie Louw, and Adrian Napper, eds. (London and New York: Routledge, 1994).
Crowhurst Lennard, Suzanne, and Henry L. Lennard. *Public Life in Urban Places* (Carmel, CA: Gondolier Press, 1984).
De Crescenzo, Luciano, *Thus Spake Bellavista* (New York: Picador, 1988).
Durant, Will, *The Age of Faith* (New York: Simon & Schuster, 1950).
Gutkind, E. A., *International History of City Development* (New York: Free Press, 1969).
Mumford, Lewis, *The City in History* (New York: Harcourt Brace Jovanovich, 1961).

Pinon, Pierre, and Caroline Rose, *Places & Parvis de France* (Paris: Imprimerie Nationale Éditions, 1999).

Rincón, Wifredo, *Plazas de España* (Barcelona: Espasa Calpe, S.A., 1999).

Simmel, Georg, "Die Gesellichkeit," in *Grundfragen der Soziologie*, Sammlung Göschen, Band 1101 (Berlin: Walter de Gruyter, 1970).

Thompson, Homer A., and R. E. Wycherley, *The Agora of Athens: The History, Shape, and Uses of an Ancient City Center* (Princeton: American School of Classical Studies at Athens, 1972).

Touring Club Italiano, *Piazze d'Italia* (Milan: Touring Club Italiano, 1998).

Webb, Michael, *The City Square* (New York: Whitney Library of Design, 1990).

Whyte, William H., *The Social Life of Small Urban Spaces* (Washington, DC: Conservation Foundation, 1980).

Zucker, Paul, *Town and Square: From the Agora to the Village Green* (New York: Columbia University Press, 1959).

4.4. ALI MADANIPOUR
Urbanism and the Articulation of the Boundary

1. This chapter draws on the author's book *Public and Private Spaces of the City* (London: Routledge, 2003).

2. For some of the key texts on public sphere, see Hannah Arendt, *The Human Condition* (Chicago: University of Chicago Press, 1958), Jürgen Habermas, *The Structural Transformation of Public Sphere* (Cambridge: Polity Press, 1989), and Richard Sennett, *The Fall of Public Man* (Cambridge: Cambridge University Press, 1976). All tend to contrast the decline of the public space with an apparently golden past.

3. See J. B. Ward-Perkins, *Cities of Ancient Greece and Italy: Planning in Classical Antiquity* (New York: George Braziller, 1974).

4. See Stanley Benn and Gerald Gaus, eds., *Public and Private in Social Life* (London: Croom Helm, 1983).

5. See Richard Sennett, "Reflections on the Public Realm," in Gary Bridge and Sophie Watson, eds., *A Companion to the City* (Oxford: Blackwell, 2000), 380–87.

6. Thomas Nagel, "Concealment and Exposure," *Philosophy and Public Affairs*, vol. 27, no.1, Winter 1998: 3–30.

7. See A. Madanipour, "Marginal Public Spaces in European Cities," *Journal of Urban Design*, vol. 9, no. 3, 2004, 267–286.

8. For a neuroscientist's interpretation, see Susan Greenfield, *The Private Life of the Brain* (London: Allen Lane, The Penguin Press, 2000). For a philosopher's interpretation, see John Searle, *Mind, Language and Society: Philosophy in the Real World* (London: Wiedenfeld & Nicolson, 1999).

9. See John Searle, *The Construction of Social Reality* (London: Penguin, 1995).

10. See a discussion of this role in ancient Greece in Arendt, *The Human Condition*, 63–4.

4.5. GEORGE BAIRD
The New Urbanism and Public Space

1. Sennett, Richard, *The Fall of Public Man* (New York: Random House, 1978), 16.

4.6. ROBERT CERVERO
Transit-Oriented Development in America: Strategies, Issues, Policy Directions

1. Cervero, R., G. B. Arrington, J. Smith-Heimter, R. Dunphy, et al., *Transit Oriented Development in America: Experiences, Challenges, and Prospects*, TCRP Report 102 (Washington, DC: Transit Cooperative Research Program, 2004),.

2. Dunphy, R., "Housing and Traffic," *Urban Land*, vol. 63, no. 2, 2004: 76–80.

3. Ibid.

4. Tumlin, M. and A. Millard-Ball, "How to Make Transit-Oriented Development Work," *Planning*, vol. 69, no. 5, 2003, 14–19.

5. Lund, H., R. Cervero, and R. Willson, *Travel Characteristics of Transit-Focused Development in California* (Oakland: Bay Area Rapid Transit District and California Department of Transportation, 2004).

6. Landis, J., S. Guathakurta, and M. Zhang, *Capitalization of Transportation Investments into Single-Family Home Prices*, Working Paper 619 (Berkeley, CA: Institute of Urban and Regional Development, University of California, 1994).

7. Cervero, R., "The Property Value Case for Transit," in *Developing Around Transit*, Robert T. Dunphy, et al. (Washington, DC: Urban Land Institute, 2004), 31–52.

8. Cervero, R., "Effects of Light and Commuter Rail Transit on Land Prices: Experiences in San Diego County," *Journal of the Transportation Research Forum* vol. 43, no. 1, 2004, 121–138.

9. Lorenz, W., *Designing Light Rail Transit Compatible with Urban Form* (San Diego, CA: San Diego Metropolitan Transit Development Board, 1996).

10. Alonso, W., *Location and Land Use* (Cambridge, MA: Harvard University Press, 1964).

11. Cervero, et al., 2004.

PART 5. THE ELEMENTS OF URBAN DESIGN

5.2. LARS MARCUS
Spatial Capital and How to Measure It—
An Outline of an Analytical Theory of Urban Form

1. Choay, 1997.

2. Hillier, 1996.

3. In the following outline of such an analytical theory it is necessary to state the debt to Bill Hillier and his research colleagues at UCL, since the following theory to a large extent builds on their work. The word "outline" furthermore implies that this is a report from work under way and not the finished thing. Work on a general theory on the relation of urban form and sustainable urban development, is presently under way at the research group Spatial Analysis and Design (SAD) at KTH in Stockholm (www.arch.kth.se/sad).

4. E.g. O'Sullivan, D. and Unwin, D. J., 2003.

5. E.g. Hillier, et al., 1993.

6. E.g. Cutini, 2001.

7. E.g. Desyllas, 2000.

8. Ståhle, A., Marcus, L., and Karlström, A., 2006.

9. For a full theoretical discussion on this shift in type of space, see Marcus, 2000.

10. The concept of capacity is chosen in analogy with the concept of capacity in computer science, the ability to carry differences.

11. It is important to stress that the population that is correlated here consists of no less than 1,700 plots, encompassing a complete inner-city district, including some pure residential areas. Against that background, the correlation for the economical index is surprisingly high rather than low. Furthermore, by excluding 17 out of these 1,700 items, the correlation rises to R2=0,60, which tells us that the correlation is fundamentally strong. Further and more detailed investigations on these promising correlations are currently under way.

12. Bourdieu, 1986.

13. De Soto, 2000.

14. See, for example, the critique put forth by Mike Davis, 2006.

SOURCES

Bourdieu, P., "The forms of capital," in Richardson, J., ed., *Handbook of Theory and Research for the Sociology of Education* (Westport, CT: Greenwood Press, 1986).

Choay, F., *The rule and the Model* (Cambridge, MA: MIT Press, 1997).

Davis, M., *Planet of Slum* (New York: Verso Books, 2006).

De Soto, H., *The Mystery of Capital* (New York: Basic Books, 2000).

Hillier, B., *Space is the Machine* (Cambridge: Cambridge University Press, 1996).

Hillier, B., Penn, A., Hanson, J., Grajewski, T. and Xu, J. "Natural movement: or, configuration and attraction in urban pedestrian movement," *Environment and Planning B: Planning and Design*, vol. 20, 1993, 29–66.

Marcus, L., *Architectural Knowledge and Urban Form—The Functional Performance of Architectural Urbanity*. TRITA-ARK academic dissertation 2000:2. KTH.

Marcus, L., "The impact of land-division on long-term occupation—the possibility of such a thing as natural occupation." *Proceedings Third International Space Syntax Symposium* (Atlanta, GA: Georgia Tech, 2001).

Marcus, L., "Urban form and Sustainable Cities," *Journal of Urban Design*, submitted 2006.

Marcus, L, Steen, J., "Physical planning for economic growth—A Study of Urban Areas," *Proceedings Second International Space Syntax Symposium*. (Brasilia: Universade de Brasilia, 1999).

O'Sullivan, D., and D. J. Unwin, *Geographic Information Analysis* (New York: Wiley, 2003).

Ståhle, A., Marcus, L. and Karlström, A., "Place Syntax—Accessibility with Axial Lines," *Environment and Planning B: Planning and Design*, submitted 2006.

5.3. SERGIO PORTA AND VITO LATORA
Centrality and Cities: Multiple Centrality Assessment
as a Tool for Urban Analysis and Design
1. Wilson, 2000.
2. Porta, et al., 2006 a, b, c; Cardillo, et al., 2006; Crucitti, et al., 2006 a, b; Scellato, et al., 2006.
3. Cardillo, et al., 2006.
4. Hillier, et al., 1993; Penn, et al., 1998.
5. Silverman, 1986; Holm, 1997.
6. Taylor, 1982.
7. Porta, et al., 2006 c.
8. Scheurer and Porta, 2006.

SOURCES
Cardillo, A., Scellato, S., Latora, V., and Porta, S. 2006. *Structural Properties of Planar Graphs of Urban Street Patterns*, Physical Review E, *Journal of the American Physical Society*, 73:6.
Crucitti, P., Latora, V., and Porta, S. 2006a. *Centrality Measures in Spatial Networks of Urban Streets*, Physical Review E, *Journal of the American Physical Society*, 73:3.
Crucitti, P., Latora, V., Porta, S.. 2006b. *Centrality in Networks of Urban Streets, Chaos*, Quarterly of the American Institute of Physics, 16:1.
Hillier, B., Penn, A., Hanson, J., Grajewski, T., Xu J. 1993. *Natural Movement; or, Configuration and Attraction in Urban Space Use*. Environment and Planning B: Planning and Design. 20:1.
Holm, T. 1997. *Using GIS in Mobility and Accessibility Analysis*. ESRI Users Conference, San Diego, CA. www.esri.com/library/userconf/proc97/proc97/to450/pap440/p440.htm.
Penn, A., Hillier, B., Banister, D., Xu, J. 1998. Configurational Modelling of Urban Movement Networks. *Environment and Planning B: Planning and Design*. 25:1.
Penn, A. 2003. *Space Syntax and Spatial Cognition: Or Why the Axial Line?* Environment and Behavior. 35:1.
Porta, S., Crucitti, P., Latora, V. 2006a. *The Network Analysis of Urban Streets: A Dual Approach*. Physical A, Statistical mechanics and its applications. 369:2.
Porta, S., Crucitti, P., Latora, V. 2006b. *The Network Analysis of Urban Streets: A Primal Approach*. Environment and Planning B: Planning and Design. 33:5.
Porta, S., Crucitti, P., Latora, V. 2006c. *Multiple Centrality Assessment in Parma: A Network Analysis of Paths and Open Spaces*, submitted.
Scellato, S., Cardillo, A., Latora, V., Porta, S. 2006. *The Backbone of a City*. European Physical Journal B, 50 1–2.
Scheurer, J., Porta, S. 2006. *Centrality and Connectivity in Public Transport Networks and Their Significance for Transport Sustainability in Cities*, paper presented at the World Planning Schools Congress, Mexico DF, July 13–16, 2006.
Silverman, B. W., *Density Estimation for Statistics and Data Analysis* (London: Chapman and Hall, 1986).
Taylor, J. R., *An Introduction to Error Analysis: The Study of Uncertainties in Physical Measurements*. Mill Valley, CA: University Science Books, 1982).

5.4. ARUN JAIN
Integrated Approaches and Dynamic Processes
SOURCES
Alexander, Christopher. "A City is Not a Tree," *Architectural Forum*, vol. 122, no. 1, April 1965, 58–62 (part 1); vol. 122, no. 2, May 1965, 58–62 (part 2).
Rittel, Horst W. J., and Melvin M. Webber, "Dilemmas in a General Theory of Planning," *Policy Sciences* 4, 1973, 155–169.
Lang, Jon, *Urban Design: A Typology of Procedures and Products* (Burlington, MA: Architectural Press, 2005).

5.5. RICK HALL
Planning for Walkable Streets
1. AASHTO Green Book, 16–17.
2. AASHTO Green Book, 4.
3. AASHTO Green Book, 7.

SOURCES
Flexibility in Highway Design (Washington, DC: Federal Highway Administration, 1997).
A Policy on Geometric Design of Highways and Streets, fourth ed. (Washington, DC: American Association of State Highway and Transportation Officials, 2001).

Duany Plater-Zyberk & Co., *Smart Code*. V 2.6. (Tallahassee, FL: Municipal Code Corporation, 2002).
Chellman, Chester, and F. Spielberg, *Traditional Neighborhood Development Street Design Guidelines* (Washington, DC: Institute of Transportation Engineers, 1999).
Duany, Andres, Elizabeth Plater-Zyberk, and Jeff Speck, *Suburban Nation: The Rise of Sprawl and the Decline of the American Dream* (New York: North Point Press, 2000).
Ewing, Reid, "From Highway to My Way," *Tech Transfer Newsletter*, Spring 2001.
Kunstler, James Howard, *The Geography of Nowhere* (New York: Simon & Schuster, 1993).
Southworth, Michael, and Ben-Joseph, Eran, *Streets and the Shaping of Towns and Cities* (New York: McGraw-Hill, 1996).
Steuteville, Robert, *New Urbanism: Comprehensive Report & Best Practices Guide*, second ed. (Ithaca, NY: New Urban Publications, 2001).

PART 6. REAL ESTATE, CITY MARKETING AND CULTURE

6.2. LAURIE VOLK AND TODD ZIMMERMAN
Confronting the Question of Market Demand
for Urban Residential Development
1. Grissom, Terry V., and Crocker, H. Liu, "The Search for a Discipline: The Philosophy and the Paradigms," in *Appraisal, Market Analysis, and Public Policy in Real Estate*, James R. DeLisle and J. Sa-Aadu, eds. (Boston: American Real Estate Society, 1994), 79.
2. Gordon, Peter, and Harry W. Richardson, "The Destiny of Downtowns: Doom or Dazzle?" *Lusk Review for Real Estate Development and Urban Transformation* 3(2), 1997, 75–76.
3. Myers, Dowell, and Kenneth Beck, "A Four-Square Design for Relating the Two Essential Dimensions of Real Estate Market Studies," in *Appraisal, Market Analysis, and Public Policy in Real Estate*, James R. DeLisle and J. Sa-Aadu, eds. (Boston: American Real Estate Society, 1994), 259.
4. Myers, Dowell, ed., *Housing Demography: Linking Demographic Structure and Housing Markets* (Madison, WI: University of Wisconsin Press, 1990).
5. Rey, Paul H., *The Integral Culture Survey: A Study of the Emergence of Transformational Values in America* (Sausalito, CA: Institute of Noetic Science, 1996).
6. Lang, Robert, James W. Hughes, and Karen A. Danielsen, "Targeting the Suburban Urbanites: Marketing Central-City Housing," *Housing Policy Debate* 8(2), 1997, 437–70.

6.3. CHRISTOPHER LEINBERGER
The Need for Patient Equity in Creating Great Places
1. Walking distance is generally considered to be approximately 1,500 feet or 1,400 meters, which translates into a district that is approximately 160–200 acres or 65–81 hectares. However, transit extends the distance that is considered walkable, either a circulator system such as in Chattanooga (small buses) or Portland (streetcar), or a short-headway light or heavy rail or bus system. Bike travel extends the distance as well. Within that district, most daily needs can be met by walking and/or there is transit to gain access to those needs and employment.
2. Floor-area ratio is a general measure of density. It is measured by dividing the square footage of the building on a parcel of land by the square footage of the parcel. For example, a 20,000-square-foot building, no matter if built as a one-story structure or a higher building, sited on a 100,000-square-foot parcel, has a FAR of 0.2.
3. The construction guarantee is the bank's assurance that if the project fails to repay the construction loan, there are additional financial assurances of repayment, in addition to the bank's assuming ownership of the project. The form of the guarantee is generally the net worth of a corporation or individual. Construction guarantees tend to "burn off" following the meeting of predetermined milestones (construction completion, lease targets met, stabilization of the project's financial performance, etc.).

6.4. ANDERS ALMÉR
A Changed Focus on Retail and its Implications on Planning
1. Slywotski, A. J., Christensen, C. M., Tedlow, R. S., and Carr, N.G., "The Future of Commerce," *Harvard Business Review*, Jan.-Feb. 2000.
2. "How US productivity pulled away," *Financial Times*. Accessed on FT.com, January 24, 2006.
3. *Productivity Growth in Swedish Retail* 1993–2004 (Stockholm: Swedish Institute for Growth Policy Studies, 2006).

4. Bernard, O., et al., *Strategic Format Management* (New York: McKinsey, 2004)

5. Bloom, N. D., *Merchant of Illusion* (Columbus, OH: Ohio State University Press, 2004).

6. Sassen, S., "The City in a Global Digital Age," *Cluster*, May 2005, 116.

7. Arvidsson, A., "Brands," *Journal of Consumer Culture*, vol. 3, no. 1, 2003.

8. Graham, S., and S. Marvin, *Splintering Urbanism* (London: Routledge, 2001).

6.5. GÖRAN CARS
The Role of Culture in Urban Development

1. Cars, G., Healey, P., Madanipour, A., and de Magalhães, C. *Urban Governance, Institutional Capacity and Social Milieux* (Aldershot, UK: Ashgate, 2002).

2. Law, C. L., *Urban Tourism—The Visitor Economy and the Growth of Large Cities. London and New York* (New York: Continuum, 2002).

3. Von Sydow, Å., "Exploring Local Governance in Urban Planning and Development: The Case of Lindholmen, Göteborg." Doctoral Dissertation, 2004. Stockholm: KTH Infrastructure.

4. Law C. L., *Urban Tourism*.

5. Jewson, N., and S. MacGregor, eds., *Transforming Cities: Contested Governance and New Spatial Divisions* (London: Routledge, 1997), 5.

6. King, A. D., *Re-presenting the City: Ethnicity, Capital and Culture in the 21st-Century Metropolis* (London: Macmillan, 1996).

7. Cars, G., "Samspelsprocesser och konflikter inom kulturmiljövården," in Pilvesmaa, M-L., A. Westerlind, and M. Paju, eds., *Plats, drivkraft, samhällsprocess: Vad gör kulturarvet till en resurs för hållbar regional utveckling?* (Stockholm: Riksantikvarieämbetet 2003), 7.; Jewson and MacGregor, *Transforming Cities*, 3; Law, *Urban Tourism*.

8. Elander, I., and M. Blanc, "Partnerships and Democracy—A Happy Couple in Urban Governance?" in van Kempen, R. and H. T. Andersen, eds., *Governing European cities: Social Fragmentation, Social Exclusion and Urban Governance* (Aldershot, UK: Ashgate, 2001); Pierre, J. and B. G. Peters, *Governance, Politics, and the State* (New York: St. Martin's Press, 2000); Gunnarsson, U. *Kultur och attraktivitet—En studie av Ales stenar och Västergötlands museum* (Stockholm: KTH., 2005); Cars, et al., *Urban Governance*; von Sydow, "Exploring Local Governance."

9. Fainstein, S. S., and D. R. Judd, "Global Forces, Local Strategies, and Urban Tourism," in Judd, D. R. and S. S. Fainstein, eds., *The Tourist City* (New Haven and London: Yale University Press, 1999).

10. Kunzmann, K. "Culture, Creativity and Spatial planning," *Town Planning Review*, vol. 75, no. 4., 2004.

11. Bianchini, F., "Remaking European Cities: The Role of Cultural Policies," in Bianchini, F. & Parkinson, M., eds., *Cultural Policy and Urban Regeneration: The West European Experience* (Manchester: Manchester University Press, 1993), 2, 15ff.

12. Law, *Urban Terrorism*.

13. Ibid.

14. Richard, G., "The Development of Cultural Tourism in Europe," in Richard, G., ed., *Cultural Attractions and European Tourism.* (Oxfordshire: CABI Publishing, 2001).

15. Bianchini F., "Remaking European Cities," 2, 15ff.; Hamnett, C. and N. Shoval, "Museums as Flagships of Urban Development," in Hoffman, L. M., S. S. Fainstein, and D. R. Judd, eds., *Cities and Visitors: Regulating People, Markets, and City Space.* (Oxford: Blackwell, 2003), 219–236.

16. Law, *Urban Terrorism*.

17. Gunnarsson, U., *Kultur och attraktivitet.*

18. Isaksson, K. *Folkoperan och kulturverksamheters villkor: Erfarenheter och effekter av en nyskapande musikteater* (Stockholm: KTH, 2004); Nilsson, E. 2004. *Stockholm Globe Arena: En studie av effekter: Publikundersökningar—ett redskap för att mäta ekonomiska effekter samt symbol- och attraktionsvärde* (Stockholm: KTH, 2004); Gunnarsson, U., *Kultur och attraktivitet.*

19. Bianchini F., "Remaking European Cities."

20. Council of Europe Publishing, *In from the Margins: A Contribution to the Debate on Culture and Development in Europe* (Strasbourg: European Task Force on Culture and Development, 1997).

21. Bianchini, F., "Cultural Planning for Urban Sustainability," in Nyström, L., ed., *City Culture—Cultural Processes and Urban Sustainability* (Karlskrona: Swedish Urban Environment Council, 2000).

22. Ibid,, 42.

23. Ibid,, 43ff.

6.6.. KRISTER OLSSON
Heritage Management in Urban Development Planning

1. Kelbaugh, D., "The New Urbanism," in *Common Place: Toward Neighborhood and Regional Design* (Seattle: University of Washington Press, 1997).

2. Casey, E. S., *The Fate of Place* (Berkeley, CA: University of California Press, 1998).

3. Olsson, K., *Från bevarande till skapande av värde. Kulturmiljövården i kunskapssamhället* (Stockholm: KTH, 2003).

4. See, e.g., von Sydow, Å. *Exploring Local Governance in Urban Planning and Development* (Stockholm: KTH, 2004).

5. Hayden, D., *The Power of Place* (Cambridge, MA: MIT Press, 1999).

6. Johansson, B. and F. Snickars, *Infrastruktur. Byggsektorn i kunskapssamhället* (Stockholm: Byggforskningsrådet, 1992).

7. Mohr, E., and J. Schmidt, "Aspects of Economic Valuation of Cultural Heritage," in Baer, N. S., and R. Snethlage, eds., *Saving Our Architectural Heritage: The Conservation of Historic Stone Structures* (Chichester: Wiley, 1997).

8. For example, Healey, P., *Collaborative Planning. Shaping places in Fragmented Societies* (London: Macmillan, 1997).

9. Olsson, K., *Från bevarande till skapande av värde. Kulturmiljövården i kunskapssamhället* (Stockholm: KTH, 2003).

PART 7. SUSTAINABILITY, TECHNOLOGY AND THE ENVIRONMENT

7.1 PETER NEWMAN
Does New Urbanism Really Overcome Automobile Dependence?

1. Lee, E. and A. Perl, *The Integrity Gap* (Vancouver: University of British Columbia Press, 2003).

2. Newman, P. W. G., and J. R. Kenworthy, *Cities and Automobile Dependence* (Aldershot, UK: Gower, 1989); Newman, P. W. G., and J. R. Kenworthy, *Sustainability and Cities: Overcoming Automobile Dependence* (Washington, DC: Island Press, 1999); Kenworthy, J. R. and F. B. Laube, *An International Sourcebook of Automobile Dependence in Cities, 1960–1990* (Niwot, Colorado: University Press of Colorado, 1999.

3. Chandra, L., *Modelling the impact of urban form and transport provision on transport-related greenhouse gas emissions*. Masters Thesis, 2006. Perth: Murdoch University Institute for Sustainability and Technology Policy.

4. Newman, P., and J. Kenworthy, "Urban Design to Reduce Automobile Dependence in Centres," *Opolis*, 2(3), 2006, 35–52.

5. Newman, P. W. G., and J. R. Kenworthy, *Sustainability and Cities.*

7.2. TIMOTHY BEATLEY
Green Urbanism: A Manifesto for Re-Earthing Cities

1. See Girardet, H., *Creating Sustainable Cities* (Devon: Green Book, 1999); Register, R. R., *Ecocities: Building Cities in Balance with Nature* (Berkeley, CA: Berkeley Hills Books, 2002); Newman, P. and J. Kenworthy, *Sustainability and Cities: Overcoming Automobile Dependence* (Washington, DC: Island Press, 1999); Platt, R., ed., *The Ecological City* (Amherst, MA: University of Massachusetts Press, 1994).

2. McDonough, W. and M. Braungart, *Cradle to Cradle: Remaking the Way We Make Things* (Northport: Northport Press, 2002).

3. See Newman and Kenworthy, *Sustainability and Cities*; also see Beatley, T., *Native to Nowhere: Sustaining Home and Community in the Global Age* (Washington, DC: Island Press, 2004), chapter 6.

4. See Beatley, *Native to Nowhere*; also see Beatley, T., *Green Urbanism: Learning from European Cities* (Washington, DC: Island Press, 2000).

5. Wilson, E. O., *Biophilia* (Cambridge, MA: Harvard University Press, 1986); Wilson, E. O., and S. Kellert, *The Biophilia Hypothesis* (Washington, DC: Island Press, 1995).

6. Kuo, F. E. and W. C. Sullivan, "Aggression and Violence in the Inner City: Effects of Environment via Mental Fatigue," *Environment and Behavior*, 33(4), 2001, 543–571; Ulrich, Roger, "View through a window may influence recovery from surgery," *Science*, 224, 1984, 420–21.

7. Louv, Richard, *Last Child in the Woods: Saving Our Children from Nature Deficient Disorder* (New York: Algonquin, 2005).

8. See Newman and Kenworthy, *Sustainability and Cities.*

9. Beatley, *Native to Nowhere*; see also Gordon, D., ed., *Green Cities: Ecologically Sound Approaches to Urban Space* (London: Black Rose, 1996).

7.3. DUSHKO BOGUNOVICH
Eco-Tech Urbanism: Towards the Green and Smart City
SOURCES

Bogunovich, D. "Eco-tech Cities: Smart Metabolism for a Green Urbanism," in *The Sustainable City II*, proceedings of the second conference on Urban Regeneration and Sustainability, Segovia, Spain, July 2002 (Wessex: WIT Press, 2002), 75–84.

Girardet, H., *Creating Sustainable Cities*. Schumacher briefing no. 2 (Devon: Green Books, 1999).

Marras, A., *Eco-Tec Architecture of the In-Between* (New York: Princeton Architectural Press, 2000).

Newman, P. and J. Kenworthy, *Sustainability and Cities* (Washington, DC: Island Press, 1999).

Russell, J. S., "Landscape Urbanism," *Architectural Record*, August 2001, 66–84.

Shane, G., "The Emergence of 'Landscape Urbanism'," *Harvard Design Magazine* 19, Fall 2003/Winter 2004.

UNEP-IETC, *Cities Are Not Cities*. Working paper (Osaka/Shiga: UNEP-International Environmental Technology Centre, 2003).

7.4. LARS LERUP
On Community (from Zoon Politikon to Multitude)

1. www.Lakewood.com. The Lakewood church, previously located outside Houston's inner loop, has at this writing moved inside the loop and so joined the general flight back to the city. The former Compaq Center, a site for sports and entertainment, has been transformed into the Lakewood International Center.

2. Giorgio Agamben, *Homo Sacer: Sovereign Power and Bare Life* (Stanford, CA: Stanford University Press, 1998), 181–182.

PART 8. URBAN DIGITAL SPACES AND CYBER CITIES

8.2. STEPHEN GRAHAM
Urban Network Architectures and the Structuring of Future Cities

1. Solnit and Schwartenberg. 2000.

SOURCES

Castells, M. and P. Hall, *Technopoles of the World* (London: Routledge, 1994).

Graham, S. and S. Marvin, *Splintering Urbanism: Networked Infrastructures, Technological Mobilities and the Urban Condition* (London: Routledge, 2000).

Markusen, A., "Sticky Places in Slippery Space: A Typology of Industrial Districts," in T. Barnes and M. Gertler, eds., *The New Industrial Geography* (London: Routledge, 1999), 98–123.

Solnit, R. and S. Schwartenberg, *Hollow City: Gentrification and the Eviction of Urban Culture* (London: Verso, 2000).

Zook, M., "The Web of Production: The Economic Geography of Commercial Internet Content in the United States," *Environment and Planning A*, 32, 2000, 411–426.

8.3. MALCOLM McCULLOUGH
Locative Media Urbanism

1. Where 2.0: http://conferences.oreillynet.com/where2006/; and International Society of Electronic Arts, www.urban-atmospheres.net/ISEA2006/.

2. Dourish, Paul, *Where the Action Is* (Cambridge, MA: MIT Press, 2001).

3. Walker, John, "Through the Looking Glass," in *The Art of Human Computer Interaction* (Reading, MA: Addison Wesley, 1989).

4. Rheingold, Howard, *Smart Mobs—The Next Social Revolution* (New York: Basic Books, 2002); also www.smartmobs.com.

5. Townsend, Anthony, "Digitally Mediated Urban Space: New Lessons for Design," *Praxis* 6, 2005.

6. Graham, Steven, and Simon Martin, *Telecommunications and the City—Electronic Spaces, Urban Places* (London: Routledge, 1996). See also Graham, Steven, and Simon Martin, *Splintering Urbanism—Networked Infrastructures, Technological Mobilities, and the Urban Condition* (London: Routledge, 2001).

7. Nardi, Bonnie, ed., *Context and Consciousness: Activity Theory and Human-Computer Interaction* (Cambridge, MA: MIT Press, 1996).

8. Ibid.

9. Suchman, Lucy, *Plans and Situated Actions* (Cambridge and New York: Cambridge University Press, 1986).

10. Ito, Mizumi, *Personal, Portable, Pedestrian: Mobile Phones in Japanese Life* (Cambridge, MA: MIT Press, 2005).

11. John Thackara, *In the Bubble—Designing in a Complex World* (Cambridge, MA: MIT Press, 2005).

12. Thackara, John, "The Design Challenge of Pervasive Computing," ACM CHI keynote, 1999; www.doorsofperception.com

13. Anderson, Chris; 2005; www.longtail.typepad.com/the_long_tail/.

l4. Engstrom, Jyri; www.zengestrom.com/blog/tagging/.

15. Vander Wal, Thomas; www.vanderwal.net.

16. www.dodgeball.com

17. Mitchell, William, *Me++: The Cyborg Self and the Networked City* (Cambridge, MA: MIT Press, 2003).

8.4. BARRY WELLMAN
What is the Internet Doing to Community—and Vice Versa?

1. Gopnik, Adam, "Bumping Into Mr. Ravioli," *New Yorker*, September 30, 2002, 80–84.

2. See the review in Wellman, Barry, and Milena Gulia. "Net Surfers Don't Ride Alone: Virtual Communities as Communities," in *Networks in the Global Village*, Barry Wellman, ed., (Boulder, CO: Westview, 1999), 331–366.

3. Ibid.; Sandwell, Barry, "Monsters in Cyberspace: Cyberphobia and Cultural Panic in the Information Age." *Information, Communication and Society* 9 (1), 2006, 39–61.

4. Quoted in Fox, Robert. "Newstrack," Communications of the ACM 38 (8), 1995, 11–12.

5. Powell, Betsy. "MySpace Used to 'Lure' Girl, 13." *Toronto Star*, July 12, 2006; www.thestar.com.

6. "Social Networking Sites Like MySpace.com Are Among the Most Popular Internet Sites." Radio broadcast, July 11, 2006. Toronto: 680 News; see also Abbott, Greg, "Testimony of Greg Abbott, Attorney General of Texas," House Energy and Commerce Committee, Subcommittee on Telecommunications and the Internet (Washington, DC: July 11, 2006).

7. Wellman, Barry, "The Community Question Re-evaluated," in *Power, Community and the City*, Michael Peter Smith, ed. (New Brunswick, NJ: Transaction, 1988), 81–107.

8. Wellman, B., ed., *Networks in the Global Village* (Boulder, CO: Westview Press, 1999).

9. Chen, Wenhong, and Barry Wellman, "Charting Digital Divides: Within and Between Countries," in *The Internet in Everyday Life*. Barry Wellman and Caroline Haythornthwaite, eds. (Oxford: Blackwell, 2005), 74–113.

10. McLuhan, Marshall, *Understanding Media: The Extension of Man* (New York: McGraw-Hill, 1964).

11. Bradner, Erin, Wendy Kellogg, and Thomas Erickson, "Social Affordances of BABBLE." Presented to the European Computer Supported Cooperative Work Conference, Copenhagen, 1998.

12. Boase, Jeffrey, John Horrigan, Barry Wellman, and Lee Rainie. "The Strength of Internet Ties" (Washington, DC: Pew Internet and American Life Project, 2006); www.pewinternet.org; Wellman, Barry, and Bernie Hogan, with Kristen Berg, Jeffrey Boase, Juan-Antonio Carrasco, Rochelle Côté, Jennifer Kayahara, Tracy L. M. Kennedy, and Phuoc Tran, "Connected Lives: The Project," in *Networked Neighbourhoods: The Online Community in Context*, Patrick Purcell, ed. (Guildford, UK: Springer, 2006), 157–211; Wellman, Barry and Caroline Haythornthwaite, eds., *The Internet in Everyday Life* (Oxford: Blackwell, 2002).

13. Bastani, Susan, "Muslim Women On-Line," *Arab World Geographer* 3 (1), 2000. 40–59.

14. Kraut, Robert, Michael Patterson, Vicki Lundmark, Sara Kiesler, Tridas Mukhopadhyay, and William Scherlis. "Internet Paradox: A Social Technology that Reduces Social Involvement and Psychological Well-Being?" *American Psychologist* 53 (9), 1998, 1017–1031.

15. Kraut, Robert, Sara Kiesler, Bonka Boneva, Jonathon Cummings, Vicki Helgeson, and Anne Crawford, "Internet Paradox Revisited," *Journal of Social Issues* 58 (1), 2002, 49–74; Bessière, Katherine, Sara Kiesler, Robert Kraut, and Bonka Boneva, "Effects of Social Resources and Internet Use on Depressive Affect Over Time." *Information, Communication, and Society,* 11 (1), 2008, in press.

16. McLuhan, Marshall, *The Gutenberg Galaxy: The Making of Typographic Man* (Toronto: University of Toronto Press, 1962).

17. Wellman, 2002; Wellman, 2003.

18. Mok and Wellman, 2007.

19. See also the studies in Quan-Haase, Anabel, B. Wellman, James C. Witte, and Keith N. Hampton, "Capitalizing on the Net: Social Contact, Civic Engagement, and Sense of Community," in *The Internet in Everyday Life*, 291–324; Carrasco, Juan-Antonio. "Social Activity Travel Behaviour: A Personal Networks Approach" (Doctoral Dissertation, 2006, University of Toronto Department of Civil Engineering); Carrasco, Juan-Antonio,

Bernie Hogan, Barry Wellman, and Eric Miller, "Collecting Social Network Data to Study Social Activity-Travel Behavior: An Egocentric Approach." *Environment and Behavior B*: 2006; Wellman and Hogan, et al. 2006.

20. For example, Kakuko Miyata, Barry Wellman, and Jeffrey Boase, "The Wired—and Wireless—Japanese: Webphones, PCs, and Social Networks," in *Mobile Communication: Re-Negotiation of the Social Sphere.* Rich Ling and Per Pedersen, eds. (London: Springer, 2005), 427–49.

21. Castells, Manuel, Imma Tubella, Teresa Sancho, and Isabel Diaz de Isla, *The Network Society in Catalonia* (Barcelona: UOC Press, 2000).

22. Kennedy, Tracy, and Barry Wellman, "The Networked Household," in *Information, Communication and Society 10*, (5), 2007, in press.

23. McPherson, Miller, Lynn Smith-Lovin, and Matthew E. Brashears, "Social Isolation in America: Changes in Core Discussion Networks Over Two Decades," *American Sociological Review* 71, 2006, 353–75.

24. Stein, Maurice, *The Eclipse of Community* (Princeton, NJ: Princeton University Press, 1960); Wellman, Barry, and Barry Leighton, "Networks, Neighborhoods and Communities," *Urban Affairs Quarterly* 14, 1979, 363–90.

25. Wellman, Barry, "Physical Place and Cyber-Place: Changing Portals and the Rise of Networked Individualism," *International Journal for Urban and Regional Research* 25, 2001, 227–52.

SEE ALSO

Boase, Jeffrey. "America Online and Offline" (Doctoral Dissertation, 2006, University of Toronto Department of Sociology).

Hampton, Keith, and Barry Wellman, "The Not So Global Village of Netville," in *The Internet in Everyday Life*, Barry Wellman and Caroline Haythornthwaite, eds. (Oxford: Blackwell, 2002), 345–371.

Hampton, Keith, and Barry Wellman, "Neighboring in Netville: How the Internet Supports Community and Social Capital in a Wired Suburb," *City and Community* 2 (3), 2003, 277–311.

PART 9. SOCIAL CAPITAL AND MUTUAL BENEFIT

9.3. KEVIN LEYDEN AND PHILIP MICHELBACH
Democracy and "Neighborly Communities:"
Some Theoretical Considerations on the Built Environment

1. Jacobs, 1961.
2. Jacobs, 1961, 56.
3. Verba, Schlozman, and Brady, 1995.
4. For an argument connecting trust to democratic citizenship, see Warren, 1999, 310. (Also Putnam, 2000; Fukuyama, 1995; Coleman, 1990)
5. But see the suggestive discussion in Hénaff and Strong, 2001. In addition, Bachelard (1969) argued that the subject's conception of space is central to the development of personality. Scott (1999, 276–82) has argued that Jacobs has the causality backwards: National politics determines neighborhood conditions, but Mansbridge (1999, 211) implies that encouraging "everyday talk" between citizens should help their capacity for democratic deliberation.
6. Putnam, 2003.
7. Oliver, 2001.
8. Leyden, 2003.
9. Emile Durkheim's foundational study *Suicide* examines precisely this question (Durkheim, 1951).
10. There have been a few recent attempts to approach this issue. For instance, see Coles, 2005. Michel Foucault has also written on the importance of architecture as both a literal and metaphorical basis for contemporary politics. (Foucault, 1979, especially chapter 3, "Panopticism")
11. Aristotle, 1996, 13.
12. Burckhardt, 1963.
13. Long, 1962.
14. Gunnell has written compellingly on the basis for this move. He argues that German émigré political theorists replaced a kind of traditional engaged American political theory with a more rarefied philosophical discourse associated with concerns imported from Weimar Germany (Gunnell, 1993).
15. Even the relationship with walking does not appear incidental. The Aristotelian tradition of political thought is known as "peripatetic" (one might say "walking philosophy").
16. Dewey, 1927, 154.
17. Westbrook, 1991, citing Dewey 1927, 146.
18. On Dewey's connection to democratic thought, see Fott, 1998.
19. Dewey, 1927, 158.
20. Ibid., 209.
21. Ibid., 211.
22. Ibid., 211-21.

23. Ibid., 213.
24. Ibid.
25. Ibid., 219.
26. Jürgen Habermas has written extensively on the development of a public sphere in modernity and its eclipse since the eighteenth century: One condition of the decline of the public sphere is the decline of public spaces and the rise of mass, media-dominated discourse (Habermas, 1991). There is a relevant discussion of the radicalized distinction between private (home) and public (the outside world) in Béteille (2003, 49). He argues that conceptions of public and private may be made complementary through a widened conception of democratic citizenship.
27. There is recent work suggesting that neighborhood design's interaction with democracy is not tied solely to the United States, or even the West. Leyden's study took place in Ireland (Leyden, 2003); see also Sellers, 2002, and Irazábal, 2005.
28. Gunnell, 1993.
29. Wertenbaker, 1947.
30. See the collection of anti-federalist writings in Ketcham, 1986. There is a helpful discussion in Fishkin, 1991.
31. Arendt, 2000, 515.
32. Duany, et al., 2000, 60-61.
33. Ibid., chapter 7.

SOURCES

Arendt, Hannah, *The Portable Hannah Arendt*, Peter Baehr, ed. (New York: Penguin, 2000).

Aristotle, *The Politics and The Constitution of Athens*, translated by Benjamin Jowett (Cambridge: Cambridge University Press, 1996).

Bachelard, Gaston, *The Poetics of Space*, translated by Maria Jolas (Boston: Beacon Press, 1969).

Béteille, André, "The Public as a Social Category," in *The Public and the Private: Issues of Democratic Citizenship*, Gurpreet Mahajan and Helmut Reifeld, eds. (Thousand Oaks, CA: Sage, 2003).

Burckhardt, Jacob, *History of Greek Culture*, translated by Palmer Hilty (New York: Ungar, 1963).

Coleman, James S., *Foundations of Social Theory* (Cambridge, MA: Harvard University Press, 1990).

Coles, Romand, *Beyond Gated Politics: Reflections for the Possibility of Democracy* (Minneapolis: University of Minnesota Press, 2005).

Dewey, John, *The Public and Its Problems* (Chicago: Henry Holt, 1927).

Duany, Andres, Elizabeth Plater-Zyberk, and Jeff Speck, *Suburban Nation: The Rise of Sprawl and the Decline of the American Dream* (New York: North Point Press, 2000).

Durkheim, Emile, *Suicide: A Study in Sociology*, translated by John A. Spaulding and George Simpson (Glencoe, IL: Free Press, 1951).

Fishkin, James S., *Democracy and Deliberation: New Directions for Democratic Reform* (New Haven: Yale University Press, 1991).

Fott, David, *John Dewey: America's Philosopher of Democracy* (Lanham, MD: Rowman & Littlefield, 1998).

Foucault, Michel, *Discipline and Punish: The Birth of the Prison*, translated by Alan Sheridan (New York: Vintage, 1979).

Fukuyama, Francis, *Trust: Social Virtues and the Creation of Prosperity* (New York: Free Press, 1995).

Gunnell, John G., *The Descent of Political Theory: The Genealogy of an American Vocation* (Chicago: University of Chicago Press, 1993).

Habermas, Jürgen, *The Structural Transformation of the Public Sphere* (Cambridge, MA: MIT Press, 1991).

Hénaff, Marcel, and Tracy B. Strong, "The Conditions of Public Space: Vision, Speech, and Theatricality," in *Public Space and Democracy*, Marcel Hénaff and Tracy B. Strong, eds. (Minneapolis: University of Minnesota Press, 2001).

Irazábal, Clara, *City Making and Urban Governance in the Americas: Curitiba and Portland* (Burlington, VT: Ashgate, 2005).

Jacobs, Jane, *The Death and Life of Great American Cities* (New York: Random House, 1961).

Ketcham, Ralph, *The Anti-federalist Papers and the Constitutional Convention Debates* (New York: Penguin, 1986).

Leyden, Kevin M., "Social Capital and the Built Environment: The Importance of Walkable Neighborhoods" *American Journal of Public Health*, vol. 93, no. 9: 2003, 1546–1551.

Long, Norton, "Aristotle and the Study of Local Government," in *The Polity*, Charles Press, ed. (Chicago: Rand McNally, 1962).

Mansbridge, Jane, "Everyday Talk in the Deliberative System," in *Deliberative Politics: Essays on Democracy and Disagreement*, Stephen Macedo, ed. (Cambridge: Cambridge University Press, 1999).

Oliver, J. Eric, *Democracy in Suburbia* (Princeton, NJ: Princeton University Press, 2001).

Putnam, Robert D., *Bowling Alone: The Collapse and Revival of American Community* (New York: Simon & Schuster, 2000).

Scott, James C., "Geographies of Trust, Geographies of Hierarchy," in *Deliberative Politics: Essays on Democracy and Disagreement,* Stephen Macedo, ed. (Cambridge: Cambridge University Press, 1999).

Sellers, Jeffrey, *Governing from Below: Urban Regions and the Global Economy.* (Cambridge: Cambridge University Press, 2002).

Verba, Sidney, Kay Lehman Schlozman, and Henry E. Brady, *Voice and Equality: Civic Voluntarism in American Politics* (Cambridge, MA: Harvard University Press, 1995).

Warren, Mark E., "Democratic Theory and Trust," in *Democracy and Trust,* Mark E. Warren, ed. (Cambridge: Cambridge University Press, 1999).

Westbrook, Robert B., *John Dewey and American Democracy* (Ithaca, NY: Cornell University Press, 1991).

9.4. KARL OLOV ARNSTBERG
Sprawling Cities

1. Ruskin, John, *Sesame and Lillies*, Gertrude Buck, ed. (New York: Longmans Green, 1905.), 73.

2. Stone, Lawrence J., *The Family, Sex and Marriage in England, 1500–1800* (New York: Harper & Row, 1977).

3. Sennett, Richard, *The Conscience of the Eye: The Design and Social Life of Cities* (New York: Knopf, 1990), 21.

4. Fishman, Robert, *Bourgeois Utopias: The Rise and Fall of Suburbia* (New York: Basic Books, 1987), 40. The villa suburbanae that wealthy Romans set outside Rome, as well as the Renaissance palazzos in Florence and Venice, could be seen as prototypes.

5. Braudel, Fernand, *The Structures of Everyday Life: The Limits of the Possible* (London: Fontana, 1979.), 503.

6. Fishman, *Bourgeois Utopias*, 6.

7. Mumford, Lewis, *The Culture of Cities* (New York: Harcourt Brace, 1938).

8. Engels, Friedrich, *The Condition of the Working Class in England* (1844) (Harmondsworth: Penguin, 1987).

9. Parkinson, Richard, *On the Present Condition of the Labouring Poor in Manchester; With Hints for Improving It* (London. 1841).

10. Jackson, Kenneth T., *Crabgrass Frontier: The Suburbanization of the United States* (New York: Oxford University Press, 1985), 79.

11. Fishman, *Bourgeois Utopias*, 115.

12. Dag, Österberg, *Arkitektur og sosiologi i Oslo: en sosio-materiell fortolkning* (Oslo: Pax, 1998), 43.

9.5. DAVID BRAIN
Beyond the Neighborhood: New Urbanism as Civic Renewal

1. See, for example, the article in the *New York Times Magazine* "The Battle for Biloxi," May 21, 2006, and other comments on the work of New Urbanists in the rebuilding of the Mississippi coastal towns in the wake of Hurricane Katrina, as well as the comments in the national press on New Urbanist proposals for New Orleans.

2. My research on changes in the social technology of place-making has been funded by grants from the Graham Foundation for Advanced Studies in the Fine Arts, and a fellowship from the National Endowment for the Humanities, Fellowships for College Teachers.

3. For the seminal discussion of social capital, see Robert Putnam, *Bowling Alone: The Collapse and Revival of American Community* (New York: Simon & Schuster, 2000). For more on the idea of civic renewal and civic innovation, see Carmen Sirianni and Lewis Friedland, *Civic Innovation in America: Community Empowerment, Public Policy, and the Movement for Civic Renewal* (Berkeley, CA: University of California Press, 2000).

4. Sirianni and Friedland focus primarily on four areas where they have found manifestations of this movement: community organizing and urban development, civic environmentalism, community health, and public journalism. They note in passing that similar processes of "reframing" have been taking place in movements focused in other areas: community justice, social services, higher education, and "New Urbanism in architecture" (241). They stop short of exploring the importance of an explicit connection to physical design.

5. Chris Leinberger has pointed out that there are nineteen standardized real estate products. See Christopher Leinberger, "The market and Metropolitanism," *The Brookings Review*, Fall, 1998.

6. For an extended discussion of convention zoning, see Jonathan Levine, *Zoned Out* (Washington, DC: RFF, 2005).

7. For more on this idea of a "quiet revolution" in regulation, see Adam Rome, *The Bulldozer in the Countryside: Suburban Sprawl and the Rise of American Environmentalism* (Cambridge: Cambridge University Press, 2001).

8. This tendency has been documented more generally by political scientists. See John R. Hibbing, and Elizabeth Theiss-Morse, *Stealth Democracy: American Beliefs about How Government Should Work* (Cambridge: Cambridge University Press 2002). See also Nina Eliasoph, *Avoiding Politics: How Americans Produce Apathy in Everyday Life* (Cambridge: Cambridge University Press, 1998).

9. For those not familiar with the current usage of the term, the charrette is an intensive design workshop, commonly of three to ten days in duration, which involves bringing a team of designers and consultants together (typically, on site). For a more detailed discussion of the techniques associated with the charrette, see Bill Lennertz and Aarin Lutzenhiser, *The Charrette Handbook* (Chicago, IL: Planners' Press, American Planning Association, 2006).

10. It is critical not to conflate the coding of urbanism with the coding of architectural style. Although architectural style is part and parcel of some form-based codes, the extent to which these codes regulate style is completely dependent on the particular community. An example of a form-based code can be seen in the Smart Code, originally developed by Duany Plater-Zyberk and Company, and now being widely distributed at no cost. See also the resources available on the web site of the Form-Based Code Institute (www.formbasedcodes.org).

11. See Duany, Andres, and Emily Talen, "Transect Planning," *Journal of the American Planning Association* 68, Summer 2002, 245–67. See also Talen, Emily, "Help for Urban Planning: The Transect Strategy," *Journal of Urban Design*, 7(3), 2002, 293–312.

12. It is often necessary, for example, to formulate trade-offs between the preservation of natural features and the realization of a quality of urbanism that is socially and economically sustainable.

13. See Sidney Brower, *Good Neighborhoods: A Study of In-Town and Suburban Residential Environments* (New York: Praeger, 2000).

14. For a more extended discussion of the transect technique, and its relationship to the politics of environmentalism in the context of growth management, see Duany, Andres and David Brain, "Regulating As If Humans Matter: The Transect and Post-Suburban Planning," 293–332, in Ben-Joseph, Eran, and Terry S. Szold, eds., *Regulating Place: Standards and the Shaping of Urban America* (New York: Routledge, 2005).

15. This idea has been pursued in a more explicit and comprehensive way in the recent work of Christopher Alexander on generative coding.

16. For an extensive review of the various criticisms of the New Urbanism, as well as the rebuttal arguments, see Cliff Ellis, "The New Urbanism: Criticism and Rebuttals," *Journal of Urban Design*, vol 7, no. 3, 2002, 261–291.

17. New urbanism has a great deal in common with what has been called "civic environmentalism," an environmental movement that implies the ability to mobilize social interests and political power in recognition of a common stake in a shared environment (Shutkin, 2000).

9.6. KNUT STRÖMBERG
Urban Design and Development in the Swedish Tradition

1. Bryson and Crosby, 1996.
2. Healey, 1997.
3. E.g., Forester, 1999; Healey, 1997)
4. Flyvbjerg, 1998.
5. Evans and Strömberg, 2001.
6. Strömberg, 2001.
7. Lindblom, 1959.
8. Forrester, 1999.
9. Schön, 1983.
10. Schön and Rein, 1994.
11. Rosenhead, 2004.
12. Friend and Jessop, 1969.
13. Friend and Hickling, 1987, 1997, 2005.
14. Strömberg, 2001.
15. Flyvbjerg, 2001; Strömberg and Kain, 2005.

SOURCES

Bryson, M. J., and B. Crosby. "Planning and the Design and use of Forums, Arenas, and Courts," in *Explorations in Planning Theory*, Mandelbaum, et al., eds. (New Brunswick, NJ: Rutgers University Press, 1996).

Evans, B., and K. Strömberg, *A New Professionalism for City Development.* Paper presented to the WPS Congress, Shanghai, 2001.

Flyvbjerg, B., *Rationality & Power: Democracy in Practice* (Chicago: University of Chicago Pressm 1998).

Flyvbjerg, B., *Making Social Science Matter: Why Social Enquiry Fails and How It Can Succeed Again* (Cambridge: Cambridge University Press, 2001).

Friend, J. K., and A. Hickling, *Planning Under Pressure: The Strategic Choice Approach* (Oxford: Elsevier, 1987, 2005).

Friend, J. K., and N. Jessop, *Local Government and Strategic Choice: An Operational Research Approach to the Processes of Public Planning* (Oxford: Pergamon Press, 1977).

Forester, J., *The Deliberative Practitioner: Encouraging Participatory Planning Processes* (Cambridge, MA: MIT Press, 1999).

Healey, P., *Collaborative Planning: Shaping Places in Fragmented Societies*. (Hong Kong: MacMillan Press, 1997.)

Khakee, A., and K. Strömberg, "Applying Future Studies and the Strategic Choice Approach in Urban Planning," *Journal of the Operational Research Society* 44(3), 1993, 213–224.

Lindblom, C., "The Science of 'Muddling Through,'" *Public Administration Review* 19, 1959.

Rosenhead, J., ed., *Rational Analysis for a Problematic World—Problem-structuring Methods for Complexity, Uncertainty and Conflict* (Chichester: Wiley, 1994, 2004).

Schön, D., *The Reflective Practitioner: How Professionals Think in Action* (New York: Basic Books, 1983).

Schön, D., and M. Rein, *Frame Reflection: Toward the Resolution of Intractable Policy Controversies* (New York: Basic Books, 1994).

Strömberg, K., "Facilitating Urban Collaborative Decision Development in Urban Planning," *Scandinavian Journal of Architectural Research* 4, 2001.

Strömberg, K., and J. H. Kain, "Communicative Learning, Democracy and Effectiveness: Facilitating Private-Public Decision-Making in Sweden," in Friend, J. K., and A. Hickling, *Planning Under Pressure: the Strategic Choice* (Oxford: Elsevier, 2005).

PART 10. COMPLEXITY SCIENCE AND NEW URBAN FORMS

10.1. MICHAEL BATTY
Hierarchy, Scale, and Complexity in Urban Design
1. Jacobs, 1961.
2. Alexander, 1964.
3. Alexander, 2003.
4. Batty, 2005.
5. Simon, 1962.
6. Alexander, 1964.
7. Batty and Longley, 1994; Salingaros, 1998.
8. Zipf, 1949.
9. West, Brown, Enquist, 1997
10. Batty, 2006; Christaller, 1933, 1966)

SOURCES
Alexander, C., *Notes on the Synthesis of Form* (Cambridge, MA: Harvard University Press, 1964).

Alexander, C., *The Nature of Order* (four vols.) (Berkeley, CA: Center for Environmental Structure, 2003).

Batty, M., *Cities and Complexity: Understanding Cities with Cellular Automata, Agent-Based Models, and Fractals* (Cambridge, MA: MIT Press, 2005).

Batty, M., "Hierarchy in Cities and City Systems," in D. Pumain, ed., *Hierarchy in the Natural and Social Sciences* (Dordrecht: Springer, 2006), 143–168.

Batty, M.. and Longley, P. A., *Fractal Cities: A Geometry of Form and Function* (San Diego: Academic Press, 1994).

Christaller, W., *Central Places in Southern Germany* (translation of *Die zentralen Orte in Süddeutschland* [1933], by C. W. Baskin) (Englewood Cliffs, NJ: Prentice-Hall, 1966).

Jacobs, Jane, *The Death and Life of Great American Cities* (New York: Random House, 1961).

Salingaros, N. A., "Theory of the Urban Web," *Journal of Urban Design* 3, 1998, 53–71.

Simon, H. A., "The Architecture of Complexity," *Proceedings of the American Philosophical Society* 106, 1962, 467–482.

West, G. B., J. H. Brown, and B. J. Enquist, "A General Model for the Origin of Allometric Scaling Laws in Biology," *Science* 276, 1997, 122–126.

Zipf, G. K., *Human Behavior and the Principle of Least Effort* (Reading, MA: Addison-Wesley, 1949).

10.2. LUCIEN STEIL, NIKOS A. SALINGAROS, AND MICHAEL MEHAFFY
Growing Sustainable Suburbs: An Incremental Strategy for Reconstructing Modern Sprawl
1. Salingaros, 2005.
2. Ibid.
3. Alexander, 2004.
4. Duany and Plater-Zyberk, 2005.
5. Alexander, 2004; Salingaros 2006.
6. Krier, 1984.
7. Salingaros, 2005.
8. Duany and Plater-Zyberk, 2005.

SOURCES
Alexander, Christopher, "A City is Not a Tree," *Architectural Forum*, vol. 122, no. 1, 1965, 58–61, and no. 2, 1965, 58–62; reprinted in Thackara, John, ed., Design After Modernism (London: Thames and Hudson, 1988), 67–84.

Alexander, Christopher, *A Vision of a Living World: The Nature of Order, Book 3* (Berkeley, CA: Center for Environmental Structure, 2004).

Duany, Andres, and Elizabeth Plater-Zyberk, *Smart Code*, Version 6.4, 2005 (www.dpz.com).

Duany, Andres, Elizabeth Plater-Zyberk, and Jeff Speck, *Suburban Nation* (New York: North Point Press, 2000).

Krier, Léon, *Houses, Palaces, Cities*, Demetri Porphyrios, ed. (London: Academy Publications, 1984).

Papayanis, Nicholas, *Planning Paris Before Haussmann* (Baltimore, MD: Johns Hopkins University Press, 2004).

Podobnik, Bruce, "The Social and Environmental Effects of New Urbanism: Evidence from Orenco Station," 2002 (www.lclark.edu/~podobnik/orenco02.pdf).

Salingaros, Nikos A., *Principles of Urban Structure* (Amsterdam: Techne Press, 2005).

———, "Compact City Replaces Sprawl," to appear as a chapter in a book by the Delft School of Design, Arie Graafland and Deborah Hauptmann, eds. (Rotterdam: 010 Publishers, 2006).

10.3. T. IRENE SANDERS
Complex Systems Thinking and New Urbanism
1. Sanders and McCabe, 2003.
2. Alexander, 2005, 2003; Bookman, 2003; Gladwell, 2000; Holland, 1995; Jacobs, 1992; Johnson, 2001; Mooney, 2004; Waldrop, 2002.
3. Sanders, 2003.
4. Sanders, 2003.
5. Ilachinski, 2001.
6. Sanders, 1998.
7. Turcott and Rundle, 2002.
8. Lorenz, 1963; Sanders, 2003.
9. Sanders, 1998; Weick, 2001.
10. Ilachinski, 2006, 2004; CSCS.
11. Axtell, Epstein, et al., 2002.
12. Bookman, 2003.
13. Aaltonen and Sanders, 2006.
14. Aaltonen and Sanders, 2006, 2005.
15. Snowden and Stanbridge, 2004.
16. Ilachinski, 2004; Johnson, 2001.
17. Ilachinski, 2004.
18. Ibid.
19. Mandelbrot, 1983.
20. Ibid.
21. Sanders, 1998.
22. Mandelbrot, 1983.
23. Sanders1998.
24. Ibid.
25. Ibid.
26. European Union Report, 2005.

SOURCES
Aaltonen, M., and Sanders T. I., "Identifying Systems' New Initial Conditions as Influence Points for the Future," *Foresight: The Journal of Future Studies, Strategic Thinking and Policy*, vol. 8, no. 3, 2006, 28–35.

———, "Complexity as a Sensemaking Framework for Methodology," in *Complexity as a Sensemaking Framework*, Mika Aaltonen, ed. (Turku, Finland: Finland Futures Research Centre, Turku School of Economics and Business Administration, 2005).

Alexander, Christopher. "Harmony-Seeking Computation." Conference paper, 2005. (www.cs.york.ac.uk/nature/workshop/Alexander Abstract.html.)

————, *The Luminous Ground: The Nature of Order, Book 4* (Berkeley, CA: Center for Environmental Structure, 2003).

Axtell, Robert L., Joshua M. Epstein, et al., "Population Growth and Collapse in a Multiagent Model of Kayneta Anasazi in Long House Valley," *Proceedings of the National Academy of Sciences of the United States of America*, vol. 9, supplement 3, May 14, 2002, 7275–7279.

Bookman, Joel D., "Building Participation and Relationships in a Complex Community: Adapting to Change in the North River Neighborhood," *Perspectives on Civic Activism and City Life*, vol. 11, Winter 2003, 9–13.

Chui, Glenda, "Unified Theory is Getting Closer, Hawking Predicts," *San Jose Mercury News*, January 23, 2000.

CSCS (Center for the Study of Complex Systems, University of Michigan), "What is the Study of Complex Systems?" (www.cscs.umich.edu)

Gladwell, Malcolm, "Designs for Working," *The New Yorker*, December 11, 2000.

Holland, John H., *Hidden Order: How Adaptation Builds Complexity* (Reading, MA: Addison-Wesley, 1995).

Ilachinski, Andrew, *Order, Disorder, Chaos and Complexity: A Physicist's/Analyst's Perspective*. Briefing, Center for Naval Analysis, Alexandria, Virginia, 2006.

————, *Artificial War: Multiagent-Based Simulation of Combat* (Singapore: World Scientific, 2003).

————, *Cellular Automata: A Discrete Universe* (Singapore: World Scientific, 2001).

Jacobs, Jane, *The Death and Life of Great American Cities* (New York: Random House, 1961).

Johnson, Steven, *Emergence: The Connected Lives of Ants, Brains, Cities and Software* (New York: Scribner, 2001).

Lorenz, Edward N., "Deterministic Nonperiodic Flow," *Journal of the Atmospheric Sciences*, March 1963, 130–141.

Mandelbrot, Benoit, *The Fractal Geometry of Nature* (New York: W. H. Freeman, 1983).

Mooney, A., "The Theory and Measurement of Community Development." Personal memorandum to Jonathan F. Fanton, president of the John D. and Catherine T. MacArthur Foundation, May 18, 2004.

Sanders, T. Irene, and Judith A. McCabe, *The Use of Complexity Science*. Report to the United States Department of Education, 2003. (www.complexsys.org/news.htm)

Sanders, T. Irene, "What is Complexity?" Catalogue essay for fine arts exhibit entitled "Complexity." (Washington, DC: Board of Governors of the Federal Reserve Board, 2003), 1–2.

————, *Strategic Thinking and the New Science: Planning in the Midst of Chaos, Complexity and Change* (New York: Free Press, 1998).

Snowden, D., and P. Stanbridge, "The Landscape of Management: Creating the Context for Understanding Social Complexity." *E:CO*, vol. 6, nos.1/2, 2004, 140–148.

Turcotte, Donald L., and John B. Rundle. Self-organized Complexity in Physical, Biological and Social Systems." Proceedings of the National Academy of Sciences of the United States of America, vol. 99, supplement 1, 2002, 2463–2465.

Waldrop, M. Mitchell, "The Management Secrets of the Brain," *Business 2.0*, October 2002, 123–125.

Weick, Karl E., *Making Sense of the Organization* (Malden, MA: Blackwell, 2001).

10.5. AYSSAR ARIDA
Quantum Urbanism: Urban Design in the Post-Cartesian Paradigm

See, for example, the work of the Hyperbody Research Group at the Technical University of Delft, or the "Doha Gardens" project "Overall Winner" and "Masterplanned Communities Winner" at the MIPIM/AR Awards 2006, by Q-DAR in collaboration with NGAP. (q-dar.com and ngarchitecture.com)

SOURCES

Arida, A., *Quantum City* (New York: Architectural Press, 2002).

Oosterhuis, K. and L. Feiress, eds., *The Architecture Co-Laboratory: Game, Set and Match II—On Computer Games, Advanced Geometries, and Digital Technologies* (conference proceedings) (Rotterdam: Episode Publishers, 2006).

Peat, F. D., *Blackfoot Physics* (Fourth Estate, 1994).

Orwell, G., "The Principles of Newspeak," in *1984* (Penguin, 1954).

Zohar, D., and I. Marshall, *The Quantum Society* (Bloomsbury, 1995).

Eco, U., *The Search for the Perfect Language (the Making of Europe)* (Blackwell, 1997).

Sennett, R., *The Conscience of the Eye* (Faber and Faber, 1991).

See also the following Web sites: www.quantumcity.com; www.quantum architecture.net; www.comparch.org/articles/; www.cityofsound.com; www.limitedlanguage.org.

PART 11. BEYOND URBANISM AND THE FUTURE OF CITIES

11.2. ROBERT FISHMAN
New Urbanism in the Age of Re-Urbanism

1. Jargowsky, Paul A., *Poverty and Place: Ghettos, Barrios, and the American City* (New York: Russell Sage Foundation, 1997).

2. Berry, Brian J. L., "Islands of Renewal in Seas of Decay," in Paul Peterson, ed., *The New Urban Reality* (Washington, DC: Brookings Institution Press, 1985), chapter 4.

3. The best account of the 1992 riots and their implications for urbanism can be found in Aseem Inam, *Planning for the Unplanned: Recovering from Crises in Megacities* (New York: Routledge, 2005).

4. For a synthetic account of Re-Urbanism, see my article "The Fifth Migration," *Journal of the American Planning Association* 71, 4, Autumn 2005, 357–367.

5. Nelson, Arthur C., "Toward A New Metropolis: The Opportunity of Rebuild America" (Washington, DC: Brookings Institution Metropolitan Policy Program, 2004).

6. Hughes, James W., and Joseph J. Seneca, "The Beginning of the End of Sprawl?" *Rutgers Regional Report*, May 2004.

7. Calthorpe Peterm and William Fulton, *The Regional City: Planning for the End of Sprawl* (Washington, DC: Island Press, 2001), 243–271.

8. For the details of this perspective, see my article "The Fifth Migration"; on "unslumming," see Jane Jacobs, *The Death and Life of Great American Cities* (New York: Random House, 1961), chapter 15; see also Richard L. Florida, *Cities and the Creative Class* (New York: Routledge, 2004).

9. Fasenfest, David, Jason Booza, and Kurt Metzger, *Living Together: A New Look at Racial and Ethnic Integration in Metropolitan Neighborhoods, 1990–2000* (Washington, DC: Brookings Institution Center on Urban and Metropolitan Policy, 2004).

10. Urban Design Associates, "East Baltimore Comprehensive Redevelopment Plan," in Congress for the New Urbanism, *Charter Awards 2003*, 12–13. For the complete plan, see http://www.urbandesignassociates.com/ project_Detail.asp?ProjectMainID=42&Section=4 [accessed August 3, 2006].

11. *Places* 17, 2, Summer, 2005, 8–67. In addition to articles by the two editors, the section includes a portfolio of projects as well as important articles by Michael Dobbins, Christopher B. Leinberger, Paul Mitchell Hess, Susan Rogers, Darren Petrucci, Lars Lerup, Renee Chow, Roger Sherman, and Michael Freedman.

12. Schaffer, Daniel, *Garden Cities for America: The Radburn Experience* (Philadelphia: Temple University Press, 1982).

13. The best recent analysis of New Town planning and design is by Ann Forsyth in *Reforming Suburbia: The Planned Communities of Irvine, Columbia, and The Woodlands* (Berkeley, CA: University of California Press, 2005).

14. As my colleague Chris Leinberger has shown, current American development practices, limited by new forms of securitized financing, have become far more standardized and oriented toward the short term than the 1920s practices that inspired Lewis Mumford's passionate protests. See Christopher B. Leinberger, "Retrofitting Real Estate Finance: Alternatives to the Nineteen Standard Product Types," *Places* 17, 2, Summer, 2005, 24–29. In the same issue, pages 54–58, Renee Chow analyzes the comparable design paralysis in "Ossified Dwellings: Or Why Contemporary Suburban Housing Can't Change."

15. Moudon, Anne Vernez, and Paul Mitchell Hess, "Suburban Clusters: The Nucleation of Multifamily Housing in Suburban Areas in the Central Puget Sound," *Journal of the American Planning Association* 66, 3, Summer, 2000, 243–265.

16. Calthorpe, Peter, "New Urbanism: Principle or Style?" in *The New Urbanism*, vol. 2 of *Michigan Debates on Urbanism*, Robert Fishman, ed. (Ann Arbor, MI: University of Michigan, 2005), 18–20.

17. The full implications of such zoning are analyzed in my colleague Jonathan Levine's important book *Zoned Out: Regulation, Markets, and Transportation-Land-Use Choice* (Washington, DC: Resources for the Future, 2005).

18. Egan, Timothy, "Vibrant Cities Find One Thing Missing: Children," *New York Times*, March 24, 2005; Booza, Jason C., Jackie Cut-

singer, and George Galster, *Where Did They Go? The Decline of Middle-Income Neighborhoods in Metropolitan America* (Washington, DC: Brookings Institution Metropolitan Policy Program, 2006).

11.3. EDWARD ROBBINS
The New Urbanism in the Twenty-first Century: Progress or Problem?

1. Norquist, 1999.
2. Kelbaugh, 2002.
3. Stern in MacCannell, 1999, 112.
4. I do not include those who limit their fundamental criticism to an attack on what they see as the New Urbanists' reliance on a neotraditionalist style.
5. Duany and Plater-Zyberk, 1994.
6. Cf., Urban Land Institute.
7. Harvey, 2000, 171.
8. Bender, 1982, 4.
9. Duany, 2002.
10. Cf., Breugmann, 2005.
11. United Nations, 2006.
12. Lewis, 2006.
13. Cf., Robbins, 2004.
14. Robbins, 2004, 229.

SOURCES
Bender, Thomas, *Community and Social Change in America* (Baltimore, MD: Johns Hopkins University Press, 1982).

Breugmann, Robert, *Sprawl: A Compact History* (Chicago: University of Chicago Press, 2005).

Calthorpe, Peter, "One," in *Charter of the New Urbanism* (New York: McGraw-Hill, 2000), 15–22.

Cervero, Robert, "Subcentering and Commuting: Evidence from the San Francisco Bay Area, 1980–1990" (Berkeley, CA: University of California Transportation Center, 1996).

Duany, Andres, "The Transect," in *Journal of Urban Design* 7(3), 2002, 251–60.

Duany, Andres, and Elizabeth Plater-Zyberk, "The Neighborhood, the District and the Corridor," in Peter Katz, ed., *The New Urbanism* (New York: McGraw-Hill, 1994), xvii–xx.

Frug, Gerald, "Urban or Suburban? A Discussion," *Harvard Design Magazine*, Winter/Spring 1997, 46–63.

Harvey, David, *Spaces of Hope* (Berkeley, CA: University of California Press, 2000).

Kelbaugh, Douglas S., *Repairing the American Metropolis: Common Place Revisited* (Seattle: University of Washington Press, 2002).

Lewis, Jim, "Battle for Biloxi," *New York Times*, May 21, 2006.

MacCannell, Dean, "'New Urbanism' and Its Discontents," in J. Copjec and M. Sorkin, eds., *Giving Ground: The Politics of Propinquity* (London: Verso, 1999).

Norquist, John O., *The Wealth of Cities: Revitalizing the Centers of American Life* (Reading, MA: Addison-Wesley, 1999).

Robbins, Edward, "The New Urbanism and the Fallacy of Singularity," in *Urban Design International*, vol. 3, no. 1, 1998, 33–42.

———, "The New Urbanism," in Rodolphe Khoury and Edward Robbins, eds., *Shaping the City: Studies in History, Theory and Urban Design* (London: Spon Press, 2004), 212–230.

Scully, Vincent, "Architecture of Community," in Peter Katz, ed., *The New Urbanism* (New York: McGraw-Hill, 1994), 221–230.

United Nations Habitat, *Cities Report 2006–2007*.

Urban Land Institute, *Shopping Center Development Handbook* (Washington, DC, 1985).

11.4. SASKIA SASSEN
Making Public Interventions in Today's Massive Cities

1. For one of the best treatments of such *terrains vagues*, see Ignasi Solá Morales, *Obra*, Vol. 3 (Barcelona: Editorial Gigli, 2004). For an example of an intervention in one of these terrain vagues, in this case in the city of Buenos Aires, see the Web site of Kermes Urbana (www.m7red.com.ar/m7-KUintro1.htm), an organization that seeks to produce public space by reactivating such *terrains vagues*.

2. There is an interesting scholarship on this issue. It is impossible to do justice to it in such a short piece. Let me just mention a few texts that show the diversity of approaches: Richard Lloyd, *Neobohemia: Art and Commerce in the Post-Industrial City* (New York and London: Routledge, 2005); Roger A. Salerno, *Landscapes of Abandonment: Capitalism, Modernity and Estrangement* (Albany, NY: SUNY Press, 2003); John Phillips, Wei-Wei Yeo, Ryan Bishop, *Postcolonial Urbanism: South East Asian Cities and Global Processes* (New York and London: Routledge, 2003).

3. See, for instance, Malcolm Miles, *Art, Space and the City* (New York and London: Routledge, 1997); George Yudice, *The Expediency of Culture: Uses of Culture in the Global Era* (Durham, NC: Duke University Press, 2003).

4. This is one of the aims of the Zaragoza (Spain) Digital Mile project (www.milladigital.es).

5. E.g., Arie Graafland, *The Socius of Architecture* (Delft: Delft School of Architecture, 2000) and Carol J. Burns and Andrea Kahn, eds., *Site Matters* (New York and London: Routledge, 2005). Of interest here is the fact that in 2006 the Venice Biennale of Architecture was focused on cities, for the first time in its history; see Ricky Burdett, ed., *Cities: People, Society, Architecture*, catalogue of the 2006 Venice Biennale of Architecture (New York: Rizzoli, 2006).

6. Two websites that provide information about a whole variety of initiatives that have these types of aims are www.generalizedempowerment.org and www.citymined.org.

6. See, for instance, the types of projects at www.transgressivearchitecture.org.

7. For a variety of representations of citiness, see, for instance, Linda Krause and Patrice Petro, eds., *Global Cities: Cinema, Architecture, and Urbanism in a Digital Age* (New Brunswick, NJ: Rutgers University Press, 2003). On architecture, see Kester Rattenbury, *This is Not Architecture: Media Constructions.* (New York and London: Routledge, 2001).

8. For one of the most original and theorized treatments of this subject, see Andre Drainville, *Contesting Globalization: Space and Place in the World Economy* (London: Routledge, 2005).

9. See, for instance, Anne Bartlett, "The City and the Self: The Emergence of New Political Subjects in London," in *Deciphering the Global: Its Spaces, Scales and Subjects*, S. Sassen, ed. (New York and London: Routledge, 2007).

10. Elsewhere I have shown in detail the complex imbrications of the digital and the material, and of flows and places. See chapter 7 in my book *Territory, Authority, Rights: From Medieval to Global Assemblages* (Princeton, NJ: Princeton University Press, 2006).

11. There are other dimensions that specify the global city; see my book *The Global City* (Princeton, NJ: Princeton University Press, 2001).

12. For a full development of this issue see chapters 5 and 7 of *Territory, Authority, Rights*.

13. See www.gnu.org for more information.

14. Indymedia is "a network of collectively run media outlets for the creation of radical, accurate, and passionate tellings of the truth." See www.indymedia.org.

15. See www.raqsmediacollective.net.

16. See also the notion of ghetto cosmopolitanism in Rami Nashashibi, "Ghetto Cosmopolitanism: Making Theory at the Margins," in *Deciphering the Global: Its Spaces, Scales and Subjects*, S. Sassen, ed. (New York and London: Routledge, 2007),

17. They are also multivalent; that is, some are "good" and some are "bad." I use the term as an analytic category to designate a whole range of dynamics and initiatives that are centered in the new capabilities for global operation coming out of the corporate global economy but used for purposes other than their original design: examples range from alter-globalization political struggles to informal global economic circuits, and, at the limit, global terrorist networks.

18. Digital City Amsterdam (DDS) was an experiment facilitated by De Balie, Amsterdam's cultural center. Subsidized by the Amsterdam Municipality and the Ministry of Economic Affairs, it allowed people to access the digital city host computer and retrieve council minutes and official policy papers, or visit digital cafés and train stations. See http://reinder. rustema.nl/dds/ for documentation; see the chapter by Lovink and Riemens in *Global Networks, Linked Cities* (New York and London: Routledge, 2002) for the full evolution, from beginning to end, of DDS.

19. An international media arts festival (www.transmediale.de).

20. A campaign carried by autonomous groups, religious initiatives, trade unions and individuals to support refugees and undocumented immigrants. For more information, see www.contrast.org/borders/.

21. London based media activists and artists (www.mongrelx.org).

22. www.metamute.com.

23. A festival that explores wireless and mobile media (www.futuresonic.com).

24. A theater festival that often includes multiple political projects (www.theaterderwelt.de).

11.6. MANUEL CASTELLS
Space of Flows, Space of Places: Materials for
a Theory of Urbanism in the Information Age
SOURCES

Ascher, F., *La Metapolis, ou l´Avenir de la Ville* (Paris: Odile Jacob, 1995).

Blakely, E. and S., *Fortress America: Gated Communities in the United States* (Washington, DC: The Brookings Institution, 1997).

Borja, J. and C., *Local and Global: The Management of Cities in the Information Age.* (London: Earthscan, 1997).

Borja, J., with Zaida, M., *L´Espai Public: Ciutat i Ciutadania* (Barcelona: Diputacio de Barcelona, 2001).

Brand, S., *The Clock of the Long Now* (New York; Basic Books, 1999).

Capra, F., *The Web of Life* (New York: Doubleday, 1996).

Castells, M., "Grassrooting the Space of Flows," in J. Wheeler, Y. Aoyama, and B. Warf, eds., *Cities in the Telecommunications Age: The Fracturing of Geographies* (London: Routledge, 2000), 18–30.

Castells, M., *The Internet Galaxy* (Oxford: Oxford University Press, 2001).

———, *The Power of Identity* (Oxford: Blackwell, 1997).

———, *The Rise of The Network Society*, revised edition (Oxford: Blackwell, 2000).

Castells, M., and Servon, L., *The Feminist City: A Plural Blueprint* (Berkeley, CA: University of California, Department of City Planning, 1996, unpublished).

Davis, M., *City Of Quartz* (New York: Vintage, 1992).

Dunham-Jones, E., "Seventy-five Percent," *Harvard Design Magazine*, Fall, 2000, 5–12.

Fernandez-Galiano, L., "Spectacle and its discontents," *Harvard Design Magazine*, Fall, 2000, 35–38.

Freire, M., and Stren, R., eds., *The Challenge of Urban Government: Policies and Practices* (Washington, DC: The World Bank Institute, 2001).

Garreau, J., *Edge City: Life On The New Frontier* (New York: Doubleday. 1991).

Gillespie, A., and R. Richardson, "Teleworking and the City: Myths of Workplace Transcendence and Travel Reduction," in J. Wheeler, Y. Aoyama, and B. Warf, eds., *Cities in the Telecommunications Age: The Fracturing of Geographies* (London: Routledge, 2000), 228–248.

Graham, S., and S. Marvin, *Splintering Urbanism: Networked Infrastructures, Technological Mobilities, and the Urban Condition* (London: Routledge, 2001).

Hall, P., *Cities in Civilization* (New York: Pantheon, 1998).

Hall, P., "Global City-Regions in the 21st Century," in Scott, A., ed., *Global City-Regions: Trends, Theory, Policy* (New York: Oxford University Press, 2001), 59–77.

Horan, T., *Digital Place: Building Our City of Bits* (Washington, DC: Urban Land Institute, 2000).

Human Development Report, United Nations Development Program, *Technology and Human Development* (New York: Oxford University Press, 2001).

Jacobs, A., *Great Streets* (Cambridge, MA: MIT Press, 1993).

Jones, S., ed., *Cybersociety 2.0* (London: Sage, 1998).

Klinenberg, E., *The Social Anatomy of a Natural Disaster: The Chicago Heat Wave of 1995.* Ph.D. dissertation, 2000, University of California, Berkeley, Dept. of Sociology; unpublished.

Kopomaa, T., *The City In Your Pocket: Birth of the Mobile Information Society* (Helsinki: Gaudeamus, 2000).

Kotkin, J., *The New Geography: How The Digital Revolution Is Reshaping The American Landscape* (New York: Random House, 2000).

Kuntsler, G., *The Geography of Nowhere* (New York: Simon and Schuster, 1993).

Massey, D., "The Age of Extremes: Inequality and Spatial Segregation in the 20th Century." Presidential address, Population Association of America, 1996.

Mitchell, W., *E-Topia* (Cambridge, MA: MIT Press, 1999).

Nel.Lo, O. *Ciutat de Ciutats.* (Barcelona: Editorial Empuries, 2001).

Putnam, R., *Bowling Alone: The Collapse and Revival of American Community.* (New York: Simon & Schuster, 2000).

Russell, J., "Privatized Lives," *Harvard Design Magazine*, Fall, 2000, 20–29.

Sassen, S., *The Global City: London, Tokyo, New York* (Princeton, NJ: Princeton University Press, 1991).

———, "Global Cities and Global City-Regions: A Comparison," in Scott, A., ed., *Global City-Regions: Trends, Theory, Policy* (New York: Oxford University Press, 2001), 78–95.

Scott, A., ed., *Global City-Regions: Trends, Theory, Policy* (New York: Oxford University Press, 2001).

Sorkin, Michael, *Variations on a Theme Park: The New American City and the End of Public Space* (New York: Hill and Wang, 1997).

Susser, I., "The Construction of Poverty and Homelessness in U.S. Cities," in *Annual Reviews of Anthropology*, 25, 1996, 411–35.

Verwijnen, J., and Lehtovuori, P., eds., *Creative Cities* (Helsinki: University of Art and Design).

Waldinger, R., ed., *Strangers at the Gate: New Immigrants in Urban America* (Berkeley, CA: University of California Press, 2001).

Wellman, B., ed., *Networks in the Global Village* (Boulder, CO: Westview Press, 1999).

Wellman, B., and C. Haythornthwaite, eds., *The Internet in Everyday Life* (Oxford: Blackwell, 2002).

Wheeler, J., Y. Aoyama, and B. Warf, *Cities in the Telecommunications Age: The Fracturing of Geographies* (London: Routledge, 2000).

CONTRIBUTORS

CHRISTOPHER ALEXANDER
Professor in the Graduate School and Emeritus Professor of Architecture at the University of California, Berkeley.

ANDERS ALMÉR
Principal of REBUS / Almér Consulting Group.

KARL OLOV ARNSTBERG
Professor of Ethnology and Planning, Stockholm University.

AYSSAR ARIDA
Urban Architect and Writer, Founder of The Centre for the Spatial Realm (CSR).

GEORGE BAIRD
Professor and Dean of the Faculty of Architecture, Landscape, and Design, University of Toronto.

MICHAEL BATTY
Bartlett Professor of Planning at University College London, where he directs the Centre for Advanced Spatial Analysis (CASA).

TIMOTHY BEATLEY
Teresa Heinz Professor of Sustainable Communities in the Department of Urban and Environmental Planning at the University of Virginia, Charlottesville.

ROBERT BEAUREGARD
Professor of Urban Planning in the Graduate School of Architecture, Planning, and Preservation at Columbia University.

DUSHKO BOGUNOVICH
Associate Professor of Urban Design, School of Architecture and Landscape Architecture, UNITEC Institute of Technology, Auckland, New Zealand.

DAVID BRAIN
Associate Professor of Sociology, Division of Social Science at the New College of Florida, Sarasota.

PETER CALTHORPE
Urban Planner and Architect, Principal and Founder of Calthorpe Associates: Urban Designers, Planners, Architects. Co-Founder of Congress for the New Urbanism (CNU).

GÖRAN CARS
Professor of Regional Planning, School of Architecture and the Built Environment, Royal Institute of Technology, Stockholm.

MANUEL CASTELLS
Professor Emeritus of Sociology and City and Regional Planning at the University of California, Berkeley, and Wallis Annenberg Chair of Communication Technology and Society at the Annenberg School of Communication at the University of Southern California.

ROBERT CERVERO
Professor of City and Regional Planning, the College of Environmental Design, University of California, Berkeley.

ANDRÉS DUANY
Architect and Urban Planner, Principal and Founder of Duany Plater Zyberk & Company (DPZ). Co-Founder of Congress for the New Urbanism (CNU).

ELLEN DUNHAM-JONES
Architect, Associate Professor, and Director of the Architecture Program at the Georgia Institute of Technology.

LEWIS FELDSTEIN
Writer and President of the New Hampshire Charitable Foundation.

ROBERT FISHMAN
Professor of Architecture and Urban Planning at the University of Michigan, A. Alfred Taubman College of Architecture + Urban Planning.

RICHARD FLORIDA
Hirst Professor of Public Policy at George Mason University and Founder and Principal of the Creativity Group Team and Catalytix Consulting.

PETER HALL
Professor of Planning at the Bartlett School of Architecture and Planning, University College London.

JAN GEHL
Principal of Gehl Architects—Urban Quality Consultants, and Professor Emeritus of Urban Design at the School of Architecture in Copenhagen, Denmark.

ROBERT GIBBS
Landscape Architect and Consultant and Principal of Gibbs Planning Group.

STEPHEN GRAHAM
Professor of Human Geography, Department of Geography at the University of Durham, and Deputy Director of the Centre for the Study of Cities and Regions.

JILL GRANT
Professor of Planning and School of Planning Director, Dalhousie University, Halifax Nova Scotia.

RICK HALL
President of Hall Planning and Engineering and Professor at the Department of Urban and Regional Planning, Florida State University.

TIGRAN HAAS
Assistant Professor of Urban Planning and Design, School of Architecture and the Built Environment, Royal Institute of Technology, Stockholm.

DOLORES HAYDEN
Professor of Architecture, Urbanism, and American Studies, Yale University.

BILL HILLIER
Professor of Architectural and Urban Morphology in the University of London and Director of the Space Syntax Laboratory at University College London.

ALLAN JACOBS
Professor Emeritus in the Department of City and Regional Planning at the University of California, Berkeley.

ARUN JAIN
Chief Urban Designer (Bureau of Planning), City of Portland, Oregon. Adjunct Associate Professor, Portland Urban Architecture Program, University of Oregon.

DOUGLAS KELBAUGH
Dean and Professor of Architecture and Urban Planning at the University of Michigan, A. Alfred Taubman College of Architecture + Urban Planning.

LÉON KRIER
Architect, Theorist, and Urban Planner.

JAMES HOWARD KUNSTLER
Author, Social Critic, and Blogger.

VITO LATORA
Assistant Professor, Department of Physics, University of Catania.

CHRISTOPHER LEINBERGER
Land Strategist and Developer, Research Fellow at The Brookings Institution, and Professor of Practice in Urban Planning at the University of Michigan, A. Alfred Taubman College of Architecture + Urban Planning.

SUZANNE CROWHURST LENNARD
Executive Director and Co-Founder of International Making Cities Livable.

LARS LERUP
Dean of the School of Architecture and William Ward Watkin Professor of Architecture, Rice University, Houston.

KEVIN LEYDEN
Associate Professor of Political Science at West Virginia University and Director of the Institute for Public Affairs.

LARS MARCUS
Director of Spacescape AB and Senior Lecturer and Researcher at the School of Architecture and the Built Environment, Royal Institute of Technology, Stockholm.

TOM MARTINEAU
Senior Manager, Evergreen Solutions, LLC and Professor Emeritus, Florida A&M University

ALI MADANIPOUR
Professor of Urban Design, School of Architecture, Planning, and Landscape, University of Newcastle-upon-Tyne.

MALCOLM MCCULLOUGH
Associate Professor of Architecture and Design at the University of Michigan, A. Alfred Taubman College of Architecture + Urban Planning.

WILLIAM McDONOUGH
Architect and Designer, Principal and Founder of William McDonough + Partners.

MICHAEL MEHAFFY
President of Structura Naturalis, Inc. and Research Associate, Centre for Environmental Structure.

PHILIP MICHELBACH
Assistant Professor of Political Science, Department of Political Science at the West Virginia University.

WILLIAM MITCHELL
Professor of Architecture, Media Arts, and Sciences at MIT and Director of the MIT Design Laboratory.

PETER NEWMAN
Professor of City Policy and Director of the Institute for Sustainability and Technology Policy at Murdoch University.

DOM NOZZI
Senior Planner, Department of Community Development, City of Gainesville, Florida.

LOUISE NYSTRÖM
Professor of Physical Planning, School of Technoculture, Humanities, and Planning, Blekinge Institute of Technology.

RAY OLDENBURG
Professor Emeritus at the Department of Sociology at the University of West Florida, Pensacola.

KRISTER OLSSON
Senior Researcher, School of Architecture and the Built Environment, Royal Institute of Technology, Stockholm.

ELIZABETH PLATER-ZYBERK
Architect and Urban Planner, Principal and Founder of Duany Plater Zyberk & Company (DPZ) and Dean and Professor at the University of Miami School of Architecture. Co-Founder of Congress for the New Urbanism (CNU).

SERGIO PORTA
Assistant Professor of urban Design and Director of the *Human Space Lab*, www.humanspacelab.com at the Department of Architecture and City Planning, Polytechnic of Milan, Italy. Adjunct Professor at the King Fahd University of Petroleum and Minerals in Dahran, Saudi Arabia. Founder of *Urban Sustainability through Environmental Design*, www.ustedurbandesign. org, an International Consortium for the Sustainable Spaces in Cities.

ROBERT PUTNAM
Peter and Isabel Malkin Professor of Public Policy at the John F. Kennedy School of Government, Harvard University.

EDWARD ROBBINS
Professor at the Institute for Urbanism and Landscape, Oslo School of Architecture and Design (AHO).

NIKOS A. SALINGAROS
Professor of Mathematics, Urbanist, and Architectural Theorist, University of Texas at San Antonio.

IRENE SANDERS
Executive Director and Founder of the Washington Center for Complexity and Public Policy.

SASKIA SASSEN
Ralph Lewis Professor of Sociology in the Department of Sociology at the University of Chicago.

DAVID GRAHAME SHANE
Adjunct Professor of Architecture at the Graduate School of Architecture, Columbia University.

EDWARD SOJA
Distinguished Professor of Urban Planning, Department of Urban Planning, School of Public Affairs, University of California Los Angeles.

DANIEL SOLOMON
Architect, Director of Solomon E.T.C., and Principal of the architecture firm WRT, Emeritus Professor of Architecture at the University of California, Berkeley. Co-Founder of Congress for the New Urbanism (CNU).

LUCIEN STEIL
Architect, Urbanist, and Writer.

KNUT STRÖMBERG
Professor of Urban Design and Development at the Department of Architecture, Chalmers University of Technology.

EMILY TALEN
Associate Professor at the Department of Urban and Regional Planning, University of Illinois at Urbana-Champaign.

LAURIE VOLK
Managing Director and Principal of Zimmerman / Volk Associates, Inc.

BARRY WELLMAN
Professor at the Department of Sociology and the Centre for Urban and Community Studies, University of Toronto.

TODD ZIMMERMAN
Managing Director and Principal of Zimmerman / Volk Associates, Inc.

ACKNOWLEDGMENTS

I am especially grateful to the authors in the book, all whom have exhibited great patience and commitment in bringing this project to life and kindly providing their latest thoughts and ideas on the subject. I am also privileged to have had the honor in moderating this amazing group. This can only happen once in a lifetime, in most cases never. Every author and editor owes intellectual debt to and draws upon the ideas, thoughts, and insights of many before him. I have been influenced and inspired by many, a large number of whom are contributing authors here.

I am deeply indebted to the co-founders of the New Urbanism movement, Andres Duany and Peter Calthorpe, not just for attending the gathering in Stockholm, but also for setting the seeds for this project (suggesting the idea that some kind of proceedings from this event would be valuable to have). Throughout the last decade they have been an intellectual inspiration for me. I am very privileged to know them. I am also grateful for the incurred intellectual and professional sustenance at my home base, the School of Architecture and the Built Environment at the Royal Institute of Technology (KTH) in Stockholm, Sweden.

Three individuals require special mention: Göran Cars, KTH; Peter Elmlund, Urban City Research, Ax:son Johnson Foundation; and Staffan Ström, the Southern Stockholm Summer University. Without them the New Urbanism & Beyond summer course and debates in Stockholm, October 2004, would have never materialized, and therefore this book, in large part the outcome of that meeting would have never seen the proper ray of light.

At Rizzoli, to David Morton, for his foresight and vision in believing that this extraordinary group of ladies and gentleman could be assembled in one place, and to Meera Deean, for patience and support during the long and tedious work of seeing this book through and bringing this whole project to a successful end. Thanks are due to all editors, expert reviewers, and various professionals that offered their valuable comments and suggestions during the way.

To Ax:son Johnson Foundation, the Sweden-America Foundation, the Swedish Research Council (Formas), and the Knut and Alice Wallenberg Foundation for generous support in enabling me to spend time in the United States, working on this book but also making my participation in pertinent conference and seminars possible. In that time, my kind hosts were William J. Mitchell, Massachusetts Institute of Technology; Douglas Kelbaugh, University of Michigan, Ann Arbor; and Robert Cervero, University of California, Berkeley. It was during those visits that this project was envisioned, created, and executed.

Finally, this is a suitable occasion to remember the late Raymond Rehnicer and present Dushko Bogunovich, who really taught me what urbanism is all about.

INDEX

Note: Pages in *italic* refer to illustrations.

A

Abbott, Greg, 221
accessibility
    centrality and, 140
    as definition of urbanity, 135–139
Adam Joseph Lewis Center for Environmental
    Studies (Oberlin College), 62
affordable housing
    mixed use, 80–84
    New Urbanism and, 78
    traditional neighborhoods and, 66, 128
    transit-oriented developments (TODs) and,
        124–125, 126
Agamben, Giorgio, 203
agora, 201, 202, 240
airports, 214, 216
Alexander, Christopher, 14–29, 20, 130, 146,
    258, 259, 287
Alexander, Maggie Moore, 14–29
allometry, 259–260
Almér, Anders, 173–175
Alonso, William, 128
alternative energy, 62, *192*, 192–193, *193*
American Association of Highway and
    Transportation Officials (AASHTO),
    153–157
American Quarterly, 88
American West, settlement and development,
    58–63
Analogical City (Rossi), 131
Anderson, Chris, 220
Andersson, Adam, 174
"Another New Urbanism" (Soja), 292–295
antirevivalism, 280–281
Appleyard, Donald, 110, 132
architectural space programing, 208–209
Arendt, Hannah, 201, 203
Arida, Ayssar, 288–291
Aristotle, 112, 203, 239
armachures, *131*, 131–132
Arntsberg, Karl Olov, 244–248
art and artists, 308
arterial roadways, 154–157
"Articles of Association Between Design,
    Technology, and the People Formerly
    Known as Users" (Thackara), 220
attractor and attraction concepts, 279, 282
Australia
    reducing auto dependency (Sydney and
        Melbourne), 186–188
    shopping center (Canberra), *188*

St. Andrews expansion area, 69
Austria
    Linz Café, 22
    Vienna and sprawl, 93, 94
automobiles. *See also* parking; streets
        and roads
    and degradation of human habitat, 89–92
    dependence on, 263–264
    dominance of, 9–10, 99, 239
    European urban squares and, 115
    factors that reduce dependence on,
        186–188
axial maps, 136, 137, *138*, 139

B

Baird, George, 120–123
Bantu Biko, Stephen, 9
Barrett, Charles, 72
Batty, Michael, 258–261
Beatley, Timothy, 189–196
Beauregard, Robert, 103–105
Beecher, Catharine, 88
Bel Geddes, Norman, 263
Belgium, Brussels New Urbanism project, *83*
Bender, Thomas, 300
Ben-Joseph, Eran, 154
Bernick, Michael, 48
Berry, Brian J. L., 296
Berry, Wendell, 112
Better Not Bigger (Fodor), 88
"Beyond the Neighborhood" (Brain),
    249–254
Bianchini, F., 177, 181
bicycles, 90, 194
big-box retailing, 173, 175, 206
Biometric Consortium, 216
biophilic urbanism, 192
Blackfoot Physics (Peat), 291
BMW plant, *44*
Bogunovich, Dushko, 197–200
Boids, 278
Borges, Jorge Luis, 280
Borja, Jordi, 320
Borys, Hazel, *71*
Bourdieu, Pierre, 139
Brain, David, 249–254
Brand, Stewart, 319
Braudel, Fernand, 245
Braungart, Michael, 61
Brazil, population growth in São Paulo, 247

Brooks, David, 206
Brown, J. H., 260
Bruno, Stephanie, *282*
Buber, Martin, 113
Burkholder, Richard, 313
Burnham, Daniel, 74
bus rapid transit (BRT), 68

C

Cadillac Desert (Reisner), 59
cafe society, 237
Cahill, Mary, 87
California
    Alma Place housing project (Palo Alto),
        125
    AvalonBay Communities, *171*, 171–172,
        172
    craigslist (Bay Area), 233
    The Crossings (Silicon Valley), 48, 49
    Davis neighborhood plan, 60
    dot-com-driven development and diversity
        (San Francisco), 215
    Fresno farmer's market, *17*
    Gap Incorporated office building
        (San Bruno), 61
    increased ridership and transit-oriented
        housing, 126–127
    Laguna West, 48, *49*
    land values and transit-oriented
        developments, 127–128
    Los Angeles growth, 247
    Los Angeles River restoration, 60–61
    Mission Valley light-rail corridor, 127–128
    reconstitution of urban core of Los
        Angeles, 293, 294–295
    San Elijo village center, 69
    Upham House, Berkeley, *25*
call-center cities, 215
Calm Streets, 154, *155*, 155
Calthorpe, Peter, 10, 48, *49*, 67–69, 296
Canada
    Cornell town center (Ontario), *83*
    Edmonton, Alberta, 48
    Garrison Woods (Calgary, Alberta), 121,
        123
    internet and local community (Toronto),
        223
    McKenzie Towne (Calgary), 81–82, *82*
    Mole Hill urban revitalization project
        (Vancouver), 194

Canada *continued*
  Toronto densities, 122
  Vancouver housing mix, 80, *81*
capital, 139
Capra, Fritjof, 318
Carmona, Richard, 74
Carpool (Cahill), 87
Cars, Göran, 176–181
Castells, Manuel, 214, 314–321
Catalonia internet users, 224
CCTV systems, 216
Celebration, 48, 85
centers. *See* urban centers (historic centers)
centrality, 140–145, 212–213, 216–217
"Centrality and Cities" (Porta, Latora), 140–145
Cervero, Robert, 48, 300
"A Changed Focus on Retail and Its Implications on Planning" (Almér), 173–175
charette process, 251–252
Charter of Athens, 110
Charter of the New Urbanism (1995), 296
Chicago. *See* Illinois
Chicago World's Fair (1893), 74–75
Chile, grid intensification in Santiago, *38, 39*
China
  patent statistics, 310
  public health and city planning, 75
  rural/urban divide, 313
Choay, Françoise, 135
Christaller, W., 260
Christenen, C. M., 173
cigar parlors, 236
circular metabolism, 193
cities, principles and attributes of good cities, 52–57, 58–63, 148–149
"The City as Growth Machine" (Molotch), 87
City Beautiful movement, 74–75
"The City is Not a Tree" (Alexander), 146
climate change, 193, 197–198
codes. *See* zoning and regulation
coffeehouses, 235–236
Cohen, Lizabeth, 88
Collage City, 121
Collage City (Rowe, Koetter), 131
collector roadways, 154–157
college campuses, 226
Collins, C., 85
Colorado, former Stapleton Airport (Denver), *41*
COLT fiber system, 213
Columbia, Santa Rosa de Cabal neighborhood, *19, 29*
common spaces, 232–233
communications. *See* information and communication technologies
community. *See also* neighborhoods
  generative codes and, 14–29
  importance of, 40
  information and communication technologies, 232–233
  internet and, 221–224
  New Urbanism, Everyday Urbanism and Post-urbanism and, 42–47
  suburban city and, 201–203
  third places and, 234–237
  traditional, and New Urbanism, 300
  virtual, 202–203, 222
Community Reinvestment Act, 297
complex adaptive systems (CAS), 275–276
complexity, 146, 258–259, 265–266, 275–279, 281–283, 289
"Complex Systems Thinking and New Urbanism" (Sanders), 275–279

"Confronting the Question of Market Demand for Urban Residential Development" (Volk, Zimmerman), 163–166
Congres International d'Architecture Moderne (CIAM), 72
Congress of the New Urbanism (CNU), 9, 42, 70–73, 296
connectivity, 208–211, 271–272, 273–274
"Connectivity and Urban Space" (Mitchell), 208–211
context zones, 157, *157*
convenience centers, *159*, 159–160
conventional development regimes, 250–251
Cooper, Alexander, 131
Corbett, Judy, 70
Cornell School, 131
Corner, James, 131
corner stores, 158–159, *159*
Crabgrass Frontier (Jackson), 86
Cradle to Cradle (McDonough), 58
craigslist, 233
"Creating Common Spaces" (Putnam, Feldstein), 232–233
Croatia, Hvar sunset, *230*
Crowhurst Lennard, Suzanne, 112–116
cultural activities
  economic impact of, 176–178
  effect on city image and identity, 178–179
  heritage management, 182–185
  role in urban development, 176–181
  Swedish case studies, 179–181
cyber districts, 214–215
Cyprus, integration analysis of Nicosia, 36, *36*

D

Dark Age Ahead (Jacobs), 47
data storage and security services, 215–216
Day, K., 85
The Death and Life of Great American Cities (Jacobs), 110, 123, 130, 281–282
De Crescenzo, Luciano, 113
deformed wheel pattern, 34, *34, 35*
Delirious New York (Koolhaas), 131
democracy. *See also* political gathering/discourse
  European urban squares and, 112
  informal gathering places (third places) and, 234–237
  neighborhoods and, 234–236, 238–243
  Swedish urban development and, 256
"Democracy and 'Neighborly Communities'" (Leyden, Michelbach), 238–243
Denmark
  bicycles (Copenhagen), 194
  traditional center (Copenhagen), 186–188
  density
  as definition of urbanity, 135–136
  diventity, 291
  incentives and disincentives, 271
  Los Angeles, 293, 294
  urban renaissance, urban villages and Smart Growth compared, 48–51
department stores, 174
de Soto, Hernando, 139
development regimes, conventional, 250–251
Dewey, John, 234–236, 240–243
Dietrick, S., 83
digital divide, 214, 217, 231
distance, definitions of, 32–33, 141
distance learning, 226
diventity, 291
diversity
  as definition of urbanity, 136–138

diventity, 291
  economic, 248
  European urban squares and, 113–114
  healthy ecosystems and, 62
  mixing uses and housing types and, 84–85
  social diversity, 78–79
  in suburbia, 86–87
Dodgeball, 202, 220
dog parks, 236
domesticity, 244–245
Douglas, Harlan, 86
Drieseitl, Herbert, *189*
Duany, Andrés
  on affordable housing, 83
  on architects, 10–11, 280
  and diversity, 60
  on gentrification, 82
  on mixed use, 84
  Seaside, 48, 80, 85, 296
  Suburban Nation (Duany, Plater-Zyberk), 154
  "The Traditional Neighborhood and Urban Sprawl," 64–66
  Traditional Neighborhood Developments, 70
  transect concept, 72, 122, 157
  urban context areas, 157
Duany Plater-Zyberk & Company, 100, 123, 269
Dunham-Jones, Ellen, 70–73, 298

E

East Baltimore Plan, 297
Eckstut, Stanton, 131
Eco, Umberto, 290
ecological cities. *See* green urbanism
economic activity, measuring, 309, 311
economies of conjunction, 216
"Eco-Tech Urbanism" (Bogunovich), 197–200
edge cities, 103
Edinburgh Garden, 283
Eishin Campus (Japan), *15, 23, 26, 27*
Electronics, 227
Ellis, C., 83
"The Emergence of Mixed-Use Town Centers in the United States" (Martineau), 98–102
enclaves, *131*, 131–132
energy crisis, 204–207, 225–226
Engels, Friedrich, 245
Enquist, B. J., 260
environmental regulations, 251–252
Etzioni, Amitai, 79
Europe. *See also specific countries*
  affordable housing, 80
  changes in retail, 175
  declining cities, 248
  multifunctional urban squares, 112–116
  pattern of night lights, *287*
  public spaces (city centers), 247
  and sprawl, 93–97
  urban village movement, 48–51, 84
Everyday urbanism, 42–43, *43*, 45, 46–47
evolutionary processes. *See* complexity science
Existence Space and Architecture (Norberg-Schulz), 131
Experience Corps, 232

F

Facebook, 222
face-to-face contact
  democracy and, 241–242

in third places, 234–237
and urban transformation, 225–227
Falconer Al-Hindi, K., 85
The Fall of Public Man (Sennett), 120
The Family, Sex, and Marriage in England, 1500–1800 (Stone), 244
farmer's markets, *17*, 115
Federal Emergency Management Agency (FEMA), 274
Feldstein, Lewis, 232–233
financial centers and services, 213–214, 307–308
Financial Times, 173
Finland, Viikki ecological district (Helsinki), 194
Fishman, Robert, 42, 88, 245, 296–298
flat-world theory, 309, 310
flexible frameworks, 147–152
Florida
    Celebration, 48, 85
    Seaside, 48, 80, 85, 296
    Winthrop (Brandon), *101*
    Winthrop mixed-use community (Brandon), 100, *100*
Florida, Richard, 309–313
Fodor, Eben, 87–88
forgiving streets, 90–91
form-based codes, 17–18, 252–253
Forrester, J., 257
fortressing, 89
fossil fuels, 192–193, 204–207, 225–226
Foucault, Michel, 132, 134, 203, 256
fractals, 258, 260, *261*, 273, 279
frameworks, urban design, 1148–152
Frampton, Kenneth, 75, 280
France, Parisian urban model, 246
Frantz, D., 85
Freedman, Michael, 109
Friedland, Lewis, 249
Friedman, Thomas, 309, 310
Frumpkin, Murray, 76
functionalism, 289
functional zoning, *54*, 54–55
Futurama, 263

G

gambling ethos, 205
Gap Incorporated office building, 61
Garde, A., 81, 85
Garden City movement, 110, 245, 263
Garreau, Joel, 225–231
gated communities, 123, 248
Geddes, Patrick, 104, 130
Gehl, Jan, 106–108
Gehry, Frank, 43
gender equality, 318
General Motors Corporation, 99
"Generative Codes" (Alexander, Schmidt, Hanson, Alexander, Mehaffy), 14–29
    definition of, 14
    developer's role, 23, 25, 27, 28–29
    experimental projects, *19, 20–22, 22, 23, 24*
    historical background, 17–18
    importance of independent project management, 24–28
    importance of sequence, 16
    procurement processes, 20, 22–24
    resulting neighborhood characteristics, 16
gentrification, 82, 215, 248, 297, 305
The Geography of Nowhere (Kunstler), 153–154
Georgia

Adair Park and Floyd neighborhoods (Atlanta), *266, 267*
deformed wheel pattern (Atlanta), *34*
grid intensification (Atlanta), *38, 39*
Suwannee Town Center (Gwinnett County), 100–101
Germany
    Eilenriede Forest (Hannover), 190, *191, 192*
    employment in cultural industries, 177
    Karow Nord (Berlin), 80
    Marienplatz, *113*
    Münsterplatz (Frieburg), *114*
    Potsdam-Kirchsteigfeld urban village, 84
    sprawl (Leipzig), *93, 94*
    water feature (Hattersheim), *189*
Gibbs, Robert, 158–162
Giles, Cris, 173
global cities, 212–217, 293–294, 306–308, 316
globalization, 293–294, 309–313
Gordon, Elizabeth, 88
Graham, Stephen, 212–217, 317
grassroots movements, 318
"Great Streets and City Planning" (Jacobs), 109–111
Green Book. See A Policy on Geometric Design of Highways and Streets (Green Book)
Green Roofs for Health Cities, 190, *191,* 192
green urbanism, 189–196
    alternatives to fossil fuels, 62, *192, 192–193, 193*
    businesses, industries, and commerce, 195
    circular metabolism, 193
    eco-tech urbanism, 197–200
    education of residents, 195
    government and, 195
    local and regional production, 193–194
    nature, 58–63, 97, 190, 192
    obstacles to, 196
    public transit, bicycles, and walking, 190, 194–195
"Green Urbanism" (Beatley), 189–196
grid intensification, *38, 39*
grid systems, 59, 67
"Growing Sustainable Suburbs" (Steil, Salingaros, Mehaffy), 262–274
Gulden, Tim, 309

H

Haas, Tigran, 9–13
Habermas, Jürgen, 256, 316
Hadid, Zaha, BMW plant, *44*
Hall, Peter, 48–51, 214
Hall, Rick, 153–157
Hampton, Keith, 223
Hannover Principles, 58, 61
Hanson, Brian, 14–29
Harvard Graduate School of Design conference (1956), 292
Haussmann, Baron, 198, 246, 247
Hayden, Dolores, 86–88, 183
herfing, 236
"Heritage Management in Urban Development Planning" (Olsson), 182–185
heterotopias, *131, 132, 133,* 134
hierarchies, *259, 259, 260, 263*
"Hierarchy, Scale, and Complexity in Urban Design" (Batty), 258–261
Hightower, Jim, 221
Hillier, Bill, 30–39, 135, 198
Holmes, Oliver Wendell *, 9

Homenet study, 223
Homestead Act (1862), 59
HOPE VI, 83, 297
House Beautiful, 88
housing. *See* affordable housing
housing bubble, 204
housing-market analysis, 163–166
Howard, Ebenezer, 49, 77–78, 245
Hungary, Budapest standard of living, 248
Hurricane Katrina, 73, 77, 274, 280, *281, 282, 284, 286–287, 287,* 300

I

idealism, 42
identity
    cultural activities and, 178–179
    diventity, 291
    heritage management and, 182
    role of urban design, 147
Illinois
    Chicago Center for Green Technology, *192*
    Chicago Principles, 61
    Chicago World's Fair "White City," 74
    libraries (Chicago), 232, 233
    rooftop gardens (Chicago), 190
    "Urban Network" for Chicago Metropolis 2020, 67, *68*
Image of the City (Lynch), 130
immigration, 294–295, 297
India
    Ahmedabad graphs, *142*
    call centers, 215
    patent statistics, 310
    rural/urban divide, 313
information and communication technologies
    call-center cities, 215
    cities as electronic communication hubs, 212–217
    and community, 232–233
    connectivity and work spaces, 208–211
    data storage and security services, 215–216
    digital divide, 214, 217, 231
    eco-tech urbanism, 197–200
    eighteen-month price-performance doubling, 227–229
    internet activities, 214, 215
    internet and community, 221–224
    and living and working space choices, 229–231
    locative media, 218–220
    and notion of locality, 306–308
    surveillance systems, 213–214, 216
    technological annoyances, 219–220
    theory of urbanism for the information age, 314–321
    virtual community, 236–237
    worldwide connectedness, 231
innovation, 309–310, *312*
INSPASS, 216
"Integrated Approaches and Dynamic Processes" (Jain), 146–152
integration analysis, 137
integration patterns, 32–36
Intel, 227
International Telecommunication Union, 231
internet. *See* information and communication technologies
Ireland (Galway City), *241, 242*
Italy
    centrality assessment (Bologna), *143, 144, 144–145*
    deformed wheel pattern (Venice), *34*
    Piazza del Campo, *115*
    Piazza del Popolo, *113*

Ito, Mimi, 220
Izenour, Steven, 132

J

Jackson, J. B., 59
Jackson, Kenneth T., 86, 88
Jackson, Richard, 76
Jacobs, Allan, 109–111, 320
Jacobs, Jane
    *The Death and Life of Great American
      Cities*, 110, 123, 130, 285, 287
    on diversity, 60
    Harvard Graduate School of Design
      conference, 292
    on local control, 258
    and modernism, 49
    on social trust, 238
    on sprawl, 47
    as traditionalist, 198, 280
    unslumming, 297
Jain, Arun, 146–152
Jamaica Digiport, 215
Japan
deformed wheel pattern (Tokyo), 34, *35*
Eishin Campus, *15*, *23*, *26*, *27*
    population growth (Tokyo), 247
    Tokyo as global finance center, 213
Jefferson, Thomas, 59, 110, 243
Jencks, Charles, 283–284
Jewson, N., 176
Johnson, Lyndon, 237
Jones, S., 317

K

Kelbaugh, Douglas, 40–47, 120
Kentlands, 48, *49*, *82*, 84, 123
Kernel Density Evaluation (KDE), *144*,
    144–145
King, A. D., 176
Klinenberg, Eric, 319
Koetter, Fred, 121, 131, 132
Koolhaas, Rem, 43, 46, 131, 198, 284
Krier, Léon, *45*, *52–57*, 72, 198, 272
Krier, Robert, 131, 198
Kunstler, James Howard, 55, 71, 153–154,
    204–207

L

Lakewood Church (Houston), 201–202
Landscape Urbanism (Infrastructure
    Urbanism), 43–44, 130–131, 200
Lang, Robert, 310
L'architettura della città (Rossi), 131
Latora, Vito, 140–145
Learning From Las Vegas (Venturi,
    Scott-Brown, Izenour), 132
least angle distance, 32–33
Le Corbusier, 49, 59–60, 75, 121, *122*, 198,
    263, 282, 288
Leinberger, Christopher B., 42, 167–172
Lerup, Lars, 201–203
level of service analysis, 155, 156
Levi-Strauss, Claude, 61
Levit, Robert, 121
Leyden, Kevin, 238–243
libraries, 236
lite hunters, 202, 203
Lithuania, Kaunas pedestrian center, *190*
Livable Communities, 104
"Lively, Attractive, and Safe Cities—But

How?" (Gehl), 106–108
local and regional commerce, 193–194,
    206–207
local roadways, 154–157
"Locative Media Urbanism" (McCullough),
    218–220
London. *See* United Kingdom
Long, Norton E., 240
long-tailed cities, 220
Los Angeles. *See* California
Louisiana, post-Katrina reconstruction, *281*,
    282, *283*, 287
Lucas, Robert, 310
Lynch, Kevin, 110, 130–131, 132, 134, 320

M

Macdonald, Elizabeth, 109
MacGregor, S., 176
MacKaye, Benton, 77–78
Madanipour, Ali, 117–119
Maitland, Barry, 132
"Making Cloth from Threads" (Solomon),
    74–76
"Making Public Interventions in Today's
    Massive Cities" (Sassen), 303–308
Malaysia, multimedia supercorridor in Kuala
    Lumpur, 214
Mandlebrot, Benoit, 279
Marcus, Lars, 135–139
Markusen, Anne, 212, 215
Marquand, David, 202
Marshall, A., 82
Martineau, Tom, 98–102
Marvin, Simon, 213, 317
Maryland
    East Baltimore Plan, 297
    Kentlands, 48, *49*, *82*, 84, 123
    Rockville Town Square (Rockville), 101
Massachusetts
    cyber districts (Boston), 214
    Fanueil Hall (Boston), 174
McCullough, Malcolm, 218–220
McDonald, Elizabeth, 320
McDonough, William, 58–63, 189
McHarg, Ian, 104, 130
McLuhan, Marshall, 212, 222
McPhee, John, 58
Mead, Carver, 227
mechanical forms, 282
mechanical worldview, 288–289
Mehaffy, Michael
    "Generative Codes," 14–29
    "Growing Sustainable Suburbs," 262–274
    "New Science, New Architecture ... New
      Urbanism?, 280–287
Mendez, M., 85
Merrick, George, 167
metric integration, 39
Meyer, Elizabeth, 59
Michelbach, Philip, 238–243
Michigan
    convenience center (Birmingham), *159*
    Simsbury Shopping Center (Bloomfield),
      160
Minnesota, Walker Art Center (Minneapolis),
    236
Mississippi, post-Katrina reconstruction, 274,
    287, 300
Mississippi Renewal Forum, 73
Mitchell, William, 208–211, 226, 316, 317
mixed use
    affordable housing and, 80–84
    reconstructing urban sprawl, 269, 272–273
    town centers, 98–102, 112–116

transit-oriented developments (TODs) and,
    124, 126
typology and, 44–45, *45*
"The Mixed Use Issue" (*Retail Traffic*), 98–99
mobility. *See also* information and
    communication technologies
    and community, 201–203
modernism, 52, 75, 198, 246, 280–281, 289
Molotch, Harvey, 87
monocentric cities, *55*, *57*
Moore, Gordon E., 227
Moore's Law, 227–229
Mormons, 59
Morocco, Marrakesh market, *231*
morphology, 258–261, 268
Moser, Eric, Katrina Cottages, *281*
Mostafavi, Mohsen, 131
Moule, ELizabeth, 70
movement patterns, 30–33
multicentered cities. *See* polycentric cities
multimedia supercorridors (MSCs), 214
Multiple Centrality Assessment (MCA), 141,
    145
multiplex urban regions, 212–213
multistrandedness, 232
Mumford, Lewis, 77–78, 245, 292, 298
museums, 236
MySpace, 221
The Mystery of Capital (de Soto), 139

N

National Real Estate Investor, 98
nature, 58–63, 97, 189, 190, 192
"The Need for Patient Equity in Creating
    Great Places" (Leinberger), 167–172
neighborhood centers, *160*, 160–161, 162,
    269, 270
neighborhoods. *See also* community
    attributes and consequences of traditional
      neighborhoods, 54, 65
    community and, 300
    as core idea of New Urbanism, 251–252
    democracy and, 234–236, 238–243
    desirable qualities of, 14, 18
    and public spaces, 118
    reconstructing suburbia, 267–269, 270–272
    retail planning principles, 158–162
neotraditionalists, 289
Neo-Traditional Town Planning, 293
Netherlands
    canal (Amsterdam), *228*
    ecological rooftops (Amsterdam), *191*
    GLW-Terrein project (Amsterdam), *194*
    Java Island (Amsterdam), *50*
    temporary communities, 202
"Netville" (Hampton, Wellman), 223
networked individualism, 224
networks, 30, 146
    future cities, 212–217
    and movement patterns, 30–33
    and reconstructing urban sprawl, 263,
      267–269, 270–272, 273–274
    the urban network, 67–69
Neuman, J., 81
Nevada, Las Vegas development, 58–59
New Mexico, Century Theatres Block
    (Albuquerque), *169*, 170–171
"New Science, New Architecture ... New
    Urbanism? (Mehaffy), 280–287
"The New Science of Space and the Art of
    Place" (Hillier), 30–39
newspapers, 232
New Tenement Law (1901), 75
New Town movement, 298

New Urbanism
  Charter of the New Urbanism (1995), 296
  Congress of the New Urbanism, 9, 42,
    70–73, 296
  criticism of, 10–11, 105, 120, 247–248,
    280, 288, 299–300
  founders of, 9, 10–11, 70, 72
  future of, 12, 299–302
  misunderstandings and
    mischaracterizations of, 253–254
  principles and philosophy of, 9–10,
    251–252
"New Urbanism: A Forum, Not a Formula"
    (Dunham-Jones), 70–73
"The New Urbanism and Public Space"
    (Baird), 120–123
"New Urbanism & Beyond" (Haas), 9–13
"New Urbanism in the Age of Re-Urbanism"
    (Fishman), 42, 296–298
New Urbanist sociology, 87–88
New York City
  Battery Park City enclave, 131
  economy, 309
  first zoning regulations, 17
  as global finance center, 213
  housing costs vs. commuting costs, 128
  internet activities, 214
  low-cost housing, 300
  New Tenement Law (1901), 75
New Yorker, 221
New York Times, 204, 206
Nichols, J. C., 167
Nigeria (Lagos), 230, 247
Norberg-Schulz, Christian, 131
North Carolina, Global TransPark, 216
nostalgia, 120, 202, 203, 249, 280
Nozzi, Dom, 89–92
Nyström, Louise, 93–97

O

obesity, 74
Oliver, J. Eric, 238
Olmsted, Frederick Law, 60, 245–246
Olsson, Krister, 182–185
"On Community" (Lerup), 201–203
Oregon
  Orenco Station (Portland), 81, 264, 265,
    268, 269, 272
  Tom McCall Waterfront Park (Portland),
    232
  urban design framework (Portland),
    147–151, 152
  Urban Growth Boundary (Portland), 48,
    67, 248
Österberg, Dag, 246

P

parking
  prices of, and rail transit, 127
  retail planning and, 161, 161–162
  transit-oriented developments (TODs) and,
    125
  urban centers and, 91
Patel, Bimal, 109–111
patent statistics, 309–310, 312
patient equity, 167–172
A Pattern Language (Alexander), 20, 130
Peat, F. David, 291
pedestrians, 66
  high-speed roads and, 90
  importance of quality public spaces, 107,
    108, 108

reconstructing urban sprawl and, 268, 269,
    271, 272
  walkable streets, 153–157, 190, 190
  walkable urbanism, 167–172
Peponis, J, 34
"Petrocollapse and the Long Emergency"
    (Kunstler), 55, 204–207
Philippines, 230
physical well-being, 74–76
place syntax analysis, 137
"Planning for Walkable Streets" (Hall),
    153–157
Plans and Situated Actions (Suchman), 220
Plater-Zyberk, Elizabeth
  on affordable housing, 82
  and diversity, 60
  Seaside, 48, 80, 85, 296
  Suburban Nation, 154
  "The Traditional Neighborhood and Urban
    Sprawl," 64–66
  Traditional Neighborhood Developments,
    70
  transect concept, 157
  urban context areas, 157
poetic urbanism, 61, 62–63
Poland
  Market Square (Krakow), 116
  retail park, 175, 175
A Policy on Geometric Design of Highways
    and Streets (Green Book), 153–157
politics and political discourse
  community and, 201–202, 203, 205,
    234–236
  in global cities, 306
  neighborhoods and, 238–243
  planning and deliberative democracy, 256
Politics (Aristotle) previous, 239
polycentric cities, 36–37, 38, 55, 57,
    212–213, 278–279, 294, 314–315
Polyzoides, Stefanos, 70
population growth, 247–248
Porta, Sergio, 140–145
postmetropolitan transition, 293–295
poststructuralism, 284–285, 289
Post-urbanism, 43–44, 44, 45–47, 120, 121
poverty, 97, 248, 294–295, 300–301, 318
The Power of Identity (Castells), 318
pragmatism, 42
private spaces, boundaries of, 117–119
privatization, 305
procurement processes, 20, 22–24
program evaluation and review technique
    (PERT), 24
The Public and Its Problems (Dewey), 243
public health, 74–76, 97
Public Land Survey System (1785), 59
public realm/public domain, 201–202, 243,
    269
public spaces
  democracy and, 238–243
  importance of quality, 106–108
  loss of, in suburban cities, 201
  making space in the in-between zone,
    303–308
  and private spaces, boundaries between,
    117–119
  reconquest of, 320–321
  streets and roads as, 120–123
  third places, 234–237
Putnam, Robert, 79, 112, 232–233, 238
Pyatok, M., 83–84

Q

"Quantum Urbanism" (Arida), 288–291

R

railroads, 207, 227–228
"Recombinant Urbanism" (Shane), 130–134
regeneration/renaissance, 48–51, 296–298
regional urbanization, 103–105, 212–213,
    293–294, 310, 314–315
regulations. See zoning and regulation
Reisner, Marc, 59
REITs (Real Estate Investment Trust), 171
relativism, 289
"Restraining Sprawl" (Nyström), 93–97
retail. See also mixed use
  big-box retailing, 173, 175, 206
  brands, 174–175
  changes in, 173–175
  local and regional commerce, 193–194,
    206–207
  planning principles, 158–162
  shopping centers and malls, 158–161,
    174–175
  surveillance, 216
  in village and town centers, 69
  Wal-Mart, 173, 206, 226
retail parks, 175, 175
Retail Traffic, 98–99, 102
"Retrofitting Suburbia" (Dunham-Jones,
    Williamson), 298
re-urbanism, 42, 296–298
revivalism, 280–281, 285
Reynolds, Craig, 278
Rheingold, Howard, 219
Rittel, Horst, 146
Robinson, Charles Mulford, 74
Rockefeller Center, 167
Rofé, Yodan, 109
"The Role of Culture in Urban Development"
    (Cars), 176–181
rooftop gardens, 61, 190, 191, 192
Ross, A., 85
Rossi, Aldo, 131
roundabouts, 68
Rouse, James, 174
Rowe, Colin, 121, 131, 132
rural/urban transect. See urban/rural
    transect
Ruskin, John, 244

S

Salingaros, Nikos A., 262–274
Sanders, T. Irene, 275–279
"The Santa Fe-ing of the Urban and Urbane"
    (Garreau), 225–231
Santa Fe (New Mexico), 225–227, 226
Sassen, Saskia, 174, 303–308, 316
Saxenian, Anna Lee, 310
scaling laws, 259–260, 261
Schmidt, Randy, 14–29
Schön, Donald, 257
Schumer, Charles, 11
Scott-Brown, Denise, 132
Scully, Vincent, 300
The Search for the Perfect Language (Eco),
    290
Seaside, 48, 80, 85, 296
segregation, 245, 248
self-organized cities/systems, 39, 142–143,
    258, 277–278, 281
Sennett, Richard, 120, 123, 244–245
Sert, José Luis, 292
"Settlements of the Future" (Krier), 52–57
Shane, David Grahame, 130–134
shopping centers and malls, 158–161,
    174–175

Shopping Mall: Planning and Design (Maitland), 132
shortest path distance, 32–33
Simon, Herbert, 259
Sirianni, Carmen, 249
Sitte, Camillo, 122, 198
slippery spaces, 213, 215–216
slums, 300–301, *301*
smart cards, 216, 217
SmartCode, 72, 269
Smart Code (Duany, Plater-Zyberk), 157
Smart Communities, 203
smart design, 197–200
smart growth, 48–51, 104, 300
social capital, 232
social communication patterns, 317
social movements, 315, 318
social objectives, 77–79, 87–88. *See also* affordable housing; diversity
Soja, Edward, 292–295
Sokol, Alan, 285
Sola-Morales, Ignasi de, 121
solar energy, 62, *192*, 192–193, *193*
Solomon, Dan, 10–11, 70, 72, 74–76
"Something Lived, Something Dreamed" (McDonough), 58–63
South Carolina, corner store (Charleston), *159*
Southworth, Michael, 154
space markets, 210
"Space of Flows, Space of Places" (Castells), 314–321
space syntax, 30–39, 137, 140–141
"Spacial Capital and How to Measure It" (Marcus), 135–139
spacial transformation, 314, 315–316
Spain, Pergola Fotovoltaica (Barcelona), *198*
Speaks, Michael, 46
Speck, Jeff, 154
"Speed, Size, and the Destruction of Cities" (Nozzi), 89–92
Spirn, Anne Whiston, 60, 62
Splintering Urbanism (Marvin), 213
sprawl. *See* suburbia and urban sprawl
"Sprawling Cities" (Arntsberg), 244–248
squares, 112–116, 121
Steil, Lucien, 262–274
Stein, Clarence, 77–78
Steiner, Yaromir, 102
sticky spaces, 213–214
Stone, Lawrence, 244
Strauss, Leo, 240–243
streets and roads
    arterials, collectors, and local, 154–157
    centrality assessment, 140–145
    characteristics of great streets, 109–111
    planning for walkable streets, 153–157
    as public spaces, 120–123
    reconstructing urban sprawl, 271–272, 273–274
    space syntax movement and, 30–39
    speed, size and urban center decline, 89–92
    Urban Networks, 67–69
Streets and the Shaping of Our Towns and Cities (Southworth, Ben-Joseph), 154
Strömberg, Knut, 255–257
structural sociology, 141
The Structures of Everyday Life (Braudel), 245
"The Suburban City" (Hayden), 86–88
Suburban Nation (Duany, Plater-Zyberk, Speck), 154
suburbia and urban sprawl
    attributes and consequences of, 64–65, 66, 93, 97, 153–154, 263–264

conventional development regimes and, 250–251
democracy and, 243, *243*
diversity in, 86–87
in Europe, 93
functional classification of roadways, 155
gasoline prices and, 204, 205–206
horizontal and vertical, *53*, *54*, 55
irresponsibility of, *54*, 55
new terms for, 88
New Urbanism and, 87–88, 103, 104–105
origins and expansion of, 86–87, *95*, 99–100, 244–247, 262–263
population growth and, 247–248
reconstruction of, 262–274
supporters of, 97
transit-oriented developments (TODs) and, 128
and urban designers, 103–105
urbanization of, 86–88, 294
victory of, 98
Suchman, Lucy, 220
supermarkets, 160, 160–161, 226
surveillance systems, 213–214, 216, 305
Susser, Ida, 319
sustainability. *See also* green urbanism
    nature and cities, 60
    reconstructing sprawl, 262–274
    of suburbs, 55, 56
Sustainable Communities strategy (United Kingdom), 51, *51*
Sweden
    axial maps (Stockholm), *136*, *138*, *139*
    cultural activities, 176, *178*, 179–181, *180*
    Hammarby Sjöstad (Stockholm), 96, 192, *193*
    high-rise apartment buildings and heritage management (Umeå), 183–184, *184*
    housing project (Stockholm), *177*
    public housing, 246–247, 255
    renewable energy (Malmö), 193, *195*
    sprawl (Stockholm), 93, 94–95, 96
    survey of preferred living areas (Ystad), 184–185, *185*
    urban planning and development, 255–257
Swedish Institute for Growth Policy Studies, 173

T

Taylor, Peter, 310
technological determinism, 222
technology. *See* information and communication technologies
technopoles, 214
Tedlow, Richard, 173
terrorism, 213–214
Texas
    Lakewood Church (Houston), 201–202
    West End neighborhood (Dallas), 229
Thackara, John, 40, 220
A Theory of Good City Form (Lynch), 110, 130
third places, 234–237
Thompson-Fawcett, M., 84
Thoreau, Henry David, 59
"Three Urbanisms" (Kelbaugh), 40–47
Tierney, John, 206
Till, K., 85
to- and through-movement patterns, 32–36
Toffler, Alvin, 212
Touraine, Alain, 202
tourism, 177–178, 180
"Toward a New Urban Design Manifesto" (Jacobs, Appleyard), 110

traditional architecture and urbanism, 52, 55–56, 280–281, 285, 287, 289
"The Traditional Neighborhood and Urban Sprawl" (Duany, Plater-Zyberk), 64–66
Traditional Neighborhood Designed (TND) communities, 158–162
transit-oriented developments (TODs), 48, 49, 104–105, 124–129, *128*
transportation modes, effects on cities, 225–231, 262–263
transportation networks, 67–69
True Urbanism, 100
"True Urbanism and the European Square" (Crowhurst Lennard), 112–116

U

United Kingdom
    aerial view (London), *31*
    Beddington Zero Energy Development (BedZED, London), *193*, 194
    Camden shops (London), *37*
    CCTV systems, 216
    deformed wheel pattern (London), *34*
    London as global finance center, 213
    Millennium Village (Greenwich), *50*
    Neo-Traditional Town Planning, 293
    origins of suburbia (London and Manchester), 244–245
    Poundbury (Dorset, England), 80
    retail hierarchy (London), 260, *260*
    Ring-of-Steel (London), 214
    Sealand web hosting, 215
    Sohonet (London), 214–215
    Sustainable Communities strategy, 51, *51*
    Upton, New Urbanism community, *84*
    urban villages, 48–51, 84
United Kingdom Urban Summit (2005), 48
University of California at Berkeley, Department of City and Regional Planning, 109
University of Phoenix, 226
University of Virginia, 110
urban centers
    centrality assessment, 140–145
    decline of, 103
    European squares, 112–116
    free parking and, 91
    high-speed roads and, 89–92
    historic centers, 52, 55–56
    mixed-use, 98–102
    reconstructing suburbia, 269, 270
    and urban designers, 103–105
    village and town centers in Urban Networks, 69
"Urban Design and Development in the Swedish Tradition" (Strömberg), 255–257
"Urban Design and the Metropolis" (Beauregard), 103–105
Urban Design Associates, 297
urban form, 147, 258
Urban Growth Boundary (Portland), 67
urban growth/urbanization, 212–213, 247–248, 300, 309. *See also* global cities; regional urbanization
urbanism, 11–12
"Urbanism and the Articulation of the Boundary" (Madanipour), 117–119
urbanity, 135–139
"Urban Network Architectures and the Structuring of Future Cities" (Graham), 212–217
"The Urban Network" (Calthorpe), 67–69

"Urban Renaissance, Urban Villages, Smart Growth" (Hall), 48–51
"Urban Retail Planning Principles for Traditional Neighborhoods" (Gibbs), 158–162
Urban Service Boundary (USB), 48
Urban Space (Krier), 131
urban sprawl. *See* suburbia and urban sprawl
urban village movement, 48–51, 84
utopianism, 11, 42

V

Vander Wal, Thomas, 220
Venturi, Robert, 132
Veregge, N., 85
Veseley, Dalibor, 131
A View from the Road (Lynch, Appleyard), 132
Viganò, Paola, 131–132
Virginia
    Arlington County parking and housing codes, 125
    Fairfax County diversity, 87
    Reston Town Center, 169–170, *171*
    Virginia (Culpepper), *227*
Virillo, Paul, 212
virtual community, 202–203, 222
Volk, Laurie, 163–166

W

walkable streets, 190, *190*
walkable urbanism, 167–172
Wal-Mart, 173, 206, 226
Warner, Sam Bass, Jr., 86
Washington
    data storage and security services, 215
    Issaquah Highlands town center, 69
Washington Post, 98
Weaver, Warren, 285
Wellman, Barry, 221–224, 316, 317
West, Cornel, 79
West, G. B., 260
"What is the Internet Doing to Community— and Vice Versa?" (Wellman), 221–224
Whittemore, Ellen, 104
Williamson, June, 298
Wilson, E. O., 192
wind power, 62
workplaces
    as community, 237
    information and communication technologies and, 208–211, 229–231
"The World is Spiky" (Florida), 309–313
Worldwatch Institute, 230
Wright, E. O., 85
Wright, Frank, Lloyd, 279

Y

Young, Brigham, 59

Z

Zimmerman, Todd, 163–166
Zipf, G. K., 260
zoning and regulation
    in conventional development regimes, 250–251
    form-based codes, 17–18, 252–253
    functional zoning, *54*, 54–55
    generative codes (*See* generative codes)
    New Urbanism, Post-urbanism and Everyday Urbanism compared, 44–46
    origins of, 17
    Recombinant Urbanism, 130–134
    reconstructing urban sprawl, 269, 270, 271, 272–273, 274
    urban/rural transect, 72, 104–105, 122, 252–253, 300
Zook, Matt, 214
zoon politikon, 202, 203

ILLUSTRATION CREDITS

PART 1. THEORIES OF URBAN FORM

1.1. CHRISTOPHER ALEXANDER
Generative Codes: The Path to Building Welcoming,
Beautiful, Sustainable Neighborhoods
Fig. 1, 2, 3, 4, 6, 7, 10, 12: Courtesy of Christopher Alexander
Fig. 5A, 5B: Kleonike Tsotropoulou
Fig. 8, 11: Hajo Neis
Fig. 9: Jim Givens

1.2. BILL HILLIER
The New Science of Space and the Art of Place:
Toward a Space-led Paradigm for Researching and Designing the City
Fig. 1, 2A, 2B, 2C, 3, 4, 5, 6, 7, 8, 9, 10, 11, 12, 13, 14, 15:
    Courtesy of Bill Hillier

1.3. DOUGLAS KELBAUGH
Three Urbanisms: New, Everyday, and Post
Fig. 1A, 1B, 4B: Courtesy of Calthorpe Associates
Fig. 2: Courtesy of Margaret Crawford
Fig. 3A: Courtesy of Zaha Hadid Architects
Fig. 3B: Courtesy of Gehry Partners, LLP
Fig. 4A: Courtesy of Leon Krier

1.4. PETER HALL
Urban Renaissance, Urban Villages, Smart Growth: Find the Differences
Fig. 1, 2, 3, 4, 5, 6: Courtesy of Peter Hall

1.6. WILLIAM McDONOUGH
Something Lived, Something Dreamed: Principles and Poetics in Urban Design
Fig. 1, 2, 3, 4, 5, 6, 7, 8: Courtesy of Léon Krier

PART 2. EXPLORING NEW URBANISM

2.1. ANDRÉS DUANY AND ELIZABETH PLATER-ZYBERK
The Traditional Neighborhood and Urban Spraw
Fig. 1, 2: Duany Plater-Zyberk & Co.

2.4. PETER CALTHORPE
The Urban Network
Fig. 1: Courtesy of Peter Calthorpe

2.3. ELLEN DUNHAM-JONES
New Urbanism: A Forum, Not a Formula
Fig. 1: © 2007 Ann B. Daigle
Fig. 2, 4: Courtesy of Ellen Dunham-Jones
Fig. 3: © 2007 Sandy Sorlien

2.6. JILL GRANT
The Challenges of Achieving Social Objectives through Mixed Use
Fig. 1, 2, 3, 4, 5, 6, 7: © Jill Grant

PART 3. SUBURBIA, SPRAWL AND URBAN DECLINE

3.3. LOUISE NYSTRÖM
Restraining Sprawl: A Common Interest to Enhance the Quality of Life for All
Fig. 1, 2, 3: Courtesy of Louise Nyström

3.4. TOM MARTINEAU
The Emergence of Mixed-Use Town Centers in the United States
Fig. 1, 2: Courtesy of Kay and John Sullivan

PART 4. STREETS, TRANSPORT AND PUBLIC REALM

4.1. JAN GEHL
Lively, Attractive, and Safe Cities—but how?
Fig. 1, 3: Courtesy of Gehl Architects
Fig. 2: Courtesy of Gehl Architects. From "Towards a Fine City," London (2004)

4.3. SUZANNE CROWHURST LENNARD
True Urbanism and the European Square: Catalyst
for Social Engagement and Democratic Dialogue
Fig. 1, 2, 3, 4, 5: Courtesy of Suzanne H. Crowhurst Lennard

4.5. GEORGE BAIRD
The New Urbanism and Public Space
Fig. 1: Courtesy of George Baird
Fig. 2: Courtesy of Wayne Copper, from *College City*, by Colin Rowe
    and Fred Koetter, published by MIT Press

4.6. ROBERT CERVERO
Transit-Oriented Development in America: Strategies, Issues, Policy Directions
Fig. 1, 2, 3: Courtesy of Robert Cervero

PART 5. THE ELEMENTS OF URBAN DESIGN

5.1. DAVID GRAHAME SHANE
Recombinant Urbanism
Fig. 1, 2, 3, 4, 5: Courtesy of David Grahame Shane. Diagram from Recombinant Urbanism (Wiley 2005)

5.2. LARS MARCUS
Spatial Capital and How to Measure It—
An Outline of an Analytical Theory of Urban Form
Fig. 1, 2, 3, 4, 5, 6: Courtesy of Lars Marcus

5.3. SERGIO PORTA AND VITO LATORA
Centrality and Cities: Multiple Centrality Assessment
as a Tool for Urban Analysis and Design
Fig. 1, 2: Courtesy of Sergio Porta and Vito Latora

5.4. ARUN JAIN
Integrated Approaches and Dynamic Processes
Fig. 1, 2, 3, 4: Courtesy of Urban Design Group, Bureau of Planning,
    City of Portland, Oregon

5.5. RICK HALL
Planning for Walkable Streets
Fig. 1, 2, 3, 4: Courtesy of Rick Hall

PART 6. REAL ESTATE, CITY MARKETING AND CULTURE

6.1. ROBERT GIBBS
Urban Retail Planning Principles for Traditional Neighborhoods
Fig. 1, 2, 3: Courtesy of Robert Gibbs

6.3. CHRISTOPHER LEINBERGER
The Need for Patient Equity in Creating Great Places
Fig. 1, 2, 3, 4: Courtesy of Christopher B. Leinberger

6.4. ANDERS ALMÉR
A Changed Focus on Retail and its Implications on Planning
Fig. 1: Courtesy of Anders Almér
Fig. 2: Courtesy of Anders Almér

6.5. GÖRAN CARS
The Role of Culture in Urban Development
Fig. 1, 2, 3, 4: Courtesy of Göran Cars

6.6. KRISTER OLSSON
Heritage Management in Urban Development Planning
Fig. 1, 2: Courtesy of Krister Olsson

PART 7. SUSTAINABILITY, TECHNOLOGY AND THE ENVIRONMENT

7.1 PETER NEWMAN
Does New Urbanism Really Overcome Automobile Dependence?
Fig. 1: Photograph by Tomas Hellberg 2005
Fig. 2: Courtesy of Peter Newman

7.2. TIMOTHY BEATLEY
Green Urbanism: A Manifesto for Re-Earthing Cities
Fig. 1, 2, 3, 4, 5, 6, 7, 8: Courtesy of Timothy Beatly

7.3. DUSHKO BOGUNOVICH
Eco-Tech Urbanism: Towards the Green and Smart City
Fig. 1, 2: Source/Photo by Relja Ferusic

PART 8. URBAN DIGITAL SPACES AND CYBER CITIES

8.4. BARRY WELLMAN
What is the Internet Doing to Community—and Vice Versa?
Fig. 1, 2: © Wellman Associates

8.5. JOEL GARREAU
The Santa Fe–ing of the Urban and Urbane
Fig. 1: Photograph by David Phillips (2005)
Fig. 2: Courtesy of Culpeper Renaissance, Inc.
Fig. 3: Photograph by Abra Grace (2007)
Fig. 4: Courtesy of Dallas Convention & Visitors Bureau

Fig. 5: Photograph by Tristan Glover (2006)
Fig. 6: Photograph R.J. Zimmerman (2006)

PART 9. SOCIAL CAPITAL AND MUTUAL BENEFIT

9.3. KEVIN LEYDEN AND PHILIP MICHELBACH
Democracy and "Neighborly Communities:"
Some Theoretical Considerations on the Built Environment
Fig. 1, 4, 5: Photo courtesy of Sherri and Kevin Leyden
Fig. 2, 3, 6: Photo courtesy of David G. Leyden

PART 10. COMPLEXITY SCIENCE AND NEW URBAN FORMS

10.1. MICHAEL BATTY
Hierarchy, Scale, and Complexity in Urban Design
Fig. 1, 2, 3: Courtesy of Michael Batty

10.2. LUCIEN STEIL, NIKOS A. SALINGAROS, AND MICHAEL MEHAFFY
Growing Sustainable Suburbs: An Incremental Strategy
for Reconstructing Modern Sprawl
Fig. 1: Reprinted with permission from the Sanborn Map Co. Inc.
Fig. 2, 4, 5: Courtesy of Satellite Images, NASA
Fig. 3 Courtesy of Lucien Steil, Nikos A. Salingaros, and Michael
    Mehaffy
Fig. 6, 7, 8: Courtesy of Michael Mehaffy

10.3. T. IRENE SANDERS
Complex Systems Thinking and New Urbanism
Fig. 1, 2: Courtesy of T. Irene Sanders

10.4. MICHAEL MEHAFFY
New Science, New Architecture . . . New Urbanism?
Fig. 1, 2, 3: Courtesy of Michael Mehaffy
Fig. 4 Nasa Goddard Space Flight Center; Scientific Visualization Studio
Fig. 5 SeaWiFS sensor on OrbView-2 satellite, August 2000. Sea WiFS
    Project, NASA/GSFC and GeoEye.
Fig. 6 Data from NOAA GOES satellite. Images produced by Hal
    Pierce, Laboratory for Atmospheres, NASA Goddard Space Flight
    Center.
Fig. 7 Courtesy of NASA. DMSP satellites, Data collected 1994-5.
    ASA/GSFC/Visualization Analysis Laboratory.

10.5. AYSSAR ARIDA
Quantum Urbanism: Urban Design in the Post-Cartesian Paradigm

Fig. 1, 2, 3: Courtesy of Ayssar Arida, from *Quantum City* (2002)

PART 11. BEYOND URBANISM AND THE FUTURE OF CITIES

11.3. EDWARD ROBBINS
The New Urbanism in the Twenty-first Century: Progress or Problem?
Fig. 1, 2: Photograph by Nabeel Hamdi

11.4. SASKIA SASSEN
Making Public Interventions in Today's Massive Cities
Fig. 1, 2, 3: Hilary Koob-Sassen, The Paraculture (Video Still).
    Courtesy T + 2 Gallery, London.